"INTO THE MAINE..."

"INTO THE MAINE..."

ONE MAINE FAMILY'S QUEST FOR LAND, 1630 - 1830

JENNIFER WIXSON

Copyright © 2025 by Jennifer Wixson
All rights reserved.

No part of this book may be reproduced or transmitted in any form or by any means, electronic or mechanical, including photocopying, recording or by any information storage or retrieval system – except by a reviewer or historian who may quote brief passages – without permission in writing from the publisher.

For more information contact:
whitewavepublishing@gmail.com

10 9 8 7 6 5 4 3 2 1

ISBN 978-0-9962237-3-7

eBook ISBN 978-0-9962237-4-4

Library of Congress Control Number: 2025912199

Images in this book used with permission (as noted) or are in the public domain.

Cover image: Map of Maine from Fielding Lucas, Jr.'s 1817 atlas, "A new and elegant general atlas: Containing maps of each of the United States."

For Dad, who always supported my writing career, no matter how crazy (or questionable) it appeared over the years.

"And land! Land! That golden word.
What trouble it has brought!
Man has sold his soul for it,
And killed without a thought.

"One wonders why it's preyed upon,
Here and all around;
For man keeps only in the end,
A little patch of ground."[1]

---
1. From, "Bedeviled America—the bicentennial poem." © Jennifer Wixson, 1976.

Table of Contents

Foreword	xiii
Author's Note	xxi
Chapter 1 – "One True Wish" ~ The First Generation	1
The Crocketts and the Churchwards of Stoke Gabriel, County Devon	4
Stoke Gabriel and the Dartmouth/Devon Fishing Industry	7
Sir Ferdinando Gorges and the Colonization of New England	9
The Stoke Gabriel Clock Tower and Yew Tree	13
Thomas Crockett Sails to the New World	14
Puritans vs. Anglicans – Shifting Tides of Power in England and New England	16
On the Ground at Pascataqua	17
Trading with the Indians at Newichawannock House	20
The Dark Years and the Devon Connection	28
Ann Crockett and Family Life in Early Kittery	31
Thomas Crockett's Last Decade	51
The Last Years of Ann Crockett	62
Chapter 2 – "The Said Land Thus Given By My Father Shall Stand Good" ~ The Second Generation	67
Longevity in New England vs. Old England	68
The Early Years of Ephraim Crockett	69
Anne Edge and the Edge Family	74
King Charles II Is Displeased – The Sale of the "Province of Mayne" to Massachusetts Bay	76
The First Indian War (1675-1678)	78
The Litigiousness of Kittery and Common "Society"	89
A (Mostly) Model Citizen	92
Kittery Land Grants and Real Estate Sales	94
Death of Ephraim Crockett	95
The Widow Anne	97
Chapter 3 – Making It To "The Short Side Front" ~ The Third Generation	99
A Youth Marred By War with the French and Indians (Second Indian War, 1688-1697)	100
John Skillin, and French and Indian Warfare	103
The Candlemas Day Massacre In York, Maine	106
Henry Barter, a Beloved Brother-in-Law, and Other Friends and Neighbors in Kittery	109
Queen Anne's War – The Third Indian War (1702-1713)	113
Marriage to Deborah Haley and Relocation to New Hampshire	116
A Founder of Stratham, New Hampshire	120
Real Estate Sales, A Yoke of Oxen, and "Bring[ing] Up the Bell"	124
The Skillin Family in Kittery	129
Father Rasles' War (The Fourth Indian War, 1722-1725)	130
The Resettlement of Falmouth	136
Massachusetts Bay Makes a Move and "Strange Ministers" in Stratham	138
The Final Years of the Brothers-in-Law	141

Chapter 4 – "Being Called 3 Times – Appearing Not" ~ The Fourth Generation	145
A Father and His Troublesome Namesake	146
Early Days in Falmouth	147
Mary Robinson	149
Massachusetts Bay Reaches Out To Maine's Native Population	151
Second Parish and a Frustrating Lack of Records	153
A Slide Into Debt and Wolves at the Door	155
Death Comes Calling	160
A Frustrated Shopkeeper	163
The Return to New Hampshire and Richard's Brothers Come to His Rescue	163
More Debt … and Father to the Rescue	168
Brother Samuel Builds a Successful Life in Falmouth	169
King George's War (The Fifth Indian War, 1744-1748)	172
Richard Crockett, Jr. Returns To Maine	175
Samuel Crockett Moves to Gorham and the Onset of the French and Indian War (1754-1763, the Sixth Indian War)	177
More Debt	181
Fall of Quebec and the End of a Century of Fear	187
Hard Times and the American Revolution	189
Relocation to Deer Isle	191
British Occupation	192
The Shaving Mill	197
Death of Richard Crockett, Jr. and a Posthumous Grant of Land	201
Chapter 5 – "At A Place Called Long Creek" ~ The Fifth Generation	205
Family Ties "at a Place Called Long Creek"	206
Too Many Richard Crocketts	207
The Roberts Family	210
King George's War in Second Parish	215
Second Parish by the Mid-18th Century	218
The Clark Controversy and Richard and Elizabeth (Roberts) Crockett	219
The French and Indian War in Greater Falmouth	221
Cape Elizabeth District	229
The March Toward Revolution	239
The Town of Cape Elizabeth Is Born	244
Susannah Westcoat and the Westcoat Family	246
Cape Elizabeth During the Revolutionary War	251
A New Day Dawns	256
Richard Crockett's 1781 Real Estate Transactions	258
Susannah's Father Slides Into Debt	261
The Crockett Family, 1785-1795	264
Death of Susannah (Westcoat) Crockett and Marriage to Elizabeth (Lewis) Masury	267
Leading Up to the War of 1812	271
The War of 1812	275
Local Effects of the War of 1812	278
Last Years of Richard and Elizabeth Crockett	281

Table of Contents

Wrapping Up the Life of Richard Crockett (III)	284
Conclusion to Chapter 5	290
Chapter 6 – The Battle Over Dawnland	**293**
Indigenous Understanding of Land vs. The Colonial English View	294
Bostoniak: Land Speculation in Maine and the Rise of the Great Proprietors	300
Massachusetts and Her Soldiers of the American Revolution	302
Chapter 7 – "In A Plea Of Land … Said Crockett Puts Himself On The Country" ~ The Sixth Generation	**311**
Ephraim's Early Years and the Influence of James Wagg, Sr. and Jr.	312
Ephraim Crockett's Service in the American Revolution	314
Marriage to Rebecca Stanford	321
The Interesting Years – 1780-1785	324
Life in the Backcountry of the Pejepscot Claim	330
Social and Religious Life in Pejepscot	337
Political Life in Pejepscot	339
Shifting Boundaries Between the Pejepscot Proprietors and the Kennebec Proprietors	341
Enter the Settlers and the Little Family	344
Proposals to "Quiet" the Settlers	351
The Pejepscot Proprietors Strike Back	356
Final Settlements	357
Conclusion to Our Crockett History	370
Quick Crockett Family Reference	**375**
Genealogical Dictionary of Thomas and Ann Crockett	**377**
Acknowledgements	**397**
List of Appendix Items	401
Bibliography	**411**
Original records	411
Periodicals, Journals, Website Articles, and Theses	416
Family Histories and Genealogies (Published and Self-Published)	419
Reference Books	421
Index	**427**
About the Author	**459**
Other Books by Jennifer Wixson	459

Foreword

Nearly half a century ago, when I was in my early twenties, I moved in with my maternal grandmother, Winona Palmer ("Nonie" to us kids). Winona lived in a dignified red brick house situated on Crockett's Ridge in Norway (Maine), where she had resided for most of her life. The ridge was named for her great-great grandfather Ephraim Crockett, Jr., who in 1812 purchased a lot of land on Lee's Grant and settled Crockett's Ridge with his wife Sally Wentworth and their family. (The brick house and much of the Crockett acreage is still owned by our family today.)

My favorite hours with my grandmother were those sitting around the old oak table, enjoying fresh-perked coffee hot off the woodstove. As I slathered fresh butter and raspberry honey on Nonie's Bakewell Cream biscuits, I listened to her stories about our ancestors. So enthralled was I by what I learned that first year living with my grandmother, I wrote a twenty-page Crockett family history, *It All Began with Ephraim*, and passed the booklet out to the family. The feedback was gratifying, and I always meant to get back to my family research, but Life got in the way.

About seven years ago, however, I returned to my Crockett history. I wanted to know more about the first Crocketts to the New World, the family that spawned our ancestors on Crockett's Ridge. Who were they? Where did they come from? Why—and when—had they come to Maine? These were questions Winona could not answer, but would have liked to have known.

This book answers those questions. What I discovered while researching and writing "Into the Maine," however, was that the answers to my questions unlocked a fascinating story about the early settlement of our state. I found I was not just following our line of Crocketts (from the first Englishman who arrived at the Pascataqua in 1630, to our Revolutionary War ancestor, the father of Ephraim who settled Crockett's Ridge), I was following the backcountry trail of the common man and woman on a quest for land in Maine.

When writing the book, my dueling natures as both novelist and amateur historian were often at war. I wanted to tell an interesting story—accurate, yet a tale not bogged down by picayune facts. While the wrestling gave me no end of trouble, it resulted in a better product: a book meant to be read on two levels. The main text carries the flow of the story. The expansive footnotes placed below the text offer good fishing to those history buffs (such as myself) who love to parse through the pickerel weeds of facts. My druthers would be to have you read the main text first, and then (if interested) reread a chapter pausing to reel in the footnotes.

Finally, this history is not meant to be a glorification of the early English colonization of New England nor an apology for the wrongs that were perpetrated by them against the indigenous First Peoples. I intend to simply put forward our family's story. My research suggests that the lives of my White ancestors in the New World exemplified the role English and Europeans played in the demise and destruction of native cultures. As individuals, my Crockett ancestors were no worse than some, and considerably better than others.

Jennifer Wixson
Troy, Maine
April 19, 2025

List of Illustrations

Chapter 1 – "One True Wish" ~ The First Generation
   Stoke Gabriel Church, 1842 Lithograph by William Spreat.   4
   17th Century Settlements in Maine   11
   Ancient yew tree and clock tower at the Church of St. Mary and St. Gabriel in Stoke
      Gabriel, keeping watch over the church's cemetery.   14
   Early map of Piscataqua (Pascataqua) Plantations and Sir Ferdinando Gorges' later
      plantation, known as Georgiana (Gorgeana).   19
   The Loosely-Knit Tribes of the Wabanaki Confederacy.   22
   Cow Cove, Vaughn Woods on the Salmon Falls River in South Berwick, looking northeast.   28
   Oath of allegiance to Massachusetts Bay Colony.   38
   Gorgeana (York) in 1652 showing the residences of the inhabitants who signed the
      "Submission" to Massachusetts Bay Colony, Nov. 22, 1652.   39
   Map of Kittery Point, 1650-1700.   46
   Lower Kittery (now, Kittery), 1635-1700.   50
   "South Side and Raynes's Neck."   61

Chapter 2 – "The Said Land Thus Given By My Father Shall Stand Good" ~
The Second Generation
   Samuel de Champlain's 1605 map of native village at the mouth of the Saco River.   81
   Mark of Ephraim Crockett.   93

Chapter 3 – Making It To "The Short Side Front" ~ The Third Generation
   Baron Jean Vincent de Saint-Castin.   102
   Kittery selectmen voted in March 19, 1694/95.   109
   Deposition of Samuel Skillin and Richard Crockett given at the Court of Common Pleas,
      York, April 4, 1704.   112
   Sketch map of Pascataqua, circa 1690.   121
   Men's seating arrangements in the First Church of Stratham (N.H.), 1718.   123
   George Clark's promissory note to Richard Crockett for a yoke of oxen dated
      April 6, 1724.   126
   Plan of land purchased of Captain Simon Wiggins by Richard Crockett.   128
   Treaty of Portsmouth, July 12, 1713, between Eastern Abenakis and the Province of
      Massachusetts Bay.   131
   Death of Father Sebastian Rasles at Norridgewock, August 23, 1724.   135
   Gravestone of Lieut. Samuel Skillin, Long Creek Cemetery, South Portland, Maine.   143
   Long Creek Cemetery, South Portland, Maine.   143

Chapter 4 – "Being Called 3 Times – Appearing Not" ~ The Fourth Generation
   Purpooduck Meeting House in Second Parish.   154
   Complaint against James Noble, innkeeper of Falmouth, June 26, 1739.   159
   1735-1736 account of Richard Crockett, Jr. at the shop of Phineas Jones.   162
   Records from the Inferior Court of Common Pleas held at Portsmouth, N.H.
      December 4, 1740.   167
   Promissory note from Richard and Samuel Crockett to Phineas Jones, shopkeeper of

Falmouth, Feb. 16, 1740 (bottom image), and writ of execution for Richard Crockett, Jr. of Stratham, N.H. for this debt.   171

1757 muster rolls for brothers Richard and Samuel Crocket, during the French and Indian War.   180

Promissory note from Richard "Crockit" to John Waite, August 1, 1758.   183

1760 List of polls and estates in the Second District of Falmouth, Maine.   186

Inset from Early Settlers Map of Deer Isle/Stonington.   194

Inset from Plan of Deer Isle, 1785.   195

The wedding of Joanna R. McFarland and Jesse Tea, July 23, 2016, Crockett's Cove, Stonington, Maine.   203

Chapter 5 – "At A Place Called Long Creek" ~ The Fifth Generation

(Partial) deed from Samuel Skillin to George and Katharine Roberts, June 8, 1753.   214

Muster roll for Richard Crocket (III), 1751.   217

Map of the French and Indian War (1754-1763).   222

Muster roll for Richard Crocket (III), 1757.   226

Muster roll for Richard's younger brother, Robinson Crockett, 1759.   227

Record of Jedidiah Preble v. Richard Crockett, Jr.   232

Record of Mountfort heirs v. Richard Crockett, Jr.   233

List of polls and estates from Cape Elizabeth, Maine, 1771. Richard Crocket (II) is first under the letter "C" and his son Richard Crockett, Jr. (III) is six lines below him.   235

Record of John Robinson v. Richard Crockett.   237

Two halves of the gravestone of Catharine Crockett.   238

The Declaration of Independence copied into the Cape Elizabeth town record.   246

Record of Susannah Westcoat before the Cumberland County Court of General Sessions of the Peace, October 18, 1768.   250

1781 deed from George Copson Roberts and Joseph Roberts to Richard Crocket, Jr.   260

1790 U.S. Census for Cape Elizabeth, Richard Crockett.   265

Plan of Township No. 2, Indian Purchase, 1835.   288

Chapter 6 – The Battle Over Dawnland

The Warumbo Deed, p. 1.   299

1764 Plan of the Pejepscot Claim by Enoch Freeman.   310

Chapter 7 – "In A Plea Of Land … Said Crockett Puts Himself On The Country" ~ The Sixth Generation

Marriage intentions filed in Cape Elizabeth with David Strout, Town Clerk, on March 12, 1777.   313

Paper signed at Falmouth December 17, 1776 by Ephraim Crockett for his third enlistment in the American Revolution.   320

"Eight lots laid out to the Pejepscot Proprietors."   328

Authorization by Pejepscot selectmen for the payment of $18 to Samuel Crockett for hiring preaching in the Free Will Baptist profession for the year of 1804.   339

1804 map of settlers on the Pejepscot Patent presented to the Massachusetts General Court.   354

Inset from 1804 map showing the lots proposed to "quiet" the Pejepscot settlers.   355

Case No. 290, Cumberland County Court of Common Pleas, March term A.D. 1812.   360

List of Illustrations

Case No. 290, Cumberland County CCP, March term, 1812 (second page).	361
Grave of Ephraim Crockett, Wagg family cemetery, Auburn, Maine.	373

Appendix
    Inventory of the estate of Thomas Crockett, 20 March 1678/79.   402
    Last Will and Testament of Ephraim Crockett, 17 July 1688 – p. 1.   403
    Last Will and Testament of Ephraim Crockett, 17 July 1688 – p. 2.   404
    Transcription of the Warumbo Deed, negotiated 7 July 1684.   405
    Petition of Josiah Crockett to the General Court of Massachusetts 11 April 1781   408

Source Abbreviations

(See Bibliography for publication and other information.)

Abbreviation	Source
AGENTBOOK	Record book belonging to an agent of the Pejepscot Proprietors.
AHS	Androscoggin Historical Society.
ANCESTRY	Original records found on Ancestry.com.
ANDHIST	"History of Androscoggin County, Maine, Illustrated." Edited by Georgia Drew Merrill.
BANKS	"History of York, Maine, Successively known as Bristol (1632), Agamenticus (1641), Gorgeanna (1642), and York 1652)." Volume I. Charles Edward Banks.
BANKS2	"History of York, Maine, Successively known as Bristol (1632), Agamenticus (1641), Gorgeanna (1642), and York 1652)." Volume II. Charles Edward Banks.
BANKSDICT	"Topographical Dictionary of 2885 English Emigrants to New England, 1620-1650." Charles Edward Banks.
BANKSPLANT	"The Planters of the Commonwealth." Charles Edward Banks.
BAXTER	"Documentary history of the state of Maine, Volume XXIV." Editor, James Phinney Baxter
BAXTER2	"Documentary history of the state of Maine, Volume XIX." Editor, James Phinney Baxer.
BAXTER3	"Documentary history of the state of Maine, Volume IV, containing the Baxter Manuscripts." Editor, James Phinney Baxter.
BAXTER4	"Documentary history of the state of Maine, Volume III, containing the Trelawny Papers." Editor, James Phinney Baxter.
BELKNAP	"The History of New-Hampshire." Vol. 1 & 2. Jeremy Belknap, D.D.
BURRAGE	"The Beginnings of Colonial Maine." Henry S. Burrage.
CANDAGE	"Crockett Genealogy 1610-1988; Some Descendants of Thomas and Ann Crockett of Kittery, Maine (with 1990 Addendum)." Charles Samuel Candage.
CAPE-E	"A History of Cape Elizabeth, Maine." William B. Jordan, Jr.
CCROD	Cumberland County Registry of Deeds.
CHAIRMAKERS	"The Case of the Chairmakers: A Problem in the Crockett Family." Merton Taylor Goodrich, M.A.
CROCKETT	"The Crockett Family of Maine." Compiled and edited by Donna Hopkins Scott.

Source Abbreviations

DEERISLE	"An Historical Sketch of the Town of Deer Isle, Maine: with Notices of its Settlers and Early Inhabitants." George Lawrence Hosmer.
DESCENDANTS	"Descendants of Richard Crockett." Dr. Carol P. McCoy. (Including Notes of Dr. David Crockett.)
DINGLEY	"The Life and Times of Nelson Dingley, Jr." Edward Nelson Dingley.
DURHAM	"History of Durham, Maine." Everett S. Stackpole.
ELP	Eastern Land Papers, Records, 1717-1860. Massachusetts Archives.
EMPIRE	"Properties of Empire: Indians, Colonists, and Land Speculators on the New England Frontier." Ian Saxine.
FHS	Falmouth Historical Society.
GOOLD	"History of Colonel Edmund Phinney's Thirty-first regiment of foot." Nathan Goold.
GORHAM	"History of Gorham, ME." Hugh D. McLellan.
GUNNISON	"Genealogy of the Descendants of Hugh Gunnison." George Gunnison.
HUBBARD	"A General History of New England, From the Discovery to MDCLXXX." The Rev. William Hubbard.
LEWISTON	"Frontier to Industrial City: Lewiston Town Politics, 1768-1863." Douglas I. Hodgkin.
LIBBYNOYES	"Genealogical Dictionary of Maine and New Hampshire." Sybil Noyes, Charles Thornton Libby, and Walter Goodwin Davis.
LIBERTY	"Liberty Men and Great Proprietors—The Revolutionary Settlement of the "Maine Frontier, 1760-1820." Alan Taylor.
LITTLE	"Genealogical and Family History of the STATE OF MAINE," Compiled under the editorial supervision of George Thomas Little, A.M., Litt.D.
MEWD	*Maine, Early Wills & Deeds* made available on American Ancestors website, by New England Historic Genealogical Society.
MHS	Maine Historical Society.
MIGRATION	"The Great Migration Begins: Immigrants to New England, 1620-1633. Vol. 1, A-F." Robert Charles Anderson.
MIGRATION2	"The Great Migration, Immigrants to New England, 1634-1635, Volume VII, T-Y." Robert Charles Anderson.
MIGRATION3	"The Great Migration, Immigrants to New England, 1634-1635, Volume I, A-B." Robert Charles Anderson, George F. Sanborn Jr., and Melinde Lutz Sanborn.
MMN	Maine Memory Network.
MPCR	"Province and court records of Maine." Vol. 1-6 (as noted). Maine Historical Society.

NEREGISTER	"The New England Historical and Genealogical Register." Volumes as noted.
NEFAMILIES	"New England Families, Genealogical and Memorial: A Record of the Achievements of Her People in the Making of Commonwealths and the Founding of a Nation." William Richard Cutter.
NOTABLE	"Notable Southern Families, Volume V: The Crockett family and connecting lines." Janie Preston Collup French.
NTLARCHIVES	National Archives.
PEMAQUID	"Beaver, Blankets, Liquor, and Politics Pemaquid's Fur Trade, 1614-1760." Neill DePaoli.
PENLEY	"Study of the Penley Family." Unknown author, AHS.
RCROD	Rockingham County (NH) Registry of Deeds.
SMALLDESC	"Descendants of Edward Small of New England : and the allied families with tracings of English ancestry." Volume II. Lora Altine Woodbury Underhill.
SMITHJOURNALS	"Journals of the Rev. Thomas Smith, and the Rev. Samuel Deane, Pastors of the First Church in Portland with Notes and Biographical Notices: and a Summary History of Portland." William Willis, editor.
STACKPOLE	"Old Kittery and her Families." Everett S. Stackpole.
STARBIRD	Various genealogies of Danville (Maine) families assembled by historian Charles Starbird.
WAYMOUTH	"True Relation of Waymouth's Voyage, 1605." James Rosier.
WGDFAMILIES	"Massachusetts and Maine Families in the Ancestry of Walter Goodwin Davis, 1885-1966." Walter Goodwin Davis and Gary Boyd Roberts.
WENTWORTH	"The Wentworth Genealogy: English and American." John Wentworth, LL.D.
WILLIS	"The History of Portland, from 1632 to 1861: With a Notice of Previous Settlements, Colonial Grants, and Changes of Government in Maine." William Willis.
YCROD	York County Registry of Deeds.

Author's Note

Reading genealogical histories such as this can be bewildering, especially when names carry over from one generation to the next. While in each generation I endeavor to be as distinct as possible, I recognize that some readers might become entangled in the plethora of repeated names. As a result, on page 377 in the back of the book you will find a "Genealogical Dictionary of Thomas and Ann Crockett" to help you untangle the characters in this history.

Also, the First Peoples of Maine had no written language, but rather a verbal history. To these Native American stories information from archaeological digs has been added over the years. But most of what we know about the eastern Algonkian-speaking tribes in Maine and New Hampshire comes from early French and English sources. I have depended upon these Euro-centric sources (or upon other historians who used them), but I regret the lack of balance they provide.

Chapter 1

"One True Wish"
The First Generation

On Friday, May 17, 1605, the explorer George Waymouth of Cockington, county Devon, England, hired by wealthy English speculators for a second voyage to the New World, dropped anchor on the north side of what is now Monhegan Island off the coast of Maine. Aboard the small sailing ship *Archangel* with Waymouth was James Rosier, chronicler of the voyage. A talented writer, Rosier noted the gooseberries, strawberries, and wild peas growing on the island, as well as an abundance of fish and fowl "of divers kinds." The chronicler also cast his gaze upon the mainland, where the Camden hills rose up behind the low shoreline, and the sight inspired hope in Rosier for "the discoverie of some good." From the small island the leviathan of land stretched "a great way (as it then seemed, and as we after found it) up into the Maine …"[1] This tantalizing view "into the Maine" promised the Englishmen an endless possibility of riches.

Not long after the *Archangel* returned to England, Rosier published his "True Relation of Waymouth's Voyage, 1605." Rosier's captivating tale of the adventures of Waymouth and his crew—including their interactions with indigenous peoples—whetted a public appetite for further exploration and colonization of what was known then as northern Virginia,[2] but officially by 1639 (and ever after) as "the Province or County of Mayne and not by any other name or names whatsoever."[3]

---

1. "True Relation of Waymouth's Voyage, 1605." (WAYMOUTH) James Rosier. P. 11 (electronic file). https://www.americanjourneys.org/AJ_PDF/AJ-041.pdf
2. American Journeys website. "Eyewitness Accounts of Early American Exploration and Settlement: A Digital Library and Learning Center." https://www.americanjourneys.org/aj-041/summary/index.asp
3. Maine Memory Network. (MMN.) "State of Mind: Becoming Maine. Sir Ferdinando Gorges." According to MMN,

Our story—a story about land ownership in Maine—begins about twenty-five years after Waymouth's 1605 voyage. My 10th great-grandfather Thomas Crockett[4] of Stoke Gabriel (a little village in Devon about eight miles from Waymouth's hometown of Cockington) sailed to the Piscataqua River about a quarter-century after the explorer's voyage. Although Thomas Crockett and his descendants were not movers and shakers in the great drama that transpired on the world stage over ownership of New England in the 17th through 19th centuries, the Crockett family's history embodies the role of the common man and woman (primarily Englishmen) in the struggle over real estate in Maine or *Wabanaki* (Dawnland).[5] From Thomas Crockett, the first Crockett who emigrated from England in 1630 (an early settler of Kittery and York), to Ephraim Crockett (my 5th great-grandfather and a Revolutionary War veteran), the driving force behind these men and others like them was the desire to acquire freehold land. Thanks to a combination of factors—initiative, wits, personal relationships, and the temporary collapsing of class from Old World to New—the Crocketts (and others) were initially successful. By the turn of the 19th century, however, that had changed. Wit and initiative were no longer enough to overcome the immutable force of the wealthy and powerful Great Proprietors (most hailing from Massachusetts), who claimed ownership of much of Maine, including the backcountry.

While this is primarily a story about the acquisition of land, it is also a story about relationships and the essential role friends and family played in the fortunes of the Crocketts and other early newcomers to Maine. In sparsely settled 17th century Maine, with its harsh climate and political and religious upheavals that rose and fell with the tide of the English Civil War, acquaintances quickly became friends, and friends became in-laws, as well as partners, benefactors, and providers of testimony. During the first generation, early friends and family members

---

England's King Charles I took a dislike to Sir Ferdinando Gorges' Somersetshire designation for his grant (named after Gorges' home county of Somerset), and proclaimed that the territory be known as "the Province or County of Mayne and not by any other name or names whatsoever." Despite the King's decree, Maine still retained Somerset County, part of the original Gorges' grant. https://www.mainememory.net/sitebuilder/site/3012/slideshow/1803/display?format=list&prev_object_id=4753&prev_object=page

4. Thomas Crockett was probably not the ancestor of the famous American frontiersman Davy Crockett. There are many different genealogies available on Davy Crockett; however, I am not sure how reliable any of them are. He seems to have originated from the Virginia Crocketts. If so, there is a possibility that Davy was a descendant of one of Thomas Crockett's brothers, who is said to have been the "father" of the Virginia Crocketts. We will likely never know for sure. NEFAMILIES, p. 1895. See also NOTABLE, p. 395.

5. The Native Americans in Maine and the land in which they lived shared the same name, "Wabanaki." The Wabanaki were loosely-connected tribes of Indians speaking similar eastern Algonkian dialects. The word "Wabanaki" translates to English as "land of the Dawn" or "People of the Land of the Dawn;" hence, Maine was also known as Dawnland. EMPIRE, p. 13.

The First Generation

of Thomas Crockett provided important depositions that helped him secure title to 188 acres of land in Kittery (a grant that he had received, but which was not recorded). In subsequent generations, as families swelled and the population of Maine grew, second sons (and third and fourth) were forced to push further eastward seeking land, almost always in the mixed company of extended relations and family groups, banding together for protection from the elements, as well as from hostile Native Americans and their French allies.

Despite the passage of four centuries since Thomas Crockett's arrival in the New World, many Crockett place names remain in Maine (and New Hampshire),[6] physical reminders of this family's history. Every time I happen upon a new Crockett place name, such as when I first learned that my sister Cheryl and her husband Phillip had purchased a home and an island in Crockett's Cove in Deer Isle, I have been struck by the coincidence. What I discovered writing this history, however, is that it is not a coincidence. Thomas and Ann Crockett, the ancestors of all New England Crocketts, had a lot of descendants! And—like other newcomers to New England—those descendants were always on the hunt for land. Indeed, Crockett's Cove in Deer Isle,[7] Crockett's Neck in Kittery,[8] Crockett's Corner in South Portland (currently the site of the Maine Mall),[9] and our family's land on Crockett's Ridge in Norway (Maine) have a direct link back to Thomas Crockett, who arrived in the New World in 1630[10] and who is the ancestor, along with his wife Ann, of the New England Crocketts. This is their story.

---

6. See Crockett's Ledge in Meredith, N.H. and Crockett's Way in Stratham, N.H., for example.

7. According to George Lawrence Hosmer's book, "An Historical Sketch of the town of Deer Isle, Maine: with notices of its settlers and early inhabitants" (DEERISLE), Crockett's Cove was named for Josiah Crockett, son of Richard Crockett (Jr.) and Mary Robinson Crockett. (Josiah was a great-grandson of Thomas and Ann Crockett.) Josiah settled 212 acres on the east side of the cove named after him, relocating there from Falmouth about 1768. The Deer Isle history says he was "a singular man," without giving any explanation as to why the author considered him odd. Josiah was joined in Deer Isle by his father Richard, Jr. (who died in Deer Isle) and brother, Captain Robinson Crockett, who came with his family. One of Robinson Crockett's sons, Richard, tended a sawmill next to Barbour Farm on the west side of Crockett's Cove, of which farm he was part owner. Currently, my sister Cheryl Wixson and her husband Phillip McFarland reside near Barbour Farm on Crockett's Cove in Stonington.

8. STACKPOLE, various pages.

9. "A Forgotten Landscape: How a Place Called Crockett's Corner Became the Maine Mall." M. M. Drymon, PhD. The Landscape History Institute, South Portland, 2017.

10. There is no certain record of Thomas Crockett's emigration date, but I believe (and will explain my reasoning in this chapter) that Thomas sailed on the *Warwick* in 1630. Kittery historian Everett S. Stackpole says depositions given by Thomas Crockett show he arrived in 1630 or 1631. (STACKPOLE, p. 20.) Many other historians believe Crockett came in 1631 on the *Pied Cow*, which Wilbur D. Spencer (PIONEERS, p. 58) notes sailed from Portsmouth, England on March 6, 1630/31, bound for Pascataqua. LIBBYNOYES, Part II, pp 171 & 172 says: "[Thomas Crockett] was brot over to the Piscataqua as a young man by Capt. Neal and app. in the 1633 accts." Robert Charles Anderson in *The Great Migration Study Project* gives an arrival date of 1633 for Thomas Crockett (likely because Thomas is first mentioned that year by Neal). MIGRATION, p. 495

The Crocketts and the Churchwards of Stoke Gabriel, County Devon

Thomas Crockett was the son of Thomas and Alse Anne (Churchward/Churchwood) Crockett. His parents were married in Stoke Gabriel, Devon, England on August 24, 1602.[11] Stoke Gabriel, a picturesque rural parish in southwest England, is situated in South Devon on a creek off the River Dart, about 200 miles south of London.

Stoke Gabriel Church, 1842 Lithograph by William Spreat.
(Image in the public domain.)[12]

Stoke Gabriel was the ancestral home of the Churchwards, the family of Thomas' mother, not his father. Sixty-four Churchwards are listed as buried (and there are probably many more) in the cemetery belonging to the Church of St. Mary and St. Gabriel, yet no Crockett (or Crechet, as the Crocketts were known) graves appear.[13] Maine historian Charles Edward Banks, who examined thousands of English baptismal records for his 1937 book, "Topographical Dictionary of 2885 English Emigrants to New England, 1620-1650," noted that the name "Crockett" was "very rare in England."[14]

---

11. "England Marriages, 1538-1973." Thomas Crechet and Alse [Ann was her middle name] Ch. [Churchward]. https://www.familysearch.org/ark:/61903/1:1:N2H7-MY2
12. Lithograph courtesy of the Stoke Gabriel Parish Church website https://stokegabrielchurch.co.uk/history/
13. "Parish Churchyard & Registers of Graves." Stoke Gabriel Parish Church website. https://stokegabrielchurch.co.uk/history/churchyard-grave-registers/ There are three graves with the family name of "Crocker," however.
14. BANKS2, p. 50. Also, Cyrus Eaton, who penned an 1865 Maine history of central Maine, claimed the Crockett family was "of the Scottish stock from the north of Ireland." (See, "The History of Thomaston, Rockland, South Thomaston, Maine," by Cyrus Eaton. Hallowell: Masters, Smith & Co., Printers, 1865.) It is entirely possible that, before relocating to Devon, our branch of Crocketts were members of the Crockett clan that originated in Strathclyde Briton (an area encompassing southern Scotland and northern England) and were "a mixture of Gaelic/Celts whose original territories ranged

The First Generation

Our Thomas was baptized at the Church of St. Mary and St. Gabriel (formerly a Roman Catholic church, but by then an Anglican church) either April 27, 1605 (according to online England baptismal records)[15] or January 13, 1610/1611 (according to Banks).[16] Thomas' brother John was baptized on December 25, 1610,[17] and so if the January 1610/11 christening date is correct for Thomas (as I suspect),[18] John and Thomas were twins (with baby Thomas less hardy than his brother and not able to be baptized on the same day). Indeed, a close connection between Thomas and John is suggested by several facts that occur later in their lives.[19]

According to "England Births and Christenings, 1538-1975,"[20] Thomas "Crechett" had the following children:

Elnore Crechett – baptized 23 December 1602
Thomas Crechett – baptized 27 April 1605
John Crechett – baptized 25 December 1610
Joan Crechett – baptized 29 April 1621
Clement Crechett – baptized 28 August 1625

---

from Lancashire in the south, northward to the south bank of the River Clyde in Scotland." From, Clan Douglas Society of North America, Crockett. http://clandouglassociety.org/crockett/#:~:text=The%20name%20Crockett%20descends%20from,King%20Edward%20I%20of%20England.

15. Thomas Crechett, son of Thomas Crechett, was christened 27 April 1605. "England Births and Christenings, 1538-1975". https://www.familysearch.org/ark:/61903/1:1:JMRG-RF7

16. BANKS2, p. 50. Banks physically saw the 13 January 1610/11 christening record for Thomas Crockett, son of Thomas and Anne in Stoke Gabriel. He notes in his "Topographical Dictionary of 2885 English Emigrants to New England, 1620-1650" (BANKSDICT, p. 29) that 175 men emigrated to New England from Devon between 1620-1650. Only two of the men listed by Banks hail from Stoke Gabriel (p. 27), Nathan Bedford, who settled in Scarborough, and Thomas Crockett.

17. Baptismal records for the family of Thomas and Ann (Churchwood) Crockett. https://freepages.rootsweb.com/~mainegenie/genealogy/CROCKETT.htm#THOMAS(2)CROCKETT

18. On April 22, 1654, Thomas Crockett "aged about 43 years" gave a deposition in the Gunnison-Shapleigh case (BAXTER, p. 108) in support of his friend Hugh Gunnison. This would support the 13 January 1610/11 baptism given by Banks. Other historians have offered different dates for the birth of Thomas Crockett. STACKPOLE says Thomas Crockett was born in either 1606 or 1610. Walter Hill Crockett of Burlington, Vt., who was a direct descendant of Thomas, in a synopsis written for Chapter IX: New England Crocketts, in "Notable Southern Families" (NOTABLE, p. 395) says Thomas was born in 1608. NEFAMILIES p. 1895 says he was born in 1608 and MIGRATION p. 497 gives his birth "by about 1615 based on service under Ambrose Gibbons."

19. John named his eldest son Thomas. Thomas Crichett, son of John Crichett, was christened at the church of St. Mary Major, Exeter, Devon, 2 August 1629. "England Births and Christenings, 1538-1975." https://www.familysearch.org/ark:/61903/1:1:NB7J-N2V In addition, John Crockett's second son, John, Jr., appears to have visited Maine in 1661, where he ended up in court on "a suspicion of felony." (See MPCR, Volume II, p. 371.) John Crichet, son of John Crichet, was christened at the church of St. Mary Major, Exeter, Devon, 13 November 1631. If this is the John Crockett, Jr. who visited Maine in 1661, he would have been thirty-years-old. "England Births and Christenings, 1538-1975." https://www.familysearch.org/ark:/61903/1:1:JWNW-58V Furthermore, two of Thomas Crockett's sons—Joseph and Joshua—had sons of their own named John, possibly after their uncle or their older cousin who came to visit. (It is also possible that the sons were named after their uncle John Andrews, Sr., husband of Thomas' sister Joane.)

20. "England Births and Christenings, 1538-1975." https://www.familysearch.org/search/record/results?f.collectionId=1473014&q.anyDate.from=1611&q.anyPlace=Stoke%20Gabriel&q.givenName=Thomas&q.surname=Crockett

Since mothers are not listed on these christening records, we cannot assume that all of Thomas Crockett, Sr.'s children were born to his wife Anne Churchwood. In fact, the eleven-year gap between the births of siblings John and Joan Crockett suggests a second marriage for Thomas' father. If so, having had different mothers would help explain the great difference in characters between the steadfast Thomas and his incorrigible younger sister Joan (Joane), who, by 1644 when she was twenty-three, had also immigrated to Maine and was living in Kittery, either with or near Thomas and his wife Ann.[21] One of my favorite stories about Thomas Crockett's bold-faced younger sister is when Joane, then wed to the stolid John Andrews twenty years her senior, was ferried up and down the Piscataqua River "about frivolous occasions" (according to the tight-laced Puritans who had recently taken over Maine) by the very married—and obviously infatuated—Gowen Wilson.[22]

The Stoke Gabriel Churchwards were of the "middling class,"[23] possessed of enough wealth to purchase a pew in the Stoke Gabriel Parish Church in the 18th century, with a brass plaque and memorial window directly behind it.[24] When Thomas was young, his father and other men from Stoke Gabriel were required to muster annually for military training with men from the surrounding parishes. Depending upon the village in which the muster was held, the men would walk five to twenty miles to train. Because of the distance between parishes, pack horses were utilized "to carry the armour and weaponry." In 1618, "Thomas Cretchet" was paid to transport the military gear to Chudleigh,[25] about eighteen miles from Stoke Gabriel. That Thomas' father was able to employ three horses to carry the heavy armor and weapons indicates that the Crocketts (or more likely the Churchwards) were well-off for commoners.

The Churchward family was proud of their position in the parish of Stoke Gabriel and did not hesitate to go to court to protect their reputation. In 1607, the Churchwards sued the local parish vicar for libel, after he refused to administer communion to them. (The vicar's refusal implied they were unworthy for some reason.) The Churchwards and the vicar were obstinate, and "the case dragged on

---

21. Information from a deposition given by Joane Andrews (her married name), February 25, 1660. MEWD, Vol. 2, p. 27.
22. Joane (Crockett) Andrews was "presented" (i.e. reprimanded) at court July 6, 1657 for dallying with Gowen Wilson (a married man), who ferried her up and down the Piscataqua River. Her stalwart husband John Andrews stood by Joane even then. MPCR, Vol. 2, p. 55-56..
23. "Early 17th Century Social History of Stoke Gabriel." Stoke Gabriel Parish Church website. https://stokegabrielchurch.co.uk/history/early-17th-century-social-history-stoke-gabriel/
24. Stoke Gabriel Parish Church website. https://www.britainexpress.com/counties/devon/churches/stoke-gabriel.htm
25. "Early 17th Century Social History of Stoke Gabriel." Stoke Gabriel Parish Church website. https://stokegabrielchurch.co.uk/history/early-17th-century-social-history-stoke-gabriel/

for years without an apparent outcome."[26] This pride in and defense of the family name were carried to New England by Thomas Crockett, who in 1660—in a case similar to the 1607 Churchward suits—sued Richard and Frances White for defamation of character in behalf of his wife Ann. On October 11, 1660, Thomas won his suit at the York County Court of Associates, and the Whites were forced to make financial restitution. Frances White was also ordered by the court to publicly acknowledge her offense (slander) against Ann Crockett, both in open court and at York County's annual Training Day. If Goody White failed to make these public acknowledgments, her husband would be liable for double the fine,[27] a sentence that certainly would have been applauded by the Churchwards back in Stoke Gabriel.

Stoke Gabriel and the Dartmouth/Devon Fishing Industry

Stoke Gabriel was a small parish when Thomas was born, having only about 60 heads of households.[28] For centuries, the village was the center of the River Dart salmon fishing industry.[29] By the 17th century, men from Stoke Gabriel were also employed in fishing the waters off Newfoundland, sailing out of Dartmouth harbor on ships owned by wealthy Devon investors and merchants. There were also jobs aplenty in support of the fishing industry for those who wanted to remain at home in Stoke Gabriel, including employment for rope- and net-makers, coopers, bakers, chandlers, and brewers. We do not know Thomas Crockett Sr.'s trade or employment, but given the irregular birth record of his children, he might have worked in the Newfoundland fishery, which from 1600-1620 depended heavily upon crews from Devon and Dorset. Despite the very real threat of losing a ship to Turkish

---

26. The vicar, in refusing to administer communion to the Churchwards, told the congregation "that there were but two or three malicious personns reddie to receave the same." Later, the Churchwards sued the vicar *and* his wife for libel. From "Early 17th Century Social History of Stoke Gabriel." Stoke Gabriel Parish Church website https://stokegabrielchurch.co.uk/history/early-17th-century-social-history-stoke-gabriel/
27. MPCR, Vol. 2, p. 367-368. Prior to this suit for libel, evidence was given at York County Court of "too much frequent familiarity between Joseph Davesse [Davis] & Ann Crockett" and an act of separation was passed on July 3, 1660 whereby a fine would be imposed if they were found alone together. (They never were.) Since Davis was occasionally employed by Thomas Crockett (who possibly was away when the act of separation was passed) it is not unreasonable that Ann and Joseph were on friendly terms. Apparently, Frances White, a shrew of a woman and often taken to court, likely called Ann Crockett a "whore" or Joseph Davis' mistress or something similar, and thus Thomas Crockett successfully sued her and her husband for defamation.
28. "Early 17th Century Social History of Stoke Gabriel." Stoke Gabriel Church website. https://stokegabrielchurch.co.uk/history/early-17th-century-social-history-stoke-gabriel/
29. "Stoke Gabriel and the Pirates of the Maghreb." Stoke Gabriel Church website. https://stokegabrielchurch.co.uk/history/stoke-gabriel-and-the-pirates-of-the-maghreb/

pirates, speculators and financiers sent hundreds of ships from England every year to the waters around Newfoundland:

> "By 1620, possibly as many as 300 English ships and vessels annually sailed to Newfoundland, with some West Country ports sending as many as 80 vessels. Many factors account for this growth: the end of the war with Spain in 1603, the elimination of the Spanish fishery at Newfoundland, bountiful fish stocks, and an availability of surplus capital."[30]

In addition, by the early 17th century colonization of the New World had become an obsession for England, as well as France and Spain. (In 1497, John Cabot, after landing in Newfoundland or Nova Scotia, had claimed North America for England.) In 1605, venture capitalists of England, not wanting France (or Spain, which had a permanent colony at San Augustin in Florida by 1565) to gain control of the New World (or beat England in finding a shortcut to the Orient) sent George Waymouth to explore the "northern coast of Virginia" (as New England was then known) and report back on "the commodities and profits of the countrey, together with the fitnesse of plantation [settlement]."[31] Waymouth had some experience in North America, having in 1602 unsuccessfully attempted to discover the fabled Northwest Passage to the riches of the Orient for the East India Company. (Waymouth's crew mutinied so he was forced to turn back.) On Easter day, Waymouth set sail with his crew from Dartmouth, Devon (about seven or eight miles from Stoke Gabriel) aboard the *Archangel*, accompanied by the chronicler Rosier, who recorded their exploration of midcoast Maine. On Friday May 17, 1605, Waymouth and his crew reached Monhegan Island, which they explored the following day. Rosier wrote glowingly of what he had seen:

> "This Iland is woody, grouen with Firre, Birch, Oke and Beech, as farre as we saw along the shore; and so likely to be within. On the verge grow Gooseberries, Strawberries, Wild pease, and Wild rose bushes. The water issued foorth downe the Rocky cliffe in many places: and much fowle of divers kinds breed upon the shore and rocks.

---
30. "The English Migratory Fishing and Trade in the 17th Century." *Heritage Newfoundland & Labrador* https://www.heritage.nf.ca/articles/exploration/17th-century-fishery.php
31. Website, American Journeys, "True Relation of Waymouth's Voyage, 1605," by James Rosier. https://www.americanjourneys.org/aj-041/summary/

"While we were at shore, our men aboord with a few hooks got above thirty great Cods and Hadocks, which gave us a taste of the great plenty of fish which we found afterward wheresoever we went upon the coast."[32]

Waymouth soon made contact with Native Americans. The explorer and his crew used trickery and force to kidnap five Abenaki[33] Indians and carry them back to England upon the *Archangel*. While unfortunate for the natives, the kidnapping played an important role in our story by securing the interest of the Englishman considered by many Maine historians to be the Father of New England colonization—Sir Ferdinando Gorges.

Sir Ferdinando Gorges and the Colonization of New England

Sir Ferdinando Gorges was one of the financial backers of Waymouth's trip. He was a well-connected military man then in command of the fort at the neighboring port of Plymouth in Devon. Upon Waymouth's return to England, the explorer made a courtesy call on Gorges, accompanied by the Native Americans he had kidnapped. Gorges was "overjoyed to see Waymouth—the knight had an almost 'childlike glee' about anything where the New World was concerned."[34] During the visit, Waymouth regaled a captivated Gorges with tales of the beauty "of the Maine" and the riches to be found there. When Waymouth departed, the explorer left Gorges with three of the five natives—Tahanedo, Amoret and Skicowaros—who, having made the best of a bad situation, had learned some English during the voyage. The three Abenakis lived with Gorges and his wife Ann and two sons, who reportedly treated them kindly. The Indians taught the knight some of their language, and over the winter Gorges pumped them for information about their home. Gorges wanted to know about their fellow tribesmen, the chiefs, the rivers and harbors, and the natural resources available in their homeland. The more he learned from the Native Americans, the more Gorges became convinced that

---
32. WAYMOUTH, p. 11 (electronic file). https://www.americanjourneys.org/AJ_PDF/AJ-041.pdf
33. The Abenaki were a group of tribes in western Maine and New Hampshire, part of the loosely-connected Wabanaki Confederacy.
34. "White Pine: American History and the Tree that Made a Nation," p. 19. Andrew Vietze. Guilford, Connecticut: Globe Pequot, 2018.

English "plantations" would thrive in the New World, and his grand vision of colonizing New England began to take shape.[35]

Despite his wealth and influence, Gorges could not realize his grand vision by himself. Sir John Popham, then Chief Justice of England, was instrumental in furthering Gorges' dream of colonizing New England.[36] Popham had received from Waymouth the other two captive Native Americans—Maneddo, and Saffacomoit—and his enthusiasm was nearly as great as Gorges' had been. The two men put their heads together, and, with the help of other wealthy investors, formed the Plymouth Company, which received a royal charter from King James I on April 10, 1606, "for the planting of colonies or plantations in North America."[37] Popham was the largest investor in the Plymouth Company, which in 1607 outfitted two large ships with enough men and supplies to plant a colony at the Sagadahock (at the mouth of the Kennebec River),[38] a site recommended by Waymouth. To his credit, Gorges sent Skicowaros and Amoret back to their people. (The sagamore Tahanedo, whom Gorges called "Dehamda," had been returned to Maine in 1606 with explorer Martin Pring.)[39]

The Popham Colony, the earliest English settlement (the second in New England after the 1604 French colony of St. Croix) was established at what is now Phippsburg, Maine in the summer of 1607. Although the Popham Colony folded in its second year, the colony's demise was not because it could not have survived. Rather, the colony was disbanded after two untimely Popham deaths: the death of its major backer, Sir John Popham, in England, and the passing of his nephew Captain George Popham, who had been elected as the first President of the Popham Colony. With only one death (Captain Popham's) known to have occurred in Maine, the settlement was much more sustainable than the failed French colony at St. Croix or the other English colony at Jamestown in Virginia. John Dyamont (Diamond)[40]

---

35. "Sir Ferdinando Gorges and His Impossible Dream of Maine." John Butman. Maine Boats: the website of the Coast. https://maineboats.com/print/issue-153/sir-ferdinando-gorges-and-his-impossible-dream-maine
36. Sir John Popham and Sir Ferdinando Gorges had a close relationship, ever since Gorges had once sprung Popham out of prison and taken him to safety. "White Pine: American History and the Tree that Made a Nation," p 24. Andrew Vietze. Guilford, Connecticut: Globe Pequot, 2018.
37. "White Pine: American History and the Tree that Made a Nation," p. 25. The Virginia Company, which settled Jamestown in 1607, was chartered at the same time as the Popham Colony. Both companies were initially chartered under the heading of "Virginia," with the Plymouth Company representing Northern Virginia, which later became New England.
38. The English translation of "Sagadahoc" from the Wabanaki is "Land at the mouth" or "mouth of the river" (in this case, the Kennebec River). "Dictionary of American-Indian Place and Proper Names in New England." Robert Alexander Douglas-Lithgow. Boston: Harvard University Press, 1909. P. 51.
39. "True Relation of Waymouth's Voyage, 1605." James Rosier. See editor Burrage's footnote at the bottom of p. 394. https://content.wisconsinhistory.org/digital/collection/aj/id/2478
40. A John Dyamont of Devon was in Kittery by 1651; however, we do not know whether he was a descendant (or related

of Stoke Gabriel was one of the select crew chosen for the Popham expedition. It is quite possible that Thomas Crockett grew up listening to Dyamont's tales (or stories told about him) of Native Americans and their ways; of the Popham Colony in New England; and of the riches of fish, fur, land, and timber; and of adventures beyond a youth's wildest dreams.

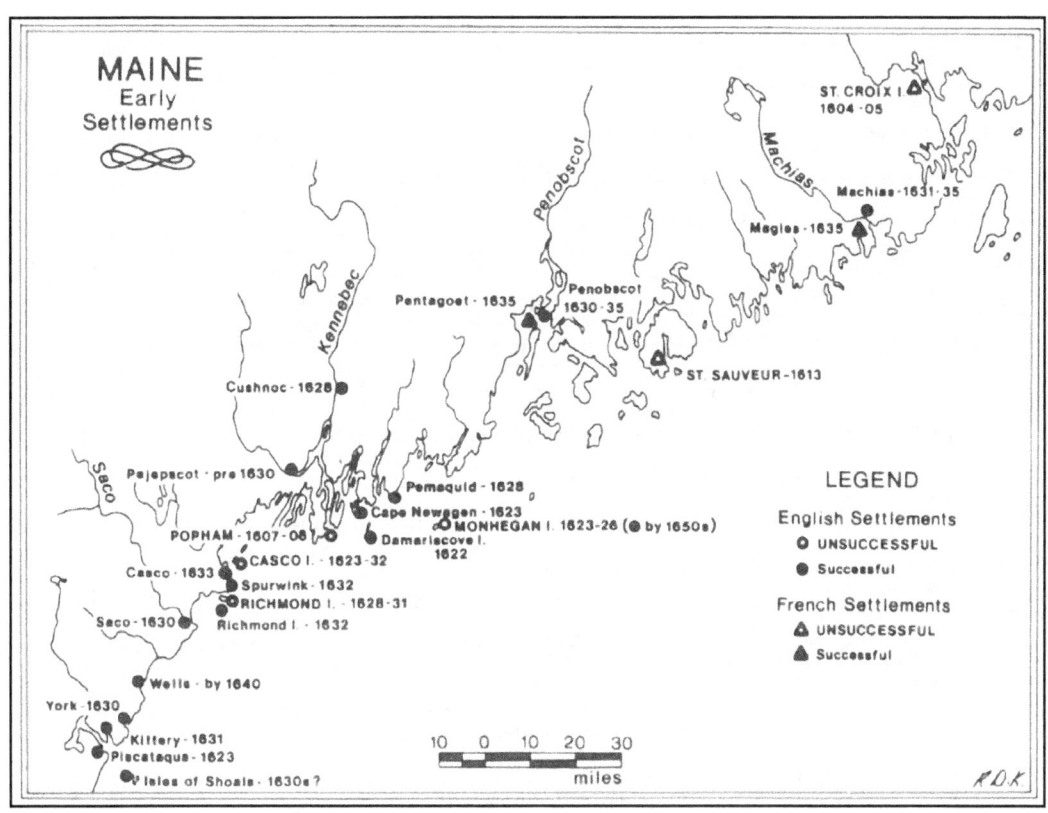

17th Century Settlements in Maine
(Map courtesy of the Maine Historical Society.)[41]

While Sir Ferdinando Gorges was somewhat discouraged by the failure of the Popham Colony, he did not give up on his dream to colonize New England. In 1620, the Council for New England was created, receiving a royal charter from James I "for the planting, ruling, ordering, and governing New England in America."[42]

---

to) the John Dyamont of Stoke Gabriel who was a member of the Popham Colony. See LIBBY/NOYES, p. 195. 3. John Diamond.
41. Kelly Jr, Richard D. *MAINE Early Settlements*. In: *The Maine bicentennial atlas: an historical survey*. Morris, Gerald E. editor. Portland, Me: Maine Historical Society, 1972, plate 5.
42. *"Maine: Early Wills and Deeds, 1640-1760" (MEWD)*. CD-ROM. Boston, Massachusetts: New England Historic

The Council of New England made several important grants (some overlapping and vague) germane to our story. In 1622, Gorges and Captain John Mason,[43] an energetic explorer and cartographer who, like Gorges, would play an important role in the life of Thomas Crockett, received a patent from the Council for all the territory situated between the Merrimac and Kennebec rivers.[44] The language in the 1622 patent to Gorges and Mason was the first official designation of the "Province of Maine" in any document,[45] and harkens back to recorder Rosier's description of the beauties of "the Maine."

In 1629, Gorges and Mason split their grant, with Mason, who was given all the land between the Merrimac and Piscataqua rivers, calling his new territory New Hampshire after his homeland in Hampshire, England. Gorges retained the land in Maine situated between the Piscataqua and Kennebec rivers,[46] and named his territory "New Somersetshire." In New Somersetshire, Gorges was "specially interested in the colony at York, first called Gorgeana, which was chartered as a city."[47] Also, on November 17, 1629, Gorges and Mason received the Laconia patent, another grant of nebulous boundaries, including "… all that land that bordering on the river and lake of the Iroquois."[48]

Mason believed that a fortune could be made trading furs with the Iroquois Indians. In addition, both Gorges and Mason were intrigued by the idea of discovering the elusive Northwest Passage, the mythical shortcut to Cathay (China), where the riches of silks and spices abounded. Mason, through some bad information

---

Genealogical Society, 2006. (Online database. *AmericanAncestors.org*. New England Historic Genealogical Society, 2009.) Vol. 1, p. 20.
43. John Mason was the second Proprietary Governor of the 1615 Cuper's Cove colony in Newfoundland and mapped that island. (See, Mason, John [M602J]. "A Cambridge Alumni Database." University of Cambridge.) He was seen by Gorges as a man who could get things done. Mason was "a man of great energy, whose readiness to embark on such undertakings had greatly strengthened [Gorges'] own hopes and aims." BURRAGE, p. 167.
44. BURRAGE, pps. 166-167.
45. BURRAGE, p. 167. The description of the land granted to Gorges and Mason reads: "… all that part of the mainland in New England lying upon the sea coast betwixt the rivers of Merrimack and Sagadahock [Kennebec] and to the furtherest heads of the said rivers and so forward up into the new land westward until three score {60} miles be finished from the first entrance of the aforesaid rivers and half way over, that is to say to the midst of the said two rivers…said portions of land with the appurtenances the said Sir Ferdinando Gorges and Captain John Mason, with the consent of the president and council, intend to name the Province of Maine."
46. STACKPOLE, p. 11.
47. STACKPOLE, p. 16-17.
48. The Laconia patent was for "… all that land bordering on the river and lake of the Iroquois for a depth of ten miles to the south and east, westward to the next great lake, and north to the main river running from the Great Lakes into the River of Canada. It was intended that this grant should convey a tract of land lying in back of the Maine grant of 1622. The Lake of the Iroquois was probably Lake Champlain, but this grant was never even located." "The Mason Title and Its Relations to New Hampshire and Massachusetts." Otis Grant Hammon. AmericanAntiquarian.org https://www.americanantiquarian.org/proceedings/44806616.pdf

he had received, believed that the Piscataqua River led to the Lake of the Iroquois (Lake Champlain, the western shore of which the Iroquois inhabited), and from there to the Orient.[49] The two men enticed other wealthy investors to join them in the Laconia Company, and plans were soon made—plans in which Thomas Crockett would participate—to plunder the wealth of New England while also discovering the shortcut to the Orient.

The Stoke Gabriel Clock Tower and Yew Tree

The old clocktower at the Church of St. Mary and St. Gabriel, where Thomas Crockett was baptized, was a notable landmark during his boyhood; however, it was not the only striking feature of Stoke Gabriel. An ancient yew tree,[50] centuries older than the Medieval church at which Thomas was baptized,[51] stood as a companion to the clock tower. The yew tree today is at least a thousand years old, one of the older trees in Britain.[52] When Thomas was born, the yew tree was already at least 600-years-old! Perhaps as a boy he made a wish, like many others according to local legend. The wish would come true if the person who made it could walk backward round the yew tree seven times without stumbling, repeating the verse:

> "Walk ye backward round about me
> 7 times round for all to see
> Stumble not and then for certain
> One true wish will come to thee."[53]

---

49. "How New Hampshire Was Settled by Mistake." SeacoastNH.com. http://www.seacoastnh.com/History/As-I-Please/how-nh-was-settled-by-mistake/?showall=1 Like many explorers before and after him, Captain Mason was doomed to failure in his quest to locate the Northwest Passage. (See Maine author Kenneth Roberts' riveting historical novel, "Northwest Passage" for other such failures.)
50. *Taxus baccata*. A yew tree is a conifer similar to a spruce.
51. "The Yew Tree." Stoke Gabriel Parish Church website. https://stokegabrielchurch.co.uk/history/the-yew-tree/
52. "The Yew Tree." Stoke Gabriel Parish Church website.
53. "Stoke Gabriel: St. Mary and St. Gabriel Church." Britain Express website. https://www.britainexpress.com/counties/devon/churches/stoke-gabriel.htm

Ancient yew tree and clock tower at the Church of St. Mary and St. Gabriel in Stoke Gabriel, keeping watch over the church's cemetery.
(Photo by Edward Lovesey, Stoke Gabriel.)[54]

If Thomas Crockett walked backward round the yew tree wishing to visit the New World someday—perhaps inspired by Popham settler John Dyamont's adventures in New England—his wish was granted in 1630 when the Laconia Company was looking for crew. At age 19, Thomas Crockett signed on with the Laconia Company to support the company's mission in New England.

Thomas Crockett Sails to the New World

In 1630, Thomas Crockett was hired as a "servant" of Captain John Mason, who with Sir Ferdinando Gorges and several other investors, outfitted the crew of the Laconia Company. The mission of the Laconia Company was to explore for the Lake of the Iroquois, that much-heralded (but erroneous) shortcut to the Orient via the waterways of North America. Most of the "adventurers" (as they were self-styled) in the Laconia Company were rather stingy men, who hoped to gain great wealth via a minimum of capital investment. These investors believed that New England's natural recourses—fish, furs, iron ore, timber, and sassafras—would net them in England some return on their investment, even if the Northwest Passage

---

54. Mr. Lovesey, the photographer, has since passed away; however, his widow graciously gave me permission to use this lovely photograph of the yew tree and clocktower and cemetery at the Church of St. Mary and St. Gabriel.

did not pan out. Gorges and Mason proved to be more open-handed than their fellow adventurers regarding funding, not coincidentally because they had other land grants from the Council for New England. Both Gorges and Mason planned to establish colonies in New England, in addition to extracting natural resources and searching for the Lake of the Iroquois.

The first ship to sail under a commission from the Laconia Company was the *Warwick*, which set sail March 28, 1630 from The Downs (where the North Sea and the English Channel meet in Deal, county Kent) with men and supplies from London. The ship docked briefly at Plymouth on April 8th to pick up Ambrose Gibbons,[55] a steward for the company, who would become Thomas Crockett's boss for the next four years. According to Wilbur Spencer, author of "Pioneers on Maine Rivers," Crockett was one of the crew of Laconia Company who came over on the *Warwick*.[56] Since Plymouth is only 25-30 miles cross-country from Stoke Gabriel, it seems plausible that Thomas Crockett boarded the ship in Plymouth with Gibbons. (Crockett could have walked cross-country or he could have caught a ride with a fishing vessel.) There might even have been some connection between Ambrose Gibbons and the family of Thomas Crockett.[57]

Aboard the *Warwick* was a military captain, Walter Neal, who had been selected by the Laconia Company at the last moment to be the first governor of their patent.[58] The company's original choice was Edward Godfrey, a future neighbor of Thomas Crockett's. By 1629, Godfrey held a high position with the Laconia Company and, although passed over for the governorship, he still came over on the *Warwick* to take charge of the fishing part of the venture.[59]

---

55. PIONEERS, p. 57.
56. PIONEERS, p. 58. Other historians have suggested that Thomas Crockett shipped aboard the *Pied Cow* in 1631 and still others believe he came even later. Since the complete crew lists for the Laconia Company vessels are not extant, historians—including this one—have had to make educated guesses as to which man shipped when (except for notable persons for whom other documentary evidence exists, such as Gibbons, who wrote a letter to Thomas Eyre, a Laconia Company adventurer, from Plymouth on April 8, 1630, the day he sailed. See Laconia Company Correspondence. BELKNAP, Appendix, p. 422). On Aug. 26, 1676, however, Thomas Crockett (and other early Pascataqua arrivals) gave depositions in the Mason case. At that time, Thomas Crocket was "aged about 70 years living in ye Countrey about 46 years." (NH Provincial Papers, xvii, p. 521-523.) This deposition appears to confirm the fact that Thomas Crockett came over with Neal and Gibbons in 1630.
57. In his pay accounts of April 23, 1634, Ambrose Gibbons unwittingly confuses Thomas' last name, denoting him as "Crockwood"—a conflation of his parents' surnames, Crockett and "Churchwood." This slip suggests that Gibbons was familiar with the Churchward family, who perhaps procured for Thomas his position with the Laconia Company.
58. "The Ancestry of Joseph Waterhouse, 1754-1837, of Standish Maine," p. 108. Walter Goodwin Davis. Portland, Maine: Anthoesen Press, 1949. Thomas Crockett's future neighbor Edward Godfrey was ready to sail with the first crew from London in the spring of 1630 "… coming over as governor, bringing the patent and authorized to take livery of seisin [physical possession of the grant] in the Co.'s behalf … but before the – Warwick – sailed, they appointed Capt. Neale gov. instead." It appears that the powers that be in the Laconia Company felt that a military man was better suited to search for the Lake of the Iroquois than Godfrey, who was a Londoner and a travelling merchant. LIBBY/NOYES, p. 267. Edward Godfrey.
59. PIONEERS, p. 126.

Puritans vs. Anglicans – Shifting Tides of Power in England and New England

The Laconia Company was also aware of the preparation of the Winthrop Fleet, a well-planned and liberally-funded mass migration of Puritans to New England organized by John Winthrop. Seven hundred Puritans emigrated to Massachusetts in 1630, with twenty thousand more to follow over the next decade in what came to be known as the Great Migration. The first three ships of the Winthrop Fleet sailed for the New World from Yarmouth, the Isle of Wight, on the same day—April 8, 1630[60]—as the *Warwick* sailed from Plymouth Harbor after picking up Ambrose Gibbons (and perhaps Thomas Crockett). The course of these two ships—with very different missions yet on parallel tracks to the New World—offers a compelling image of the competing forces in the life of Thomas Crockett and his future friends and neighbors in Maine.

Sir Ferdinando Gorges, Captain John Mason, and the men of the Laconia Company were Royalists who supported the Anglican Church, the church of the English monarchy. By contrast, Winthrop and his fleet were Puritans, who supported the overthrow of the monarchy and the establishment of a Puritan church and Parliment. Thomas Crockett, an Anglican by birth (as were most of the early settlers of Maine and New Hampshire), attempted to fashion a life in the New World within shifting tides of power, from Royalist to Puritan, then back to Royalist again, ending with the Puritans in control of Maine. These shifting tides mirrored in the New World the power struggle that occurred in the Old World during the English Civil War (1642-1651), and the decades immediately following.

The difference between the common Englishmen who settled Maine and New Hampshire, and the Puritans of Massachusetts, could not have been starker. The two groups—hard scrabble fishermen, farmers, and fur traders on the one-hand and well-heeled Puritans on the other—were motivated by different aspirations. The Puritans wanted to organize their lives (and the lives of everyone else in their realm) around their own religious beliefs, while most Mainers were actuated by the desire to own land. Charles Edward Banks, in his "History of York, Maine," describes this contrast:

---

60. "The Winthrop Fleet in 1630." The Macy-Colby House website. https://www.macycolbyhouse.org/Winthrop-Fleet/#:~:text=The%20first%20ship%20arrived%20in,to%20Boston%20and%20other%20settlements.

"Possession of the soil in fee simple, or freehold, was one of the principal incentives of emigration to Maine. The religious factor was negligible, as most of the emigrants were adherents of the Church of England, conforming to its doctrine and ritual, and they had never been troubled by the ecclesiastical authorities. It was not so with a majority of the emigrants to Massachusetts who were influenced by the religious unrest of the period, and led by the Puritan clergy believed themselves 'persecuted' and driven overseas to escape the 'cruel Archbishop Laud,'[61] as they were pleased to characterize this church dignitary."[62]

Like many early arrivals to Maine, Thomas Crockett bought, sold, and was granted real estate. His primary motivation during his life—in addition to protecting and supporting his family—appears to have been to own land outright, known as fee simple ownership. In England, real estate was reserved for the class of landed gentry, not the common man. The New World, however, offered an opportunity to gain something that could not be had in the Old.

Thomas Crockett's decision to join the crew of the Laconia Company and sail to America turned out to be highly advantageous. Thanks to his early arrival in New England, his steady hand on the tiller throughout his life, and the long-time relationships he formed in New England, Thomas Crockett eventually ended up owning more than 228 acres of Ferdinando Gorges' land in Maine.[63]

On the Ground at Pascataqua

The *Warwick* sailed to what was known as "Pascataqua" or "Pascataquack" in the common vernacular,[64] a general designation for the area of land on both sides of the Piscataqua River, which now serves as a boundary between Maine and New Hampshire. The Laconia Company crew arrived safely at Pascataqua on May 31,

---

61. William Laud, a bishop of the Church of England and later Archbishop of Canterbury under Charles I, was a foe of the Puritans and was known to use the Star Chamber (a secret English court) to try and condemn them. Yorke, Philip Chesney (1911). *Laud, William*. In Chisholm, Hugh (ed.). "Encyclopaedia Britannica" Vol. 16 (11th ed.). Cambridge University Press, pp. 276-278.
62. BANKS, p. 131.
63. The 228 acres represents the 40 acres Thomas Crockett was granted by the town of York in 1653 plus the 188-acre tract in Kittery, a grant from Thomas Gorges on behalf of his cousin Sir Ferdinando Gorges. In addition, Thomas Crockett bought and sold other real estate during his lifetime and likely received at least one other grant, in Brave Boat Harbor.
64. Many documents and early depositions indicate that "Pascataqua" or "Pascataquack" was the name by which the early arrivals denoted the general area around the Piscataqua River where they settled and where ships landed.

1630,[65] landing at Little Harbor (now Rye, N.H.)[66]—a small harbor to the south of what is now Portsmouth Harbor. Little Harbor became the first stop for early sailing ships bound for the Pascataqua region. From there, individuals and groups relocated via water to New Hampshire settlements upriver or along the southern Maine coast. The Winthrop Fleet was an exception, sailing further south to land at Salem, Massachusetts on June 13, 1630. The Puritans proceeded to spread out from Salem to Boston and surrounding towns, where Winthrop established his power center.[67] (The Pilgrims, also a Puritan sect but not part of Winthrop's faction, had settled at Plymouth in 1620.)

Captain Neal set up his headquarters at David Thomson's former fishing site at Pannaway Manor at Little Harbor.[68] (Later, some of the men would move up to Sanders' Point,[69] the outer edge of the settlement that would morph into Strawbery Banke, reportedly named for the wild strawberries that grew on banks of the Piscataquis River.) No portrait exists of Captain Neal, the colony's first governor, who was a professional soldier.[70] J. Dennis Robinson in his article, "How New Hampshire Was Settled by Mistake," gives a general description of Neal:

> "Neal likely dressed and acted the part of an ex-Tudor soldier. Sporting a bushy beard, ruffled collar, armor breastplate, sword and helmet, he was likely a figure of authority in the earliest days when Strawbery Banke was little more than a single large house and a few huts along the river surrounded by dense and dangerous wilderness."[71]

---

65. PIONEERS, p. 57.
66. STACKPOLE, p. 19.
67. "The Winthrop Fleet in 1630." The Macy-Colby House website.
68. David Thomson first settled Pannaway Manor at Little Harbor in 1623, but moved to Boston by about 1630. SeacoastNH.com. "How New Hampshire Was Settled By Mistake," by J. Dennis Robinson. http://www.seacoastnh.com/how-nh-was-settled-by-mistake/?start=1 STACKPOLE says Thomson's grant to the land was an infringement on Gorges and Mason's grant, which preceded that to Thomson and his three partners by two months, and was possibly the reason Thomson moved on, leaving his crude home and fishing operation at Little Harbor for Captain Neal and company. STACKPOLE, p. 18-19. Thomson was a gentleman from Plymouth in county Devon, who, along with three other Plymouth merchants (Abraham Colmer, Nicholas Sherwill, and Lenoard Pomery, all of whom stayed in England) set up a fishing operation on the New Hampshire coast. The location of their 6,000-acre grant is not specifically denoted in David Thomson's Indenture, a copy of which was published in 1905 by *The New England Genealogical Register* (NEREGISTER) Vol. 2, No. 1, July 1904-April 1905. Dover, N.H.: Charles W. Tibbetts, Editor and Publisher, 1905. https://scholars.unh.edu/cgi/viewcontent.cgi?article=1001&context=genealogical_record
69. "Sanders' Point is one of the oldest names in New Hampshire. It was given to the promontory which lies between Little Harbor and Sagamore Creek and now forms the southerly approach for the bridge to Great Island." PIONEERS, p. 39-40.
70. MIGRATION, Walter Neale, p. 1324-1326.
71. SeacoastNH.com. "How New Hampshire Was Settled By Mistake," by J. Dennis Robinson.

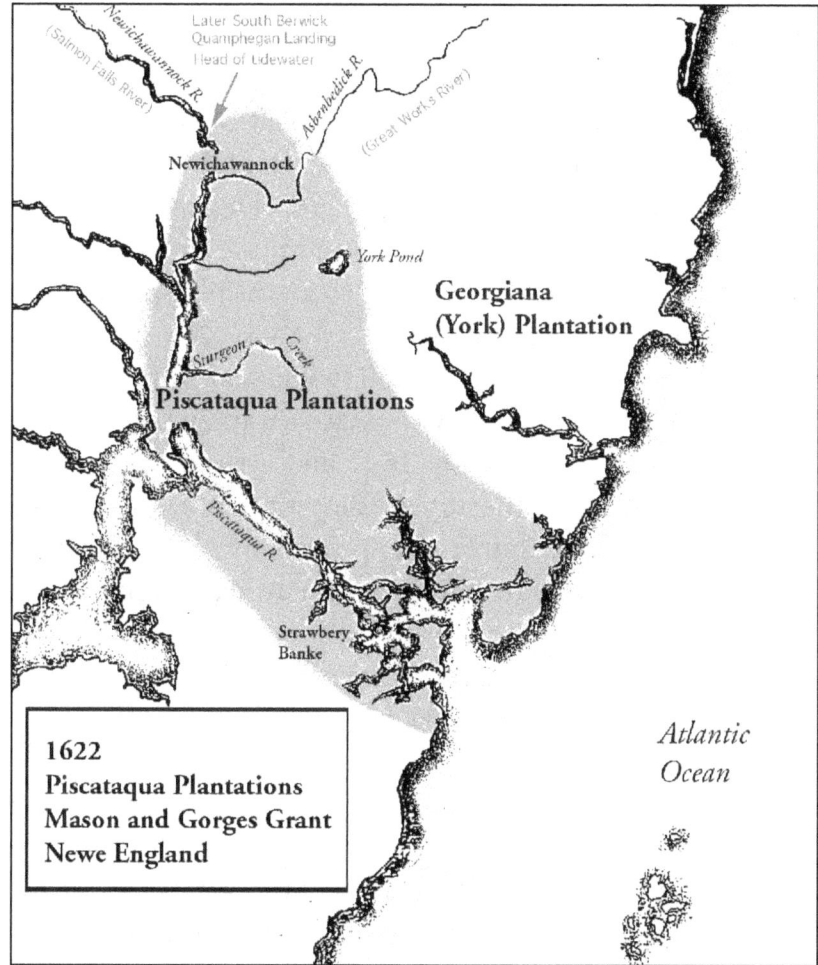

Early map of Piscataqua (Pascataqua) Plantations and Sir Ferdinando Gorges' later plantation, known as Georgiana (Gorgeana). (Map courtesy of Old Berwick Historical Society.)[72]

Captain Neal's mission was to discover the Lake of the Iroquois, which he soon set out for not long after landing. Neal took with him on his mission some of the crewmembers, former soldiers like himself. Those who did not go with Neal (including Thomas Crockett) spent the summer and fall preparing for the upcoming New England winter. Ambrose Gibbons was tasked with setting up a trading post with the Native Americans. On July 21, 1630, Gibbons, the steward, wrote to Laconia Company investor Thomas Eyre, complaining "for want of the trade

---

72. Old Berwick Historical Society website. https://www.oldberwick.org/history-articles/places-landmarks/deepwater-anchorages-near-the-head-of-tide-salmon-falls-river-1600s-and-1700s.html

goods." Eyre replied in a letter dated from London May 1631 that "… if you send us returnes, doubt you not but that you shall be supplied from time to time unto your owne contents."[73] One can see from this (and from other letters between Gibbons and Laconia Company investors, including Mason and Gorges), that for those safely in London the company's efforts in New England were little more than a romantic adventure. For Ambrose Gibbons and the Laconia Company crew on the ground at Pascataqua, however, the experience was physically and emotionally demanding, almost a matter of life and death.

The ship the *Pied Cow* returned the following year with new recruits[74] and more supplies for the Laconia Company crew at Pascataqua. The small ship sailed from Portsmouth, England on March 6, 1631 and arrived at Pascataqua on June 25th.[75] The vessel was described in Boston at Winthrop's Massachusetts Bay Colony as a "small English ship[76] come thither with provisions, three (3) wives, and some Frenchmen to make salt."[77] One of the wives aboard was Gibbons' wife Rebecca. That fall, the London investors also sent the *Warwick* back to Pascataqua to pick up goods received in trade from Native Americans (beaver and other animal pelts) and from English settlers (wooden staves) and to drop off supplies.[78]

Gibbons awaited the return of the *Warwick* and fresh supplies. After restocking his inventory, the steward, accompanied by his wife and daughter (named Rebecca after her mother), as well as Thomas Crockett and seven other men, used an incoming tide to sail a smaller vessel up the Piscataqua River watershed. At Newichawannock (see Piscataqua Plantations map on page 19), the little group "planted" a new trading settlement with the Indians.[79]

Trading with the Indians at Newichawannock House

Ambrose Gibbons selected a likely site upon the Newichawannock River, a tributary of the Piscataqua, upon which to build the Laconia Company's new trading center. The site, which the English crew called Newichawannock House, was the

---

73. "No. 2. An original letter from Thomas Eyre, one of the adventurers or company of Laconia, to Mr. Gibbins [sic], their factor." BELKNAP, Appendix, p. 422.
74. Several historians believe that Thomas Crockett shipped aboard the *Pied Cow* in 1631.
75. PIONEERS, p. 58.
76. While the *Pied Cow* sailed from England, it was a Danish ship.
77. CANDAGE, p. 1.
78. PIONEERS, p. 59.
79. PIONEERS, p. 85-86.

home base of the Newichawannock Indians, who (like many other Native American tribes) took their name from the river with which they most associated.[80]

Maine historian Wilbur Spencer believed Newichawannock House "stood upon the point of land that lies opposite the mouth of the Great Works River, in the Town of Rollinsford, New Hampshire."[81] Archaeology digs in Spencer's day uncovered evidence that Newichawannock House appeared to have been situated in Rollinsford. Spencer notes in "Pioneers on Maine's Rivers," that "In the theory of Indian nomenclature the former [Newichawannock] embraced both sides of the northerly branch of the Piscataqua, because it was applied by the natives to the streams instead of the contiguous region. The name means 'My wigwam place.'"[82]

Newichawannock House was much more suitable for trade than at the head of the Piscataqua River, since it was not only frequented by the Newichawannocks, but also by other bands of Abenakis that populated what is now eastern Maine and New Hampshire. ("Abenaki" and "Wabanaki" are often used interchangeably; however, the Abenaki were a family of tribes within the loosely-knit Wabanaki Confederacy. See map on page 22.)

Wabanaki Indians of the various tribes spoke related dialects of the eastern Algonkian language family. Pre-contact with Europeans, there were about 25,000 Native Americans living in what is now the state of Maine. "They were hunters, fishers, and gatherers who moved seasonally along the coast and across the interior waterways in birchbark canoes during open water season."[83] It is impossible to know, however, how many Native Americans resided in Maine and New Hampshire when Thomas Crockett arrived at Newichawannock, due to severe population decline from European diseases, including diphtheria, smallpox, and influenza, to which illnesses the natives had no natural immunity.

---

80. The fact that Native Americans shared their tribal names with water bodies (particularly rivers) is widely assumed and has been for centuries; however, I do wonder if the early English (and French) explorers and colonizers might not out of convenience endowed the tribes with names utilizing this simple nomenclature. Since the indigenous people did not have a written history, we will likely never know for sure.
81. PIONEERS, p. 86. Old Berwick Historical Society says on its website the location of Newichawannock House was either South Berwick, Maine, or Rollinsford, N.H.
82. PIONEERS, p. 86. I have seen other translations of Newichawannock, including the likely "river with many falls."
83. "Maine Native American Pre-European History (or Maine Pre-History)." Maine Historic Preservation Commission website, State of Maine. "Prehistoric Archaeology." https://www.maine.gov/mhpc/programs/education/prehistoric-archaeology#:~:text=About%2025%2C000%20Native%20American%20made%20their%20living,and%20may%20have%20visited%20the%20coast%20periodically.

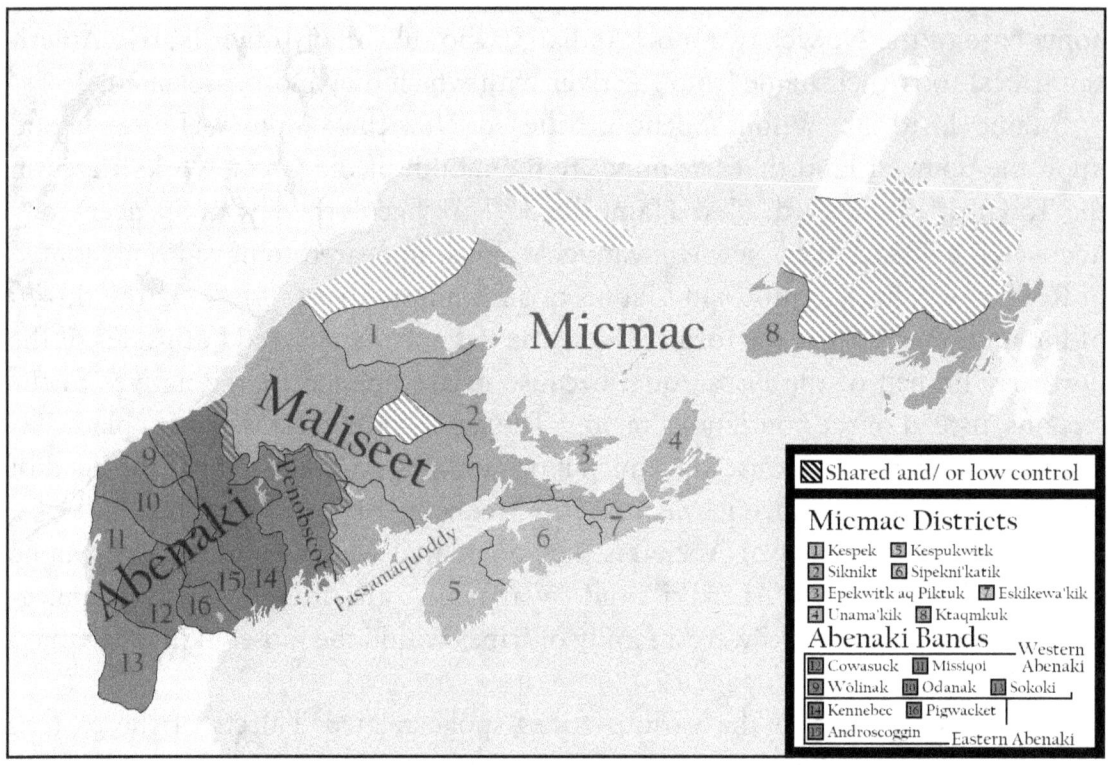

The Loosely-Knit Tribes of the Wabanaki Confederacy.
Abenaki bands are in darker ink to the left, followed by the Penobscot, Passamaquoddy, Maliseet, and Micmac tribes in eastern Maine and Canada. Eastern Abenaki bands are: 14. Kennebecs, 15. Androscoggins, and 16. Pigwackets. Western Abenaki bands are: 9. Wolinaks, 10. Odanaks, 11. Missiquois, 12. Cowasucks, and 13. Sokokis.
(Image by Grug-Jack from Wikipedia, in the public domain.)

Historian Spencer gives us a description of Newichawannock House, where Gibbons and his family, Thomas Crockett, and at least three other men resided for nearly three years:

> "The main buildings [at Newichawannock] consisted of a large mansion and storehouse, fenced with a strong palisade and fortified with six guns, described in an inventory as two robenets,[84] two murderers[85] and two chambers. Gibbons reported that he had dug a well within the palisade and proposed to enclose it with timber. His men were engaged 'to pale [fence] in ground for corne and garden.' "[86]

---

84. A robinet was a piece of military equipment used for throwing darts or stones.
85. A murderer was a breech-loading swivel gun that used gunpowder and projectiles, with one or more chambers. In this case, the weapon had two chambers.
86. PIONEERS, p. 89.

The weapons mentioned in the inventory were necessary because at times dozens of Native Americans descended upon Newichawannock, setting up temporary wigwams, to fish, plant corn, and trade with Gibbons and his crew. When in 1633 the Laconia Company wanted to downsize employees, Gibbons warned that while he could maintain the trading post with fewer assistants, he could not do so safely: "You may perhaps think that fewer men would serve me but I have sometimes on C [one hundred] or more Indians and [am] far from neybors."[87]

According to the Old Berwick Historical Society, Newichawannock[88] House did a "brisk trade with the Indians of the Piscataqua River region, exchanging items such as liquor, blankets, hatchets, kettles, coats, shirts, and shoes for beaver pelts and furs and moose, bear, and otter skins."[89] One can imagine how the colorful sight of a dozen or more wigwams with a hundred Native Americans cooking, keeping an eye on rambunctious children, netting fish, and milling around Newichawannock House affected the young Thomas Crockett. Although only a general laborer (Crockett likely helped build the great house and palisade), he might also have mingled some with the natives. In a letter sent to the Laconia Company investors June 24, 1633, Ambrose Gibbons reported the weight and types of furs he received from the Indians and turned over to the company's agent: "I have delivered unto Mr. John Raymon 76lb and 4 ounses of beaver, 10 otters, 6 musquashes and on[e] martin more…"[90] If Thomas, while walking backward round the yew tree in Stoke Gabriel, had wished for an exciting adventure in the New World, he was likely not disappointed at Newichawannock House!

After hearing of the impressive volume of fish at Newichawannock, the Laconia

---

87. Letter from Ambrose Gibbons to John Mason, Newichwanicke, July 13, 1633. "No. 5. Copy of another [letter] from Gibbins to the [Laconia] company." BELKNAP, Appendix, p. 425. The nearest English neighbor to be found was at Dover (then called Bristol), more than ten miles away by boat over two water courses.
88. The Old Berwick Historical Society says that the name "Newichawannock" was used in several ways by the natives: "'Newichawannock' was the Indian name of the river flowing through Milton Three Ponds (New Hampshire) to the sea -- we call it the Salmon Falls River. One translation of the name is 'river with many falls.' The river does indeed have numerous waterfalls all along its length. The waterfalls at Quamphegan and at the Salmon Falls, and undoubtedly, at Great Falls, further north, were significant, for native people from all over the region came to this area to catch salmon and other fish that migrated up the river in the spring, the visitors setting up temporary wigwams across the river in the fields of Rollinsford." From, "South Berwick's First People." Old Berwick Historical Society website. https://www.oldberwick.org/history-articles/people/17th-century/south-berwicks-first-people.html
89. "Berwick Begins:1631-1713." Old Berwick Historical Society website. The trading house was set up at an excellent site, according to the website, being a place where Native Americans had gathered for thousands of years in the spring to fish the "salmon, shad, alewives, and eels that made their annual migratory runs up Maine's coastal rivers. By the time English explorers such as Martin Pring (1602) and John Smith (1614) sailed along the coast of southern Maine, the Indians of Newichawannock and Quamphegan had established planting grounds of corn and beans along the Salmon Falls River."
90. "No. 4. Copy of a letter from Ambrose Gibbins to the company." From Newichwanicke, this 24th of June, 1633. BELKNAP, Appendix, p. 424.

company investors sent over a vessel to secure a share for themselves. But the ship arrived too late in the season, and the fish that had swum upriver to spawn had already returned to the ocean.[91] Gibbons was unimpressed by the captain and crew, pointing out in a letter to John Mason with no little disdain that they were all Londoners:[92]

> "A Londoner is not for fishing, neither is there any amity betwixt the West countrimen and them. Bristo or Barnstable is very convenient for your fishing shipes. It is not enough to fit our shipes to fish but they must be sure (God will) to be at their fishing place the beginning of February and not to come to the land when other men have half their viage."[93]

Thomas Crockett would have been one of the "West countrimen" who had little use for the London newcomers. Having grown up on the River Dart in Devon amid a thriving salmon fishery, Thomas would have understood the ludicrousness of sending a fishing vessel too late to catch fish.

But life at Newichawannock was not all fun and adventure. As time went by and supplies dwindled, Gibbons rationed the meat and drink, not sparing himself or his family. Clothing became scarce and the crew had to make do—or do without. Gibbons' letters to company headquarters back in London requesting appropriate supplies fell mostly on deaf ears. Except for Mason and Gorges, most of the Laconia Company investors were armchair adventurers, expecting returns on their money without the proper investment. Only Mason and Gorges, with grand visions of establishing permanent colonies in New England (Mason in New Hampshire and Gorges in Maine), were willing to invest larger amounts of capital.

On December 5, 1632, the Laconia Company investors as a group wrote back to Gibbons, which missive he did not receive until six months later, on June 7, 1633. The adventurers told Gibbons they had directed Captain Neal (who had returned from a fruitless search for the River of the Iroquois) to dismiss the household.

---

91. "Unlike Pacific salmon, which always die after spawning, Atlantic salmon often survive spawning and may migrate back out to sea with the chance of returning to spawn again." "The King of Fish." U.S. Fish and Wildlife Service website. https://www.fws.gov/story/life-cycle-atlantic-salmon#:~:text=Unlike%20Pacific%20salmon%2C%20which%20always,produce%20larger%20eggs%20with%20a

92. Captain John Mason resided in London, where it was easier for him to recruit sailors and dock workers than to secure fishermen. Mason's poor choice of crew in 1632 suggests that Ferdinando Gorges of Plymouth in Devon (or his agent, perhaps Gibbons) had more of a hand in selecting the earlier 1630 and 1631 crews, which included Thomas Crockett.

93. Letter from Ambrose Gibbons to John Mason, Newichawannock, July 13, 1633. "No. 5. Copy of another from Gibbins to the company." BELKNAP, Appendix, p. 425.

The First Generation

Only men who were able to live by themselves were to be allowed to stay on. In addition, Neal (perhaps because of his failure) was being called back to England. To placate and retain Gibbons, however, the steward was told he could settle at Sanders' Point.[94] "Wee doe take notice of your care and paines in our plantation," the investors[95] wrote, "and doe wish that others[96] had bine that way the same that you are and wee hope soe continew."[97]

Thomas Crockett was not one of the men who was dismissed after the downsizing instructions were received. Instead, Gibbons, in his July 13, 1633 letter to John Mason reported that "Crockit" was one of the four men who would remain with him at Newichawannock.[98] Gibbons took the opportunity to unburden himself to Mason, further elucidating upon the sufferings of himself and his remaining crew (and family), including their lack of basic necessities. He also chastised Mason for expecting immediate profits from what the investors had provided to date:

> *"You complain of your returnes ; you take the coorse to have little ; a plantation must be furnished with cattle and with good hir'd hands, and necessaries for them, and not thinke the great lookes of men and many words will be a meanes to raise a plantation.*[99] Those that have been here this three year some of them have neither meat, money, nor clothes, a great disparagement. I shall not need to speak of this, you shall hear of it by others. For myself, my wife and child and four men we have but half a barrel of corne ; beefe and porke I have not had but on[e] peese this three months, nor beare this four months ; for I have for two and twenty months had but two barrels of beare and two barrels and four booshel of malt, our number commonly hath bin ten. I nor the servants have neither money nor clothes, I have been as sparing as I could, but it will not doe."[100]

By the end of 1633—after less than four years—the Laconia Company investors

---

94. Gibbons had previously expressed an interest in settling at Sanders' Point. The house there was then in the custody of Laconia Company investor Thomas Wannerton, but would be turned over to Gibbons. PIONEERS, p. 88.
95. This letter from Laconia Company investors is signed by John Mason, Henry Gardiner, George Griffith, Thomas Wannerton, and Thomas Eyre.
96. The company is likely referring to Captain Walter Neal, who seems to have been a disappointment to them and was recalled to England, probably because he had failed to set out upon another search for the Lake of the Iroquois the previous fall.
97. "No. 3. An original letter from the company to Ambrose Gibbins." London, 5th December, 1632. BELKNAP, Appendix, p. 423.
98. "No. 5. Copy of another from Gibbins to the company." Newichwanicke, July 13, 1633. BELKNAP, Appendix, p. 425.
99. The italics are from the BELKNAP text, not added by the author.
100. "No. 5. Copy of another from Gibbins to the company." Newichwanicke, July 13, 1633. BELKNAP, Appendix, p. 425.

decided to fold the company. The men met in London on December 6, 1633 to divvy up the territory (on paper) on the northeast side of the Piscataqua River.[101] The three properties owned by the company—at Little Harbor, Sanders' Point, and Newichawannock—were also parceled out.[102]

On April 23, 1634, Thomas Crockett was paid for his services the prior year. Denoted as "Crockwood" by Gibbons in papers that contain this payment report, Thomas was paid 6 pounds for service of one year to Mason. Because money was in short supply (barter was the main form of monetary exchange), Thomas was paid in beaver skins, from which more than half his pay—3 pounds, 18 shillings, and 4 pence—was deducted for his provisions[103] (which, considering the poor quality and scarcity of the provisions described by Gibbons in his letter to Mason, seems hard).

Gibbons learned in a letter from Gorges and Mason dated from Portsmouth, England, May 5, 1634[104] that they had bought up shares of the other Laconia Company investors and planned to proceed with their colonization efforts. (Probably the rapid expansion of the Puritan Massachusetts Bay Colony hastened Gorges' and Mason's transition from speculators to colonizers.) Mason also penned an individual letter to Gibbons on the same day, explaining how the Laconia Company inventory in New England was to be divided up. He asked the steward to make room at Newichawannock House for Henry Jocelyn, the new manager he was sending out, and the eight-man crew[105] of carpenters and skilled workers accompanying Jocelyn. Mason then directed Gibbons to discharge the remaining Laconia Company "servants," which would necessarily include Thomas Crockett. Gibbons was to pay their wages "out of the stocke of beaver in your hands at the rate of 12s. [shilling] the pound..."[106] Since the letters were sent aboard the *Pied Cow* along with Jocelyn, the new manager, and Jocelyn's workmen (and parts for two

---

101. PIONEERS, p. 88. In 1631, Mason, Gorges, and the other investors had received a grant of land on the northeast side of the river "to reimburse the Laconia Adventurers for the expense of operations at Pascataqua...". PIONEERS, p. 86.
102. Edward Godfrey (who had been passed over for Laconia Company governor in 1630, but was still sent over to New England) was to continue to run a fishing operation out of the Great House at Little Harbor (with a fishing shack across the river in York, Maine); Ambrose Gibbons, for his services, was to have the house at Sanders' Point; and Newichawannock House would be turned over to new overseer Henry Jocelyn to manage.
103. "The Crockett Family of Maine." Compiled and edited by Donna Hopkins Scott. Provo, Utah: BYU Press, 1968. CROCKETT, p. 313-316.
104. "No. 7. An original letter from Sir Ferdinando Gorges and Capt. John Mason to Messrs. Wannerton and Gibbins," and "No. 8. An original letter from Capt. John Mason to Ambrose Gibbins." May 5, 1634. BELKNAP, Appendix, p. 428-429.
105. According to Spencer (PIONEERS, p. 91-92), the "eight hands" was incorrectly transcribed as "eight Danes" in a deposition of Francis Small. In addition to new overseer Henry Jocelyn, the men who arrived on the Pied Cow were: William Chadbourne and sons Humphrey and William; John Goddard; Thomas Spencer; James Wall; and John Wilcockes.
106. "No. 8. An original letter from Capt. John Mason to Ambrose Gibbins." Portsmouth [England], May 5th, 1634. BELKNAP, Appendix, p. 429.

saw mills), Gibbons received his instructions at the same time he received the extra bodies he was to afford "some house roome in Newichewannocke house."[107] The order to dismiss the poorly-clad, ill-supplied men who had been with Gibbons for three years in the wilderness must have struck him as boorish and thoughtless. Nevertheless, the steward obeyed orders and discharged the men under his employ at Newichawannock—except possibly Thomas Crockett.

The *Pied Cow* arrived at Little Harbor on July 8, 1634.[108] Gibbons, getting word of the ship's arrival, traveled down the Piscataqua River to meet it and guided the vessel upriver to a cove below Salmon Falls.[109] Gibbons reported back to Mason in a letter dated August 6th that the ship was unloaded on July 18th.[110] The first cows on Maine soil were unloaded from the *Pied Cow* in addition to the men and equipment. While we cannot say for certain that Thomas Crockett helped unload the first cows in Maine, he was likely still with Gibbons at the time. The interesting story of the first cows in the Pine Tree State (as well as the first two sawmills)[111] was captured in a short vignette written in 1974 in "Maine Parks Campgrounds and Historic Sites:"

> "There is a tiny cove along the riverbank called 'Cow Cove.' It is very unimpressive, especially if seen at low tide. But it was here that the first cows were landed

---

107. "No. 8. An original letter from Capt. John Mason to Ambrose Gibbins." Portsmouth, May 5th, 1634. BELKNAP, Appendix, p. 429
108. PIONEERS, p. 91.
109. Two hundred and fifty years after Thomas Crockett first trod the old Native American trails at Salmon Falls and Newichawannock, author Sarah Orne Jewett, a South Berwick, Maine native, described the ancient footpaths in her charming 1884 story, "The White Rose Road." Jewett wrote: "… where the highway made a long bend eastward among the farms, two of us left the carriage, and followed a footpath along the green river bank and through the pastures, coming out to the road again only a minute later than the horses. I believe that it is an old Indian trail followed from the salmon falls further down the river, where the up-country Indians came to dry the plentiful fish for their winter supplies. I have traced the greater part of this deep worn footpath, which goes straight as an arrow across the country, the first day's trail being from the falls (where Mason's settlers came in 1627, and built their Great Works of a sawmill with a gang of saws, and presently a grist mill besides) to Emery's Bridge. I should like to follow the old footpath still farther. I found part of it by accident a long time ago. Once, as you came close to the river, you were sure to find fishermen scattered along, sometimes I myself have been discovered; but it is not much use to go fishing any more… Years ago, there were so many salmon that, as an enthusiastic old friend once assured me, 'you could walk across on them before the falls;' but now they are unknown, simply because certain substances which would enrich the farms are thrown from factories and tanneries into our clear New England streams." From, "The White Rose Road." Sarah Orne Jewett. "Selected Stories and Sketches," pp. 585-587. 1884: Barnes and Noble edition published electronically. Jewett's note of concern for the health of New England rivers was certainly prescient, and reveals the depth of her love of nature.
110. "No. 9. Answer to the foregoing." Letter from Ambrose Gibbons to John Mason. Newichawannock, the 6th of August 1634. BELKNAP, Appendix, p. 429-431.
111. As mentioned, the *Pied Cow* carried components for two sawmills. According to BANKS, by July 22, 1634, only sixteen days after having landed at Cow Cove, "the carpenters began about the mill(s)." The mill for "Pascataquack" (Mason's mill) was set up on the "Assabenbedick" (Great Works River) and the other sawmill (Gorges') was set up at "Aguamenticus" (Old Mill Creek, a branch of the York River). BANKS, p. 64-65.

in Maine from a tiny Danish vessel called the *Pied Cow*. The same ship also brought in parts for a sawmill which was constructed about a mile upriver from the site. This all happened in the 1630s. You ponder this, then look at the cove which looks barely large enough for a rowboat and wonder about what sort of seamen those early sailors were to dare the rough Atlantic in their tiny craft."[112]

Cow Cove, Vaughn Woods on the Salmon Falls River in South Berwick, looking northeast. (Photo courtesy of Old Berwick Historical Society.)

The Dark Years and the Devon Connection

In the letter that Ambrose Gibbons received from John Mason on July 8, 1634, the steward was directed to discharge the four men who were still working for him at Newichawannock House. While the other three men appear to have been let go, Thomas Crockett was not immediately released. (Again, this points to a close connection between Gibbons and Thomas Crockett or his family.) Rather, around

---
112. "Maine Parks Campgrounds and Historic Sites." Victor A. Schlich. Copyright 1974- J. Weston Walch, Publisher Portland, Maine.

The First Generation

mid-August Gibbons sent Crockett down to Strawbery Banke, where Thomas Pickering was renovating for the steward the house at Sanders' Point.[113] The carpenter had already taken a year or more on Gibbons' house and Gibbons was likely getting anxious for its completion. Thomas Crockett, who boarded with the carpenter, was sent to assist Pickering or hurry him along. On September 6, 1634, when Gibbons finally settled his account with Pickering, the steward was charged "with three weeks' diet for Thomas Crockett, his employee..."[114]

From the fall of 1634 to 1640, Thomas Crockett's whereabouts remain a mystery. The next historical reference to Crockett finds him at Kittery Point, Maine by 1640, where he ran a ferry.[115] Historians have speculated that after leaving Gibbons, Thomas went to work in the fishing industry, possibly for Edward Godfrey. (Godfrey claims to have built the first house in Maine, at York in 1630; however, historian Spencer says this was likely a fisherman's shack, easily accessible to the Isle of Shoals and other nearby fishing grounds.)[116] Considering that Crockett and Godfrey later became neighbors in York, it seems reasonable that he and Godfrey had a connection that continued after Thomas left Newichawannock House. It seems just as likely, however, that Thomas Crockett ended up in Kittery thanks to the Devon connection that dominated the area by the early to mid-1630s.

Two well-born sons of Devon—Francis Champernowne and Nicholas Shapleigh—emigrated permanently to Kittery, Maine. The Shapleighs built the first house and warehouse on Kittery Point,[117] and Francis Champernowne and Nicholas Shapleigh each managed extensive properties in Kittery. Both men became magistrates, and as such they affected the lives of Thomas Crockett and his family, as well as many others who settled the area. Champernowne and Shapleigh hailed from ancient estates on the River Dart. The Champernowne family[118] was from

---

113. Once Ambrose Gibbons learned the house that he wanted was to be his, "he removed the corporate property from the premises to the other two houses [at Little Harbor and Newichawannock]..." PIONEERS, p. 88.
114. PIONEERS, p. 93.
115. MIGRATION, p. 497.
116. PIONEERS, p. 126.
117. The first documented "real" house in Kittery was built in 1637 or 1638 by James Treworgy for his father-in-law Alexander Shapleigh. Near this house Treworgy built a brewhouse on leased land for the use of the fishermen employed on Shapleigh's ship, the *Bachelor*. Thomas Crockett might have been fishing for Treworgy at this time. PIONEERS, p. 115.
118. In 1622, Arthur Champernowne (father of Francis and head of the family) was given fishing and trading privileges in New England by Sir Ferdinando Gorges. (The wives of the two men at the time were sisters.) Champernowne turned these privileges over to his sixth son, a soldier, Captain Francis Champernowne, who by 1631-32 was shipping fish from the New World in the *Hercules*. (LIBBY/NOYES, p. 135. Capt. Francis Champernowne.) By 1634, Francis Champernowne, then only twenty, purchased a tract of land from Gorges' agent Thomas Bradbury, Champernowne's Island (later, Cutt's Island) and 500 acres across the stream that separated the island from the mainland. The deed was officially signed (by Gorges to Arthur Champernowne) in England Dec. 12, 1636. According to Libby/Noyes, "Apparently, Mr. [Arthur] Champernowne sent over

Dartington, situated at the headwaters of the Dart, and the Shapleighs[119] were located at Kingsweare, at the mouth of the river. The village of Stoke Gabriel, from which Thomas Crockett emigrated, lies about half way between Dartington and Kingsweare. Given the wealth and influence of both the Champernownes and Shapleighs, it would be highly unlikely that the Crocketts—including Thomas— were unfamiliar with both families.

Meanwhile, back in England, the simmering issues which led to the English Civil War (the power of the Sovereign versus the power of the Puritan Parliament), began breaking out into the open. The differences in the New World mirrored those in the Old, with lines drawn between Puritans and Royalists. Almost all of those who resided in Maine during the early 17th century, including Thomas Crockett, were Anglicans (the others belonged to minor Protestant sects, such as Quakers and Baptists, who were not welcome in Puritan Massachusetts Bay Colony).

In 1640, when Thomas Crockett operated the ferry at Kittery Point, [120] he was safe (for the time being) from the narrow-mindedness of the Puritans in Massachusetts. We do not know whether Thomas owned the vessel he used to ferry people (the inventory of his estate after his death shows Thomas owned an old canoe)[121] or whether he borrowed a shallop or pinnace belonging to one of the Devon fishing

---

his youngest son, barely of age, with a cargo of cattle, to set up a branch of his family in the new world." Although Francis Champernowne would settle in Greenland, N.H. (near Strawbery Banke) by 1640, he always had an influence in Kittery, as well as what he called his "lower house" at Kittery Point, to which he returned to live. (Champernowne also had a prior house, an early house in Kittery, that he lost to Edward Saunders for a debt.)

119. In 1635, Alexander Shapleigh, father of Nicholas and the pioneer of the American branch of the Shapleigh family (see, "Alexander Shapleigh's Family Tree – the first four generations in America." Shapleigh Family Association website. https://shapleigh0.tripod.com/shapleighfamilyassociation/id3.html) purchased 500 acres of land in Kittery. Shapleigh's home at Kingsweare was known as Kittery House, and it was from this—according to the Shapleigh family—that the town of Kittery gets its name. *The New England Historic, Genealogical Register* describes Alexander Shapleigh as a "merchant, ship-owner, and interested in the primitive plantations and trading establishments in Maine and New Hampshire, where he found a market for his goods sent over in his own ships." Shapleigh bought his 500-acre tract from Captain Thomas Cammock, who had purchased the property from Sir Ferdinando Gorges and John Mason in 1634. (*The New England Historical and Genealogical Register*, p. 346, "The Shapleigh Family.") Alexander Shapleigh presented the deed from Cammock on July 20, 1642 to the Court in York (Maine). It was recorded by Roger Gard. Thomas Gorges, Ferdinando Gorges' cousin, was then Deputy Governor of Maine. According to the *The New England Historical and Genealogical Register*, Shapleigh, who was also an agent of Ferdinando Gorges, had probably "visited the country" prior to his purchase. After buying the property from Cammock, Alexander Shapleigh—who remained in England—sent his son-in-law, James Treworgye, to establish a fishing and trading outpost in Maine and build a warehouse at what would become known as Warehouse Point on Kittery Point. Later, Shapleigh's son Nicholas would buy back his father's rights to the property in Kittery, where he became the most prominent early citizen.

120. MIGRATION, p. 497. Charles Taylor Anderson does not document the source behind Thomas Crockett running a ferry at Kittery Point as early as 1640. While this information might be helpful in establishing a further connection between Crockett and the Shapleigh-Treworgy families of Devon, given the thoroughness of Anderson's "Great Migration" project, I am not inclined to doubt the accuracy.

121. "An Inventory of the Estate formerly Thomas Crocketts, now deceased as it was shewed unto vs whose names are vnderwritten, [Francis Hooke, William Scrivine] this 20th day of March 1678/79." MEWD, Vol. 5, Page 85-86.

operations. The ferry at Kittery Point was important because it "connected the Point with Great Island and Strawberry Bank, and the ferry boat sometimes ran up the Pascataqua to Sturgeon Creek and Dover Point."[122] Since most of those who wanted to travel from one location to another did not own boats, and there were few roads, ferries (or shanks' mare)[123] were the main means of transportation in early New England. Thanks to his position as ferryman (and his residence at the Point), Thomas Crockett became known to local fishermen, traders, trappers, and all the English gentry, former soldiers, merchants, and adventurers who worked, resided, or passed through this busy and exciting English settlement in southern Maine. One of those was the woman who was to become Thomas Crockett's wife, and the mother of their eight children.

Ann Crockett and Family Life in Early Kittery

Historians have long speculated about the identity of Thomas Crockett's wife Ann. Her maiden name and parentage are not known. Ann's last name has been surmised as "Lynn" or "Gunnison," mostly because she was believed to have been related to early Boston innkeeper Hugh Gunnison or his second wife, Sarah, the widow of Henry Lynn of York.

Much of this speculation stems from the fact that the Crocketts had close ties to Hugh and Sarah Gunnison and their combined family.[124] (It appears to me, however, that the close connection between the Crocketts and Sarah Lynn preceded Sarah's marriage to Hugh Gunnison.)[125] York County Court records reveal that

---

122. STACKPOLE, p. 54.
123. On foot.
124. Together, the Crocketts and Gunnisons had three children who shared the same given name: Ephraim, Elihu, and Joseph. (Ephraim Lynn was Hugh Gunnison's stepson, not his son.) In addition, Thomas and Ann Crockett named a son "Hugh," who was born not long after Hugh and Sarah Gunnison relocated to Kittery from Boston (Sarah was in Kittery prior to her second marriage), and they also named a daughter "Sarah," both probably as compliments to the Gunnisons. See Robert Charles Anderson's column "Editor's Effusions" (Great Migration Newsletter July-September, 2002, p. 18 and 24) for the connection between the Gunnisons and Crocketts.
125. On April 22, 1654, Thomas Crockett gave the following deposition in the Gunnison-Shapleigh case:
"The Deposition of Thomas Crocket aged aboute 43 yeares [saith] for the tearme of 3. or 4. Years that Sarah Linn widow was Tenant to mr. Nicholas Shapleigh in an old house at the Rivers mouth at Puscataquah, & that the [said] Sarah had not any priviledge to the house, but the bare house onelie nott Could not Cut any wood without the Leave of Lauender [Lander] & Billin [Billing]..." (BAXTER3, p. 108. The Gunnison-Shapleigh Case.) From this deposition we learn that Sarah (and her four young children) removed from York after the death of her first husband, and lived near the Crocketts on the Point in Kittery. The old house referred to was the original Shapleigh house, which, after Sarah married Gunnison and moved to Boston, Nicholas Shapleigh renovated and leased to another innkeeper until the Gunnisons returned to Kittery in 1651. In his deposition Thomas calls the widow Lynn by her given name, "Sarah," which indicates there was a very close connection between them as he certainly would not have taken the liberty otherwise.

Ann Crockett and Sarah Gunnison spent time together[126] and that Thomas was employed by or helped Hugh Gunnison with a garden the first spring after the innkeeper relocated to Kittery,[127] although the Crockett family then lived in neighboring York.

Was Ann a sister of Hugh Gunnison?[128] (Their estimated ages probably preclude Ann from being Hugh's daughter.) Was she Sarah's sister? Or was Ann a sister or relation of Henry Lynn, Sarah's first husband (perhaps Sarah's sister-in-law)? We will likely never know for sure, although I lean toward the theory that Ann was a sister to Henry Lynn.[129]

---

126. On July 30, 1656 a complaint against Magdeline Wiggin, wife of James Wiggin, was brought in and agreed upon by the Grand Inquest at a Court held in York, for the county of York. The complaint was that Magdeline said she saw her mother Frances White in the act of adultery with William Moore. This was reported by witnesses Miss (Sarah) Gunnison, Ann Crockett, and Joane Andrews (Thomas Crockett's sister), and signifies that the four women were together someplace where Magdeline told them the lie about her mother. Magdeline was censured by the Court to have 20 lashes on the bare skin or pay 5 pounds to the County Treasury. MPCR, Vol. 2, p. 52.

127. BAXTER3, p. 108. The Gunnison-Shapleigh Case.

128. I do not believe that Ann Crockett was related to Hugh Gunnison. Firstly, Ann's son Ephraim appears to have been named as a compliment to Ephraim Lynn, the son of Sarah and Henry Lynn, years before Gunnison relocated to Kittery. Secondly, Ann gave a deposition on January 27, 1679 about the late Hugh Gunnison's desire that the land he had leased to his stepsons should revert to his natural sons. In that deposition (MEWD, Vol. 3, p. 248) Ann refers to her deceased friend as "Mr. Hugh Gunnison." Had they had a closer connection—or been related in any way—Ann would have mentioned it, naming him as "my father" or "my brother" or even "my cousin," as she does in a deed from her son Hugh Crockett to Henry Barter, calling Barter (who was married to her granddaughter, and thus her grandson-in-law) "my cousin Barter" (MEWD, Vol. 7, p. 192-193).

129. Part of the challenge with unraveling Ann's identity is lack of information. While ships' records exist for the Puritans who emigrated to New England, many women, especially those who settled in Maine, came over as supercargo aboard supply ships sent over by merchants from Devon, Bristol, and London. These women were typically brought to New England to be with their husbands (such as Rebecca Gibbons, who joined her husband Ambrose at Pascataqua), fathers, and even brothers. If the women were noted at all, it was as "wife of so-and-so," and not by name. Ann could have emigrated to join a brother, such as Henry Lynn in York, where she would have been an important helper for Sarah and their four young children. (Indeed, fondness for her nephew Ephraim Lynn might be why Ann and Thomas gave their eldest son that birth name.) In addition, marriages in Maine were often performed by sea captains or local magistrates, whose records (if any) are no longer extant. And while the Puritans in Massachusetts did keep marriage and birth records, once a woman was married or remarried (especially if she was wed prior to arrival in New England) her maiden name was lost. Due to the scarcity of women in the New World, a widowed female was often quickly remarried. In fact, Sarah Lynn Gunnison was married four times. While we know Sarah's first husband was merchant Henry Lynn, with whom she immigrated to Boston in 1630 as part of the Winthrop fleet (PIONEERS, p. 119), we do not know her maiden name or who were her relations in England, which information might have helped us identify Thomas Crockett's wife. Early historians believed Sarah to have been the daughter of William Tilley, a Boston merchant; however, later historians have speculated that due to their ages (Tilley was not old enough to have been her father) William was Sarah's stepfather. Robert Charles Anderson of the *Great Migration Project* believes Sarah was the daughter of Alice (Frost) Blower, a prominent Boston midwife (whose second husband was William Tilley) and Thomas Blower, a sailmaker from Stanstead, county Suffolk, England. (See MIGRATION2, William Tilley, p. 51 for Anderson's conclusion that Sarah was likely the daughter of Thomas and Alice Blower.) Historian Mary Beth Norton comes to the same conclusion in her excellent article about midwife Alice (Frost) Blower Tilly, " 'The Ablest Midwife That Wee Knowe in the Land': Mistress Alice Tilly and the Women of Boston and Dorchester, 1649-1650." *William and Mary Quarterly*, 3d Series, Volume LV, Number 1, January 1998. Because Sarah Lynn Gunnison Mitchell Morgan appears to share many of the same characteristics as Alice Frost—confident, outspoken, independent, possibly vain about her age (like her mother, Sarah married a much younger man in her fourth husband)—I agree Sarah was most likely the daughter of Alice and Thomas Blower; however, this cannot be squared with her early arrival in Boston in 1630, unless Sarah was their first child (Alice and Thomas were married in Stanstead, 19 November 1612, per Anderson, MIGRATION3, Thomas Blower, p. 338), or she would have been a child in 1630 when she accompanied Henry Lynn as his wife to Boston.

Data about Ann Crockett gleaned from court and real estate records provides us with an estimation of her character, if not her identity. From these tantalizing tidbits we learn that Ann was warm-hearted, generous, and loyal, and possibly a bit silly[130] or naive[131] in her younger years, but intelligent and steady in maturity.[132] She loved her family and took pains to treat her children fairly after the death of their father.[133] Ann was a good helpmeet for Thomas Crockett and a woman of whom any descendant could be proud.

The first home Thomas Crockett owned was a house and four acres on Kittery Point that he purchased from William Wormwood,[134] a trader[135] who was in the area by 1639. Wormwood was given two acres of land each from John Billing and John Lander,[136] fishermen who had absconded from the Trelawny Plantation at Richmond Island. Although Wormwood traded on the Isle of Shoals, he evidently built the house on the Point that Crockett purchased. The four acres ran "up into the woods" and was later fenced in, likely by Thomas. (Fences were necessary to protect one's garden and crops from the depredations of loose livestock.) This real estate transaction was not recorded, which was not unusual since until March of 1643 land conveyances in Maine were entered into the records of the General Court in Boston,[137] if they were recorded at all. Possession would have been given by "Turf and Twig" (also known

---

130. On March 5, 1651/52, Edward Godfrey in behalf of his wife Ann, filed an action of defamation and slander in court in York against Mr. Francis Raynes and Ellen, his wife, and the same against Thomas Crockett and his wife. (The three parties were neighbors in York at the time.) This action was because the two women—Ann Crockett and Ellen Raynes—had made fun of Ann Godfrey, claiming that "it was the pride of her heart to wear her husband's hat about and a waistcoat." (MPCR, Vol. 1, p. 174.) The issue was settled out of court, apparently amicably, although with a caution from the Grand Inquest two weeks later that the women would be bound to their good behavior if such inappropriate (and scandalous) joking occurred again. MPCR, Vol. 1, p. 177.
131. On July 5, 1660, evidence was presented in Court that there was "too much frequent familiarity between Joseph Davesse [Davis] and Ann Crockett" and an act of separation was passed between the two, whereby they would be fined if they "be found privately, frequently or unseasonably together." MPCR, Vol. 2, p. 93.
132. After Thomas Crockett's death, the Court felt that Ann was capable of managing his property on Crockett's Neck, and gave her the right to sell some of the real estate if she needed money for the support of herself and/or her children. This decision signifies that the magistrates not only thought Ann intelligent enough to handle the responsibility (not usually accorded a woman), but also steady and dependable. MPCR, Vol. 3, p. 59.
133. Ann Crockett did not deed over to their son Ephraim (and his heirs) all the lands on Crockett's Neck (granted to Thomas Crockett by Sir Ferdinando Gorges) until May 20, 1688, after Ephraim had paid the legacies in his father's will, including 12 pounds to his brother-in-law Elisha Barton (husband of his sister Mary Crockett). MEWD, Vol. 4, p. 303.
134. MEWD, Vol. 1, p. 64-65.
135. Wormwood was accused of improper dealings with sailors on Star Island (one of the Isle of Shoals) and ordered to the mainland in 1647. The date suggests that he might have lived at the Point first before relocating to the Isle of Shoals. LIBBY/NOYES, p. 771. William Wormwood.
136. MPCR, Vol. 1, p. 104. On March 26, 1647, Goodwife Thomas, widow of John Billing (who had married Rice Thomas), testified at Court at Pascataqua that her late husband and John Lander each gave two acres on the Point to William Wormwood "... & it is to go up into the woods as the pales [fences] now stand." This testimony was likely to protect the home and land of Thomas Crockett against the execution against John Lander's home and land the prior day. See also MPCR Vol. 1, p. 112.
137. MEWD, Vol. 1, p. 30.

as "Livery of Seisin")[138] whereby full real estate rights (fee simple) transfer from one person to another during a ceremony on the property with sod and sticks.

We do not know the year Thomas and Ann were married, although 1643 is a good guess (since the couple's first son, Ephraim, was born in 1644). Around the year he was wed, another important event occurred in Thomas Crockett's life—he was granted a tract of land near Kittery Point, which property came to be known as Crockett's Neck. The grant was made by Thomas Gorges, then Deputy Governor of Maine and a cousin of Sir Ferdinando Gorges. Like the property purchased from William Wormwood, the grant from Gorges was not recorded and as a result would later come into dispute between Crockett and his friend Rice[139] Thomas. So many people came forward to give depositions supporting Thomas Crockett's ownership right, however, that the grant was able to stand, and Crockett's Neck became Thomas' legacy to Ann and their children.

The first clue of Thomas and Ann Crockett's early family life is found in a deposition given in 1660 by Thomas' sister Joane, who was then married to John Andrews of Kittery. At the time the deposition was taken, Thomas was attempting to prove that Crockett's Neck belonged to him. Joane's deposition is one of many given by friends and family to support Thomas' claim. She is about forty when her deposition was taken by court recorder Edward Rishworth, making Joane mid-twenties when this incident to which she refers occurs:

> "… about 15 or sixteen years agone [1644 or 1645], having occasion to be at Thomas Crockett's when his wife was ready to lie down, of one of her children, & she being in want of help at that time, desired this deponent to call her husband who was at work in his ground, whereupon she went into Thomas Crockett's field, & called over to him who was chopping of wood, & burning of brush on the Neck of Land on the other side of Spruce Creek, over against his field on this side of the said creek, & this Deponent demanding of him what he was doing, he answered he was clearing that Neck of Land, for a field & if he lived intended to set a house there."[140]

---

138. "Turf and Twig" or "Livery of Seisin" was a feudal English way of transferring full property ownership rights from one person to another. Early Englishmen brought this ceremony with them to New England, where it continued until the late 19th century. Early York County Maine property transfers contain many references to "Turf and Twig" real estate transfers.
139. "Rice" is short for Richard.
140. MEWD, Vol. 2, p. 27. Note: I have corrected the grammar in this (as I occasionally have elsewhere) in order that the text is easier to read.

From this testimony we learn that Joane[141] was present in Maine at the birth of Thomas and Ann's child, and that by 1644 Thomas Crockett was already planning and preparing a future for his family on Crockett's Neck. In addition, the fact that Joane feels able to "demand" of Thomas Crockett what he is doing, at such a critical time as the birth of his first child, bespeaks a very close relationship between Thomas and Joane. This, combined with the fact that the child born in 1644—son Ephraim—grows up to become one of Joane's biggest helpers (next to her steadfast husband),[142] *and* considered alongside the fact that Thomas had a sister Joan baptized in 1621, almost certainly confirms the relationship between Thomas Crockett and Joane Andrews as brother and sister. We also learn from this deposition that by the mid-forties Joane was already part of the Crockett's circle of family and friends in Kittery.

The life of Thomas and Ann Crockett dovetailed with the life of their good friend Sarah Lynn and her second husband Hugh Gunnison. After Hugh's first

---

141. Joane Crockett likely emigrated to New England from Stoke Gabriel as supercargo on one of the Champernowne or Treworgy (Shapleigh) vessels that sailed out of Dartmouth and into Kittery Point. She might have come to help her brother Thomas and his new wife, and at the same time to find a husband in New England where wives were in short supply. There is also the interesting possibility that—if Ann was Sarah Lynn's sister-in-law (as I suspect)—Joane came over to take Ann's place upon her marriage to Thomas Crockett. By 1640, Sarah and Henry Lynn were living permanently in York; however, Henry, as a coastal trader, was away from home for prolonged periods of time. It is not likely that Lynn would leave his wife without a companion, someone to help her with their young children. Around 1642, Henry Lynn left York for Virginia. He never returned. He died in Virginia in 1643, leaving Sarah with four young children to support. (See MIGRATION, p. 1220. Henry Lynn.) If Ann Crockett was indeed Henry Lynn's sister, she almost certainly could not be induced to leave the home of her sister-in-law and nephew and nieces until a woman was provided (or a second husband) who could take her place. In fact, early court records reveal that the widowed Sarah Lynn *did* have a woman living with her. On October 21, 1645, Sarah Lynn took Edward Saunders to General Court for slander and harassment. In court, which was held at Saco, Sarah claimed that Saunders had pressed his attentions on her, even in her bedroom *when another woman was with her*. From the court records: "The plaintiff [Sarah Lynn] cometh into Court & declareth against the defendant [Edward Saunders] to witt: that the said defendant hath sclandered [sic] her by calling her whore & base whore & punk & going abroad & declareth her excessive Lasivious carriage towards him and in his presence by divers times enticing him to her bed, yea though another woman in bed with her, by coming to bed to him, by putting her hand in his codpiece, by shifting herselfe openly before him, soe that he hath discerned a secrett marke in her body in such parte as were very immodest. And alsoe declareth that he hath divers times threatened her life and hath assaulted her & stroke her along the house & this hath beene his practice almost this two years, to her greate feare & damage and alsoe reproach in the mouthes of many, & hinderance of her preferment in any match which might otherwise have beene attained to the great comfort & to the preventing this great cost for the vindicating her name, and damage to 100li sterling." (MPCR, Vol. 1, p. 90-91. Entered into the court record this date was also the record from the court of Aug. 12, 1644 in which it was noted that Henry Lynn had died and left his wife [Sarah Lynn] and children in very mean condition. MPCR, Vol. 1, p. 92-93.) Sarah's case went to the jury, who found for her. Edward Saunders was ordered to pay Sarah 30 pounds in damages and pay court costs of 40 shillings. (MPCR, Vol. 1, p. 90-91.) Since there is no evidence indicating Joane Crockett and John Andrews were married before 1648, it is possible that Joane was the woman referred to in Sarah's testimony. In addition, future events in the lives of these two women suggest that Joane had at one time a close relationship with Sarah and her daughters.

142. John Andrews, Joane's faithful husband, was about 20 years older than his pert and outspoken wife. (LIBBY/NOYES, p. 65. John Andrews.) Because of their age difference and because she resided in Kittery as a single woman many years prior to their marriage, I suspect that Joane was granted great license by her husband as a condition of their union. In addition, Andrews relocated not long after their marriage from his home in the Eliot part of Kittery to Brave Boat Harbor, where they could be near his wife's brother and family. A perusal of MPCR reveals that John steadfastly paid fine after fine for Joane's incorrigible behavior, of which he might even have been proud. (Andrews was no shrinking violet himself.)

wife (Elizabeth)[143] died in January of 1646, Hugh and the widowed Sarah formed an attachment.[144] When in 1647 Sarah Lynn married Gunnison[145] and relocated with her four children to Boston, Thomas Crockett decided to sell his house and four acres on Kittery Point to Robert Mendum.[146] The Crocketts did not relocate to York (where Thomas was given the ferry privilege for Brave Boat Harbor in 1648),[147] until after Sarah had moved to Boston. Probably not coincidentally, Thomas Crockett's sister Joane and her husband John Andrews also relocated to Brave Boat Harbor the same year.[148]

The Crocketts might even initially have lived with Joane and John Andrews, who are credited with building the first house on the Kittery side of Brave Boat Harbor in 1648 (although the Kittery/York boundary, which is at Brave Boat Harbor, was in dispute for many years). At some point, Thomas, Ann, and their family moved across the harbor to York (or Gorgeana, as Gorges' settlement was then still known). In 1653, Thomas was granted 40 acres of land to plant by the town of York.[149] The grant occurred after Crockett and the other townsmen (including Edward Godfrey) voted in November of 1652 (under pressure) to submit to the civil and religious authority of the Massachusetts Bay Colony.[150] The Bay had taken the

---

143. Hugh Gunnison's first wife was possibly Elizabeth Boaneo, who, as "one of our brother Richard Bellinghams maid servants," was admitted to the First Church of Boston about four months after Hugh Gunnison (also once one of Richard Bellingham's servants). Boston, MA: Church Records, 1630-1895. First Church volume, p. 9. https://www.americanancestors.org/databases/boston-ma-church-records-1630-1895/image?volumeId=7625&pageName=9&rId=8658980

144. I am unsure how Sarah Lynn and Hugh Gunnison connected, since Hugh was living in Boston and Sarah in Kittery, although it is possible the Gunnisons knew the Lynns prior to the Lynns relocating to Maine. It is also possible that the couple's relationship was forwarded by Sarah's stepfather, William Tilly, who was a close friend of Gunnison and a traveling wine merchant.

145. George Gunnison, a descendant of Hugh, states in his "Genealogy of the Descendants of Hugh Gunnison" (GUNNISON) that the couple was married on May 23, 1647; however, Sarah was welcomed to the First Church of Boston as Gunnison's wife May 15, 1647. MIGRATION, p. 173. PIONEERS, p. 118 confirms George Gunnison's date, possibly because Spencer used Gunnison's genealogy.

146. The property transfer from Crockett to Mendum, written up by Mendum, was dated Sept. 21, 1647. Mendum was to pay Crockett a total of 9 pounds, 10 shillings for the house and four acres that Thomas Crockett had purchased from William Wormwood. The payment was set forth as follows: "Three pounds In money, & the rest in Commoditys at Michelmas next, in the yeare 1648." John Seely and Thomas Bestone (a proprietor of Kittery by 1642) were witnesses to the transaction. MEWD, Vol. 1, p. 64-65. See also Vol. 2, p. 46. After this sale, on Nov. 11, 1647, Crockett purchased from Joseph Miles eight acres of land formerly belonging to fishermen John Billing and John Lander; however, he turned around and sold this property in December to Rice Thomas, who had married Billing's widow. MPCR, Vol. 1, p. 114-115

147. LIBBY/NOYES, p. 172. Thomas Crockett. The ferry ran from the York side to the Kittery side of Brave Boat Harbor, making it easier (until a bridge was built a few years later) to travel on foot between the two settlements.

148. On March 21, 1648, John Andrews, husband of "Joanie" Crockett, moved from upper Kittery (Eliot) to Brave Boat Harbor. STACKPOLE, p. 94. With the consent of his wife Joan, Andrews sold via indenture his current house and some land in Kittery. MEWD, Vol. 1, p. 52. This signals that he and Joane (Crockett) were married at least by this date.

149. At a Town Meeting in York Jan. 10, 1653, Thomas Crockett was granted 40 acres of planting ground by the town of York located between Mr. Edward Godfrey and Mr. Francis Raynes. MEWD, Vol. 1, p. 93.

150. On Monday, Nov. 22, 1652, a General Court was held at Gorgiania (York), now Aggamenticus. MPCR, Vol, II, p. 6-7. "The inhabitants appeared, asked questions of the representatives from Massachusetts Bay Colony, raised objections, and finally 'with a full & joynt consent' acknowledged they were subjects of MA, with Mr. Godfrey holding out until last." The

opportunity presented by the English Civil War to grab the Royalist Sir Ferdinando Gorges' land in Maine. Puritan Massachusetts utilized a carrot and stick approach with the resident Royalists of Maine: the Bay sent armed representatives to speak to the people, which representatives also offered townsmen the opportunity to become free men if they submitted to the authority of Massachusetts Bay Colony.

---

recording of the submission by the townsmen of York leaves out a few details, including the fact that weapons were carried by the Bay's representatives. Upon their submission, however, Thomas Crockett and the others became freemen per the Massachusetts Bay Colony. (See MA Census Substitutes 1630-1788, p. 4796.) Edward Godfrey, a staunch Royalist and supporter of Gorges' rights to Maine, also signed the submission: "Whatever my body was enforced unto," he said afterward, "heaven knows my soul did not consent unto." Godfrey knew his submission to the Puritans of Massachusetts would cost him and Gorges land. Godfrey's submission should be taken as proof that he felt he had very little choice in the matter.

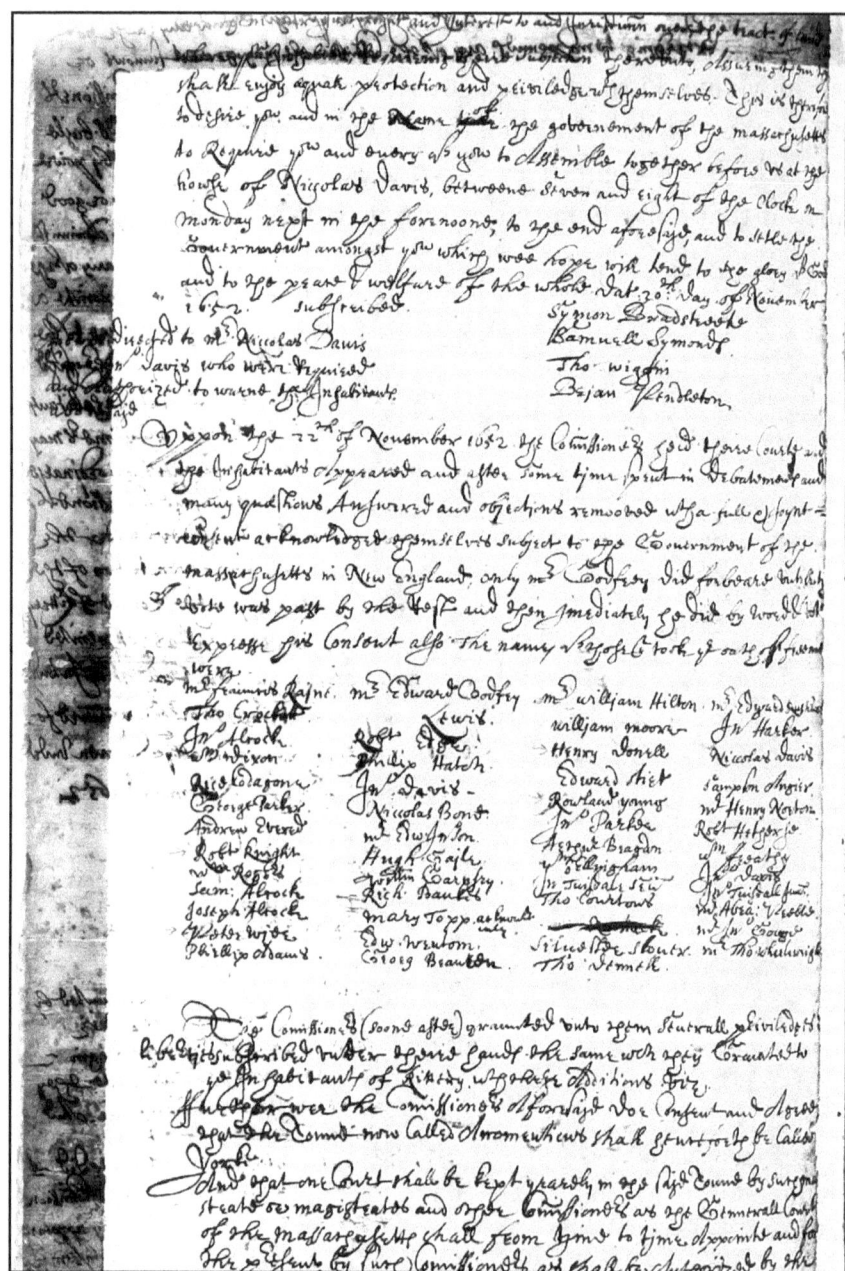

Oath of allegiance to Massachusetts Bay Colony.
Thomas Crockett and other men of York signed an oath of allegiance to Massachusetts Bay Colony on Nov. 22, 1652. Thomas' name is second in the left-hand column (middle of the page), appearing under that of his neighbor, Mr. Francis Raynes.
(Image in the public domain.)

The First Generation

It is unclear whether Thomas built a house on his 40-acre grant in York, the planting ground "next the sea-side"[151] south of York River, situated between the homes of Edward Godfrey and Francis Raynes. (See map below.) It is possible that Crockett only tended crops on this grant of land, upon which Abenaki Indians had once planted corn. If so, he likely built a house at Brave Boat Harbor, where in 1653 Thomas also received a grant of land "of marsh he improves at Brave Boat Harbor."[152] It would make sense that if Thomas was operating the ferry, he would reside near Brave Boat Harbor, which was separated from his planting ground by Raynes' property.

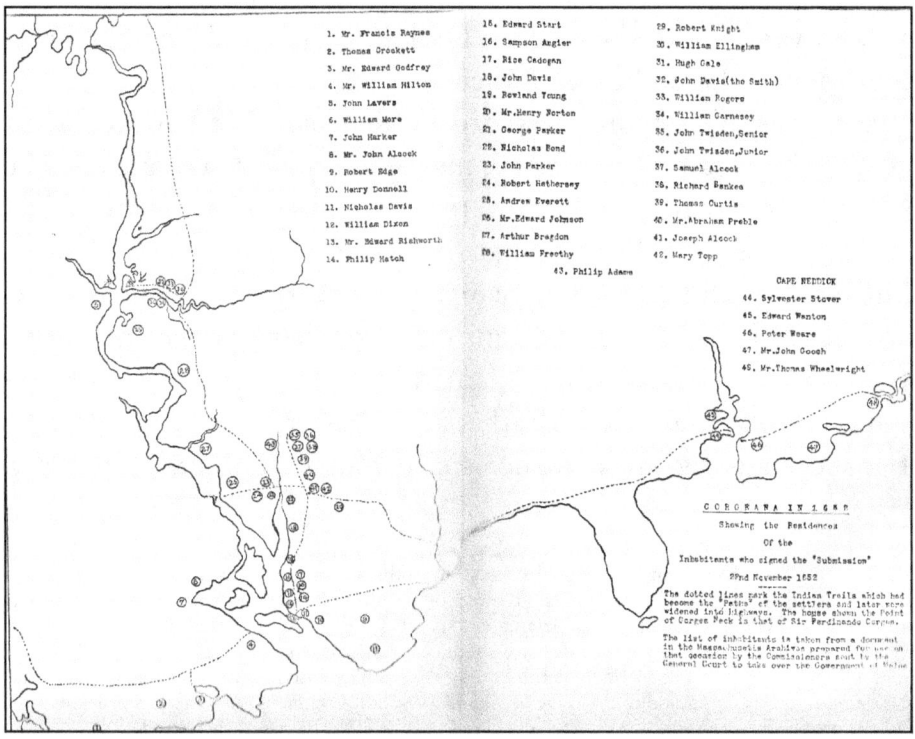

Gorgeana (York) in 1652 showing the residences of the inhabitants who signed the "Submission" to Massachusetts Bay Colony, Nov. 22, 1652. (Charles Edward Banks, "History of York, Maine, Vol. I.")[153]

---

151. BANKS2, p. 50. (Deeds I, 36.)
152. LIBBY/NOYES, p. 34, List 298.
153. BANKS, p. 187-188. Banks notes that the dotted lines represent Native American trails used by the settlers, which later became roads. Most of the residents of York settled on the east side of the river; however, Francis Raynes (1) and Thomas Crockett (2) had property in south York near Brave Boat Harbor (bottom left of map). This location likely brought the Crocketts and Raynes families into Kittery more often than the others from York, who would have had to cross the York River, as well as cross (or go inland around) Brave Boat Harbor. (Image in the public domain.)

During their five years residing in York, the Crocketts reached the height of their social status. They owned land between two educated gentlemen, the physician Francis Raynes and former fellow Laconia Company employee Edward Godfrey, both of whom were almost always denoted in records by the deferential "Mr." This rise in prominence brought more trouble than it was worth, however. Ellen Raynes, wife of Francis, became a close companion of Ann Crockett's, which unfortunately landed Ann in legal jeopardy. Ellen, who appears to have been young and immature, gossiped with Ann that their neighbor Elizabeth Godfrey (Edward's wife) liked to wear her husband's hat and waistcoat. When this scandalous tidbit about Elizabeth's predilection became public, the Godfreys were humiliated. Edward Godfrey sued both Francis Raynes and Thomas Crockett for defamation and slander on behalf of their wives.[154]

The fracas was made more awkward by that fact that Crockett worked for Raynes tending his cattle.[155] Eventually, the legal controversy was settled amicably with no fines paid, but the gossipers were ordered by the court not to repeat the offense or the women would be bound (by a sum of money) "to their good behavior." In addition, during the five years the Crocketts resided in York, Thomas' incorrigible sister Joane was a constant embarrassing presence at York County Court. Joane was herself sued for defamation and slander;[156] sued for selling a firkin of butter containing stones rather than butter;[157] and, in addition, when in court Joane regularly unleased her sharp tongue. She once abused a grand

---

154. MPCR, Vol. 1, p. 174. "The Plaintiff [Godfrey] Cometh in to this Court & Complaineth that they have lived in this place many years in good report & fame, booth in Church & Commonwealth, his wife being a Church member, the wife of the said Francis Raynes did in most slanderous & defamatory speeches, Revile the said Ane with the word: Ly and base Ly: & twas the prid of her hart to wearer her husbands hatte about & a waskoat which Consernd them not. And not onely soe but Mr. Raynes did in & att a publique meting one the Lords day Complayne ther of to the whole Congregation, whereby the plaintive is damnifid in his reputation to the value of 50li & ther upon Commenseth his action of defamation & slander & desyreth a legal proceeding: the same against Tho. Crocket & his wife, the names onely altered."

155. On March 6, 1650/51, William Hilton gave a deposition to Basil Parker (then court recorder) saying he heard Francis Raines say "he was to alowe Thomas Crocket for keeping therteene head of Cattell" MPCR, Vol. 1, p. 131.

156. MPCR, Vol. 2, p. 20. On Oct. 25, 1653 at the County Court held at York for York Shire, John Andrews on behalf of his wife Joane, was sued for defamation and slander by Rice Thomas to the value of 20 pounds. The summons was served Oct. 20, 1653; however, the charges were withdrawn prior to going to court. Andrews likely was able to amicably settle the issue with Thomas. At Court, Andrews acknowledged himself indebted to the County for 10 pounds in behalf of his wife Joane "...who is bound to the peace with all persons more especially Ryce Thommasse who hath sworne the peace agnast her."

157. MPCR, Vol. 2, p. 22 On Oct. 25, 1653 at the County Court held at York for York Shire, Joane Andrews was presented for selling a firkin of butter to Mr. Nicholas Davis (an innkeeper), which had two stones in it containing 14 pounds 2 oz. weight. Joane owned the substitution, and her husband was bound in a bond of five pounds that Joane would stand in Town Meeting at both York and Kittery for two hours with her offense written on paper in capital letters attached to her head. (The fondness of the Puritans for shaming those who colored outside their narrow lines was captured brilliantly by Nathaniel Hawthorne in his classic novel "The Scarlet Letter.")

juryman with "many threatening and reviling speeches."[158] At that point, Thomas must have felt that Ellen Raynes and his sister Joane might not be the best companions for his wife, and lamented the loss of Sarah Lynn Gunnison, who was an educated woman of superior qualities.[159]

Fortunately, less than five years after Sarah removed to Boston (where she helped her second husband operate the King's Arm Tavern), the couple returned to Kittery.[160] Hugh and Sarah Gunnison sold their popular inn[161] and they and their combined family relocated to Kittery by June of 1651.[162] They were granted leave to run an ordinary (tavern) in the old Shapleigh house, upon which Gunnison took a long-term lease. (The house was possibly the same as that in which the widowed Sarah Lynn and her children had lived, and where she, too, might have fed and provided drink for travelers after her first husband's death.) On November 16, 1652, the residents of Kittery, including Hugh Gunnison and John Andrews (Joane's husband), submitted to the authority of Massachusetts Bay Colony,[163] six days prior to the submission by the men of York. Land grants by the town of Kittery to Hugh Gunnison (and others) shortly followed.

But not all was smooth sailing for the Gunnisons upon their return to Kittery. Hugh Gunnison and Nicolas Shapleigh (both Alpha males with big egos) soon had

---

158. MPCR Vol. 2, p. 12. On June 30, 1653, Joane was "presented" (indicted) by the Grand Inquest held at York for abusing a grand juryman. She owned her guilt and was given an admonition by the court and ordered to pay the officer's fee.
159. A deep dive into the life of Sarah (Blower) Lynn Gunnison Mitchell Morgan has convinced me that she was not only educated, but also a woman of superior qualities. Sarah, who appears to have been popular with townspeople in Kittery, was regularly granted the privilege of running a tavern, revealing that the men in power had great confidence in her abilities, especially for a woman. Also, when her hot-headed husband Hugh Gunnison was embroiled in a property dispute with Nicholas Shapleigh, Sarah (according to Kittery constable Robert Mendum and resident Joseph Miles) acted as a reasonable intermediary. (BAXTER3, p. 109.) In addition, when Benjamin Gilliam and Mark Munns approached Sarah with an offer to pay for the copper destroyed by Shapleigh in order to settle the dispute, she gave a thoughtful and prudent reply. According to their deposition: "...She thanked us for our love, but she could not accept of it [their offer] because it would mar or wrong her case and her husband was not at home." BAXTER3, p. 113. Sarah was wise enough not only to *not* harm her husband's lawsuit, but also to not damage her relationship with her husband.
160. GUNNISON. "The King's Arms Tavern formerly as early as two centuries ago was the principal place of entertainment in the town [Boston], at the corner of Col. Shrimpton's Lane, now called Exchange St. Afterwards called States Arms Tavern, in State Street, then known as Water St."
161. On April 1651, Hugh Gunnison of Boston, Vintner, and Sarah his wife, deeded to John Sampson, Henry Shrimpton, and William Brenton, all of Boston, Merchants, for 600 Sterling, his house and personal property described in an inventory of 18 rooms, halls and closets. GUNNISON.
162. On June 7, 1651, Nicholas Shapleigh of Kittery leased Hugh Gunnison for 21 years "all his edifices, lands, accommodations & privileges at the Point where Mr. William Hilton now dwelleth containing five hundred acres." The Gunnisons were already residents of Kittery when this indenture was made, although not at the house occupied by William Hilton, who was apparently still there. MEWD, Vol. 1, p. 67-68.
163. On Nov. 16, 1652, Commissioners Simon Bradstreet, Samuel Symonds, Thomas Wiggin, and Bryan Pendleton held court at Kittery (after summoning the people to appear there). Residents did not want to submit to the authority of Massachusetts Bay and there was long agitation. The people of Kittery wanted their own articles and conditions, which were wholly denied. Finally, they submitted to Massachusetts. MPCR, Vol. 2, p. 5-6.

a falling out over the boundaries of the property Gunnison had leased, and a legal dispute ensued in 1653-1654.[164] Gunnison eventually prevailed, but, disgusted by Shapleigh's behavior, he gave up his lease and bought out rival innkeeper Robert Mendum on Kittery Point. Mendum's real estate included two houses, one of which was formerly Thomas Crockett's.

By 1656, the Crockett family returned permanently to Kittery, where they lived near the Gunnisons on the Point.[165] We do not know why the Crockett family returned to Kittery,[166] but in addition to providing Ann with a better daily companion than Ellen Raynes, the move might have been because Hugh Gunnison was then in poor health[167] and needed assistance. In addition to having a license to run an ordinary, Gunnison had also been granted the Piscataqua River ferry privilege. On June 30, 1653, however, he was "presented" at court (a public shaming that carried a penalty) for "not providing beare & Victualls for strangers

---

164. See BAXTER3 (p. 98-121) for documents related to the Gunnison-Shapleigh case. Thanks to the intervention of the Massachusetts General Court, Gunnison eventually prevailed and recovered most of the property appropriated by Shapleigh (housing, lands, coppers, guns, and pewter to the value of 107 pounds), as well as a financial settlement.

165. On Oct. 11, 1656, John Billine [Billing] (a minor) with his mother Elizabeth, widow of John Billine Sr., sold to Thomas Crockett and Rice Thomass [young Billing's stepfather], a house and land in Kittery at the point near the Harbor's mouth, a part of the neck of land that Major Shapleigh's store house stood on. John Billing, Jr. was paid 12 pounds—6 pounds each by Crockett and Rice Thomas. MEWD, Vol. 3, p. 172-173. (This second deed was drawn up Aug. 12, 1661 because John Billing was a minor at the time of the original sale.) In his 1661 deed, Billing, Jr. says he delivered this house up to Thomas Crockett in 1656. The later deed appears to clear title to this land and house, part of which Thomas apparently sold to his son Ephraim, for the seven-pound debt from Ephraim that showed on the inventory of Thomas Crockett's estate.

166. Another possible motivating factor for the move could have been to remove the Crockett family from the proximity of the Stover family in York. Sylvester Stover was a fisherman (and ferryman) in York with stages at Cape Neddick River. (LIBBY/NOYES, p. 667. Sylvester Stover) Stover and his shrew of a wife Elizabeth were frequently in court for fighting and not attending religious meetings (see MPCR). On July 28, 1655, Stover and his wife were "presented" at court for "complaining one of another on a Lords day in the morning; in saying his wife did abuse him & bade him go to Thomas Crockett's to his bastard & carry some bread & cheese; & the said wife of Stover said her husband did commonly call her 'whore'." MPCR, Vol. 2, p.46. York historian Charles Edward Banks says a John Stover "in his youth lived with Thomas Crockett..." Although John Stover called Sylvester Stover his "uncle," Sylvester might have been his father rather than his uncle, and thus John was the bastard to whom Elizabeth refers in 1655. (BANKS2, P. 52.) I could find no indication in the MPCR the identity of the mother of John Stover, nor how or why the boy came to be connected to the Crocketts. No later information connects him to the Crockett family, and it is possible the boy was simply bound out to Thomas Crockett in exchange for his food and clothing.

167. In his deposition given March 15, 1654, Mark Munns, who was present during the Shapleigh-Gunnison confrontations, noted that Hugh Gunnison commented upon his fatigue, leading one to believe he might have been ill. "...So Mr. Shapleigh went forth ... and when he came in again he said, If you will not end the business now I will take my Course: whereunto Mr. Gunnison answered Mr. Shapleigh, If you will stand to what hath been tendered so: if not you may take your Course for it is very late & I am very weary and cannot at this time agitate any longer, & forthwith went to bed..." BAXTER3, p. 115. In addition, on May 6, 1657, Hugh Gunnison, who had been elected Deputy Constable of Kittery, was judged unmeet for service, and discharged from whatever "employments he hath had, both in Military and Judicial affayres." Gunnison's descendant George Gunnison (who shares this fact in GUNNISON) assumes this dismissal is related to his ancestor's religious beliefs, which were known to stray from that of the Puritans of Massachusetts Bay Colony; however, another possibility is that Gunnison suffered from a debilitating long-term illness and as a result was physically unable to fulfill his duties. But if so, his illness did not prevent the litigious and erudite Gunnison from pursuing his financial or personal grievances in court, where he was both a frequent plaintiff and defendant.

The First Generation

& for his neglect in not attending the ferry."[168] Gunnison's lack of attention to his business—the family's main source of income—and to the ferry (the popular mode of travel between Kittery and Strawbery Banke/Portsmouth), suggests that he might have been ill. By 1659, the ferry situation had become so dire that on July 4th the York County Court reprimanded the town of Kittery for not ensuring that the Piscataqua River ferry from Gunnison's to Bryan Pendleton's in Portsmouth was maintained, "whereby Travellers are much Damnifyd by unnecessary stays." The Court ordered Kittery to "putt in Tho: Crockett to keepe the Ferry."[169] This was a lifetime appointment for Crockett (provided he proved fit, and, one assumes, wanted the position). Ferry rates were set at "six pence a person for ferriage."[170] After losing the ferry privilege, Hugh Gunnison was again presented at court for keeping a house of common entertainment without a license. Since Gunnison was acutely aware of the law, this also suggests that he might have been unwell. Not long after this presentment, on March 14, 1659, Hugh Gunnison entered into a 21-year agreement with his stepsons-in-law, William Seely (husband of Sarah's daughter Elizabeth Lynn) and William Rogers (husband of Sarah's daughter Sarah Lynn) for his land on Gunnison's Neck.[171] By April of 1660, Hugh Gunnison was dead[172] and Sarah Lynn Gunnison was again a widow. She appears to have continued to run the tavern with the help of Richard and Frances[173] White,[174] but their relationship fell apart and ended up in court in October of 1660.[175] Sarah soon mar-

---

168. MPCR, Vol. 2, p. 13. The presentment was brought into York County Court by the Grand Inquest held at York on the same day (June 30, 1653). Gunnison was discharged with an admonition from the court and required to pay officer's fees.
169. MPCR, Vol. 2, p. 80 and p. 82. The Court told the town of Kittery that it would be charged five pounds for their neglect if they failed to secure Thomas Crockett for the ferry.
170. MPCR, Vol. 2, p. 80.
171. MEWD, Vol. 1, p. 157-158. The lease to Seely and Rogers also included the little island Gunnison owned, but excluded 2 acres of land Hugh had previously sold to Francis Trickey. Seely and Rogers were to pay Gunnison or his heirs 10 shillings annually for the lease, which might (in addition to providing for his stepdaughters) have been an attempt to help net his current family with some regular income after his death. Interesting enough, the deed was acknowledged before magistrate Nicholas Shapleigh, with whom Gunnison had previously had the property dispute. Shapleigh, who was always a friend to Sarah Lynn Gunnison, was likely the closest magistrate at hand.
172. On April 12, 1660, Richard Davenport, who had purchased a (likely discounted) bill from Francis Knight to Hugh Gunnison, reassigned this bill to "Sarah Gunnison, Administratrix to the estate of Hugh Gunnison," signifying Gunnison was deceased by this date. Sarah was possibly related to Francis Knight, hence the loan of money in the first place. The assignment, which was probably to protect Knight from prosecution, was witnessed by William Tilly (Sarah's stepfather) and Robert Howard, Notary Public. MPCR, Vol. 1, p. 252.
173. Frances was the widow of William Hilton. Hilton had previously held the license for the tavern at the Point in Nicholas Shapleigh's house.
174. On July 5, 1660, Richard White of Kittery was presented at York County Court by the Grand Inquest for keeping a public ordinary without a license and for selling wine and beer and giving entertainment by virtue of Mr. Gunnison's license. White was acquitted, suggesting that the court recognized the business relationship into which he and Sarah Gunnison had entered. MPCR, Vol. 2, p. 90.
175. On Oct. 11, 1660, at the Court of Associates for the County of York, Sarah Gunnison was the plaintiff in an action of defamation to the value of 60 pounds against Richard White. (White had previously said that Sarah and "Skipper Jacobs"

ried for a third time, Captain John Mitchell,[176] possibly calculating that a husband might be easier to manage than someone she hired to help run the business.

In the meantime, Thomas Crockett had troubles of his own. Evidence was given by the Whites and others at York County Court on July 5, 1660, suggesting that there was "two [too] much frequent familiarity between Joseph Davesse [Davis] & Ann Crockett."[177] Davis, who at one point was a constable of Kittery, worked occasionally for Thomas Crockett.[178] He might also have been employed by Sarah Gunnison.[179] If Ann also helped Sarah at the tavern, it makes sense that the Whites saw them there together. If the evidence in the case against Ann and Joseph Davis had been given solely by Richard and Frances Whites, who were known troublemakers, the Grand Inquest would likely not have taken the matter up. But Magistrates Nicholas Shapleigh and John Davis (possibly Joseph's uncle)[180] also provided evidence that Joseph and Ann were spending too much time together. As a result, the Court ordered an Act of Separation between Ann and Davis, which carried a 10-pound penalty for each of them if they "shall hereafter bee found privately, frequently or unseasonably together."[181] (They never were.)[182] Davis, who

---

were having an affair or had slept together.) The Court found for Sarah and ordered White to acknowledge in open court the wrong he had done to her (which he did that day) and make a public acknowledgement at the next Training Day at Kittery. Sarah also sued White for detaining several buildings and goods from her (possibly her business) to the value of 60 pounds. That case went to a jury, which found for the defendant (White) costs of court. MPCR Vol. 2, p. 366-368.

176. The date of Sarah's marriage to Captain Mitchell is not known, however, it was prior to July 1, 1661, when Nicholas Shapleigh was presented at York County Court by the Grand Inquest for marrying the couple before publication of the banns, contrary to law. MPCR, Vol. 2, p. 106.

177. MPCR, Vol. 2, p. 93.

178. On July 5, 1658, at York County Court, Rice Thomas charged both Thomas Crockett and Joseph Davis with trespass "for cutting and destroing Tymber upon his Land..." MPCR, Vol. 2, p. 61-62. As this court case was related to the neck of land then in dispute between Crockett and Rice Thomas, Davis, who was also sued, must have been working for Crockett at the time. In both cases the jury found for the defendants (Crockett and Davis). Crockett was awarded costs of court and Davis 16 shillings and 6 pence.

179. At the same court, Richard White and his wife Frances were charged with (among other things) "backe bitting of their neighbors & slandering them & for their great disorder In falling out & feighting one with another & for beateing Company in their house & for beateing Mis Gunnison & Joseph Davesse his servants..." MPCR, Vol. 2, p. 91. An initial reading suggests that Davis worked for White; however, the early recorders never used the pronoun "her" when referring to a woman, and so Davis could have been Sarah Gunnison's servant (i.e., worked for her, when it was recorded "him"). It is also possible that the house referred to was Sarah's own, but that she had hired the Whites to run or let it, and that both she and Davis were working there as well.

180. According to LIBBY/NOYES (p. 184, Major John Davis) Davis, who would become one of the most prominent men in Maine, was possibly a brother of Nicholas Davis, a tailor and innkeeper of York, who had a son named Joseph. The historians say Joseph died young (p. 187), without giving more information about the man, who was baptized in 1621 (and thus would have been about forty—around Ann Crockett's age—when the Act of Separation was passed). Since Joseph Davis never prosecuted the appeal of his case against Richard White and those who posted bond for him were never charged for this failure, he likely died prior to that opportunity. In addition, the last mention of Joseph Davis in MPCR (Vol. 2, p. 373) is Sept. 17, 1661.

181. MPCR, Vol. 2, p. 93.

182. Nothing in the MPCR suggests that Ann Crockett and Joseph Davis ever violated the Act of Separation. The bonds posted were never forfeited.

was present at court, posted his own 10-pound bond. Thomas Crockett was not at court, and Captain Francis Raynes of York, husband of Ann's immature friend Ellen, stepped forward and posted the bond for Ann's good behavior.[183]

The fact that Thomas Crockett—always quick to defend his family and his property—was not present at court when the accusation against his wife was made (especially since the session was held in York and not at Saco or Wells) was extremely unusual. His absence, combined with the accusation itself, leads one to wonder if Thomas was away from Kittery for a prolonged period. Even if he was loath to leave the ferry, Thomas would have found someone to operate it for him for the day so he could defend his wife and post her bond. In addition, the lives of those with whom Thomas Crockett was most closely connected went "to Hell in a handbasket" during this time.[184] If he was off on an extended trip (perhaps visiting England), Thomas was back in Kittery by the fall. In October of 1660 he charged Richard White (on behalf of White's wife Frances) with defamation, probably for asserting that Ann and Joseph Davis had an affair. Thomas won his case and five pounds damages from the Whites. More importantly, however, Frances White was ordered to make an acknowledgement in open court and at the next Training Day (an annual public event) that she had wronged Ann Crockett.[185]

From evidence provided in the court records, there appears to have been no cooling of the relationship between Thomas Crockett and Joseph Davis, no hint that Thomas ever suspected his wife or Davis of any inappropriate behavior. The following year Joseph Davis, then a Constable for Kittery, was charged by Richard White of taking away his goods and account books, and not returning them. When White took Davis to court and won his case, Thomas stepped forward to help Joseph post a bond ensuring that he would prosecute his appeal.[186] This

---

183. MPCR Vol. 2, p. 93. A year later, on July 2, 1661, Raynes' bond was taken off and Thomas Crockett entered into a bond of ten pounds in behalf of his wife for the continuance of her good behavior unto the next County Court. MPCR, Vol. 2, p. 93. Reading between the lines as to why Raynes stepped forward for Ann Crockett, one must also consider the possibility (long shot though it is) that he (or his wife) and Ann were related. I did some research on this possibility; however, not finding any reasonable lead, I discontinued it. Perhaps others who take up the Raynes' connection will be more prosperous.
184. In the same court as Ann was tried, Joane, Thomas' sister, was accused of drunkenness (MPCR, Vol. 2, p. 92); Sarah Gunnison was abused and beaten by the Whites; and Ann and Joseph Davis were presented for spending too much time together. One wonders if all these lapses would have occurred had Thomas Crockett been present in Kittery.
185. MPCR, Vol. 2, p. 367. On Oct. 11, 1660, Thomas Crockett, in behalf of his wife Ann Crockett, was plaintiff in an action of defamation to the value of 60 pounds versus Richard White, in behalf of his wife, Frances White, defendant. The Court found for the plaintiff costs of court, and ordered Goody White make a public acknowledgment of her offence given to Ann Crockett in open Court, as well as at the next Training Day at Kittery (or otherwise). Richard White was also ordered to pay five pounds damages.
186. MPCR, Vol. 2, p. 99-100. Thomas Crockett, Davis himself, and Jonathan Thing "engaged themselves in a bond of 200 pounds that the said Davis shall prosecute his appeal according to law." In addition, on Aug. 12, 1661, Joseph Davis

appeal never happened, probably because Joseph Davis passed away prior to his court date.[187]

Another challenge on Thomas Crockett's plate was the defense of the land grant he had received from Sir Ferdinando Gorges. Although Thomas had begun work clearing the land in 1644 in preparation for building a house (according to sister Joane's deposition), his work on Crockett's Neck appears to have been sporadic, especially after the family relocated to York. Unaware of Thomas Crockett's right of possession, the town of Kittery granted the land to Rice Thomas. This act might also have initiated the Crockett family's return to Kittery, so that Thomas could defend his property.

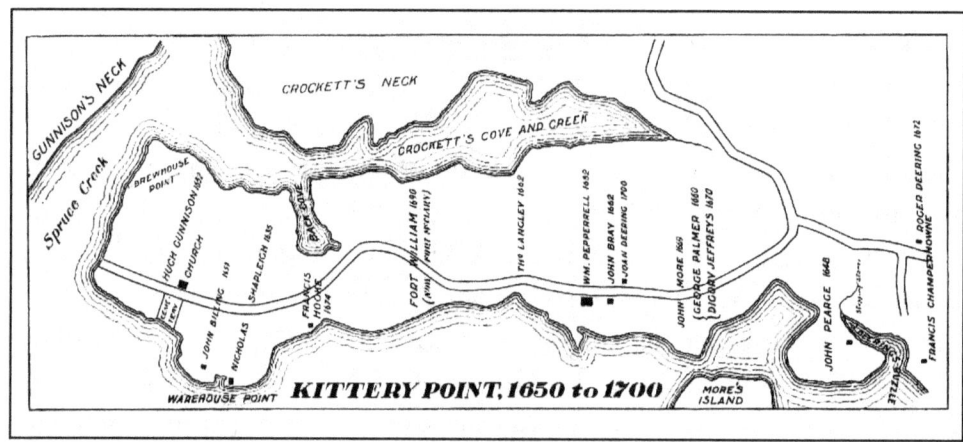

Map of Kittery Point, 1650-1700.
Crockett's Neck is across Spruce Creek in the area known as Crockett's Creek and Cove.[188]
(Map from "Old Kittery and her families," Everett S. Stackpole.)[189]

---

witnessed the replacement deed from John Billing, Jr. to Thomas Crockett for the house and land he had purchased from Billing (a minor when the sale occurred) in 1656. MEWD, Vol. 3, p. 172-173. This evidence supports the fact that there remained a strong relationship between Thomas Crockett and Joseph Davis after the Act of Separation between Davis and Ann Crockett was passed.

187. On Sept. 7, 1661, Thomas Crockett disowned before the Court of Associates held at Wells for York County "that ever Joseph Davis had any testimony of his concerning Davis' appeal to the last Court of Associates in the case between the said Davis & Richard White, so as to say, much less swear, that Joseph Davis was enforced by the County Court last at York to Join issue with Richard White." MPCR, Vol. 2, p. 373. This sounds as though Davis was deceased, and Richard White was attempting to make it appear as though Davis had agreed with White at the last County Court (in August). Sometime between Aug. 12, 1661, when Davis witnessed the deed from Billing to Crockett, and Sept. 7, 1661, the date of this court, Joseph Davis must have died. He does not appear in any real estate or court records after July 2, 1661, when he and George Palmer posted a bond in court for 40 pounds that Palmer, who had gotten drunk and verbally abused several people, would "bee of good behaviour towards all persons until the next County Court." MPCR, Vol. 2, p. 107.

188. The water body was known as Crockett's Cove during high tide and Crockett's Creek during low tide. Later it became known as Barter's Creek, named after Henry Barter, who married Thomas and Ann Crockett's granddaughter Sarah Crockett (daughter of Ephraim and Ann Edge Crockett). Barter was a shipbuilder and launched his vessels in the cove.

189. STACKPOLE, p. 44. (Image is in the public domain.)

The First Generation

The original grant to Rice Thomas, who had arrived in the area around the same time as Thomas Crockett,[190] was made by the town of Kittery in 1652 (the year the townsmen submitted to Massachusetts Bay Colony, when the Bay appropriated Ferdinando Gorges' land in Maine). Like many others, this grant was not recorded. No doubt at the instigation of Rice (who might have been aware that the Crocketts were planning to return to Kittery), the Selectmen of Kittery made a second grant to him on December 4, 1655. This grant to Rice Thomas read:

> "That whereas there was a certain neck of land granted by the Select Townsmen for Kittery, in the year 1652, : unto Ryce Thomas & was not recorded, it was therefore then granted by the Select Townsmen, the 4th day of December 1655 : unto the said Ryce Thomas, his heirs or assigns forever, the neck of land lying within the Spruce Creek, & upon the south west side, & is the neck of land that lieth on the further side of the creek, that runs behind Mr. Gunnison's house/ *provided it be in no former grant/.*"[191]

In 1658, the dispute over the neck of land came to a head, when on July 5th Rice Thomas brought a charge of trespass against Thomas Crockett "for cutting & destroying timber upon his land" before York County Court.[192] Depositions from Nicholas Frost[193] and Robert Mendum,[194] then both men of property and distinction, must have been provided to the jury, because despite the town grant to Rice Thomas the jury found for Thomas Crockett (the defendant), also awarding Crockett costs of court in the amount of 10 shillings.

Undeterred, Rice Thomas decided if he could not improve the property, he would sell it. In 1659 or 1660, Thomas approached Bryan Pendleton of Portsmouth, N.H., a prominent innkeeper, selectman, and military man, who was then buying up real

---

190. On April 21, 1654, Rice Thomas gave a deposition in the Gunnison-Shapleigh case about early property lines in Kittery. According to PIONEERS (p. 173) Rice Thomas was a "husbandman, Kittery, came at an early day; worked for John Treworgy, brewing for the fishermen, to this he deposed in the Gunnison case 21 April 1654, being of the age of 38 years." Rice Thomas was thus about five years younger than Thomas Crockett.
191. MEWD, Vol. 2, p. 28. I have added the italics at the end for emphasis.
192. MPCR, Vol. 2, p. 61-62.
193. Nicholas Frost gave his deposition to magistrate Nicholas Shapleigh on April 4, 1658. Frost's deposition stated that about sixteen or seventeen years ago Thomas Crockett had possession of a neck of land on Spruce Creek, lying on the northside of the creek, against his field that he now owned. "His possession was had by felling timber and clearing ground, and made preparation to build an house upon the said land." MEWD, Vol. 2, p. 26. The deposition was entered into the land records Feb. 12, 1665, by Edward Rishworth, the long-time recorder.
194. Robert Mendum gave his deposition to magistrate Thomas Withers on April 29, 1658. Mendum said that about twelve or thirteen years earlier Thomas Crockett and Thomas Beeson "did fall Tymber to Saw upon the necke of land over against Thomas Crockett's field." MEWD, Vol. 2, p. 26-27.

estate in Maine.[195] At the time, Thomas Crockett, who operated the ferry from the Gunnison's to Pendleton's in Portsmouth, was also occasionally employed by Pendleton in his brew house. In a deposition given by John White years later, White said he overheard Crockett and Pendleton talking about the land that Pendleton was going to buy from Rice Thomas (Crockett's Neck), and Crockett asked Pendleton "not to meddle with that land ... because it was his land, & it would breed a great difference between them." According to White, Pendleton replied: "God forbid I should do any man wrong. I will not meddle with it."[196] Despite this proclamation, Pendleton did take Thomas Crockett to court over the neck of land in Kittery, however. (Pendleton might have already purchased the property from Rice Thomas and could not get his money back.) On September 17, 1661, at the Court of Associates held at Wells for York County, Pendleton, charged Crockett with trespass. This time, the court found for the plaintiff (Pendleton) the trespass done and costs of court. Thomas Crockett appealed from the judgment of the court to the next County Court, and posted a bond that he would prosecute his appeal.[197]

What occurred next to secure the disputed neck of land for Thomas Crockett was a freak fluke of history or luck—or both. Although the English Civil War had been settled by 1653 and a Protectorate established (after the beheading of King Charles I), the Puritans did not long retain their hold on power. Lord Protector Oliver Cromwell died in 1658 initiating a political power vacuum that created a crisis in Great Britain. Eventually, the royal heir to the throne, Charles II, was invited to return to Britain and the monarchy was restored in 1660. The power shift that occurred in Great Britain from Puritans to Royalists was mirrored on the ground in New England. After a Privy Council in England was appointed in May of 1661 to settle affairs in Maine, Ferdinando Gorges (the grandson of Sir Ferdinando Gorges), who had inherited his grandfather's extensive holdings in Maine, which had been usurped by the Puritans of Massachusetts, lost no time in resurrecting his claims. He appointed Crown loyalists Nicholas Shapleigh and Francis Champernowne—the Devon men— "to reorganize the government of Maine."[198] Most Mainers, although

---

195. LIBBY/NOYES, p. 537. Major Brian Pendleton.
196. Deposition of John White, given June 24, 1669. MEWD, Vol. 2, p. 212.
197. MPCR, Vol. 2, p. 371. Thomas Crockett and Robert Wadleigh acknowledged themselves in a bond of 40 pounds each that Crockett would prosecute his appeal. There is no evidence that this appeal ever occurred—nor the bonds forfeited—likely due to the reversal in the legal control of Maine from Massachusetts Bay Colony to Gorges' men under the restoration of the monarchy in Great Britain.
198. MEWD, Vol. 1, p. 39. See also "Documentary History of the State of Maine," Vol. 4 (BAXTER3), p. 230-231 and 242-247.

tolerating the Puritans while they had been in power (as did Shapleigh and Champernowne), had remained loyal to the Crown. After Thomas Crockett lost his case against Pendleton at the Court of Associates September 17, 1661, "no sessions of the Court of Associates were held, as most of the [magistrates] bench had gone over to Gorges."[199]

During the period that Gorges' representatives were in the ascendant, Thomas Crockett took the opportunity to obtain another important deposition that helped him secure Crockett's Neck to himself and his descendants. On April 16, 1662, Nicholas Frost gave a second deposition[200] to magistrate Nicholas Shapleigh stating that "Mr. Thomas Gorges did give unto Thomas Crockett the neck of land that lyeth over against the field of Thomas Crockett, within Spruce Creek, within the town of Kittery, Which land was given by Mr. Thomas Gorges eighteen or nineteen years since, or there about."[201] Since the grant by the town of Kittery to Rice Thomas was on the condition that the land "be in no former grant," Crockett's prior grant from Gorges now took precedence. Thomas Crockett proceeded to clear the land on Crockett's Neck and build his house. Although Pendleton and his son made other attempts in court to get back the land, they were unsuccessful.[202]

Around the year 1667, Thomas Crockett's house was completed and he and Ann—and their growing family—relocated across Spruce Creek to Crockett's Neck.

---

199. MPCR, Vol. 2, p. 375. On December 22, 1661, Shapleigh and Champernowne met at Wells with the commissioners and public notice was given that the commissioners "had taken into their own hands the rentals and properties of Gorges." MPCR, Vol. 1, p. 39. In January of 1662, a warrant was issued for the towns to send deputies to Wells May 25 to act as deputies for Gorges. "The inhabitants of the province were instructed to present the title deeds to their lands at the same time and place ..." Demand was made (and apparently complied with) for all the books, rolls, etc. of the province. MEWD, Vol. 1, p. 39. On May 27, 1662, commissioners from Massachusetts Bay appeared at Wells, met with the Gorges' men, and eventually a gentlemen's agreement was struck to hold court mutually at York in July. MPCR, Vol. 1, p. 59. Massachusetts Bay did not long keep up their end of the agreement.
200. Because a grant from Gorges would have meant nothing prior to the Restoration of the monarchy, Nicholas Frost's 1658 deposition claimed Crockett's possession was because he had felled timber and cleared ground there. After Gorges' rights were restored by the Crown under the return of Charles II, however, Frost came forth with the information that Thomas Gorges, on behalf of Sir Ferdinando Gorges, had granted the land to Crockett.
201. MEWD, Vol. 2, p. 27. Prior to Crockett's appearance at the Court of Associates to answer the charge of trespassing brought by Captain Pendleton, Richard Burgess had given a deposition claiming he overheard Thomas Gorges and Richard Vines give a grant of land to Thomas Crockett on the north side of Spruce Creek. Burgess claimed they ordered Roger Gard to record the transaction. (MEWD, Vol. 2, p. 27.) The recording obviously never occurred. Frost's second deposition about the grant from Gorges, combined with Burgess' testimony, helped confirm Thomas Crockett's claim to Crockett's Neck.
202. On July 9, 1667, around the time that the Crocketts moved into their new home on Crockett's Neck, Captain James Pendleton (Pendleton's son) brought a charge of trespass against Thomas Crockett before the Court held at York for the Western Division (of Maine). This time the jury found a *non liquet*, a deferment of the case for lack of information. MPCR, Vol. 1, p. 282-283. On July 2, 1672, Major Bryan Pendleton was plaintiff in an action concerning a title of land v. Thomas Crockett at York County Court. After hearing the case, the court gave the decision to Crockett, awarding him his costs of 1 pound, 16 shillings, and effectively title to the property. MPCR, Vol. 2, p. 230-233. The Pendletons must have given up after this last attempt, because there is no further record of the case at court. If Pendleton paid Rice Thomas for the property, it is highly unlikely he ever recovered his money.

Lower Kittery (now, Kittery), 1635-1700.
(Map from "Old Kittery and her families," Everett S. Stackpole.)[203]

---

203. STACKPOLE, p. 65. Henry Barter, the only person noted on Crockett's Neck on this map, was married to Thomas and Ann Crockett's granddaughter Sarah, daughter of Ephraim and Anne (Edge) Crockett. NOTE: Brave Boat Harbor, the dividing line between Kittery and York where Thomas Crockett once operated a ferry, can be seen in the bottom right of the map. (Image in the public domain.)

Thomas and Ann Crockett had eight children who lived to adulthood: Ephraim, Ann (or Anne), Sarah, Elihu, Joseph, Joshua, Hugh, and Mary. All eight children received a share of Sir Ferdinando Gorges' 1643 grant to their father, either in land on Crockett's Neck or in money for their share of those 188 acres. Please refer to the "Genealogical Dictionary of Thomas and Ann Crockett" beginning on page 377 for more information on Thomas and Ann's children. (Ephraim Crockett's life will be covered in Chapter 2.)

Thomas Crockett's Last Decade

The last decade of Thomas Crockett's life was filled with the rise of his and Ann's children, particularly eldest son Ephraim, and the diminishment of older family members and friends. As Thomas watched his children mature and his eldest son take a place in Kittery society, he also witnessed his sister Joane and friend Sarah Gunnison decline in health and social status.

Ephraim had come of age prior to Thomas Crockett's move to Crockett's Neck in 1667. Arrangements between father and son suggest that Ephraim helped his father build the family's new home, perhaps in exchange for land and/or a house in Brave Boat Harbor.

Thomas helped his eldest son raise cash by transferring to Ephraim some land on Kittery Point. In 1667, Ephraim and Thomas *both* sold property to Abraham Corbett, a distiller from Portsmouth.[204] Corbett purchased from the Crocketts the former Billing's house and land that Thomas had bought from John Billing, Jr. in 1656, and where he and Ann had raised their family after returning from York. Prior to the Corbett sale, Thomas sold (via a seven-pound loan)[205] a portion of the Billing's land to Ephraim, which real estate on April 16, 1667, Ephraim turned around and sold to Corbett. Ephraim Crockett sold the distiller six acres for 17

---

204. LIBBY/NOYES, p. 162. Abraham Corbett. The historians note that while Corbett owned property in Portsmouth, he "app. generally liv. on his 11 a. homestead on Kit. Point, where he had a warehouse, kept tavern and ran ferry to Great Isl. and Portsm." The Kittery Point real estate was likely that which Corbett purchased from Thomas and Ephraim Crockett.
205. On July 13, 1680, Edward Rishworth, recorder, entered into the York land records the deed from John Billing, Jr. to Thomas Crockett. Underneath the Billing's deed is written the following: "Further, each of us do allow of the sale of yt Land formerly sold by our father unto our brother Ephraim Crocket, only he is to allow unto the Estate seven pounds, mentioned in the Inventory [of Thomas Crockett's estate] unto all which We do set our hand this day and year above written [July 21, 1679]," followed by: the mark of Ann Crockett; the mark of Ephraim Crockett; the mark of Hugh Crockett; the mark of Joseph Crockett; and the mark of Joshua Crockett. "Acknowledged this 21st of July – 1679 – before me, Francis Hooke, Commissioner." MEWD, Vol. 3, page 173.

pounds,[206] thus netting 10 pounds on the property transfer (although Ephraim did not pay the seven pounds he owed his father until after Thomas' death). On May 29, 1667, Thomas Crockett, "husbandman," followed with the house and balance of the Billing's property (2 ½ acres) on Kittery Point, selling that to Corbett for 32 pounds.[207]

Thomas Crockett also appears to have sold his Brave Boat Harbor real estate (an unrecorded grant of land), to son Ephraim prior to his death. The property might have had a house on it and could be where the Crocketts lived when Thomas ran the ferry (and where Ephraim Crockett resided in 1667, rather than with his parents on Crockett's Neck). If the Brave Boat Harbor property had no house, Ephraim would have used the money from his sale of land to Corbett to build one.

Ephraim was married by 1671 (and probably before). He and his wife Anne Edge resided in Brave Boat Harbor, where Ephraim worked as a tailor. Ephraim and Anne's son, Ephraim Crockett, Jr., was likely born before Thomas Crockett's death, and thus the Crockett patriarch would have known the laughter and love of at least one grandchild prior to his death.

Although Thomas and Ann Crockett's offspring were rising in prominence during the last decade of his life, their friends were falling. By the spring of 1664, Sarah Gunnison's third husband, Captain John Mitchell, was deceased,[208] and she was once again running a tavern. On July 5, 1664, Sarah Mitchell was admonished by the Grand Jury at York County Court for selling wine and beer without a license.[209] Sarah wasted no time in marrying again. This time the Crockett's old friend—then in her mid-forties (if not older)—wed a man much younger than herself, Francis Morgan, who had just come of age.[210]

Perhaps because Sarah was old enough to be her fourth husband's mother she thought she could manage him; however, this proved a tragic mistake. Thomas and Ann Crockett had to watch helplessly as Sarah was beaten by her husband (who, when confronted about his spousal abuse, admitted "he had struck his wife & would do it [again]"), and taken advantage of by Morgan throughout her final

---

206. MEWD, Vol. 2, p. 137-138. Thomas Crockett witnessed the deed, as did William Cotton.
207. MEWD, Vol. 2, p. 134-135. This deed was witnessed by Francis Champernowne, Henry Greenland, and Ephraim Crockett. Ann Crockett signed off on her dower rights; both Thomas and Ann Crockett acknowledged to Justice Francis Champernowne (the scion of Devon Champernownes) that this was their free act and deed on the day the deed was signed.
208. The inventory of the estate of Capt. John Mitchell was taken May 8, 1664. The estate was valued at a considerable amount, much of which was probably accrued by his predecessor, Hugh Gunnison, second husband of Sarah Lynn Gunnison Mitchell. MPCR, Vol. 1, p. 227-228.
209. MPCR, Vol. 2, p. 152-153. The license previously was probably under Capt. Mitchell's name, and ended with his death.
210. LIBBY/NOYES, p. 491. Francis Morgan.

years.[211] Morgan began liquidating Hugh Gunnison's estate,[212] which had been folded into that of Sarah's third husband, Captain Mitchell. In addition, family squabbles between Morgan and his stepchildren frequently played out embarrassingly in court. (Sarah's son, Ephraim Lynn, was about five years older than his stepfather, and thus he was understandably protective of his mother.)[213] One wonders what Thomas and Ann Crockett must have thought to have seen their old friend fallen in social status to such a degree.

By the spring of 1673, Sarah Morgan was reduced to begging for help. On April 1, 1673, Sarah requested financial assistance via a petition to the Court of Associates held at Wells. The Court, which was sympathetic to her plea, acknowledged her "weak condition" and ordered the Kittery Selectmen to "take some effectual course for supply of what is needful for her convenient maintenance out of her husband's estate according to what he is able to allow her …"[214] After this date, no

---

211. In addition to liquidating the estates of Hugh Gunnison and Capt. John Mitchell, Morgan was a vile-tempered man who was abusive to his wife. Sarah apparently tried to hold her own against this hot-headed young man, causing physical fights that ended the couple up in court. An example of this occurred in Oct. 22, 1667, when Sarah Morgan complained in court against her husband "for such abusive speeches & Actions as tend to her great Injury, if not the apparent Hazard of her life." When examined about the charge, Morgan confessed "he had struck his wife & would do it, for it was below him to complain to Authority against his wife." Morgan failed to repent, and "obstinately said that he repented not of what he had done & for all this he should be the worse for it." MPCR, Vol. 1, p. 300. The Court was so bothered by Morgan's attitude—and worried about Sarah's safety—that they prohibited him from "keeping her company under any pretense whatsoever upon the penalty of the breach of one hundred pound until the next Court held in November." By then, however, the couple had either made up, or—more likely—Morgan had found a way to threaten his wife, for at court Nov. 12th Morgan acknowledged his "obstinate carriage" and at an adjournment of the court the couple expressed "their desire to live together as becometh their relation." The Court acquitted Morgan of his 100-pound bond, which left him free to continue to liquidate his wife's resources and those of her prior husbands. MPCR, Vol. 1, p. 300.
212. On April 22, 1665, Francis Morgan, surgeon, and wife Sarah sold to John Cutt of Portsmouth, merchant, for 111 pounds, 6 shillings and 10 pence, 110 acres of the 300-acre grant Hugh Gunnison received from the town of Kittery. On the same date, the couple also sold to Cutt two acres of marsh at Brave Boat Harbor near Christopher Mitchell's, which land was bought of John Lander (probably by Capt. Mitchell, who was likely related to Christopher). Morgan received 11 pounds for the marsh land. MEWD, Vol. 2, p. 39-42.
213. On March 8, 1670/71, Capt. Richard Walden, Commissioner, Edward Rishworth and Capt. John Wincoll, Associates, dealt with several matters in an impromptu court held at the house of John Bray in Brave Boat Harbor. A complaint was made by Mr. Francis Morgan against Ephraim Lynn and Elihu Gunnison (Sarah's sons and Morgan's stepsons) for "abusing the said Morgan by throwing him down in his own house & for striking of his man Watt for endeavoring to rescue him out of their hands." Lynn and young Gunnison owned their actions to the magistrates, and Ephraim Lynn was fined 40 shillings and required to post a bond for 20 pounds that he would be on his good behavior toward all men, especially his stepfather. Elihu Gunnison was fined 20 shillings (10 shillings to Watt, Morgan's servant, and 10 shillings to the County). No bond for good behavior was required of Elihu, possibly because he was still a minor. MPCR, Vol. 2 p. 417. This is only one instance of multiple times Francis Morgan ended up in court with extended family members. Morgan, although a man with some education, was hot-headed and often abusive. The following month after this incident occurred, on April 25, 1671, Morgan was brought before the Court of Associates (at an adjournment at Saco to Newichawannock) for "profane swearing." He was fined 20 shillings and court costs. The Court also ordered a special warrant sent for Sampson Penley, prison keeper of Falmouth, to call Penley before the County Court to know "a reason of Francis Morgan's release." Apparently, Morgan had been jailed in Falmouth for some other infraction. MPCR, Vol. 2, p. 427.
214. MPCR, Vol. 2, p. 467-468. The estate referred to was the fruit of Sarah's labors, not that of Sarah's current husband. Although Francis Morgan did have some income from his dubious medical practice, most of his money likely came from the Gunnison/Mitchell estates and income Sarah earned from tavern keeping.

mention is made of the woman known as Sarah Lynn Gunnison Mitchell Morgan in any deed or court record and so it is assumed by historians that she must have died not long after her petition for help.

Francis Morgan remained in the area for several more years. After some of the Saco, Androscoggin (Ammoscogon), and Penobscot Indians began raiding English homesteads and killings settlers in Maine during the First Indian War (1675-1678, King Philip's War in southern New England), however, Morgan shipped for England in August of 1677 and "is seen little thereafter."[215] The Crocketts would likely have thought: "Good riddance!"

Much like Sarah Morgan, Thomas' sister Joane also experienced a diminishment of her social status in Kittery in her later years. The lives of these two women highlight the dangers facing widows in early New England. Widows needed a man to protect and defend them, as well as to provide them with clothing and sustenance, and agency in court to manage their late husbands' estates. Once remarried, however, power and resources were transferred to their new husbands.

Joane Crockett's first protector and defender was her husband, John Andrews, an early settler (around 1640) and farmer in the Eliot portion of Kittery.[216] Andrews was twenty years older than Joane and obviously devoted to her. During his lifetime, John Andrews stood by his incorrigible wife through thick and thin, paying fine after fine for her bold and often outrageous behavior (which mimicked Andrews' own disdain for authority). But in 1666, when Joane needed money for clothes and necessities, it was to her nephew Ephraim Crockett she turned for assistance, perhaps because her husband, then in his mid-sixties,[217] was ill or infirm. Ephraim helped Joane borrow money from Captain Richard Lockwood of Kittery to cover her basic needs and likely those of her husband and unmarried children.[218]

---

215. LIBBY/NOYES, p. 491. Francis Morgan.
216. LIBBY/NOYES, p. 65. John Andrews.
217. LIBBY/NOYES, p. 65. John Andrews.
218. On Dec. 11, 1666, Joane Andrews promised to pay Richard Lockwood 1 pound, 1 shilling and 6 pence on the last of June upon demand and to pay double damages if she failed. This debt was witnessed by Ephraim Crockett and recorded. MEWD, Vol. 2, p. 165-166. Also, Joane Andrews, wife of John Andrews, promised to deliver to Richard Lockwood (for clothing "to supply my necessity") one steer and one calf. This debt was also witnessed by Ephraim and John Puddington. Vol. 2, p. 166. Since Joane had a negative history in court with the Lockwoods—in June of that same year Joane was administered 10 lashes on the bare skin as punishment for her words against Mrs. Lockwood (Deborah Gunnison, daughter of Crockett friend Hugh Gunnison and his first wife Elizabeth) MPCR, Vol. 1, p. 264—it is not likely that she herself would have sought them out to borrow from them money or necessities, nor would they have been inclined to provide that to her. This leads one to suspect that Ephraim Crockett—nephew to one party and childhood friend of the other party (Deborah Gunnison Lockwood)—played a major role in bringing them together. Unfortunately, Joane failed to pay Lockwood the money and bovines due, and ended up in court with the Lockwoods several more times. For some reason, there was bad blood between Deborah (Gunnison) Lockwood and Joane (Crockett) Andrews, which might have occurred when Deborah

The First Generation

By July 4, 1671, John Andrews was dead and Joane was granted administration of his estate.[219] For her next husband, Joane selected Philip Atwell,[220] a fisherman who was much younger than her first husband. On April 2, 1672, at a Court of Associates held at Wells, letters of Administration were granted Philip Atwell for the estate of John Andrews. Christopher Mitchell (Joane's son-in-law) and Ephraim Crockett posted a bond of 300-pounds that Philip would make a true account of the estate within twelve months.[221] The inventory of Andrews' appreciable estate was taken January 15, 1671/72 by Rice Thomas and Jeremiah Gutteridge, and included 18 acres of valuable marsh land (valued at 54 pounds); a house with orchard, garden, outhouses and fencing (20 pounds); nine score (180) acres of outland (20 pounds); five cows (21 pounds, 5 shillings); a mare, two colts, and a horse (16 pounds); and a variety of other stock, plus household goods, a gun and a rapier. The total of John Andrews' estate was valued at 151 pounds and 12 shillings,[222] which, considering Joane's tart tongue, is probably what had enticed her second husband to tie the knot.

By March 23, 1673, however, Philip Atwell and Joane had had a falling out and "he had taken his chest out into the bushes."[223] Although Joane was still legally married to Atwell—who as her husband should have managed Andrews' estate—that fall, the Court appointed magistrate Francis Hooke to be Administrator of the estate of John Andrews (Sr.)[224] (Possibly the Court considered Atwell, an uneducated fisherman, incapable of settling the estate.) Ephraim stepped forward to assist his aunt again in 1675, appearing on the Great Island (where women were prohibited) to swear an oath that he had witnessed a deed from her and his cousin John Andrews, Jr. for three acres of marsh land, which they had sold to John Bray, shipwright of Kittery.[225]

---

was a young girl. (Deborah was nine when Gunnison moved his combined family to Kittery.) Possibly Deborah worked for or was bound out to Joane and her husband prior to her marriage to Lockwood. The antagonism could also have stemmed from a personality clash, the two viragos being very much alike.
219. MPCR, Vol. 2, p. 214.
220. STACKPOLE, p. 294.
221. MPCR, Vol. 2, p. 449. Ephraim was acquitted from his bond and John Billing (another of Joane's sons-in-law) replaced him.
222. MPCR, Vol. 2, p. 452.
223. LIBBY/NOYES, p. 68. Philip Atwell. Joane's son John Andrews, Jr. remained friendly with his stepfather, with whom he might have fished. He and Philip Atwell appeared together at the Court of Associates held at Wells on April 1, 1673, where they owned a judgment to Henry Deering of one barrel and a half of mackerel and 4 shillings. MPCR, Vol. 2, p. 465.
224. MPCR, Vol. 2, p. 475. The Court of Associates directed Hooke to take an inventory of the debts due to and from John Andrews, Sr.'s estate and report back at the next County Court.
225. MEWD, Vol. 2, p. 338-339. This must have been a valuable piece of marsh in Brave Boat Harbor because Bray paid 100 pounds sterling for the property. (Jeremiah Gutteridge also appeared with Ephraim Crockett on the Great Island to swear an

Joane appears to have lived the next decade quietly upon the money she received from her first husband's estate. The last mention of Thomas Crockett's sister occurs in June of 1688, when at the Court of Quarter Sessions held at York on June 13, 1688, Edmund Gage was bound over to answer for "his beating and evil in treating Joan the wife of Philip Atwell."[226] The beating, which occurred about a month prior to the date Ephraim Crockett made his last will and testament,[227] suggests that Joane had fallen further in social status, and had no man to protect and defend her. (Her brother Thomas Crockett was deceased by then.)

No death record exists for Joane, so we have no way of knowing how long she lived after this beating. Since she did not reside with her husband, Joane probably lived in Brave Boat Harbor with one of her daughters, likely Sarah, who was also a widow.[228] The two women would have had to depend on Joane's rather simple son John Andrews, Jr. (Sarah's brother) for protection and defense. (John Andrews, Jr. appears to have been more of an agreeable "yes-man" to his mother than a protector, defender, and helper, as his father had been.) Ephraim Crockett, who had been stepping up to help prior to the death of his uncle John Andrews, Sr., passed away himself in September of 1688.

The last few years of Thomas Crockett's life were also marred by Indian troubles. King Philip's War broke out in Rhode Island in 1675 between the Wampanoags (another eastern Algonkian language speaking tribe) and the Plymouth Colony, after the English hung three Wampanoags for killing another Wampanoag. (Chief Metacom of the Wampanoag, known as King Philip by the English, refused to acknowledge English authority over his tribe.) This abuse of power and other English offenses against the Native Americans (notably, the continued expansion into

---

oath to the same.) In addition, Ephraim witnessed an indenture of the same date in which Joane and her son John Andrews, Jr. deeded the balance of the land and marsh to Bray for 33 pounds sterling. Vol. 2, p. 340-341.

226. MPCR, Vol. 3, p. 270. Gage was fined 30 shillings or could elect instead five lashes on the bare skin as punishment for beating Joane. The Court did not award her anything for her pain and suffering, although it does not appear that Joane pressed charges. If her mainstay, nephew Ephraim, was ill and/or on his deathbed, Joane might not have had anyone to press charges for her. The mention of Philip Atwell in court was likely to clarify who Joane was, not that the two of them lived together as man and wife.

227. Ephraim Crockett made his last will and testament July 17, 1688. MEWD, Wills, p. 71-72. Although he made his will in July, Ephraim did not die until after Sept. 26, 1688, when he and his wife Anne appeared in person in front of Francis Hooke, Just. Quo, probably bringing the reversion (voiding) of the deed from Ephraim to Richard White for 50 acres in Brave Boat Harbor. (The transfer of this real estate was covered in a new deed dated April 27, 1686. See MEWD, Vol. 5, p. 145.)

228. Sarah Mitchell, widow, was one of the petitioners against the surveying and granting of their lands in Brave Boat Harbor to Walter Barefoot, Aug. 15, 1688. LIBBY/NOYES, List 292, p. 33. Other signers of the petition were: John Bray, Dygory Jeffrey (then husband of Ann Crockett), John Andrews, Jr., John Billing, Jr., Ephraim Crockett, and Joseph Couch. List 292 is pretty much a Who's Who of the extended Crockett-Andrews family, with the exception of latecomer and shipbuilder John Bray, and Joseph Couch, who was Bray's apprentice. See MEWD, Vol. 2, p. 114-115 for Couch's indenture.

Indian territory) resulted in Wampanoag raiding parties throughout southern New England. The English colonists responded with deadly force, attacking not just the Wampanoags, but also peaceful tribes.[229]

A second theatre of King Philip's War opened in Maine in the summer of 1675. Known in Maine as the First Indian War, the conflict between the English and disaffected Native Americans lasted until 1678, the year before Thomas Crockett's death.

After learning of the Wampanoag raids on Swansea in June of 1675, English colonists, who until then had lived peaceably in Maine for half a century with the various Wabanaki tribes, marched up the Kennebec River and demanded the Kennebec (Kennebis) Indians surrender their guns. This—and the banning of the sale of powder and shot to all Native Americans—led to a dire food shortage amongst the Indians the following winter, since the natives had become dependent upon their guns for shooting game.[230]

In their ignorance, most of the English colonists lumped the loosely-connected Wabanaki tribes together as one common enemy—rather than treating the tribes as individual entities—thereby alienating those (such as the Kennebecs) who wanted peace with the English and might otherwise have remained neutral:

> "Ironically, it was the English vision of a monolithic Indian enemy that was key to the success of Maine's Wabanakis in this war. The English of Massachusetts Bay and Maine retaliated against Wabanaki depredations as if all Wabanakis were subject to a central authority, that all Wabanakis were geared for war. This blanket attitude toward the Indians, held by many (not all, but many) Englishmen from Maine, New Hampshire, and Massachusetts Bay, would be self-fulfilling."[231]

While King Philip's War proved a disaster for Native Americans in southern New England, the opposite was true in Maine, where "the Wabanakis won an

---

229. In December of 1675, fearful that the Narragansett tribe of Rhode Island (with whom Roger Williams had inked a treaty) would join the Wampanoags, an armed force of 1,000 Englishmen from Massachusetts Bay, Plymouth, and Hartford colonies attacked the Narragansett in their winter settlement. During what became known as the Great Swamp Massacre, approximately 700 Narragansett men, women and children were killed. After the massacre the remaining Narragansett *did* join forces with King Philip against the English. National Park Service website, Roger Williams National Memorial, Rhode Island. "King Philip's War (1675-1678)." https://www.nps.gov/rowi/learn/historyculture/kingphilip.htm#:~:text=The%20army%20invaded%20Rhode%20Island,American%20men%2C%20women%20and%20children.
230. PEMAQUID, p. 185. "To make matters worse, several Machias and Cape Sable Indians were kidnapped and sold into slavery in spring 1675 by a Boston-based trading vessel sailing along the Maine coast."
231. "Creating an Indian Enemy in the Borderlands: King Philip's War in Maine, 1675-1678." Christopher J. Bilodeau. "Maine History." Vol. 47, Number 1. Jan. 1, 2013. p. 13.

astounding victory, pushing English settlers and traders almost entirely out of the province."[232] Nine out of thirteen Maine settlements were destroyed, and more than 7% of the colonists—men, women, and children—were killed (260 out of an estimated population of 3,500).[233] Those in the eastern settlements who survived relocated south to the Pascataqua region or to Massachusetts. Although the Crockett family survived the raids that occurred during the First Indian War, many other families, mostly to the eastward, experienced tragic losses, and the sad and horrific stories about their deaths (or captivity) were well-known by the survivors. (More on the First Indian War in Chapter 2.)

Thomas Crockett would see peace with the Wabanakis in Maine before he died, but he must have known—as probably both the colonists and Native Americans did—that the peace would not hold. Few Englishmen bothered to get to know the natives and their unique culture, and this lack of understanding and respect resulted in fear and distrust. As he faced his final days, Thomas would have worried and wondered what the future would bring for his children and grandchildren.

Thomas Crockett died in February or March of 1678/79. If he was born in 1610/11, Thomas was approximately sixty-eight when he died. The inventory of his estate was taken March 20, 1678/79 by magistrate Francis Hooke and William Scriven, a planter and shipwright of Kittery. Scriven also founded the Baptist church in Maine[234] (and later in South Carolina)[235] and it is possible that prior to Thomas Crockett's passing he and his family (like many others in Kittery seeking spiritual solace during the First Indian War) came under the influence of the intelligent and articulate Scriven, who espoused believer baptism and more forgiving religious tenants than that of the Puritans, who were strict Calvinists.

---

232. "Creating an Indian Enemy in the Borderlands," p. 13.
233. IBID.
234. LIBBY/NOYES, p. 615. William Scriven. On Jan. 31, 1681/82, William "Scrivine" was brought before the Court of Sessions held at Wells to respond to "rumors and reports from a common fame of some presumptuous if not blasphemous speeches about the holy ordinance of baptism." Scriven was examined and did not deny that he believed in "believer's baptism," (i.e. when a believer knowingly submits to accept Jesus Christ, typically in adulthood) and claimed "infant baptism was an ordinance of the Devil…an invention of man." Scriven demanded the magistrates to prove "by any positive command in the gospels or scriptures that there was infant baptism." Magistrate and recorder Edward Rishworth told Scriven he was "mincing the matter" and Scriven replied "mincing was to put it in better terms than it deserved." Scriven was required by the Court to give in security sufficient to the Treasurer of the Province a bond of 100 pounds to answer his charge at the next Court of Pleas held for this Province, or the magistrates would send him to the goal. Scriven refused, and he was sent to jail. John Davess (Davis) was Deputy President of the court and Edward Rishworth and Francis Hooke were the other two justices. MPCR, Vol. 3, p. 161-162. (NOTE: The Baptist minister's last name is also spelled "Screven," as well as "Scrivine," in some records.)
235. Scriven was eventually forced out of Maine (around 1698) by the Puritans of Massachusetts Bay Colony. He and his family (and other followers) relocated to Charleston, S.C., where he founded the Baptist church there. See MEWD, Vol. 3, p. xxxiv-xxxix.

Thomas Crockett's estate was valued at 170 pounds, 10 shillings and 6 pence.[236] Most of the value came from his real estate on Crockett's Neck, described as "one Necke of Land near unto Spruse Cricket bounded at the head with a little Ysland, & doth Containe as we do judg one hundred eighty eight Acres [188 acres] or [thereabouts] at 50 [shillings] per acre" (141 pounds in total). Thomas also owned about six acres of marsh (probably at Brave Boat Harbor), valued at 10 pounds, and a modest assortment of homestead and household inventory, including:

One horse, 50 shillings; one heifer, 3 pounds
Two iron pots, a pot hook, & crooks at 1 pound
3 chests and things in them, 2 shillings; earthen & wooden ware, 13 shillings
A spit; two old axes; betle rings and other iron at 10 shillings
A frying pan, 4 shillings; and other several old Calkes, 6 shillings
4 pewter dishes, one cup, basin, and candlesticks at 11 shillings
One grindstone, two baskets, 3 shillings, 6 pence; a cupboard, 2 shillings, 6 pence
Two wedges, 2 shillings, 6 pence; clothing, linen and woolen, 40 shillings
A debt due from Ephraim Crockett – 7 pounds[237]
An old canoe at 16 shillings

At some point after Thomas returned to live in Kittery, he sold to friend and former neighbor Francis Raynes thirty of the forty acres of the planting ground he received as a grant from the town of York in 1653.[238] What happened to the balance ten acres (and perhaps a house) in York we do not know.

On April 1, 1679, the Court of Associates held at York granted administration of Thomas Crockett's estate to his wife Ann and son Ephraim. William Scriven, the nascent Baptist minister, posted a bond that Ann and Ephraim would give a legal

---

236. An inventory of Thomas Crockett's estate was taken March 20, 1678/79 by Francis Hooke and William Scriven. MEWD, Vol. 5, Page 85-86. (See Appendix, page 402, for the Inventory of Thomas Crockett's estate from York Deeds Book 5.)
237. This debt of seven pounds was for some of the Billing's property, which both Thomas and Ephraim sold to Abraham Corbett. See MEWD, Vol. 3, p. 172-173.
238. Will of Francis Raynes. MEWD, Wills, p. 95. Raynes made his will Aug. 21, 1693; however, he did not die until 1706 at "nearly one hundred years of age." BANKS2, p. 46. In his will, Francis Raynes left "a tract of land I bought of Thomas Crockett of thirty Acres lying Betwene my [two] Farms" to his grandson Nathan, son of Nathaniel Raynes. This was raw land. If there had been a house on the property at the time of the purchase (or a farm with a house) Raynes would likely have noted that in his will.

and accurate account of his estate.[239] (Scriven's posting of the bond also indicates a close relationship with the Crocketts by this date.) Although we do not have a copy of his last will and testament, we know Thomas had one because the will is mentioned in a later deed.[240] Perhaps because Thomas' will stated it, the Court of Pleas on June 30, 1680—in response to a petition from Ann Crockett—ordered that "the whole Neck of Land remain in her own hands for her maintenance during her natural life, according to her desire, and if the necessity of her condition do require it she hath hereby power to sell the whole or any part thereof for her future maintenance."[241] The court empowering Ann to dispose of her late husband's major asset as she saw fit was unusual for a time in which women had no rights of property ownership. Considering that Ann Crockett must still have had four or five minor and/or unmarried children at home, however, the court's decision seems highly logical even if the request was not specified in Thomas' will.[242]

---

239. MPCR, Vol. 2, p. 532.
240. MEWD, Vol. 4, p. 303.
241. MPCR, Vol. 3, p. 59. The Deputy President of the Court was then Bryan Pendleton, who had gone to court with Thomas Crockett over this same neck of land. It must have pinched Pendleton a bit to award Crockett's Neck to Crockett's widow Ann.
242. The court did not give Ann the right to leave the property to her heirs upon her death (although this might have been covered in Thomas Crockett's will) and it is not entirely clear what would have happened had she not deeded the balance of Crockett's Neck to her son Ephraim and his heirs.

The First Generation

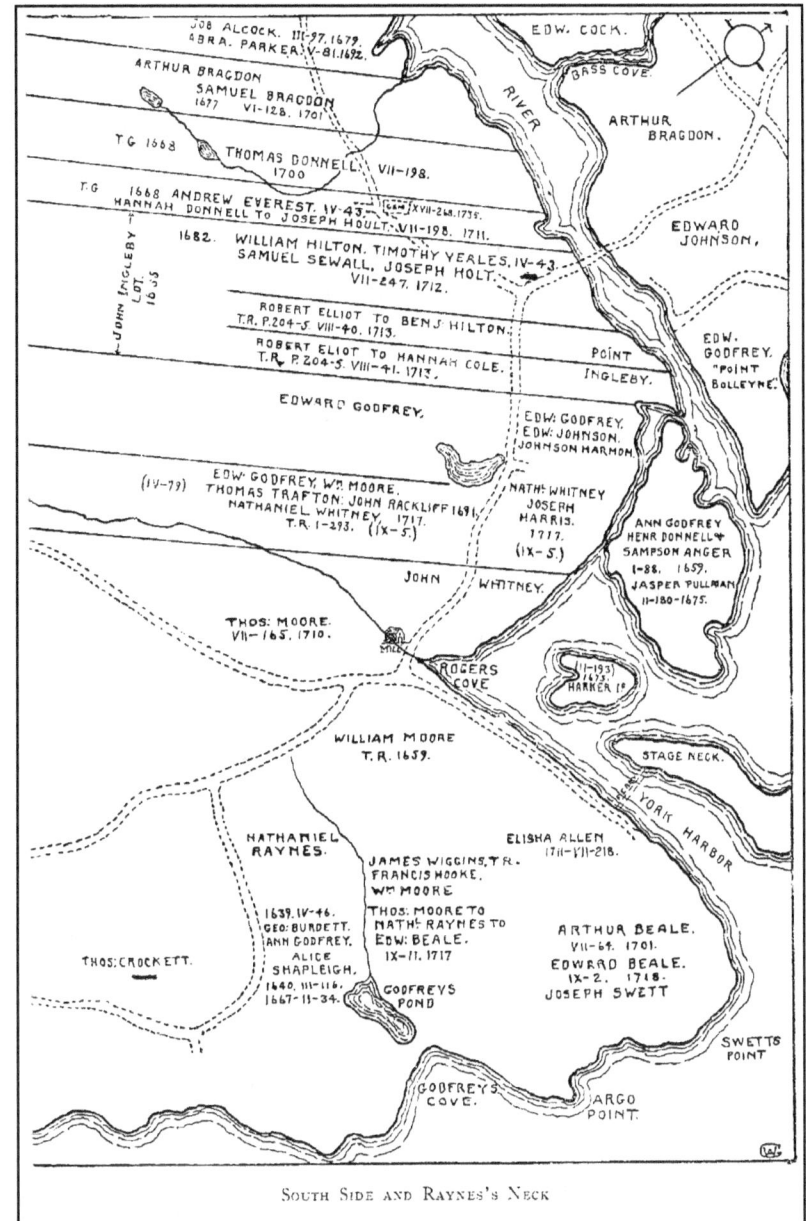

"South Side and Raynes's Neck."
Map of early York showing Thomas Crockett's 40-acre grant (bottom left) on what became known as Raynes' Neck. Thomas sold 30 acres of his land to Francis Raynes (grandfather of Nathaniel, shown on map). What happened to the remaining 10 acres owned by Crockett remains a mystery.
(Map from "History of York, Maine, Vol. II," Charles E. Banks)[243]

---

243. BANKS2, p. 56. "South Side and Raynes's Neck." (Image in the public domain.)

The Last Years of Ann Crockett

Everett Stackpole reports in his history of Kittery that Ann Crockett lived until 1712.[244] If so, she outlived her husband by 33 years. Assuming that Ephraim was her first child[245]—and that Ann was approximately twenty in 1644 when Ephraim was born—the 1712 date means she would have lived to be nearly ninety. Stackpole is the only historian to suggest Ann lived that long, however.

The "Genealogical Dictionary of Maine and New Hampshire" says Ann was living as late as 1701.[246] No reference is given for that date, regrettably. The last mention of Ann in any records I could find was in the land records. On July 7, 1697, Ann took her deed giving son Ephraim the real estate known as Crockett's Neck to William Pepperrell, Justice of the Peace, to swear that this was done by her free act and deed.[247] Since her eldest son had been dead for nine years when Ann appeared before Pepperrell, Ann must have been helping her daughter-in-law Anne (Edge) Crockett organize Ephraim's estate. With an eye to her own impending demise, Ann might also have been attempting to settle or clarify the disposition of Thomas Crockett's real estate on Crockett's Neck.

Whether Ann died in the first or second decade of the 18th century is immaterial, because no matter which date is correct we know that she lived a full life for at least another generation after Thomas' death in 1679. Ann lived to see all their children mature to adulthood. She witnessed the marriages of some of her grandchildren, who went on to have children of their own, whom Ann would know. Ann became a great-grandmother many times over before she died.[248]

In addition, Ann, who might still have been in her fifties when her husband died, found a new life with a second husband. By 1683, four years after the death of Thomas Crockett, Ann was remarried. She wed Dygory (Digory) Jeffrey,[249] a

---

244. STACKPOLE, p. 330. One must also consider the possibility that Stackpole confused Thomas Crockett's widow Ann with her daughter-in-law Anne (Edge) Crockett, widow of Ephraim.
245. Some historians believe Thomas and Ann's first child was possibly Anne (see CANDAGE, p. 1), born as early as 1642. Except for Ephraim and Joseph (whose births are calculated from ages given in their depositions), there is little factual evidence for the birth years or order of the Crockett's children. As a result, historians are all over the map with both.
246. LIBBY/NOYES, p. 375, Digory Jeffrey.
247. MEWD, Vol. 4, p. 303.
248. Ann's granddaughter Sarah, daughter of Ephraim and Anne (Edge) Crockett, married the Welshman Henry Barter. The couple had at least seven children, most of whom would have been known by their great-grandmother, including: Elizabeth Barter (unknown birth year), Sarah Barter (born 1693), Eleanor Barter (born 1695), Henry Barter II (born 1697), Richard Barter (born 1700), William Barter (born 1703) and Martha Barter (unknown birth date). See CANDAGE p. 4-5. In addition, Ann might also have known the grandchildren of her daughter Ann (Crockett) Roberts, including William Roberts II (born 1701) and George Roberts (born 1704). See CANDAGE, p. 4.
249. Online database. *AmericanAncestors.org*. New England Historic Genealogical Society, 2008. Originally published as:

carpenter who had moved to Kittery in 1663,[250] and who was a widower (possibly twice over).[251] Jeffrey appears to have been well-acquainted with the family prior to Thomas Crockett's death. In 1678, Dygory Jeffrey and Ephraim Crockett, both of whom resided in or near Brave Boat Harbor at the time, were witnesses to George Burrin's deed to Nicholas Shapleigh of a house and land at Brave Boat Harbor.[252]

Ann made a much better selection for a second husband than did her sister-in-law Joane and her friend (and possible former sister-in-law) Sarah, whose fourth and final husband dissipated the estates of Hugh Gunnison and Captain Mitchell. Jeffrey appears to have been a steady, good-tempered man,[253] who raised no objections when Ann deeded the balance of Crockett's Neck to son Ephraim in May of 1688[254] or when she deeded the land in Brave Boat Harbor to her widowed daughter-in-law Anne Crockett and Ephraim's heirs in July of 1695.[255] In fact, Jeffrey's ambition (if he had any) seems to have been closely-aligned with the ambitions of the Crockett family. In 1695, Dygory Jeffrey sold a 30-acre grant he had received from the town of Kittery (near the York line) to Henry Barter,[256] husband of Ann's granddaughter Sarah (Crockett) Barter. In 1688, prior to his marriage to Ann, Dygory Jeffrey and Ephraim Crockett both signed a petition of landowners at Brave Boat Harbor against "surveying and granting their lands to Walter Barefoot…"[257]

Ann lived to see Massachusetts purchase Maine from Ferdinando Gorges (the younger) in March of 1677/78,[258] and the extinguishment of the annual rent

---

"New England Marriages Prior to 1700." Boston, Mass.: New England Historic Genealogical Society, 2015.
250. LIBBY/NOYES, p. 375. Digory Jeffrey.
251. Online database. *AmericanAncestors.org*. New England Historic Genealogical Society, 2008. Originally published as: "New England Marriages Prior to 1700." Boston, Mass.: New England Historic Genealogical Society, 2015. Mention of Jeffrey's wife Mary is made in a deed from him to John Moore, Sr. in 1669, in which Mary signs off on her dower rights. See MEWD, Vol. 3, p. 204-205. Mary is not mentioned in 1680 when Jeffrey takes the deed before Magistrate Francis Hooke to swear it was by his free act and deed. At that time, Mary must have been deceased. She was the daughter of Robert Mussell of Newcastle and widow of a man named Rowe. (LIBBY/NOYES, p. 375, Digory Jeffrey.) Jeffrey married his second (or third) wife Ann Crockett by 1683.
252. MEWD, Vol. 3, p. 93-94.
253. LIBBY/NOYES (p. 375, Digory Jeffrey) suggests that prior to his marriage to Ann, Jeffrey had an improper relationship with Mary (Pearce) Jones, and possibly had a child out of wedlock. The historians do not give their source and no mention is made of any lapse from Puritan laws by Jeffrey in MPCR. Whether he did or did not have an earlier relationship outside of marriage is immaterial to our story as he did in fact later marry Ann Crockett.
254. MEWD, Vol. 4, p. 303. Henry Barter, who married Ephraim Crockett's daughter Sarah and would go on to own much of Crockett's Neck, witnessed the deed. The deed was conditioned upon Ephraim paying the legacies required in his father's will, which he did.
255. MEWD, Vol. 4, p. 303-304. This 80-acre tract was land previously sold by Ephraim Crockett to Richard White and this deed was likely a formality to clear up the title to the property, most (or all) of which was originally Thomas Crockett's.
256. MEWD, Vol. 7, p. 191-192. Hugh Crockett, Ann's son, was one of the witnesses to the transaction. The next deed in the record (Vol. 7, p. 192-193) was that of Hugh Crockett to Henry Barter. Hugh sold his house and land to his niece Sarah's husband. Ann Crockett Jeffrey, to whom the Court had granted the disposition of Crockett's Neck, also signed off on the sale.
257. LIBBY/NOYES, p. 33, List 292.
258. On March 13, 1677/78, Ferdinando Gorges (Sir Ferdinando Gorges' grandson) sold his patrimony in Maine to John

payments (established by Sir Ferdinando Gorges, the elder) that had been carried over in the deeds to Massachusetts.[259] She also lived through the horrors of King William's War (the Second Indian War, 1688-1697),[260] during which French nobleman Baron de Saint-Castin and his Native American allies raided many English settlements in Maine. Closest to home for Ann was the Candlemas[261] Massacre at neighboring York, January 24-25, 1691/92, during which 150 residents of York (out of approximately 500) were killed, wounded, or captured and carried north to Canada by Indian warriors led by Chief Madockawando (Saint-Castin's father-in-law).[262] If Ann lived until 1712, as Stackpole suggests, she also lived through Native American attacks during Queen Anne's War (the Third Indian War, 1702-1713).[263] Some of these raids also hit close to home. In 1704, Thomas and Ann's son Joseph Crockett had his taxes abated along with about thirty-five other Kittery residents, due to ravages of the Indians during Queen Anne's War.[264]

Usher for 1,250 pounds sterling. (MPCR, Vol. 3, preface p. x.) On March 15, 1677/78, John Usher deeded the Gorges property (i.e. most of Maine inhabited by the English) to the colony of Massachusetts Bay. (MPCR, Vol. 3, preface p. x.) The King of England, unhappy with the Gorges sale, sent a letter to Massachusetts Bay on July 24, 1679, demanding the colony reimburse Ferdinando Gorges for the sale of his patrimony and surrender the deeds to Maine. (MPCR, Vol. 3, preface, p. xi.) Massachusetts basically ignored this request, sending the King some wooden masts to placate him instead. The colony also wrote various letters to the King, hoping to drag the issue out, to which goal they were ultimately successful.

259. Most of Sir Ferdinando Gorges' deeds/grants contained language that included a small annual payment to him for the land. Thomas Crockett, whose deed from Gorges of Crockett's Neck was not recorded, was therefore probably not paying any annual compliment to Gorges, nor were his heirs likely paying any to Massachusetts. Others in Kittery, however, were. On Oct. 12, 1681, the Massachusetts General Court held at Boston (MPCR, Vol. 3, p. 154-155), in response to proposals put forth at a Maine General Assembly in July, agreed to stop the annual rents, if the Province of Maine promised to pick up the tab for running Fort Loyal, and pay the back due on costs of the fort and soldiers. For this extra burden and expense, Maine was to have the revenue from trade with the Indians toward the maintenance of Fort Loyal in Casco (Falmouth). This became moot in 1690 when Fort Loyal was destroyed by Native Americans, led by Frenchman Baron de Saint-Castin, during the Battle of Fort Loyal. Two hundred settlers were massacred on May 16, 1690, eventually leading to a depopulation of Englishmen in Maine during King William's War. Those who remained moved to southern settlements, where even there the settlers were not safe from French and Indian raids.

260. Known as the Nine Years War in Europe.

261. Candlemas Day was an ancient festival marking the half-way point of winter, now celebrated February 2nd. In the 17th century the Christian significance would have been the ritual purification of Mary 40 days after the birth of Jesus. Website, Project Britain, "Candlemas Day." http://projectbritain.com/year/candlemas.html#:~:text=2nd%20February%20is%20Candlemas%20Day,birth%20of%20her%20son%20Jesus.

262. On Sunday, January 24, 1691/92, Candlemas Day, Shubael Dummer, the minister of the York church preached a sermon per usual, not knowing that 200-300 Indian warriors under the leadership of Chief Madockawando (Baron de Saint-Castin's father-in-law) and the Jesuit priest Father Louis-Pierre Thury, were camped at the base of Mt. Agamenticus, plotting a surprise attack on the town. Monday morning, despite the snow, the Indians decided to attack. Father Louis-Pierre and Chief Madockawando split their war party into two groups, attacking simultaneously both settlements at York (then known as Scotland and Scituate). By the end of the day, about 150 souls in the town of 500 had been killed, wounded, and/or carried away by the Indians (including Rev. Dummer) in what turned out to be one of the worst Indian raids during King William's War. (Synopsis from various sources.)

263. Known as the War of Spanish Succession in Europe.

264. STACKPOLE, p. 175. Joseph Crockett's taxes were abated six shillings. His loss appears to have been material (i.e. property-related), not physical, as Joseph lived until 1715. (On Jan. 3, 1716, Hannah Crockett petitioned the Court of General Sessions of the Peace, stating that she was the relict of Jospeh Crockett, lately deceased. MPCR, Vol. 5, p. 186.)

The First Generation

Despite wars with the French and Indians that persisted throughout the balance of Ann's life, none of Ann's children or grandchildren appear to have been killed, wounded, or captured during the many Native American raids or battles. In fact, in contrast to the general depopulation of Maine during this time, Ann witnessed a dramatic expansion of her family. She also lived to see several of her sons receive land grants in Kittery, as well as grandsons, sons-in-law, and grandsons-in-law.[265]

Everett S. Stackpole, whose history of Kittery was published in 1903, concludes the biographical information of the family of Thomas and Ann Crockett by saying: "The descendants of the Crocketts are many."[266] As I write this story of the Crockett family in Maine more than 120 years after Stackpole published his history, I cannot even begin to fathom how many tens of thousands of us descendants of Thomas and Ann Crockett there have been!

---

265. On July 28, 1679, the town of Kittery granted Joshua Crockett 10 acres of land on Crockett's Plain, abutted by William Godsoe. Joshua sold this land to Francis Avant on the same date for 40 shillings. (MEWD, Vol.4, p. 305-306.) Avant also bought 10 acres from Joseph Crockett, likely granted to Joseph on the same date. On May 10, 1703, Joseph Crockett, Sr. was granted 40 acres (in what is now Berwick) by the town of Kittery. (MEWD, Vol. 7, p. 325.) The same day his brother Hugh Crockett was granted 50 acres by the town of Kittery. (MEWD, Vol. 6, p. 326-327.) Also, on May 24, 1699, at a legal Town Meeting in Kittery, William Roberts (husband of Thomas and Ann's daughter, Ann Crockett), Joseph Crockett, Jr. (Joseph Crockett's son and Ann's grandson) and Hugh Crockett were all granted land (40 acres to Roberts; and 30 acres each to Joseph, Jr. and his uncle Hugh Crockett), if they could find the land free and clear of other grants. All three sold their interest in these grants to William Pepperell, Sr. (MEWD, Vol. 6, p. 264-266.) On the same date in 1699, Richard Crockett (Ephraim Crockett's son and Ann's grandson) was granted 30 acres by the town of Kittery. Richard sold this land Dec. 11, 1719 to his "well-beloved" brother-in-law Henry Barter. Barter received a 50-acre grant the same date, May 24, 1699. (MEWD, Vol. 10, p. 17.) These last two land grants were also in Berwick, then part of Kittery. See Vol. 16, p. 220 where Barter sells his and Richard's grants in Berwick to William Pepperell, Jr., son of William Pepperell, Sr., who would go on to become Sir William Pepperell, the richest man in Maine (some say the richest in America), a merchant, real estate baron, and slave owner, who became famous for defeating the French at Fort Louisbourg in Cape Breton, Nova Scotia in 1745 during King George's War. (Grants to Ephraim Crockett will be covered in Chapter 2. More on Richard Crockett in Chapter 3.)
266. STACKPOLE, p. 53.

Chapter 2

"The Said Land Thus Given By My Father Shall Stand Good" The Second Generation

Our story follows six generations of the Crockett family (through the author's line), from Thomas Crockett, the first Crockett to the New World, down to Ephraim Crockett, Sr., a veteran of the American Revolution.[1] This line contains two Ephraim Crocketts and three Richard Crocketts, as shown below. (See also pages 375–376 for my "Quick Crockett Family Reference" of the direct descendants Thomas and Ann Crockett.)

> First Generation – Thomas Crockett, b. 1610/11; d. 1678/79 at age 68
> **Second Generation – Ephraim Crockett, b. 1644; d. 1688 at age 44**[2]
> Third Generation – Richard Crockett, b. 1682; d. 1757 at age 75
> Fourth Generation – Richard Crockett, Jr., b. circa 1706; d. by 1786 at age 79 or 80
> Fifth Generation – Richard Crockett (III, also known as Richard, Jr.), b. circa 1733; d. 1821 at age 87
> Sixth Generation – Ephraim Crockett, b. 1755; d. 1835 at age 79

---
1. Ephraim Crockett and his wife Rebecca Stanford were the parents of my fourth-great grandfather Ephraim Crockett, Jr., who settled Crockett's Ridge in Lee's Grant (Norway, Maine) in 1812. Much of the land purchased by Ephraim, Jr. and his brother-in-law Nathan Morse still remains in our extended family. See my 2024 book, "A History of the Crockett Family of Crockett's Ridge, Norway, Maine."
2. The bold type indicates which generation we are covering in each chapter.

In this chapter, we will explore the life of Ephraim Crockett of the second generation and his wife Anne Edge.

Longevity in New England vs. Old England

A quick glance at the age at death of the first six generations of Crocketts on the prior page reveals that Ephraim died unusually young (age 44) compared to his father and his descendants. Ephraim's father lived into his seventh decade and Ephraim's descendants (in the line we are following) lived at least into their eighth decade. Ephraim's great-grandson Richard (III), who was nearly eighty-eight when he died, came close to reaching his tenth decade!

It might seem counterintuitive that early English settlers in the New World lived longer than those they left behind in the Old World, but such is the case. Studies have shown that early New England immigrants, despite starting from scratch in a colder climate and having to contend with Indian troubles, experienced better health and led longer lives than their counterparts back in England. In fact, the climate probably played a role in their longevity:

> "Because of its cold winters and low population density, New England was perhaps the most healthful region in the world [in the 17th century]. After an initial period of high mortality, life expectancies quickly rose to levels comparable with our own. Men and women, on average, lived about 65 to 70 years, 15 to 20 years longer than in England. One result was that seventeenth-century New England was the first society in history in which grandparents were common."[3]

The Great Migration Study Project undertaken by the New England Historic Genealogical Society (directed by Robert Charles Anderson) also found the "remarkable health and longevity of the population [of early New England] noteworthy."

> "Many colonists lived to the age of seventy, and a substantial number lived to be eighty. Both male and female settlers in New England lived significantly longer than their English counterparts. This longevity is no doubt due to a variety of factors: dispersed settlement patterns, lack of epidemic disease, the healthful effects

---

3. "Regional Contrasts." Digital History ID 3580. https://www.digitalhistory.uh.edu/disp_textbook.cfm?smtid=2&psid=3580

of 'a little ice age,'[4] clean air and water, possibly a better diet, and the original good health of most immigrants. Also, infant and childhood mortality rates were lower in New England, and the settlers produced large and healthy families—most having seven or more children. Accordingly, New England experienced tremendous population growth within the lifetime of first generation settlers."[5]

The Early Years of Ephraim Crockett

Ephraim Crockett was the eldest son and first-born child of Thomas and Ann Crockett. According to a deposition given by Ephraim on June 19, 1672, when he was "aged 28 years or thereabouts,"[6] he was born around 1644[7] and was likely the child whose imminent birth was recollected in the deposition given by his aunt Joane (Crockett) Andrews in 1660.[8]

---

4. The Little Ice Age, 1300 C.E. to 1850 C.E., was a period of cooling in the northern hemisphere during which many glaciers expanded.
5. "New England's Great Migration." Lynn Betlock. *New England Ancestors* 4 (2003): 2:22-24.
6. MEWD, Vol. 2, p. 222. Ephraim gave a deposition about Francis Champernowne laying out some of his former land to Abraham Corbett. At one point, Champernowne asked for 10 acres of land on either side of Walter Knight's house or he would not proceed any further. According to Ephraim, Corbett was unwilling to have any difference with Champernowne and complied with the Devon "curled darling's" request, selling Champernowne 10 acres of land for 10 pounds. (For the reference to "curled darlings" see Shakespeare's "The Tragedy of Othello, Moor of Venice," Act I, Scene II.)
7. STACKPOLE, p. 330, says Ephraim was born about 1641. CANDAGE, p. 1, agrees with the 1644 birthdate.
8. On Feb. 25, 1660, Joane Andrews, about 40 years of age, said in a deposition that fifteen or sixteen years earlier she was with Thomas Crockett's wife when she was ready to give birth, and went over and called across Spruce Creek to Thomas to come and help his wife and child. The deposition was given to provide evidence that Crockett's Neck belonged to Thomas Crockett. MEWD, Vol. 2, p. 27.

Direct Descendants of Thomas and Ann Crockett
(Author's line, which we are following.)

1. First Generation – Thomas Crockett
b. 1610/1611, Stoke Gabriel, Devon, England; d. Feb. or March, 1678/79, Kittery, Maine, m. by 1644
Ann (unknown surname, possibly Lynn or Gunnison)
b. unknown; d. after 1697, Kittery, Maine

2. Second Generation – Ephraim Crockett
b. 1644, Kittery, Maine; d. Sept. or Oct. 1688, Kittery, Maine
m. between 1667 and 1671, probably Kittery
Anne Edge
b. unknown; d. by 1713, probably Kittery

3. Third Generation – Richard Crockett
b. 1682, Kittery, Maine; d. Jan. 7, 1757, Stratham, N.H.
m. between 1704-1708, probably Kittery
Deborah Haley
b. birth date unknown, probably Kittery or York; d. by May 1719 (and probably earlier), Stratham, N.H.

4. Fourth Generation – Richard Crockett, Jr.
b. around 1706, probably Kittery, Maine; d. by Jan. 1, 1786, Deer Isle, Maine
m. Aug. 20, 1731, First Parish, Falmouth, Maine
Mary Robinson
b. Jan. 22, 1712, Gloucester, MA; d. probably by 1759, Second Parish (Cape Elizabeth), Falmouth, Maine

5. Fifth Generation – Richard Crockett (III, also known as Richard, Jr.)

b. around 1733, Falmouth, Maine; d. 1821, Cape Elizabeth, Maine

m. 1. 1754, Second Parish, Falmouth, Maine

Elizabeth Roberts

b. 1736, Falmouth, Maine (probably Second Parish); d. by November 1776, Second Parish, Falmouth, Maine

(Richard also had two other marriages not relevant to our story.)

6. Sixth Generation – Ephraim Crockett

b. July 12, 1755, Second Parish, Falmouth, Maine; d. April 9, 1835, Danville, Maine

m. June 20, 1777, Cape Elizabeth, Maine

Rebecca Stanford

b. July 20, 1760, Falmouth (probably Second Parish); d. Dec. 6, 1839, Durham, Maine

By age twenty-eight, Ephraim Crockett was a tailor in Kittery. Ephraim alludes to his occupation only once, in a 1672 deed,[9] which he and his wife Anne jointly executed. In the 17th century, the occupation of a tailor required a period of apprenticeship, usually around seven years. Since tailors were not numerous in Kittery, it is possible that the young man learned his trade from Nicholas Davis,[10] an innkeeper from neighboring York, who had been a tailor at Wapping Hall in London prior to emigrating to Massachusetts in 1635.[11]

Davis, born around 1595,[12] would have been a grandfather figure for Ephraim. Davis and his family relocated to York by 1650, not long after Thomas Crockett received the ferry privilege at Brave Boat Harbor in 1648 and moved his family there from Kittery Point. Although the Crocketts returned to live permanently in Kittery, a bond between the Crockett and Davis families remained.[13] Therefore, it is entirely plausible that as a teenager (if not before) Ephraim was apprenticed to Nicholas Davis, who might have worked as a tailor, in addition to his innkeeping, during those early years.

Ephraim is first mentioned in court records on June 12, 1666, when he was twenty-two. On this date, his aunt Joane Andrews was "presented" (a form of shaming) at court[14] for breaking the King's peace and abusing "Mis Lockewood."[15]

---

9. On Sept. 16, 1672, Ephraim Crockett, tailor, with the consent of his wife Anne, sold the 10 acres on Spruce Creek granted to him by the Town of Kittery. Ephraim and Anne sold the land to Charles Ogradoe (O'Grady) of Portsmouth for 11 pounds, 10 shillings. Mary Stileman and Richard Stileman, ser. (possibly servants of Ogradoe) witnessed the deed. MEWD, Vol. 7, p. 93-94. This is the only mention of Ephraim Crockett's occupation in deeds and depositions.
10. The surname of Davis was usually written into the old records as "Davess."
11. LIBBY/NOYES, p. 187. Nicholas Davis. Ephraim might also have learned something about the trade from Sylvester Harbert, a tailor, who bought from Walter Barefoot 30 acres and a house in Kittery in 1661, when Ephraim was about seventeen (MEWD, Vol. 10, p. 27). Harbert remained in Kittery less than a year, however. (See MEWD, Vol. 2, p. 202-203.)
12. LIBBY/NOYES, p. 187. Nicholas Davis. The historians note Davis came over on the *Planter* in 1635 when he was about 40.
13. Joseph Davis, probably Nicholas' son, worked for Thomas Crockett (and possibly worked for Sarah Lynn Gunnison Mitchell Morgan, as well). In addition, in 1660 the Court passed an Act of Separation between Ann Crockett (Thomas' wife) and Joseph Davis, because it was thought they were spending too much time together. (See Chapter 1.)
14. Court was held at York by his Majesty's Justices of the Peace for the Western Division. At that time, the courts were under the auspices of the King (not Massachusetts Bay Colony) and divided into eastern and western divisions. Four years elapsed after the last Court of Associates held at Saco Sept. 12, 1664 before the County Court and Court of Associates under Massachusetts Bay held sessions, the government of the Province in the meantime being in the hands of Justices of the Peace appointed by the Commissioners of Charles II. See MPCR, Vol. 2, p. 162, note by Charles Thornton Libby and again on p. 400.
15. MPCR, Vol. 1, p. 264. For her offenses, Joane was sentenced by the Court to "bee carried to the poast & there to have 10 lashes on the bare skine." The punishment was administered the same day by John Parker, prison keeper at York, after which Joane's husband John Andrews was discharged from his bond of ten pounds. Court records do not reveal the reason Joane abused Deborah Lockwood, although "Mis Lockewood, wife of Mr. Lockwood" (Deborah) was "presented" for lying before the Court of Pleas held at Saco Nov. 7, 1665. MPCR, Vol. 1, p. 235. There was bad blood between Deborah Lockwood and Joane (Crockett) Andrews for some reason, which possibly occurred when young Joane cared for Deborah and her siblings as children, prior to Joane's marriage to Andrews.

Witnesses to Joane's infraction (i.e. those who reported her) were her nephew Ephraim Crockett, John Billing, Jr. (her son-in-law to be), and Elizabeth (Lynn) Seely (daughter of Sarah Lynn Gunnison and her first husband Henry Lynn). While it might appear that this youthful trio ganged up on Aunt Joane, the reverse is likely true. The "Mis Lockewood" (Mrs. Richard Lockwood) whom Joane had abused was Deborah Gunnison, daughter of Hugh Gunnison and his first wife Elizabeth. After Hugh married Crockett friend Sarah Lynn (his second wife), their combined family returned to Kittery, where the young people—Crocketts, Gunnisons, and Lynns—grew up together. Although Ephraim in adulthood became one of his Aunt Joane's most faithful protectors (second only to her husband John Andrews),[16] during this episode he appears most concerned with protecting his childhood chum Deborah from what was probably a nasty tongue-lashing (if not worse) from his volatile and voluble aunt. (This incident reveals that Ephraim Crockett associated with the archetype of the Protector or Defender from a young age.)

In 1667, when he was twenty-three, Ephraim sold six acres of land on Kittery Point to Abraham Corbett, a distiller from Portsmouth.[17] Since Ephraim had not purchased any real estate, nor yet received any in a town grant, he must have received the six acres he sold (for 17 pounds) from his father, to whom he promised a payment of 7 pounds[18] at some future date. The property sold by Ephraim was part of John Billing's real estate on the Point that Thomas Crockett had bought[19] and where he and Ann had raised their children in Kittery. Thomas finished building his house on Crockett's Neck in 1667 and moved his family there that year. Ephraim might have used the 17 pounds from the Corbett sale to build a house for himself and his wife (or wife-to-be) in Brave Boat Harbor, where he and his family resided until after the death of his father.

---

16. Later that same year, on Dec. 11, 1666, Ephraim helped his Aunt Joane secure two loans from Deborah's husband Richard Lockwood. One loan was for 1 pound, 1 shilling and 6 pence (MEWD, Vol. 2, p. 165-166) and another in which Joane promised to deliver to Lockwood for supplies and necessaries given, one steer and one calf (MEWD, Vol. 2, p. 166). Ephraim was witness to both recorded transactions, and it is difficult to see any circumstances under which Lockwood would have advanced Joane money or supplies without Ephraim's reassurances. Joane's husband John Andrews must have been ill or infirm at the time and she needed money and supplies.
17. LIBBY/NOYES, p. 162. Abraham Corbett.
18. MEWD, Vol. 2, p. 137-138. The loan was noted in the inventory of Thomas Crockett's estate taken in 1679, signifying that Ephraim had not yet paid it.
19. Thomas Crockett sold the house at Kittery Point and the balance of land to Corbett the same year.

Anne Edge and the Edge Family

Between 1667 (the year Thomas Crockett moved his family across Spruce Creek to Crockett's Neck)[20] and 1671, Ephraim was married to Anne Edge. We know the couple was married by the fall of 1671 because at the Court of Associates held at York, September 19, 1671, "Ephraim Crockett's wife" is mentioned in the accounts given as owing 10 shillings (in fines and fees) from the last Court of Associates.[21] (Anne's offense is not noted in the records.) Ephraim's aunt Joane Andrews is also mentioned at the same court as owing 8 shillings, 4 pence (in fines and fees), and so it is possible that the incorrigible Joane had led her nephew's young wife astray. If so, Anne Edge Crockett never again followed Joane's lead, because Anne never again appeared in court for any infraction.

Anne was the daughter of Robert and Florence Edge. Robert Edge sailed to the New World on the vessel *Hopewell* in 1635 at the age of twenty-five.[22] For the next fifteen years after his arrival, however, Edge's whereabouts remains a mystery. Genealogists have speculated that Edge returned to England on another ship, perhaps to fetch his wife and family.[23] Edge shows up again in York in 1650 (where some sources say he married his wife Florence). In York, he received a grant of three acres of land—confirmed by York on July 3, 1653—in the lower part of the town, near the ocean, where Edge built his house.[24]

Florence Edge, Anne's mother, had a ready wit and was unafraid to use it, regardless of potential ramifications. (Unlike reticent Puritan women of Massachusetts Bay Colony, the women of Maine appear to have freely expressed themselves.) While under a bond to compel better behavior (which she ignored), Florence commented in public about "the admiration which Goody Parker, wife of John Parker, later the keeper of the York gaol ... felt for the manly charms of Richard Banks."[25] Her lewd remarks—whether malicious or not—landed Florence in court, where she was sued for slander. She was found guilty and sentenced to receive ten lashes "on

---

20. MIGRATION, p. 497, says that Ephraim was married to his wife by 1667. This seems reasonable, since Thomas Crockett finished his house on Crockett's Neck in 1667 and moved there. Both Thomas and Ephraim sold the Billing's property to Abraham Corbett in 1667, which would have given Ephraim capital to build a house in Brave Boat Harbor on land belonging to his father. Having his own home and money in his pocket, Ephraim would be well-positioned to marry.
21. MPCR, Vol. 2, p. 441.
22. LIBBYNOYES, p. 214. Robert Edge.
23. WGDFAMILIES, p. 475.
24. WGDFAMILIES, p. 475.
25. WGDFAMILIES, p. 475.

the bare skine" or pay a 10-pound fine.[26] Florence was let off, however, paying only 5 shillings, which was the amount of the officer's fee.[27]

Robert Edge, Florence's husband, could not stay out of trouble with the authorities, either. A complaint was lodged against Robert in June of 1655 (after he had been in York about five years) that he "did not seek to apprentice his children" and that "the selectmen should see it done."[28] Perhaps thinking that there would be less interference in his personal life in Kittery, home to fishermen, sailors and the like, Edge removed his family from York (home of more educated and well-heeled English gentry) to Kittery in 1661. In Kittery he continued his self-willed ways, squatting on land owned by Captain Walter Barefoot, without Barefoot's consent. The "Genealogical Dictionary of Maine and New Hampshire" reports that by 1661 Edge had moved to "the Kittery side of the creek running into Braveboat Harbor, where he lived ever aft."[29] In the 18th century, depositions about Robert Edge's home in Kittery were given as part of a case before the Supreme Judicial Court, but no deeds of the property were recorded so it is possible Edge never bought the land upon which he built his new home (probably not much more than a shack).[30]

In 1662, while living in Kittery, Robert Edge, with his wife Florence (and their oldest child Peter), sold "the three acres of marsh lying on the western-most branch of the York River," which had been granted to Edge by the town of York.[31] In that deed Edge describes himself in this interesting fashion: "now of Kittery, sometyms of York."[32] The date of Robert Edge's death is not known, although he was alive as late as 1672, when he was sued by abutter Richard Lockwood (husband of Deborah Gunnison) regarding property lines.[33] Anne's mother Florence Edge lived until

---

26. It is difficult to know the value of 10 pounds at the time (i.e. how many acres of land the sum would have purchased, for example); however, 10 pounds would have been a significant amount of money, entirely beyond the ability of Robert Edge to pay.
27. WGDFAMILIES, p. 475.
28. WGDFAMILIES, p. 475 Also, LIBBYNOYES (p. 214, Robert Edge) says Anne was one of the children not "apprenticed." While we often think of apprentices—those who work with a craftsman to learn a trade—as being male, WIKI, referencing Apprenticeship indentures stored in the Cambridge University Library Archives and the Cambridge St. Edward Parish Church Archives notes that "…female apprentices were found in crafts such as seamstress, tailor, cordwainer, baker and stationer," with apprenticeships beginning around ten to fifteen years of age. It appears the town of York expected parents to raise their children to be able to support themselves.
29. LIBBYNOYES, p. 214. Robert Edge.
30. WGDFAMILIES, p. 476.
31. WGDFAMILIES, p. 475.
32. WGDFAMLIES, p. 475.
33. WGDFAMILIES, p. 476. Edge was awarded costs in the property lines suit because Capt. Lockwood "failed to enter the writ."

at least 1690, when she was noted as "Gamar Eage" living in "the care of Anne Crockett of Kittery."[34] (Ephraim's widow).

Robert and Florence Edge probably had four children, with Anne perhaps the youngest.[35] At the time of the Edge family's removal to Kittery, Thomas Crockett was running the ferry at Brave Boat Harbor. The two families would thus have lived in proximity, with Ephraim Crockett and his future wife Anne Edge coming into regular contact.

Ephraim and Anne (Edge) Crockett had four children, all probably born in Kittery or York:[36] Ephraim, Jr. (the eldest), Sarah, Mary, and Richard. Please refer to the "Genealogical Dictionary of Thomas and Ann Crockett" beginning on page 377 for more information about Ephraim and Anne's children. (Richard Crockett's life we will cover in Chapter 3.)

King Charles II Is Displeased – The Sale of the "Province of Mayne" to Massachusetts Bay

In Chapter 1, we covered the early land grants of New England (then, Northern Virginia), including the grants made by King James I to Sir Ferdinando Gorges (reconfirmed by Charles I), from whom Thomas Crockett had received Crockett's Neck. In 1649, after the Puritans in England had overthrown the crown and beheaded Charles I, the Puritans of Massachusetts Bay Colony took the opportunity to expand into the Royalist Gorges' territory in Maine by claiming that the Bay's original 1628/29 charter from Charles I had included this area. (The Puritans thus offer a lesson in how to treat your enemies—behead them and claim their land.) In 1652, buttressed by this (illegitimate) claim, Massachusetts Bay strongarmed residents of Kittery, York, and other Maine settlements to submit to their authority. (For a good summary of the tug of war over the possession of Maine, see "Note By

---

34. WGDFAMILIES, p. 476. Apparently, the care of Anne's mother, "Gamar Eage" ("Grandma Edge") was paid for (i.e. money was given to Anne for her mother's care) by a man named Joshua Downing, who was possibly the husband of one of Florence Edge's grandchildren.
35. LIBBYNOYES, p. 214. A Rootsweb ancestry chart says Anne was born in Kittery to Robert and Florence Edge about 1647. See also the Edge genealogy given on page 476 in "Massachusetts and Maine Families in the Ancestry of Walter Goodwin Davis, 1885-1966," (WGDFAMILIES), which notes: "Of the Edge children only the son Peter (the eldest) is certain." (Most likely Davis notes this because Peter signed the deed when his father sold some of his land in York, thus there is an official record of him.)
36. CANDAGE, p. 2. Basic information about Ephraim and Anne's children comes from Candage; however, I have also added new material I uncovered. We do not know the birth order of the children, except that Ephraim, Jr. was likely first-born and Richard probably last-born.

the Commissioner on the Sources of Land Titles In Maine" in the Revised Statutes of the State of Maine, Fourth Revision, 1883/84.)[37]

When the English monarchy was revived in 1660 during the Restoration, however, Gorges' grandson (also named Ferdinando Gorges) appealed to Charles II and to Parliament to restore the Province of Maine to him. (Captain John Mason's heirs in New Hampshire also attempted to reclaim their land.) Massachusetts Bay was ordered to surrender Maine to Gorges (the younger) in 1664 or explain why they would not return the property to its rightful owner. Distance and the political adroitness of Massachusetts Bay (including the sending of thirty "great masts" to the King)[38] enabled the Puritans in Massachusetts to stall turning over Maine for many years. Finally, in 1676, the Privy Council extinguished "the claims of Massachusetts Bay to Maine, but [left] the rightful owner of the Province [of Maine] undetermined."[39]

Massachusetts Bay, seeing the writing on the wall and realizing that the loss of Maine represented not only valuable real estate but also the loss of significant resources, hired John Usher, a Boston trader who was then in England, to buy Maine from Ferdinando Gorges. On May 6, 1677, Gorges assigned "the Province of Mayne for £1,250 sterling" to Usher, including all the rights and privileges that had been granted his grandfather Sir Fernando Gorges in the charter from King Charles I. Usher in turn sold Maine to Massachusetts Bay (for the same price). King Charles II, who himself was in negotiations to purchase the Province of Maine from Gorges, was angry that Massachusetts Bay had beaten him to the punch:

> "The purchase of Maine by the colony of Massachusetts Bay displeased Charles II, who was himself, at the time, in treaty with Gorges for its purchase for his natural son, the Duke of Monmouth, (afterwards executed by Charles' brother James) and he remonstrated with the colonial government on their conduct, and even required the colony's agents to assign [Maine] to the crown upon payment of the purchase money; to this demand little attention was paid [by Massachu-

---

37. Introduction to the "Fourth Revision. The Revised Statutes of the State of Maine, passed August 29, 1883, and taking effect January 1, 1884." Portland: Loring, Short and Harmon and William Marks, Printer, 1884. https://lldc.mainelegislature.org/Open/RS/RS1883/RS1883_f0005-0017_Land_Titles.pdf#:~:text=The%20purchase%20of%20Maine%20by%20the%20colony,remonstrated%20with%20the%20colonial%20government%20on%20their
38. MPCR, Vol. 3, p. ix.
39. "Notes by the Commissioner on Sources of Land Titles in Maine," p. xiii. Introduction to the "Fourth Revision. The Revised Statutes of the State of Maine, passed August 29, 1883, and taking effect January 1, 1884." Portland: Loring, Short and Harmon and William Marks, Printer, 1884.

setts Bay], and at the October session the General Court resolved to keep the Province."[40]

The King's dissatisfaction with Massachusetts Bay deepened as the colony continued to ignore his commands. Only when it became apparent that the Bay might lose its *own* charter by defying the King did the Massachusetts General Court instruct its agents in England in 1683 to turn over to the crown the title deeds of Maine. By then, however, it was too late. By 1684, "the Royal Charter granted to the Colony of Massachusetts Bay by Charles I in 1628 was promptly adjudged to be forfeited and the liberties of the colonies were seized by the crown."[41]

It is difficult to tell from the records how much effect this shifting tide of power—from the crown to Massachusetts Bay Colony and back to the crown again—was felt by the Crockett family and other English settlers on the ground in Maine. The most obvious difference would have been the fealty of the magistrates who sat at the various courts, with Royalists (supporting the crown) giving way to Puritans (supporting Massachusetts Bay), and vice versa. Most likely the daily life of men like Ephraim Crockett, whose first duty would have been to provide for his family (and help his friends and neighbors), was little affected. When in power, the Puritans demanded strict observance of their narrow religious beliefs, which most residents generally obeyed, albeit grudgingly. Likewise, the King demanded loyalty to the crown. In Maine, English colonists probably pivoted from one to the other with about an equal showing of allegiance.

The First Indian War (1675-1678)

During Ephraim Crockett's childhood (1644-1665), the English, Scotch, and Irish settlers in Maine coexisted peaceably (for the most part) with Native Americans, and had done so for nearly forty years, since 1628 when the first English trading post (at Cushnoc) was established on the Kennebec River by the Plymouth Colony.

---

40. "Notes by the Commissioner on Sources of Land Titles in Maine," p. xiii. Introduction to the "Fourth Revision. The Revised Statutes of the State of Maine, passed August 29, 1883, and taking effect January 1, 1884." Portland: Loring, Short and Harmon and William Marks, Printer, 1884.
41. "Notes by the Commissioner on Sources of Land Titles in Maine," p. xiv. Introduction to the "Fourth Revision. The Revised Statutes of the State of Maine, passed August 29, 1883, and taking effect January 1, 1884." Portland: Loring, Short and Harmon and William Marks, Printer, 1884.

That peaceful coexistence would undergo a dramatic change when Ephraim reached his early thirties, however.

In 1675, King Philip's War broke out in southern New England. Native American hostility toward the English spilled over into Maine, initially because some Wampanoags, Narragansetts, and other warring braves from Rhode Island came north seeking help from their Wabanaki brethren. This infectious hostility might have been tamped down by savvy Englishmen, had the English been smart enough not to lump all Indians into one amorphous group of "savages." Fear and ignorance on the part of the English led to what became known as the First Indian War in Maine (an extension of King Philip's War in southern New England).

Despite the attempts of southern Indians to stir up animosity against the English, most Maine Wabanaki tribes were wary of helping Metacom, the sachem of the Wampanoag tribe (called King Philip by the English). The native peoples depended upon trade with the English and while relations in 1675 were not perfect, they were not worth fighting about. But hope of keeping the violence from spreading to Maine was probably doomed in the summer of 1675 by the stupidity of a group of English sailors. The seamen (whether local sailors or not is unknown) attempted to discover if the tale that Native Americans could swim from birth was true by tossing an Indian baby into a river. Unfortunate as the incident was, it was made worse by the fact that the baby was a child of Squando, a sagamore of the Saco Indians. An account of the incident was given by William Hubbard, a Puritan minister of Ipswich, in his 1676 narrative of the Indian wars in New England:

> "Some little color or pretense of injury was alleged before those eastern [Maine] Indians began their outrage, both in the former [1675], as well as the present year [1676]; the chief actor or rather the beginner of all the aforesaid mischiefs eastward, is one Squando, the Sagamore of the Saco Indians, whose squaw, as is said, was abused by a rude and indiscreet act of some English seamen, the last summer, 1675, who either overset the canoe wherein the said squaw with her child were sailing in the river thereabouts, or else to try whether the children of Indians, as they had heard, could swim as naturally as any other creatures, wittingly cast her child into the water; but the squaw immediately diving into the water after it, fetched it up from the bottom of the river, yet it falling out within a while after the said child died (which is might have done if no such affront had been offered)

the said Squando, father of the child, hath been so provoked that he hath ever since set himself to do all the mischief he can to the English in those parts, and was never as yet, since that time, truly willing to be reconciled ..."[42]

Hubbard, who describes the murder of the Indian child as a "rude and indiscreet act," nevertheless blames Squando for the hostilities that broke out between the two groups. The Saco sagamore was understandably outraged, not just at the murder of his son, but also by the crude and disrespectful treatment of his wife. Squando "vowed not to let the act go unpunished, and he convinced a number of Wabanakis of western Maine and eastern New Hampshire (surely his fellow Sacos, but possibly some allied Pigwackets [Pequawket][43] and Androscoggins as well) to join him in harassing English settlements along the northeastern frontier."[44]

The tribes that belonged to the very loosely-knit Wabanaki Confederacy did not rush to join the aggrieved Squando, the Saco sagamore, in his war against the English. The Kennebecs, Penobscots, and some of the Androscoggins (Ammoscongons)[45] were hesitant, having peaceably coexisted with the English for two generations. During this time, Englishmen in Maine, including the Crocketts, had hugged the extreme southern coast around the Pascataqua region (for the most part), leaving the vast interior of forests and rivers, as well as most of the eastern coast, to the domain of the Indians. A brisk trade occurred on the borderland between the two groups, which benefitted both the English and the natives. Even when the English, fearful of King Philip's War spreading to Maine, demanded that peaceful Kennebecs and Androscoggins disarm (and refused to sell the Indians powder and shot for their guns), these Wabanakis (although not turning over many of their weapons) still clung to hope that war could be avoided.

---

42. "A narrative of the Indian wars in New-England, from the first planting thereof in the year 1607, to the year 1677. : Containing a relation of the occasion, rise and progress of the war with the Indians, in the southern, western, eastern and northern parts of said country." William Hubbard, A.M. Minister of Ipswich. Boston: Printed and sold by John Boyle in Marlborough-Street, 1775. P. 301-302.
43. A Wabanaki tribe situated around the headwaters of the Saco River, which tribe moved between Oxford County in Maine and Carroll County in New Hampshire.
44. "Creating an Enemy in the Borderlands: King Philip's War in Maine, 1675-1678," p. 7. Christopher J. Bilodeau. Maine History. Volume 47, Number 1. *The Maine Borderlands*.
45. The Ammoscongon peoples were an Abenaki tribe whose home base was around the Androscoggin River. Since the Anglicized name, "Androscoggin," is more common today, I have utilized it in this book.

The Second Generation

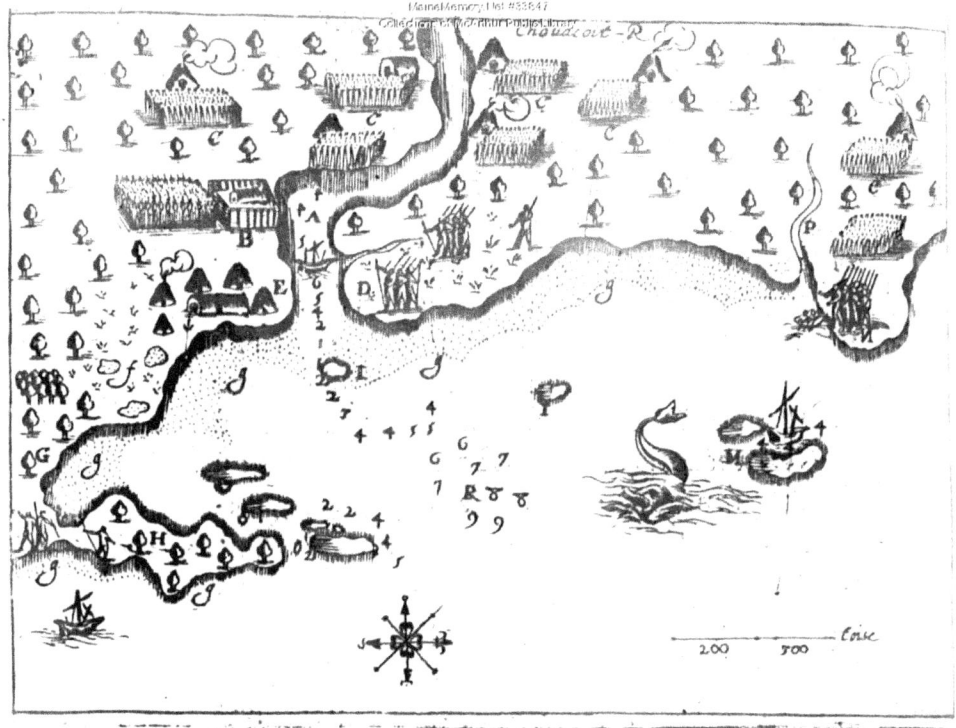

Les chifres montrent les braſſes d'eau.

A La riuiere.
B Le lieu ou ils ont leur forteresse.
C Les cabannes qui sont parmy les champs ou auprés ils cultiuent la terre & sement du bled d'Inde.
D Grāde compaigne sablonneuse, neantmoins templie d'herbages.
E Autre lieu où ils font leurs logemēs tous en gros sans estre separez aprés la semence de leur bleds estre faite.
F Marais où il y a de bons pasturages.
G Source d'eau viue.
H Grande pointe de terre toute defrichee horsmis quelques arbres fruitiers & vignes sauuages.
I Petit islet a l'entree de la riuiere.
L Autre islet.
M Deux isles où vesseaux peuuent mouiller l'ancre à l'abry d'icelles auec bon fons.
N Pointe de terre defrichee où nous vint trouuer Marchim.
O Quatre isles.
P Petit ruisseau qui asseche de basse mer.
Q Basses le long de la coste.
R La rade où les vaisseaux peuuent mouiller l'ancre attendant le flot.

Samuel de Champlain's 1605 map of native village at the mouth of the Saco River.
In 1676, sailors tossed a baby of Squando, a Saco sagamore, into the river to see if the infant would know how to swim. The murder of his child moved Squando to declare war against the English.
(See French translation of this document next page.)
(Image courtesy of Maine Memory Network.)

Translation of the French from Samuel de Champlain's 1605 Map[46]

AUTHOR'S NOTE: Champlain's map (prior page) showing a village of Saco Indians, reveals that indigenous Americans were not savages who lived like animals in the wilderness (as thought by early English colonists), but rather enjoyed a complex agricultural society by 1605 (and probably long before).

(French writing directly beneath the map): "The numbers show the fathoms of water."

- A. The river.
- B. The place where they [the natives] have their fortress.
- C. The huts which are among the fields where the Indians cultivate the land & sow wheat.
- D. Sandy beach nevertheless filled with grassland.
- E. Other place there are their lodgings all roughly without being separated after the seed of their corn is made.
- F. Marshes where there is good pasturage.
- G. Sighted water source.
- H. Large point of land, empty road apart from a few fruit trees & wild vines.
- I. Little islet at the entrance of the river.
- L. Other islet.
- M. Two isles – vessels can anchor in the shelter of these without good sounds.
- N. Point of cleared land where Marchim came to find us.
- O. Four isles.
- P. Small stream which flows from the base of the sea.
- Q. Bases along the coast.
- R. The harbor where ships can drop anchor waiting for the tide.

---
46. The translation is done by the author using her minimal French and AI and so might contain inaccuracies.

Some disaffected Androscoggins, however, did join up with Squando. The warring Indians began by attacking English trading houses on the Pejepscot and Kennebec rivers (and raided nearby ships filled with stores of corn). They killed livestock and made off with some plunder. But the First Indian War began in earnest after the militant Indians attacked the family of Thomas Wakely, an "ancient man" who lived at Casco Bay far from any neighbors. Wakely, his wife, son, pregnant daughter-in-law, and three grandchildren were likely the first English victims of the war. (A daughter of Wakely and a granddaughter were taken into captivity.) Ipswich minister Hubbard relates this outrage against the English, which attack September 12, 1675 is largely credited by (English and American) historians with initiating the First Indian War in Maine:

> "Lieut. Ingersoll, of Casco, the next day with a file of men, repaired to the place where [Wakely's] house stood, to see what was the reason of the fire they discerned the day before; where they found the house burnt to ashes, the body of the old man half consumed with the fire, the young woman killed, and three of the grand-children having their brains beat out and their bodies laid under some oaken planks not far from the house; one girl of about 11 years old was carried captive by them, and having been carried up and down the country some hundred of miles, as far as Narragansett fort, was this last June [1676] returned back to Major Waldern's [Waldron's] by one Squando, the Sagamore of Saco; a strange mixture of mercy and cruelty."[47]

The gruesome details of the attack on the Wakely family were soon known throughout Maine (and New England), and must have been a shocking wake-up call to settlers such as the Crockett family. English men and women in Maine, while generally looking down upon Native Americans as lesser beings, nevertheless had come to accept the presence of the Indians among them. Now, everything had changed. Anger, and distrust led most of the English to fear *all* Wabanakis, whether the Indians belonged to a tribe that was still peaceable or not. For even after the

---

47. "A narrative of the Indian wars in New-England, from the first planting thereof in the year 1607, to the year 1677. : Containing a relation of the occasion, rise and progress of the war with the Indians, in the southern, western, eastern and northern parts of said country." William Hubbard, A.M. Minister of Ipswich. Boston: Printed and sold by John Boyle in Marlborough-Street, 1775. P. 279-280. https://www.google.com/books/edition/A_Narrative_of_the_Indian_Wars_in_New_En/VaLqoJ6DpZcC?hl=en&gbpv=1&bsq=Wakely

Wakely attack, many Native Americans still hoped to prevent all-out war. When Squando and his warriors planned to attack garrison (fortified) houses in Saco, "...a Saco Wabanaki named Scossaway and a group of pro-peace Androscoggins warned English settlers of Squando's plans,"[48] thus saving English lives.

Regrettably, very few Englishmen understood that the Indians were not one group acting in concert, but rather were separate tribal entities with their own motivations for war (or peace). Nor could the English understand that even within a particular tribe, such as the Sacos, feelings could be divided. There were a few exceptions to English blindness, however, such as the trader Thomas Gardiner of Pemaquid, who understood and trusted the Indians.[49] But most did not. For safety reasons, the English retreated, leaving Pemaquid (then, the most eastern point settled by English), Casco Bay, and Saco to the natives. Unappeased, the Wabanakis bent on war also dropped down, and sporadically attacked vulnerable targets in southern Maine and New Hampshire around the Piscataqua River, including an attack at Kittery where the Crocketts resided.

The harsh winter of 1675/76 caused a temporary cessation of hostilities, after which the English and the Indians entered into peace talks. In the summer of 1676, the talks resulted in a peace treaty signed by seven important warring Native Americans, including the Saco sagamore Squando,[50] whose child had been murdered. But the treaty was broken almost immediately by Bostonians Henry Lawton and John Leverdure, who sailed up the coast of Maine and, through trickery, captured seventeen natives to sell into slavery (slaves being more valuable at the time than the animal pelts traded by the Indians). An outcry went up from the peaceful Native Americans, who naturally demanded an explanation and accountability. Unfortunately, the accountability was slow to materialize, which tardiness only exacerbated tensions, sinking the nascent peace treaty.[51]

---

48. "Creating an Enemy in the Borderlands: King Philip's War in Maine, 1675-1678," p. 19. Christopher J. Bilodeau. Maine History. Volume 47, Number 1. *The Maine Borderlands*.
49. Gardiner, writing to the governor of Massachusetts Bay, John Leverett, suggested that hostilities with the Indians were the result of "our owne Acctings." He noted that the Indians with whom he traded were peaceful until the English demanded they give up their guns. "And seeing these Indians in these parts did never Apeare dissatisfied untill their Armes weare Taken Away, I doubt of such Actions whether they may not be forced to go to the french for Releife," he warned. If any Wabanakis did seek aid from the French, either at Acadia (Downeast Maine) or in Canada, as Gardiner warned, that support never materialized. The French were careful to keep out of this conflict (although the French and Indians would band together against the English in the wars to come). "Creating an Enemy in the Borderlands: King Philip's War in Maine, 1675-1678," p. 8 and p. 20. Christopher J. Bilodeau. Maine History. Volume 47, Number 1. *The Maine Borderlands*.
50. "Creating an Enemy in the Borderlands: King Philip's War in Maine, 1675-1678," p. 21. Christopher J. Bilodeau. Maine History. Volume 47, Number 1. *The Maine Borderlands*.
51. In 1677, the two men finally went to trial in Boston, where Leverdure was acquitted and Lawton fined £20 for the kidnapping and sale of Indians. "Creating an Enemy in the Borderlands: King Philip's War in Maine, 1675-1678," p. 21-22.

The Second Generation

Despite the best efforts of some peaceful Indians to tamp down violence, hostilities between Native Americans and the English soon broke out again. Many attacks and raids on both sides resulted in death and destruction, and much weeping and gnashing of teeth.[52] According to Hubbard, "upwards of fifty" English settlers died between August and November of 1676, and "above 90 [Native Americans], partly in the aforesaid skirmishes, and partly in their joining the Indians to the westward, whither it is said many were invited to repair, to help destroy the English, in hopes to enjoy their possessions afterwards …"[53]

It is not possible in a story such as this to detail the depredations on both sides (such as the taking of scalps)[54] that occurred during the First Indian War, until peace was finally struck in 1678. (King Philip's War ended in the south in the summer of 1676, after the death of Metacom and his braves; however, the fighting in Maine continued for two more years.) Two incidents stand out as noteworthy, however: one perpetuated by Native Americans against the English and the other by the English against Native Americans. The awful nature of these incidents reveals the terror of the times, which terror was felt by English settlers and Indians alike.

The first incident occurred at Casco (Falmouth) in August at Anthony Brackett's homestead. One of Brackett's cows was killed August 9, 1676 by Native Americans, possibly for food, but more probably as a deliberate trick. (Even though the English allowed their livestock to run loose, the Indians were not supposed to kill them, no matter how hungry they were or how much damage the livestock caused.) An Indian by the name of Simon (later discovered to be Simon the Yankee Killer of Metacom's tribe, who had escaped jail in Dover) offered to bring the guilty party to Brackett (a captain in the English militia). Brackett agreed, but nevertheless sent an emissary with a missive down to Major Richard Waldron in Dover, who had command of English soldiers there. According to the Puritan minister Hubbard, Simon kept his promise to return with the cow killers, but the situation did not go as Brackett might have expected.

Christopher J. Bilodeau. Maine History. Volume 47, Number 1. *The Maine Borderlands*.
52. Common phrase in "The New Testament" describing the agony experienced (or prophesied to be experienced) by the people. See for example, Matthew 8:12 and Luke 13:28.
53. "A narrative of the Indian wars in New-England, from the first planting thereof in the year 1607, to the year 1677. : Containing a relation of the occasion, rise and progress of the war with the Indians, in the southern, western, eastern and northern parts of said country." William Hubbard, A.M. Minister of Ipswich. Boston: Printed and sold by John Boyle in Marlborough-Street, 1775. P. 297.
54. The taking of scalps was a practice perpetuated not only by Native Americans, but also by Englishmen. Over the years the Massachusetts General Court offered a bounty on Native American scalps. Prices on the scalps varied; however, the scalps of young braves paid more than those of women, children, and the elderly.

"... very early in the morning on the 11th of August, Simon with a party of Indians came to Anthony Bracket's house, and told him there were the Indians that had killed his cow; but as soon as they said that, the Indians went further into his house and took hold of all the guns they could see : Bracket asked what was the meaning of that, Simon replied, that so it must be, asking him withal, whether he had rather serve the Indians, or be slain by them; to which [Brackett] answered, that if the case were so, he would rather chuse to serve them than be killed by them ..."[55]

It was a wise decision on Brackett's part to submit to the natives. Brackett, his wife Ann, and a "negro" (likely an enslaved African American) were tied up; however, Brackett's brother-in-law resisted and was killed on the spot. Five children and the bound adults were taken captive. The Indian warriors (probably a loose coalition of disaffected braves from Maine and southern New England) continued to attack and kill settlers, and plunder English homes in the greater Falmouth area. By the end of the day, approximately thirty-four English colonists were killed or carried off into captivity. (Some captives would be ransomed later.)[56] No Native American account of the raids exists, so we do not know how many Indians were killed. Possibly none.

Once known, the details of the Indian raids at Casco shocked English settlers in Maine (and throughout New England). Ephraim and Anne Crockett, then living at Brave Boat Harbor, had at least two children born at the time of the attacks (Ephraim, Jr. and Sarah). No doubt after hearing of the grisly details of the raid the couple (like other English families) kept careful track of their children (and their

---

55. "A narrative of the Indian wars in New-England, from the first planting thereof in the year 1607, to the year 1677. : Containing a relation of the occasion, rise and progress of the war with the Indians, in the southern, western, eastern and northern parts of said country." William Hubbard, A.M. Minister of Ipswich. Boston: Printed and sold by John Boyle in Marlborough-Street, 1775. P. 307.

56. Anthony and Ann Brackett (and some of their children) survived. thanks, it is told (in a rather romantic tale) to Ann's ability to sew repairs to an old Indian canoe, which they found next to the river and in which the family made their escape. (As was customary at the time, Ann reportedly had her needle—fashioned from whalebone or iron—pinned to her dress so she would not lose this valuable household necessity.) "Ann Mitton Brackett—Needlewoman to the Rescue," by Pat Higgins. The Maine Story website https://www.mainestory.info/maine-stories/ann-mitton-brackett.html Ann lived only a year after escaping from the Indians, perhaps dying from childbirth. Anthony Brackett remarried and returned to Casco, but lived just over a decade longer. He was killed by Native Americans during the opening salvos of the Second Indian War (King William's War, 1689-1697), probably not far from where he, Ann, and their family had been captured in the 1676 attack. See also "A narrative of the Indian wars in New-England, from the first planting thereof in the year 1607, to the year 1677. : Containing a relation of the occasion, rise and progress of the war with the Indians, in the southern, western, eastern and northern parts of said country." William Hubbard, A.M. Minister of Ipswich. Boston: Printed and sold by John Boyle in Marlborough-Street, 1775. P. 307.

guns). The unexpected nature of these sporadic Indian attacks terrified the settlers (as did the barbarity that often accompanied the raids). For the next ninety years the English would live in fear—even during times of peace with Native Americans—expecting that at any moment hostile Indians would jump out from behind the trees and attack them.

The second noteworthy incident occurred at the end of King Philip's War, not long after Metacom (King Philip) had been killed. This incident reveals that the English could be every bit as duplicitous as the Native Americans.

When King Philip's coalition fell apart after his death in the summer of 1676, many Wampanoag, Narragansett, and Nipmuck braves fled north and sought refuge among the peaceful Penacook Indians of New Hampshire. (The Penacook had not taken sides during King Philip's War.) Under a directive from the Massachusetts General Court, Major Waldron of Cocheco (Dover), along with Major Charles Frost of Kittery and about 130 soldiers, met with 350-400 natives (men, women, and children), ostensibly to "reinvigorate the peace talks."[57] But Waldron and others recognized some of the Indian warriors from previous battles. Because the English were outnumbered, Waldron devised a trick to disarm and trap the natives. The major proposed the two groups participate in a sham battle, which war games also included a good deal of alcohol. During the sham battle, the English soldiers (who did not disarm as promised) proceeded to surround and capture the unarmed, intoxicated Native Americans, who until that point believed they were not only playing games, but also were meeting for peace talks with the English.

About 200 Native Americans (possibly more) who were captured at Cocheco were sent to Boston, where eight were hanged (for crimes committed during King Philip's War) and the rest were "sold into slavery in places as far away as the West Indies, the Azores, and Tangier (in Morocco). The Penacooks …were separated out and set free, but most never forgot what they considered Waldron's betrayal."[58] This betrayal by the English shocked the Penacooks, who until then had not taken up arms against the colonists. In addition, peaceable Kennebecs and Penobscots in Maine were also shocked by Waldron's duplicity. Ironically, if Major Waldron (and the Massachusetts General Court) hoped to prevent further bloodshed (as

---

57. "Creating an Enemy in the Borderlands: King Philip's War in Maine, 1675-1678," p. 25. Christopher J. Bilodeau. Maine History. Volume 47, Number 1. *The Maine Borderlands*.
58. "Timeline of New Hampshire History, 1676." New Hampshire Historical Society website. https://www.nhhistory.org/Timeline?id=1676.1

some historians suggest), his betrayal of the Penacooks and their guests had the opposite effect:

> "With this blow the war reached a new phase, as it galvanized Indian opposition like never before. As the Kennebecs and Penobscots had recently joined the war, the Wabanakis throughout Maine finally presented a unified front against the English. Now, Pigwackets, Kennebunks, Sacos, Androscoggins, Kennebecs, and Penobscots all took part in the violence, and many of the New Hampshire Penacooks felt alienated, at the least from their English allies. The homogenizing vision of Massachusetts Bay officials had created the pan-Wabanaki enemy it had always believed existed."[59]

Major Waldron later led soldiers in an expedition into Maine, where—while under a flag of truce with a cohort of friendly Indians—fearing he and his men were about to be attacked, he killed or captured them all. Waldron continued his wanton killing of Native Americans in Maine. After he returned to Dover he believed (wrongly, as it turned out) that he had "scattered and broken" the warring natives in Maine.[60] (Waldron's duplicity would not be forgotten by the Indians, however, and he received his just deserts in 1689 during King William's War.)[61]

Oddly enough, peace between the English and Native Americans during the First Indian War came about through the involvement of their nemeses. First, the English asked the Mohawks, who had helped them defeat King Philip in southern New England, to support them in their war with the Indians on the Maine frontier. When the Wabanakis heard that the Mohawks, their long-time foes to the west of whom they were terrified, were allied with the English (which never actually came about) they became much more interested in striking a peace deal. Second, Massachusetts Bay Colony learned that Governor Edmund Andros of New York, in order to further the claim of the Duke of York to the Sagadahoc region (the area east of

---

59. "Creating an Enemy in the Borderlands: King Philip's War in Maine, 1675-1678," p. 25-26. Christopher J. Bilodeau. Maine History. Volume 47, Number 1. *The Maine Borderlands*.
60. "Creating an Enemy in the Borderlands: King Philip's War in Maine, 1675-1678," p. 32. Christopher J. Bilodeau. Maine History. Volume 47, Number 1. *The Maine Borderlands*. The Indians in Maine and New Hampshire never forgot Waldron's duplicity.
61. When King William's War broke out in 1689, Waldron's garrison at Cocheco was attacked first by Native Americans. The English soldier was taken from his bed, tortured, and killed. Major Charles Frost of Kittery, who participated with Waldron in the trickery at Cocheco in 1676, would also be killed by Indians during King William's War, as we will see in Chapter 3.

the Kennebec River),[62] had sent ships to Pemaquid to initiate peace talks with the Wabanakis, they became alarmed. The powers-that-be in Boston "recognized the difficulty of retaining any authority in Maine without peace, so Massachusetts Bay officials pushed for their own diplomatic negotiations with the Wabanakis."

"The two sides eventually came to terms April 12, 1678 [with the Treaty of Casco]. The Wabanakis agreed to release all English captives, and they gained one peck of corn for every settlement household in Maine. The English settlers were then allowed to go back to their homes [to the eastward]. War in Maine was over, for the time being."[63]

The Litigiousness of Kittery and Common "Society"

One would think that Maine settlers of this time had enough to worry about, what with trying to eke out a living in a New World; following the shifting tides of power from Massachusetts Bay Colony to the English Crown (and back again); and wondering whether the 1678 Treaty of Casco with the Wabanaki would hold; however, court records reveal frequent squabbles between neighbors, some appearing (to us now, not to them) picayune in nature. Kittery (and York) residents, including Ephraim Crockett, were a litigious bunch! In fact, Ephraim's name appears often in the Province and Court Records of Maine (MPCR). Through Ephraim Crockett's court appearances, we learn a lot about the lives of the common men and women of 17th century Maine.

Not long after the ending of the First Indian War (and his father's death in the spring of 1679), Ephraim Crockett was a defendant at York County Court. On July 1, 1679, the thirty-five-year-old was in court to answer a charge of trespass, lodged by Francis Raynes. A surgeon and venerable resident of York, Raynes was also an old family friend and former neighbor of Thomas Crockett's. (In 1660, Raynes had stepped forward and posted bond for Ephraim's mother, when Ann was charged with spending too much time in the company of Joseph Davis). Despite this closeness between the two families, and Raynes' seniority and status as a gentleman

---
62. In 1664, King Charles II had granted Sagadahoc to his brother the Duke of York (later King James II), although much of the territory had previously been granted to others.
63. "Creating an Enemy in the Borderlands: King Philip's War in Maine, 1675-1678," p. 36. Christopher J. Bilodeau. Maine History. Volume 47, Number 1. *The Maine Borderlands*.

and leading citizen, Ephraim committed enough of an offense that the elder man charged him with trespass.

It is possible that the two men might have had a boundary dispute (Thomas Crockett having sold abutter Raynes 30 of his 40 acres in York); however, it seems more likely that the dustup simply related to who owned a particular cow. The jury, after hearing the case (and deciding for Raynes) awarded that gentleman a three-year-old heifer or the equivalent, 2 pounds, 5 shillings, in damages. (Bovines were still a valuable commodity in Maine.) The fracas represented an expensive lesson for Ephraim, who not only had to return the heifer (or pay the equivalent in cash), but as the loser he was also required to cover the court costs of 1 pound, 1 shilling and 6 pence.[64]

Ephraim did not learn his lesson, either. Six years later he appeared again in court as a defendant. At a Court of Sessions held at Kittery on March 31, 1685, John Morrill, plaintiff, charged Ephraim Crockett for non-payment of 4,500 bricks. Ephraim, not to be outdone, charged Morrill (at the same court) with detaining a heifer. Which came first—the unpaid for bricks or the "detained" heifer—we do not know. The two men were able to work out their differences, however, coming to a mutually agreeable settlement so that the case was not heard at court.[65] (Again, note the value of bovines—4,500 bricks for a heifer!)

Many historians often lump the settlers of Maine in with residents of Massachusetts Bay Colony, as if the two groups were cut from the same broadcloth. And while Mainers were of British origin (for the most part), as were the people of Massachusetts (and most Mainers *did* eventually submit to the authority of Massachusetts Bay in 1652), Maine was not settled (like Massachusetts) by Puritans seeking religious liberty, but rather by fisherman, farmers, fur traders, and merchants seeking land and opportunity. For the second group (to which Ephraim Crockett belonged) the flame of religion did not burn very bright (nor, for some, their intellectual flame).

During his short life, Ephraim Crockett appears to have been most comfortable among the common folk. He never reached for higher society, as his father had done (briefly) in York when Thomas Crockett owned land (and possibly dwelt) between Mr. Frances Raynes and Mr. Edward Godfrey.[66] Ephraim's proletarian

---

64. MPCR, Vol. 2, p. 346.
65. MPCR, Vol. 3, p. 211.
66. The term "Mr." was used in the early records to note a man of distinction, usually someone with education, who typically came from a landed family in England.

bent is revealed in two other court cases, during which he stood up for ordinary men and women.

On July 6, 1675, Ephraim Crockett stood bound with Jeremiah Gutteridge in a bond of 10 pounds for Gutteridge's security in York. The two men must have been close friends, because at the time the 10-pound bond was worth about the equivalent of ten acres of land.[67] If Gutteridge had absconded, Ephraim Crockett would have been stuck paying the bond for his friend. (Gutteridge, who was probably a fisherman, had accompanied Ephraim Crockett to the Great Island in April of that same year on behalf of Ephraim's aunt Joane Andrews and her real estate sale.)

The fisherman had been charged by the Grand Jury of the York County Court for being an idle person and for not providing for his family. In addition, Gutteridge was charged with giving "reproachfull Languidg" to Captain Nathaniel Fryer (captain of a sea coaster[68] and then selectman of Kittery)[69] after Fryer reproved the man for his idleness. (One can almost hear *that* exchange, which would likely go over about as well today if a selectman told a local resident he was too idle.) The Court declared that Gutteridge should receive 20 lashes at the post,[70] either that or to bring in security that he would be on better behavior in providing for his family by using more diligence in his calling for the future.[71] Whether Gutteridge chose the lash or made his payment we do not know, although there is no record that Ephraim Crockett had to come up with the 10 pounds to pay the fisherman's bond.

Others Ephraim stood up for included people of questionable character, such as his cousin Ann (Andrews) Billing (daughter of Joane and John Andrews) and her paramour Ambrose Boaden, another fisherman. At the Court of Pleas held at Wells, June 30, 1680, the Court considered the "unchast and Lascivious carages of Ambrose Boaden with Ann Billine." Boaden, then likely married (to another woman), had apparently "carried on" in public with Ann, the wife of John Billing. (Ann's behavior is reminiscent of her mother's escapade decades earlier when bold-faced Joane Andrews allowed herself to be ferried up and down the Piscataqua River by the married Gowen Wilson.)

Boaden appears not to have been present at court, where he was sentenced

---

67. In 1672, Ephraim Crockett sold 10 acres of land in Kittery for 11 pounds, 10 shillings. MEWD, Vol. 7, p. 93-94.
68. A sea coaster was a packet that ferried goods between ports, probably in Fryer's case between Kittery, Portsmouth, and Boston.
69. LIBBY/NOYES, p. 249.
70. The whipping post was typically in a public place and the punishment was meant to be a form of shaming as well as bodily punishment.
71. MPCR, Vol. 2, p. 305.

to receive 15 stripes at the post on the bare skin "well layd on" (a not-to-subtle directive not to spare the rod). Perhaps in lieu of the thrashing, Ephraim stepped forward for his friend. He promised that Boaden would pay the Treasurer of York County four pounds in money within three months and "further to pay seaven pounds in fish or red oake pipe staves, at 40s per M [thousand] within the tearme of three Moenths afterwards."[72] No mention of punishment for Ann Billing appears in the court record, although her husband was present at court, possibly because he expected to pay a fine for her.[73] Since Ephraim had no business before the Court of Pleas—and did not just drop in for the entertainment value, having to travel from Kittery to Wells to attend—Ephraim must have been there solely on Boaden's or his cousin Ann's behalf (or both).

A (Mostly) Model Citizen

With a few exceptions, such as swearing[74] and the disputes over the bovines, Ephraim Crockett's life represents that of a mostly model citizen (by Maine standards, anyway). By 1672, Ephraim (then married to Anne) was earning his living as a tailor.[75] He was appointed Constable of Kittery (along with William Love) in 1672,[76] and served on the jury in 1675[77] and in 1680.[78] In addition to witnessing several deeds for his aunt Joane Andrews, Ephraim also witnessed deeds over the

---

72. MPCR, Vol. 3, p. 61.
73. At the same court John Billing "owned" a judgment of four pounds to Nathaniel Fryer, according to a bill left in court. Billing promised to pay in "Merchantable red oake pipe staves at 45s per thousand." According to MPCR editor Robert Moody, "This paragraph [about Billing's debt] was crowded in later by the Recorder," so Billing was either late or was at court for another purpose, possibly this infraction of his wife's. MPCR, Vol. 3, p. 60.
74. On July 4, 1671, at a Court held at York for York County, "Nicholas Frost the beaver trader and Ephraim Crockett" were "presented" for swearing by God and giving of Capt. Charles Frost several abusive speeches. Nicholas Frost was marked with a non-appearance at this court; however, he later appeared in front of magistrate Edward Rishworth, where he owned his presentment (acknowledged his offense) and paid a fine. There is no indication that Ephraim Crockett appeared in court or paid a fine—or was docked for the lapse—which suggests the elder Frost was the true culprit. (MPCR, Vol. 2, p. 222.)
75. Ephraim is described as "taylor" in his deed to Charles O'Grado. This is the only reference (in recorded deeds or depositions) to an occupation for the first son of Thomas and Ann Crockett. MEWD, Vol. 7, p. 93.
76. On July 2, 1672, at York County Court Ephraim Crockett and William Love were appointed Constables for Kittery for the ensuing year. MPCR, Vol. 2, p. 238.
77. On Aug. 18, 1675, Ephraim Crockett and his brother Joseph were both on the jury during the Inquest of John Cox. LIBBY/NOYES, p. 33, List 287.
78. On June 30, 1680, at a Court of Pleas held in Wells for the Province of Maine under the authority of the heirs of Sir Fernando Gorges, Ephraim was on the jury that heard the case of John Fergison, accused of taking and detaining a horse from James Warrens. (Warrens had requested a jury trial, and since Ephraim was in court that day to help his mother petition that the management of Crockett's Neck remain in her hands, he was likely selected for the jury or volunteered.) MPCR, Vol. 3, p. 59.

years for people with whom he had no obvious connection,[79] possibly because as a tailor he could regularly be found at home (as opposed to local fishermen and sailors, who were often at sea). Or possibly because Ephraim was just a good guy. In addition to posting bonds for his friends, Ephraim also helped friends and neighbors post bonds relating to their ability to justly administer an estate after the death of a loved one.[80]

Although Ephraim signed legal documents with a mark—a rather interesting capital "E" (see below)—it is probable that as a tailor he had some ability to read and write. Ephraim almost certainly was able to do sums, since in 1678 he was appointed as one of the appraisers of the large estate of Joseph Pearce.[81] In 1688, Ephraim also inventoried the estate of Christopher Mitchell,[82] the husband of his cousin Sarah (Andrews) Mitchell (sister to the wayward Ann, who had carried on with Andrew Boaden). Ephraim took the inventory of Mitchell's estate shortly before his own death (in fact, when Ephraim believed he was dying), signifying that for him it was an important commitment.

Mark of Ephraim Crockett.
(See Appendix, pages 403–404, for a transcription of Ephraim's will, from which this mark was taken.)

---

79. On July 22, 1672, Robert Marshall, mariner, acknowledged a debt to John Bray, the shipbuilder from Brave Boat Harbor, which was witnessed by Ephraim Crockett and Jonathan Pett. (MEWD, Vol. 2, p. 332.) On Nov. 30, 1678, Ephraim Crockett and his stepfather-to-be Dygory Jeffrey witnessed a deed of a house and land in York at Brave Boat Harbor for George Burrin, who sold to Nicholas Shapleigh. (MEWD, Vol. 3, p. 93-94.) On Feb. 14, 1679, Ephraim Crockett witnessed a deed for Stephen and Catherine Paul of Kittery. (MEWD, Vol. 3, p. 184.) On Aug. 24, 1686, Ephraim Crockett witnessed a deed for Samuel Knight of Kittery. (MEWD, Vol. 6, p. 30.)
80. On Feb. 8, 1678/79, Ephraim Crockett and Roger Dearing posted a 200-pound bond for John Bray and Francis Hooke, Administrators of the estate of Joseph Pearce, to ensure they shall give a just account of the estate. (MPCR, Vol. 2, p. 531.) On June 30, 1681, Ephraim Crockett and Henry Brooking stood bound in a bond of 40 pounds that William Palmer would bring in a true inventory/account of the estate of Henry Brooking. (MPCR, Vol. 3, p. 14.) On May 18, 1686, John Dyamont (Diamond) and Ephraim Crockett mutually stood bound with Sarah Trickey that she should administer her son John's estate as law requires, in a bond of 300 pounds. (MEWD, Vol. 5, p. 81.)
81. MEWD, Vol. 5, p. 68.
82. Information on the inventory of Christopher Mitchell's estate taken from "The Mitchells from Kittery: a reprint from Descendants of Edward Small and their families." Lora Atline Woodbury Underhill. Riverside Press, Cambridge, 1911. P. 1302. Christopher Mitchell died in April 1688. Ephraim Crockett died in September or October of 1688.

Kittery Land Grants and Real Estate Sales

Although Maine settlers were not fond of Puritan laws and religious tenents, they did receive two important benefits from the Bay's confiscation of Sir Ferdinando Gorge's real estate. First, Massachusetts Bay granted men who submitted to their authority the status of freemen (which promise, along with the guns wielded by the Bay's commissioners, no doubt helped encourage the men to submit). Second, Massachusetts Bay was only too happy for the towns to dole out land that (until 1677, anyway) belonged to Sir Ferdinando Gorges or his grandson. (These overlapping land grants obviously caused title issues and headaches that cropped up later, however, none of these are germane to our story.)

Like many men of the time, Ephraim received two grants of land from the town of Kittery. The first grant occurred in 1672 when Ephraim was twenty-eight. On June 3, 1672, the town of Kittery laid out 10 acres of land for him on the west side of Spruce Creek, between the land of John Shapleigh and John Shephard.[83] With his wife Anne's consent, Ephraim sold this real estate in September of that same year to Charles Ogrado (O'Grady)[84] of Portsmouth for 11 pounds, 10 shillings.[85] The second grant was given by the town of Kittery in 1679 when Ephraim was thirty-five. On July 28, 1679, Kittery granted Ephraim 40 acres of land between Long Reach and Spruce Creek. On October 2nd surveyor John Wincoll (Winchell) laid out the 40-acres, which land Ephraim left to his youngest son Richard upon his death.[86]

Ephraim and Anne Crockett and their family lived in Brave Boat Harbor from 1667 until 1683 (or a few years later), when his mother married Dygory Jeffrey. By 1683, Ann and Thomas's children were grown and married (or on their own),[87] and after her second marriage Ephraim's mother lived with Jeffrey at his house in

---

83. MEWD, Vol. 5, p. 190.
84. Early English scribes, who did not use apostrophes, had difficulty spelling names for which we now use contractions.
85. MEWD, Vol. 7, p. 93-94. Mary Stileman and Richard Stileman, possibly servants of Ogrado, witnessed the deed. Abutter John Shephard coveted this property, and after the 10 acres was sold twice more Shephard ended up in a decades-long dispute over it with the newest purchaser Nathaniel Kene. Kene ultimately prevailed, thanks in part to depositions provided by Ephraim's younger brothers Joseph and Joshua Crockett. See MPCR, Vol. 4, p. 25-28. While Kene was in the right in this instance, he was a notoriously litigious and unseemly person, to whom one's sympathy would not normally be given. See the many instances Kene is negatively mentioned in the MPCR.
86. MEWD. The information about this 40-acre grant to Ephraim, including dates, comes from the deed of sale of the same real estate to John Fernald, given by Richard and Deborah (Haley) Crockett in 1708.
87. Last to leave the Crockett nest was probably daughter Mary, who was married to Elisha Barton before October 28, 1684, when Ephraim owned in court how he was going to pay his brother-in-law Barton Mary's inheritance of 12 pounds from her father Thomas Crockett's estate. MPCR, Vol. 3, p. 203.

Kittery,[88] freeing up the house on Crockett's Neck for Ephraim's family. On April 27, 1686, Ephraim and Anne sold to Richard White for 46 pounds sterling, 90 acres of upland and marsh in Brave Boat Harbor.[89] At the time of the sale, Ephraim and his family appear to have relocated to the house his father built on Crockett's Neck, where Ephraim lived only a short period of time until his own death.

Death of Ephraim Crockett

Ephraim Crockett died in September of 1688, only nine years after his father Thomas passed away. He was forty-four years of age. A few months before his death, in May of 1688, his mother deeded to him (and more importantly to Ephraim's heirs) all the lands on Crockett's Neck, where Ephraim and his family resided. The property was bounded by Spruce Creek; by land of Ann and Thomas' son Hugh Crockett; and by the property of sons-in-law William Roberts (husband of daughter Ann) and John Parrot (husband of daughter Sarah).[90]

Ephraim left behind his widow, Anne, and their four children (Ephraim, Jr., Sarah, Mary, and Richard), none of whom had reached the age of maturity (twenty-one) by the time of his death.[91] Ephraim apparently knew his death was approaching. He was either seriously ill or had suffered an accident, for in his last will and testament dated July 17, 1688, Ephraim writes that he is in "dayly expectacon off" his death (although he lived another two months) and that he was making the will to settle his affairs "for the prevention of distraccon after my decease."[92] Ephraim passed away after September 26, 1688,[93] when he and Anne appeared

---

88. On Sept. 1, 1694, Dygory Jeffrey, with the consent of his wife Ann (Crockett), sold to Henry Deering (Dearing) his home and outbuilding and 100 acres of land in Kittery. The sale was subject to his and Ann's right to peaceably enjoy the house and land for the rest of their natural lives. The property formerly belonged to George Palmer. After Palmer, the real estate was owned by Dr. Henry Greenland, then William Broad, and then Jeffrey. MEWD, Vol. 6, p. 95-96.
89. MEWD, Vol. 5, p. 144-145. This replaces a prior deed for 50 acres at Brave Boat Harbor, which White acknowledges (see Vol. 5, p. 145). There is no mention of a house in the deed, but a house is noted in a later mortgage given Sept. 27, 1692 by White to Henry Dearing, to whom the property eventually passes. MEWD, Vol. 8, p. 76+. We do not know when the house was built or who built it; however, I surmise the house was built by Ephraim Crockett using the 17 pounds from the sale of his father's land to Abraham Corbett in 1667. (See Chapter 1 for more information on the Brave Boat Harbor real estate.)
90. MEWD, Vol. 4, p. 303. Henry Barter, who would marry Ephraim's daughter Sarah (perhaps named for her aunt Sarah or Sarah Lynn Gunnison), was one of the witnesses.
91. CANDAGE, p. 2.
92. Last Will and Testament of Ephraim Crockett. Probate Office 1, 10. Maine Wills, 1640-1760.
93. Many historians, including CANDAGE, p. 1, state that an inventory of Ephraim's estate was taken Sept. 10, 1688. I think this is a mistake that continues to live on. According to MEWD, Vol. 5, p. 145, Ephraim and Anne appeared in person before Francis Hooke on Sept. 26, 1688, more than two weeks after the inventory was supposedly taken. The couple brought Hooke the new deed to Richard White for the 90 acres of land at Brave Boat Harbor (replacing a deed for 50 acres) and both swore before Hooke that this was their free act and deed. Richard White also nullified the deed for the 50 acres, and Ephraim and Anne signed that document, too.

in person in front of magistrate Francis Hooke to clear up the two deeds to Richard White for land sold to White in Brave Boat Harbor. (If Ephraim's death was imminent and he was bedridden, Hooke might have come to Crockett's house to perform this service.)

Ephraim's will, which he signed with his mark, is beautifully written, full of the heartfelt emotions one would expect from someone who knew he was shortly going to be separated forever from his loved ones. He describes Anne as "my well beloved wife" and reveals confidence in her abilities by leaving her in charge of "both Lands and moveables" until their eldest son Ephraim came of age (which appears not to have happened). Although he bequeaths the bulk of his estate—his house and land (including a piece of salt marsh at Broad Boat[94] Harbor that he purchased as an investment from Francis Champernowne)—to his eldest son, Ephraim generously provided for Anne, dictating in his will that after young Ephraim comes of age "my now wife Anna Crockett shall have possesse and quietly enjoy the one halfe of my house and Land and Marsh during her Naturall life."[95] (The typical widow's portion of the time was one-third.)

To his two daughters, Sarah and Mary (around age seventeen and thirteen, respectively) Ephraim left "twenty pounds a peece to be paid to them by my Eldest son Ephraim Crocket att the decease of my wife."[96] To his youngest child, Richard Crockett, Ephraim left the 40 acres of land granted to him by the town of Kittery "lyeing neare the Mast way to him and his Heires for ever./ And one Cow."[97] (Reading this line of Ephraim's will reminded me not only of his court cases over bovines, but also of his father Thomas, who had helped land the first cow in Maine at Cow Cove fifty-four years earlier. Cows were still important to the Crocketts at the time of Ephraim's death.)

Significantly, in his will Ephraim reaffirmed the marriage portions of land on Crockett's Neck given by their father to his sisters Ann and Sarah. He asserts: "That Wheras my father Thomas Crockett did in his life tyme give Lay out and bound a peece of his Neck of Land which was in his owne possession to my sister An Roberts[98] as alsoe a peece of sd Neck of Land to my Sister Sarah Parrett as their

---

94. Brave Boat Harbor.
95. Last Will and Testament of Ephraim Crockett. Probate Office 1, 10. Maine Wills, 1640-1760.
96. Last Will and Testament of Ephraim Crockett. Probate Office 1, 10. Maine Wills, 1640-1760.
97. Last Will and Testament of Ephraim Crockett. Probate Office 1, 10. Maine Wills, 1640-1760.
98. On September 23, 1706, Ann's husband William Roberts mortgaged this property (including the house and one shallop) to his and Ann's son George Roberts, of Ipswich, Massachusetts Bay. The mortgage enabled Roberts pay a bond due to Francis Wainwright, also of Ipswich. (MEWD, Vol. 7, p. 304-305.) On July 17, 1708, the younger Roberts sold the mortgage to

Marriage portions my Will is the said Land thus given by my father shall stand good to my Sisters and their Heires forever/."[99] It says a lot about the character of the man that—when Ephraim knew he was dying—he ensured that the dowries of his sisters would stand against any potential future challenge.

The Widow Anne

Despite the fact that women were still in short supply in Maine, Anne (Edge) Crockett appears never to have remarried. Her mother, Grandma Edge, resided with the widow and her children in 1690 (and likely until Florence Edge's death) in the house that Thomas Crockett built on Crockett's Neck. In records of 1695, seven years after Ephraim's death, Anne Crockett was listed simply as a widow.[100]

We do not know when Anne died. In September of 1722, when Anne would have been approximately seventy-five-years-old, the selectmen of Kittery met with local military officers and ordered many houses made "Defencible"[101] from attacks by Native Americans, once again on the warpath. (This occurred at the beginning of Father Rasles' War, which we will cover in Chapter 3.) In case of an attack by warring Norridgewock, Mi'kmaq, and Maliseet Indians, the "widow Crockett and her family" were ordered to lodge in the 32nd house on the list, which belonged to Henry Barter.[102] Since Barter was Anne Crockett's son-in-law (the husband of her daughter Sarah), some historians and genealogists have assumed the reference is to Ephraim's widow; however, because Anne's children were grown, it makes more sense to me that the woman on this list—"the widow Crockett and her family"— was a generation younger than Anne, one who would still have children at home.

By my calculations, Anne (Edge) Crockett was deceased by 1713, if not before.[103] Ephraim provided for his widow in his will by giving her the right to half

---

William Pepperell, Sr. (MEWD, Vol. 7, p. 305-306.) In 1715, after William Robert's death, Pepperell took the widow Anne/Anna/Nan (possibly a second wife and not Ann Crockett) to court, where she owned the judgment against her husband. Pepperell foreclosed and the widow was removed. (MPCR, Vol. 5, p. 57.) On Feb. 10, 1729, Henry Barter, Jr. (son of Henry and Sarah Crockett Barter) bought the former Roberts' homestead from Pepperell for 135 pounds, paying nearly ten times the 14+ pound-debt that Pepperell had against the property. (MEWD, Vol. 18, p. 110-111.)

99. Last Will and Testament of Ephraim Crockett. Probate Office 1, 10. Maine Wills, 1640-1760.
100. CANDAGE, p. 2.
101. NOTABLE, p. 411.
102. NOTABLE, p. 411.
103. A case could be made that Anne (Edge) Crockett was deceased by Sept. 23, 1706, when William Roberts (husband of Anne Crockett and son-in-law of Thomas and Ann) mortgaged his Crockett's Neck property to his son William. (See MEWD, Vol. 7, p. 304-305.) Roberts' property, which was cut from Thomas Crockett's grant on Crockett's Neck, was bounded on one side by Thomas' old homestead, which is described in Roberts' deed as "northeast by land of Richard Crockett." No reference is made in this deed to Richard's mother Anne (or to older brother Ephraim, Jr.), which such reference *had* occurred

his house, land, and marsh during her natural life. If Anne was still alive in May of 1713, her son Richard Crockett would not have sold the balance of Crockett's Neck (about 40 acres, which likely included his grandfather Thomas Crockett's house) to his brother-in-law Henry Barter on May 26, 1713.[104] Even if Anne had remarried—and given her son her blessing for the sale—she would still have had to sign away her dower rights in the deed. Instead, it was Richard's wife, Deborah (Haley) Crockett, who signed off on her dower rights when the property was sold.

This concludes the story of Ephraim and Anne (Edge) Crockett, the second-generation of the Crockett family we are following. Despite his short life, the historical record about Ephraim is rich. I wish, however, that there was more information about Anne (although it is good she did not appear in court as often as Ephraim's aunt Joane did!). Most of all, though, since the lifespan for these early English colonists had increased significantly over their counterparts back in the old country, I wish that Ephraim Crockett had lived to meet his grandchildren, as many—if not all—of his siblings lived to do.

---

in 1695, when Hugh Crockett sold his adjoining property to Henry Barter and noted in his deed a boundary line as being by "land of my sister-in-law," Anne (Edge) Crockett. (See MEWD, Vol. 7, p. 192-193.) Also, Ephraim Crockett, Jr. must have been deceased by 1695. Had Ephraim, Jr. been alive in 1695, he should have been mentioned as an abutter in Hugh's deed to Barter, rather than his mother. His father left Ephraim, Jr. the homestead in his 1688 will, and the young man would have reached or been near the age of majority by 1695. Richard was then about thirteen, and so he would naturally not be referenced as the owner of the property. By 1706, however, when Roberts' deed was executed, Richard was twenty-four, and the legitimate owner of his father's estate as the only remaining son after the death of his older brother Ephraim.

104. MEWD, Vol. 8, p. 105-106. Henry Barter borrowed 100 pounds from William Pepperell, Jr., then still a minor, to buy out his brother-in-law Richard Crockett. No mention is made in the deed of the 20 pounds apiece that Ephraim Crockett, Sr. states in his will that eldest son Ephraim, Jr. was to make to his two sisters after the death of their mother. Barter, who was married to Sarah Crockett, would have been due 20 pounds and it seems as though the sum would have been referenced as part of the purchase price had the payment been made (or the sum subtracted from the total paid). Instead, Barter borrows the entire 100 pounds paid to his brother-in-law. Richard was not obligated to make the payments, however, since his father in his will directed Ephraim, Jr. to make them, not Richard.

Chapter 3

MAKING IT TO "THE SHORT SIDE FRONT" THE THIRD GENERATION

First Generation – Thomas Crockett
Second Generation – Ephraim Crockett
Third Generation – Richard Crockett, 1682-1757
Fourth Generation – Richard Crockett, Jr.
Fifth Generation – Richard Crockett (III, also known as Richard, Jr.)
Sixth Generation – Ephraim Crockett

Richard Crockett, the third generation of Crocketts we are following, was the grandson of Thomas and Ann Crockett. His father died when Richard was six years old, leaving the boy in the care of his mother, older siblings, and extended Crockett relations. It appears that Richard's elder brother, Ephraim Crockett, Jr., died before inheriting the estate left to him by their father's will and thus Richard inherited not only 40 acres and a cow (his share from the will), but also the house built by Thomas Crockett and land on Crockett's Neck (his brother Ephraim's share). Despite this bounteous inheritance, however, Richard chose to leave Kittery and make a life for himself and his family in New Hampshire, the only Crockett in our line *not* to make his home in Maine. But his long-time friendship with brother-in-law Samuel Skillin, who remained in Maine, affected not only Richard's life, but also the lives of his children and grandchildren.

Richard's youth was blighted by war with the French and Indians. While war appears to have shaped young Richard's decisions about his future, he did not allow the hostilities to define his life. Like most of the Crockett men, Richard's adulthood was driven by a quest for land. Unlike his father, however, who appeared satisfied during his short life with his social status, Richard's life was marked by a rise to prominence as one of the founders of Stratham, New Hampshire.

A Youth Marred By War with the French and Indians (Second Indian War, 1688-1697)

Richard Crockett was born in Kittery to Ephraim and Anne (Edge) Crockett in 1682, about four years after the Treaty of Casco was signed (April 12, 1678) ending the First Indian War (King Philip's War in southern New England). He was the younger of the couple's two sons, and possibly the youngest child.

In the fall of 1688, when Richard was six, his father, Ephraim Crockett, Sr., died. Richard and his siblings and their mother were then living in the home that Thomas Crockett (Richard's grandfather) had built on Crockett's Neck. Prior to Ephraim's death, this property had been deeded to him by his mother, Ann Crockett Jeffrey[1] (Richard's grandmother, who had remarried and was living with her second husband). Richard grew up surrounded by Crockett aunts, uncles, and cousins.[2] In addition, Richard's maternal grandmother, Grandma Edge, appears to have resided with the family until her death.

Richard's childhood was marred by a second grisly war with the Indians, this time joined by their new French allies. The year of his father's death—1688—saw the opening salvos of King William's War,[3] the first (of four) wars fought globally by France and England. (See chart on opposite page for a list of the Indian wars.) On the ground in Maine, the French were aided by their Wabanaki allies. The war, which broke out here even before England had declared war on France,[4] was known in Maine as the Second Indian War.

---

1. Ann might have known that her son was dying and transferred the property to him prior to his death to facilitate ownership for Ephraim's heirs.
2. Richard's uncle Hugh Crockett's property abutted the house in which Richard lived, as did the homesteads of aunts Ann (Crockett) Roberts and Sarah (Crockett) Parrett.
3. King William's War was known in Europe as the Nine Year's War. In New England, it was also known as the Second Indian War (King Philip's War was the First Indian War).
4. England declared war on France May 17, 1689. "History of King William's War." History of Massachusetts blog https://historyofmassachusetts.org/king-williams-war/

> ### Indian Wars in Maine
>
> First Indian War (King Philip's War) – 1675-1678
> Second Indian War (King William's War) – 1688-1698
> Third Indian War (Queen Anne's War) – 1702-1713
> Fourth Indian War (Father Rasles' or Dummer's War) – 1722-1725
> Fifth Indian War (King George's War) – 1744-1748
> Sixth Indian War (French and Indian War) – 1754-1763

In April of 1688, Sir Edmund Andros, then governor of the Dominion of New England, led an expedition against the French nobleman Baron Jean Vincent de Saint-Castin at his home and trading center in Acadia in eastern Maine. Saint-Castin was away at the time, however, and in a fit of pique at not capturing his prey, Andros plundered and destroyed the baron's longtime home, trading post, and orchard.[5] (To justify his actions since France and England were not then at war, Andros declared Saint-Castin's trading center was within English jurisdiction, which the French denied.) Andros' ill-advised act sparked immediate retaliation from Saint-Castin and his Wabanaki confederates.

Saint-Castin was popular with the Indians thanks to his fair treatment of Native Americans at his trading post. (Unlike many English traders, Saint-Castin did not get the natives drunk and take advantage of them.) More importantly, the Frenchman was also married to the daughter of Madockawando, a Penobscot sagamore. In August of 1688, while Richard's father was dying, Saint-Castin and his Indian allies raided and attacked unsuspecting English settlers at New Dartmouth (Newcastle) and Yarmouth.[6]

---

5. Some Maine historians have suggested that the atrocities that occurred during this nine-year war against French expansionism might have been averted or lessened in New England, had it not been for the stupidity of Sir Edmund Andros, who destroyed Saint-Castin's home and trading post when he was away. (At the time, France and England were not at war.) Andros had been knighted for his service in King Philip's War and was appointed governor of the Dominion of New England in 1686 (much to the disgust of the Puritans in Massachusetts), who were also appalled by the Catholic king, James II. Andros' governance in New England lasted only until James was overthrown in the Glorious Revolution.
6. "History of King William's War." History of Massachusetts blog https://historyofmassachusetts.org/king-williams-war/

Baron Jean Vincent de Saint-Castin.
(Etching created by Charles E. Banks circa 1890, and is in the public domain.)[7]

While Saint-Castin and his Native American allies were organizing a formal campaign against the English in New England,[8] some in England were plotting to overthrow their Catholic king, James II. On November 6, 1688, William of Orange landed in Devon with 20,000 soldiers, sending James II into exile. In April of 1689, England's Parliament made Mary (James' eldest child) and William (her husband) joint monarchs. They restored the Protestant religion, and—in an historic move—placed the English Parliament above the Crown. Back in Boston, a mob on April 18, 1689, after hearing the news of the "Glorious Revolution," tossed out the Dominion of New England government of the hated and trouble-making Edmond Andros, and restored Puritan law and order to New England (albeit still under the authority of England).

On December 20, 1689, Major John Davess (Davis) of York was sworn back in as Deputy Governor of Maine. Other justices were also sworn in, and regular court

---

7. Bank's etching of St. Castin via Maine Memory Network https://www.mainememory.net/record/20760
8. This campaign was known as the Northeast Coast Campaign of 1688.

dates set.[9] Regrettably, that spring after Andros and his government were thrown out, Massachusetts soldiers who had been guarding the "Eastward" (as Massachusetts Bay called settlements in Maine) returned home, leaving the frontier exposed to Saint-Castin and his Native American allies.[10]

John Skillin, and French and Indian Warfare

One early victim of warring bands of French and Indians was probably John Skillin of Falmouth, the father of Samuel Skillin, the youth who would become Richard Crockett's best friend (and later his brother-in-law). In 1675, during the First Indian War, John Skillin had abandoned his Casco Bay homestead for the safety of Salem in Massachusetts. When hostilities ceased, however, Skillin returned to Casco by 1680 with his wife Elizabeth (Ingersoll) and their family.[11] In the spring of 1689 when Saint-Castin and his Wabanaki allies began their reprisal campaign against English settlers, Skillin prudently removed his wife and children south to Kittery.[12] John Skillin died not long after ensuring the safety of his family, from what has been presumed to have been an Indian attack.

After her husband's death, the widow Skillin married Elihu Gunnison[13] (son of Crockett family friends Hugh and Sarah Gunnison), who was also widowed. Young Samuel Skillin was ten or twelve[14] when his mother remarried and the combined Gunnison-Skillin family resided on Spruce Creek near the Crocketts. One can imagine the two boys—Samuel and Richard—discussing the horrors of French and Indian raiding parties to the northeast (including depredations that occurred

---

9. MPCR, Vol. 3, p. 287.
10. "King William's War, 1689-1697." Colonial Society of Massachusetts https://www.colonialsociety.org/node/1869
11. "Descendants of Edward Small of New England : and allied families with tracings of English ancestry." (SMALLDESC) See p. 1134-1142, "The Roberts Family," for Skilling information. John Skillin's father, Thomas Skillin, settled in Falmouth as early as 1651, purchasing a farm at Back Cove from George Cleeves in 1658, where he died in 1666 (prior to the First Indian War). When John Skillin returned to Falmouth in 1680, he was granted a house lot near where his own house stood, a parcel of meadow, and his late father's property. "[Portland historian William] Willis says the principal farm of John Skillings was at Stroudwater, about a mile northwest of Long Creek." More properties are described, as well.
12. Information that Samuel Skillin returned to Kittery before the Battle of Falmouth came from a deposition given by him in 1744. Then, at age 66, Samuel said he had lived in Falmouth until the spring before Fort Loyal was taken. LIBBY/NOYES, p. 636.
13. See STACKPOLE, p. 731 "Skillin" and p. 478, "Elihu Gunnison." Elihu was the son of Hugh Gunnison and Sarah Lynn Gunnison. His first wife was Martha Trickey. According to Stackpole, Gunnison had also lived in Falmouth prior to Kittery (possibly when the Skillins first resided there), and he and his then wife Martha (Trickey) had a child killed by Indians around 1677. STACKPOLE, p. 478.
14. STACKPOLE, p. 731, says Samuel Skillin was born July 25, 1679 to John and Elizabeth Skillin. His gravestone in Long Creek Cemetery, South Portland, however, suggests Samuel was born in 1677. The inscription on his gravestone reads: "here lyes Buried the Body of Lieu. Samuel Skilling, Who departed this Life Jany the 2, 1757 in the 80th year of His Age." (Info from personal visit to the cemetery by the author.)

during the First Indian War). But the two boys would learn that even Kittery was not safe.

During the winter of 1689/90, Count Louis de Buade de Frontenac, Governor of New France (Canada), planned and equipped three expeditions against the English, one into New York, one into New Hampshire, and one into Maine. On March 18, 1690, Francois de Hertel with a force of about 50 Wabanaki warriors and French soldiers, destroyed Salmon Falls (South Berwick), then part of Kittery, only 10-12 miles from where the Crocketts lived on Crockett's Neck. According to Kittery historian Stackpole,[15] the number of residents killed or captured during this raid vary—from 30 people killed and 64 captured to 34 killed and 54 captured. In addition, approximately 27 houses were burned and 200 cattle were killed at Salmon Falls. During this French and Indian attack on Kittery, the townspeople of York were called upon for help and a volunteer from that community also perished.[16]

In early May of 1690, Maine native Sir William Phips[17] (then famous for recovering a fabulous treasure from a sunken Spanish galleon) was sent from Boston with a fleet of seven ships and 736 New England soldiers and sailors to retaliate against the French. Phips was to attack Port Royal, the capital of French Acadia (now Nova Scotia). The Battle of Port Royal lasted two days (May 9-11, 1690), during which Phips captured and destroyed France's newly-built fort there. After the French governor surrendered, he and his troops were imprisoned, and residents were made to swear an oath to King William of England. This triggered immediate retaliation by the French. On May 16th, French soldiers, joined by warriors from some of the loosely-knit Wabanaki tribes, attacked and burned the English Fort Loyal during the Battle of Falmouth (Battle of Fort Loyal, May 16-20, 1690). Hundreds of Englishmen, women, and children were killed, many slaughtered after surrendering. The more fortunate residents of Falmouth were taken as captives to Canada, some never to return.[18] After this destruction and death, a generation would pass before the greater Falmouth area of Maine was resettled by the English.[19]

On July 16, 1690 (when Richard Crockett was about eight-years-old), the Court

---

15. STACKPOLE, p. 162-164.
16. BANKS, p. 283. Banks does not say specifically, but this attack was probably the attack at Salmon Falls.
17. Sir William Phips went from becoming an uneducated shepherd boy in Maine to Governor of Massachusetts Bay Colony. In addition to his successful attack on Port Royal, Phips is most known for recovering a Spanish treasure on a sunken galleon and for establishing the court of the Salem witch trials.
18. WILLIS. See Chapter X, "The Second Indian War."
19. Richard Crockett's friend Samuel Skillin would be one of those who resettled Falmouth, returning to the site of his childhood home where his father was killed in 1689. Two of Richard Crockett's sons (Richard and Samuel) would join their uncle Samuel Skillin there. Their lives will be covered in Chapter 4.

of Common Pleas held at York appointed a day of solemn fasting and prayer to be observed throughout the Province on the "24th day this instant July."[20] The day of fasting and prayer might have brought comfort to the remaining English settlers in Maine, but it did not bring relief. A month later, on August 22nd, two men and their wives, travelling between York and Kittery, were set upon by a band of French and Indians and were killed.[21]

On September 11, 1690, Major Benjamin Church of Plymouth Colony, who formed the first ranger force in America during King Philip's War,[22] landed at Casco Bay with a force of 300 men, on his second foray into Maine. The force attacked Fort Pejepscot (at present day Brunswick), which had been taken over by Indians, before moving on to attack another native settlement at Purpooduck[23] (Cape Elizabeth). Church and his soldiers then returned to Massachusetts,[24] leaving the eastern frontier vulnerable once again.

In the Fall of 1690, Massachusetts Bay Colony, encouraged by Phips' success at Port Royal, sent two more expeditions against the enemy, one to attack the French at Montreal and the other to attack Quebec. (Phips led the assault on Quebec.) Both expeditions failed, and the forces returned home despondent. French and Indian raids continued in Maine throughout the autumn. Charles Banks, in his history of York, notes that the large number of estates inventoried and reported in October 1690 led him to surmise that the deceased were probably victims of Indian attacks, then occurring daily.[25]

On February 25, 1691, the Court of Common Pleas held at York appointed a Day of Public Humiliation to be kept throughout the Province on the third Wednesday of March (March 21st). All servile labor was forbidden on that day.[26] On July

---

20. MPCR, Vol. 3, p. 294.
21. BANKS, p. 284.
22. "The First Way of War: American War Making on the Frontier." John Grenier. Cambridge University Press. 2005. p. 33 and 35.
23. There is some disagreement among Maine historians as to the meaning of the Native American word "Purpooduck." WILLIS, p. 96, says that Purpooduck was an "aboriginal name for Spring Point, but it afterward was extended over the whole northern shore of Cape Elizabeth" and in his footnote on p. 191 claims that the word meant a place "often frozen over" or the "burial place." This translation of Purpooduck is stoutly contradicted by William Jordan, Jr. who on p. 27 of his history of Cape Elizabeth claims: "The name, Purpooduck, is of Indian origin, meaning a place that conspicuously juts out into the water and is little frequented. Unfortunately there is no basis for the traditional meanings of 'often frozen over' and 'burying place'." CAPE-E, p. 27. (Regrettably, Jordan, who obviously has done painstaking research, offers few sources for the information in his otherwise fine history; however, since Willis has been found to have made many errors and since Jordan's description appears more like a Native American name, my money is on Jordan.)
24. "History of King William's War." History of Massachusetts blog.
25. BANKS, p. 284-285.
26. MPCR, Vol. 3, p. 298. It is hard to know the meaning of "servile labor" in this context. The term probably does not mean work performed by slaves or servants; however, because few in Maine could afford them. Perhaps, since the day of public

1, 1691, the Court of Common Pleas, due to continuous attacks by the French and Indians, adjourned the Court of Sessions until October. Many settlers to the northeast had abandoned their homesteads, some just escaping with their lives, leaving their belongings and livestock behind. The Court ordered that the local militia of York and Wells were empowered to impress and take any "fat cattle" for the supply of their soldiers from any person whatsoever, especially "from such persons as desert the Province, them giving a true account of what cattle they take."[27] That fall, a Day of Public Thanksgiving was held November 5, 1691. The Court of Sessions also appointed January 14, 1692 as a Day of Solemn Fasting and Prayer.[28]

The Candlemas Day Massacre In York, Maine

The strait-laced Puritans of Massachusetts Bay did not celebrate Christmas, which tended to be a rowdy time of drunkenness and debauchery among the fishermen and sailors in Maine.[29] Instead, the religious day marked for distinction in Puritan New England was Candlemas Day, held about the halfway point of winter.[30] Candlemas Day was the religious holiday celebrating the day the baby Jesus was presented in the Temple in Jerusalem.[31] On Sunday, January 24, 1692, Candlemas Day, the Reverend Shubael Dummer, minister of the York church, preached a sermon as usual. Neither Reverend Dummer nor churchgoers that day (nor others in town), were aware that 200-300 warriors under the leadership of Chief Madockawando (Saint-Castin's Penobscot father-in-law) and the Jesuit priest Father Louis-Pierre Thury, were camped at the base of Mt. Agamenticus in York plotting a surprise attack.

Monday morning, despite the snow, the Indians attacked, splitting their war party into two factions. By the end of the day, about 150 residents in the town of 500 souls had been killed, wounded, or carried away, including the minister. York was devastated. Residents of neighboring Kittery were shocked and horrified when they heard the news. Richard Crockett would have been ten years old when nearly

---
humiliation was set for a Wednesday, the work referred to was one's ordinary employment, from which one would desist on a Sunday. It would be hard to feel the full effect of humiliation if one was carrying on as though the day was like any other.
27. MPCR, Vol. 3, p. 300.
28. MPCR, Vol. 3, p. 305.
29. "Christmas in Early New England, 1620-1820: Puritanism, Popular Culture, and the Printed Word." Stephen W. Nissenbaum. American Antiquarian Society https://www.americanantiquarian.org/proceedings/44539478.pdf
30. Today we celebrate the halfway point of winter as Groundhog Day.
31. "Candlemas." Claire Ridgway. The Tudor Society https://www.tudorsociety.com/candlemas/

one-third the population of neighboring York was wiped out. The Candlemas Massacre, as the attack came to be known, was one of the worst raids on Maine settlers during the Second Indian War.[32]

Following the massacre at York, an even larger force of French and Native Americans (about 500) attacked Wells on June 10-11, 1692, marking "the most critical stages of a war which lasted ten years and cost the inhabitants of Maine severe losses." After a forty-eight-hour battle, the French and Indians finally retreated.[33]

For English settlers, the most terrifying type of attacks were ambushes or attacks of opportunity conducted by roving bands of Native American warriors against individual settlers or small groups of settlers. The English were used to war being conducted by armies that faced each other on a battlefield, but the sporadic and seemingly random attacks on families kept the colonists on edge, fearful even of going to the field to tend their crops and livestock. (The colonists' fears were also magnified by the memory of the gruesome killings that occurred during the First Indian War.)

In 1694, Indians effected a raid on Kittery, from the Berwick area to Spruce Creek (where the Gunnisons lived), during which young Sarah Nason was captured and held for nearly five years before she was ransomed.[34] On August 20, 1694, several other settlers on Spruce Creek were killed, and four days later eight were killed or captured at Long Reach.[35] On July 6, 1695, Captain Joseph Hammond of Kittery was captured by Indians while in the woods searching for a lost cow. (Hammond was later ransomed.)[36] These raids occurred close to where the Crocketts lived and must have been terrifying for young Richard Crockett and his family.

One raid that was both terrifying *and* targeted was that against Indian fighter Major Charles Frost of Kittery. Native Americans had long held a grudge against Frost for being part of a trick employed by Major Richard Waldron at Coheo (Dover) in 1676 during the First Indian War, when via trickery 350-400 Indians were captured while attending what they believed was a peace conference. (About 200 of the natives were taken to Boston and sold into slavery.) Kittery historian Everett Stackpole describes how, on July 4, 1697, the Indians finally took their revenge against Frost:

---

32. Information on the Candlemas Massacre came from several sources, including BANKS.
33. MPCR, Vol. 4, Preface xxxii.
34. STACKPOLE, p. 166.
35. STACKPOLE, p. 167.
36. STACKPOLE, p. 167.

> "As [Frost] was returning from church at Great Works, about a mile north of his garrison house [in Berwick] he fell into an ambush. Dennis Downing was shot with him and also Phebe, wife of John Heard…The night after Frost's burial the Indians opened his grave, took out the body, carried it to the top of Frost's hill and suspended it upon a stake."[37]

The last major skirmish of the Second Indian War, the battle of Damariscotta, occurred September 9, 1697, during which 25 Native Americans were slain.[38] In Europe, the Peace of Ryswick was signed September 30th, bringing an end to the War of the League of Augsburg (King William's War in America), "but hostilities in Maine continued until into the next spring [1698].[39] By then the eastern settlements were virtually prostrate as a result of a decade of constant warfare and alarms."[40] In addition to the lives lost during this period, the war was costly in other ways:

> "This long war reduced the population of Kittery to extreme poverty. The houses and barns of many were burned and their cattle killed. The schools were discontinued for fear that the children in going and coming would be exposed to hostile attacks. If religious services were held, they were attended by armed men. Petitions were sent [by Kittery Selectmen] to the General Court every year from 1694 to 1697, asking for relief from taxation and aid in paying the minister at Berwick."[41]

---

37. STACKPOLE, p. 168.
38. "History of King William's War." History of Massachusetts blog.
39. On May 9, 1698, "Enoch Hutchins was killed by the Indians at Spruce Creek, as he was at work in his field, and 3 of his sons carried away. The same day Joseph Pray of York was wounded." STACKPOLE, p. 170.
40. MPCR, Vol. 4, Preface xxxii.
41. STACKPOLE, p. 170.

Kittery selectmen voted in on March 19, 1694/95.
Newly voted selectmen were: John Shapleigh, Elihu Gunnison, William Pepperrell, Joshua Downing, William Fernald, Richard King, and James Emery. Every year from 1694 to 1697, Kittery selectmen petitioned the Massachusetts General Court for relief from taxation and aid in paying the minister at Berwick (then part of Kittery).
(From the records of Maine, County of York, Court of Sessions, April Term, 1695.) [42]

Henry Barter, a Beloved Brother-in-Law, and Other Friends and Neighbors in Kittery

If Richard's childhood was marred by war with the French and their Native American allies, his family's trials were steadied by the advent on Crockett's Neck of a much beloved brother-in-law, Henry Barter, who married Richard's older sister

---

42. Records, Maine, County of York, Court of Sessions, April 1695 https://www.familysearch.org/ark:/61903/3:1:3QS7-893N-WD88?i=217&cat=1923498

Sarah. Barter, a Welshman, came to New England around 1675,[43] probably as a young man. Like Richard's uncle Hugh Crockett, Barter was a fisherman on the Isle of Shoals, and it was likely through Hugh that he met the extended Crockett family.

Henry Barter married Sarah Crockett by 1692. Their daughter Sarah Barter was born March 26, 1693.[44] In 1694, Dygory Jeffrey (the second husband of Richard's grandmother Ann Crockett) sold Barter the 30-acre grant Jeffrey had received from the Town of Kittery.[45] The following June, Barter purchased Hugh Crockett's house and land on Crockett's Neck.[46] Barter and his family moved next door to Richard, where the Barter family remained for generations. (Although the land deeded to Thomas Crockett by Sir Ferdinando Gorges is still known as Crockett's Neck, over the years Crockett's Creek became Barter's Creek.)

Henry Barter appears to have assumed the role of elder brother to the fatherless Richard Crockett. (Richard's older brother Ephraim had passed away by 1695.) Barter was a steady, dependable man, whom Richard came to love and trust. In addition to his fishing, Barter served as a selectman of Kittery;[47] was a juror (at least once);[48] and was on the Grand Inquest.[49] Henry Barter also owned a quarter interest in a sawmill on Crockett's Back Creek until 1709.[50]

Richard Crockett was sixteen when the Second Indian War, which had dominated his childhood, came to an end. As a young man, in addition to performing his own chores, Richard appears to have done pick-up work for friends and relatives. Richard and best friend Samuel Skillin helped Elihu Gunnison (Samuel's stepfather) build a fence on the west side of Spruce Creek. In 1704, when Elihu Gunnison and

---

43. STACKPOLE, p. 282. According to Stackpole, Henry Barter arrived on the same vessel that brought William Pepperell to Kittery.
44. CANDAGE, p. 4. We do not know the year that Henry Barter and Sarah Crockett were married; however, there is no evidence they were not married when their first child was born (i.e. they were not "presented" at court for fornication, as was Hugh Crockett and his wife-to-be).
45. MEWD, Vol. 7, p. 191-192. Richard's grandmother, Ann Crockett, signed off on her dower rights. Uncle Hugh Crockett was one of the witnesses.
46. MEWD, Vol. 7, p. 192-193. Henry Barter purchased Hugh Crockett's house and eight or nine acres on June 22, 1695. Hugh calls Barter his "cousin" in the deed, although Barter was his nephew-in-law. Ann Crockett signed off on the deed as well, because after the death of Thomas Crockett, the Court had left the Crockett's Neck property in her hands. Nicholas Tucker was one of the witnesses and William Roberts, husband of Ann Crockett (Hugh's sister) was the other.
47. On April 5, 1709, at the Court of General Sessions of the Peace held at York, Henry Barter and Lieut. Roger Dearing, selectmen of the Lower Parish of Kittery, were summoned to answer their neglect of duty in not apportioning a tax for support of the minister. (Money was tight, and the selectmen regularly requested relief from the Massachusetts General Court.) Barter and Dearing were convicted and ordered to pay a fine of 40 shillings apiece and fees of Court. MPCR, Vol. 4, p. 364.
48. MPCR, Vol. 5, p. 5. Henry Barter was one of 12 jurors Oct. 2, 1711 at the Court of Common Pleas held at York.
49. Henry Barter served as a member of the Grand Inquest 1711-1712. (MPCR, Vol. 5, p. 125 and p. 127.) The Grand Inquest were the group of men who decided whom to "present" to the Court for religious and/or immoral social offenses.
50. MEWD, Vol. 7, p. 331-332. Barter sold his ¼ share of the sawmill and appurtenances to Joseph Wilson of Kittery in 1709.

Samuel Winkley disputed the location of this boundary-line fence on Gunnison's Neck, Richard and Samuel gave a joint deposition to the court. The two young men testified that they had helped build (or repair) the fence for Gunnison across his neck of land next to Samuel Winkley's house, and that during the process Gunnison and Winkley together had run a course for that fence. Richard and Samuel's testimony combined with the testimony of others, helped Elihu Gunnison win his case.[51] (See deposition on the following page.)

Also living near the Crocketts and Gunnisons when Richard and Samuel Skillin were growing up was the Haley family, from which family (after the turn of the century) both young men would select wives. Andrew Haley, father of the two young ladies, was an early fisherman who came to be known as the King of the Shoals (the islands off the Maine and New Hampshire coast).[52] In 1662, Haley purchased (with another man) a homestead in York.[53] Prior to 1684, Andrew Haley wed Deborah Wilson, daughter of Gowen Wilson, an early Kittery settler (who, while married, had once dallied with Richard's great-aunt, Joane Andrews). Wilson gave Andrew Haley eleven acres on Spruce Creek for Deborah's marriage "portion" of his estate.[54] Andrew and Deborah Haley made their home at Spruce Creek, in the vicinity of the Gunnison and Crockett households, where they raised their children, including Andros (also known as "Rhoda"), who would marry Samuel Skillin,[55] and Deborah, who would marry Richard Crockett.

---

51. MPCR, Vol. 4, p. 164. Elihu Gunnison and Samuel Winkley went to court over the location of a boundary fence between their properties. The fence was originally built by Gunnison's step brothers-in-law William Rogers and William Seely (stepsons-in-law of Hugh Gunnison). Also helping to build the original fence, which Richard and Samuel repaired for Gunnison years later, was Winkley's father-in-law Francis Trickey. (Trickey had purchased his small acreage from Elihu's father Hugh Gunnison prior to Hugh's leasing Gunnison's Neck to his two stepsons-in-law. Trickey later received a grant of land never laid out. Winkley attempted to establish boundaries after Trickey's death, but there was not enough land without taking some of Gunnison's.) After Gunnison won his case at the Inferior Court of Common Pleas held at York, April 4, 1704, Winkley appealed to the Superior Court of Judicature, heard in Boston May 2, 1704. This court also found for Gunnison, reaffirming the Inferior Court's decision. MPCR, Vol. 4, p. 162-164.
52. STACKPOLE, p. 483.
53. This property Haley sold in 1684 when he was deeded land by his wife's father.
54. MEWD, Vol. 4, p. 191-192. The eleven acres include an orchard and was part of a 45-acre grant Wilson had received from the selectmen of Kittery two decades earlier.
55. LIBBY/NOYES, p. 297. Andrew Haley. At first seeing several different names on legal documents—among them Andros and Rhoda—I suspected that Samuel Skillin's first wife had died and that he had remarried; however, Libby/Noyes suggests otherwise. Also, in a deed executed in 1722, Samuel's wife, signs off on the deed as "Richord" (MEWD, Vol. 11, p. 47-48), which suggests that, whatever her name was, it was challenging to spell, but that Samuel only had one wife.

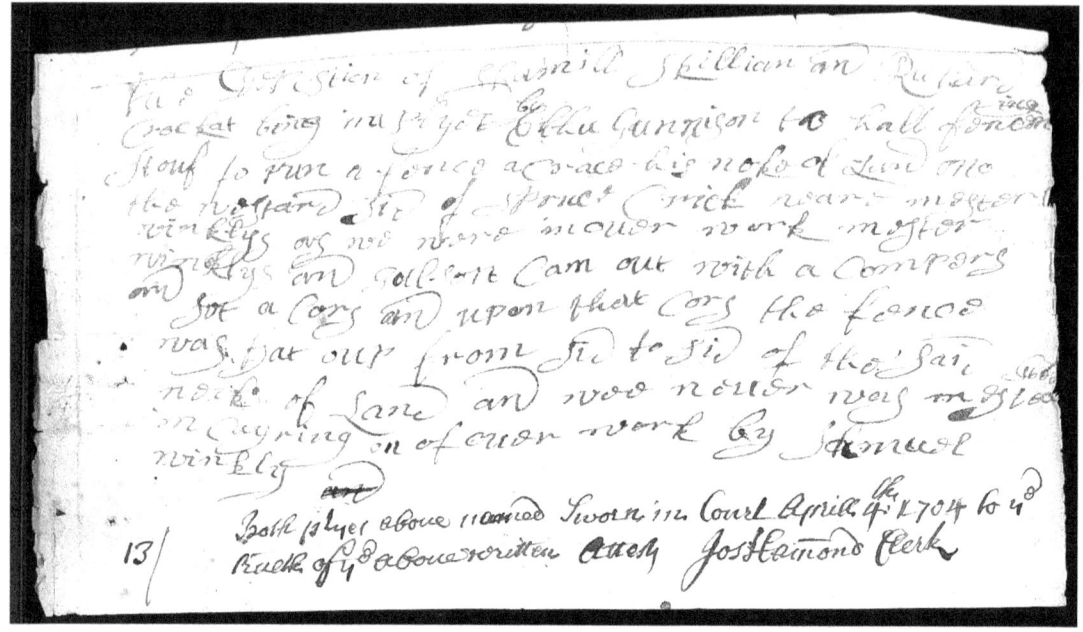

Deposition of Samuel Skillin and Richard Crockett given at the Court of Common Pleas, York, April 4, 1704.
(Notes from York County Court of Common Pleas, April term, 1704.)[56]

Transcription of the Deposition:

"The depostien of Samill Skillian and Richard Crokat being imployd by Elihu Gunnison to hall [the word "fencing" is crossed out] stouf to run a fence across his neke of Land on the northerd sid of Spruce Crick neare mester Winklys ous [house] we were in ouer work mester[s] Winklys and Gullison[57] cam out with a compers [compass] and set a cors and upon that cors the fence was set out from sid to sid of the said neck of Land and wee never was [stopped?] on cayring on of ouer work by Samuel Winkly.

Both parties above named Sworn in Court April 4th 1704 to ye truth of ye above written [Attested to by] Jos. Hamond, Clerk [of Court]."

---

56. Records from Maine, County of York, Court of Common Pleas, April term 1704. https://www.familysearch.org/ark:/61903/3:1:3QSQ-G93N-WK89?i=20&cat=1923498
57. The two surnames, Gullison and Gunnison, were interchangeable during this time.

The Third Generation

When he was about seventeen, Richard received a grant of 30 acres of land from the town of Kittery. Also receiving grants at the same Town Meeting, held May 24, 1699, were three of Richard's uncles.[58] (Richard's best friend Samuel Skillin appears not to have received a land grant in 1699, although he did later.)[59] The land grants were situated in the Berwick section of Kittery, and might have been given as an inducement to keep the young men in town. If so, the device did not work with Richard. Despite hanging onto his grant longer than most of his relations, Richard Crockett would remove permanently to New Hampshire.

On March 8, 1702, King William of England died. Since he and his deceased wife Mary were childless, Mary's sister Anne (William's cousin) became Queen of England, Scotland, and Ireland. On December 25, 1702 (the end of the year in which Anne became Queen), Richard's friend and neighbor Samuel Skillin was married to Rhoda Haley, daughter of the late Andrew Haley, Sr. and Deborah (Wilson) Haley.[60] After they were wed, the couple initially made their home on Crooked Lane (an aptly named waterway in Kittery).[61]

Queen Anne's War – The Third Indian War (1702-1713)

After the end of the Second Indian War (King William's War), relief from ambushes and attacks by the French and Indians was short-lived, lasting only about five years. The War of Spanish Succession (Queen Anne's War in New England and the Third Indian War in Maine) began when England declared war against France and Spain in 1702. New England was shortly drawn into the war, and during the summer and fall of 1703, the French and Indians began their first major campaign against the

---

58. Receiving grants on the same day as Richard were three of his uncles: Hugh Crockett (who received a grant of 30 acres), Joseph Crockett, Sr. (also 30 acres), and William Roberts (husband of aunt Ann Crockett, 40 acres). Richard's cousin Joseph Crockett, Jr. was also granted 30 acres and Richard's brother-in-law Henry Barter received a 50-acre grant. Three of these grants were later sold to William Pepperell, a Kittery lawyer and magistrate, merchant, and money lender, who avidly bought up property in Maine. On June 27, 1701, Joseph Crockett, Jr. sold his grant to Pepperell for a "valuable sum of money" (MEWD, Vol. 6, p. 265); on June 18, 1702, William Roberts sold his grant to Pepperell, as did Hugh Crockett on the same day (MEWD, Vol. 6, p. 264-265). Joseph Crockett, Sr. sold his grant to Joseph Curtis, and Richard eventually sold his land to his brother-in-law Henry Barter, who would resell the property to William Pepperell, Jr. Richard's future brother-in-law, Andrew Haley, Jr., also received a grant from the town of Kittery in 1699. LIBBY/NOYES, p. 297.
59. Samuel Skillin does not appear to have received a land grant from the town of Kittery in 1699 (perhaps because *his* father, John Skillin, had settled Falmouth, not Kittery); however, he did receive a 50-acre grant from Kittery in 1703, the year after he and Rhoda Haley were married. Samuel sold 30 acres of his 50-acre grant on July 1, 1714 to William Wilson for 40 shillings. See MEWD, Vol. 8, p. 104.
60. LIBBY/NOYES, p. 297.
61. On July 26, 1706, Samuel Skillin of Kittery purchased for 60 pounds from James and Katharine Waymouth and Elizabeth and Mary Lidden, heirs of Edward Lidden, a house and about ten acres of land on Crooked Lane in Kittery. YCROD, Vol. 7, p. 199-200. (The "lane" was a waterway, not a road.)

English in Maine, attacking settlements between Wells and Casco Bay. Casualties from these raids totaled 73 killed, 2 wounded, and 94 taken prisoner from settlements at Wells, Cape Porpus, Winter Harbor and Saco, Black Point (Scarborough), Spurwink (a Falmouth-area settlement), and Casco.[62] One of those killed at Casco was probably Sarah (Gunnison) Tucker (daughter of Crockett friends Hugh and Sarah Gunnison), the wife of Lewis Tucker. On January 18, 1704, there was also a surprise Indian attack on Andrew Neal's garrison house in lower Berwick.[63]

In January of 1704, the Court of General Sessions of the Peace held at York, upon instructions from the Massachusetts General Court, ordered that a tax of 30 pounds be apportioned to help pay for the war effort,[64] despite the general poverty of Maine residents. There was another attempt to raise taxes later in the year, but on December 28, 1704, Kittery selectmen petitioned the General Court of Massachusetts for relief. That Court resolved that 38 pounds was to be abated to the poor of Kittery, according to the disposition of the selectmen, "they [the selectmen] being most capable to relieve such as they Know have met with most sufferings by the Heathen."[65] Among those whose 1704 taxes were abated due to "sufferings by the Heathen" were many of Richard's relatives, including Joseph Crockett (Richard's uncle) abated 6 shillings; William Roberts, Jr. (Richard's cousin) abated 5 shillings; Widow Mitchell (Sarah Andrews Mitchell, daughter of Joane Crockett and John Andrews) abated 5 shillings; Lewis Tucker (brother-in-law to Elihu Gunnison, whose wife Sarah was killed by Indians) abated 10 shillings; and Widow (Deborah) Haley (soon to be Richard's mother-in-law) abated 5 shillings. The Third Indian War had hit painfully close to home.

On May 4, 1704, "many persons were surprised by the Indians at Spruce Creek and York," with several killed and the rest carried away into captivity.[66] Also at Spruce Creek, in June of 1707, Philip Carpenter and his wife and children were slain about midday by a small band of Indians.[67] These two tragic events at Spruce Creek in Kittery likely led to one even more tragic—the accidental shooting of

---

62. Maine Genealogy Trails website, Queen Anne's War, "The Northeast Coast Campaign of Queen Anne's War." http://genealogytrails.com/maine/queenanneswarcasualties.html#:~:text=The%20Northeast%20Coast%20campaign%20of%20the%20Queen%20Anne's%20War,-10%20August%20%2D%206&text=They%20attacked%20English%20settlements%20on,capturing%20more%20than%20150%20people
63. STACKPOLE, p. 172.
64. MPCR, Vol. 4, p. 300. Of the 30 pounds tax to be raised, Kittery's share was 17 pounds; York's share 9 pounds and 4 shillings; and Wells' share 3 pounds 16 shillings.
65. STACKPOLE, p. 174.
66. STACKPOLE, p. 173.
67. STACKPOLE, p. 173.

The Third Generation

Grace Wentworth by Joseph Gunnison. In the fall of 1707, only a few months after the Carpenter attack, sixteen-year-old Joseph Gunnison,[68] son of Elihu Gunnison and his second wife Elizabeth (Ingersol) Skillin Gunnison, was standing guard duty at his father's garrison house on Spruce Creek during an early snowstorm. Hostile Indians had been reported in the area and young Gunnison was posted as a sentinel. He was instructed to hail any person who approached three times, and if no response he was to shoot. Gunnison descendant George Gunnison describes what happened next:

> "Now it happened that a boatload of persons from Portsmouth landed near by, among whom was Grace, the wife of William Wentworth, who had left a young child at home [in Kittery] and was hurrying on in advance of the rest of the company, past the Garrison house, muffled up in her cloak, facing the driving snow storm. She was hailed, and not replying, was fired upon by Joseph Gunnison, and mortally wounded. Before she died, she acquitted him of all blame in the matter, but his own conscience refused to pronounce him guiltless."[69]

Joseph Gunnison was tried at a Court of Oyer and Terminer held at Kittery on January 8, 1707/08. He pleaded not guilty and asked for trial by jury. After hearing the evidence, the jury found young Joseph not guilty. He was ordered to pay damages of 40 shillings and fees of court.[70] George Gunnison in his family genealogy says: "[Joseph] was himself always under the impression that he was guilty of murder. During the rest of his life he was melancholy, and at times deranged."[71]

---

68. There is disagreement among historians as to the identity of Joseph Gunnison. STACKPOLE (p. 474-475) and GUNNISON both believe Joseph was the son of Hugh and Sarah Gunnison. STACKPOLE says this Joseph was born Jan. 31, 1649 (MIGRATION agrees), making Joseph in his late fifties at the time of the accidental shooting incident. By contrast, "North American Family Histories 1500-2000," *Gunnison*, (available on Ancestry.com) says the Joseph Gunnison who killed Grace Wentworth was the son of Elihu Gunnison and Elihu's second wife, Elizabeth (Ingersol) Skillin Gunnison (making him a grandson of Hugh and Sarah Gunnison). This Joseph was born Oct. 14, 1690 (according to STACKPOLE) and thus was just shy of his seventeenth birthday when he shot Grace Wentworth. While we might never know the truth of Joseph's identity, the fact that Samuel Skillin (son of John Skillin and Elizabeth Ingersol) was one of Joseph's bondsmen suggests that the Joseph in question was Samuel's half-brother, not a brother of his stepfather. Also, it seems more likely to me that an untested youth might be more apt to shoot accidentally than an older man who had lived through two previous Indian wars. The other bondsman was Elihu Gunnison, who would have been the father of the younger Joseph or the brother of the older Joseph.
69. GUNNISON. See p. 4 for the incident related here.
70. MPCR, Vol. 4, p. 347-348.
71. GUNNISON, p. 4.

Marriage to Deborah Haley and Relocation to New Hampshire

Sometime between 1704 and 1708, Richard Crockett and Deborah Haley were wed.[72] Crockett genealogist Charles Candage reports that the couple's first child was Ephraim (named for his grandfather), born circa 1708.[73] My research has led me to believe that their son Richard was born in 1706 or 1707[74] and thus might have been Richard and Deborah's first child. (Richard, Jr.'s birthdate also suggests an earlier marriage for the couple.) The family initially resided in Kittery, where several of their children were likely born. They lived in the home on Crockett's Neck built by Thomas Crockett.

Depredations by roving bands of Native American were still occurring in the local area when Richard and Deborah were married, which raids continued through the births of their first children. In September of 1708, Robert Reed, a schoolmaster, and another man "ventured too far into the woods at Spruce Creek on the Sabbath, fell into an ambush and were slain. A lad who was with them escaped."[75]

A month after the attack on the schoolmaster, Richard sold the 40 acres of land between Long Reach and Spruce Creek that was left to him in his father's will. Sporadic attacks by French and Indians had been occurring in and around Kittery during most of Richard's life and possibly this latest attack was the straw that broke the camel's back. Richard needed money to relocate to a place where it might be safer for his family to live. On Oct. 14, 1708, Richard Crockett, yeoman of Kittery, sold his 40-acre lot for fifty pounds to John Fernald, yeoman, also of Kittery. Deborah signed off on her dower rights.[76]

The possibility of relocating had already occurred to Richard's friend and

---

72. Richard and Deborah were married by Oct. 14, 1708, when Deborah Crockett signed off on her dower rights from the 40 acres that Richard sold to John Fernald of Kittery. (MEWD, Vol. 7, p. 228)
73. CANDAGE, p. 4. The first Ephraim (son of Thomas and Ann Crockett) must have been a well-loved person—as well as his namesakes—for the name "Ephraim" continued for many generations in the extended Crockett family, making genealogy in Maine often challenging. A quick glance at some Ephraim Crockett family trees on Ancestry.com reveals how easy it is to mistake one Ephraim for another. Deeds play an important role in distinguishing which Ephraim is which, since the documents often reveal, in the signing away of dower rights, the name of a particular Ephraim's wife (although even then sometimes the wives and daughters-in-law possess the same given name).
74. Testimony provided to the General Court of Massachusetts in April of 1781 by Josiah Crockett (son of Richard II) noted that his father was then "being above 75 years of age" (meaning he was born by 1706.) Also, an affidavit by Nathaniel Thomas presented to the General Court of Massachusetts (same month and year) stated that Richard Crockett (II) was "above Seventy Three Years of Age," which also points to a 1706/07 birth. (More on these two affidavits in Chapter 4.)
75. STACKPOLE, p. 174.
76. MEWD, Vol. 7, p. 228. Both Richard and Deborah appeared before Justice of the Peace William Pepperrell to own that the instrument was their free act and will. Witnesses to the transaction were Richard Keats (unknown) and Margery Pepperrell (Pepperrell's wife).

brother-in-law Samuel Skillin (who had married Deborah's sister Rhoda). While we cannot be sure that the two couples discussed moving from Kittery, it seems reasonable to conclude that they did, since that this is exactly what happened. The Skillin family relocated first.

By the summer of 1710, Samuel had sold his home in Kittery, and he and his family were living in Exeter, New Hampshire.[77] Although Exeter, which was situated at the confluence of the Exeter and Squamscott[78] rivers,[79] experienced occasional attacks from the French and Indians, thanks to its location further from the war front the population suffered "not as much as settlements farther East in New Hampshire and in the more exposed Maine settlements."[80] Exeter was a busy port where the freshwater Exeter River met the tidal water coming in from Great Bay and the Piscataqua River basin, which waters carried "schooners, wherries, and gundalows back and forth to the Atlantic Ocean."[81] Skillin, a shipwright by trade (likely trained by his stepfather, shipwright Elihu Gunnison), would have had no difficulty finding employment at Exeter.

Whether Richard and Deborah immediately followed the Skillin family to Exeter is not entirely clear. I have found no documentary evidence one way or another.[82] Richard was in Kittery in May of 1712 to swear that he witnessed Nicholas Tucker's deed to Tucker's son William,[83] however, given the relative ease of travel

---

77. On June 13, 1710, Samuel Skillin, shipwright of Exeter, sold for 85 pounds to his brother Josiah Skillin (also a shipwright) his house, land, and orchard on Crooked Lane in Kittery. MEWD, Vol. 7, p. 200. Rhoda Skillin signed off on her dower rights.
78. Squamscott "gets its name from the Algonquin sub-tribe, the Squamscott Indians, who called it Msquam-s-kook, translated as 'at the salmon place' or 'big water place.' " From "Exeter is a Seaport," by Carol Walker Aten, Exeter (NH) Historical Society website. https://www.exeterhistory.org/exeter-history/2016/6/24/exeter-is-a-seaport
79. The freshwater Exeter River becomes the tidal Squamscott River at the falls. The religious leader the Reverend John Wheelwright made two purchases of land here from Wehanownowit, a sagamore of the Piscatoquake, after being exiled by the strict Puritans of Massachusetts Bay Colony. https://www.exeterhistory.org/exeter-history/2016/6/24/early-exeter-history-1638-1887
80. "Early Exeter History 1638-1887." Nancy Carnegie Merrill. From Exeter (N.H.) Historical Society website. https://www.exeterhistory.org/exeter-history/2016/6/24/early-exeter-history-1638-1887
81. "Exeter is a Seaport," by Carol Walker Aten. Exeter (N.H.) Historical Society website. https://www.exeterhistory.org/exeter-history/2016/6/24/exeter-is-a-seaport
82. Birth records for the children of Richard and Deborah would prove helpful at documenting where the family lived. One historian noted that all but their last child was born in Kittery, however, he provided no evidence. Possibly there are New Hampshire birth records that have not yet come to light.
83. On May 13, 1712, Richard Crockett appeared in Kittery before Justice of the Peace William Pepperrell to swear that he saw Nicholas Tucker sign and seal the deed of Tucker's property to his son William, and saw Hugh Tucker witness the deed of Mar. 20, 1707/08. MEWD, Vol. 7, p. 413. There might have been some difficulty with the transaction since Hugh Tucker, the other witness to the deed, was not present and/or available to confirm it. Instead, Hugh's wife Bridget swore that she saw Nicholas sign the deed and her husband witness it. Hugh was captured by the Indians in 1706, but was returned in time to witness the original deed. It is possible Hugh was deceased. In October of 1717, Samuel Penhallow took Hugh Tucker to Inferior Court for non-payment of a debt. He did not show up then, either. MPCR, Vol. 5, p. 95.

by boat between the two locales, his presence there does not necessarily mean the family was residing in Kittery at the time.

On April 10, 1713, Richard purchased a large tract of land in the Squamscott Patent, then part of Exeter. He and Samuel Piper[84] of "Quamscott in the township of Exeter," together paid Hannah Wiggin 420 pounds "good and lawful New England Money" for a large tract of land and marsh along the Squamscott River (the saltwater portion of the Exeter River). Hannah was a single woman who resided in Ipswich, Massachusetts Bay Colony.[85] She was a great-granddaughter of Captain Thomas Wiggin, an early arrival at Pascataqua whom Thomas Crockett would have known.[86]

On the following day, April 11, 1713, Captain Simon Wiggin (another descendant of Captain Thomas Wiggin) of Quamscott sold to Richard Crockett for 76 pounds and 10 shillings, 102 acres and some rods of land in the Quamscott Patent. Richard was also given the right of free passage down to the salt water (the Squamscott River) from this parcel. Samuel Skillin was on hand with the Crocketts to witness the deed.[87] Richard's brother-in-law, who would go on to buy and sell a significant amount of real estate in Maine, might even have helped Richard arrange for his two land purchases. There is every reason to consider that, in addition to buying a place to homestead, Richard purchased the real estate for investment purposes. From the day of his second purchase forward, Richard never paid for another acre. He either was granted land or he sold his real estate.

Three days after witnessing Captain Wiggin's deed to Richard Crockett, Samuel Skillin was back in Kittery, where he made two similar real estate purchases on

---

84. Samuel Piper was probably the cordwainer of Stratham (formerly Squamscott Patent, then part of Exeter), per LIBBY/NOYES, p. 557. Piper was in Exeter by 1698. I cannot see any relationship between Richard Crockett and Piper; however, because Piper was a cordwainer in an area where Samuel Skillin worked as a shipwright the two men were likely known to each other. Skillin might even have brought Richard Crockett and Samuel Piper together to facilitate the large real estate transaction.

85. RCROD, Vol. 9, p. 378-379. Hannah Wiggin's mother and stepfather Mathew and Martha Whipple, signed off on the deed. Richard likely teamed up with Samuel Piper to make this large land purchase. (Hannah probably wanted to sell the entire piece.) One property line of land the duo purchased was ½ mile in length. The land and marsh were described as "lying in Quamscott and is bounded upon ye N-East by ye land of Thomas Road [unsure spelling] and Thomas Wiggins marsh and bounded on ye Southwest part by a Creek commonly known as and called House Creek near to ye house called Quamscott House…" The property was bounded by the river on the northwest. Quamscott House was likely an inn or an ordinary owned by Jonathan and Mary (Emery) Wiggin (a descendant of Capt. Thomas Wiggin via another branch of the same family). See https://www.newmarketnhhistoricalsociety.org/docs/genealogy/perkins-family/

86. Hannah Wiggin's property was originally part of the Council of New England's 1632 grant to Captain Thomas Wiggin, her great-grandfather. Hannah inherited the property from her father Thomas Wiggin, one of Captain Wiggin's grandsons. LIBBY/NOYES, p. 752-753.

87. RCROD, Vol. 9, p. 379-380. Again, I can see no relationship between Captain Wiggin and Richard Crockett; however, Samuel Skillin, Richard's brother-in-law, as a shipwright, would have known the captain. Benjamin Hoag and John Gilbert were the other two witnesses to the transaction. Probably both men were from the local area.

Spruce Creek.[88] Reviewing the large real estate purchases of the two brothers-in-law—Richard Crockett and Samuel Skillin—one gets the impression that the young men put their heads together and decided upon a similar course of action, albeit in two different locations. Richard, as a husbandman, needed acreage upon which to farm, which real estate was cost prohibitive in long-settled Kittery. Samuel needed water access upon which to build and float his ships, which he secured on Spruce Creek. The distance from Stratham to Portsmouth, from which the ferry regularly ran across the Piscataqua River over to Kittery, was only about 10 miles. (See "Sketch map of Pascataqua, 1690" on page 121.) Although the Crocketts resided in Stratham and the Skillins in Kittery, the two families stayed close for the remainder of their lives. In February of 1717, Deborah gave birth to a son, which she and Richard named Samuel as a compliment to a beloved brother-in-law.[89]

To pay for his real estate purchases from the Wiggins, Richard needed to raise more capital. On April 19, 1713, Richard sold for 72 pounds 72 acres of the land he had just purchased from the Wiggins.[90] More significantly, on May 26, 1713, Richard sold the Thomas Crockett homestead on Crockett's Neck to his brother-in-law Henry Barter for 100 pounds. Barter, who years earlier had purchased Hugh Crockett's house and few acres, was likely happy to add the 40 acres onto his adjoining small lot, even though he had to mortgage his own home and the purchased property to get it.[91] The following year, on Nov. 20, 1714, Richard Crockett and Samuel Piper split the property they had purchased jointly from Hannah Wiggin, dividing it equally, except part of the orchard that was on Piper's land, to which

---

88. Samuel Skillin bought land and a home from the brothers Nathaniel and Jonathan Mendum. These two transactions gave Skillin a three-quarter share of the property on Spruce Creek that was left to Robert Mendum (Nathaniel and Jonathan's brother, recently deceased) by his grandfather of the same name (another former crony of Thomas Crockett's). MEWD, Vol. 8, p. 15-16 and Vol. 8, p. 51-52. Samuel Skillin paid Nathaniel Mendum 34 pounds for his quarter-share of the property and Jonathan Mendum 60 pounds for his one-half share. Two months later Skillin purchased the last quarter-share from the brothers' sister Dorothy. YCROD, Vol. 8, p. 8. Samuel Skillin purchased for 29 pounds this last quarter share from Dorothy (Mendum) Frost, also a sibling (as were Jonathan and Nathaniel) of the late Robert Mendum (the grandson). A small parcel had been sold from the property prior to Robert's death.
89. CANDAGE, p. 4. The child's full name was Samuel Haley Crockett, the middle name being Deborah and Rhoda's family name.
90. RCROD, Vol. 9, p. 667. Richard sold the property to Joseph Hoag. Witnesses to the transaction were John Gilbert, Jr., Simon Wiggin, and Benjamin Hoag.
91. MEWD, Vol. 8, p. 105-106. Richard Crockett, husbandman, of Exeter, sold to Henry Barter, fisherman on Piscataqua River, 40 acres of upland and swamp on Crockett's Neck, formerly Thomas Crockett's, deceased, and then Ephraim Crockett's, deceased. Richard's wife Deborah signed off on her dower rights. The deed was witnessed by Diamond Sargeant, William Pepperrell, Sr. and William Pepperrell, Jr. (the younger Pepperrell was then just sixteen years old). It is possible that the elder Pepperrell was beginning the education of his new heir after the death of oldest son Andrew in 1713. Young Pepperrell took the mortgage on the property from Barter, an old family friend. Barter agreed to pay Pepperrell, Jr. back the 100 pounds over the course of six years with interest of six pounds per year. Richard Crockett witnessed this transaction. MEWD, Vol. 8, pl. 73-74.

Richard was to have access, as long as the trees remained standing.[92] On Jan. 26, 1714/15, Richard sold 30 more acres of the former Wiggin land in Squamscott.[93]

A Founder of Stratham, New Hampshire

On January 26, 1715/16, Richard Crockett was one of about 60 inhabitants of the Squamscott Patent who petitioned New Hampshire's Lieutenant Governor George Vaughn for that settlement to be set off from Exeter as a separate township. In their petition, residents decried the travel distance for worship services and lack of a school for their children:

> "The very sad circumstances we lay under by reason of our great distance from the publick Worship of God and having no benefit of any School, notwithstanding we have ever paid our proportion to the School of Exeter, and are now by the Province of God increased to such a number as we hope we are able of ourselves to maintain a Minister & a school & other public charges as shall necessarily fall upon us …"[94]

The petitioners were successful, and on March 20, 1716, Governor Vaughn denoted the settlement as a township by the name of Stratham. The Lieutenant Governor directed a meeting house be built as soon as possible so that a "learned and orthodox" minister could preach there by the following March.[95]

---

92. RCROD, Vol. 9, p. 652-653. Deborah Crockett signed off on her dower rights. James Kenison and James Jeffrey witnessed the deed.
93. RCROD, Vol. 11, p. 93. Richard sold this property to Phillip Door of Portsmouth for 8 pounds. Deborah signed off on her dower rights. The deed was witnessed by William French and Thomas Crockett. Thomas was Richard's cousin, who lived in Portsmouth. He was the son of Elihu Crockett and his wife Mary Winnock.
94. "History of Stratham, New Hampshire, 1631-1900." Compiled and Written by Charles B. Nelson. Stratham, NH: Town of Stratham, c1987. P. 9-11.
95. Website, Town of Stratham, N.H. "History of Stratham." https://www.strathamnh.gov/historical-society/pages/history-stratham

The Third Generation

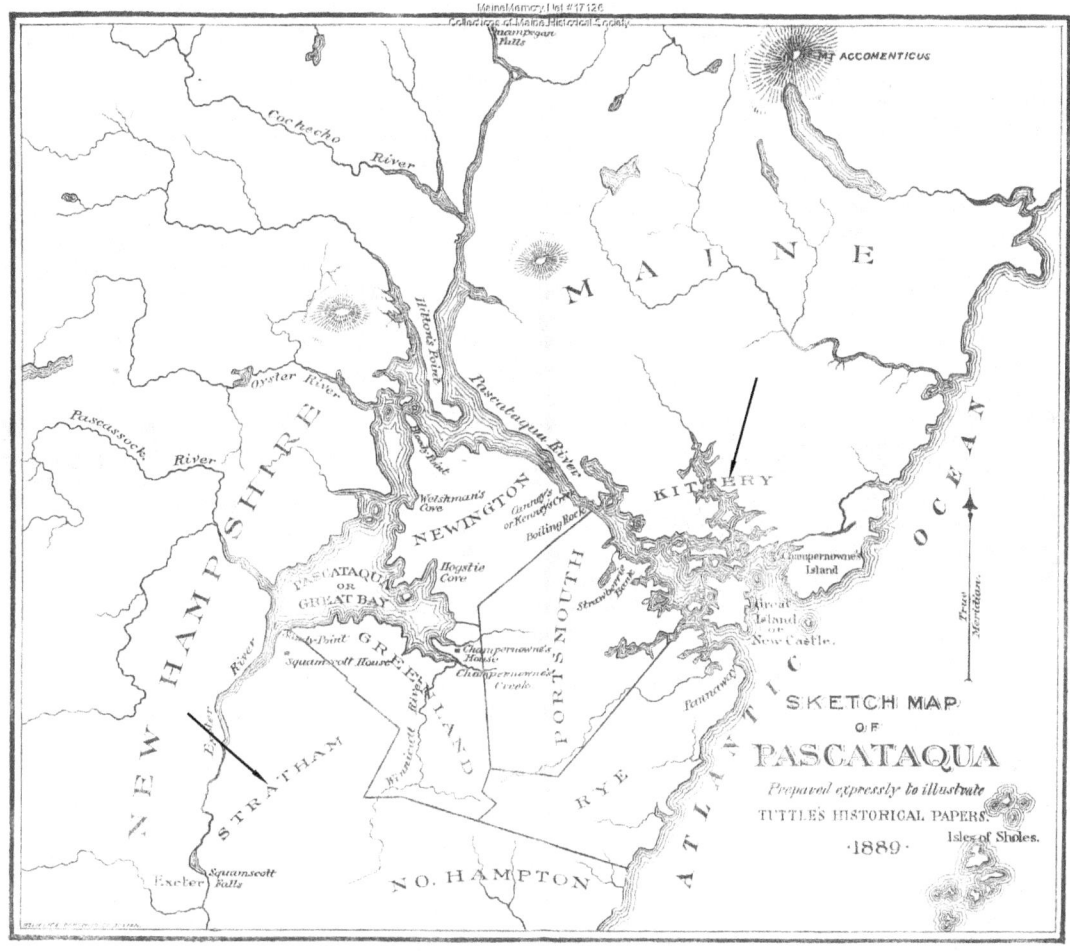

Sketch map of Pascataqua, circa 1690.
This map of the Pascataqua region shows the proximity of Richard and Deborah Crockett's new home in Stratham, N.H., to the town of Kittery, where the couple was born and raised. Travel by waterway made keeping in touch with Samuel Skillin and his wife Rhoda (Deborah's sister), as well as other Crockett family members, relatively easy. Richard's grandfather, Thomas Crockett, had arrived at Pascataqua in 1630.
(Map courtesy of the Maine Historical Society, from the John H.S. Fogg autograph collection. The map was created circa 1889, although the subject matter of the map was 1690. Image is in the public domain, accessed via Maine Memory Network.)

That June, possibly to help pay for his share of the new meeting house, Richard sold 30 acres of upland and two parcels of marsh to Jeremy Folsom of Exeter for 73 pounds. Richard reserved the right for himself and his heirs to pass through the land with a sled or cart to access his orchard or to haul hay. Richard also reserved the right to fence a small cove of marsh for himself, as well as the right to access that marsh.[96]

In 1717, the Town of Stratham "called" (invited) Mr. Henry Russ (Rust) to serve as pastor. That fall the new meeting house was finished enough for use, and on September 18, 1717, at a Town Meeting in Stratham, Thomas Veasey, Thomas Rollins, and Jonathan Wiggin were chosen as "sufficiently fearless, impartial and competent to award the seats."[97] (Later, two other men were added to the committee to assign seats in the meeting house.) The awarding of seats was a difficult task:

> "Doubtless, this duty required fine discrimination and some firmness. An individual's own estimate of his relative consequence and that made by an impartial committee might differ considerably ... By consulting the record, we can ascertain the exact relative rank of every man from Captain Andrew Wiggin, who was the recognized foremost citizen, down to humble Holdridge Kelley, who was awarded the remotest seat in humility row. By vote of the town, Captain Andrew Wiggin was given 'liberty to sit in what seat he pleaseth in the meeting house.' The others were assigned by [the] committee."[98]

Richard "Krocket"[99] was assigned to "the Short side front," a fairly-prominent position just below "The first chief seat" (assigned to Mr. Thomas Wiggin and Mr. William Scammon) and the "Second short seat" (assigned to Jonathan Chase, David Robinson, Jr. and Jonathan Dearborn).[100] Richard's assignment to

---

96. RCROD, Vol. 20, p. 501-502. Deborah Crockett signed off on her dower rights. Witnesses to the transaction were Cyprian and James Jeffry.
97. "History of Stratham, New Hampshire, 1631-1900." Compiled and Written by Charles B. Nelson. Stratham, NH: Town of Stratham, c1987. P. 114-117.
98. "History of Stratham, New Hampshire, 1631-1900." Compiled and Written by Charles B. Nelson. Stratham, NH: Town of Stratham, c1987. P. 114-117. The town also voted that people were required to sit in their designated seats. If any person "set out of there seatts in a disorderly manner to advance them selves higher in the meeting house" that person would receive a stiff fine of five shillings a day. Stratham, N.H. Town Records via Family Search. https://www.familysearch.org/ark:/61903/3:1:3QS7-899K-DT9L?i=15&cc=1987741&cat=393768
99. "Krocket" is how Richard's last name was spelled in the original record. Stratham, N.H. Town Records https://www.familysearch.org/ark:/61903/3:1:3QS7-899K-DT9L?i=15&cc=1987741&cat=393768
100. "History of Stratham, New Hampshire, 1631-1900." Compiled and Written by Charles B. Nelson. Stratham, NH: Town of Stratham, c1987. P. 114-117. Also in the short-side front with Richard Crockett was Benjamin Jones, William French, Israel Smith, and John Clark.

"the Short side front" bespeaks an upward movement in social status from Kittery to Stratham. Likewise, in the women's section "Mrs. Crocket"[101] was assigned an important seat in "The long front," which was below "The chief fore seat" (assigned to Mrs. Sarah Wiggin, Mrs. Leavitt, Mrs. Wright, Jr., and Sarah Wiggin) and below six ladies in the "Front gallery," which included two widows.[102]

Men's seating arrangements in the First Church of Stratham (N.H.), 1718.
Richard "Krocket" is seated in the short side front. Seating arrangements were decided by committee and approved by the voters of Stratham on December 30, 1718.
(State of New Hampshire, Stratham Town Records 1716-1783, Vol. 1.)[103]

Deborah Crockett did not long enjoy the advantages of her new social prominence in the long front seat at church. By May of 1719 (and probably earlier) she

---
101. Spelling in original record. Stratham Town Records.
102. "History of Stratham, New Hampshire, 1631-1900." Compiled and Written by Charles B. Nelson. Stratham, NH: Town of Stratham, c1987. P. 114-117.
103. Stratham, N.H. Town Records.

was deceased.[104] Richard was left a widower with the responsibility of raising their young children.

Richard and Deborah had at least five—and possibly seven—children: Richard, Jr., Ephraim, Samuel Haley, William, Elizabeth, and possibly Sarah and Mary. (Little information is available about Sarah and Mary.) The first two boys, Richard and Ephraim, and probably Elizabeth, were born in Kittery, prior to the family's removal to Stratham in 1713. Samuel and William were likely both born in New Hampshire. For more information about Richard and Deborah's family, please refer to the "Genealogical Dictionary of Thomas and Ann Crockett" beginning on page 377.

Real Estate Sales, A Yoke of Oxen, and "Bring[ing] Up the Bell"

On December 6, 1719, Richard Crockett sold 40 acres of land to George Clark, a joiner of Stratham, for 120 pounds current money of New England. This parcel abutted the Exeter River and the road, and came within six feet of Richard's orchard fence.[105] A little less than two years later, on September 2, 1721, Richard (described as a "planter" in this deed) sold his new neighbor Clark a tract of marsh, 3 acres and 100 rods, for 36 pounds, 5 shillings,[106] taking a promissory note for the whole.

Clark agreed to pay Richard double the amount of the purchase price (72 pounds), unless the joiner paid the entire 36 pounds, 5 shillings in full before March of 1722. John (Jonathan) Sinkler, who was one of the witnesses to the deed, stood surety for Clark. As it turned out, Clark made a small payment, but did not pay the whole amount due. Richard took Clark's promissory note to magistrate Theodore Atkinson, who issued a writ of execution for both Clark and Sinkler on August 18, 1722. Shortly thereafter a Deputy Sheriff "apprehended the body of George Clark" and attached a chair of Johnathan Sinkler ("not finding his person or any other") and left a summons at his dwelling house to appear at the next Inferior Court of

---

104. On May 28, 1719, Richard Crockett appeared before Justice of the Peace Andrew Wiggin (Captain Andrew Wiggin, who was given liberty to sit where he pleased in the meeting house) to swear that the deed he executed to Jerremy Folson on June 14, 1716 was his free act and deed. Deborah did not appear, even though she had signed off on her dower rights in 1716. In fact, she never again appeared to sign off on any deed Richard executed, including one to her brother. This leads me to believe that Deborah (Haley) Crockett was deceased by 1716, and possibly before. Deborah, like so many women during this time, might have died in childbirth or from an infection that occurred during or after giving birth.
105. RCROD, Vol. 4, p. 202-203. Witnesses: William and Thomas French. Again, Deborah (Haley) Crockett did not sign off on her dower rights, and Richard declares that the property is free and clear of dower rights, so she is deceased by this date.
106. RCROD, Vol. 12, p. 449-451. Witnesses: John Sinkler, Chase Wiggin, and Thomas Wiggin.

The Third Generation

Common Pleas held at Portsmouth.[107] The case does not appear to have gone to court, however, so Clark (or Sinkler) must have satisfied the debt to Richard.

But Richard did not learn his lesson about Clark, apparently. On April 6, 1724, Crockett sold the joiner a yoke of oxen, taking as payment another promissory note from Clark for 24 pounds, unless Clark paid the full sum of the oxen (12 pounds) by September 5th. (See copy of Clark's promissory note on page 126.) Clark did not pay up, and once again a writ of execution and summons were issued for Clark. This time the case *did* end up in court. On December 3, 1724, at the Inferior Court of Common Pleas held in Portsmouth, Clark was called three times, and, failing to appear, Richard Crockett was granted judgement against him by default. Richard won the 12 pounds, plus interest on his money in the amount of 3 pounds, 6 shillings. Clark was also ordered to pay 3 pounds, 13 shillings, and 6 pence in costs.[108] (In 1727, Clark sold his land, dwelling house, barn and shops to Benjamin Jewett, a tanner from Rowley, county of Essex, Massachusetts Bay, providing Richard with a new neighbor and likely making the neighborhood a more comfortable place in which to reside.)[109]

---

107. Colonial Records of New Hampshire, 1638-1722. File No. 18306.
108. Colonial Records of New Hampshire, 1638-1722. File No. 18307.
109. RCROD, Vol. 15, p. 292. Clark sold his property to Jewett for 365 pounds. John Sinkler, who had once (but not twice) stood surety for one of the joiner's promissory notes, was one of the witnesses.

George Clark's promissory note to Richard Crockett for a yoke of oxen dated April 6, 1724. (Colonial Records of New Hampshire, 1638-1722. File No. 18307.)

The Third Generation

In 1724, a survey of the land sold by Simon Wiggins to Richard Crockett in 1713 was performed by James Jeffrey. Captain Wiggins had sold Richard 102 acres; however, after surveying the parcel, Jeffrey reported that "... [I] can but make eighty-seven acres in the whole."[110] Why the survey was done, we do not know, although Richard had made several cuts from the parcels he purchased from the two Wiggins and it is possible boundary issues might have cropped up. Whatever the reason, it appears that the land he bought from Captain Wiggins was fifteen acres short. (See "Plan of land purchased of Captain Simon Wiggins by Richard Crockett" on page 128.) The adage, "Buyer beware," was likely adhered to as no further action appears to have been taken.

In 1725, Richard was paid 10 shillings by the selectmen for some work he did on the meeting house.[111] (He would have made more money by killing a wolf, the selectmen then paying 1 pound per wolf.) Richard earned 7 pounds, 6 shillings from the town of Stratham in 1734 for "bring[ing] up the bell" that the town had sent to London to have recast (a crack having formed). Richard probably hauled the bell with his team of oxen. Accounts of the selectmen suggest the town paid Captain Rindage for the meeting house bell, likely not for the bell itself, but for sailing the repaired bell to London and back.[112] (Bells were not cast in the American colonies until later in the 18th century.)[113] The repaired bell[114] cost the growing town the sum of 81 pounds, 18 shillings, plus the money paid to Richard for transportation to (and maybe from) Stratham.[115]

---

110. RCROD, Book 13, p. 459.
111. Stratham, N.H. Town Records. https://www.familysearch.org/ark:/61903/3:1:3QS7-L99K-86J3?i=110&cc=1987741&cat=393768
112. In 1734, when the bell was returned, John Levett was paid one shilling by Stratham selectmen to ring the bell. Stratham, N.H. Town Records of Expenses.
113. "Early Church Bell Founders," Connecticuthistory.org https://connecticuthistory.org/early-church-bell-founders/#:~:text=During%20the%2017th%20and%20early,such%20as%20Mexico%20or%20Peru.
114. Permission to send the meeting house bell to London to be recast was given to Stratham selectmen at a Town Meeting held Dec. 31, 1733. (In 1737, selectmen were given the authority to repair the bell's clapper.) Stratham, N.H. Town Records.
115. The money to pay for the original meeting house bell was raised by the sale of the town's common land. At a Town Meeting held March 25, 1727, a committee was designated to sell some of the Commons, and to also arrange for the purchase of a bell. Stratham, N.H. Town Records.

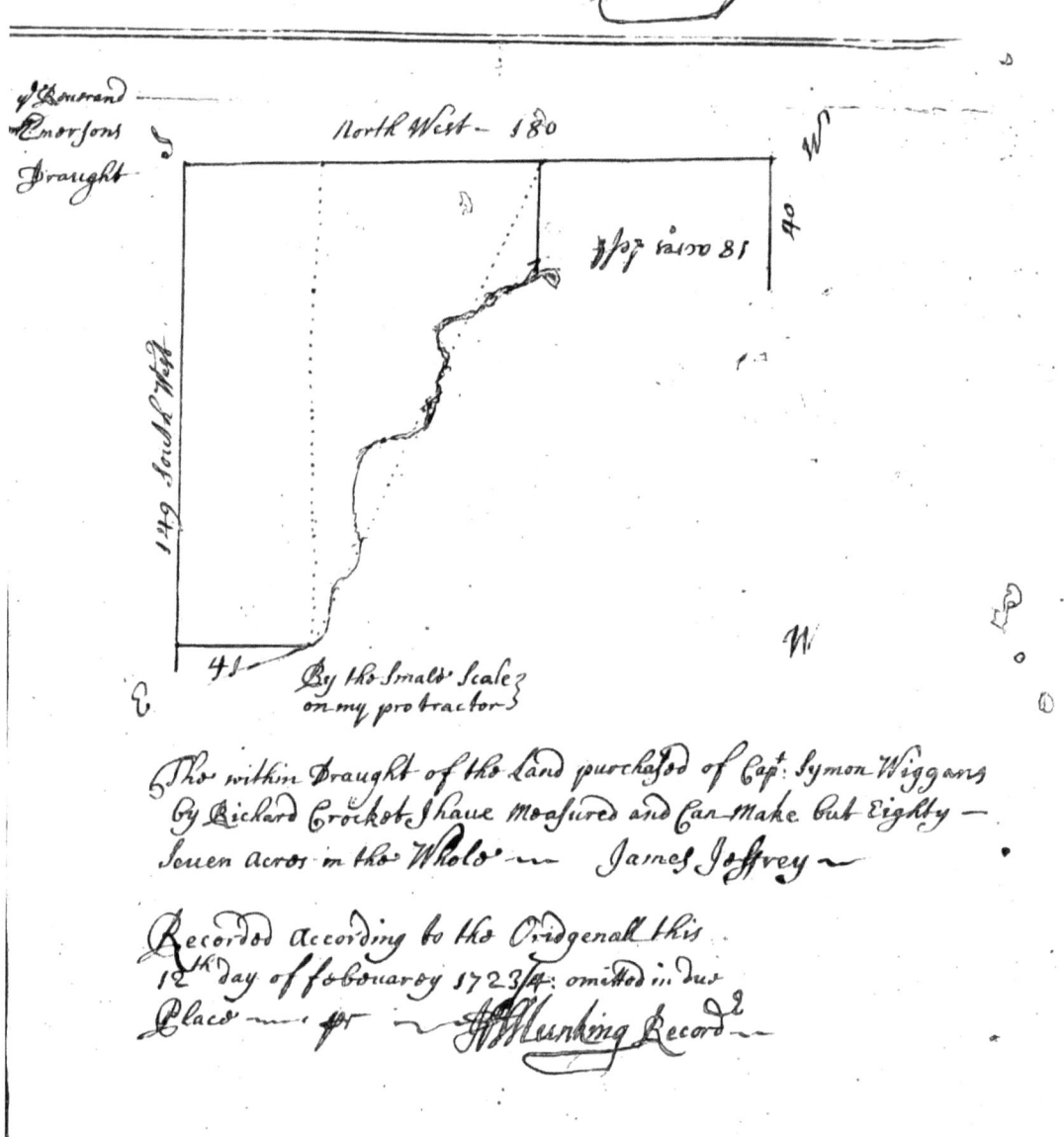

Plan of land purchased of Captain Simon Wiggins by Richard Crockett. (Rockingham, N.H., County Registry of Deeds, Book 13, p. 459.)

The Third Generation

The Skillin Family in Kittery

In Kittery, Samuel Skillin's life mirrored his brother-in-law's life as an upstanding citizen of Stratham. Although Samuel was more successful financially than Richard (he eventually became wealthy enough to buy enslaved African Americans),[116] the main difference between the lives of the two men was that Samuel's wife outlived him, so he was not, like Richard was, left a widower with the care of young children.

In 1714, a Congregational church was organized in Kittery and Samuel Skillin was one of eighteen original male members, which also included his step-father Elihu Gunnison. Richard Crockett's brother-in-law Henry Barter served as Deacon of the new church. Unlike her sister in Stratham, Rhoda (Haley) Skillin was *not* one of twenty-five original female members of the church, which included two unnamed Barter women (likely Richard's sister Sarah, Henry's wife, and one of their daughters), two Crockett women, and probably Samuel's mother, noted as " __ Gunnison."[117] Samuel also served as a juror[118] and was a member of the Grand Inquest.[119] In April of 1718, Skillin and his brother-in-law Andrew Haley swapped some land.[120]

In 1724, Richard—and Samuel and Rhoda (and other Haley siblings)—released to their brother and brother-in-law Andrew Haley, their share of Andrew Haley, Sr.'s estate in Kittery.[121] Deborah and Rhoda's father had passed away in 1697, probably without a will, and nearly three decades later Andrew, Jr. was attempting to settle the estate, possibly so that he could sell or pass the property on. Richard signed off by virtue to his marriage to Deborah. She did not sign off (as Rhoda did), another signal that Deborah was deceased. Nathaniel Kene and William Godsoe, both of Kittery, witnessed Richard's deed, indicating he was in Kittery in June of 1724 when the transaction occurred. No money changed hands during these

---

116. On July 20, 1753, "Jewel, a Negro Slave of Lieut. Samuel Skillins Entered his name and Purpose of Marriage with Phillis a Neggo Slave of Mr. James Millers. July 20th, 1753. Per Stephen Longfellow, [Falmouth] Town Clerk." Falmouth, Maine Town Records, Book 2, 1728-1773, p. 47. https://archive.org/details/falmouth-maine-town-records-book-2-1728-1773/page/47/mode/1up?q=Skillin&view=theater
117. STACKPOLE, p. 189-191.
118. MPCR, Vol. 5, p. 86. Samuel was on the jury April 2, 1717. He also served on other occasions.
119. MPCR, Vol. 6, p. 34. Samuel Skillin was one of sixteen men sworn onto the Grand Inquest for the year on April 5, 1720.
120. MEWD, Vol. 10, p. 110 and Vol. 10, p. 230-231. In the land swap, Skillin received six acres of land in Kittery that Haley bought from John Follet, and Haley netted some of the land Skillin purchased from one of the Mendums, which land abutted Haley's property on the east side of Spruce Creek.
121. On May 4, 1724, Samuel Skillin, Shipwright of Kittery, who married Arodas [Rhoda], daughter of Andrew Haley, deceased, deeded to Andrew Haley, Jr. their share of Haley, Sr.'s estate. YCROD, Vol. 11, p. 232. On June 4, 1724, Richard Crockett of Stratham, but formerly of Kittery, who married Debra Crockett, the young daughter of Andrew Haley, deceased, released to his brother-in-law Andrew Haley all rights/titles to any of Haley, Sr.'s estate by virtue of his marriage to Deborah. MEWD, Vol. 11, p. 546-547.

transactions with Haley, Jr. The releases occurred due to the goodwill and affection that existed between the extended family members.

Father Rasles' War (The Fourth Indian War, 1722-1725)

In 1713, the Peace of Utrecht ended the War of Spanish Succession (Queen Anne's War in New England and the Third Indian War in Maine), ushering in a time of peace between France and Great Britain. In the treaty, France ceded French Acadia (part of Maine and Canada) to Britain; however, the eastern Wabanaki tribes that had peaceably shared Acadia with the French for nearly a century were not a party to the treaty. In addition, the actual boundaries of Acadia were still a point of dispute between New France and New England, including land east of the Kennebec River in Maine and what is now the Canadian Province of New Brunswick.

Having been left in the lurch by the French, eastern Indians met at Portsmouth with officials from Massachusetts Bay Colony (including Governor Joseph Dudley) and New Hampshire Province to negotiate their own peace. On July 13, 1713, the English and some Native Americans agreed to a new treaty, which basically renewed the tenets of a treaty struck in 1693 at Pemaquid between Sir William Phipps (then Governor of Massachusetts Bay) and various tribes, including the Penobscot and Norridgewock. Eight Native American representatives from the Penobscot, St. John, and Kennebec tribes signed the 1713 Treaty of Portsmouth. (The Mi'kmaq, also known as the Tarratines, did not sign.)

The treaty was written in English, which the Indians could not read, and so it was interpreted to them. In the treaty the natives agreed (among other things) to submit to the authority of the English Queen Anne and her representatives. They also apologized for breaking earlier peace treaties; agreed to trade only at established English trading houses; and promised not to associate with the French again. More important for the English in Maine, the Indians promised to cease all acts of hostility against them and to allow the settlers to return to their frontier homes in eastern Maine "without any molestation or claims by us [the Indians][122] or any other Indians…" Also, in order to "prevent mischiefs and inconveniences" the Indians agreed not to venture near English settlements below the Saco River. In return, the English agreed to reserve ("save") for the Indians "… their own Grounds, and

---
122. Claims by the Indians that the English settlers were encroaching upon their territory.

free liberty for Hunting, Fishing, Fowling, and all other their lawful liberties and privileges [as in the 1693 treaty]."[123]

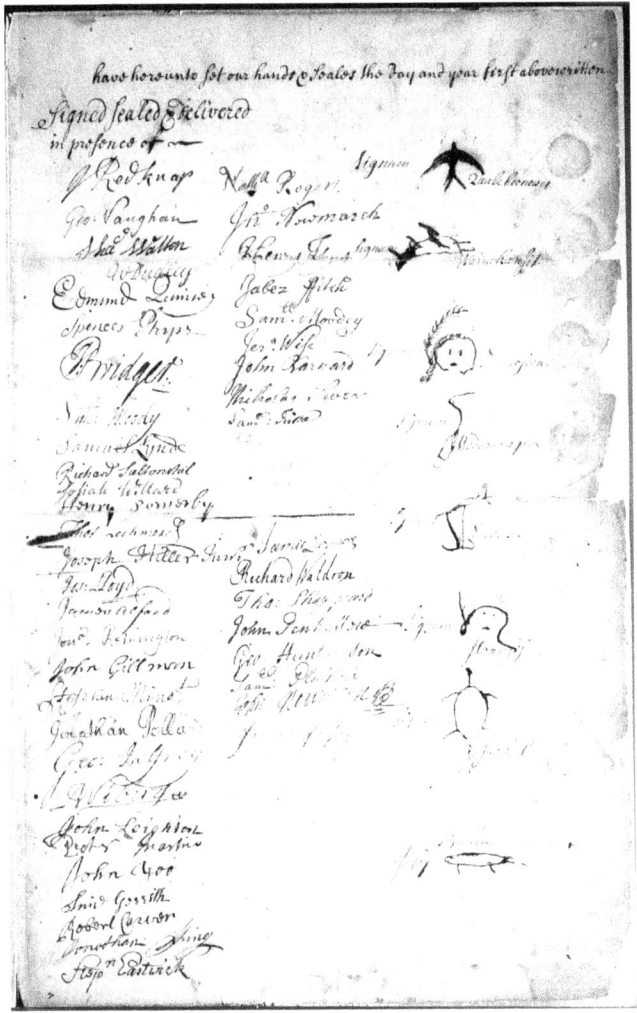

Treaty of Portsmouth, July 12, 1713, between Eastern Abenakis and
the Province of Massachusetts Bay.
The image above is the 3rd page of the treaty showing the signatures of Massachusetts Bay and New Hampshire officials, as well as the totemic pictographs (right side) of the eight representatives from the Penobscot, St. John, and Kennebec tribes.
(Levi Woodbury Papers, Library of Congress, Washington, D.C.)[124]

123. Treaty of Portsmouth, 1713. P. 1. Levi Woodbury Papers. U.S. Library of Congress. http://www.1713treatyofportsmouth.com/treaty1.cfm#:~:text=That%20is%20to%20say:,Treaty%20of%20Portsmouth%2C%20page%20tw0.
124. Treaty of Portsmouth, July 12, 1713. By Eastern Abenakis and the Province of Massachusetts Bay. - Levi Woodbury Papers, courtesy of the Library of Congress, Washington, D.C., USA., Public Domain, https://commons.wikimedia.org/w/index.php?curid=20253515

The end of hostilities between the English and warring Native American saw a revival of interest in resettling Maine's eastern towns, those which had been abandoned or destroyed during the war with the French and Indians:

> "In 1713, the [Massachusetts] General Court revived the old 'Committee of Eastern Claims and Settlements.' The committee was now enlarged from seven to nine members and empowered to examine all claims to the abandoned lands and confirm those it found valid. At the same time, the Court designated five towns for resettlement: Saco, Scarborough, Falmouth, North Yarmouth, and Arrowsick. The legislators required that the abandoned towns be replanted by groups of twenty to thirty families. Each family was to live on a small home lot of three or four acres, and each settlement was to take the form of an easily defensible cluster of houses located near the seacoast."[125]

Benjamin Skillin, Samuel Skillin's cousin, who had been living in Portsmouth, was one of the first to return to Falmouth (formerly, Casco). Anxious to claim the land previously belonging to his father, Benjamin and his family relocated to Falmouth by 1715, settling on what had been Thomas Skillin, Jr.'s farm. This homestead was situated in Back Cove, near what had been the original farm of Benjamin and Samuel's grandfather, Thomas Skillin, Sr.[126] In 1719, Benjamin Skillin was elected one of the first selectmen of the newly reorganized Falmouth.

The English soon broke the 1713 Treaty of Portsmouth, however. Settlers pushed into territory reserved for Native Americans, destroying in the process their hunting and fishing grounds. In truth, the English believed that the territory to the Eastward *all* belonged to them (after France withdrew her claims to the territory), and that the Indians, by signing the Treaty of Portsmouth, had agreed to become English subjects. (This claim of subjection to the English crown the natives vehemently denied.) Not all Native American tribes in eastern Maine had been parties to the Treaty of Portsmouth, either, which caused confusion amongst the English, which regularly lumped the loosely-connected Wabanaki tribes into one group. The

---

125. ELP, p. 3. https://www.sec.state.ma.us/arc/arcpdf/eastland.pdf
126. Benjamin's father, Thomas Skillin, Jr., and Samuel's father, John Skillin, were brothers, both sons of Thomas and Deborah Skillin. Skillin, Sr. had a younger son also named Benjamin, who is often confused with his nephew Benjamin. See "Descendants of Thomas and Deborah (?) Skillings of Cumberland Co., Maine" by Arlene L. Brown Ackerman for Skillin facts and source materials. https://freepages.rootsweb.com/~arlene/genealogy/Skillings/index.htm WILLIS appears to make this mistake in his "Journals of the Rev. Thomas Smith and the Rev. Samuel Deane, Pastors of the First Church in Portland, with Notes and Biological Notices: and a summary, History of Portland." Wm. Willis, author. Portland: Joseph S. Bailey, 1849.

Indians claimed later that the written document did not accurately represent the verbal terms to which the two parties had agreed. Some Native Americans pointed out that those who signed the treaty for the natives did not have the authority to speak for "any other Indians" (as the language in the 1713 Treaty of Portsmouth proclaimed), but rather only for their individual tribe.

The aggrieved Indians found a sympathizer for their renewed hostility toward the English in Father Sébastien Rasles ("Rales"), a French Jesuit priest who had (reportedly) lived with the Norridgewock Indians on the Kennebec River since 1694. In 1689, the French priest had volunteered for missionary work among the American Indians and, departing his home country, sailed to the New World. The thirty-two-year-old Jesuit arrived at Quebec on July 23, 1689, where over the next few years he was one of the Black Robes (as the natives called the priests) who converted the St. Francis Indians to Catholicism.[127] Rasles had a special interest in the language spoken by the Native Americans, and after he went to live with the Norridgewocks, he not only learned their language but also created an important dictionary of the Abenaki language.[128]

Rasles, as a devout Catholic, had no love for the Puritan English. (The feeling was mutual—the English Protestants hated and distrusted the priests.) He marshalled the Norridgewocks and other Wabanaki Indians around Quebec, and on July 28, 1721, Rasles and 250 Indian warriors arrived at Georgetown via a flotilla of canoes. In a letter (likely penned by Rasles) they demanded that the English abandon Native American territory or they would be killed and English property and livestock destroyed. Massachusetts Bay Colony was given two months to respond to these demands. Infuriated, Massachusetts immediately ordered traders to stop selling guns and powder to any Native Americans. The English authorities also plotted an attack on Norridgewock to put down the rebellion by capturing the troublemaking priest Rasles.

---

127. Some of the information about Father Rasles might have been a romantic biography contrived for political reasons after his death, and published as two letters reported to have been written by the Jesuit, one to his brother and one to his nephew. The validity of these letters has been called into question. For a good exposition of this see, "The Attack on Norridgewock, 1724," by Fannie Hardy Eckstrom, published in *The New England Quarterly*, Vol.7, No. 3, (Sept. 1934), pp. 541-578. https://penelope.uchicago.edu/Thayer/E/Journals/NEQ/7/3/Attack_on_Norridgewock*.html#:~:text=He%20says%20that%20twenty%2Deight,the%20best%20retreat%20they%20could

128. Rasles' "A Dictionary of the Abnaki Language in North America" was taken in a raid upon Norridgewock and now belongs shamefully to Harvard University. (A more appropriate place for the dictionary would be the Abbe Museum in Bar Harbor, a Smithsonian affiliate whose mission is "To illuminate and advance greater understanding of and support for Wabanaki Nations' heritage, living cultures, and homeland.") An English publication of the dictionary is available online at Digital Maine https://digitalmaine.com/cgi/viewcontent.cgi?article=1102&context=books

In January of 1722, while most of the Norridgewocks were away on a hunting trip, Colonel Thomas Westbrook surrounded the Indian settlement on the Kennebec River (at what is now Madison). The wily priest, however, had been warned of the impending arrival of the English soldiers and escaped into the woods. Papers found in Rasles' strongbox at Norridgewock revealed that officials in New France, although currently at peace with Great Britain, probably sanctioned and supported the Indians in their raids upon English settlements. That October Rasles (reportedly) wrote a letter to his nephew, claiming that in the raids upon the English, which had begun as threatened, the Indians "...took care not to harm the settlers, but to destroy only their property." The priest continued:

> "This moderation of the savages[129] did not have the effect which they had hoped. Thus we have a new signal of the war which is likely to flame forth between the English and the savages. The latter look for no support from the French ... but they have a resource in all the other savage nations, who will not fail to enter into their quarrel and take up their defense."[130]

Indian raids upon English homesteads and settlements in Maine, originating from Norridgewock, began again in 1723. During the Indian's Northeast Coast Campaign of 1724, the Native Americans raided English settlements on the coast of Maine, from Berwick to Mount Desert Island (including Falmouth, where Benjamin Skillin had settled.) The fearful and bloody raids continued through 1724 and came to be known as Father Rasles' War (also, Dummer's War[131] and the Fourth Indian War). During this warfare more than 30 English settlers were captured or killed. Many houses and outbuildings were burned and livestock destroyed. An unknown number of Native Americans were also killed, captured, or wounded during the uprising.

---

129. Although the Jesuit priest Rasles lived with the Indians at Norridgewock, where he built a church and converted the natives to Catholicism, it appears (from this letter, anyway, which might not be authentic) that he still regarded them as lesser beings or "savages," much as the English did. This point of view is contested, however, by those who claim that Rasles was a martyr (not an instigator) and that he loved—and was beloved by—the Norridgewock Indians.

130. Letter of Sébastien Rasles to his nephew, October 1722. "Father Rasles, the English, and the Indians." Candace Kanes. Maine Memory Network https://www.mainememory.net/sitebuilder/site/820/page/1230/display?use_mmn=1 Fannie Hardy Eckstrom, in her article, "The Attack on Norridgewock, 1734," claims that this letter of Rasles and that of another he sent to his brother were written by others for political purposes after the priest's death, in order to obscure the truth of French involvement in the Indian uprising (and to whitewash Rasles' character).

131. Father Rasles' War was also known by residents of Massachusetts Bay as Dummer's War, after Lieutenant Governor William Dummer, who was then in power at Boston.

On Aug. 22, 1724, a second English attack (this one a surprise) upon the Indian settlement at Norridgewock, resulted in Rasles' death and the destruction of the village there.[132] The Catholic church the priest had built was burned. The attack was led by Captain Jeremiah Moulton and Captain Johnson Harmon, and included a number of Mohawk warriors, sworn enemies of the Wabanaki. Conflicting reports about the raid claim as few as 28 Indians were killed and as many as 80, including women and children. The Norridgewocks who survived the massacre at their village slipped away to Canada (for the time being), and once again the frontier was open to English expansion. The death of the controversial French priest Rasles, whom some Native Americans later claim had deliberately incited the Norridgewocks (and other Indians) to violence with the English (to protect New France territory), once again opened eastern Maine to English expansion.[133]

Death of Father Sebastian Rasles at Norridgewock, August 23, 1724.
The lithograph is the frontispiece from "Indian Good Book" by Eugene Vetromile.[134]
(Image in the public domain.)

---

132. I have often visited the site of the Norridgewock village in Madison where today a monument to Father Rasles stands in a little clearing surrounded by trees. Walking along the banks of the Kennebec River contemplating Rasles' death and the massacre of many Norridgewocks is a powerful experience. This sacred site is a reminder of the bloody and tragic struggle over Dawnland.
133. For a good exposition of the conflicting claims of what happened during the attack at Norridgewock, see "The Attack on Norridgewock, 1724," by Fannie Hardy Eckstrom, published in *The New England Quarterly*, Vol.7, No. 3, (Sept. 1934), pp. 541-578.
134. Thomas W. Strong, lithograph publisher, 98 Nassau Street, New York.

The Resettlement of Falmouth

By 1727, another attempt to resettle Falmouth was initiated. Emigration to Falmouth included inhabitants from those who had settled there after the 1713 Treaty of Utrecht (like Benjamin Skillin), as well as the children (now grown) of former landowners who had fled to Massachusetts and southern Maine for safety decades earlier during the Second Indian War (King William's War). Among those who returned to Falmouth this year was Benjamin York[135] of Gloucester, Massachusetts, son of early eastern settler Samuel York.[136] This resettlement was prompted by the need for land in New England, combined with the desire on the part of the emigrants to reclaim family property:

> "The natural increase in population together with the constant stream of new comers produced a scarcity of farming land. Consequently, in 1727 and 1728 a tide of emigration [from Gloucester, MA] set toward what is now Maine, then a part of Massachusetts. The motive to better material conditions prompted their ancestors to make uncertain venture in American, and today, the ruling passion, strong, impels their descendants to seek new and enlarged fields of endeavor."[137]

Another settler who became interested in returning to Falmouth during this time was Samuel Skillin, whose father had been killed there by Indians in 1689, prior to

---

135. Benjamin York and his older brother Samuel (ten and thirteen respectively) were living on Falmouth Neck when Fort Loyal was besieged and taken by the French and Indians in May of 1690. Both boys survived, but Samuel was captured and carried to Canada, where he spent 10 years making masts for the French Navy before escaping. The following is an excerpt from an account Samuel York penned for the Earl of Belmont, Capt. General and Governor in Chief of the Province of New York: "The memorial of Samuel Yorke, Caprenter, sheweth, That I was taken prisoner at Casco Bay by a party of French and Indians under the command of Monsieur de Portneuf in the month of May, 1690, and carried to Canada, where, and in the hunting Indians countries, I have lived ever since till the 29th day of this last July [1700], that I made my escape to come hither, and during the last ten years and a half I was employed in cutting masts for the use of the French king navy." From, "The Siege and Capture of Fort Loyall, Destruction of Falmouth, May 20, 1690 (O.S.). A paper read before the Maine Genealogical Society, June 2, 1885. By John T. Hull. Printed by Order of City Council of Portland. Portland, ME: Owen, Strout & Co., Printers. 1885. See p. 107-108. Benjamin also provided in his "memorial" to the Earl of Belmont a description of the western Indians with whom he had lived.

136. On June 20, 1670, Samuel York purchased a large tract of land—600 acres in Topsham—from the Indians Jeromkin, Daniel, and Bobin, in partnership with James Thomas. York and his family settled there, but during the First Indian War, he removed to Cape Porpus. Once hostilities ceased, like the Skillin family, the Yorks returned to the greater Falmouth area (Mussel Cove; today, Falmouth Foreside) by 1680. During the Second Indian War, hostilities with Native Americans drove the elderly York to Gloucester, Massachusetts Bay Colony; however, his sons Samuel and Benjamin, remained in Falmouth. LIBBY/NOYES, p. 775, Samuel York (3).

137. "History of the Town and City of Gloucester, Cape Ann, Massachusetts. James R. Pringle. Gloucester, Mass: Published by the Author, 1892. See p. 59-60, where Benjamin York is listed among those who emigrated from Gloucester to Falmouth in the 1727-1728 wave of settlers.

The Third Generation

the destruction of Fort Loyal. Skillin, now over fifty and a successful shipwright, appears to have become consumed by the idea of reestablishing himself upon his father's family land, much as his cousin Benjamin had reclaimed *his* father's farm in 1715. On Nov. 10, 1730, Samuel sold his homestead on Spruce Creek in Kittery for the impressive sum of 800 pounds[138] and he and his family relocated permanently to Falmouth, where he eventually reacquired some (if not most) of John Skillin's properties, including his father's grist and saw mills.[139] (Samuel deeded the mills to his son and daughters prior to his death, reserving Rhoda's right to receive income from the mills during her lifetime.)[140]

On November 23, 1736, Samuel Skillin sold his 4/5th share of the Commons in Falmouth (apportioned to him as a descendant of an "ancient" settler, one who had been driven away by the Indians in the 17th century) to his son-in-law George Roberts,[141] who was a grandson of Richard's aunt and uncle, Ann (Crockett) and William Roberts. Roberts had married Samuel and Rhoda Skillin's daughter Katharine. The families resided at Long Creek in that area of Falmouth on the south side of the Fore River that became known as Second Parish (later, Cape Elizabeth, and eventually South Portland). Richard and Deborah Crockett's son, Richard, Jr., joined his aunt and uncle (and cousins) in Second Parish, where in 1731 he married Mary Robinson, a granddaughter of ancient settler Samuel York.[142] The resettlement of Falmouth—and in particular of Second Parish where Samuel Skillin

---

138. YCROD, Vol. 14, p. 30. Rhoda ("Richord") signed off on her dower rights.
139. The rights to the property John Skillin (Sr.) owned in Falmouth and eastern Maine were divided amongst his children, with eldest son John receiving a 2/5th share. (John sold his share to Thomas Westbrook.) Son Samuel, in addition to his 1/5th share, also bought up the remaining shares of his other siblings (and their offspring). See, for example, YCROD, Vol. 13, p. 93, where Rebecca (Skillin) Frink and her husband George sold to her brother Samuel Skillin her share in their father John Skillin's estate in Falmouth, except for personal property and moveables at Scarborough (which suggests there was still some personal property that remained in the house abandoned by the Skillins after John's death). Samuel Skillin's deeds to property in Falmouth and to the rights to his father's property are too numerous to mention in this history of the Crockett family. A good place to start for interested parties, however, is to search the link between Thomas Westbrook and Skillin. On Sept. 2, 1732, Westbrook of Falmouth, signed an indenture to Lieut. Samuel Skillin, Shipwright of Falmouth, for property at Long Creek (including a ¼ part of a saw mill and ten acres Westbrook purchased from Samuel's older brother John Skillin) in Falmouth for 400 pounds, payable in bills for 1,000 pounds. See YCROD, Vol. 15, p. 190. On May 4, 1739, Skillin discharged the 1,000-pound mortgage he had of Westbrook, and bound himself (for 1,000 pounds) against any claims that might be brought against Westbrook's 4/5th share of a 60-acre lot in Falmouth by right of inheritance. See YCROD, Vol. 21, p. 91 and Vol. 21, p. 121.
140. See YCROD, Vol. 28, p. 119 and p. 126, and Vol. 31, p. 32. See also YCROD, Vol. 33, p. 218.
141. YCROD, Vol. 18, p. 126. George Roberts, a laborer, paid 20 pounds (a small amount compared to the property's value) for the 4/5th share in the 60-acre lot to be laid out from the Commons, as well as Skillin's 4/5th right to a 10-acre lot laid out to John Skillin (Sr.). Samuel promised to warrant and defend the title against the heirs, assigns, etc. of his late brother John Skillin, which suggests there might have been some issue between Samuel and his older brother John, the firstborn son of John Skillin and Elizabeth (Ingersoll) Skillin (later, Gunnison).
142. Keeping it all in the family, Richard and Mary's son, Richard III (known as Richard, Jr.) would grow up and marry Elizabeth Roberts, a daughter of George and Katharine (Skillin) Roberts. After Elizabeth died, for his second wife, Richard, Jr. selected Susannah Westcoat, another granddaughter of Samuel Skillin. (See Chapter 5.)

and other interconnected families dwelt at Long Creek—represents an important development for our line of Crocketts. The story of these families at Long Creek will be covered in Chapter 4.

Massachusetts Bay Makes a Move and "Strange Ministers" in Stratham

Meanwhile, back in New Hampshire, there was treachery in the works. Someone had taken around Stratham a petition directed to the King of England for "sundry people" to sign, which petition asked for the Province of New Hampshire to be put under the government of Massachusetts Bay Colony (like Maine was), rather than remain an independent province. Many people had been "unwarily prevailed upon to Signe the Same without considering the fatal consequences that will attend the same if granted." The petition and the way in which it was circulated represented an undermining of local government that residents would not stand for.

On July 21, 1739, sixty-nine freeholders in Stratham called for a Town Meeting to discuss the petition. The meeting was held July 24th, during which the petition was protested and disallowed, and a representative was selected to convey the *true* sentiments of Stratham residents to the King. Richard Crockett and his son Ephraim both voted against going under the Puritanical thumb of Massachusetts Bay.[143] If the move to subsume New Hampshire into Massachusetts occurred elsewhere in the Province (and it likely did), the attempt was unsuccessful because New Hampshire remained an independent Province.

By 1743, not everyone in Stratham was happy with the preaching and theology of long-time pastor, the Reverend Henry Rust, who had received a lifetime call from the townspeople in 1717. A move to expand the religious offerings of the community surfaced at a Town Meeting held March 25, 1743. At the meeting, the selectmen were given the power to see what other ministers might be available to preach a weekly lecture (and, one presumes, to pay the weekly "lecturers"). This falling away in fealty to Reverend Rust was seen as a "grievance" against him and was not without dissent. Town Clerk David Robinson notes in his official record:

> "Because the two Last votes being without any Liberty from the Reverend Mr. Henry Rust and a greavince unto him and Conterry to us whose names are hear

---

143. Stratham, N.H. Town Records. https://www.familysearch.org/ark:/61903/3:1:3QS7-899K-DRPB?i=43&cc=1987741&cat=393768

underwritten wee have seen fit to Enter our decents against the two last votes ... for Strange ministers to Preach."[144]

Thirty-two men registered their dissent against having "Strange ministers" preach in Stratham, including Richard Crockett and his son, Richard, Jr. (who, because of debt, had temporarily taken up residence with his father, along with his family), as well as various Wiggins and Town Clerk Robinson. Rust had been preaching in Stratham for more than twenty-five years, with an annual salary of 200 pounds old tenor[145] (not always paid in full), plus firewood provided to him. While many residents were satisfied with this divine's work, apparently the majority was not. Notably, Richard's son, Ephraim, who was likely more independent of his father than Richard, Jr. (Ephraim was not constantly in debt like his brother) was not one of the dissenters.[146]

The move to hire another minister in Stratham persisted and on April 5, 1745, at the annual Town Meeting (adjourned from March to consider the issue), it was voted to call Mr. Dudley Leavitt "for preaching in the town of Stratham." (Both Richard Sr. and Jr. once again dissented, and Ephraim did not.)[147] By March of 1746, however, a case had been brought against Dudley Leavitt, who asked the town to pay his legal fees. This infuriated dissenters, but did not discourage those who sought an alternative to Reverend Rust. Once again, a committee was formed to look for another minister to settle in Stratham. At a special Town Meeting held June 24, 1746, the town elected to call and ordain Mr. Joseph Adams. Richard Crockett, Sr. was again one of the dissenters. (Richard, Jr. either did not oppose Mr. Adams or did not attend the meeting, which was held during the busy summer farming season.)

Probably much of the objection against the second settled minister in Stratham

---

144. Stratham, N.H. Town Records. https://www.familysearch.org/ark:/61903/3:1:3QS7-899K-DRPB?i=50&cc=1987741&cat=393768
145. Paper money issued in bills of credit was long used in New England; however, in 1737 Massachusetts issued new money (i.e. "new" tenor), each pound being worth three pounds of "old" tenor. Therefore, Rev. Rust's 200-pound salary in old tenor was equal to about 67 pounds new tenor.
146. I suspect that Ephraim and his wife Rebecca were Baptists, as was probably Rev. Adams. Three of Ephraim and Rebecca's sons who later relocated to Gorham, Maine—Peletiah, Andrew and Jonathan—were members of the East Baptist Church, with Andrew at one point serving as Elder. Gorham Town Records, 1770-1805, via Family Search. https://www.familysearch.org/ark:/61903/3:1:3QS7-L9NW-6Q33?view=explore&groupId=TH-1942-41592-29035-27
147. We are not able to tell if Ephraim Crockett was present at the Town Meeting, however, as only those opposed to calling Mr. Leavitt to the ministry are noted in the record. Stratham, N.H. Town Records via Family Search. https://www.familysearch.org/ark:/61903/3:1:3QS7-899K-DR2X?i=54&wc=M6CV-HWL%3A265836301%2C266022101%2C266022102%3Fcc%3D1987741&cc=1987741&cat=393768

was the cost of carrying two preachers. Those who objected to the second minister petitioned the General Assembly of the Province of New Hampshire that they be exempted from paying the second salary. At a Town Meeting held in Stratham June 15, 1747, the dissenters carried their point—and voters decided to exempt the petitioners from taxation for Mr. Adam's salary while Reverend Rust was also preaching in the town.[148]

Reverend Rust died soon after the exemption was voted,[149] however, and his son submitted an extravagant claim to the town (which even took into consideration the devaluation of money) for salary not paid to his father over the years: 1594 pounds, 13 shillings.[150] The Town refused to pay the bill and a committee was established to negotiate with the younger Rust. Negotiations failed and the matter ended up in court.

The egregious lawsuit with the younger Rust no doubt affected the disposition of the townspeople, because at Stratham's annual Town Meeting held March 25, 1752, the town voted to pay the Reverend Adams 300 pounds old tenor. Dissenters were notably less, and this time Richard Crockett, Sr. was not one of them.[151] (By then, Richard, Jr. and his family had returned to Falmouth to live.) By 1756, enough of the dissenters "of the Standing Church of Stratham [the late Reverend Rust's church] that have lately adheared to the Reverend Mr. Adams ministry" acquiesced to his ministry, and the Town voted to join the two congregations as one under the leadership of Reverend Adams.[152]

Stratham continued to experience similar growing pains. By 1755, residents requested that other schools be established in more remote locations of town. Selectmen were given the authority to select locations for four schools.[153] New residents had settled in the outskirts of Stratham and while nearly impossible for their children to attend school on a regular basis because of the distance, they were still expected to pay their share of the cost of education. The request reflected

---

148. Stratham, N.H. Town Records.
149. According to Stratham, N.H. Cemetery Records (via Family Search) the Rev. Henry Rust died March 20, 1749 at age 63.
150. The back salary Rust's son claimed was due his father was likely quoted in new tenor, thus would have been about 532 pounds old tenor (still an outrageous amount).
151. Richard might not have attended Town Meeting; however, he had been always present (as a dissenter) at prior meetings when the issue was discussed. (The following year, 1753, the town failed to pass a rate to pay Rev. Adams, despite an attempt to reconcile dissenters.) https://www.familysearch.org/ark:/61903/3:1:3QS7-899K-DRL5?i=77&wc=M6CV-HWL%3A265 836301%2C266022101%2C266022102%3Fcc%3D1987741&cc=1987741&cat=393768
152. Stratham, N.H. Town Records. https://www.familysearch.org/ark:/61903/3:1:3QS7-899K-DRH4?i=86&wc=M6CV-H WL%3A265836301%2C266022101%2C266022102%3Fcc%3D1987741&cc=1987741&cat=393768
153. Stratham, N.H. Town Records. https://www.familysearch.org/ark:/61903/3:1:3QS7-L99K-DRSY?i=83&wc=M6CV-

the reality of the situation. Stratham, an unincorporated part of Exeter known as Squamscott Patent when Richard Crockett had settled there nearly four decades earlier, was now bursting at the seams. Richard and his late wife Deborah had contributed to this growth spurt, having raised their five (at least) children there. While several of their sons had relocated to greener pastures (William to Epping, N.H.; Richard, Jr. and Samuel back to Maine), Ephraim and his extended family had remained in Stratham. Like other married couples of the time, Ephraim and his wife Rebecca had at least six children, and probably ten.[154] No wonder more schools were needed!

The Final Years of the Brothers-in-Law

Samuel Skillin continued to buy and sell real estate throughout the rest of his life. His later property deeds describe the former shipwright simply as a yeoman (a very modest term, considering his wealth). Samuel also continued to supervise his mills, and served in the local militia, where he rose to the rank of Lieutenant, probably during King George's War (the Fifth Indian War, 1744-1748). *The Maine Historical and Genealogical Recorder* writes of Samuel (some of which information is conflated with that of his son, Samuel, Jr.):

> "Samuel Skillings was prominent in Indian affairs, and rendered especially good service toward Wells. He was called Captain,[155] and besides his military rank, had attained distinction as a selectman. His possessions were extensive, and by their influence he was quite the dominating member of the [Skillin] family during

---

154. CANDAGE, p. 6. Ephraim's son David Crockett and his wife Sarah "Sally" Thompson, who also remained in Stratham, had thirteen children. (CANDAGE, p. 10-11.)

155. The *Recorder* here conflates the life of Lieutenant Samuel Skillin with his son, Captain Samuel Skillin, Jr. The deeds that the senior Skillin executed and his gravestone clearly denote his highest military rank was that of Lieutenant. Willis writes of a Captain Skillin who, during the French and Indian War (1754-1763) rendered a service to Windham. Because this incident occurred in 1756, eight months before Samuel Skillin's death at age 80, the service was performed by Samuel, Jr., who would have been fifty and in 1757 was captain of a militia at Stroudwater: "In May, 1756, a report having been brought to town that a body of one hundred and twenty Indians were coming upon the frontier and were about spreading themselves from Brunswick to Saco, four companies of volunteers were immediately raised from among our people and under the command of Captains Milk, Ilsley, Skillings, and Berry, went out in pursuit of them. Capt. Skillings marched in the direction of Windham and succeeded in saving the people and property of that place ..." WILLIS, p. 431-432. The confusion was likely caused by the fact that in Capt. Skillings' company of 1757 there was a private named Samuel Skillings, Jr., who was (in actuality) Samuel Skillin III. This son of Samuel Skillin, Jr. and Rebecca Sawyer was born March 21, 1735 and died Nov. 22, 1817 (per his gravestone, Long Creek Cemetery, Cape Elizabeth, Maine): "In memory of Mr. Samuel Skillin who died Nov. 22, 1817 aged 82 years." Nevertheless, it was Samuel Skillin (the first) who was the selectman of Falmouth and who built saw and grist mills and invested heavily in real estate.

his lifetime. His sagacity and foresight in securing mill privileges on the Creek and the connecting fertile acres show him worthy to be considered the second founder of the family."[156]

Samuel Skillin died at Long Creek[157] on January 2, 1757, at 80 years of age.[158] Lieutenant Samuel Skillin is buried at the historic Long Creek Cemetery, situated behind the Air National Guard on Western Avenue in South Portland.[159] Some of the Crocketts and Skillins remain together in death, as they had done in life. Near Samuel's slate gravestone in Long Creek is the (now broken) marker of Catharine Crockett, who died January 11, 1761, at two months of age.[160] Catharine was the daughter of Elizabeth (Roberts) and Richard Crockett (III), making her the great-granddaughter of *both* Samuel Skillin and Richard Crockett (and the great-granddaughter of their wives, sisters Rhoda and Deborah Haley). Many other Crocketts and Skillins are presumed buried in Long Creek Cemetery, as well.

---

156. *The Maine Historical and Genealogical Recorder*, vol. 2: 103, *et. seq*. I found this passage in "Descendants of Edward Small of New England : and allied families with tracings of English ancestry." Lora Altine Woodbury Underhill. Boston/New York: Houghton Mifflin, 1934. See p. 1134-1142, The Roberts Family for Skillin genealogy. The first founder of the family to which this passage refers was Samuel's grandfather Thomas Skillin, one of the original early settlers of Falmouth.
157. Long Creek was a settlement in Falmouth that was set off as part of the district of Cape Elizabeth in 1765, and in 1895 became part of South Portland.
158. According to birth and death records Samuel Skillin was 77 years at his death; however, his gravestone reads: "here lyes Buried the Body of Lieu. Samuel Skilling, Who departed this Life Jany the 2, 1757 in the 80th year of His Age."
159. To see this historic cemetery, ask at the gatehouse of the Maine Air National Guard. My experience at Long Creek Cemetery was made easy by the courtesy of the Guard. After I received permission, a guard member came out and escorted me out back where the cemetery is located. (Because my visit was during the COVID pandemic, I drove my own car out.) I found the cemetery, where many of my ancestors lie at rest, to be a deeply moving place.
160. See Chapter 5, page 238, for photo of Catharine's gravestone.

The Third Generation

Gravestone of Lieut. Samuel Skillin, Long Creek Cemetery, South Portland, Maine.
"*Here lies Buried the Body of Lieu. Samuel Skillings who departed this Life Jan the 2 1757 in Ye 80th Year of His Age.*"
(Photo by Jennifer Wixson.)

Long Creek Cemetery, South Portland, Maine.
This ancient cemetery is situated behind the Maine Air National Guard.
Access is provided by the Guard.
(Photo by Jennifer Wixson, June 3, 2022.)

Before he died Richard Crockett also sold more real estate in Stratham,[161] but reserved his homestead for his son Ephraim. In addition, at some point Richard had become a proprietor of the town of Bow, N.H., although he never lived there. (After his father's death, Ephraim sold off the Bow lot.)[162] In 1733, Richard had conveyed to his youngest son William one-half acre on the west side of his orchard, reserving enough land for a family burial ground.[163] William appears not to have lived on this lot (although he might once have planned to build a house there). Since Richard specifically wanted to save space on this small lot for a cemetery, his late wife, Deborah (Haley) Crockett, was probably laid to rest near the orchard.

On January 7, 1757—five days after the death in Maine of his childhood friend and brother-in-law Samuel Skillin—Richard Crockett, Sr. died in Stratham, N.H. He was likely buried in the family plot next to his wife.[164] Richard was about seventy-five when he passed. His death was recorded as that of "old Mr. Richard,"[165] the epithet a sign of affection and distinction from the town he helped found.

---

161. On Feb. 28, 1744/45, Richard Crockett, yeoman of Stratham, for 60 pounds bills of credit in the old tenor paid by Benjamin Jewett, tanner (his neighbor that had bought out George Clark), sold four acres of land in Stratham. RCROD, Vol. 75, p. 72-74. Witnesses to this deed were Ephraim Crockett (Richard's son) and Richard Young.
162. On July 4, 1760, Ephraim Crockett of Stratham sold to Joseph Barker of Pembroke, town of Bow, for 150 pounds of old tenor, his father Richard Crockett's original lot in Bow. The parcel was about 40 acres, and was situated in the 5th range of lots in the first division, the 8th lot in that range. According to the deed, the lot was laid out to Richard Crockett as shown in the town Books. RCROD, Vol. 145, p. 79. Witnesses were Andrew and Dorothy Wiggin. Since the town of Bow was granted to Jonathan Wiggin and others in 1727, when Richard was already established in Stratham, he likely became one of the proprietors to secure real estate for future sales. Although Richard never lived in Bow, his eighth great-grandson, my brother Wesley E. Wixson, and his wife Lori, have resided in that community many years.
163. RCROD, Vol. 23, p. 77. This conveyance is a bit of a headscratcher, since if Candage's birth dates are at all accurate, the deed, dated July 13, 1733, was executed when William was about sixteen years of age. Richard added the caveat that if ever William wanted to sell the lot, he was first bound to offer it to his brothers Ephraim and Richard, Jr.
164. I have found no record of Richard or Deborah Crockett's burial in any of the Stratham, N.H. cemeteries.
165. Online database, *The New England and Historical Genealogical Register*. Boston: The New England Historical Society.

Chapter 4

"Being Called 3 Times – Appearing Not"
The Fourth Generation

First Generation – Thomas Crockett
Second Generation – Ephraim Crockett
Third Generation – Richard Crockett
Fourth Generation – Richard Crockett, Jr., circa 1706-circa 1786
Fifth Generation – Richard Crockett (III, also known as Richard, Jr.)
Sixth Generation – Ephraim Crockett

Richard Crockett, Jr., the fourth generation of Crocketts in the line we are following, is one of the more colorful of the Crockett men. So many facts are available about his life—such as his perpetual debt and court non-appearances—yet, maddeningly, so little about the man's character is truly known. That Richard or "Dick"[1] Crockett, Jr. must have been a likeable fellow is evident by the fact that, in addition to family members who signed promissory notes for him, many affluent and respectable men were willing to lend Richard money. Because debt dogged him most of his adult life, Richard Crockett, Jr. never owned much real estate or settled permanently in one location. He shuffled between Stratham, N.H and Falmouth (Cape Elizabeth), before ending his days in Deer Isle.

---

1. In a court execution against Richard Crockett, Jr. in 1740 he is styled "alias Dick or Richard Crockett of Falmouth," and so it is evident Richard, Jr. utilized the nickname "Dick" for a time, at least in Maine, anyway.

A Father and His Troublesome Namesake

Richard Crockett, Jr. was born around 1706, probably in Kittery,[2] and might have been the first-born son of Richard and Deborah (Haley) Crockett, even though his brother Ephraim appears to have been treated as the eldest by their father. Although early Maine homesteads usually passed to the elder son, this tradition was by no means set in stone in egalitarian New England, as was the rule of primogeniture in Old England.[3] Ephraim could have inherited their father's property in Stratham, N.H. for no other reason than simply he was the oldest son who remained at home, whereas brothers Richard, Jr. and Samuel returned to Maine, and William settled in Epping, N.H. (There could have been other, more compelling reasons for Richard, Sr. to leave his homestead to Ephraim, too.)

While Richard Crockett, Sr. gifted three of his four sons property or rights to property,[4] he never gave anything to his namesake Richard, except for an early right of refusal (given also to son Ephraim) on the ½ acre of cemetery land he conveyed to son William in 1733 (see prior chapter). This oversight stands out as noteworthy. Initially, I suspected the oversight was the result of a father hurt by the abandonment of an elder son, and a namesake at that. A little more digging, however, has led me to believe that the reason was much more banal: Richard, Jr. had perpetual money troubles. His father appears to have bailed Richard, Jr. out of debt on at least one occasion, and probably more. If so, it would have been understood between Richard, Sr. and Richard, Jr. that the monies paid by the father on the son's behalf were part of the son's inheritance.

Whether young Richard was sent to Falmouth by his father to be with his aunt and uncle Rhoda and Samuel Skillin, or whether the youth came back to Maine on his own initiative we do not know. If Richard, Sr. sent his namesake to profit from the steadying influence of his uncle, however, that strategy failed miserably. Richard, Jr. seems as little influenced in his life by Samuel Skillin as he was by his father.

---

2. I have seen interesting locations for Richard, Jr.'s birth, including the island of Vinalhaven; however, there is no evidence to support these records and no reason to believe he was born anyplace other than Kittery.
3. The one exception to primogeniture in England occurred in the county of Kent. "In Kent the dominant inheritance code was 'gravelkind,' by which all sons inherited equally. However the predominant inheritance rule throughout the rest of England in the medieval period and afterward was male-preference primogeniture, whereby estates passed in total to the eldest son." University of Nottingham, Manuscripts and Special Collections, "Inheritance." https://www.nottingham.ac.uk/manuscriptsandspecialcollections/learning/medievalwomen/theme2/inheritance.aspx#:~:text=In%20Kent%20the%20dominant%20inheritance,total%20to%20the%20eldest%20son
4. Richard Crockett (senior) conveyed his rights to any division of the Commons in Kittery and Berwick to sons William and Samuel.

As it turned out, Richard's younger brother Samuel (namesake of Samuel Skillin), who soon joined him in Falmouth, was the one most influenced by (and probably favored by) their uncle.

<u>Early Days in Falmouth</u>

The earliest documented record of Richard Crockett, Jr. in Falmouth is that of his 1731 marriage in that town to Mary Robinson, when (by my calculations) he was about twenty-five. Richard probably joined his aunt and uncle, and several of his adult Skillin cousins at least a year prior to his marriage, however. The Skillins resided on the south side of the Fore River in the settlement known as the Second Parish of Falmouth or Purpooduck Parish.[5] Prominent among those who dwelt in the same neighborhood around Long Creek in Second Parish (in addition to the Skillins) were the York, Jordan, Roberts, and Sawyer families, including brothers Jacob and John Sawyer. These Second Parish families contributed to Falmouth's population explosion during its resettlement period in the second quarter of the 18th century, a time of peace with the French and Indians, after the ending of Queen Anne's War (the Third Indian War) and Father Rasles' War (the Fourth Indian War).

John Sawyer had the important ferry privilege over the Fore River to First Parish on Falmouth Neck (now, downtown Portland) "… he keeping a good canoe for the accommodation of passengers."[6] (Sawyer was also appointed to take care of the parishioners' horses during the church services until their return.) The ferry ran from "…the southern side of Long Creek nearly opposite the landing on the Neck…"[7] The Sawyers were prominent members of the Second Parish community, where Richard likely resided. Second Parish families supported one another and often intermarried.

In 1735, about four years after Richard and Mary were married, his younger brother Samuel arrived in Falmouth. On November 8, 1735, Samuel (then about

---

5. At a Town Meeting held at the Meetinghouse in Falmouth on May 7, 1733, it was voted that "as many of the people and estates as desire the same lying on the South side of the Fore River running up said River to Stroudwater River and so into ye country as Stroudwater River runs shall be set off & to be a separate parrish and shall be discharged from paying any part of the Rev. Dr. Mr. Smith's salary or his successor's when they have built a meetinghouse and settled an orthodox minister on the south side of said River …" Falmouth (Maine) Town Records, Book 2, 1728-1773. https://archive.org/details/falmouth-maine-town-records-book-2-1728-1773/page/106/mode/1up?q=Skillin&view=theater
6. WILLIS, p. 342. John Pritchard was granted the ferry privilege over the Fore River from the Neck to Purpooduck in 1719; however, because it was difficult to call over the river from the Purpooduck side to Pritchard, John Sawyer was granted the ferry privilege on that side.
7. CAPE-E, p. 29.

eighteen) charged a hat, some flour, and powder (probably gunpowder) to his brother Richard's account at shopkeeper Phineas Jones' establishment in Falmouth.[8] Opportunity was likely the motivation behind Samuel's return to Maine, not only for employment, but also the for the acquisition of land.

By the 18th century, chairmaking was a trade unto itself, separate from other woodworking trades, such as cabinetry.[9] The rapid growth of Falmouth spurred a house building boom, as well as a companion demand for furniture. Richard appears to have taken advantage of this demand and become a chairmaker. When Samuel arrived in Falmouth, he, too, went into the chairmaking trade. (Samuel would later go on to become a shipwright like uncle Samuel Skillin.)

Admittance to the town of Falmouth required a payment of ten pounds, and accorded new (male) proprietors town "privileges,"[10] which included a lot of land laid out by the Proprietor's Committee and a right to a share of the Commons. There is no evidence that Richard paid his ten pounds or received a lot of land as a new proprietor.[11] (Samuel's name is not listed in the "Original Record of the Proprietors of Falmouth," either.)[12] Although he was not a proprietor, Richard was still counted as a resident of Falmouth. At the annual Town Meeting in March of

---

8. The total charged by Samuel to Richard's account was 2 pounds, 9 shillings and 9 pence. Because Samuel later made a payment to Richard's account (more than what he had bought), his purchase would not become part of the debt Richard owed to the shopkeeper. (Phineas Jones later won a judgment against Richard Crockett, the chairmaker, for 19 pounds, 17 shillings, and 2 pence. This was at the Inferior Court of Common Pleas held at Portsmouth in December of 1740. See Colonial Records of N.H., 1638-1772. Case File No. 21052, Phineas Jones v. Richard Crockett, Jr.)
9. Sheraton, Thomas. "The Cabinet Dictionary, containing An Explanation of all the Terms used in the Cabinet, Chair, and Upholstery Branches." London: W. Smith, 1803.
10. Falmouth, Maine Town Records frequently note a 10-pound admittance fee. See, for example, Record Book 2, p. 131: "Falmouth 6: May 1728. Received of Sam 11. Cobb Town Clerk Twenty Seven Notes or Bills given by sundry Persons for Ten Pounds each Payable to this Town for their admittance in to said Town & Priviledges of Inhabitants which I promise to be accountable for to the Town as also for said money when Received. Received Pr Mr. Benjamin Ingersoll. Received & Recorded, July 25th 1739 Pr. Samuell Moody Town Clerk." https://archive.org/details/falmouth-maine-town-records-book-2-1728-1773/page/131/mode/1up?q=Skillin&view=theater
11. There was a distinction between new proprietors, who made up the 1717/18 and later settlement of Falmouth, and the original or "ancient" proprietors (such as Samuel Skillin's father John Skillin) of the Casco Bay area. Rights of these ancient proprietors, who had been killed by Indians or were forced to relocate south for safety) were claimed by their descendants. The struggle over lots and land rights between these two groups—new and ancient proprietors—does not affect the course of our story and thus I have chosen not to elucidate upon it.
12. "Original Records of the Proprietors of Falmouth For the Years 1718 to 1826." Three volumes in one. Portland: Copied by F.A. Gerrish, 1861. https://archive.org/details/proprietors00falmouth_202105/mode/1up?q=Crocket&view=theater

The Fourth Generation

1736,[13] Richard was voted one of six field drivers,[14] responsible for rounding up loose animals.

Mary Robinson

On August 20, 1731, Richard Crockett, Jr. married Mary Robinson,[15] then of Falmouth,[16] but formerly of Gloucester, county of Essex in Massachusetts Bay Colony. Their wedding was during a time of peace that occurred after Father Rasles' War (the Fourth Indian War, 1722-1725). Mary was nineteen when she was married, having been born January 22, 1712 in Gloucester to Abraham Robinson III and Sarah (York) Robinson.[17] Mary's mother died when she was six[18] and her father died a month before her thirteenth birthday.[19] Because of the loss of both her parents, Mary might have come to Maine to live with (or for a long visit to) her uncle Benjamin York (her mother's brother), who was part of the 1727-1728 emigration to

---

13. On March 16, 1735/36, "At an annual Meeting held [in Falmouth] March the 16th 1735/6 Voted That Benjamin Larraby, Joseph Thornes, Robert Mitchell, Joseph Sawyer Richard Crockett and Richard Pomeroy be Field Drivers." Falmouth, Maine Town Records, Book 2, 1728-1773, p. 115 https://archive.org/details/falmouth-maine-town-records-book-2-1728-1773/page/115/mode/1up?q=Skillin&view=theater When Richard relocated back to Stratham, N.H., because of debt, he also served as field driver there. At the annual Town Meeting in Stratham on March 25, 1741/42, Richard Crockett and Nathaniel Ambreas were voted field drivers for the ensuing year. Although Richard is not noted as "junior" in this record, anyone reading the record (back then) would have understood that it was not his sixty-year-old father who was selected to chase hogs, sheep, and horses. Stratham N.H. https://www.familysearch.org/ark:/61903/3:1:3QSQ-G99K-D5B3?i=49&cc=1987741&cat=393768

14. A field driver was much like a hog reeve (and sometimes they were the same person), except that while a hog reeve was responsible for rounding up loose swine and assessing damages caused by these marauders, a field driver's duties extended to other loose animals, such as horses, sheep, and even dogs.

15. I always wondered when and how the interesting name "Robinson" entered our family lineage, knowing that in Norway my great-great-great-grandfather's full name was William Robinson Crockett. After learning who Richard of the fourth generation married, I believe the name was carried forward in memory of a beloved matriarch, Mary (Robinson) Crockett. The name is carried on in Richard and Mary's son, Captain Robinson Crockett; grandson, Robinson Crockett, Jr.; as well as their great-great grandson William Robinson Crockett.

16. CANDAGE, p. 7.

17. "Massachusetts Births and Christenings, 1639-1915," database, FamilySearch https://familysearch.org/ark:/61903/1:1:V5N4-HWY There has been much confusion over Mary Robinson's parentage. Some historians and genealogists claim that her father Abraham was a descendant of the Rev. John Robinson, pastor to the Pilgrims and organizer of the Mayflower Expedition. (See Pringle's "History of the Town and City of Gloucester, Cape Ann, Massachusetts," p. 49.) According to Dr. Carol McCoy in her genealogy of Richard Crockett, Mary was the eleventh child (of fourteen) of Abraham "Peter" Robinson: "The Robinson family was Dutch in origin and had migrated to America in the early 1600's. [Mary's] parents were born in MA. Her father, Abraham Peter Robinson was born in 1655 and her mother Experience Manter in 1677." (DESCENDANTS, p. 3.) Given Mary's connection to the York family, however, (Mary and Richard sold her rights of inheritance as a descendant of Samuel York) I feel confident that her mother was Sarah (York) Robinson and *not* Experience Manter. This would necessarily suggest that Dr. McCoy has selected the wrong Abraham Robinson for Mary's father. I am unsure whether this eliminates the connection to the Rev. John Robinson, though, not having taken my research in that direction.

18. Sarah (York) Robinson died in Gloucester on Aug. 9, 1718, at the age of 36. Massachusetts, Town and Vital Records, 1620-1988, Gloucester, Births, Marriages and Death.

19. Abraham Robinson III died in Gloucester Dec. 28, 1724, at the age of 48. Massachusetts Deaths and Burials, 1795-1910," database, FamilySearch https://familysearch.org/ark:/61903/1:1:FH1T-665

Falmouth from Gloucester. This would explain how Mary was already residing in Falmouth when she and Richard were married there.[20] (There was a John Robinson in Falmouth by 1728, however, I have been unable to determine his relationship to Mary, although it does not appear from the dates that he could have been her younger brother John.)[21]

The same month that Richard and Mary were married—August of 1731—the Skillin's granddaughter Rhoda,[22] daughter of Katharine (Skillin) and George Roberts, was baptized at the First Church of Falmouth. Soon, baby Rhoda had a playmate. Richard and Mary's first child, Mary Crockett, was born March 28, 1732 in Falmouth.[23] (Since Richard Crockett, Jr. and Katharine Skillin were first cousins, their children were first cousins once removed.) Baby Mary was baptized by the Reverend Thomas Smith of First Church[24] on August 20, 1732, [25] the same day her parents accepted the covenant of that church.[26] Accepting the covenant alongside Richard and Mary were Richard's cousins, Samuel Skillin, Jr. and Katharine (Skillin) Roberts and their spouses.[27] (Baby Josiah Skillin, son of Samuel, Jr. and his

---

20. It is possible the couple met in Stratham, N.H., Richard's hometown, where a man by the name of David Robinson was chosen as the first Town Clerk in 1716. (Town of Stratham, N.H. website, "Facts and Firsts." https://www.strathamnh.gov/historical-society/pages/facts-firsts) He appears to have been no relation to Mary, however, being from a different Robinson family altogether. (See LIBBY/NOYES, p. 591-592, John Robinson (4) and Jonathan Robinson (8).)
21. This John Robinson, whose children were baptized at the First Church of Falmouth in 1728, was too old to have been Mary's younger brother. Records from the First Church of Falmouth, p. 95. https://archive.org/details/baptismsadmissio00lcfirs/page/95/mode/1up?view=theater
22. Mary's older sister Sarah might have married the ferryman John Sawyer of Second Parish (another reason for Mary's presence there), but I have not done the necessary research on this line to confirm the relationship. The baby was named after her grandmother Rhoda (Haley) Skillin, who was Katharine Skillin's mother and Richard Crockett, Jr.'s aunt.
23. Vital Records of Falmouth. Vital Records from *The New England Historical and Genealogical Register*. Online database. AmericanAncestors.org. New England Historic Genealogical Society, 2014.
24. First Church of Falmouth, a Congregational church, was organized in Falmouth (now Portland) March 8, 1726/27. The Rev. Thomas Smith was called as the church's first pastor. "Baptisms and Admission From the Records of First Church in Falmouth, Now Portland, Maine, with Appendix of Historical Notes." Compiled by Marquis F. King, President of the Maine Genealogical Society. Portland, Maine: Maine Genealogical Society, 1898. https://archive.org/details/baptismsadmissio00lcfirs/page/n10/mode/1up?view=theater
25. "Baptisms and Admission From the Records of First Church in Falmouth, Now Portland, Maine, with Appendix of Historical Notes." Compiled by Marquis F. King, President of the Maine Genealogical Society. Portland, Maine: Maine Genealogical Society, 1898. P. 65. https://archive.org/details/baptismsadmissio00lcfirs/page/65/mode/1up?view=theater
26. The original covenant of the First Church of Falmouth, a typical Christian covenant of the time, can be found in "Baptisms and Admission From the Records of First Church in Falmouth." Accepting the covenant was necessary prior to admission to the church. https://archive.org/details/baptismsadmissio00lcfirs/page/n14/mode/1up?view=theater
27. Katharine, daughter of Samuel and Rhoda (Haley) Skillin, was married to George Roberts. Her brother Samuel Skillin, Jr. was married to Rebecca Sawyer. All three couples—Richard and his two cousins and their spouses (Richard and Mary Crockett, Katharine and George Roberts, and Samuel, Jr. and Rebecca Skillin), accepted the covenant of the First Church of Falmouth on Aug. 20, 1732. "Baptisms and Admission From the Records of First Church in Falmouth, Now Portland, Maine, with Appendix of Historical Notes." Compiled by Marquis F. King, President of the Maine Genealogical Society. Portland, Maine: Maine Genealogical Society, 1898. P. 9. https://archive.org/details/baptismsadmissio00lcfirs/page/9/mode/1up?view=theater

wife Rebecca Sawyer, was baptized August 30, 1732,[28] and so the three children—Rhoda, Mary, and Josiah—were about the same age, with Rhoda being a year older.) Mary's aunt and uncle, Mary and Benjamin York, would have been present for the occasion, as they were already members of First Church.[29] Uncle Benjamin York had been made deacon of the church in 1729.[30] Despite the population growth of the area, it was still a very small world.

Massachusetts Bay Reaches Out To Maine's Native Population

In July of 1732, a noteworthy event occurred: the Governor of Massachusetts Bay Colony, Jonathan Belcher, sailed to Falmouth from Boston with a large group of other dignitaries—"gentlemen from all parts of the country"[31]—to meet with representatives from various Wabanaki tribes. Governor Belcher took the opportunity during this time of peace to attempt to foster better relations with the Native Americans. One wonders, however, about the feelings of those former Falmouth residents such as Samuel Skillin, who had lost friends and family members during the French and Indian destruction of Falmouth in 1690 during the Second Indian War, as well as those settlers who had suffered from the depredations that occurred (on both sides) during Father Rasles' War.

The gathering must have presented a grand spectacle, with English dignitaries sailing into the harbor in man-of-war ships accompanied by dozens of canoes bearing hundreds of colorfully-clad Native Americans paddling up. An initial setback occurred on July 26th because the Indians bore French colors. The governor was insulted and refused to see them. The natives were promptly presented English colors, however, which ameliorated the situation. The two groups convened on Munjoy Hill beneath a "spacious great tent, with seats and benches."

During the meeting, complaints about English aggression were raised (by the

---

28. Rebecca, a daughter of Samuel Skillin, Jr. and Rebecca (Sawyer) Skillin, was baptized at First Church two years later in 1734.
29. Mary York was admitted as a member of the First Church of Falmouth on August 13, 1727, five months after the church was founded in March. Her husband Benjamin York was admitted to the church March 23, 1729. "Baptisms and Admission From the Records of First Church in Falmouth, Now Portland, Maine, with Appendix of Historical Notes." Compiled by Marquis F. King, President of the Maine Genealogical Society. Portland, Maine: Maine Genealogical Society, 1898. P. 7. https://archive.org/details/baptismsadmissio00lcfirs/page/7/mode/1up?view=theater
30. Benjamin York was chosen deacon Sept. 8, 1729. "Baptisms and Admission From the Records of First Church in Falmouth, Now Portland, Maine, with Appendix of Historical Notes." Compiled by Marquis F. King, President of the Maine Genealogical Society. Portland, Maine: Maine Genealogical Society, 1898. P. 7. https://archive.org/details/baptismsadmissio00lcfirs/page/7/mode/1up?view=theater
31. SMITHJOURNALS, p. 75. https://archive.org/details/journalsofrevtho00smit_0/page/75/mode/1up?view=theater

natives) and promises of reparation and friendship were made (by the English).³² Portland historian William Willis offers further insight into what must have been an extraordinary event:

> "There were one hundred of the Penobscot tribe present, represented by *Loron*,³³ their Chief and Speaker. There were also present *Toxus*, chief Sachem of the Norridgewocks;³⁴ *Adiawando*, of the Pigwackets;³⁵ *Medaganesset*, of the Ameriscoggins [Androscoggins], *Wahway* and *Wiwurna*, prominent speakers in the Conference. The Indians had their quarters on Hog Island, and the Conference was held under a large tent on Munjoy's hill. The signal for meeting was a gun from the man of war, and hoisting the King's Jack at the main top…The Indians brought presents of furs at the opening of the Conference, and at its close received English presents in return."³⁶

Before the conference ended, Governor Belcher, eager to assimilate Native Americans into English society (to further erode Wabanaki culture), urged tribal representatives to educate their children in the "English religion." The Governor even offered to provide appropriate Protestant Christian instruction for the native children. Not surprisingly, the various Indian chiefs "very cooly and politely evaded the proposition." After retiring to sleep on the offer, Penobscot Chief Loron sagaciously informed Belcher the following day:

> "Friend! We have been thinking of what your Excellency said to us, yesterday… We are too few to enter into this dispute [about religion], which is a weighty affair. There are other tribes to be discoursed with; and when we know their minds we will be better able to answer. We had the advice of the other tribes about the Peace, and therefore think it proper to have their advice in this affair."³⁷

---

32. SMITHJOURNALS, P. 75.
33. Italics in this passage were in the original text.
34. This meeting must have been especially challenging for the Norridgewock Indians, their settlement on the Kennebec having been destroyed by Captain Jeremiah Moulton and Captain Johnson Harmon in August of 1724 (only eight years prior to this meeting with the English), during which raid the French Jesuit priest Father Rasles was killed. The English continued to pursue the Norridgewocks through the balance of 1724.
35. The Pigwackets, more commonly known as the Pequawkets, resided near the headwaters of the Saco River.
36. SMITHJOURNALS, p. 76. https://archive.org/details/journalsofrevtho00smit_0/page/76/mode/1up?view=theater
37. SMITHJOURNALS, p. 76, footnote 1.

The Fourth Generation

Second Parish and a Frustrating Lack of Records

Crockett genealogist Charles Candage claims that on November 18, 1733, Richard and Mary left the First Church of Falmouth and joined the Congregational Church in Scarborough.[38] Regrettably, Candage does not cite his source. I have searched the records of the First Congregational Church in Scarborough[39] for evidence of their admission or the baptism of the Crockett children, but in vain. Rather than attend meeting in Scarborough, I think it is more likely that Richard and Mary went to meeting in Second Parish (Cape Elizabeth).

By the 18th century, English settlers in Maine, especially those who had recently immigrated from Massachusetts, were much more sophisticated than the Province's original fisherman, sailors, trappers, and traders. The Puritan religion had taken hold and was an important part of daily life. On September 18, 1733, residents of the Second Parish of Falmouth "held a meeting, at which they voted to build a meeting-house." The meeting house was built upon what is known as Meeting House Hill in (now) South Portland, the site of Mount Pleasant Cemetery. The timber for the frame of the meeting house was white oak, cut upon the spot.[40] Residents then invited the Reverend Benjamin Allen to be their minister. He accepted, and Reverend Allen was installed at the church on November 10, 1734.[41]

Portland historian Willis notes that "there are no records of [Second] parish for the first twenty years of its existence, and but imperfect ones afterward."[42] The lack of Second Parish records explains why there are no birth or baptism records for Richard and Mary Crockett's children, except for their first child, Mary, who was baptized at First Church (across the Fore River on Falmouth Neck). After Reverend Allen was established at Second Parish, the children would have been baptized by him. Allen either did not keep records or his records have been lost to vagaries of time.

---

38. CANDAGE, p. 7.
39. Church records, 1728-1859, First Church in Scarborough, Me. Congregational Library & Archives. New England's Hidden Histories. https://congregationallibrary.quartexcollections.com/Documents/Detail/church-records-1728-1859-first-church-in-scarborough-me./60215?item=60230
40. WILLIS, p. 383.
41. WILLIS, p. 382.
42. WILLIS, p. 385.

Purpooduck Meeting House in Second Parish.
(Image courtesy of the South Portland Historical Society.)

Falmouth birth records for Richard and Mary's children might also be non-extant because around 1737 or 1738 (we do not know exactly when), Richard and his family returned to Stratham, N.H. to live. (Richard was fleeing his creditors.) Some of Richard and Mary's children must have been born in Stratham, but I have been unable to locate birth records for them there, either.

Richard, Jr. and Mary (Robinson) Crockett had at least nine (possibly ten) children: Mary, Richard (III, also known as Richard, Jr.), Joshua, Sarah, Hannah, Daniel, George, Robinson, Josiah, and possibly Joseph. Please refer to the "Genealogical Dictionary of Thomas and Ann Crockett" beginning on page 377 for more information about Richard and Mary's children. (Richard Crockett III's life will be covered in the next chapter.)

We do not know exactly where in Falmouth Richard and Mary—and their growing family—initially resided. A search of the land records at the York County[43] Registry of Deeds from 1728-1750 yielded no real estate purchases for Richard. Although the land records are not complete, it seems probable that had Richard, who was regularly in debt, owned any real estate, his creditors would have forced a sale of some of his land to provide them with satisfaction. The lack of such evidence suggests Richard and his young family either lived with a relative in Second Parish or on land owned by a friend or relative.

On June 4, 1734, Richard Crockett witnessed a deed for John Sawyer[44] (the

---

43. Cumberland County in Maine was not established until 1760. Until that time, Falmouth (and the settlements that made up what was then Falmouth) was part of York County, the only county then in existence in Maine.
44. John Sawyer was the father of Rebecca Sawyer, who married Samuel Skillin, Jr.

ferryman and possibly Mary's brother-in-law) and Benjamin York (Mary's uncle). The two men sold a tract of meadow in Scarborough to Robert Brooks.[45] Richard's presence as witness reveals that he remained physically close to the York and Sawyer families, corroborating my theory that he and his family lived in Second Parish, as did the York, Sawyer, and Skillin families.[46] On October 29th of that same year, Benjamin York of Falmouth sold to Phineas Jones 154 acres on the Fore River in Falmouth, buying from Jones on the same day 17/20th of 100 acres of land in Falmouth.[47] (Jones, described in this deed as a "yeoman," was also a surveyor who traded in real estate and a shopkeeper. Benjamin York is described in the two deeds as a "husbandman" and a "gentleman.")[48] That the families who settled around Long Creek in Second Parish were intertwined can be seen by the fact that on December 23, 1736, Richard's cousin Joanna Skillin (daughter of Samuel and Rhoda Skillin), married Samuel York, Benjamin York's son.[49]

A Slide Into Debt and Wolves at the Door

On September 17, 1734, Richard Crockett, Jr. signed a promissory note to Captain Samuel Jordan, gentleman, of Biddeford, for 24 pounds, 17 shillings upon demand,

---

45. MEWD, Vol. 17, p. 571.
46. Uncle Samuel Skillin (and his extended family) lived at what was known as Long Creek in Purpooduck (Second Parish), where he had grist and saw mills. On March 26, 1734, at a Town Meeting held at the meetinghouse in Falmouth, Lieutenant Skillins was voted one of three surveyors of the highways on the Purpooduck side of the Fore River Falmouth. Also, at that same meeting, residents voted to accept the location of a road laid out from Long Creek to the County Road at Purpooduck, viz: "To begin at a white oak tree about ten Rods to the southward of George Roberts House marked W, from thence East Northerly to a Hemlock tree marked W: from thence East south East to a Beech tree standing by the Road which leads from the Grist Mill To Black Point [Scarborough] thence as the Road goes to Stephen Randles barn from thence East and be South to the place agreed on for setting the Meeting house, from thence East and North to the County Road which leads to Spurwink [Falmouth Neck]." Falmouth, Maine Town Records, Book 2, 1728-1773, p. 109. https://archive.org/details/falmouth-maine-town-records-book-2-1728-1773/page/109/mode/1up?q=Skillin&view=theater George Roberts, who was married to Samuel's daughter Katharine Skillin, was the future father-in-law of Richard and Mary's son, Richard Crockett, III.
47. The 100 acres that Benjamin York purchased from Jones was "formerly belonging to Lewis Tucker, where he lived many years between the First and Second Indian Wars."
48. YCROD, Vol. 17, p. 39 and Vol. 2, p. 463. Phineas Jones also served as a representative from Falmouth to the Massachusetts General Court, selected after some initial "trials" (i.e. difficulty in choosing a representative) in 1739. "At a Legall Town Meeting held at the Meeting house in the First Parrish in Falmouth May the Twenty Fourth 1739. The Selectmen being present they opened the Meeting and desired the votes to be brought in for a Representative which was done and after Sundry Tryalls there could be no choice then the Meeting was adjourned for an hour. The Town, being mett according to adjournment and Sundry Tryalls more there could be no choice made Then the Meeting was adjourned till to morrow morning at Ten of the Clock . The Town being mett according to adjournment. Then Mr. Phinehas Jones was made choice of to represent the Town in the Great and General Court this present Year." Falmouth, Maine Town Records, Book 2, p. 131 https://archive.org/details/falmouth-maine-town-records-book-2-1728-1773/page/131/mode/1up?q=Skillin&view=theater In a later Town Meeting, Sept. 17, 1739, Jones, as representative to the General Court, was tasked with getting a fort built "for the defense of that part of the Eastern Country." See p. 134.
49. STACKPOLE, p. 731.

"for value received this day."⁵⁰ (The note was probably to cover goods purchased from Jordan, who was a trader and shopkeeper.) Captain Jordan, then about fifty years of age, was a prominent resident of Maine and a man of some distinction. He ran a general store out of his old garrison house in Biddeford, where he "had a large trade in general merchandise with the neighboring settlers, the location being most accessible by boat from all points."⁵¹ Samuel Jordan's father, Dominicus Jordan, was killed by Native Americans during the Second Indian War (King William's War). During the attack, young Samuel, his mother, and four siblings, were all carried off to Canada by the French and Indians. (All but one of the captives, a sister who married a Frenchman and remained in Canada, were eventually returned to Maine.) Over the ensuing years, Richard made a few sporadic attempts to repay his debt to Jordan, paying a total of five pounds toward the 24 pounds, 17 shillings. But he failed to pay the balance due and eventually Captain Jordan took legal action.⁵² The early debt with Captain Jordan was the beginning of Richard's slide into insolvency.

In 1735, wolves presented such a problem to the agrarian life of the citizens of Falmouth that at Town Meeting in March it was voted to pay the princely sum of 10 pounds for every head of a mature wolf⁵³ or 3 pounds for every wolf's welp ("other than such as shall be taken out of the belly of any Bitch wolf").⁵⁴ Had he been a great hunter, Richard could have cleared his debt to Captain Jordan by killing a couple of wolves. The selectmen paid a man named Buxton 30 pounds for killing wolves in 1735. To facilitate payment, rather than track down selectmen, the wolf killers nailed the heads of their trophies to the outer wall of the meetinghouse, a

---

50. At the time, promissory notes or notes of hand were often written for twice the amount of money borrowed, no doubt as an inducement for the borrower to repay the debt. When these notes ended up in sympathetic courts, judgment was often only for the actual amount borrowed, plus interest, not the amount on the promissory note. In Richard's case, however, because the court (later) ordered Richard to repay the balance due, it appears that the promissory note to Captain Jordan was for the actual amount borrowed, suggesting the money was for goods purchased from the trader rather than money borrowed.
51. "Goldthwaite genealogy: descendants of Thomas Goldthwaite, an early settler of Salem, Mass., with some account of the Goldthwaite Family in England." Goldthwaite, Charlotte. Hartford: Hartford Press, 1899. P. 127-128. https://archive.org/details/goldthwaitegenea00gold/page/127/mode/1up?view=theater
52. Colonial Records of NH, 1638-1772. Case File No. 21040.
53. According to Cape Elizabeth historian Marian Peabbles Johnson, the wolf heads were nailed to the church. "Any person who killed a wolf brought the head to the meeting-house and nailed it to the outer wall; the fierce looking head and splotches of blood made a grim and horrible decoration. The early settlers could spare little time for traveling to assemble except to church and so it was here that they brought their trophies for which they received a bounty." "A History of Cape Elizabeth, Maine. Submitted by Marian Peabbles Johnson in Partial Fulfillment of Requirements for the Degree of Master of Education, 1954." Boston University School of Education Library. See p. 83. Via the University of Maine, DigitalCommons@UMaine. https://digitalcommons.library.umaine.edu/cgi/viewcontent.cgi?article=1172&context=mainehistory
54. Falmouth, Maine Town Records, Book 2, 1728-1773, p. 112. https://archive.org/details/falmouth-maine-town-records-book-2-1728-1773/page/112/mode/1up?q=Skillin&view=theater

"grim and horrible decoration." (Three wildcats were also killed in Falmouth that year, each earning their slayer 1 pound per predator.)[55]

A predator of a different sort was also on the loose in Falmouth in 1735—innkeeper James Noble, whose questionable practices earned him the ire of Second Parish residents, including the Sawyers. According to six citizens who signed a complaint against the innkeeper in 1739, Noble took financial advantage of some of the customers at his tavern after getting them intoxicated. (See copy of complaint, page 159.) Although the complainants do not name the unfortunates who were taken advantage of, the document might have been describing Richard Crockett, Jr., who, on December 15, 1735, signed a bond to Noble for the considerable amount of 53 pounds.[56] The complaint against Noble reads:

> "May it please your honor we beg leave humbly to inform your honor that James Noble by keeping tavern and taking advantage of sundry of his neighbors[57] when in drink have ruined them and [their] families as to their present outward circumstances and still goes on in the same tract entertaining his neighbors with drink to excess, from hour to hour, day to day, nay even from week to week so that unless some step is put to such his unlawful proceedings we are afraid that many of those who now support themselves & families will in a short time be a public charge to the town therefore [we] humbly pray your honor in your wisdom would prevent any such proceedings for the future – and we as ever in duty bound shall pray [signed] Mary Jordan (her mark), George Welch, John Sawyer, Jacob Sawyer, Jeremiah Jordan, and Robert Jordan. Falmouth, June 26th, 1739."[58]

In January of 1740, Isaac Parker charged innkeeper James Noble with forging a deed. The petition from the concerned citizens (written the prior year) was included with the paperwork for the case Parker brought against Noble, likely as a testament to the innkeeper's character (or lack thereof). A warrant was issued for

---

55. Falmouth, Maine Town Records, Book 2, 1728-1773, p. 156 https://archive.org/details/falmouth-maine-town-records-book-2-1728-1773/page/156/mode/1up?q=Skillin&view=theater
56. Colonial Records of NH, 1638-1772. Case File No. 10821.
57. The petition could also be describing John Jordan, Jr., who sold off part of his home farm to James Noble in several installments. Although in his deeds Jordan says the sale of the tracts of land is for consideration of money in hand, it could possibly have been to pay his debts to Noble. See for example, YCROD, Book 21, Pages 33 & 34 (two separate deeds, and there are others). It would certainly make sense that Jordan's relations were worried about his sales of real estate to Noble, especially if agreed to while Jordan, Jr. was intoxicated and/or the sale was to pay a large liquor bill.
58. York County, Maine, Court of General Sessions of the Peace case files, Box 85. Apr 1740 term. Accessed via FamilySearch https://www.familysearch.org/ark:/61903/3:1:3QS7-L93N-Z6P5?i=400&cat=1923498

Noble to appear before the Court of General Sessions of the Peace, held in York on the first Tuesday of April 1740, to answer the forgery charge.

Noble's answer to the Court was that he had not forged the deed, rather he had found the instrument amongst some papers in the house of the late Dr. Allen, whose property he had purchased. Noble said he had simply forwarded the deed along to be recorded, "not knowing who claims the Lands in Said Deed mentioned."[59] The Court was still skeptical, however, and the case was eventually sent on to the Massachusetts Superior Court of Judicature. There, at the June 1740 term, the verdict was decided as "Ignoramus"[60] (i.e. the Court did not know why Noble should be indicted on the charges, likely accepting his excuse that he only forwarded the deed he discovered and did not forge it). The case against Noble disappeared, and the innkeeper remained in Falmouth, no doubt to the detriment of many other young men like Richard Crockett, Jr.

---

59. York County, Maine, Court of General Sessions of the Peace case files, Box 85. Apr 1740 term. https://www.familysearch.org/ark:/61903/3:1:3QS7-L93N-Z6P5?i=400&cat=1923498
60. Superior Court of Judicature records, Suffolk County, Massachusetts, 1738-1740. Film #007943514, image #337.

> To the Honorable the Justices of His Majesty's General Sessions of the peace to be held at York within and for the County of York in July next.
>
> May it please your Honors, We begg leave humbly to informe your honors that James Noble by keeping tavern and taking the advantage of sundry of his neighbours when in Drink have ruined them and familys as to their present outward Circumstances and still goes on in the same tract Entertaining his Neighbours with Drink to excess from hour to hour from day to day nay Even from week to Week so that unless Some Stop is put to such his unlawfull proceedings we are afraid that many of those who now support themselves & familys will in a short time become a publick Charge to the Town therefore Humbly pray that yettones in your wisdome would prevent any such proceedings for the future and we shall as in Duty bound ever pray ———
>
> Falmouth June 26th 1739 — George Veach
>
> John Sayer
> Jacob Singer
> Jeremiah Jordan
> ...

Complaint against James Noble, innkeeper of Falmouth, June 26, 1739. (York County, Maine, Court of General Sessions of the Peace case files, Box 85. April 1740 term.)[61]

---

61. Accessed via FamilySearch https://www.familysearch.org/ark:/61903/3:1:3QS7-L93N-Z6P5?i=400&cat=1923498

Death Comes Calling

In 1736, a "terrible distemper" was visited upon Falmouth, which "swept away such multitudes of the children and younger people, and which since it has come into the houses of this town has become greatly mortal."[62] The epidemic, a "throat distemper" (probably diphtheria), which particularly affected children and young adults, had begun to circulate the prior year in New Hampshire (where the disease killed 1% of the population) and gradually spread to Massachusetts, Maine, and Connecticut.[63] On June 16, 1736, during the Maine outbreak, the First Church of Falmouth marked a day of fasting and prayer, at which "a very few women were absent."[64] On September 14, 1736, the First Church of Scarborough adjourned their regular meeting until October 20th noting it was "a time of great Calamity and distress with us by reason of the Epide-pical [sic] mortal Sickness among us."[65] Twenty-six people died just in Purpooduck (Second) Parish,[66] including five members of the Reverend Benjamin Allen's family.[67]

Richard and Mary did not escape the pain of loss. On September 13th Mary purchased four yards of silk crape at the shop of Phineas Jones in Falmouth, probably to sew herself a mourning dress. (Crape, which was black, was worn by women in mourning.) This material was unlike the other yard good purchases charged to Richard's account the prior year, which consisted of everyday broadcloth and calamanco.[68] The crape purchase was even more unusual in that Mary bought it

---

62. "Baptisms and Admission From the Records of First Church in Falmouth, Now Portland, Maine, with Appendix of Historical Notes." Compiled by Marquis F. King, President of the Maine Genealogical Society. Portland, Maine: Maine Genealogical Society, 1898. P. 9. https://archive.org/details/baptismsadmissio00lcfirs/page/9/mode/1up?view=theater
63. "Great Sorrows, the Deadly 'Throat Distemper' of 1735." Historic Ipswich website. https://historicipswich.net/2021/02/05/the-deadly-throat-distemper-of-1736/#:~:text=The%20epidemic%20spread%20south%20through,under%20the%20age%20of%20ten.
64. "Baptisms and Admission From the Records of First Church in Falmouth, Now Portland, Maine, with Appendix of Historical Notes." Compiled by Marquis F. King, President of the Maine Genealogical Society. Portland, Maine: Maine Genealogical Society, 1898. P. 9. https://archive.org/details/baptismsadmissio00lcfirs/page/9/mode/1up?view=theater
65. SMITHJOURNALS.
66. "A History of Cape Elizabeth, Maine. Submitted by Marian Peabbles Johnson in Partial Fulfillment of Requirements for the Degree of Master of Education, 1954." Boston University School of Education Library. See p. 91. Via the University of Maine, DigitalCommons@UMaine. https://digitalcommons.library.umaine.edu/cgi/viewcontent.cgi?article=1172&context=mainehistory
67. WILLIS, p. 383 in his footnote says that this loss of five members of Rev. Allen's family occurred in September of 1738; however, given his tendency to make mistakes, this is almost certainly a reference to the deadly throat distemper that occurred September 1736.
68. Calamanco was "... a thin fabric of worsted wool yarn which could come in a number of weaves: plain, satin, damasked, and was even brocaded in floral, striped and checked designs ... calamanco's heyday was from the end of the 17th century to the end of the 18th century. It was a popular fabric for women's gowns and petticoats and men's waistcoats..." The DreamStress website. ""Terminology: What is calamanco?" 18th Century, Textiles & Costume. https://thedreamstress.com/2012/02/terminology-what-is-calamanco/

herself. In the twelve months prior, Richard had made all the purchases at Jones' shop (except the items bought by his brother Samuel, previously mentioned). Although we do not know if Richard and Mary lost a child (because we do not have a good list of their family or deaths in Second Parish), we learn from this purchase that someone beloved by them perished during the epidemic. (See Richard Crockett's 1735-1736 account at Phineas Jones' shop on the following page.)[69]

---

69. In addition to this unknown death in 1736, Mary lost a young cousin, Samuel York, who died in Ipswich, Massachusetts of the "throat distemper" on Nov. 27, 1735. Samuel was the son of Samuel and Mary (Dutch) York of Ipswich, Mary (Robinson) Crockett's aunt and uncle. Website, Historic Ipswich. "Great Sorrows, the Deadly 'Throat Distemper' of 1735." https://historicipswich.net/2021/02/05/the-deadly-throat-distemper-of-1736/#:~:text=The%20epidemic%20spread%20south%20through,under%20the%20age%20of%20ten

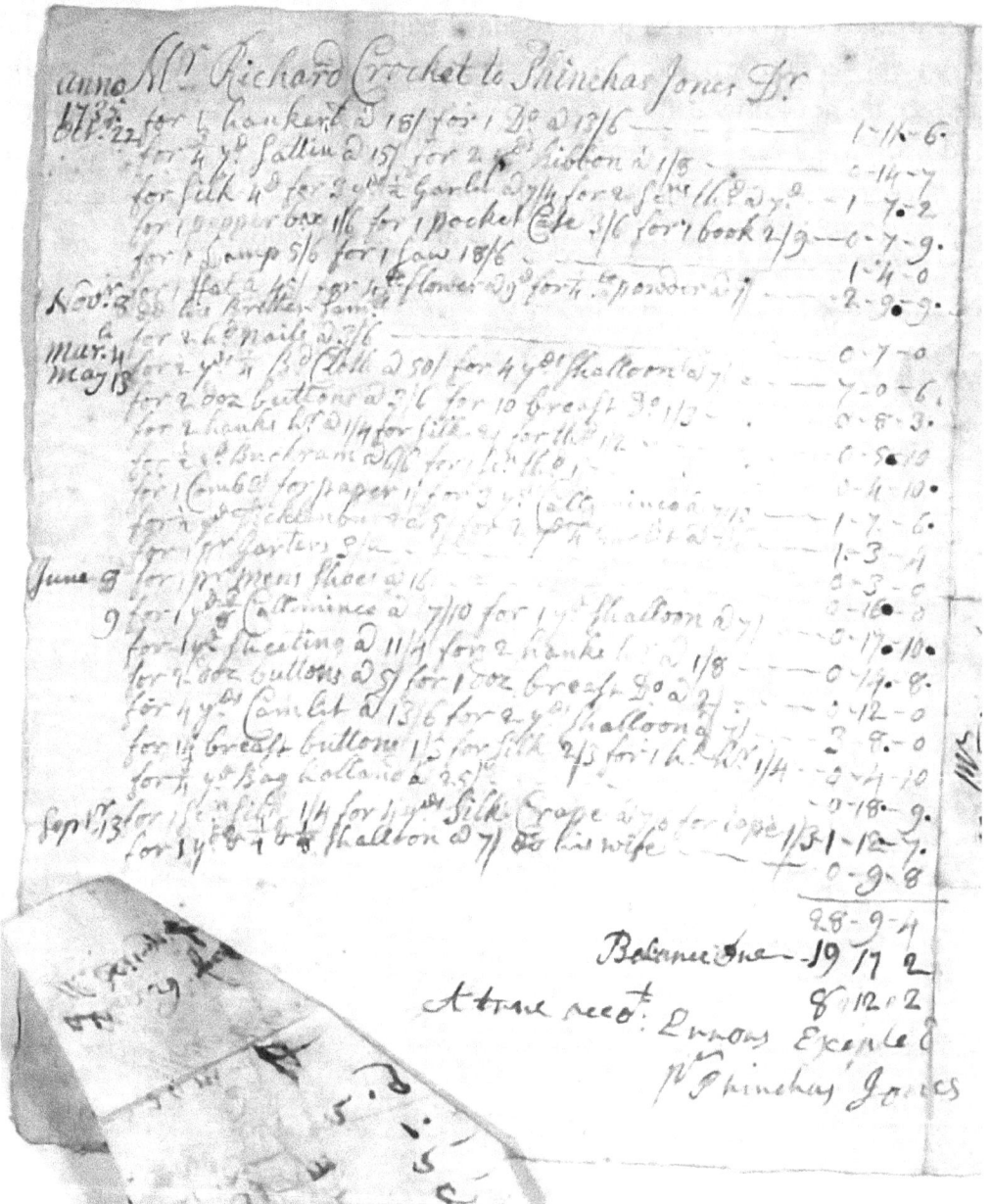

1735-1736 account of Richard Crockett, Jr. at the shop of Phineas Jones.
The September 13, 1736 entry (last entry before the total at bottom) shows a purchase by "his wife" of 4 yards silk crape, among other items.
(Colonial Records of N.H., 1638-1772. Court records. Case File No. 21052. Phineas Jones v. Richard Crockett, Jr.)[70]

---

70. Jones' account for Richard Crockett, Jr. was included with other documentation for his suit against Crockett heard before the Inferior Court of Common Pleas at Portsmouth, N.H. on Dec. 4, 1740.

The Fourth Generation

A Frustrated Shopkeeper

Mary's purchase was the last recorded for Richard Crockett, Jr. in Phineas Jones' account book for the 1735-1736 year, which had begun the prior October. The total charged to Richard from October 22, 1735 to September 13, 1736, was 28 pounds, 9 shillings and 4 pence. On April 29th, Samuel had made a payment of 8 pounds, 1 shilling and 3 pence (more than covering the 2 shillings, 9 pounds and 9 pence he charged for his hat and other items the prior November) and some buttons had been returned for a small credit. But Richard had not paid anything toward alleviating his debt, leaving him with a balance due at Phineas Jones' shop of 19 pounds, 17 shillings and 2 pence. On April 4, 1737, Jones finally accosted Richard about his debt, and the chairmaker promised to pay.[71]

Whether Richard's chairmaking business did not provide enough income for his family's lifestyle or whether he was spending too much time and money imbibing at James Noble's tavern, we cannot know. But by 1737, Richard's financial condition was dire. He was in debt a total of 92 pounds, 14 shillings, and 2 pence[72] to the following men:

Captain Samuel Jordan – 19 pounds, 17 shillings
James Noble, innkeeper – 53 pounds
Phineas Jones, shopkeeper – 19 pounds, 17 shillings, 2 pence

The Return to New Hampshire and Richard's Brothers Come to His Rescue

Sometime after April of 1737, Richard and his family left Falmouth and returned to Stratham, N.H. Richard was probably fleeing from his debt (and perhaps the temptations of alcohol provided by innkeeper Noble). He returned to the town of his youth, likely to his father's house. While in New Hampshire, Richard, Jr. worked as a joiner, rather than as a chairmaker.

Although Richard returned to Stratham, his younger brother Samuel remained in Maine, and continued in the chairmaking business. On March 10, 1738, marriage

---

71. Colonial Records of NH, 1638-1772. Case File No. 21052, Phineas Jones v. Richard Crockett, Jr.
72. Colonial English used the same monetary system as did Great Britain, where 1 pound = 20 shillings; 1 shilling = 12 pennies or pence. Hopefully, I have calculated correctly to net the total of Richard's debt to the three men.

intentions were published in Falmouth between Samuel Crockett and Sarah Cobb, daughter of Jonathan Cobb, formerly of Middleboro, Massachusetts, but lately of Falmouth.[73] In 1740, Samuel and Sarah Crocker [sic] accepted the covenant of the First Church of Falmouth.[74] Their daughter Sarah was baptized at First Church that same year.[75]

On August 25, 1740, "Samuel Crockit, chairmaker of Falmouth," purchased for 130 pounds old tenor 30 acres in Falmouth (half of a 60-acre proprietor's lot) from Phineas Jones and Jones' brother Stephen, and Jonathan Wait.[76] (If we compare the 130 pounds Samuel spent for 30 acres of land to Richard's debt of 92+ pounds, we can see the burden of the elder brother's financial situation.) Despite Richard's issues with these three men (all three—Phineas and Stephen Jones and Jonathan Wait—were or would become Richard's creditors), Samuel Crockett appears to have been well-regarded by them and not considered a financial risk.

On February 16, 1740 (or prior to this date), something critical happened that forced Richard, Jr. to sign (at Portsmouth) promissory notes and a bond for nearly 50 pounds. To accomplish this, Richard recruited his younger brothers William and Samuel to cosign with him. Falmouth shopkeepers Phineas and Stephen Jones[77] happened to be in Portsmouth on that day and, although Richard already owed Phineas over 19 pounds on account, the shopkeeper lent Samuel 30 shillings on his brother's behalf, accepting a promissory note (signed by both Richard and Samuel) for six pounds plus interest "for value given"[78] due February 16th "next" (i.e. in

---

73. CANDAGE, p. 7.
74. "Baptisms and Admission From the Records of First Church in Falmouth, Now Portland, Maine, with Appendix of Historical Notes. Compiled by Marquis F. King, President of the Maine Genealogical Society. Portland, Maine: Maine Genealogical Society, 1898." P. 11. https://archive.org/details/baptismsadmissio00lcfirs/page/11/mode/1up?view=theater
75. "Baptisms and Admission From the Records of First Church in Falmouth, Now Portland, Maine, with Appendix of Historical Notes. Compiled by Marquis F. King, President of the Maine Genealogical Society. Portland, Maine: Maine Genealogical Society, 1898." P. 65. https://archive.org/details/baptismsadmissio00lcfirs/page/65/mode/1up?view=theater
76. YCROD, Vol. 28, p. 3. Phineas and Stephen Jones, in addition to being shopkeepers, were also land speculators, who "speculated largely in purchasing the titles of ancient settlers…" In 1738, Phineas purchased for 484 pounds a four-acre tract of land on Falmouth Neck and proceeded to develop this tract, selling off small lots until his early death (at age thirty-eight) in 1743. WILLIS, p. 316.
77. Stephen Jones was also a surveyor who worked for the proprietors of Falmouth Township. "Copy of the Original Records of the Proprietors of Falmouth [Maine] for the years 1718 to 1826." Three volumes in one. Portland: Copied by F.A. Gerrish, 1861. See p. 22. https://archive.org/details/proprietors00falmouth_202105/page/n67/mode/1up?view=theater
78. Promissory notes were often written for more than the amount of money borrowed by the debtor, likely as an inducement to pay. The Colonial Courts appear to have sagaciously awarded judgments in the amount of the sum borrowed, plus interest, however, as can be seen in the judgments in the cases of both Phineas Jones and Stephen Jones v. Richard Crockett, Jr. At the N.H. Court of Common Pleas June 9, 1743, Phineas Jones recovered judgment against Richard Crockett, Jr., joiner of Stratham, 30 shillings principle in damages, and 4 shillings interest. At the same court, Stephen Jones recovered judgment against Richard for 1 pound, 2 shillings and 11 pence damages, and 2 shillings and 11 pence interest. (Richard was also charged with court fees on both cases.) N.H. Court Records, Court of Common Pleas records 1734-1745.

The Fourth Generation

one year, in 1741. See page 171 for a copy of Richard and Samuel's promissory note to Phineas Jones.)[79] Stephen Jones, perhaps not having the experience with Richard that his brother Phineas had, personally took a promissory note from Richard Crockett, Jr. for four pounds, ten shillings, "for value given." In addition, Portsmouth attorney Matthew Livermore accepted a bond for 39 pounds from Richard Crockett Jr., joiner of Stratham, and William "Crocket," husbandman of Exeter, in exchange for 39 pounds bills of credit[80] of the Province of New Hampshire. The bond was payable upon demand.[81]

What was all this money for?

An educated guess would be that Richard wanted the money to pay his dubious 53-pound debt to the scallywag Noble, who (in legal trouble himself at the time) was probably pressing Richard hard to pay his debt. By August of 1740, James Noble had taken his promissory note from Richard to a magistrate in Portsmouth and a writ of execution was issued against Crockett on August 16th. The sheriff (or one of his deputies) was commanded to "attach the goods or estate of Richard Crockett Jr. of Stratham, within the Province of New Hampshire, chair-maker, alias Dick or Richard Crockett of Falmouth in the County of York in New England, chair-maker, to the value of 106 pounds," and to leave a summons for the next Court of Common Pleas to be held at Portsmouth in September 1740. On August 19, 1740, Deputy Sheriff James Marston served the writ of execution, scribbling on the back of the writ: "then attached a Chair of the Def. [defendant] value three shillings. I left a summons at his xxxxxxxxx[82] Dwelling house."[83] Records from the September 1740 Court of Common Pleas held at Portsmouth[84] reveal no information on the case—nor was there any further action from Noble—so it is probable that Crockett's debt to Noble was satisfied, probably with the money and bills of credit Richard and his brothers borrowed on February 16th.

Not long after Richard's debt to Noble went away, both Phineas Jones and

---

79. Colonial Records of N.H., 1638-1772. Case File No. 28168, Phineas Jones v. Richard Crockett, Jr.
80. "Bills of credit were notes issued by provincial governments that were similar in many ways to modern paper money: they were issued in convenient denominations, were often a legal tender in the payment of debts, and routinely passed from man to man in transactions." "Money in the American Colonies." Ron Micheneur, University of Virginia. EH.net https://eh.net/encyclopedia/money-in-the-american-colonies/
81. Colonial Records of N.H., 1638-1772. Case File No. 8778, Matthew Livermore v. Richard Crockett, Jr. and William Crockett.
82. While writing up his record on the back of the writ, Deputy Sheriff Marston appears to have crossed out Richard's name ("Richard Jr.'s") prior to the words "Dwelling house," which suggests that the house at which Richard resided did not belong to him. This adds some corroboration to my suspicion that Richard, Jr. and his family were back living with his father.
83. Colonial Records of NH, 1638-1772. Case File No. 10821, James Noble v. Richard Crockett, Jr.
84. N.H. Court Records, Court of Common Pleas records 1734-1745. September 1740.

Captain Samuel Jordan, perhaps learning of Noble's satisfaction, sought payment for what Crockett owed them. On September 24, 1740, two writs of execution were issued at Portsmouth against Richard Crockett, Jr., chairmaker of Stratham. In one, the Sheriff was ordered to attach the goods or estate of Richard Crockett to the value of 38 pounds (for Richard's unpaid account at the shop of Phineas Jones, his personal debt to Jones not having come due yet),[85] and in the other case the value was for 36 pounds (for Captain Jordan).[86] On October 11, 1740, Fitzwilliam Sargeant, Deputy Sheriff of New Hampshire, "…Tuck [took] the Body of the Def. [the defendant, Richard, Jr.] and Tuck William Crockett bail"[87] money for both cases. The summons included in the two writs was for Richard to appear at the next Court of Common Pleas held in Portsmouth. On December 4, 1740, both cases—Jones' and Jordan's—against Richard Crockett, Jr. were heard at the Court of Common Pleas.[88] Richard, the defendant, did not appear at court in Portsmouth[89] (not unusual in debt cases) and the judgements defaulted to the plaintiffs. Phineas Jones was awarded 19 pounds, 17 shillings and 2 pence damages. (Court costs in the amount of 2 pounds 9 shillings were also assessed against Richard Crockett, Jr.) Jordan won a judgment against Richard for 19 pounds and 17 shillings damages. (Costs in Jordan's case were 2 pounds, 7 shillings.)[90]

---

85. Colonial Records of N.H., 1638-1772. Case File No. 21052, Phineas Jones v. Richard Crockett, Jr.
86. Colonial Records of N.H., 1638-1772. Case File No. 21040, Samuel Jordan v. Richard Crockett, Jr.
87. This was written on the back on the writ of execution, which was included with the court papers. I am not sure whether "Tuck William Crockett bail" meant that William paid up so he did not go to jail or that the bail money was used to liberate his brother Richard (the actual debtor).
88. N.H. Court Records, Court of Common Pleas records 1734-1745. December 4, 1740.
89. Richard Crockett, Jr. "being called 3 times – appearing not …" was the language from the court records in both cases.
90. In neither case was interest added to the balance due to the creditors, adding more weight to the possibility that the debt to Captain Jordan was for good purchased at his store, as was the case with Richard's debt to Phineas Jones.

Records from the Inferior Court of Common Pleas held at Portsmouth, N.H. December 4, 1740. On this date the cases of Samuel Jordan v. Richard Crockett, Jr. and Phineas Jones v. Richard Crockett, Jr. were both heard (right hand page, middle). "The Defendant three times called appeared not" and judgment was for the plaintiffs in both cases.
(N.H. Court of Common Pleas records, 1734-1745. December 1740.)[91]

---

91. This record, and many others that were locked online, the author viewed at the FamilySearch Center operated by the Church of Jesus Christ of Latter-Day Saints, 639 Grandview Avenue, Bangor, Maine. My thanks to Laura Hurst and her husband for their kind assistance over my many weeks of research.

More Debt ... and Father to the Rescue

Two new executions were issued for the sums due to Phineas Jones and Captain Jordan, and Richard was either to satisfy the debts or appear before the Court of Common Pleas in June of 1741. Once again, Richard appears to have borrowed from St. Peter to pay St. Paul, as the saying goes. On May 12, 1741, Richard borrowed money from Nicholas Perryman, gentleman from Exeter, giving him a note of hand in which he promised to pay 56 shillings (2 pounds, 16 shillings) before July 1st.[92] On May 28th, Richard paid 10 pounds, 19 shillings as partial payment against his judgment to Captain Jordan, and agreed to pay the remainder 11 pounds, 7 shillings to the creditor's attorney, Matthew Livermore. The attorney signed off on November 5, 1741, signifying that Livermore had received full satisfaction for Crockett's debt to Jordan.[93] On June 4, 1741, Livermore, who was also attorney for Phineas Jones, signed an acknowledgement that he had received full satisfaction from Richard Crockett for the 19 pounds, 17 shillings, and 2 pence due Jones.[94]

Richard, having paid off what he owed shady innkeeper James Noble, as well as to shopkeepers Phineas Jones and Captain Samuel Jordan, was still left with the smaller debts to Jones and his brother Stephen; a large debt to the attorney Matthew Livermore; and the new debt to Nicholas Perryman of Exeter. Probably to help pay some of these debts, Richard, on March 17, 1742, borrowed money from Samuel Duely, husbandman of Newmarket, N.H. Richard promised to pay Duely 11 pounds in money or bills of credit on or before "the first day of November next" (November 1, 1743).[95] Needless to say, Richard did not pay this new debt (initially).[96] From the summer of 1740 through December 1744, deputy sheriffs of

---

92. Colonial Records of N.H., 1638-1772. Case File No. 25054, Nicholas Perryman v. Richard Crockett, Jr. On Nov. 9, 1741, a writ of execution of was issued for Richard Crockett, Jr. of Stratham, joiner, to the value of 5 pounds on behalf of creditor Nicholas Perryman of Exeter, gentleman. On November 13, 1741, Deputy Sheriff John Folson attached a chair belonging to Richard Crockett, Jr. to the value of 3 shillings and left a summons for him to appear before the Court of Common Pleas at Portsmouth on "the first Thursday next following the first Tuesday in December" 1741. Colonial Records of N.H., 1638-1772. Case File No. 25054, Nicholas Perryman v. Richard Crockett, Jr. Because this case was not heard at the December 1741 Court of Common Pleas—and yet Perryman had another case that *was* heard then—this debt must have been satisfied (or arrangements made to satisfy it) prior to court. N.H. Court Records, Court of Common Pleas records, 1734-1745. December 1741.
93. Colonial Records of N.H., 1638-1772. Case File No. 20140, Samuel Jordan v. Richard Crockett, Jr.
94. Colonial Records of N.H., 1638-1772. Case File No. 21052, Phineas Jones v. Richard Crockett, Jr.
95. Colonial Records of N.H., 1638-1772. Case File No. 16501, Samuel Duely v. Richard Crockett, Jr.
96. On November 15, 1742 a writ of execution was issued for Richard Crockett (the "jr." was inadvertently left off) of Stratham, N.H., joiner, to the value of 22 pounds old tenor on behalf of creditor Samuel Duely of Newmarket, husbandman. On November 22nd Deputy Sheriff Benjamin Bitman attached a hat of Richard's (he must have had a lot of hats!) to the value of three shillings and left a summons with him to appear before the Court of Common Pleas at Portsmouth "the first Thursday next following the first Tuesday in December" 1742. Colonial Records of N.H., 1638-1772. Case File No. 16501,

New Hampshire were kept busy traveling to Stratham from Portsmouth (and back) with writs of execution (and summonses) for Richard Crockett, Jr. from his various creditors.[97]

On February 28, 1745, Richard's father, Richard Crockett, yeoman of Stratham, sold to Benjamin Jewett, a tanner also from Stratham, four acres of his land in that town for 60 pounds, paid in bills of credit.[98] Given the dates that Richard, Jr.'s creditors acknowledged satisfaction, Richard, Sr. must have utilized the 60 pounds from the land sale to discharge his son's debts. On March 25, 1745, less than a month after Richard, Sr. sold the property to Jewett, Matthew Livermore, attorney to Richard, Jr.'s creditor Stephen Jones, signed off on the last writ of execution issued from Portsmouth against the younger Crockett, signifying that all but 3 shillings of the court costs were paid on that debt.[99]

Brother Samuel Builds a Successful Life in Falmouth

While Richard was living in Stratham, trying to evade creditors, younger brother Samuel made a life for himself and his family back in Falmouth. Samuel and Sarah Crockett's second daughter, "Betty" (Elizabeth), was baptized at the First Church of Falmouth in 1741,[100] followed by daughter Susanna in 1743.[101] Samuel initially

---

Samuel Duely v. Richard Crockett, Jr. No further information is available on this case, which did not appear in the records of the Court of Common Pleas in either December 1742 or March 1743, so one assumes the debt was satisfied. N.H. Court Records, Court of Common Pleas records, 1734-1745. December 1742 and March 1743.
97. Matthew Livermore, the attorney for Phineas and Stephen Jones, was also a creditor of Richard Crockett, Jr.'s, having lent him and William 39 pounds in bills of credit on February 16, 1740. On May 11, 1742, a writ of execution was issued against Richard Crockett, Jr. of Stratham, "joyner," and William Crockett of Exeter, husbandman, ordering the Sheriff to attach the goods or estate of either of them on behalf of creditor Livermore. On May 15th Deputy Sheriff Fitzwilliam Sargent attached a hat of Richard's to the value of 5 shillings and left a summons in Stratham for him and William to appear before the Court of Common Pleas at the June term in Portsmouth. Because this case did not come up when the court sat in June—and because there is no further record of the debt—it must have been satisfied prior to court, possibly by William. Colonial Records of N.H., 1638-1772. Case File No. 8778, Matthew Livermore v. Richard Crockett, Jr. and William Crockett. See also N.H. Court Records, Court of Common Pleas records, 1734-1745. June 1742.
98. RCROD, Book 75, p. 72-74.
99. Colonial Records of NH, 1638-1772. Case File No. 22353. No date is given in court records for the satisfaction of Richard's personal debt to Phineas Jones (Case File No. 28168), for which Phineas recovered judgment at the June 1743 Court of Common Pleas in the amount of 30 shillings principle and 4 shillings interest; however, a note written into that record reveals that an execution (and summons) was issued against Richard for that amount on October 31, 1743; another execution issued in December (with a summons) was received "too late to leave;" and that eventually, "This judgment satisfied." Because Matthew Livermore was attorney for both Phineas and Stephen Jones, the judgment to Phineas was likely collected at the same time as the judgment to Stephen, i.e. on March 25, 1745, less than a month after Richard's father, Richard Crockett, Sr., sold his property to Jewett. See N.H. Court Records, Court of Common Pleas records, 1734-1745, June 1743.
100. "Baptisms and Admission From the Records of First Church in Falmouth, Now Portland, Maine, with Appendix of Historical Notes." P. 65. https://archive.org/details/baptismsadmissio00lcfirs/page/65/mode/1up?view=theater
101. First Church records note another "Sarah" was baptized in 1743; however, this was likely a mistake for Susannah, who was born circa 1743 to Samuel and Sarah Crockett. "Baptisms and Admission From the Records of First Church in Falmouth,

worked as a chairmaker, but in less than ten years he became a shipwright, which was a much more lucrative career. He also invested successfully in real estate. With such good fortune falling upon him, one can almost see the beneficial hand of an approving uncle—Samuel Skillin—in Samuel Crockett's affairs. Not only did Skillin have just one son (also named Samuel) to his six girls, but Samuel Crockett was his namesake. (One can understand, knowing something of Samuel Skillin's personal history, why he might have preferred his hard-working nephew Samuel to his ne'er-do-well nephew Richard, Jr., and refused to rescue Richard from financial difficulties.)

Now Portland, Maine, with Appendix of Historical Notes." P. 65. https://archive.org/details/baptismsadmissio00lcfirs/page/65/mode/1up?view=theater

The Fourth Generation

Promissory note from Richard and Samuel Crockett to Phineas Jones, shopkeeper of Falmouth, Feb. 16, 1740 (bottom image), and writ of execution for Richard Crockett, Jr. of Stratham, N.H. for this debt.
The writ of execution was issued by New Hampshire magistrate Hunking Wentworth[102] on May 20, 1743. Although the promissory note to Phineas Jones was co-signed by Richard's younger brother Samuel Crockett, there is no evidence that Jones held Samuel accountable. This was likely because Jones knew that Richard was the one who received the funds.
(Colonial Records of N.H., 1638-1772. Court records. Case File No. 28168.)

---
102. (Mark) Hunking Wentworth was the brother of Benning Wentworth, first Royal Governor of N.H.

In May of 1742, Samuel Crockett sold the 30 acres in Falmouth he purchased in 1740 for 200 pounds, making a tidy profit of 70 pounds in less than two years.[103] On October 11th, Samuel (now styled a "shipwright of Falmouth") bought for 50 pounds a small lot on Middle Street on Falmouth Neck (downtown Portland) from shopkeeper Phineas Jones, as well as a one-third part of five rods of flats,[104] which led down to the low water mark.[105] Samuel set up shop in the business district, either for chairmaking or ship building (or both). In August of 1743, Samuel sold off 1/8th of an acre of the lot to Samuel Clark, a tailor from Falmouth, netting 5 pounds, 15 shillings.[106] Samuel added to his holdings on the Neck in 1747, buying from Thomas Cook of Falmouth for 60 pounds old tenor a small lot of land on Middle Street, which also included five rods of flats.[107]

King George's War (The Fifth Indian War, 1744-1748)

In 1744, England was drawn into the European War of the Austrian Succession. The hostilities spilled over into the American colonies where it was known as King George's War (the Fifth Indian War in Maine).[108] Fighting again erupted in Maine between the English and the French and their Wabanaki tribal allies. So much for the beneficial relations with the Indians that Governor Belcher had attempted in Falmouth in 1732!

Initially, the Penobscot tribe pledged that they would remain neutral in the conflict. But when the St. John and Cape Sable Indians elected to side with the French, and the English colonists declared war on those tribes, the Penobscots (understandably) ended up siding with the French during King George's War.[109]

---

103. On May 11, 1742, Samuel "Crockit," chairmaker of Falmouth, sold the 30 acres he purchased from Phineas and Stephen Jones and Jonathan Wait. YCROD, Vol. 23, p. 42.
104. "Flats" were what we in Maine now call clam flats, but which back then were much more valuable, since the flats enabled access to the water and harbor.
105. YCROD, Vol. 24, p. 70.
106. YCROD, Vol. 25, p. 154. Sarah Crockett signed off on her dower rights.
107. YCROD, Vol. 26, p. 235-236. Samuel purchased the property from Cook, who had purchased the parcel from trader Phineas Jones, on Sept. 29, 1747.
108. King George's War was the third of the four so-called French and Indian wars and was also known in Maine as the Fifth Indian War. King Philip's War, 1675-78 (which did not involve the French and very little Wampanoags under their sagamore King Philip) was known in Maine as the First Indian War; King William's War (1689-1697) was the Second Indian War; Queen Anne's War (1702-1713) was the Third Indian War; Father Rasles' War (or Dummer's War, 1722-1725) was the Fourth Indian War; and King George's War (1744-1748), the Fifth Indian War; and the French and Indian War (the Seven Years' War, 1754-1763), the Sixth Indian War. The four French and Indian wars are: King William's War, Queen Anne's War, King George's War, and the French and Indian War.
109. WILLIS, p. 413. Willis, writing in the mid-19th century, makes no attempt to hide his contempt of Native Americans. "... these children of the forest [the Penobscots], by a natural attraction, were soon found fighting by the side of their red

The Fourth Generation

This time around, however, residents of Falmouth (and in New England, in general) were more prepared for war, having learned their lessons from prior French and Indian conflicts. Even before England had joined the War of Austrian Succession, breastworks had been built in Falmouth and garrison houses established.[110] In addition, the increase in population in the greater Falmouth area helped ensure the people's safety. Native American warriors tended to rove in small bands, preying upon families (and their livestock) in more isolated situations. The Massachusetts General Court began offering an eye-popping bounty of 400 pounds old tenor[111] per native scalp, which incentive to genocide had the effect of clearing the territory of Indians, according to Portland historian Willis:

> "This sort of merchandise [native scalps] was indeed rather difficult and hazardous to obtain, but the temptation was so strong that four companies of volunteers were raised in [Falmouth] in September, and others in the neighboring towns to go in quest of it. They were all however unsuccessful; for scarce had the presence of the enemy created alarm upon the whole frontier, than they suddenly retired far beyond the reach of an observation quickened by the strongest passions of our nature."[112]

Although there were some sporadic Native American attacks in Second Parish in 1746, the greatest alarm occurred that fall when a large French fleet that included "frigates, fire-ships, and transports," carrying more than 3,000 troops under the Duke d'Anville set sail from France to New England.[113] D'Anville's fleet threatened not just Falmouth, of course, but the rest of New England, including Massachusetts.

---

brethren against the English." Willis even goes so far in his history of Portland to describe Native Americans as "our natural enemies, if I may so call the aboriginal inhabitants, whose very existence as an independent people was incompatible with the growing population and power of the colonies…" (p. 411).
110. WILLIS, p. 412.
111. Willis (p. 414), writing in the mid-19th century, says the 400 pounds "old tenor" bounty was the equivalent to $165 in silver. The bounty upon Native American scalps was resurrected again in 1755 during the French and Indian War (1754-1763). One of those most eager to exterminate Native Americans was the Rev. Thomas Smith, long-time pastor of First Church of Falmouth. According to the Maine Historical Society (via Maine Memory Net), in 1757 "Smith and prominent members of the First Parish Church equipped a posse of 16 men. These 'scouters and cruisers' were sent to 'kill and captivate the Indian Enemy' to the east of Falmouth in the area between the Kennebec and Penobscot Rivers. Shortly after, Reverend Smith noted in his journal the receipt of 198 British pounds for 'my part of the scalp money'—equal to one-quarter of his salary." "Parson Thomas Smith, ca. 1795." https://www.mainememory.net/record/48487 Assuming the bounty was still 400 pounds old tenor, the 16-man-crew from First Church must have killed and scalped about 8 Native Americans.
112. WILLIS, p. 414-415. Willis notes that one company even went as far north as the Penobscot River searching for Indians, but "returned without seeing any."
113. WILLIS, p. 416.

Fifteen thousand men quickly sprang to the colony's defense, marching into Boston for its protection. In Maine (as elsewhere on the New England coast) residents in seaside communities began moving inland for safety from the French invaders, and Falmouth even shipped the town's records down to Newbury, Massachusetts, to secure them. A public fast was held October 10th to pray that the danger "might be averted ... [when] news was received that an epidemic prevailed in the French fleet, that their admiral was dead, and that a violent gale of wind had dispersed the fleet and had destroyed some of the best ships."[114] The French fleet having been debilitated, the colonists were relieved of their fear of attack from that direction.

Richard Crockett, Jr. and his family appear to have remained safely in Stratham during the four years of King George's War. On Nov. 5, 1747, Richard and Mary Crockett of Stratham sold for ten shillings[115] any land in Falmouth and "to the Eastward" to which they might have a rightful share as heirs of the estate of her grandfather Samuel York.[116] The couple sold their rights to this potential estate (from a division of the Commons or land that might be granted posthumously to Samuel York as an ancient proprietor of Falmouth) to John Robinson, Jr., a mariner from Falmouth and likely a relation of Mary's.[117] (John Robinson, Jr. also purchased the same rights from Samuel Robinson,[118] Mary's older brother, as well as from two York descendants.)[119]

On October 18, 1748, the Treaty of Aix-la-Chapelle was signed, bringing an end to the War of the Austrian Succession, but not King George's War. While the European treaty ended the hostilities between England and France, the treaty did not end the hostilities between the English colonists in New England and warring Wabanaki tribes. Governor William Shirley of Massachusetts Bay Colony wasted

---

114. WILLIS, p. 416.
115. Although Mary was a grandchild of Samuel York, the value (10 shillings) of her rights to any potential land grant or division of the Commons made in Maine in the name of her deceased grandfather was worth less than her brother Samuel's right (2 pounds) because she was a woman.
116. YCROD, Vol. 26, p. 236. Witnesses were Joshua Woodbury Sr. and Jr.
117. Mary had a younger brother, John Robinson, born in Gloucester, Mass., Dec. 31, 1714. (Massachusetts Vital Records, 1620-1988, via Ancestry.) He possibly had a son named for himself, who ventured to follow-up a claim against his great-grandfather York's estate; however, if so, John, Jr. was a very enterprising young man.
118. On Oct. 27, 1748, Samuel Robinson of Gloucester, County of Essex, fisherman, sold to John Robinson, Jr., Falmouth, County of York (Maine) for 2 pounds, all the land in Casco Bay or to the Eastward that may be coming to him from the estate of his grandfather Samuel York, Gloucester, shoreman, deceased. YCROD, Book 27, p. 61. Less than three weeks earlier, on Oct. 7, 1747, John Robinson, mariner of Falmouth, for the sum of 4 pounds 10 shillings each (in two separate deeds), purchased from Samuel York (of Ipswich) and Thomas York (of Gloucester), both cordwainers, their "rights and Title to any Lands lying in said Falmouth or in any other part of ye Eastern Country; which was formerly belonging to Samuel York, [our] honored grandfather, deceased..." YCROD, Vol. 26, p. 236.
119. Samuel Robinson was born in Gloucester, Mass., Sept. 15, 1706, to Abraham and Sarah Robinson. (Massachusetts Vital Records, 1620-1988, via Ancestry.)

The Fourth Generation

no time in getting word to the Indians that the war was over. He requested a meeting with some eastern chiefs to discuss peace between the tribes and the colonists. The two-day meeting was held in Falmouth on October 14-16, 1749, during which peace talks the tenets of Dummer's Treaty of 1726 (that concluded Father Rasles' War or Dummer's War) were largely agreed upon. According to Willis, this treaty was signed by "six chiefs of the Wawenock,[120] eight of the Norridgewock, and five of the Penobscot tribes."[121]

Richard Crockett, Jr. Returns To Maine

By 1750, Richard, Jr. and his family had returned to Maine. On January 21, 1750, Richard purchased from John Sawyer, Jr., yeoman (son of the ferryman Sawyer) "a small piece of land where the said Richard Crockett's dwelling house now standeth in Falmouth containing by estimation two thirds parts of one quarter of an acre."[122] I can find no record of Richard buying any real estate prior to this parcel from John Sawyer, Jr., so it appears that Richard was living on this very small lot—with a house on it that he or someone had built—before buying the parcel. The property was situated in Second Parish,[123] and so once again Richard and his family were installed in the neighborhood of his aunt and uncle Skillin (and their extended family), interspersed with Sawyer and York families.

At the time of Richard's return to Maine, his brother Samuel was living "on the corner of Middle and Plum [streets]"[124] on Falmouth Neck. By 1750, Samuel's wife had died, and on December 8, 1750, the shipwright remarried, taking for his second wife the widow Mrs. Priscilla (Swett) Jackman, daughter of John and Martha (Noyes) Swett of Falmouth.[125] Because of Samuel's more prominent location in the business district, Richard (and his family) might have lived at his house in

---

120. The Wawenocks were a subgroup of the Penobscots.
121. WILLIS, p. 424. The spirit of peace "did not prevail in our country," says Willis, as English colonists had not learned how to live peacefully with their native brethren, as did the French. As a result, within five years the English would be at war again with the French and Indians.
122. York County Registry of Deeds, Book 35, Page 77a. Richard Crockett paid 20 shillings for the property, a very reasonable price for this miniscule lot. John Sawyer, Jr. was brother to Rebecca Sawyer, who had married Samuel Skillin, Jr. His father, John Sawyer, was one of those who signed the 1739 complaint against Falmouth innkeeper James Noble. The senior Sawyer's wife might have been Mary Robinson's sister (i.e. Richard, Jr.'s sister-in-law). If so, John Sawyer, Jr. was Richard's nephew by marriage.
123. In 1760, Richard Crockett was on a list of polls and estates from Second Parish. Massachusetts State Archives collection, colonial period, 1622-1788. Volume 130, p. 26. Valuation of Second Parish, Falmouth, Maine. https://www.familysearch.org/ark:/61903/3:1:3Q9M-C9Y5-37K7?i=832&cat=1055547
124. GORHAM, p. 452.
125. CANDAGE, p. 7.

Second Parish and he worked or sold chairs at his brother's shop across the Fore River on the Neck.

In the summer of 1751, Samuel sold 20 square rods out of the tract he had purchased from Thomas Cook in 1747 (which included a barn) and 30 feet 8 inches of the flats he purchased from Phineas Jones.[126] That fall, Samuel and brother William sold their father's proprietor's rights in the town of Kittery to Moses Hanscom for 2 pounds, 2 shillings and 2 pence.[127] (Unlike brothers Samuel and William, Richard, Jr. was not added to the deed from their father for Richard Crockett, Sr.'s proprietor's rights. This omission represents another hint that Richard's debts were likely paid by his father from the sale of property in 1745. If this had not been the case, it would have made more sense for Richard, Sr. to have granted his proprietor's rights in Kittery and Berwick to Richard, Jr. rather than to William, since Richard, Jr. lived in Maine and William did not.)

Despite his earlier difficulties in Falmouth—debt and possible slide into alcoholism—Richard Crockett, Jr. seems to have been accepted back into the fold. At the annual Falmouth Town Meeting (which included Second Parish) held March 13, 1753, Richard was voted one of four "tything men" for the ensuing year.[128] Richard's job as a tithingman, in addition to collecting the offering, would have been to sit at the back of the meetinghouse during the service and, utilizing a long rod, run herd over the younger boys (several of whom—Daniel, Robinson, Josiah, and George—were his and Mary's sons). He would also have used the rod to wake up those parishioners who nodded off during the service.[129] (One suspects Richard might have enjoyed his tithingman duties.) At an annual town meeting held four years later, on March 8, 1757, Richard was one of sixteen men (including Samuel Skilling, Jr.) of Falmouth voted as surveyors of highways.[130]

---

126. YCROD, Vol. 30, p. 84. Samuel sold the tracts to Samuel Atwood for 6 pounds, 13 shillings, and 4 pence. Shopkeeper Phineas Jones is often styled a "trader" in deeds; however, anyone who searches Falmouth land records during this era will come across Jones' name a lot and realize that he was a land speculator as much as a shopkeeper.
127. YCROD, Vol. 31, p. 165. William Crockett, yeoman of Epping, N.H. and Samuel Crockett, shipwright of Falmouth, sold to Hanscom "... four rights or shares that they own of the common lands belonging to the Proprietors of the Town of Kittery, but since divided among the sd. Proprietors, which four shares lie in that part called Pudding Hole Commons in Division No. 3 and is a 6 acre lot."
128. Falmouth, Maine Town Records, Book 2, 1728-1773, p. 208 https://archive.org/details/falmouth-maine-town-records-book-2-1728-1773/page/208/mode/1up?q=Skillin&view=theater
129. "The Tithingman at the Ipswich Meeting House." Historic Ipswich website. https://historicipswich.net/2020/01/24/tithingman/
130. Falmouth, Maine Town Records, Book 2, 1728-1773, p. 231. https://archive.org/details/falmouth-maine-town-records-book-2-1728-1773/page/231/mode/1up?view=theater

Samuel Crockett Moves to Gorham and the Onset of the French and Indian War (1754-1763, the Sixth Indian War)

In the 1750s, Richard's brother Samuel relocated to Narragansett Township No. 7, also known as Gorham Town (and later, Gorham). This township, situated in a sparsely-settled area to the west of Falmouth, was a new creation of the Massachusetts General Court, one of seven townships granted to the men (and their heirs) who had fought in King Philip's War of 1675. In 1753, Samuel Crockett purchased two, 30-acre lots—Lot No. 79[131] and Lot No. 103[132]—in Narragansett Township No. 7. By 1755, Samuel and his family were permanently living in Gorham Town, where he "built and occupied the two story house on Main St. in this village..."[133] On Nov. 14, 1755, Samuel purchased from Christopher Strout a 30-acre lot, which adjoined the 30-acre lot upon which he lived. In this deed Samuel is described as a husbandman,[134] suggesting that when he relocated inland to Gorham, Samuel intended to phase out his ship building and become a farmer, like his and Richard's father was in Stratham.

There is no evidence that Richard, like Samuel,[135] purchased property in Gorham. Historian Merton Taylor Goodrich, however, claims that it is certain "[Richard] lived in Gorham and had a shop in what is now Portland."[136] According to Goodrich, the two brothers resided in Gorham and maintained their businesses on Falmouth Neck, Richard working as a chairmaker and Samuel as a shipwright. (Falmouth was still a sprawling township, not yet having been chopped up to create Portland, South Portland, Cape Elizabeth, Deering, Westbrook, *and* Falmouth.) This undocumented claim by Goodrich seems rather sketchy. Richard could not have leased a home in Narragansett Township No. 7, since few houses existed when the brothers would have relocated there. There is also evidence that

---

131. On Jan. 15, 1753, Samuel Crockett, shipwright of Falmouth, purchased from Wheeler Riggs for 34 pounds, 13 shillings, and 4 pence, a lot of land in York County laying in Narragansett Township No. 7, a.k.a. Gorham Town, a 30-acre lot in the first division, Lot No. 79. YCROD, Vol. 33, p. 4.
132. On Oct. 24, 1753, Samuel Crockett, shipwright of Falmouth, purchased from Joseph Bangs for 53 pounds, 6 shillings, and 8 pence, a lot of land in York County laying in Narragansett Township No. 7, alias Gorham Town, 30 acres, lot No. 103. YCROD, Vol. 30, p. 370.
133. GORHAM, p. 452-453.
134. CCROD, Vol. 2, p. 508. Samuel Crockett paid "forty pounds current money of the Province" for the 30-acre lot, upon which a man by the name of Charles Hall was living. Strout was from Falmouth and possibly inherited the lot or purchased it as an investment.
135. In addition to deeds showing Samuel in Gorham, he was also on a three-man committee to repair the old fort there that had been built during King George's War and was now needed during the French and Indian War. GORHAM, p. 46.
136. CHAIRMAKERS, p. 141.

Richard did *not* move to Gorham. Marriage intentions for three of his and Mary's children (Sarah in 1754; Richard in 1755; and Hannah in 1756) were not only filed in Falmouth, but also list Falmouth—not Gorham—as the home of these children.[137] (Gorham residents like Samuel's children who filed marriage intentions in Falmouth were noted as being from Gorham.)

Goodrich's supposition that Samuel and Richard commuted from Gorham into Falmouth to their shops rings hollow, as well. The idea of commuting ten-plus miles daily by horseback or on foot seems like an unnecessary waste of time, energy, and resources. In addition, by 1754, hostilities between Great Britain and France had erupted again. Although war was not officially declared until 1756, the shaky 1749 treaty struck in Falmouth between Native Americans and Massachusetts Bay Colony had not held, all of which led to what became known as "the old French war"[138] (and later, the French and Indian War or the Sixth Indian War in Maine).

In 1757, Richard Crockett was on the alarm list of Captain Loring Cushing's militia company from Cape Elizabeth (Second Parish).[139] Early Colonial law required "all male persons from sixteen years of age to sixty [with some exceptions] … shall bear arms and always be provided with a well fixed firelock musket, of musket or bastard bore,[140] a knapsack, a collar with twelve bandoleers,[141] or cartouche box,[142] one pound of good powder, twenty bullets fit for his gun, and twelve flints, a good sword or cutlass, a worm and priming wire fit for his gun."[143] The alarm list was for aged men, usually fifty and older (or men who were less able-bodied). At the

---

137. On September 6, 1754, "Richard Obrion Entered his Name and Purpose of Marriage with Sarah Crokit both of Falmouth September 6th 1754 Per Stephen Longfellow Town Clerk." Falmouth, Maine Town Records, Book 2, 1728-1773, p. 52. https://archive.org/details/falmouth-maine-town-records-book-2-1728-1773/page/52/mode/1up?q=Skillin&view=theater Richard and Sarah were married Sept. 24, 1754 by the Rev. Thomas Smith of Falmouth. See p. 72. On November 14, 1755, "Richard Crockit Entered his Name and Purpose of Marriage with Elizabeth Roberts both of Falmouth Nov 14 1755 Per Stephen Longfellow Town Clerk." Falmouth, Maine Town Records, Book 2, 1728-1773, p. 55. https://archive.org/details/falmouth-maine-town-records-book-2-1728-1773/page/55/mode/1up?q=Skillin&view=theater On January 26, 1756, "John Briant of Biddeford Entered his Name and Purpose of Marriage with Hannah Crokit of Falmouth January 26th 1756 Per Stephen Longfellow Town Clerk." Falmouth, Maine Town Records, Book 2, 1728-1773, p. 56 https://archive.org/details/falmouth-maine-town-records-book-2-1728-1773/page/56/mode/1up?q=Skillin&view=theater
138. GORHAM, p. 65. This fourth and last of the so-called "French and Indian wars" was known as the Seven Years War in Europe. The war raged from 1754 to 1763, although war was not formally declared between England and France until 1756 (hence the seven years).
139. Maine Genealogy Archives, "Falmouth Militia Members, 1757." https://archives.mainegenealogy.net/2010/02/falmouth-militia-members-1757.html
140. A "bastard bore" was an 18th century long-barrel fowling gun 69 caliber or smaller. (A "club butt" fowling gun was 70 to 80 caliber.)
141. A shoulder belt used to hold ammunition.
142. Cartridge box.
143. "Baptisms and Admission from the Records of First Church of Falmouth, now Portland, Maine. With Appendix of Historical Notes." Compiled by Marquis F. King, President of the Maine Genealogical Society. Portland, Maine: Maine Genealogical Society, 1898. Pgs. 171-177 https://archive.org/details/baptismsadmissio00lcfirs/page/171/mode/1up?view=theater

time, Richard would have been about fifty (by my calculation). His brother Samuel, who was younger (about forty), was a private in Captain Cushing's list of regulars in his training band.[144]

George Roberts of Second Parish, a son-in-law of Samuel Skillin, was one of four lieutenants in Captain Cushing's Company.[145] (By then, Roberts was also father-in-law to Richard and Mary Crockett's son, Richard III, who had married Elizabeth Roberts.) Samuel Skillin, Jr. was captain of the company from Stroudwater,[146] in which young Richard Crockett (about age 23) and his brother Joshua (about 21) were privates. Another Crockett relation, Abraham Crockett (about 23), was also in the Stroudwater company.[147]

---

144. "Baptisms and Admission From the Records of First Church in Falmouth, Now Portland, Maine, with Appendix of Historical Notes." Compiled by Marquis F. King, President of the Maine Genealogical Society. Portland, Maine: Maine Genealogical Society, 1898. Appendix, p. 175. https://archive.org/details/baptismsadmissio00lcfirs/page/175/mode/1up?view=theater
145. "Baptisms and Admission From the Records of First Church in Falmouth, Now Portland, Maine, with Appendix of Historical Notes." Compiled by Marquis F. King, President of the Maine Genealogical Society. Portland, Maine: Maine Genealogical Society, 1898. Appendix, p. 175. https://archive.org/details/baptismsadmissio00lcfirs/page/175/mode/1up?view=theater
146. "Baptisms and Admission From the Records of First Church in Falmouth, Now Portland, Maine, with Appendix of Historical Notes." Compiled by Marquis F. King, President of the Maine Genealogical Society. Portland, Maine: Maine Genealogical Society, 1898. Appendix, p. 183 https://archive.org/details/baptismsadmissio00lcfirs/page/183/mode/1up?view=theater
147. Abraham was probably the son of John and Mary (Knight) Crockett (grandson of Joshua and Sarah Trickey Crockett), since his father John Crockett was on the alarm list for Captain Skillin's company. "Baptisms and Admission From the Records of First Church in Falmouth, Now Portland, Maine, with Appendix of Historical Notes." Compiled by Marquis F. King, President of the Maine Genealogical Society. Portland, Maine: Maine Genealogical Society, 1898. Appendix, p. 183. https://archive.org/details/baptismsadmissio00lcfirs/page/183/mode/1up?view=theater

1757 muster rolls for brothers Richard and Samuel Crocket, during the French and Indian War. Samuel (then about forty) was a private in the Second Parish regulars under Captain Loring Cushing. Richard (about fifty) was on Cushing's alarm list.
(Courtesy Massachusetts Archives.)[148]

---

148. Massachusetts Archive Collection, 1603-1799. Index to French and Indian War Muster Rolls. Mass. Archives. Vol. 91-99. Film #008731870.

More Debt

After Samuel relocated to Gorham, Richard found himself once again pressed for funds. Around 1754 he borrowed a small amount of money from Jedidiah Preble of Falmouth. Preble, a respected Lieutenant Colonel (who would go on to become a Brigadier General),[149] had also been buying up land in Falmouth. Possibly because the sum was so trifling and because Preble had recently married Mehitable (Bangs) Roberts,[150] the widow of John Roberts, Jr. (the Roberts and Crockett families having many connections), Preble did not take a promissory note from Crockett. While Preble was off on a military expedition northward to assess potential danger from the French, however, his son, Jedidiah Preble, Jr., asked Richard to repay the loan to his father. Since Richard could not then repay, at the instigation of Preble, Jr., he signed a promissory note to Preble, Sr. on April 30, 1754 for "…Seven Pounds, fourteen Shillings and one Peney [penny] Lawful money on Demand and with Lawfull Interest till Paid for value Recd."[151] Although Richard was later again asked for the money owed the Lieutenant Colonel, he failed to pay. But Preble, Sr. apparently was not a hard-nosed creditor (and likely too busy with military matters), for he let the matter ride for several more years.

On January 2, 1757, Richard and Samuel's uncle Samuel Skillin, Sr. died. Five days later their father passed away in Stratham. Whether Richard, Jr. expected to receive an inheritance from his father (or suggested to his creditors that he expected an inheritance)—and did not—we do not know, but not long after Richard, Sr.'s death, George Knight, the son-in-law of Lieutenant Colonel Preble, began pressing for Richard's promissory note to be paid. Once again, Richard was unable to make any payment.

---

149. Preble played important roles during both the French and Indian War and the American Revolution. He led a colorful life and was reportedly the first white man to climb Mt. Washington. "Genealogical Sketch of the First Three Generations of Prebles in America: with an account of Abraham Preble, the Emigrant, their Common Ancestor and the grandfather of Brigadier General Jedidiah Preble and his Descendants." George Henry Preble, Captain, U.S.N. Boston: Printed for Family Circulation, David Clapp & Son, 1868. P. 41. https://archive.org/details/genealogicalsket00preb/page/n64/mode/1up?view=theater
150. Mehitable, a childless widow, married Jedidiah Preble May 9, 1754, the second marriage for him, as well. Mehitable was known as a "bustling, energetic, business woman," who looked out for her husband's property and business interests while he was away on military expeditions. During the burning of Falmouth in 1775 she "hastened, with an axe, and with her own hand humanely liberated the pigs, &c., from their confinement, by knocking down the piggery in which they were confined…" "Genealogical Sketch of the First Three Generations of Prebles in America: with an account of Abraham Preble, the Emigrant, their Common Ancestor and the grandfather of Brigadier General Jedidiah Preble and his Descendants." George Henry Preble, Captain, U.S.N. Boston: Printed for Family Circulation, David Clapp & Son, 1868. P. 57. https://archive.org/details/genealogicalsket00preb/page/n84/mode/1up?view=theater
151. Maine, Court of Common Pleas, Case Files, Oct. 1757. York County. Case No. 14-348. https://www.familysearch.org/ark:/61903/3:1:3QS7-893N-D9D3-W?i=241&cat=1923498

On September 16, 1757, York County Magistrate Sir William Pepperrell (now a wealthy baronet, but who as a youth had loaned money to Elihu Gunnison to buy the Thomas Crockett homestead from Richard Crockett, Sr.) issued a writ of execution against Richard Crockett (Jr.) in the case of George Knight (for Knight's father-in-law Jedidiah Preble, Sr.). Pepperrell summoned Richard to appear at the next Court of Common Pleas. The next day, Deputy Sheriff John Marston attached "one chair of the within named Richard Crockit to the Value of four shillings and left a Summons at [the] usual place of his abode."[152]

The case of George Knight v. Richard Crockett was heard at the Court of Common Pleas held in York for York County on October 4, 1757. Initially, Richard did not appear, and the Court awarded Knight a judgment (for his father-in-law Preble, Sr.) of 9 pounds, 14 shillings and 6 pence damage, and 1 pound, 11 shillings and 4 pence for cost of suit. Richard must have made his appearance prior to the end of the court session, however, because the text entered into the record about him not appearing is struck out. The following notation was added to the record: "The Deft. [defendant, i.e. Richard Crockett] appealed from this Judgment to the next Supr. Court of Judicature to be held in said County & entered into Recognizance with Sureties as the Law directs to prosecute his appeal with Effect."[153]

The next Massachusetts Superior Court of Judicature was held in York County on June 20, 1758. Information about Richard's case does not appear in the court's records, however. Nor was mention made of Richard having lost the bond money he posted to ensure his appearance at the court of Judicature.[154] We can guess—given what happened next—that Richard had been up to his old trick of robbing Peter to pay Paul.

On August 1, 1758, Richard signed a promissory note to John Waite for 12 pounds, 6 shillings and 9 pence for "value recd,"[155] a sum that would have just paid off his promissory note to Jedidiah Preble, Sr. and court fees. Why Richard did not approach his brother Samuel to pay off the debt to Preble—but rather sought out Waite—is a mystery, although one can understand Richard might have been embarrassed to ask his brother for money. (Or Samuel might have refused.) Waite,

---

152. Maine, Court of Common Pleas, Case Files, Oct. 1757. York County. Case No. 14-348.
153. Records of the Courts, Maine Court of Common Pleas, v. 14, 1753-1759, p. 348. https://www.familysearch.org/ark:/61903/3:1:9392-FMSX-18?i=358&cc=1877829&cat=1911177
154. Massachusetts Court Records, Superior Court of Judicature, 1755-1759 https://www.familysearch.org/ark:/61903/3:1:3Q9M-CSZC-B23C?i=641&cat=301381
155. York County, Maine, Court of Common Pleas case files, Box 129, Oct. 1758-Jan 1759 (cont); Case No. 14-504.

The Fourth Generation

then in his mid-fifties,[156] was a well-heeled Falmouth merchant and "coaster," captain of a packet that ferried goods between Falmouth and Boston. Waite also lent out money[157] and was unabashed about taking defaulters to court. Richard's note was payable on demand (with interest), yet when Waite demanded payment, Richard (not surprisingly) failed to pay. On December 7, 1758, a writ of execution against Richard Crockett of Falmouth, chairmaker, was issued to the value of 20 pounds. The Sheriff was ordered to attach the goods or property of Crockett (or take him physically if enough value could not be found) so that he could answer the charge at the next Court of Common Pleas held in York for York County. On December 9th Deputy Sheriff John Marston "attached the House and all the Land of the within named Richard Crockit to the value of 15 pounds at the same time left a summons at the usual place of his abode."[158]

Promissory note from Richard "Crockit" to John Waite, August 1, 1758.
(Maine Court of Common Pleas case files, Box 129, Oct 1758-Jan 1759 (cont); Case (or Folder) No. 14-504.)[159]

Ironically, Samuel was certainly able to lend his brother money or provide him with bills of credit. On December 2, 1758—five days before Waite's writ against Richard was issued—Samuel and William Crockett sold for 160 pounds old tenor

---
156. WILLIS, p. 850. Willis says that Waite lived "on the road fronting the beach below India street" in downtown Portland, although also noting he relocated to Peaks' Island in his later years.
157. At the same Court of Common Pleas in January 1759, Waite also brought a case against Thomas Ficket for debt. York County, Maine, Court of Common Pleas case files, Box 129, Oct 1758-Jan 1759 (cont); Case No. 14-504 #59. https://www.familysearch.org/ark:/61903/3:1:3QSQ-G93N-631H?i=748&cat=1923498
158. Maine Court of Common Pleas case files, Box 129, Oct 1758-Jan 1759 (cont); Case No. 14-504.
159. https://www.familysearch.org/ark:/61903/3:1:3QS7-893N-6S1Q?i=741&cat=1923498

in Bills of Credit their rights to the Commons in Berwick, which rights had been deeded to them by their father, Richard Crockett of Stratham.[160] (This is another example of Richard, Jr. being left out of a legacy from his father,[161] which confirms my belief that Richard Crockett, Sr. paid his son's earlier debts as his share of inheritance.)

The summons left at "the usual place of his abode" by Deputy Sheriff Marston ordered Richard Crockett to appear at the next Court of Common Pleas held in York at the January 1759 session. Richard's name was called aloud at this court, but this time he did not appear at all, thus defaulting. The judgment for Waite was a total of 13 pounds, 13 shillings (Richard's original debt of 12 pounds, 6 shillings and 9 pence plus 6 shillings and 3 pence for interest charges of five months and seven days). Richard was also ordered to pay the costs associated with recovering the debt, as well as court costs, for an additional sum of 2 pounds 17 shillings.[162]

On March 15, 1759, to satisfy these debts, Richard gave Waite a mortgage upon the tiny Falmouth lot (with his house upon it) he had purchased from John Sawyer, Jr. The mortgage amount was 17 pounds, 4 shillings—more than what he owed Waite—which leads one to suspect that Richard also borrowed from his creditor the court and recovery costs. (All this because Richard had failed to pay his original debt to Jedidiah Preble for 7 pounds, 14 shillings and 1 penny, not all of which he probably received in cash!) According to the mortgage to Waite, if Richard paid the 17 pounds, 4 shillings within a year—by March 16, 1760—the note would be null and void.[163] I can find no evidence in the land records that Richard paid the debt by that date, and the mortgage remained on the property (and, in fact, the lien appears never to have been discharged). In the conveyance to Waite, Richard's wife Mary (Robinson) Crockett did not sign off on her dower rights, making it all but certain she was deceased by 1759. (Mary would have been 47, had she lived until this time.)

---

160. YCROD, Vol. 35, p. 248. The two Crockett brothers—William, described as a husbandman from Epping, and Samuel, a shipwright from Gorham Town—sold their father's rights to the Commons in Berwick to Nathan Lord, Jr.
161. Even brother Ephraim, who inherited Richard Crockett, Sr.'s homestead, netted a share of their father's bounty from early land claims. On July 4, 1760, Ephraim Crockett of Stratham sold the lot granted to his father by the town of Bow to Joseph Barker for 150 pounds old tenor. The parcel was 40 acres in the 5th range of lots in the first division, the 8th lot in number, laid out to Richard Crockett (but upon which Richard never lived) as shown in the town books. RCROD, Vol. 145, p. 79. Richard was the only son of Richard Crockett, Sr. never to receive an inheritance or gift of real estate deeded to him by his father.
162. York County, Maine, Court of Common Pleas case files, Box 129, Oct 1758-Jan 1759 (cont); Case No. 14-504 #58. https://www.familysearch.org/ark:/61903/3:1:3QS7-893N-6S1Q?i=741&cat=1923498
163. York County Registry of Deeds, Book 35, Page 77a-78.

If Mary *was* deceased, Richard would have had sole custody of five minor boys: Daniel (seventeen), George (fifteen), Robinson (around fourteen), Josiah (eleven or twelve), and Joseph (if he existed, age nine). The older boys would have been apprenticed out, in the usual custom, but the younger ones would have been at home or with relatives. (The fact that Robinson Crockett initially became a chairmaker suggests that he either learned his trade from his father or from his older brother Richard, also a chairmaker, who was then married and out of the house.)

In 1760, Richard "Crocket" was included on a list of polls (one—himself) and estates in the Second District of Falmouth. The list of his estate shows that Richard was very poor. No land, pasture, orchard, or salt marsh accompanied his house. He owned no oxen or swine, although Richard did have one cow and a horse, both above three years of age. If he commuted to the Neck where his shop might have been situated (from his house in Second Parish), the horse certainly would have come in handy, enabling Richard to take the long way around through Stroudwater, where there was a bridge and thus saving the ferry charge. The final category on the list asked for the sum total of rents, and Richard reported an annual rent of 1-pound. This rent might be what Richard paid to lease his shop or it could be what he paid annually against his mortgage to Waite.

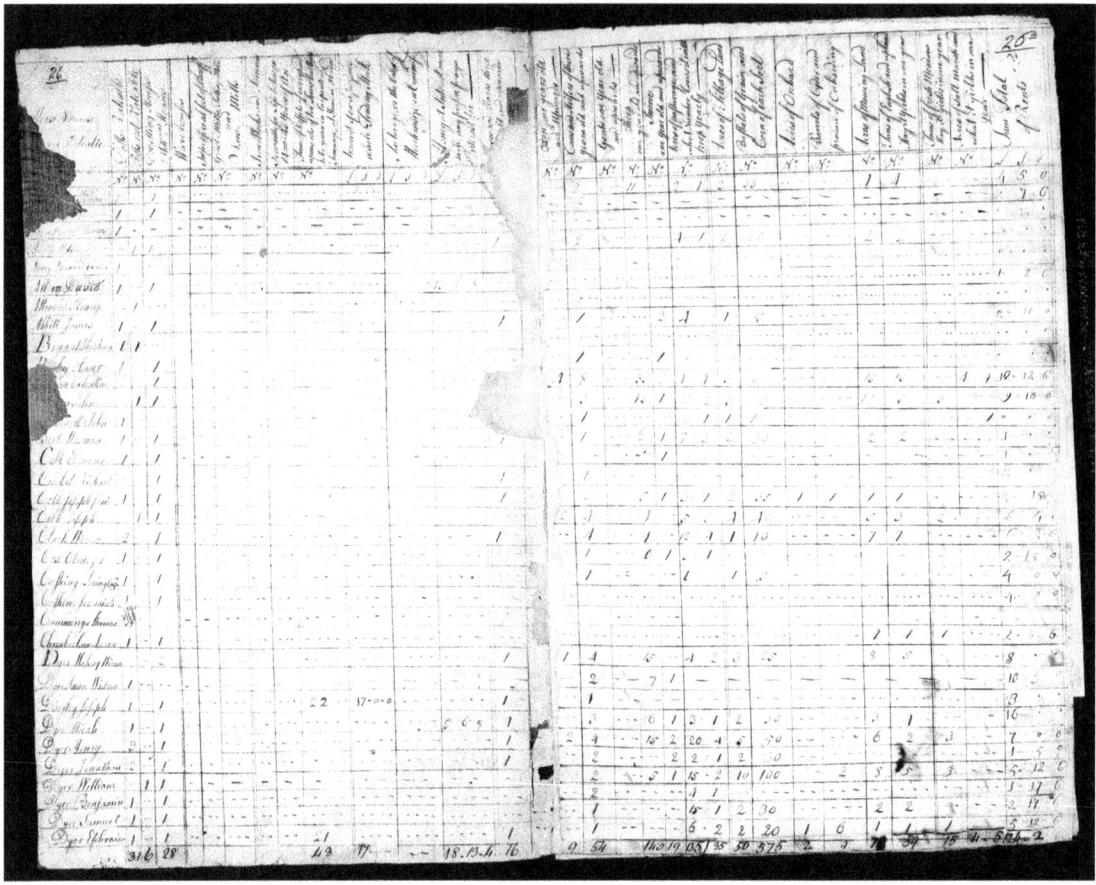

1760 List of polls and estates in the Second District of Falmouth, Maine. Richard Crocket is the second man listed under the letter "C," beneath Ebenezer Cobb. (Massachusetts State Archives, colonial period 1622-1788. Volume 130. Valuations of towns 1760.)[164]

The Fourth Generation

Fall of Quebec and the End of a Century of Fear

In 1759, an event of great consequence for all Mainers occurred. After more than a century of living in fear of ambushes and attacks by Native American warriors and their French allies, English settlers were overjoyed to learn that the reign of terror had come to an end—permanently. On September 13, 1759, the French lost their northern fortress, the city of Quebec, to the English during the Battle of the Plains of Abraham (also, Battle of Quebec).[165] The battle, which lasted only about an hour, culminated a months-long siege of the city by British forces, and resulted in the deaths of both commanders, the English General James Wolfe, and the French General Marquis de Montcalm. The relief felt by the English in Maine (and elsewhere) at hearing of the news of the fall of French Quebec cannot be overstated. Reverend Smith of First Church in Falmouth gives voice in his journal to the elation of the populace after learning (about a month later) of the fall of Quebec:

"Oct. 14. [1767] We have news that Quebec is taken, and that General Wolfe and Montcalm are killed.

[Oct.] 16. The canon were fired at the fort yesterday and to day. Mr. Mayhew's house was illuminated and small arms fired in the evening, upon further and more authentic news of the victory at Quebec.

[Oct.] 18. The country is all in ecstacy, upon the surprising news of the conquest of Quebec. General Wolfe, with an army of 5000 men, on the 13th of last month, having got above the city and landed on the north side, attacked the French behind the city, who after a terrible engagement of 15 minutes, fled into the city, which surrendered the 17th.

"[Oct.] 25. Public Thanksgiving for the reduction of Canada and Quebec particularly."[166]

After their French allies were defeated, Native Americans who remained in Maine—the Penobscot, Passamaquoddy, St. John, and Nova Scotia tribes—were

---

165. John Waite's son, John Waite, also a sea captain, "commanded one of the transports in the expedition under General Wolfe to Quebec, and saild from Louisburg, June 4, in company with eight sail of the line, several frigates, and about one hundred transports for the St. Lawrence. He remained near Quebec until the city fell, and returned to Falmouth in November of the same year [1759]." WILLIS, p. 851.
166. SMITHJOURNALS, p. 182. https://archive.org/stream/journalsofrevtho00smit_0/journalsofrevtho00smit_0_djvu.txt

forced to enter into treaties with the English.[167] The official end to the French and Indian War (the Seven Year's War) occurred several years after the fall of Quebec, on February 10, 1763, when Great Britain (under the new king, King George III) ratified the Treaty of Paris, which had been inked the prior year. Under this treaty, "France gave up all its territories in mainland North America, effectively ending any foreign military threat to the British colonies there."[168] For residents of Maine, however, the war ended with the fall of Quebec in 1759. This ushered in the long hoped-for period of peace and security from surprise attacks by the enemy.

After the fall of Quebec, Maine experienced a population explosion, much as occurred earlier after the end of Queen Anne's War (the Fourth Indian War) and Father Rasles' War (the Fifth Indian War). A census taken in 1764 (five years after the battle of Quebec), revealed that there were now 54,020 people residing in the District of Maine. The population had more than quadrupled since 1743, when the population of Maine was only 12,000.[169] According to the 1764 census, about seven percent of Maine's population—3,770 people—resided in Falmouth, 585 families occupying 460 houses (an average of eight people per household.)[170] This number included 566 souls from Second Parish (Cape Elizabeth), where Richard Crockett and his family resided.

Among those who came to Maine after the fall of Quebec, helping to swell the population, were three of Richard's nephews from New Hampshire. Between 1762 and 1764, Peletiah,[171] Andrew,[172] and Jonathan[173] Crockett (sons of Richard's

---

167. CAPE-E, p. 38. Cape Elizabeth historian William B. Jordan claims these treaties remain "unbroken to this day." This fact is incorrect, as we will see in the next chapter, when Maine forces the Penobscots to sell two unorganized townships that the Native Americans had received from Massachusetts in various treaties. In 1835, Richard's son Samuel received a 200-acre land grant from the state of Maine for his Revolutionary War service. Samuel's 200-acre lot was in Township No. 2 in the "Indian Purchase." Maine Land Office, Land Grant Application, Samuel Crockett (Cape Elizabeth). Courtesy of the Maine Archives. Now available via DigitalMaine Repositories. https://digitalmaine.com/revolutionary_war_me_land_office/222/
168. Office of the Historian, U.S. Secretary of State website, "Treaty of Paris, 1763." https://history.state.gov/milestones/1750-1775/treaty-of-paris#:~:text=The%20Treaty%20of%20Paris%20of,well%20as%20their%20respective%20allies.
169. In 1743, just prior to King George's War (which preceded the French and Indian War) there were less than 12,000 people in Maine. State of Maine website, "History of Maine (3)." By contrast, only a few thousand souls resided in Maine by the end of Queen Anne's War (the Third Indian War) in 1713.
170. SMITHJOURNALS, p. 203.. https://archive.org/stream/journalsofrevtho00smit_0/journalsofrevtho00smit_0_djvu.txt
171. On May 31, 1762, Peletiah Crockett of Stratham, N.H. bought one-half of the hundred-acre lot #25 in Gorham. GORHAM, p. 454. "He also purchased, of Abel Whitney in 1764, five acres of land 'on the northerly side of sd Crockett's land' … On this latter lot he probably lived when he first came to town." Whitney was the man whose widow Samuel Crockett married in 1763, so he must have passed away not long after this real estate sale.
172. On Oct. 19, 1764, Andrew Crockett bought the eastern half of the 100-acre lot #26 in Gorham. GORHAM, p. 455.
173. On Dec. 11, 1764, Jonathan Crockett bought from Solomon Lombard the 100-acre lot #28 in Gorham. "He came to Gorham from Falmouth, where his oldest child [David, b. Dec. 7, 1775] was born." GORHAM, p. 455.

brother Ephraim Crockett and his wife Rebecca Frink),[174] relocated to Gorham from New Hampshire.[175]

Hard Times and the American Revolution

On March 7, 1763, Samuel Crockett's second wife Priscilla died. Their last child (Abigail) had been born in 1758, so Priscilla's death does not appear to have been from complications related to childbirth. Samuel, left with five young children (his and his first wife's three daughters were already married) remarried immediately. On June 10, 1763, Samuel wed for his third wife Mary (Cane) Whitney, the widow of Abel Whitney of Gorham.[176]

On January 3, 1765, the Reverend Thomas Smith of Falmouth noted in his diary that, "The country from Boston to Portsmouth is entirely blocked with snow." Food was scarce in Falmouth that winter. In addition to a few church and death notices, Smith writes mostly in his diary about welcome deliveries of corn. On February 25th Smith noted, "A vessel from Newbury [MA] brought in 500 bushels of corn, and Dyer of Purpoodock [brought in] 1000, with which the flour in town are a wonderful relief to the people."[177] On March 10th Smith also jotted down, "One Davis brought from Boston 1000 bushels of corn; and neighbor Mayo and Lieut. Thomes, 1000 more," and on the 14th he added that another 3,400 bushels had arrived in Falmouth.[178] But by April 9, 1765, Smith noted the first robin appeared in Falmouth, bringing hope and a spring serenade.[179]

The peace and serenity of the robin proved short lived. While the 1763 Treaty of Paris officially ended the Seven Years' War (the French and Indian War here), the ramifications of years of war led to a fight over taxes between the American colonies and the King and Parliament in Great Britain. The mother country was anxious to tax her American citizens for a return on monies discharged during decades of warfare with the French (and Indians), which had depleted England's treasury:

---

174. Rebecca was the daughter of George and Rebecca (Skillin) Frink and the granddaughter of Samuel and Deborah (Haley) Skillin. Ephraim's wife was thus his first cousin once removed (or his second cousin, as we say in Maine.) CANDAGE, p. 6.
175. See CHAIRMAKERS, p. 141, for information on Richard Crockett, Jr. and Samuel Crockett. See, GORHAM, p. 452-455 for information on Samuel, and nephews Peletiah, Andrew, and Jonathan. (In his history of Gorham, McLellan does not realize that the Crocketts *are* related. See CANDAGE p. 4 and p. 6 for the connection.)
176. CANDAGE, p. 7.
177. SMITHJOURNALS, p. 204.
178. SMITHJOURNALS, p. 204.
179. SMITHJOURNALS, p. 205.

"Decades of war with France left England deeply in debt. To raise funds, the Crown levied a series of unpopular taxes upon the colonists. In 1765, residents of New Casco joined their neighbors on the Neck to protest a proposed tax on all printed paper. By 1775, in a show of resistance to colonial rule, Falmouth voted to support several boycotts of British goods. Tensions between the elite merchant class on Falmouth Neck, local militias, and the British grew, culminating in the burning of Falmouth [Portland] by British forces that same year."[180]

In mid-October of 1775, after the upstart colonists in Maine had boycotted English goods and made their resistance to British tyranny known, a fleet from the English Royal Navy under the command of Captain Henry Mowatt sailed into Falmouth harbor. Mowatt was not only familiar with the harbor, but also harbored resentment in his bosom toward the locals, who had captured and briefly detained him in May.[181] Mowatt gave the townspeople a two-day warning (so that they could evacuate) and then proceeded to bombard Falmouth Neck with incendiary shot. He also sent in landing crews of marines to physically light the town afire. Between 300-400 homes were destroyed (as well as most businesses), leaving about 1,000 people on the Neck homeless before the onset of winter.[182] Portland historian Willis describes the scene:

"On Wednesday morning, October 18th, a clear, calm, Indian Summer day, a British naval force, including the Canceau, with some of the very guns from old Fort Pownal, began shooting fire bombs into the helpless town.

Into the night the fires raged. Before daylight it rained. A cold, pitiless October rain fell for three days all along the coast as the stricken people of Falmouth sought food and shelter.

---

180. Falmouth, Town of, "History of Falmouth, Maine" (2019). *Maine History Documents*. 191.
181. WILLIS, p. 507-510. The capture of Mowatt occurred about two weeks after the British attacks at Lexington and Concord, when feelings toward the Red Coats were running hot in Maine (and New England); however, his brief detainment—although occurring in Falmouth—was not accomplished by locals. Many local men *wanted* to take Mowatt, whose ship was in the harbor; however, cooler heads in Falmouth prevailed. Instead, on May 7, 1775, when Captain Mowatt, the surgeon from his ship, and the Rev. Wiswell were walking uphill toward town they were encircled and captured by Col. Samuel Thompson of Brunswick, who, with a company of his militia, had come down from Brunswick to destroy Mowatt's ship. Mowatt was detained a short period before giving his parole that he would surrender the next day. Instead, Mowatt returned to his ship without surrendering, breaking his parole. His escape to his ship left many on the Neck and in the surrounding towns angry. (Mowatt later excused himself by claiming his life had been threatened and that is why he did not surrender as he had promised.) After Mowatt was safe on his ship, local militia groups, raised after the attacks on Lexington and Concord, wanted to strike the ship; however, the British officer eventually sailed safely away, only to return in the fall and in a fit of revenge destroy Falmouth Neck.
182. Website, Founder of the Day. "Mowatt's Revenge: The Burning of Falmouth." https://www.founderoftheday.com/founder-of-the-day/falmouth

The men of Falmouth wept, they admitted, in helpless rage and despair, to see the women and children huddled among the rocks and trees at the outskirts of the steaming, hissing, soot-stinking ruins in the night and the rain."[183]

Relocation to Deer Isle

The burning of Falmouth might have been the last straw for Richard Crockett, Jr. Not long after Falmouth Neck burned to the ground, he emigrated to Deer Isle, where his son Josiah then was living.

The exact year that Richard Crockett moved to Deer Isle is not known. We can track, however, his further fall into poverty before he left the greater Falmouth area. In 1771, Richard was on a list of polls and estates in Cape Elizabeth (taken September 23). He still owned one cow, but he no longer owned a horse. The annual value of Richard's real estate was reported to be a very modest 1 pound, 4 shillings.[184] After the destruction of Falmouth—and along with it much of the wealth of its residents—Richard's financial prospects would only have been further diminished.

While some Crockett historians suggest (without documentation) a 1780 date for Richard's relocation to Deer Isle, it makes more sense that he emigrated to Deer Isle after the destruction of Falmouth. Although Cape Elizabeth was spared by Mowatt (the town did not have a harbor deep enough for British ships to sail into), if Richard rented or leased a shop on Falmouth Neck (which seems plausible given that the Neck was Falmouth's business center of its day),[185] that shop most likely was destroyed by the fire. In addition, by 1775, all of Richard's younger sons had reached the age of maturity (or close to it) and were likely out of the house. Combined, these factors could have caused the kind of existential crisis necessary to prompt a man in his seventh decade to make a major relocation.

In addition, Deer Isle, a rural island to the eastward, presented Richard with a new frontier, one that had recently been made available to colonists after the fall of Quebec. (After their French allies were defeated, warring Native Americans fled to Canada for safety, abandoning central and eastern Maine.) Opportunities for

---

183. "When Revolution Came: The Story of Old Deer Isle In the Province of Maine During the War For American Independence," p. 23. Vernal Hutchinson. Ellsworth, Maine: The Ellsworth American, 1972.
184. Massachusetts State Archives collection, colonial period, 1622-1788. Volume 132. Town valuations, Cape Elizabeth. P. 165. https://www.familysearch.org/ark:/61903/3:1:3Q9M-C9YR-V6Q2?i=235&cat=1055547
185. WILLIS, p. 438.

land ownership via grant (something that always appealed to the Cricketts as to almost every settler), would have been a sweet enticement. Plus, by 1775, Richard and Mary's son Josiah had been living on Deer Isle for seven years. If Richard lost his shop when Falmouth burned—and did not even own his small bit of land and house in Cape Elizabeth because it was mortgaged to John Waite—he had nothing to gain by staying in the Falmouth area, and everything to gain by leaving.

A "First Settlers List" for Deer Isle shows that Josiah Crockett immigrated to Deer Isle in 1768.[186] He would have been twenty-one (or twenty-two) when he moved from Falmouth to Deer Isle. (Deer Isle historian George Hosmer says Josiah hailed from "Portland, then known as Falmouth, or that vicinity.")[187] Josiah built and operated a sawmill at what became known as Crockett's Cove, where he lived with his wife Sarah Dow and their family.[188] (Today, my sister Cheryl Wixson and her husband Phillip McFarland live on the east side of Crockett's Cove, opposite where Josiah, and later, his father Richard, settled.)

If Richard relocated to Deer Isle in late 1775 or early 1776, he would have been about seventy years of age. Initially, he would have lived with Josiah and his family in their home on the west side of Crockett's Cove, while he (probably with help from his son or sons) built a house, also located on the west side of the cove. After Richard immigrated to Deer Isle, he again worked as a joiner,[189] which he had done decades earlier while living in Stratham, N.H. (Probably chairs were not in high demand in the backcountry of Deer Isle, settlers there unlike the once affluent residents of Falmouth.)

British Occupation

Unluckily for Richard, the Revolutionary War years were particularly trying for settlers in eastern Maine. If after the burning of Falmouth Richard had initially hoped by relocating to Deer Isle to enjoy his later years beyond the reach of British tyranny, he was doomed to disappointment. Instead, he experienced rather

---

186. DEERISLE, p. 24-25.
187. DEERISLE, p. 103.
188. I have taken the liberty of ascribing the sawmill to Josiah Crockett, since the mill was located on his property. In addition, it is doubtful the sawmill would have appeared on the 1785 Plan of Deer Isle by Peters, Stone, Titcomb and Mathews, unless it had been operational sometime prior to the arrival of Josiah's father and brother.
189. Affidavit of Nathaniel Thomas presented to the General Court of Massachusetts. Falmouth, April 13, 1781. BAXTER2, p. 198-199. This affidavit, which expressly says that Richard is a joiner, testifies to the attack and beating Richard Crockett suffered at the hands of American privateers March 6, 1781. Richard survived the attack.

the reverse. In addition to suffering from food and supply shortages from British blockades, Deer Isle residents (and other settlers Down East) soon became cut off from their own countrymen.

On June 17, 1779, British troops landed on the Bagaduce peninsula in Penobscot Bay (at what is now Castine) where they commenced to build a fort (Fort George). The British occupation of eastern Maine during the Revolutionary War caused no little distress to American patriots living in the area. They were now separated from the rest of Maine and New England by the enemy plunking down amongst them.

Inset from Early Settlers Map of Deer Isle/Stonington.
The map shows Crockett's Cove and the homestead of Josiah Crockett,
son of Richard Crockett, Jr. and Mary (Robinson) Crockett.
("Deer Island." Map drawn by George L. Hosmer.)[190]

---

190. Hosmer's "Deer Island" map, from which this section was taken, shows the location of first settlers. Copyright 1905 by Abel Hosmer. (Now in the public domain.) The map was glued to the Contents page in Hosmer's "An Historical Sketch of the Town of Deer Isle, Maine: with Notices of Its Settlers and Early Inhabitants." Reprinted by the Courier-Gazette, Inc., 1976.

The Fourth Generation

Inset from Plan of Deer Isle, 1785.
Plan shows Crockett's Mill, situated at the head of what was known as Crockett's Cove (named for Josiah Crockett, son of Richard Crockett, Jr. and Mary Robinson Crockett).
(Plan courtesy of the Digital Maine Repository, Maine State Library.)[191]

---

191. The plan, created by Jonathan Peters, Jonathan Stone, Samuel Titcomb, and Jonathan Mathews, was recorded at Lincoln County Registry of Deeds in Plan Book 11, Page 50. (Hancock County was not split from Lincoln County until 1789.) https://digitalmaine.com/planbook_11/51/ We know that this mill was a sawmill because Hosmer writes in his history of Deer Isle (DEERISLE, p. 111) that Rufus York (a grandson-in-law of Captain Robinson Crockett, Josiah's brother) "was drowned in 1844, in endeavoring to escape from his vessel which took fire in the night, while lying loaded with wood in Crockett's Cove." Also, from p. 21 of Hosmer's History of Deer Isle: "Another [sawmill] was maintained several years, known as 'Crockett's Mill,' till about 30 years ago."

In July of 1779, the Provincial Congress of Massachusetts Bay, outraged by the audacity of the British to invade its territory, raised a joint expedition (a land and sea operation) to drive the Red Coats from eastern Maine. The Penobscot Expedition included 44 ships (19 warships and the rest support ships) carrying 1,000 troops and supplies. Once in Maine waters, ego and ineptitude precipitated a squabble over command of the expedition. This caused a delay long enough for the British to send for a relief fleet, which chased the American ships up the Penobscot River and destroyed the fleet. Surviving soldiers and sailors from the sunken and burnt American vessels fled into the surrounding woods, where they made their way home through the wilderness as best they could.

The Penobscot Expedition was rated the worst naval defeat for the United States until Pearl Harbor, 162 years later.[192] One of those soldiers who took to the woods was Richard Crockett's grandson, Samuel Crockett,[193] the son of Richard Crockett (III) and Elizabeth (Roberts) Crockett. Samuel might have gone to his grandfather's or uncle's house in Deer Isle first, from where, under the cover of darkness, he could have been surreptitiously sailed back down to Second Parish (then known as Cape Elizabeth).

Following this naval victory, British soldiers and sailors maintained a stout hold over eastern Maine for the balance of the Revolutionary War. Great Britain even had the brass to declare that section of Maine to be once again part of the British Empire. Guns belonging to the settlers were confiscated, and Americans (including the Crocketts) were forced to submit to British authority, although little was offered in return for their submission.

For four long years, from 1779 to 1783 when the Treaty of Paris was signed ending the American Revolution, those who resided in eastern Maine were largely abandoned. British soldiers, who had military possession of the area, did not particularly care what happened to these American settlers, and Massachusetts Bay, which still (on paper, anyway) had political and social control of the territory, was not in any position to offer protection to its residents. (Some settlers were Tories, too, although the Crocketts certainly were not.)

Because of the lack of any formal law and order, the area in which the Crocketts resided presented a tempting target. Residents became vulnerable to raids

---

192. "Redcoats, and Rebels: The American Revolutionary War." H. Bicheno. London: Harper Collins, 2003. P. 149.
193. U.S., Revolutionary War Pension and Bounty-Land Warrant Application Files, 1800-1900. https://www.ancestry.com/discoveryui-content/view/14508:1995?tid=118893465&pid=312138417148&queryId=4e15a43a4965aa4ecb-58f03099bbd335&_phsrc=zoc23&_phstart=successSource

perpetrated against them by both American and British miscreants. Deer Isle historian Hosmer describes the unenviable position of coastal settlers (including Josiah and Richard Crockett), who were easy prey for scallywags on both sides of the war, although more often than not by Americans preying upon other Americans:

> "One great cause of annoyance was the practice that there was of plundering the inhabitants of the seacoast in this vicinity; by persons who went about for that purpose in boats which were then styled 'shaving mills.' They committed their depredations in places where they were not known. They would land upon the shore, visit the houses of the inhabitants, and steal whatever they could lay their hands on, which was a cause of distress to the persons plundered, as they had but little, and that little they wanted themselves. It was useless to make any complaint, as there was then no redress to be had."[194]

<u>The Shaving Mill</u>

On March 6, 1781, Richard Crockett (then in his mid-seventies) and his son Josiah (about thirty-five) and Josiah's family, were subjected to a shaving mill. The raid was led by Nathaniel Thompson of Falmouth, who had command of a privateer, the *Roebuck*,[195] and was known to be "engaged in some questionable operations."[196]

Prior to attacking the Crocketts, Thompson and fifteen of his men raided the Deer Isle home of John Campbell and his wife Mary, who, unsuspecting of treachery, had fed the hungry crew the day before. During that visit, Mary had made the mistake of showing off to the men a trunk of inherited fine linens and garments, which collection so impressed Thompson and his crew that they returned at night to steal the trunk, taking along with it John Campbell's watch and "fifteen hard dollars."[197] The thieves sailed off with the loot and hid away in Crockett's Cove, where early on the morning of March 6th Thompson and his crew rowed ashore. The thugs raided Josiah's house and then proceeded to Richard's home, where they beat, threatened, and robbed the septuagenarian.

---

194. DEERISLE, p. 30-31.
195. "When Revolution Came: The Story of Old Deer Isle In the Province of Maine During the War For American Independence," p. 148. Vernal Hutchinson. Ellsworth, Maine: The Ellsworth American, 1972.
196. Deposition of S.P. Mayberry, sworn before Enoch Freeman, J.P., in Falmouth, April 13, 1781. "Deposition in the Time of the Revolutionary War. Deer Isle." *Bangor Historical Magazine*, Vol. 2, 1887. P. 84.
197. "When Revolution Came: The Story of Old Deer Isle In the Province of Maine During the War For American Independence," p. 149. Vernal Hutchinson. Ellsworth, Maine: The Ellsworth American, 1972.

Thanks to the affidavit of Nathaniel Thomas, a carpenter and neighbor of Richard's, who was at Richard's house not long after the raid occurred, we know what happened during the shaving mill. (Thomas' deposition was taken in Falmouth April 13, 1781 and was presented to the Massachusetts General Court at the same time Josiah Crockett petitioned for redress after the attack.) Thomas' deposition reveals the physical abuse and contumely Richard Crockett received:

> "… And about sunrise of said sixth of March [1781] there entered the house of the said Richard, three armed men viz. Beniah Low, Kemp, and Daniel Marston, who were part of a boat crew commanded by Nathaniel Thompson of Falmouth in the County Cumberland. Mr. Crocket, attempting to go out of his door, Kemp, Low, and Tobey struck him several violent blows with the butts of their guns, and one of them, viz. Marston, presented the muzzle of his gun (the gun being cocked) at the said Crocket–the others continuing to beat and wound the said Crocket tearing his clothes and abusing his person. Rummaging his house and taking from thence a gun and bullet bag,[198] which they carried away with them. When Mr. Crocket cried Murder and for help–they said 'Damn him. Kill him.' and Damn you–speaking to the said Crocket, 'We mean to kill you'–in consequence of all which abuse and ill-usage the said Crocket was confined to his house for above a fortnight…"[199]

Richard's son Josiah happened to be away visiting a neighbor when *his* house was attacked. Josiah's wife, while caring for a sick child, was beaten, and rum and tobacco stores were taken by the intruders. Upon Josiah's return, he was captured by the miscreants, and taken out to the *Roebuck* against his will. We learn the particulars of the attack on Josiah and his family from a petition he later filed with the Massachusetts General Court:

> "… Yet in addition to their distress as though it were not already sufficient, in total disregard of the feelings of humanity, prompted by avarice and a desire of plunder a certain Nathaniel Thomson of Falmouth in the County of Cumberland in a boat with fifteen men from said Falmouth on the sixth day of March last past

---

198. Although the British in Castine demanded the colonists surrender their guns, it is obvious that not everyone did so. Guns would have been necessary to help provide food for the table and for protection. Richard Crockett, apparently taken by surprise, was not able to grab and load his weapon.
199. *Affidavit of Nathaniel Thomas*, April 13, 1781. BAXTER2, p. 198-199. I have edited the deposition for easier reading.

The Fourth Generation

landed at said Deer Island abused robbed and plundered some of the inhabitants thereof. They entered the house of your petitioner, struck and abused his wife there being, broke in the window where a child was laying then dangerously sick and thereby greatly hazarded its life;–They took and carried away from your petitioners store rum tobacco &c and meeting your petitioner as they left his house as he returned from his neighbour's, they insulted and abused him; took from him eleven gallons of molasses he then had with him, and forced him on board their boat, where they detained him a considerable time. They also entered the house of Mr. Richard Crockett your petitioners father, being above 75 years of age, and with a loaded gun placed at his breast threatened to take away his life, they otherwise insulted him, and beat and wounded him so that he was unable to follow his business for the space of fourteen days.[200]

Because of the way the raid unfolded, Captain Thompson probably did not know that the Crocketts—who formerly were part of the greater Falmouth community to which Thompson belonged—resided in this obscure cove.[201] Nevertheless, Thompson and some of his crewmen were recognized by the Crocketts and their friends. Josiah Crockett (whom historian Hosmer describes as "singular," without offering any more detail on how he was odd)[202] was particularly infuriated by the attack upon himself and his father by fellow Americans. Shortly after the raid Josiah sailed his sloop down to Falmouth (with fellow victim Mary Campbell and witness Nathan Thomas aboard) to confront Thompson and attempt to regain the stolen goods. When Thompson refused to return his plunder, Josiah petitioned the Massachusetts General Court requesting relief.[203] (See Appendix, pages 408–409

---

200. Petition of Josiah Crockett to the General Court of Massachusetts, April 11, 1781. BAXTER2, p. 195.
201. Vernal Hutchinson in his book "When Revolution Came" implies that the Crocketts (and neighbors, the Campbells) were attacked due to their fealty or supposed fealty to England. Like all Americans living on Deer Isle, Josiah Crockett was forced to sign an oath of loyalty to the King of England to procure supplies from the British with which to feed his family. He and the Campbells attempted to remain neutral during the Revolution; however, I doubt whether Thompson knew one way or another whether Josiah was a Tory or not; he was likely just looking for an opportunity to plunder. In fact, Thompson probably stumbled onto the Crocketts by accident when hiding his ship from British detection in Crockett's Cove. The Crocketts were not Torys. Many (if not all) of Richard Crockett's grandsons served in the Continental Army. (See Chapter 7.)
202. DEERISLE, p. 103. In his petition, Josiah Crockett seems not only intelligent and well-spoken, but also righteously indignant (rightly so).
203. Having no type of political or social government in place, British troops allowed these types of civil complaints and squabbles between American settlers to proceed before the General Court of Massachusetts so that they would not have to deal with them. For its part, the General Court treated Deer Isle and the surrounding towns as American territory temporarily occupied by the enemy. Josiah, Mary Campbell, and Nathan Thomas gave their depositions to magistrate Enoch Freeman of Falmouth, who presented the petitions to the Massachusetts General Court on their behalf. "When Revolution Came: The Story of Old Deer Isle In the Province of Maine During the War For American Independence," p. 155-156. Vernal Hutchinson. Ellsworth, Maine: The Ellsworth American, 1972.

for a copy of Josiah's petition, which provides details about the raid, as well as information about the onerous conditions under which eastern Mainers were then living—having neither the protection of the Americans nor the British.)

Josiah's petition was read in the Massachusetts Senate on April 19, 1781 and was likely accompanied by the deposition given by Nathan Thomas about the attack upon Richard Crockett. (A *Certificate in Favor of Josiah Crockett* signed by thirty-three Deer Isle residents, including Richard, also accompanied Josiah's petition.)[204] It was then ordered that two men from the Senate (Increase Sumner and Jonathan Greenleaf) should join with House members to consider the petition and report "what may be proper to be done thereon."

The Massachusetts House concurred with the Senate on April 23, 1781, and Representatives General Titcomb, Colonel Coffin, and Mr. Leggate joined the Senate's committee. After receiving the committee's report, a decision was rendered in the Senate April 26, 1781, during which it was reaffirmed that "the Inhabitants of said Island [Deer Isle] have been, and now are considered in such a Situation as that they ought to have and enjoy the same Protection, Security, and Advantage from the laws of this Commonwealth, as the other Subjects thereof do, or may exercise and enjoy…," by which it was understood that Josiah Crockett had the "Right to prosecute to final Judgment and execution such persons, as have or may be Guilty of plundering or in any Way or Manner Abusing" him. In addition, Josiah was granted the privilege of transporting fifty bushels of much-needed Indian corn back to the inhabitants of Deer Isle, as he had requested. The House concurred with slight amendments on April 27, 1781, to which the Senate concurred the same day.[205]

Josiah Crockett probably never received the legislated justice from the damage of Thompson's raid. Living between two national enemies during the prosecution of a war would have made it difficult for Josiah to sue Thompson. According to Vernal Hutchinson in "When Revolution Came: The Story of Old Deer Isle In the Province of Maine During the War For American Independence," Mary Campbell "recovered a few of [her stolen items], from owners and crew of the *Roebuck*. Josiah recovered nothing."[206] The politicians of the Massachusetts General Court

---

204. *Certificate in Favor of Josiah Crockett.* Signed in Deer Isle March 9, 1781 (three days after the raid) by thirty-three residents. BAXTER2, p. 223-224.
205. *Resolve Granting Privilege of Transporting Corn.* Massachusetts General Court, April 26, 1781. BAXTER2, p. 220-221.
206. "When Revolution Came: The Story of Old Deer Isle In the Province of Maine During the War For American Independence," p. 159. Vernal Hutchinson. Ellsworth, Maine: The Ellsworth American, 1972.

provided only empty words to those who suffered the Deer Isle shaving-mill. The only satisfaction Josiah Crockett received was the privilege of hauling 50 bushels of corn back to his hungry neighbors.

Death of Richard Crockett, Jr. and a Posthumous Grant of Land

Some Crockett genealogists date Richard's death as March 6, 1781, the day of the shaving mill; however, we know that Richard not only survived, but was still among the living when the depositions were given to the Massachusetts General Court. Despite Richard's advanced age, and the injuries he suffered during the shaving mill, he was back at his regular joiner work within two weeks, according to the depositions. Given his apparent resiliency, Richard Crockett, Jr. could have lived several years after the 1781 raid. While we do not know the actual date of his death, Richard Crockett, Jr. was deceased by January 1, 1786, when a posthumous grant of 100 acres of land to Richard's heirs and assigns was drawn up. (The grant was not officially awarded until 1788.)

After the American colonists defeated the British, Great Britain ceded her land in the United States to the fledgling nation, including the occupied territory of eastern Maine. In 1788, the General Court of Massachusetts, as compensation for the abuses these Americans on Deer Isle experienced during the war, voted to grant land on the island (for a nominal sum) to the settlers there. The Court "passed a resolve granting one hundred acres of land to each of the persons who had settled on Deer Island … previous to the first day of January, 1784."[207] The men who received these grants were styled "proprietors."[208] (Both Richard and Josiah Crockett received grants as proprietors.)[209] Those who settled Deer Isle after that date—and proprietors' sons who came of age after January 1, 1784—were known as "young settlers."[210] (Robinson Crockett, Richard and Mary's son and Josiah's brother, received a grant as a young settler.)[211] The difference between the two groups was the price paid for the granted land. Proprietors, most of whom were on Deer Isle during the occupation by the British, paid only thirty shillings for their

---

207. DEERISLE, p. 34.
208. DEERISLE, p. 35.
209. DEERISLE, p. 103. According to Deer Isle historian Hosmer, Josiah's lot was 212 acres, not 100. "Why he had one so large is not known to us," he writes.
210. DEERISLE, p. 35. Richard's son Robinson (two years older than Josiah) received a grant of 100 acres as a "young settler."
211. DEERISLE, p. 103-104.

100 acres. Young settlers paid $1 per acre, a significantly higher sum.[212] Had Richard Crockett been alive at the time his grant was awarded, he—a man perpetually in debt—would have appreciated the lower price to be paid for his land. The grant to Richard's heirs was as follows:

> "Pursuant to a Resolve of the General Court, we have laid out and appropriated unto the heirs and assigns of Richard Crockett as a compensation for settlement before the first day of January A.D. 1786, one hundred acres of land on Deer Island bounded as follows, at a bound mark at the shore, opposite to Crockett falls, on the Western side of the Cove, thence runs East two hundred and forty rods, thence South seventy-eight rods, thence West to the shore to the bound mark begun at. We have made allowance for roads, and have received thirty shillings as stipulated by said resolve."[213]

The deed was dated January 1, 1789 (as were all the proprietors' deeds, according to Deer Isle historian Hosmer); however, all the deeds were drawn up on January 1, 1786, so we know Richard was deceased by that date. If one of Richard's motivations for relocating to Deer Isle was to secure land, he was ultimately successful, albeit after his death.

We do not know where Richard was buried. Possibly this colorful Crockett was laid to rest in an unmarked grave near his home on Deer Isle. Just as likely, however, he lies in the old cemetery atop the hill overlooking Crockett's Cove at what became known as Barbour Farm, of which his grandson Richard (one of Robinson's sons) became a part owner.[214] If so, the peaceful presence of the remains of Richard Crockett, Jr. added historical profundity to the marriage of his seventh-great granddaughter Joanna R. McFarland to Jesse Tea. The marriage took place at Barbour Farms on July 23, 2016, more than two hundred and twenty-five years after Richard's death. He was remembered on that day.

---

212. DEERISLE, p. 34-35.
213. Hancock County Registry of Deeds, Book 4, pages 236-237.
214. DEERISLE, p. 104.

The Fourth Generation

The wedding of Joanna R. McFarland and Jesse Tea, July 23, 2016,
Crockett's Cove, Stonington, Maine.
The wedding occurred at high tide at the head of Crockett's Cove, down the hill from the old cemetery in which Joanna's ancestor Richard Crockett, Jr. possibly lies at rest. To the left of Joanna and Jesse is the bride's grandmother, Rowena Palmer, who was Richard Crockett, Jr.'s fifth-great granddaughter.
(Photo courtesy of Joanna McFarland.)

Chapter 5

"AT A PLACE CALLED LONG CREEK"
THE FIFTH GENERATION

First Generation – Thomas Crockett
Second Generation – Ephraim Crockett
Third Generation – Richard Crockett
Fourth Generation – Richard Crockett, Jr.
Fifth Generation – Richard Crockett (III, also known as Richard, Jr.), circa 1733-1821
Sixth Generation – Ephraim Crockett

This Richard Crockett, the third Richard in the line we are following, resided in Cape Elizabeth for his entire adult life. Richard was born around 1733, the son of Richard Crockett, Jr. and Mary (Robinson) Crockett. At the time of his birth, Richard's family lived in what was known as Second Parish, the Falmouth settlement situated on the south side of the Fore River. In 1765, when Richard was in his early thirties, Second Parish became Cape Elizabeth District, with the right to govern itself under Falmouth's political umbrella (still part of the Province of Massachusetts Bay). A decade later, at the beginning of the American Revolution, the town of Cape Elizabeth was established by the Provincial Congress of Massachusetts, with the privilege of sending a representative to the General Court. Richard is unique among his Crockett ancestors in that—rather than chase after land and opportunities elsewhere when he reached the age of maturity—he remained where he was born, making a commitment to the town of Cape Elizabeth.

Family Ties "at a Place Called Long Creek"

The whole cloth of the community into which Richard was born, married, lived and died was woven of threads from interconnected families of English ancestry. These consisted of the Roberts, Crockett, Skillin, Sawyer, Robinson, Westcoat (Wescott), York, and Dunn families. Most of the threads led back to Rhoda (Haley) and Samuel Skillin, Sr., Richard's great-aunt and uncle, although other Second Parish families were interwoven as well. When Samuel Skillin, Sr. returned to Falmouth he settled at Long Creek, the large stream that flows into the Fore River where his late father John Skillin had formerly established a mill. Samuel Skillin operated both a saw mill and a grist mill ("the Great Mill")[1] at Long Creek. Many deeds that were executed by (and among) the connecting threads of family members over the decades describe the various properties that were traded, gifted, bought, and sold as being situated "at a place called Long Creek."

Richard's first two wives—Elizabeth Roberts and Susannah Westcoat—were both granddaughters of Samuel and Rhoda Skillin. (Elizabeth and Susannah were first cousins.) Elizabeth was the daughter of George Roberts and Katharine Skillin. Richard's second wife, Susannah Westcoat, was the daughter of William Westcoat and Dorcas Skillin. Katharine and Dorcas were two of the many daughters of Samuel and Rhoda (Haley) Skillin. (Richard's third wife, Elizabeth Lewis Masury appears to have been no direct relation to the Skillin family, although we cannot tell for sure since we do not know if Lewis was her maiden name.) Because of Samuel Skillin's generosity in endowing his children and their spouses with real estate at Long Creek, the extended families remained physically close and naturally intermarried.

Although Richard spent most of his life at Long Creek, by the time of his death in 1821 many of the younger members of the interconnected families (such as Richard's eldest son Ephraim Crockett) had departed for greener pastures. They were replaced by an inflow of disparate people. In 1898, the greater Long Creek area, no longer dominated by descendants of Samuel and Rhoda (Haley) Skillin, was spun off into the separate town of South Portland. If he was alive today, Richard would not recognize the little settlement once fondly known as Long Creek. Even the

---

1. Following various deeds through generations of Skillin, Roberts, and Westcoat families we learn that the Great Mill often referred to was a grist mill.

name, "Long Creek," is now most associated—not with a water body—but with a secure juvenile detention facility.

Too Many Richard Crocketts

To assemble an accurate timeline with which to recreate the life of this Richard Crockett, we must first dispose of a superfluous Richard Crockett—Richard IV—the reported son of this Richard and his first wife Elizabeth Roberts. Having spent several years studying various records—birth, marriage, death, land, military, valuation, and court and town records—I have concluded that Richard IV never existed. Historians who have reported otherwise (including Crockett genealogist Candage) have been confused, understandably so, by the plethora of Richard Crocketts. This confusion, which led to the spawning of an extra Richard Crockett, Jr., has three major causes.

The first issue that caused the confusion was that Richard (III) and his father (Richard II) were both known during their lives as "Richard Crockett" *and* "Richard Crockett, Jr." Secondly, both men resided for decades in Second Parish in which they were intimately known by the same set of people. Since Richard the elder lived well into his mid-seventies, many in Cape Elizabeth utilized the suffix "junior" to distinguish Richard (III) from his father (although it appears that Richard himself might have preferred not to use the suffix).[2] Thirdly, both Richard (III) and Richard (II) had the same vocation—they were chairmakers. Merton Taylor Goodrich does a good job untangling the ancestry of the Crockett family in his 1941 article in

---

2. Two deeds, both executed Sept. 12, 1781, offer a good example of how the use of the suffix "Jr." has confused historians. In the first deed (CCROD, Book 15, p. 99) Richard Crockett, chairmaker of Cape Elizabeth, assigns two-fifths of a parcel of land formerly belonging to "my father Mr. George Roberts" to Mr. George Roberts. We know this is Richard Crockett (III) because George Roberts was his father-in-law. In another deed executed the same day by Richard's brothers-in-law George Copson Roberts and Joseph Roberts (selling to Richard III for 20 pounds the remainder of their parent's estate, with a few exceptions) the brothers describe the buyer as "Richard Crockett, Jr.," chairmaker of Cape Elizabeth (CCROD, Book 11, p. 408). Naturally, when considering the two deeds side by side, one might assume that the Roberts brothers are selling the property to their nephew, Richard Crockett, Jr. (IV), who (if he existed) would be of an age to purchase real estate; however, this assumption does not take into consideration that facts that, a. George and Joseph have known their brother-in-law Richard Crockett III as "Richard, Jr." their entire lives, and b., Richard III's father, Richard II, is still alive on this date, and the Roberts know this. But because his father has relocated to Deer Isle, Richard III has dropped the "Jr." from his name in his deed (or possibly he preferred not to be known by that designation in the first place). His brothers-in-law, for the reasons given, have retained the suffix in their deed. Thus, both deeds relate to the same man—Richard Crockett (III)—and do not present evidence for the existence of a son of Richard and Elizabeth named Richard, Jr. (IV). In two other deeds he executes in 1781, Richard (III) also denotes himself simply as "Richard Crockett" a chairmaker of Cape Elizabeth. On April 23, 1781, Richard buys 30 acres of land in Cape Elizabeth from Samuel Mountfort (CCROD, Book 11, p. 281) and on Sept. 13, 1781, Richard sells 25 acres of land at Long Creek to his brother Robinson Crockett (CCROD, Book 11, pg. 329. Some historians have suggested these deeds relate to Richard II, claiming he sold the property to his son, Robinson; however a careful tracing of the Mountfort property reveals the buyer and seller could only have been Richard (III).

The American Genealogist, "Case of the Chairmakers: A Problem in the Crockett Family;"[3] however, Goodrich made mistakes, which errors have contributed to the confusion.[4]

Also, there is no birth record for the excess Richard. This by itself would not necessarily consign him to the dustbin of historical fiction since there is no birth record for his purported father, either. (Lack of a birth record for Richard Crockett IV forced Crockett genealogist Candage to squeeze him into the birth order of Richard and Elizabeth's children between Deborah and Samuel, so he would be old enough to have married Susannah Westcoat.) Birth records for Second Parish or Cape Elizabeth during the 18th century are scarce. Indeed, the only known birthdate for any of the eight children of Elizabeth Roberts and Richard Crockett (III) is that of their eldest son, Ephraim. His birth is known—not from any birth record—but from other sources, including the record of Ephraim's death[5] and his Revolutionary War pension application.[6]

Also, while there is a perfectly good explanation for the lack of Richard IV's birth record, there is no explanation for the lack of a military service record during the American Revolution. Had this extra Richard existed—unless he was deaf, dumb, blind, or infirm (which we have no reason to suspect)—he would have fought in that great battle for liberty, as did his (supposed) brothers Ephraim and Samuel Crockett; his male cousins and uncles; and, indeed, most of the young men from Cape Elizabeth and Falmouth.

Perhaps the most compelling reason to suspect that Richard IV never existed, however, is that he was not the Richard Crockett who, in 1776, married Susannah Westcoat. On November 7, 1776, Cape Elizabeth Town Clerk David Strout entered

---

3. CHAIRMAKERS, p. 138-143. https://archive.org/details/sim_american-genealogist_1941-01_17_3/page/138/mode/1up?view=theater

4. Goodrich's most notable mistake is to declare that brothers Samuel and Richard Crockett are operating together in the prior generation, when the historical record shows otherwise. Goodrich assumes that the property Richard (II) purchases from John Sawyer, Jr. (perhaps because of its size) is on Middle Street in Falmouth (downtown Portland) where Samuel purchased property; however, Richard's deed gives no street name or location other than Falmouth. (See YCROD 33, p. 77a.) Also, Goodrich asserts that Richard accompanies his brother Samuel when he removes to Gorham, again, without providing evidence from deeds or other records. Falmouth town records clearly show that several of Richard's children were of that town when married, not Gorham. In addition, there are no property records for Richard in Gorham, and several for his brother Samuel. Valuation records for Falmouth reveal that Richard lived (and owned property) in Second Parish/Cape Elizabeth District.

5. Maine Death Record, 1761-1922 https://www.ancestry.com/discoveryui-content/view/1322685:1962?ssrc=pt&tid=118893465&pid=312093739007

6. U.S. Revolutionary War Pension and Bounty=Land Warrant Application Files, 1800-1900. Crockett, Ephraim. https://www.ancestry.com/imageviewer/collections/1995/images/MIUSA1775D_135275-00084?pId=14814 We do get an idea of when Ephraim's younger brother Samuel was born from his Revolutionary War pension application, too.

into his record book the marriage intentions for "Mr. Richard Crocket, Jur & Miss Suzanna Waistcoat both of Cape Elizabeth."[7] Given the date—four months before eldest son Ephraim filed his marriage intentions—combined with the suffix "junior," most historians (including Candage) have concluded that this notice relates to a son of Richard and Elizabeth, also named Richard (i.e. Richard IV). But in 1776, Richard—the father of Ephraim and this superfluous Richard—was himself still known in Cape Elizabeth as "Richard, Jr.," *his* father then being still alive. Had he and Elizabeth produced a son named Richard, to whom this marriage intention referred, Strout most certainly would have identified the young man as "Mr. Richard Crocket, 3." Anyone who has spent time scrolling through old town and court records in Maine has found them replete with clerks utilizing the number "3" (and even, on occasion, "4," signifying the fourth male in a line bearing the same name).

Finally—and decidedly—our extraneous young Richard *would not have married Susannah Westcoat*. Not only was Susannah a generation ahead of him (albeit on the younger end of that generation), but also she would have been considered "damaged goods" by aspiring young beaus of the day. Susannah, who was charged with fornication in October 1768,[8] gave birth to son[9] out of wedlock the last day of February of that year.

But if not the wife of our superfluous Richard Crockett, who did Susannah Westcoat marry? The answer to that is easy: Susannah Westcoat married Richard Crockett, Jr., just as town clerk Strout says.[10] While Susannah's indiscretion from prior years (now an eight-year-old boy) would have been an anathema to a young man just coming up in the world, her youthful stumble would not have kept a widower with two young daughters from offering marriage to his late wife's cousin. In fact, just the opposite. Where else could Richard, if he *was* widowed (no death

---

7. "A Book of Records For the Second Parish in The town of Falmouth containing 212 pages." New P. 13 (image 41) South Portland, Maine Town Records, 1765-1823.
8. Cumberland County records, Court of General Sessions of the Peace, Oct. 18, 1768, p. 167-168. https://www.familysearch.org/ark:/61903/3:1:3Q9M-CS73-LWRQ-8?i=88&cat=554097
9. The Court of General Sessions of the Peace termed Susannah's son "a male bastard child born of her body in Evil Example to Others in Like Cases." Cumberland County records, Court of General Sessions of the Peace, Oct. 18, 1768, p. 167-168. https://www.familysearch.org/ark:/61903/3:1:3Q9M-CS73-LWRQ-8?i=88&cat=554097
10. Sharp-eyed skeptics will question why—if Richard (III) was known locally as Richard, Jr.—he was styled as "Richard Crockit" (not, Crockett, Jr.) on November 24, 1755, when Falmouth Town Clerk Stephen Longfellow entered his and Elizabeth Robert's marriage intentions? The reply that springs to mind is that Longfellow, of Falmouth, was not as familiar with the Crockett family as was Town Clerk Stout, who was from Cape Elizabeth, where the Richard Crocketts resided. https://www.familysearch.org/ark:/61903/3:1:3Q9M-C9B2-VZSF

record exists for Elizabeth Roberts Crockett),[11] find a wife so well-known and so close at hand as from the house of William Westcoat, his relative[12] and neighbor?

Having sufficiently disposed of our extra Richard (we hope), let us proceed to tell the story of Richard Crockett—the third Richard Crockett in the line we are following—as well as that of his wives and their families and friends, and Cape Elizabeth, the town in which they all lived.

The Roberts Family

When in 1737 Richard's father fled with his family to Stratham, N.H. (to his father's house) to escape his creditors, young Richard, then about four, likely went, too. Because Richard became a chairmaker like his father, he probably learned his trade at his father's knee. Whether he spent his entire youth in Stratham, however, returning to Maine with the family by 1750 after his father's debts were paid, we cannot know. As a youth Richard might have apprenticed with his uncle Samuel Crockett in Falmouth, who was also a chairmaker (and a shipwright). By 1754, however, when he reached the age of maturity and married Elizabeth Roberts, Richard began to be influenced by his father-in-law George Roberts, a husbandman, and an established member of the Cape Elizabeth community. In many ways, Richard Crockett's life mirrors that of his father-in-law's life in Cape Elizabeth. In addition, Richard ended up with much of George and Katharine (Skillin) Roberts' real estate at Long Creek, certainly because of his relationship with the extended Roberts family.

As a man, George Roberts—also a descendant of Thomas and Ann Crockett—was worth emulating. Roberts was born in Kittery on March 30, 1704, the son of William Roberts (II) and Sarah (Creasey) Roberts.[13] His grandfather, William Roberts (I), was the husband of Ann Crockett, the eldest daughter of Thomas and Anne Crockett. George married Katharine Skillin, a daughter of Samuel and Rhoda

---

11. Since no death record or gravestone exists for Elizabeth (Roberts) Crockett, it is reasonable to suppose she died after the couple's last child, Lucy, was born on June 24, 1765 (according to CANDAGE, p. 11, although I have not found a birth record for Lucy). Elizabeth would have been thirty-five in 1765 (SMALLDESC, p. 1140) and, had she been alive, would have continued to bear children, as did other married women of her day. Some historians have pointed to an 1808 deed in which Richard's wife Elizabeth signs off on her dower rights as proof she was still alive (see CCROD, Book 94, p. 54, executed January 18, 1808); however, if we dispose of Richard IV (because he never existed), then it must be Richard (III) who marries Elizabeth Magenry in 1797 and she is the Elizabeth Crockett who signed away her dower rights in 1808.
12. William Westcoat, who was married to Dorcas Skilling, was also an uncle (by marriage) to Richard Crockett, Jr. and thus the great-uncle of Richard (III).
13. SMALLDESC, p. 1134. Roberts was probably born in that part of Kittery now known as South Berwick.

The Fifth Generation

(Haley) Skillin. When by 1730 the Skillins returned to Falmouth (where Samuel's father John Skillin had been killed by Native Americans in 1689), George and Katharine accompanied them. On July 31, 1731, George and Katharine Roberts acknowledged the covenant of the First Church of Falmouth.[14] Daughter Rhoda (named for her grandmother) was baptized at First Church in August of that same year.[15] The following year, on August 20, 1732, Katharine Roberts was accepted into full communion of the church.[16]

The Roberts and Skillins families (and Richard Crockett, Jr. and his family) resided across the river from the larger settlement at Falmouth Neck, in Second Parish, known also at various times as Purpooduck or Cape Elizabeth District. This historic area had a tragic history, having been attacked in 1675 during the First Indian War and destroyed in 1703 during Queen Anne's War (the Third Indian War).

Getting across the river to Falmouth Neck to attend services or meetings held at First Church was time-consuming and cumbersome. Residents applied for relief and on May 7, 1733, the General Court of Massachusetts established Second Parish on the south side of the Fore River. On September 18, 1733, "… the inhabitants of Purpooduck had a Parish meeting and voted to build a meeting-house, and chose Mr. [Benjamin] Allen as their minister."[17] The first meetinghouse was built the following year and Reverend Allen was installed as pastor. Allen served the families of Second Parish from 1734-1754.[18] Because only Rhoda Roberts, the firstborn of George and Katharine's children, was baptized at First Church, we can surmise the other Roberts children (and many of the Crocketts) were baptized by Reverend Allen in Second Parish, who either did not keep records or whose records did not survive.

The first mention of George Roberts in official records occurs March 26, 1734, when at a town meeting in Falmouth (held across the river at the Neck) the town voted to lay out a highway in Purpooduck, "To begin at a white oak tree about ten Rods to the southard of George Roberts House marked Ws from thence East Northerly to a Hemlock tree marked W: from thence East south East to a Beach

---

14. SMALLDESC, p. 1135.
15. SMALLDESC, p. 1140.
16. SMALLDESC, p. 1135.
17. "History of Cape Elizabeth Maine." P. 68. Major Project submitted by Marian Peabbles Johnson, In Partial Fulfillment of the Master of Education, 1954, Boston University. The University of Maine, DigitalCommons. *Maine History Documents*. 173. https://digitalcommons.library.umaine.edu/mainehistory/173 The quote originated from the journal of the Rev. Thomas Smith, pastor of First Church.
18. Website, First Congregational Church, United Church of Christ, South Portland, Maine. https://fccucc.org/about/history/

tree standing by the Road which leads from the Griss mill To Blackpoint [Scarborough] thence as the Road goes to Stephen Randles barn from thence East and be South to the place agreed on for setting the Meeting house from thence East and be north to the Countey Road which leads to Spurwink."[19]

Not long after Falmouth was resettled, the town began parceling out lots, some granted to new settlers and some to "ancient" settlers (or their descendants) of the prior colonies in the Casco Bay area destroyed by the French and Indians. (Initially, there were squabbles over new grants being laid upon former grants; however, these disagreements were soon ironed out.) Like elsewhere in southern Maine where population was on the rise, land speculation became rampant and granted lots were soon sold (and resold). George Roberts became one of those who profited from the purchase and sale of property in Second Parish. Most of the real estate Roberts held onto, including land given to him and his wife Katharine by her father Samuel Skillin, was purchased after their deaths by son-in-law Richard Crockett (III), the subject of this chapter.

On July 4, 1734, George Roberts, husbandman, paid 42 pounds[20] for thirty acres of land in Falmouth. Robets purchased this parcel from Phineas Jones—speculator, shopkeeper, and creditor of Richard Crockett, Jr. (II)—whom we met in Chapter 4. (Jones was also on the Falmouth Proprietors Committee, which doled out the grants.) The lot was located in Second Parish "about twenty rods Southerly from the now dwelling House of the said Roberts" and was half of the sixty-acre lot formerly laid out to James Crocker.[21] On November 23, 1736, the Falmouth Proprietor's Committee laid out to George Roberts, as an assign of his father-in-law Samuel Skillin, "… gentleman, one of the heirs of John Skillings late of Falmouth, carpenter, deceased, fifty-four acres and fourteen rods of land lying in Falmouth aforesaid and at a place called Long Creek…"[22] (Skillin had purchased the rights to his late father's share of granted land from his other siblings, except that belonging to his eldest brother John.) Also assigned to Roberts this day was "…four fifths of sd. John Skillings ten acres lott belonging to the right voted to him by

---

19. Falmouth, Maine Town Records, Book 2, p. 109. (Spurwink was a settlement on the west side of Second Parish on the Spurwink River.) https://archive.org/details/falmouth-maine-town-records-book-2-1728-1773/page/109/mode/1up?q=Skillin&view=theater
20. One wonders if it was George's father-in-law Samuel Skillin who provided the significant sum for this land purchase.
21. YCROD, Book 16, p. 195. Witnesses: Caleb Preble and Samuel Leighton.
22. "Copy of the Original Records of the Proprietors of Falmouth for the years 1718 to 1826." Three volumes in one. PORTLAND: Copied by F.A. Gerrish, 1861. P, 166. https://archive.org/details/proprietors00falmouth_202105/page/n211/mode/1up?view=theater

The Fifth Generation

the Proprietors of Falmouth mentioned above, provided the same has not already [been] laid out; and the land above laid out, to be free from former grants."[23] On November 23, 1736, Samuel Skillin made the land transfer official by deeding these two lots to his son-in-law George Roberts for twenty pounds.[24]

In the 1740s, Roberts made two sales of real estate to his brother-in-law William Westcoat, the husband of his wife's sister, Dorcas (Skillin) Westcoat. (William and Dorcas were the parents of Susannah Westcoat, Richard Crockett III's second wife.) On September 4, 1742, George Roberts, yeoman of Falmouth, sold to Westcoat for 35 pounds "... Five Acres of Land at Long Creek & near to my now Dwelling House being part of Thirty Acres of Land which I purchased of Phineas Jones of Falmouth."[25] (Roberts had previously sold 25 acres from the same lot to William's brother Richard Westcoat.)[26] Five years later, on May 30, 1745, Roberts sold to William Westcoat for 46 pounds and 15 shillings approximately eleven acres of land at Long Creek.[27] These deeds reflect the close physical relationship of the Westcoat and Roberts families, and later (after Richard Crockett purchased his late father-in-law's property), Richard and the Westcoats.

On July 23, 1745, George Roberts, yeoman of Falmouth, sold for 172 pounds old tenor to Thomas Cummins, husbandman of Falmouth, thirty acres of land in Falmouth "... bounded as followeth viz: beginning at a Red Oak tree Standing near Long Creek by a place called the Indian Spring ..."[28] George's wife Katharine also signed the deed to Cummins.

On June 8, 1753, Samuel Skillin of Falmouth, gentleman, "for & in consideration of the Love and Good will that I have for my Daughter Katharine Roberts the wife of George Roberts of Falmouth" granted the couple forty acres of land at

---

23. "Copy of the Original Records of the Proprietors of Falmouth for the years 1718 to 1826." Three volumes in one. PORTLAND: Copied by F.A. Gerrish, 1861. P. 166. https://archive.org/details/proprietors00falmouth_202105/page/n211/mode/1up?view=theater
24. YCROD, Vol. 18, p. 126. George Roberts is described as a "laborer" by Samuel Skillin in this deed. Possibly he worked at the mill for his father-in-law at the time.
25. YCROD, Book 24, p. 28. Witnesses: Bejamin Allen and Hannah Allen.
26. On Nov. 23, 1736, George Roberts of Falmouth, husbandman, sold for 60 pounds, 10 shillings in Bills of Credit to Richard Westcoat "...a certain Tract of Land Containing Twenty-five acres lying about Twenty Rods Southerly from the now Dwelling House of sd. Roberts the nearest part thereof it being Twenty Five Acres out of thirty acres which I the said Roberts bought of Phineas Jones as by a Deed bearing date July 4, 1734, which thirty acres being the one half of a sixty acre Lot which was laid out to James Crocker of Falmouth aforesaid and is in Width and one hundred & sixty rods in length and is Bounded Westerly on John Cox his Sixty Acre lot and Easterly on Bayley lot ..." YCROD, Book18, p. 191. The location of this property near Roberts' house is notable because it shows the proximity of the Roberts and Westcoat families, and, later, the Richard Crockett (III) and Westcoat families.
27. YCROD, Book 25, p. 205. Witnesses: Charles Frost and Joanna Frost.
28. YCROD, Book 26, p. 54. Witnesses: Noah Mayo and Will: Strout.

Long Creek, as well as "the one Quarter Part of my Great Mill Standing upon Long Creek ... after my Decease and the Decease of my Wife Rhoda Skillen."[29]

> To all People to whom these Presents Shall Come Samuel Skillin of Falmouth in the County of York in New England Gent. Sendeth Greeting & Know that I the S. Skillin for & in Consider. of Love and Good will that I have for my Daughter Katharine Roberts the Wife of George Roberts of Falmouth have Given and Granted unto him the S. George Roberts & Katharine his wife and to their heirs and Assigns forever a Certain Tract or Parcell of Land lying at Long Creek in S. Falmouth Containing about Fourty acres of the Same being the same Tract or Parcell of Land which I Bought of Isaac Winter which was Laid out to him by the Proprietors Com.tee in Lieu of Forty acres of Land he Purchased of Elijah Glerin which Proved to be Laid out Before only inasmuch as I have Sold a Small Tract of Land to George Copton on Webbers Line so Called if it Should Cut any Part of this Land off then I Except that Small part Otherwise I make no Exception as to the Quentity of Land also I Give unto my S. Son in Law George Roberts and Katharine his Wife the one Quarter Part of my Great mill

(Partial) deed from Samuel Skillin to George and Katharine Roberts, June 8, 1753.
(York County Registry of Deeds, Book 33, p. 218.)

Samuel Skillin died in January of 1757 (as did his brother-in-law Richard Crockett in Stratham, N.H.). There is no known date of death for his wife Rhoda (Haley) Skillin, although she outlived her husband.

George and Katharine Roberts had eight children: Rhoda (baptized 1731); William (born 1733); Elizabeth (Richard Crockett's first wife, born 1736); George Copson (born 1738); Benjamin (born about 1741); Joseph[30] (born between 1739 and 1745); Joshua (born about 1742); and Lydia (unknown birth year).[31] After Richard Crockett and Elizabeth Roberts were married, her siblings, and in particular her brother George Copson Roberts, became his closest friends.

---

29. YCROD, Book 33, p. 218. Witnesses: Benjamin Allen and Priscilla Allen. Skillin notes in the deed that he had previously sold off a small portion of the land to George "Copton," for whom George and Katharine Roberts' son George Copson Roberts was probably named.
30. SMALLDESC, p. 984-985 says George Copson and Joseph were twins.
31. SMALLDESC, p. 1140-1142.

The Fifth Generation

King George's War in Second Parish

King George's War (War of the Austrian Succession in Europe and the Fifth Indian War in Maine) became personal in Cape Elizabeth when sporadic attacks from Native Americans hit close to home on several occasions. We do not know if Richard was living and apprenticing in Second Parish at the time (his father was then in Stratham, N.H.), although his future wife, eight-year-old Elizabeth Roberts, and her family—as well as the greater Skillin connections—were affected. During the first year of the war, an Indian was fired at from Long Creek, where Samuel Skillin had his saw and grist mills, and a "son of Col. Cushing of Purpooduck was killed by them."[32]

In 1745, the Massachusetts General Court offered a 400-pound old tenor bounty on Native American scalps, which bounty had the initial effect of dispersing the enemy. But bold Native American warriors returned to the greater Falmouth area in 1746, continuing their guerilla warfare. The uncertainty and worry about potential raids forced settlers to stick close to garrison houses, negatively affecting the tending of crops, as well as the harvesting of timber, a lucrative trade upon which many coastal communities depended. On June 6, 1746, the Reverend Thomas Smith of First Church of Falmouth recorded in his diary a brazen daytime attack in Cape Elizabeth:

> "Two soldiers were killed by the Indians at the side of Westcoat's field, (at Long Creek).[33] There were twenty-five soldiers in the field, besides Westcoat's own folks, and only seven Indians drove them all; scalped the two men, took their clothes and three guns; (after Skillin, Stephen Irish, and one or two more of our men had courageously stood and made a few fires) the Indians never supposed there were so many men there, only Westcoat's hands."[34]

On Sunday June 15th the Falmouth minister noted in his journal that, "An Indian was seen and fired at by N. Crocket,[35] near the Causeway, by Chapman's

---

32. WILLIS, p. 414.
33. Parenthesis added here by Rev. Smith, not the author.
34. SMITHJOURNALS, p. 123. https://archive.org/details/journalsofrevtho00smit_0/page/123/mode/1up?view=theater&q=Crocket+
35. "N. Crocket" was probably Nathaniel Crockett, son of John "Jonathan" Crockett and Mary (Knight) Crockett. (John was the son of Joshua Crockett and Sarah Trickey.) Nathaniel was born in Portsmouth in 1717 and would have been about twenty-nine at the time. He married Oct. 29, 1740, in Scarborough, Margaret Andrews, and was then probably living in

(near what is now called the Horse Tavern) upon which account a great number of our men were absent from meeting, and pursuing him."[36]

In Europe, the War of the Austrian Succession ended October 18, 1748 with the Treaty of Aix-la-Chapelle. This treaty, however, did not include the Native American tribes that had fought in Maine on the side of the French. To fix this deficiency, Governor William Shirley of Massachusetts invited warring Wabanakis to a peace conference. The conference was held in Falmouth on October 14-16, 1749. At this two-day peace conference, the earlier tenants of Dummer's Treaty of 1726 were largely agreed upon by both the natives and the English.

Although a treaty with the warring Native Americans had been struck, the agreement produced an uncertain peace. In Maine, settlers had learned not to trust the Indians. (For their part, Native Americans certainly had ample reason not to trust the English, who broke almost every treaty they ever signed.) The settlers kept their guard up and maintained stores of gunpowder and shot.

In 1751, Richard, then about seventeen, performed sentinel service as part of Captain Bryant Morton's[37] company. (Because Richard was still a minor, his father, Richard Crockett, Jr. likely had to sign for him when Richard enlisted.)[38] Richard served five weeks and four days, from July 22nd to August 30th. Captain Morton's company was "engaged in scout & guard service."[39] Richard's guard duty was probably performed in the greater Falmouth area.

Scarborough or Falmouth. See CANDAGE p. 5 (John Crockett) and p. 8. (Nathaniel Crockett).
36. SMITHJOURNALS, p. 124. https://archive.org/details/journalsofrevtho00smit_0/page/124/mode/1up?view=theater&q=Crocket+
37. Spelled Capt. "Briant Morten" on Richard Crockett's muster roll.
38. Richard's muster role record is linked to that of his father, Richard Crocket.
39. Massachusetts Archive Collection, 1603-1799. Index to French and Indian War Muster Rolls. Mass. Archives, Vol. 91-99. Film #008731870.

The Fifth Generation

> 35089
>
> Richard Crocket
>
> Appears on
>
> **A Muster Roll**
>
> dated Falmouth, Sept 5, 1751,
> of a company in His Majesty's service under the command of
>
> Capt. Bryant Morten
>
> Quality, Centinel
>
> Residence, Falmouth
>
> Entered service, July 22
>
> Served until, Aug 30
>
> Length of service, 5 weeks 4 days
>
> Remarks: Year not given — probably 1751.
>
> Co. engaged in scout & guard service
>
> Reported. Son of Rich'd Crocket
>
> Mass. Archives: Muster Rolls.
> Vol. 93, page 52.

Muster roll for Richard Crocket (III), 1751.
(Massachusetts State Archives.)[40]

---

40. Massachusetts Archives Collection, 1603-1799. Index to French and Indian War Muster Rolls. Mass Archives Vol. 91-99. Film #008731870.

This uneasy peace with the French and their Wabanaki allies lasted only five years. The final territorial dispute, known as the French and Indian War, erupted in earnest in New England in 1754.

Second Parish by the Mid-18th Century

Falmouth Neck in First Parish was the locus of activity and importance during the resettlement period after the turn of the century, with major trade and commerce centered there. Over the ensuing decades, however, Second Parish gained not only in population, but also in commerce. By 1745, "… five schooners and five sloops hailed the settlement as their home port."[41] Colonel Ezekiel Cushing (whose son was killed by Indians during the first year of King George's War) was one of the prosperous men who owned ships, a wharf and warehouse (and home) in Second Parish. Cushing was engaged in the West Indies trade "… bringing home rum, sugar, and molasses, in exchange for lumber and fish."[42] William Simonton, who also owned ships and a wharf and warehouse in Second Parish, was Cushing's main competitor in the West Indies trade. According to Cape Elizabeth historian William B. Jordan, Jr., "More commercial business was carried on in the Second Parish previous to 1760 than on the Neck."[43]

By 1749, the population of Second Parish had "increased to approximately 900 including 150 families."[44] Included in the swelling population were a number of Scotch Irish families, who, like Colonel Cushing, were Presbyterians. Thanks to the Skillin sawmill (and other sawmills in the area) and a brisk timber trade, most of the houses were built of sawn local wood. The homes were modest and unpainted, with few of them more than one-story. The most notable exception was the house of Colonel Cushing's at Cushing's Point (where his home, wharf and warehouse stood), which was the first two-story home built in Second Parish.[45]

By the mid-18th century, the occupation of farming had taken a back seat to other more lucrative trades in Second Parish:

"Lumber, wood, and fishing still provided the principal business pursuits. Those

---
41. CAPE-E, p. 36.
42. CAPE-E, p. 36.
43. CAPE-E, p. 37.
44. CAPE-E, p. 36.
45. CAPE-E, p. 36-37.

engaged in the lumber trade specialized in the procurement of masts, spars, timber, and deal for the British Navy. The farming interest remained much neglected, so much so, that the people were almost entirely dependent upon importations from the South."[46]

Into the greater Second Parish community, which now consisted of an amalgamation of peoples (some new and some who had been there since the resettlement of Falmouth) young Richard Crockett took his place by 1754, if not before. Although he and his family resided amongst a tightly-knit group of intermarried families at Long Creek, they were not immune from changes and controversies arising from outsiders.

The Clark Controversy and Richard and Elizabeth (Roberts) Crockett

Elizabeth Roberts, who was born to George and Katharine Roberts in Second Parish on March 5, 1736,[47] was eighteen-years-old when, on November 14, 1754,[48] Richard Crockett filed his intention to marry her with Falmouth Town Clerk Stephen Longfellow.[49] Richard had probably turned twenty-one this year, the age of majority.

The couple was likely married not long after their intentions were filed by the Reverend Ephraim Clark, the Congregational divine then being considered to fill the vacancy left by the Reverend Benjamin Allen, who had died May 6, 1754.[50] Clark's ministry in Second Parish was tenuous, to say the least. Not only was Clark

---

46. CAPE-E, p. 37.
47. SMALLDESC, p. 1140.
48. While Town Records show the marriage intentions of Richard and Elizabeth were entered in 1755, I believe this is a mistake, either by Falmouth Town Clerk Stephen Longfellow or (more likely) by someone copying over his record. My reasons for suspecting this record are many. First, Elizabeth would have been 18 in 1754 (an age when most girls were married). Second, men were usually married around age 21. If Richard were born at the end of 1733, he would have turned 21 late in 1754 and thus a date of November 14, 1754 seems reasonable for filing their marriage intentions. Third (and most importantly), son Ephraim's death record and his application for a Revolutionary War pension list his birthdate as July 12, 1755, before the couple was married (if the 1755 date is accurate). But there is no way that Ephraim was born out of wedlock—months before his parents even filed their marriage intentions—without Richard and Elizabeth being charged with fornication, of which there is no record. Finally, fourth, it seems highly probably that, given the controversy over the Rev. Ephraim Clark in Second District, Ephraim was named as a compliment to the minister. The height of the controversy occurred around the time of Ephraim's birth, in the summer of 1755. Adding up the prior information, we can be fairly sure that Richard and Elizabeth were married in 1754, not 1755.
49. Falmouth, Maine Town Records, Book 2, 1728-1773, p. 55. Again, I believe this record is off by one year, and was likely a mistake made by the person copying from Longfellow's record. https://archive.org/details/falmouth-maine-town-records-book-2-1728-1773/page/55/mode/
50. CAPE-E, p. 38.

not the parish's first choice, he was vehemently opposed by the newly-arrived Presbyterian faction of Second Parish:

> "Almost immediately [after Reverend Allen's death] a bitter controversy broke out between the Presbyterian and Congregational elements over a successor. The first choice was the Reverend Eleazer Holyoke of Harvard College, who, due to the controversy, declined the call. Soon after, the Reverend Ephraim Clark began to preach in the second Parish and accepted the call to settle there. Whereas a majority of the inhabitants were in favor of Mr. Clark, the vociferous Presbyterian minority, led by Colonel Ezekiel Cushing, railed against him."[51]

Where Richard and Elizabeth stood in relation to the disagreement over the proposed the new minister is quite clear. Their support for Reverend Clark was made manifest in their first child, a son, born July 12, 1755, during the height of the Clark controversy.[52] The couple elected to name their son "Ephraim" as a compliment to[53]—and vote of confidence for—the Reverend Ephraim Clark.

Reverend Clark was known as "a man of great energy and determination."[54] He carried on his ministry in Second Parish, even after three councils refused to install him. A fourth council was shut out of the meetinghouse where services typically were held, forcing Clark to become installed in William Simonton's apple orchard:[55]

> "The meeting-house was closed against them and Mr. Clark was installed in Simonton's orchard. Five days afterward, a convention of ministers in Boston testified unanimously against this installation, as irregular. The year after [Clark's] installation, twenty-four of his parishioners were sent to jail for refusing to pay the Parish rates. This opposition gradually subsided, and in the course of a few years, he seems to have won the respect and the confidence of the people."[56]

---

51. CAPE-E, p. 38.
52. In August of 1755, Col. Cushing and his cronies even had Rev. Clark arrested on a trumped-up charge of lying; however, the minister was quickly acquitted by a jury. CAPE-E, p. 38.
53. While "Ephraim" was an old Crockett family name, it had not surfaced as a given name in this direct line for more than a hundred years—not since Ephraim Crockett of the second generation.
54. "The centennial of the Cumberland Association of Congregational Ministers, at the Second Parish Church in Portland, Maine, Monday and Tuesday, May 28 and 29, 1888." Cumberland Association of Congregational Ministers. P. 19-20. (Via N.H. Historical Society.)
55. "The centennial of the Cumberland Association of Congregational Ministers, at the Second Parish Church in Portland, Maine, Monday and Tuesday, May 28 and 29, 1888." P. 19-20.
56. From Rev. E.A. Harlow's historical address, 150th anniversary of the Cape Elizabeth Church. "The centennial of the Cumberland Association of Congregational Ministers, at the Second Parish Church in Portland, Maine, Monday and

The Fifth Generation

The Cushing faction petitioned the Massachusetts General Court to allow them to return to religious services held at First Parish. Their petition was approved, but after Colonel Cushing's death in 1765, most of the errant parishioners petitioned to be returned to Second Parish to sit under Clark's ministry. (This petition was granted in 1767.)[57] The Reverend Ephraim Clark became the longest-serving pastor in Cape Elizabeth, serving for forty-one years. During that time, Clark performed many baptisms, weddings, and (no doubt) funerals for Richard and Elizabeth Crockett and their extended family.

The French and Indian War in Greater Falmouth

The French and Indian War (also known as the Seven Years War, and, in Maine, the Sixth Indian War) was the final great conflict on this continent between Great Britain and France, and France's Native American allies. The war was a territorial battle for control of a large swath of disputed land, from eastern and northern Maine, spilling down the St. Lawrence seaway into the Great Lakes and Ohio River Valley region, all the way down to the Gulf Coast. At the conclusion of the war, France ceded vast acres of land to Great Britain, including eastern and northern Maine.

Tuesday, May 28 and 29, 1888. Portland, Maine: Cumberland Association of Congregational Ministers, 1888." Pg. 19-20. Rev. Clark did not get rich at his profession, either. In 1780, when a bushel of corn cost four pounds Sterling, he earned only a seventy-pound annual salary.
57. CAPE-E, p. 293.

Map of the French and Indian War (1754-1763).
The dark color represents land in British possession and the light color represents French possession, with the land in between disputed territory.
(Map by Hoodinski via Creative Commons, and is in the public domain.)

During the French and Indian War, the greater Falmouth area was mostly spared the bloodshed and depredations that had occurred during earlier clashes with the French and their Wabanaki allies.[58] Unlike during King George's War, when settlers had remained close to home (or at fortified garrison houses), Falmouth town records reveal that residents appear to have gone about their business as usual. New roads were surveyed and laid out; old roads were repaired; voters approved money to repair the bridges at Long Creek and Stroudwater (now, Westbrook); children went to school; and the meetinghouse was repaired.[59] Although in 1756 there was an article on the Falmouth annual town meeting warrant to see if the town would divide the stock of ammunition among its several militia companies, the article was

---
58. CAPE-E, p. 38.
59. Falmouth, Maine Town Records, Book 2, 1728-1773, various pages from 1755-1760.

voted down, apparently as unnecessary.[60] This evidence points toward a progressive march forward unimpeded by sporadic attacks—or the expectation of sporadic attacks—from roving bands of Native Americans taking pot shots at or the scalps of Falmouth area settlers.

Not all Indians were considered hostile, either. Some Native Americans contributed to the English war effort by serving as scouts or spies. At the annual Falmouth town meeting held March 13, 1759, one of the items on the warrant was to see how much the town would allow Colonel Cushing for the support of Sias Penas, a poor Indian. Although the town regularly provided for indigent White people, this was an unusual request because Penas was Native American. The warrant item was initially passed over, but at a follow-up meeting Selectmen were asked to look into Cushing's request. After "waiting on" Colonel Cushing, Selectmen William Cotton, John Robinson, Jr., and William Bucknam presented a report March 1, 1760, which stated: "We report that we think it reasonable [Colonel Cushing] be allowed Six Pounds Thirteen Shillings and Four Pence for supporting said Indian."[61] It was voted to accept this report (and the proposed payment) at the annual town meeting March 11, 1760. Although the record does not reflect any particular service performed by Sias Penas, Colonel Cushing's eldest son, Loring, was captain of the militia in Cape Elizabeth and it is possible that Penas had rendered some type of service against the French and their native allies (either in this conflict or a previous one), especially considering that voters approved the payment knowing Cushing could certainly have afforded to support the Indian himself. To have approved such a sum the town must have felt that the obligation belonged to the community at large, not to Colonel Cushing.

In 1757, after receiving word that a hostile group of Indians potentially threatened frontier settlements in Maine, Falmouth organized five companies of militia. Captain Loring Cushing commanded the Cape Elizabeth militia; Captain James Milk headed the company at Falmouth Neck;. Captain Isaac Ilsley commanded the militia at Back Cove; Captain Dominicus Jordan headed the company at Spurwink (situated on the southwest end of Cape Elizabeth); and Samuel Skillin's son,

---

60. Falmouth, Maine Town Records, Book 2, 1728-1773, p. 227. The vote not to divide the town stock of ammunition was taken at an adjournment of the annual Falmouth town meeting held March 15, 1756. https://archive.org/details/falmouth-maine-town-records-book-2-1728-1773/page/227/mode/1up?view=theater

61. Falmouth, Maine Town Records, Book 2, 1728-1773, p. 249. https://archive.org/details/falmouth-maine-town-records-book-2-1728-1773/page/249/mode/1up?view=theater

Samuel, Jr., captained the company formed at Stroudwater (the settlement to the north of Long Creek).

Richard Crockett, then about twenty-three, was a private in Captain Skillin's company. Richard's service with the Stroudwater company under Captain Skillin is somewhat perplexing. We do not know why he joined young Skillin's regiment, when his family and relations belonged to Captain Loring Cushing's Cape Elizabeth company. Richard's father-in-law George Roberts (who was brother-in-law to Captain Skillin), was one of four lieutenants in Captain Loring Cushing's company. Three of Roberts' sons—George C., Benjamin, and Joseph—were privates in Cushing's company, too.[62] In addition, Richard Crockett's father (Richard Crockett, Jr.) was on Cushing's alarm list (comprised of men over fifty or infirm).

It is possible that proximity to where the Stroudwater militia drilled might have played a role in Richard's decision to join Captain Skillin's company. (Richard's brother Joshua, recently married to Hannah Babb, was a private in Skillin's company, as well.)[63] We do not know exactly where Richard lived in 1757. He is not listed (as his father is) on the list of ratable[64] polls and valuations for Second Parish taken three years later in 1760. Either Richard did not have enough of an estate to entitle him vote and/or he and his family lived with someone else during the early years of their marriage.[65] An equally plausible explanation for why Richard joined Captain Skillin's company and not Captain Cushing's, however, could be hard feelings resulting from the on-going feud with the Cushing faction over the ministry of the Reverend Ephraim Clark. (Richard and Elizabeth and their family were definitely Clark-ites.) Despite his militia membership, there is no evidence that Richard saw any active duty during the French and Indian War.

Two of Richard's brothers-in-law, George Copson Roberts and Benjamin Roberts, played a small role in the building of a fort on the Penobscot River during

---

62. "Baptisms and Admission From the Records of First Church in Falmouth, Now Portland, Maine, with Appendix of Historical Notes." Compiled by Marquis F. King, President of the Maine Genealogical Society. Portland, Maine: Maine Genealogical Society, 1898. Appendix, p. 175. https://archive.org/details/baptismsadmissio00lcfirs/page/175/mode/1up?view=theater
63. Maine Genealogy Archives, "Falmouth Militia Members, 1757." https://archives.mainegenealogy.net/2010/02/falmouth-militia-members-1757.html
64. A ratable poll was a male resident who met the requirements to vote. He had to be at least age 21 and have a freehold (annual income) of 3 pounds or own an estate valued at 60 pounds or more. The numbers of ratable polls in a township helped determine the number of representatives that town sent to the General Court. In 1760, Second Parish was still under the umbrella of Falmouth, not having its own representation to the Court, but rather contributing to Falmouth's number.
65. Unfortunately, some of the residents of Second Parish appear to be missing from the 1760 valuation, including Richard's father-in-law George Roberts, as well as William Westcoat, Roberts' brother-in-law. Massachusetts State Archives collection, colonial period, 1622-1788. Volume 130. Town valuations, Second Parish of Falmouth, 1760. P. 25-33. https://www.familysearch.org/ark:/61903/3:1:3Q9M-C9Y5-3QBW?i=831&cat=1055547

the French and Indian War. In 1759, then Massachusetts Bay Governor Thomas Pownall led an expedition to Wasaumkeag Point at the mouth of the Penobscot (now Cape Jellison in Stockton Springs) to build a fort there to protect against frontier raids from the French and Indians.[66] (The Tarratine[67] and Penobscot Indians were active around the Penobscot River.) Governor Pownall took pains to ensure the area was safe before landing his four companies of men. "There was no enemy," Pownall notes in his journal, "nor did I expect any. But I could not have justified myself if anything had happened, if I did not take all the same precaution as though there were."[68]

---

66. WILLIS, 434-435. Brigadier General Samuel Waldo, who accompanied Governor Pownall, died of "apoplexy" (a heart attack) during this mission. Waldo had a vested interest in the fort since it was situated in his Waldo Patent land.

67. Rev. Richard Pike, who in 1759 wrote an account of the building of Fort Pownall, was callous in his description of the once-proud Tarratine (Mi'kmaq) Indians, without acknowledging the role Englishmen played in their demise: "The Tarratines were a powerful nation then, a foe to be feared and dreaded; and they roamed the wilderness, and launched their canoes on the rivers and bays, sovereigns of the land, and a terror to all daring adventurers. Now they are a degenerate race, scarcely able to muster three score and ten warriors. A small island in the upper Penobscot the only territory they can call their own." "Building and Occupancy of Fort Pownall." A paper read before the New England Historic-Genealogical Society, Oct. 5, 1859. By Rev. Richard Pike of Dorchester, Mass. *The New England Historical and Genealogical Register*, Volume XIV, p. 6. Boston: Samuel G. Drake, Publisher, 1860. Today, the Mi'kmaq number about 30,000 (29 bands) in Maine and Atlantic Canada. "While the tribe has no reservation lands, it owns 2,674 acres of fee and trust land in the vicinity of Presque Isle [Maine]—north as far as Stockholm and south as far as Littleton. https://fourdirectionsmaine.org/about-four-directions/wabanaki-tribes/#:~:text=The%20Mi'kmaq%20are%20a,whom%20reside%20in%20Aroostook%20County.

68. "Building and Occupancy of Fort Pownall." A paper read before the New England Historic-Genealogical Society, Oct. 5, 1859. By Rev. Richard Pike of Dorchester, Mass. *The New England Historical and Genealogical Register*, Volume XIV. Boston: Samuel G. Drake, Publisher, 1860. See p. 4-10. During the American Revolution when the British occupied Castine, Col. Cargill "… came from New Castle to complete the destruction of Fort Pownall [to keep the fort from the hands of the British]."

> 35091
>
> Richard Crocket
>
> Appears on
>
> **A List**
>
> dated Falmouth, Aug. 11, 1757 of the men of Capt. Samuel Skillens' Co.
>
> Mass. Archives: Muster Rolls.
> Vol. 95, page 151.

Muster roll for Richard Crocket (III), 1757.
(Massachusetts State Archives.)[69]

---

69. Massachusetts Archive Collection, 1603-1799. Index to French and Indian War Muster Rolls. Mass. Archives Vol. 91-99.

The Fifth Generation

> 35108
>
> Robinson Crockett
>
> Appears on
>
> **A Muster Roll**
>
> dated Boston, Oct. 24, 1759.
>
> of a company in His Majesty's service under the command of
>
> Capt. George Berry.
>
> Quality, Private.
>
> Residence,
>
> Entered service, April 1, 1759.
>
> Served until, July 23, 1759.
>
> Length of service, 16 weeks 2 days.
>
> Remarks: Also reported Major Berry
>
> Not given
>
> Endorsed Co. at Penobscot.
>
> Mass. Archives: Muster Rolls.
> Vol. 97. page 217.

Muster roll for Richard's younger brother, Robinson Crockett, 1759.
(Massachusetts State Archives.)[70]

---

70. Massachusetts Archive Collection, 1603-1799. Index to French and Indian War Muster Rolls. Mass. Archives Vol. 91-99.

George C. and Benjamin Roberts are listed as sentinels on Captain James Cargill's muster roll in service on the Penobscot in preparation for the arrival of Governor Pownall's expedition from Boston. The company was comprised of twenty-four young men from Falmouth serving under Captain Cargill:

> "[Cargill's company] first went to Pemaquid to collect whale-boats, by order of Brigadier-General [Jedidiah] Preble,[71] and had them on the Penobscot when Governor Pownall arrived. The boats, with their crews, were sent out with surveying parties, and were retained at the Fort some time after the departure of the troops for Boston."[72]

Both George C. and his younger brother Benjamin were underage when they volunteered to help Pownall's expedition to the Penobscot region to build Fort Pownall (later, Fort Point), and had to be signed for by their father George Roberts. George Copson Roberts served from March 31st to July 23, 1759. Benjamin enlisted in Captain Cargill's company the same day as his brother, but was released a week earlier.[73] That autumn, George C., now twenty-one, published his intentions of marriage with Deborah York (his first cousin), daughter of Samuel and Joanna (Skillin) York.[74]

Richard's younger brother, Robinson Crockett, might also have served on the Penobscot during the building of Fort Pownall. His muster roll reports that Robinson served sixteen weeks and two days (from April 1, 1759 to July 22, 1759) under Captain George Berry's company at the Penobscot. (See copy of muster roll for Robinson Crockett on page 227.)

On September 13, 1759, the French lost the city of Quebec to the English during the Battle of the Plains of Abraham (Battle of Quebec). Both opposing

---

71. After Pownall's departure, Preble, of Falmouth, was put in charge of the fort.
72. SMALLDESC, p. 1140-1141. https://www.ancestry.com/imageviewer/collections/14388/images/dvm_GenMono000511-00696-0?pId=1203
73. SMALLDESC, p. 1141-1142. https://www.ancestry.com/imageviewer/collections/14388/images/dvm_GenMono000511-00696-1?pId=1204
74. George Roberts entered his name and intention to marry Deborah York with Falmouth Town Clerk Stephen Longfellow on October 20, 1759. Longfellow wrote the young man's name as "George Roberts Junr," even though George was George Copson Roberts, not George Roberts, Jr. In most deeds and official records, the younger George Roberts is distinguished from his father by his middle initial, "C" (i.e. George C. Roberts). Longfellow's mistaken use of the "junior" designation seems to offer further proof that the Falmouth town clerk was not as familiar with the families of Second Parish as he was with those from First Parish, and certainly not as knowledgeable as (later) Cape Elizabeth Town Clerk David Strout. Falmouth, Maine Town Records, Book 2, p. 67 https://archive.org/details/falmouth-maine-town-records-book-2-1728-1773/page/67/mode/1up?q=Skillin&view=theater

generals—James Wolfe and Louis-Joseph de Montcalm—were mortally wounded during the battle. After the French loss at Quebec, the major Wabanaki tribes, the Penobscot, Passamaquoddy, St. John, and Nova Scotian, "…finding they could not unaided by French power and influences, resist the English arms, entered into a treaty of peace, and from that time forever ceased to become formidable in the northern colonies."[75] Maine settlers believed their troubles were finally over.

In 1760, however, the French briefly attempted to retake Quebec. Richard's brother-in-law Benjamin Roberts reenlisted on February 25, 1760, "for the total reduction of Canada."[76] In September of 1760, the French governor of Canada capitulated to British General Jeffrey Amherst. This treaty finally brought an end to almost a century of warfare with the French and their Native American allies. In February of 1763, the Treaty of Paris was signed in which France ceded all her land in Canada to the British.

Cape Elizabeth District

Almost from the beginning of the second settlement of Purpoodock, residents of Second Parish petitioned to be set off from Falmouth as a separate township:

> "As early as 1742 they petitioned the [Massachusetts] General Court for an act of separation. The petitioners stressed the fact that poor roads, faulty ferry service and a lack of sufficient boats prevented the attendance of the inhabitants at the town meetings on the Neck. Due to this inability to attend to their particular interests they were not properly represented at the meetings. They also objected to supporting a school that their children were unable to attend for want of suitable transportation."[77]

The response from the Massachusetts General Court was for the residents of Falmouth and Second Parish to settle the dispute among themselves. Falmouth initially protested separation, believing that the residents of Second Parish were attempting to escape their financial obligation for repair of the Stroudwater bridge.[78]

---

75. WILLIS, p. 437.
76. SMALLDESC, p. 1141-1142. https://www.ancestry.com/imageviewer/collections/14388/images/dvm_GenMono000511-00696-1?pId=1204
77. CAPE-E, p. 38.
78. CAPE-E, p. 39.

The issue waxed and waned over the ensuing decades, but was never entirely forgotten.

By the early 1760s, however, the inhabitants of Second Parish began exercising some local control. At a meeting held in Second Parish on June 21, 1762, the inhabitants voted to divide their parish into three districts and that "each Destrect draw thear proportion of the money voted by this Town [Falmouth] for the use of Schools…and any [person] may have the previledge of sending to the school next to his house."[79] The first district was laid out "from Pond Cove to Ebenezer Sawyers and from thence to Richard Crocketts bridge…"[80] Whether this bridge relates to Richard Crockett (III) or his father, we do not know, nor do we know the size or location of the structure. Richard might have built the bridge, from which it took its name. It is just as probable, however, that the bridge was located near where Richard, Jr.'s small house was situated in Second Parish.[81]

But divvying up school districts was not enough local control for Second Parish. The residents persisted to petition for separation from Falmouth. In 1765, the General Court officially created the District of Cape Elizabeth. The new district was granted all the rights of an independent township, except legislative rights (i.e. the right to send a representative to the General Court).[82] Because of ongoing agitation in the American colonies, King George III had decided not to create any new townships in the colonies that might further erode England's political and religious authority over them.

Richard and Elizabeth's children were born between the years 1755 and 1765, when Second Parish officially became Cape Elizabeth District and began establishing schools. By 1773, Cape Elizabeth had established and was operating four separate school districts, situated at: Purpooduck, Long Creek, Spurwink, and Barron Hill. With four schools spread across Cape Elizabeth, it is likely the Crockett children were able to receive some sort of education, especially as one was established at Long Creek. Both sons Ephraim and Samuel signed their Revolutionary War

---

79. Cape Elizabeth, Town and vital records 1760-1900. "Meeting minutes, 1760-1765, of the Second Parish of the Town of Falmouth; town and vital records of Cape Elizabeth: town officers, strays, intentions of marriage and marriage records 1773-1865, births and deaths prior to 1879 arranged in families." (Via FamilySearch.)
80. Cape Elizabeth, Town and vital records 1760-1900. "Meeting minutes, 1760-1765, of the Second Parish of the Town of Falmouth; town and vital records of Cape Elizabeth: town officers, strays, intentions of marriage and marriage records 1773-1865, births and deaths prior to 1879 arranged in families."
81. The main bridge at Long Creek was regularly described as "Long Creek Bridge" in the records of both Falmouth and Second Parish. No further mention of Richard Crockett's bridge is made in either record.
82. CAPE-E, p. 39.

The Fifth Generation

pension applications in a fair hand.[83] Forty pounds was voted to be apportioned to the schools in 1773. Two tax collectors were appointed, one to collect the Province and County tax and the other to collect the taxes for local use in Cape Elizabeth District.[84]

In March of 1770, Richard Crockett (III) borrowed money from Jedidiah Preble of Falmouth. He failed to pay the money back, however, and Preble took Crockett to court. (Preble, who had once loaned money to Richard's father, was regularly in court or had agents appearing for him to sue for money owed.) Richard Crockett, Jr. (III), the defendant in the case, failed to appear before the Court of Common Pleas held in Falmouth for the newly-established Cumberland County on April 17, 1770. Judgment was by default for Preble, the plaintiff, in the amount of 2 pounds, 13 shillings, and 4 pence. Richard was also charged with costs of suit in the amount of 2 pounds, 3 shillings and 10 pence.[85] Crockett paid his debt to Preble. In the margin of the record is written: "Rec'd full satisfaction for above judgment. Jedidiah Preble." (See "Record of Jedidiah Preble v. Richard Crockett, Jr." on page 232.)

What possibly triggered the initial default to Preble was Richard's purchase of real estate. Around 1770 or 1771, Richard appears to have bought 30 acres of land in Cape Elizabeth District from the heirs of Edmund Mountfort of Falmouth. (Edmund Mountfort, who died in 1737,[86] received as an early settler a 30-acre lot in Falmouth, situated in Second Parish.)[87] Richard must not have paid the full amount for the property, however, because he ended up in court.

In April of 1771, Richard Crockett, Jr. (III), yeoman of Cape Elizabeth, was a defendant at the Court of Common Pleas held in Falmouth for Cumberland County. His accusers were the Mountfort heirs: Edmund and Samuel Mountfort, shipwrights of Falmouth; Elizabeth Mountfort, a single woman of Falmouth; and Gersom Rogers on behalf of his daughter Esther (daughter of Esther Mountfort

---

83. Ephraim's signature is a bit shaky, but he was 77 when he applied for his pension. U.S. Revolutionary War Pension and Bounty-Land Warrant Application Files, 1800-1900. https://www.ancestry.com/imageviewer/collections/1995/images/MIUSA1775D_135275-00084?pId=14814 Samuel's handwriting at around age 60 is steady. https://www.ancestry.com/imageviewer/collections/1995/images/MIUSA1775D_135275-00184?pId=14508
84. Town Records, South Portland, Maine, 1765-1806. https://www.familysearch.org/ark:/61903/3:1:3Q9M-C3HY-ZS4W-D?i=32&cat=300073
85. Maine, Cumberland County Court of Common Pleas records, 1764-1839. Court records, v. 3, 1768-1772. https://www.familysearch.org/ark:/61903/3:1:3QSQ-G93S-R93Q-K?i=239&cat=1881394 A case could be made that Richard's father is the debtor; however, it appears at this point in his life Richard (III) was known as Richard Crockett, Jr. See the Mountfort case following, which was definitely Richard (III).
86. FamilySearch, Edmund Mountfort, Jr. 1694-1737. https://www.familysearch.org/tree/person/details/MK4H-7BX
87. "Copy of the Original Records of the Proprietors of Falmouth for the years 1718 to 1826." Three volumes in one. PORTLAND: Copied by F.A. Gerrish, 1861. Index. Mountfort, Edmund. https://archive.org/details/proprietors00falmouth_202105/page/n23/mode/1up?view=theater

Rogers). The case was a plea on the part of the Mountfort plaintiffs that Richard "…render them thirty Acres of Land as in the Writ on File Dated March 30th 1771."[88] (See opposite page.) Richard requested that the case be continued to the October term. Between April and October, Richard must have worked out his differences with the Mountfort heirs, because the case, when it came up again at the October 1771 term of the Court of Common Pleas held in Falmouth, was dismissed.[89] (Since a decade later this same lot is deeded to Richard Crockett by Samuel Mountfort, one surmises that Richard offered to lease the land from the heirs or the parties had worked out a lease-purchase agreement.)

Record of Jedidiah Preble v. Richard Crockett, Jr.
Cumberland County Inferior Court of Common Pleas, April term, 1770.[90]

---

88. The year on this writ of execution is possibly 1770. I am unable to distinguish clearly from the copy or from the meaning of the record.
89. Maine, Cumberland County Court of Common Pleas r1764-1839. Court records, v. 3, 1768-1772, p. 392. https://www.familysearch.org/ark:/61903/3:1:3QSQ-G93S-R939-J?i=403&cat=1881394
90. Maine, Cumberland County Court of Common Pleas records, 1764-1839. Court records, v. 3, 1768-1772. https://www.familysearch.org/ark:/61903/3:1:3QSQ-G93S-R93Q-K?i=239&cat=1881394

Record of Mountfort heirs v. Richard Crockett, Jr.
Court of Common Pleas, October term, 1771.[91]

---

91. Maine, Cumberland County Court of Common Pleas records 1764-1839. Court records, v. 3, 1768-1772, p. 392. https://www.familysearch.org/ark:/61903/3:1:3QSQ-G93S-R939-J?i=403&cat=1881394

In 1771, Massachusetts asked for another assessment of polls and estates from its various cities and towns for taxation purposes. This time, Richard Crockett, Jr. (III) was on the list of ratable polls (one—himself) and estates for Cape Elizabeth. The assessment was taken September 23, 1771. (His father was also listed; see Chapter 4.) Richard would turn thirty-eight later that fall. Under the category, "Dwelling Houses and Shops under the same Roof or adjoining them," it is noted that Richard owned a one-quarter share of either a house or shop. This suggests that Richard might have been in the process of building a home. Later deeds indicate that Richard had a house situated on his father-in-law Roberts' property. There was likely an understanding between Richard and his father-in-law that a certain amount of real estate would come to Richard (on behalf of his wife Elizabeth) after George and Katharine Roberts' deaths, which is exactly what happened.

The 1771 assessment also shows that Richard had one acre of tillable land, which produced eight bushels of wheat or corn per year. He owned three acres of fresh meadow ground, from which Richard harvested a ton of hay annually, probably for the consumption of his one cow. The whole annual worth of Richard's taxable real estate was valued at 1 pound, 10 shillings.[92] Since his estate was valued at less than 60 pounds, Richard must have earned an annual income of more than 3 pounds in order to vote (i.e. to meet the requirements of a ratable poll).

From the 1771 assessment we learn that Richard's father-in-law George Roberts (one ratable poll) owned half of a dwelling and his wife Katharine owned (presumably) the other half. Katharine also owned one-quarter of a mill, a gift from her father Samuel Skillin (from whom she also might have received her portion of the house). Katharine also had one cow and her husband had another. Although not wealthy, by Cape Elizabeth standards (especially compared to both Richard Crocketts), the Roberts family had a comfortable living. George Roberts had a yoke of oxen and two swine. He owned 14 acres of pasture that was able to carry three cows. Richard's father-in-law also had 2-½ acres of tillable land that produced 25 bushels of grain or corn annually. In other taxable real estate, Roberts had one acre of English upland mowing land that produced a ton of hay, and two acres of fresh meadow that produced 1-½ tons of fresh hay per year. For taxation purposes, George Roberts' real estate was valued at 4 pounds, 19 shillings and 2

---

92. Massachusetts State Archives collection, colonial period, 1622-1788. Volume 132. Town valuations, Cape Elizabeth. P. 165. https://www.familysearch.org/ark:/61903/3:1:3Q9M-C9YR-V6Q2?i=235&cat=1055547

pence; Katharine's share was valued at 1 pound, 10 shillings.[93] (By contrast, Samuel Skillin, Jr., who inherited more of his father's estate, including Samuel, Sr.'s house, owned real estate in 1771 valued at 36 pounds, 13 shillings, and 4 pence.)[94]

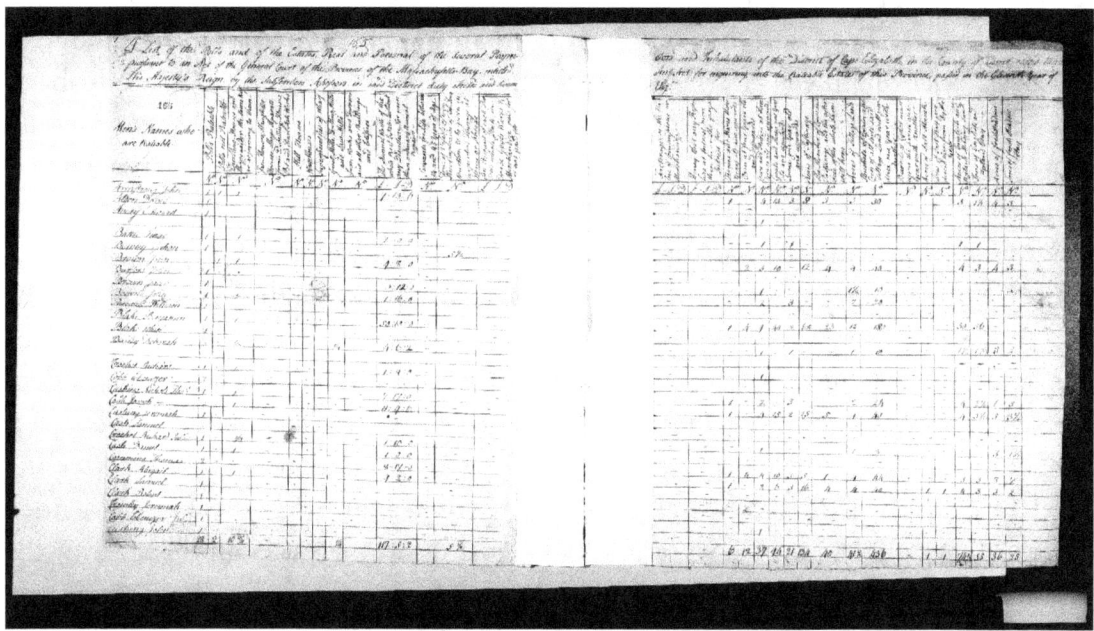

List of polls and estates from Cape Elizabeth, Maine, 1771. Richard Crocket (II) is first under the letter "C" and his son Richard Crockett, Jr. (III) is six lines below him.
(Massachusetts State Archives)[95]

During the mid-1760s to mid-1770s, when Cape Elizabeth was being formed into a separate entity, "Richard Crockett" appears only once in town records as serving in any official capacity. At the annual Town Meeting held March 10, 1767, Mr. Richard Crockett (probably Richard's father, Richard, Jr.) was voted surveyor of highways with Samuel Dunn, Joseph Cobb, Jr. and Isaac Dyer.[96] (Samuel Skillin, Jr. held prominent roles in early Cape Elizabeth, including Selectman, Surveyor of Lumber, and Deer Reeve.)[97] This supports an inference that the Crocketts were not

93. Massachusetts State Archives collection, colonial period, 1622-1788. Volume 132. Town valuations, Cape Elizabeth. P. 169. https://www.familysearch.org/ark:/61903/3:1:3Q9M-C9YR-V67X?i=240&cat=1055547
94. Massachusetts State Archives collection, colonial period, 1622-1788. Volume 132. Town valuations, Cape Elizabeth. P. 171. Because his father is deceased, Samuel Skillin has dropped the suffix "junior," which is now attached to his son, Samuel Skillin, Jr. In 1771, Skillin owned one-half of a mill (probably his father's saw mill). https://www.familysearch.org/ark:/61903/3:1:3Q9M-C9YR-V63N?i=242&cat=1055547
95. Massachusetts State Archives collection, colonial period, 1622-1788. Volume 132. Town valuations, Cape Elizabeth. P. 165. https://www.familysearch.org/ark:/61903/3:1:3Q9M-C9YR-V6Q2?i=235&cat=1055547
96. South Portland, Maine, Town Records 1765-1823, p. 13.
97. South Portland, Maine, Town Records, 1765-1823.

in a position—either because of lack of financial resources or lack of time due to family-raising—to volunteer to serve the town. Richard Crockett (III)'s father-in-law, George Roberts, filled various small but necessary roles in town government during these years. In 1768, Roberts was voted field driver and fence viewer for the following year.[98] For two years running, 1769 and 1770, Roberts was voted one of the surveyors of highways in the newly-formed District.[99] In 1772, George Roberts was elected as one of three men to collect the tithes for the church.[100] Richard would later emulate his father-in-law by stepping into some of these same town roles.

In the early years of Cape Elizabeth, most of the town resources went into the making and repairing of roads, rather than into education. (Today, in small town Maine, more money is spent on education than roads, although roads consume the second largest share of a typical town's annual budget.) A taxation rate for roads was voted at the annual Town Meeting held in March. Men of means (such as Samuel Skillin, Jr.) paid their road tax; however, others not so richly endowed by their fathers were allowed to work off their tax. In 1772, at the annual Town Meeting April 14th (adjourned from March 30th) it was voted that the highways be mended (for the year) by a rate of 250 pounds assessed upon the polls and estates in the District. A man could work off his road tax at 4 shillings per day. A yoke of oxen (such as George Roberts owned) was worth 2 shillings, 8 pence a day. In addition, a cart was worth 1 shilling a day and a plow was credited at 2 shillings per day.[101]

In 1773, Richard Crockett (III) was again a defendant at the Court of Common Pleas. On March 13, 1773, John Robinson of Falmouth, gentleman, was plaintiff in a plea of the case against Richard Crockett, Jr., defendant, chairmaker of Cape Elizabeth.[102] The court had a writ on file dated the same day for a small sum of money. Richard's name was called, but as he did not appear, Robinson received a judgment by default in the amount of 3 pounds, 11 shillings in damages, and costs of suit 1 pound, 9 shillings.[103] An execution against Richard for the total amount

---

98. South Portland, Maine, Town Records, 1765-1823.
99. George Roberts was voted surveyor of highways at the annual Town Meetings held March 21, 1769 and March 20, 1770. South Portland, Maine, Town Records, 1765-1823.
100. South Portland, Maine, Town Records, 1765-1823.
101. South Portland, Maine, Town Records, 1765-1823. https://www.familysearch.org/ark:/61903/3:1:3Q9M-C3HY-ZSWY-7?i=29&cat=300073
102. John Robinson was likely a relation of Richard's mother, Mary (Robinson) Crockett. There is a possibility that the Richard in this case is Richard, Jr. (II), not Richard (III). The relatively small size of the debt, however, leads me to believe the defendant was the son, rather than the father. In addition, at the time Robinson was one of the Deputy Sheriffs of Cumberland County. Given Richard's father's history of impecunity, it is not likely Robinson would have lent the older man money.
103. Maine, Cumberland County Court of Common Pleas records, 1764-1839. Court records, v. 4, Mar. 1773-Oct. 1785, p. 41. https://www.familysearch.org/ark:/61903/3:1:3QSQ-G93S-R93K-J?i=45&cat=1881394

was issued July 31, 1773. Since he did not reappear in court, the sum must eventually have been paid.

Record of John Robinson v. Richard Crockett.
Cumberland County Court of Common Pleas, March 13, 1773.[104]

Richard and Elizabeth (Roberts) Crockett had eight children, all likely born in Second Parish/Cape Elizabeth. In pulling together my list of their children, I utilized Crockett genealogist Candage's list, from which I subtracted the superfluous Richard Crockett (Richard IV) and to which I added daughter Catharine, whom Candage attributes to Richard and Mary (Robinson) Crockett (as do many other Crockett genealogists). Catharine's gravestone, however, clearly identifies her mother as Elizabeth Crockett and her father as Richard Crockett, Jr. (III). The children of Richard and Elizabeth are: Ephraim, Anna, Sarah, Deborah, Samuel, Mary, Lucy, and Catharine. (Since only son Ephraim's birthdate is known, this list is not necessarily in order of the children's births.) Please refer to the "Genealogical

---

104. Maine, Cumberland County Court of Common Pleas records, 1764-1839. Court records, v. 4, Mar. 1773-Oct. 1785, p. 41. https://www.familysearch.org/ark:/61903/3:1:3QSQ-G93S-R93K-J?i=45&cat=1881394

Dictionary of Thomas and Ann Crockett" beginning on page 377 for more information about Richard and Elizabeth's family. (Son Ephraim Crockett's life is covered in Chapter 7.)

There is no evidence that Elizabeth (Roberts) Crockett lived much beyond the birth of her last child, Lucy, born June 24, 1765.[105] There is no death record for Elizabeth Roberts, either. Given the fact that Richard remarried in 1776, we can guess that Elizabeth passed away sometime between 1765 and 1776. She is probably buried with her daughter Catharine at Long Creek Cemetery, although no stone has been found for her in this ancient cemetery.

Two halves of the gravestone of Catharine Crockett.
Catharine was the daughter of Richard Crockett, Jr. (III) and Elizabeth (Roberts) Crockett.
Catharine died at 22 months[106] on January 11, 1761 and was buried in Long Creek Cemetery
with her great-grandfather Samuel Skillin and other relations.
(Photo credit: Becca Tibbetts. From Find-A-Grave, Long Creek Cemetery, South Portland, Maine.)

---

105. CANDAGE, p. 11. Unfortunately, Candage does not give a source for this birth date, although since the genealogist was so specific, presumably he must have had one.
106. In 1887, D.W. Clark transcribed the headstones in Long Creek Cemetery. His transcription for this stone reads: "Catharine Crocket, dau. of Mr. Richard Crocket Junr. died Jany, 11, 1761 Ag'd 22." Clark omitted to mention Elizabeth Crockett, whose name is clearly on the headstone in this later photograph, as well as the word "months" after "22" (also legible). These omissions (and the frequent confusion between Richard and his father due to the "junior" designation both used) have led many historians over the years (including Candage) to believe Catharine was the daughter of Richard Crockett, Jr. (II) and Mary (Robinson) Crockett. See a list of Clark's inscriptions on the South Portland Historical Society website https://sphistory.pastperfectonline.com/archive/B89D5F67-03D6-466D-9412-051366501517#gallery-3

The March Toward Revolution

The inevitable march toward revolution was triggered by the British Parliament's passage of the Stamp Act on March 22, 1765. The Stamp Act, which followed the unpopular Sugar Act of 1764,[107] was a tax upon colonists in an effort to recharge England's coffers after the immense financial drain of the French and Indian War. This new direct tax imposed a severe burden upon colonists:

> "The act required the colonists to pay a tax, represented by a stamp, on various forms of papers, documents, and playing cards. It was a direct tax imposed by the British government without the approval of colonial legislatures and was payable in hard-to-obtain British sterling, rather than colonial currency."[108]

The Stamp Act was to go into effect on November 1, 1765. On October 14th at a legal meeting of freeholders in Falmouth, it was voted that the town's representative to the Massachusetts General Court was "… hereby directed to use his utmost efforts to prevent the Stamp Act taking place in the Province."[109] Colonial resistance to the Stamp Act (including an unruly mob that threatened the custom-house in Falmouth), combined with pressure from "… merchants and manufacturers on both sides of the water, whose pecuniary interests were in danger," brought about the repeal of the tax in March of 1766.[110] At the same time Parliament repealed the Stamp Act, however, it declared Parliament and the King held full authority to govern and tax the colonies. Parliament proceeded to levy new duties known as the Townshend Acts, a series of taxes and regulations levied upon the American colonies, initially instituted by (and named for) the Chancellor of the Exchequer, Charles Townshend.

---

107. The Sugar Act was a tax on sugar, coffee, wine, and some textiles.
108. The Gilder Lehrman Institute of American History. History Resources. "The Stamp Act, 1765." https://www.gilderlehrman.org/history-resources/spotlight-primary-source/stamp-act-1765#:~:text=The%20act%20required%20the%20colonists,sterling%2C%20rather%20than%20colonial%20currency
109. Falmouth, Maine Town Records, Book 2, 1728-1773, p. 281. Samuel Waldo (son of the late Brigadier-General Samuel Waldo) then represented Falmouth and Cape Elizabeth District at the Massachusetts General Court. He might have been one of the representatives who gathered in New York City from October 7-25, 1765 at what was known as the Stamp Act Congress. This extra-official gathering acknowledged "that while Parliament has a right to regulate colonial trade, it does not have the power to tax the [American] colonies since they were unrepresented in Parliament." Website, The Gilder Lehrman Institute of American History. History Resources. "The Stamp Act, 1765." https://www.gilderlehrman.org/history-resources/spotlight-primary-source/stamp-act-1765#:~:text=The%20act%20required%20the%20colonists,sterling%2C%20rather%20than%20colonial%20currency
110. WILLIS, p. 482.

At a town meeting held in Cape Elizabeth on May 25, 1768, Jedidah Preble of Falmouth (who had distinguished himself during the French and Indian War) was voted to be the District's representative to the Grievance Committee that was to meet at Faneuil Hall in Boston to discuss these unfair taxes levied by the British.[111] Two years later on March 27, 1770, at the annual Town Meeting held in Falmouth, that community attempted to get around England's tax upon certain textiles by offering to pay "any person well skilled in weaving cotton velvet with all his tools necessary for that business," and even to provide that person with an advance if he did not have the tools necessary, so he could buy the equipment. It was also voted at the same meeting that "This Town will do what lies in their power to discountenance the purchasing of foreign Tea, and to discourage the use of it in their several families."[112]

Residents of Cape Elizabeth initially hoped that issues with the British could be worked out peacefully. They rather naively believed that the King (and Parliament) would eventually come round and provide representation to the colonists. Just in case, however, the District of Cape Elizabeth voted on May 30, 1770 to spend 6 pounds to purchase "a Town Stock of ammunition."[113] Hope for a peaceful resolution remained as late as December 1772, when the District appointed a committee of correspondence to reply to a list of grievances received from Boston.[114] But all hope had faded by December 16, 1773, when the Sons of Liberty organized the Boston Tea Party to protest Parliament's tax upon tea in the colonies. The Boston Tea Party was roundly applauded in Maine:

> "When the citizens of Boston took the bit in their teeth and proceeded to dump the tea into Boston Harbor, the news was received here in Falmouth with great joy. A militia was enlisted at once to aid the people of Boston should the need arise."[115]

At a town meeting held in Cape Elizabeth on December 30, 1773, several

---

111. South Portland, Maine, Town Records 1765-1823.
112. Falmouth, Maine Town Records, Book 2, 1728-1773, p. 307.
113. South Portland, Maine, Town Records, 1765-1823.
114. The Committee of Correspondence was voted to be: Deacon Henry Dyer, Mr. Joseph Mariner, and Dr. Nathanial Jones. In addition to thanking Boston for their zeal in defending the District's rights, the new committee was told to encourage the District's representative to get relief by petitioning the King and Parliament, "... and by any other legal method the House of Representatives may think proper," however, the representative was to be encouraged "... not [to] give up any of Our Invaluable Charter Rights of Privileges."
115. CAPE-E, p. 40.

additional men, including Captain Samuel Skillin, were added to the already-formed Committee of Correspondence.[116] Early in 1774, in response to the Boston Tea Party, the British Parliament began passing a series of acts, known in the colonies as the Intolerable Acts (or the Insufferable Acts), to punish Massachusetts. These four acts (known as the Coercive Acts in Great Britain) basically eliminated Massachusetts right of self-governance. The passage of the acts elicited outrage throughout the colonies, including, naturally, in Maine, which was part of Massachusetts.

A town meeting was called in the District for February 23, 1774. During this meeting, residents expressed their anger, which was recorded in the minutes: "At Such an Alarming & Crtitical a Time of our Publick affairs as this when our Enemies in Great Britain are using every Stratigam in their power to Wrest from us that best of blessings Liberty, We think ourselves and all the Sons of Freedom loudly called upon to express our Abhorrance of such measures, & our willingness at all times to join our Brethren upon this Continent in preventing their deep laid Schemes taking Effect by all lawfull Constitutional methods."[117]

In March of 1774, the British Parliament passed the Boston Port Act, effectively closing the port of Boston to commerce. This was another retaliatory act for the Boston Tea Party. In June, the Quartering Act, the last of the four Intolerable Acts was passed by Parliament. This act entitled the British to house troops in private homes and was the only Intolerable Act to apply to all the American colonies, not just Massachusetts.

A rupture with Great Britain was now a certainty. On September 6, 1774, at a town meeting held in the District of Cape Elizabeth, residents voted to send

---

116. South Portland, Maine, Town Records, 1765-1823.
117. Voters passed nine resolves stating the position of Cape Elizabeth District at the February 23, 1774 meeting: "That the District's beliefs cannot be better expressed than that recently expressed by Boston."
    1. That "... the disposal of their own property is the inherent right of Freemen" and that right cannot be taken without consent, and that the taxing of us by Parliament is the claiming of such a right.
    2. That the duty on tea is such a tax without our consent.
    3. That the tax levied supports the British government by which it "renders assemblies useless and [introduces us to] Arbitrary government and slavery."
    4. That "a virtuous and steady opposition to this ministerial Plan of governing America is absolutely necessary to preserve even the Shadow of liberty, and is a duty which every freeman in America owes to his country to himself & to his Posterity."
    5. That the resolution of the East India Company to tax their tea is a part of this ministerial government and a violent attack upon the liberties of America.
    6. That it is the duty of every American to oppose this attempt.
    7. That anyone who directly or indirectly countenances their attempt or in any way aids or abets the unloading or sale of East India tea is an Enemy.
    8. That "we will not buy or sell in our families this tea that is taxed." (South Portland, Maine, Town Records, 1765-1823.)

representatives to the newly-formed County of Cumberland Congress. They also unanimously voted that the District would abide by the charter of William and Mary (as opposed to abiding by the laws and regulations passed by the British Parliament). In a more ominous sign, Cape Elizabeth voted to spend 17 pounds to purchase a stock of gunpower, balls and flints. On Friday, October 21, 1774, a committee was chosen to pick and commission "Patriotic Gentlemen" to lead two companies of soldiers for Cape Elizabeth. This committee elected Nathaniel Jordan, Jr. as captain and Dr. Clement Jordan as lieutenant of the Spurwink Company, and Daniel Strout as captain and Samuel Dunn as lieutenant of the "Papoodock" (Purpoodock) Company. The captains and their companies were given the right to choose their ensigns and other officers.[118]

On April 19, 1775, the "shot heard round the world" opened the American Revolution with the battles of Lexington and Concord, fought between red-coated British soldiers and Massachusetts minutemen and militia members. News of the battles reached Cape Elizabeth the following day.[119] On Monday, April 24, 1775, at a town meeting held in Cape Elizabeth, a watch was established. Eight men would be on the watch every night; two at the Cape and two at Portland; and four men were to be stationed between Spring Point and the ferry. If any danger from the British presented itself, the minutemen were to post directly to the captain of the company in charge, who was to muster his company and march immediately to fight the enemy. It was voted to provide the militia when called to march to the "Westward or elsewhere" with provisions for a fortnight and one dollar per man, and to provide arms and bayonets to those men who did not have them. (The weapons were to be returned to the town stock when the men were dismissed.) The town voted to borrow the necessary funds from any person who would lend it, with the selectmen to give surety for their town.[120]

That same day—April 24, 1775—Captain Samuel Dunn of Cape Elizabeth mustered his company of militia into the Provincial Army for active service.[121] Sixty-two men (counting Dunn) were mustered in for a period of eight months,

---

118. South Portland, Maine, Town Records, 1765-1823.
119. The information that the news of the attack on Lexington and Concord reached Cape Elizabeth on April 20, 1775 came from information collected by historian Charles Starbird (STARBIRD) on William Dingley, a fellow Cape Elizabethan who settled near Ephraim Crockett in Pejepscot following the Revolutionary War. See STARBIRD's file on Dingley at the Androscoggin Historical Society, Auburn, Maine.
120. South Portland, Maine Town Records, 1765-1823. https://www.familysearch.org/ark:/61903/3:1:3Q9M-C3HY-ZSHV-1?i=41&cat=300073
121. CAPE-E, p. 45.

including Ephraim Crockett, the oldest child of Richard and Elizabeth (Roberts) Crockett. Captain Dunn was well-regarded in Cape Elizabeth. He was born in 1735, the son of Nathaniel Dunn and Deborah (Bailey) Dunn. A shipwright as well as militia leader, Dunn was also one of those chosen by Cape Elizabeth to attend the Cumberland County Congress.[122] He was married to Sarah Skillin, daughter of Samuel Skillin, Jr. and Rebecca (Sawyer) Skillin.[123] Ephraim Crockett served his first enlistment (of three) in the American Revolution under the command of Captain Samuel Dunn, the husband of his mother's first cousin.[124] (See Chapter 7.)

General Jedidiah Preble of Falmouth, who was no longer able to serve in the military because of his age and poor health, nevertheless was requested to attend a Provincial Congress held in Cambridge to give recommendations for the raising of troops in Maine. By April 26, 1775, Preble had been given authority to raise a regiment (although he would not lead it) in Cumberland County, the first regiment to be raised in Maine. He appointed Edmund Phinney of Gorham as Colonel.[125] Captain Dunn's company was incorporated into Phinney's regiment. The regiment was delayed from marching to Cambridge, where the Provincial Army of Massachusetts was situated, when it was discovered that another regiment was being formed in Maine. Citizens were worried that the loss of so many local soldiers would make the Maine coast vulnerable to attack by the British navy. As a result, Dunn's company was initially posted in the greater Falmouth area.

On June 27, 1775, at a town meeting held in Cape Elizabeth it was voted to supply Captain Dunn's Company with provisions, including one fortnight's allowance of the District's flour, provided the company was on active duty in the District at the time. At this meeting a Committee of Inspection was chosen to settle any disputes that might arise in town,[126] a judicious way of settling arguments and controversies until the fledgling nation could work out a court system.

The Battle of Bunker Hill occurred June 17, 1775. Although a loss by the new Continental Army,[127] the Americans distinguished themselves well, and the battle cost the British a great number of soldiers. This encouraged the colonial rebels with

---

122. GOOLD, p. 52.
123. Maine Vital Records, 1670-1921. Samuel Dunn and Sarah Skillin were married July 19, 1757.
124. Sarah (Skillin) Dunn was the daughter of Samuel Skillin, Jr. and Rebecca (Sawyer) Skillin. Elizabeth Roberts was the daughter of George Roberts and Katharine Skillin (Samuel, Jr.'s sister).
125. GOOLD, p. 8-10.
126. South Portland, Maine, Town Records, 1765-1823.
127. On June 14, 1775, the Second Continental Congress voted to unite the former colonial militias into one national fighting force under Commander-in-Chief General George Washington. This established the Continental Army, into which the Provincial Army of Massachusetts (already fighting the British in the Boston-area) was folded.

new hope in their quest for Liberty. After Bunker Hill, General George Washington was anxious to have as many soldiers under his command as possible, and he requested Phinney's regiment be sent down. In early July, Captain Dunn's company (and most of the other companies in Phinney's regiment) marched to Cambridge, where they joined the Continental Army as part of General William Heath's brigade. (To allay concerns about British attack, about two hundred men from Phinney's regiment were left behind to guard the coast, although these soldiers joined the army in Cambridge later.) Captain Dunn's company marched about twenty miles a day until the men reached Cambridge (probably a five- or six-day march), stopping for food at local taverns along the way.[128]

As it turned out, residents of Falmouth had good reason to worry about the lack of local defense. On October 18, 1775, the English Royal Navy under the command of Captain Henry Mowat, shelled and burned Falmouth. (See prior chapter.) Cape Elizabeth was spared incendiary shot from the ships' cannons, thanks to its shallower harbor that kept the frigates from getting close enough to fire. Nevertheless, residents were shocked by the destruction that occurred to the homes and businesses of their friends and family across the Fore River. (Some time after the burning of Falmouth, Richard's father relocated to Deer Isle, where brother Josiah Crockett resided.)

The Town of Cape Elizabeth Is Born

Upon a Resolve of the Provincial Congress of Massachusetts passed August 23, 1775, Cape Elizabeth became a town separate from Falmouth.[129] At a town meeting held in Cape Elizabeth on December 13, 1775, after the burning of Falmouth, residents voted to appoint a Committee of Safety for the town. Five members were voted onto the committee, which would meet in Falmouth on December 19th with other Committees of Safety from Cumberland County. The Cape Elizabeth Committee of Safety was given the right to "transact any business for the Safety of said Town and County."[130]

On December 31, 1775, the eight-month term of enlistment for those soldiers in Captain Samuel Dunn's company ended (as did many other volunteer

---

128. GOOLD, p. 15.
129. CAPE-E, p. 46.
130. South Portland, Maine, Town Records, 1765-1823.

The Fifth Generation

companies at Cambridge). General Washington, attempting to turn his army from volunteer to professional, disbanded Colonel Phinney's regiment and formed the 18th Continental Regiment, with Phinney appointed as its commander.[131] Some of the eight-month Cape Elizabeth men reenlisted in Phinney's new regiment. Most, like Ephraim Crockett, returned home, much to General Washington's chagrin. Washington, who needed every man, had been hoping these early volunteers would re-up. But after the burning of Falmouth that October, it is easy to understand that these men felt strongly about protecting the home front first. Many of the soldiers who returned home (including Ephraim Crockett) joined other companies serving in Maine.

On February 21, 1776, Cape Elizabeth voted for the first time to send a representative to the Massachusetts General Court, electing James Leach to represent the town.[132] At a legal town meeting held in Cape Elizabeth May 20, 1776, it was voted to comply with "the Hon. Congress Concerning Independence." The Second Continental Congress unanimously adopted the *Declaration of Independence* in Philadelphia on July 2, 1776, and on July 4th the *Declaration* was published. Printed broadsides of the *Declaration* were sent throughout the colonies. Massachusetts Provincial Congressman Richard Derby, Jr. ordered extra copies of the document be printed and sent to the ministers of every parish in Massachusetts (no matter their denomination) for them to read aloud to their parishioners after Sunday service. After this task was completed, the clergymen were to give a copy of the *Declaration* to the town clerk to be written into the record. Cape Elizabeth proudly inscribed a copy of the *Declaration of Independence* into its official town record that summer.[133]

---

131. CAPE-E, p. 46.
132. South Portland, Maine, Town Records, 1765-1823.
133. South Portland, Maine, Town Records, 1765-1823.

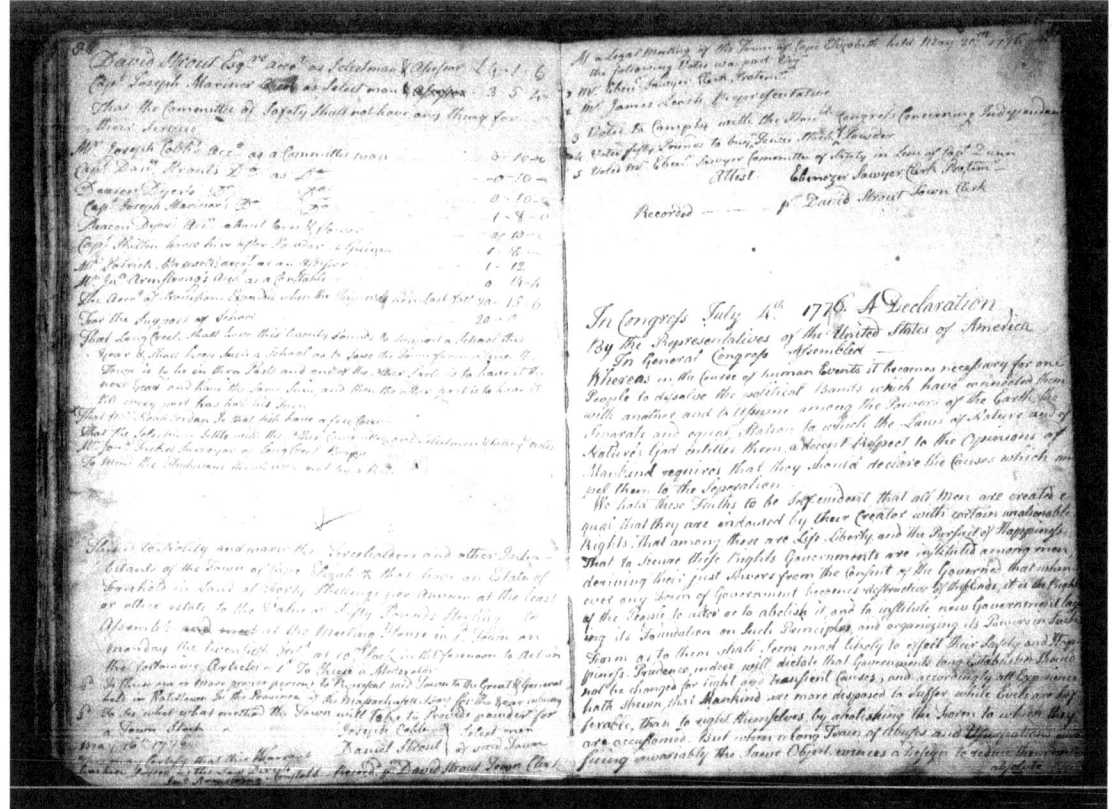

The *Declaration of Independence* copied into the Cape Elizabeth town record.
(The text begins on the right-hand page.)
(South Portland, Maine, Town Records, p. 81, Image #48.)

Susannah Westcoat and the Westcoat Family

Richard Crockett's second marriage occurred late in the year 1776, after the signing of the *Declaration of Independence*. These were uncertain times for every American, especially for those who had sons fighting the British, such as Richard's sons Ephraim and Samuel Crockett. This fact might have contributed to the widower's decision to marry again. In addition, Richard's eldest daughter, Anna, was soon to be married to John Parker of Portland.[134] When Anna departed her father's home, Richard would be left with the responsibility of a household that included two young daughters. In addition to caring for these children, he also had to earn a living.

---
134. Anna Crockett and John Parker were married January 29, 1777, in Portland. CANDAGE, p. 11.

The Fifth Generation

On November 7, 1776, Richard Crockett filed marriage intentions for himself and Susannah Westcoat. Richard was then about forty-three. Susannah, who was second to the youngest of William and Dorcas (Skillin) Westcoat's ten children, was twenty-four, having been born in 1752.[135] There is no marriage record for Richard and Susannah, however, we know they were not married by the Reverend Ephraim Clark, who was away at Cambridge serving as a chaplain for Maine companies in the Continental Army. (Reverend Clark performed no marriages in Cape Elizabeth from May 31, 1776 to June 11, 1777.)[136]

Susannah was most likely still living at home with her parents when the couple was wed. Her father, William Westcoat, who had purchased land from George Roberts, was one of the Crockett's nearest neighbors at Long Creek. Whether at the time of her marriage Susannah's illegitimate eight-year-old son was alive and living with her and her parents, we do not know. If so, the boy would have been melded into Richard Crockett's household, which (after his daughter Anna's departure) consisted of daughters Mary (about twelve) and Lucy (eleven).

Susannah would have moved into a home less affluent than that of her father; however, she probably preferred being mistress of her own household, rather than continuing to live under her mother's thumb. (Her older sister Dorcas was also still unmarried and at home.)[137] From all appearances, it was a prudent marriage for both Susannah and Richard.

Susanna's father, William Westcoat, was about seventy-six when she was married. Her mother, Dorcas (Skillin) Westcoat, was sixty-six. William and Dorcas were first cousins. They were also both related to the Crockett family.[138]

As with all of Samuel Skillin's children, Dorcas inherited property (and other resources) from her father, including one-quarter of a corn mill. In 1771, the value of

---

135. Abstract from *Skillings 8 Generations*, pp. 24-25. https://freepages.rootsweb.com/~arlene/genealogy/Skillings/d0/i0004172.htm#i4172
136. Maine Genealogy Archives. "Marriages by Rev. Ephraim Clark of Cape Elizabeth, 1756-1797." Cape Elizabeth historian William B. Jordan, Jr. says Rev. Clark served as chaplain for only a month; however, the minister's lack of marriage records for an entire year suggests that he served much longer in Cambridge.
137. Dorcas Westcoat, daughter of William and Dorcas (Skillin) Westcoat, is mentioned in a 1777 deed from William to his son Richard Westcoat, as being unmarried. On April 16, 1777, William sells to Richard 41 ½ acre of land in Scarborough abutting his brother William's land. William retains the privilege of deciding how much wood can be cut on the property, as long as he and his wife are alive, and until the marriage of his daughter Dorcas. She was then about 27 years old. CCROD, Book 13, Page 540.
138. William Westcoat's mother, Hannah Haley, was a sister of Dorcas Skillin's mother, Rhoda Haley. Both Hannah and Rhoda were sisters of Deborah Haley, the mother of Susannah's new father-in-law, Richard Crockett, Jr. (II), who had recently relocated to Deer Isle. There is a possibility that Richard (III) and his father lived together, and that Richard's marriage to Susannah occurred after his father relocated to Deer Isle. There certainly would have been more room in the home with her new father-in-law gone.

William Westcoat's real estate, including his share in the corn mill, was 21 pounds. This valuation was significantly higher than that of Richard Crockett's, whose real estate was valued at 1 pound, 10 shillings in 1771. (To be fair, Richard was a generation behind William Westcoat.) In addition, that year Westcoat had one horse, five oxen, three cows, five sheep (or goats) and three pigs. He owned 20 acres of pasturage that was able to support seven cows. William Westcoat's five-acres of tillable ground could produce 50 bushels of grain or corn per year, and his 10 acres of English upland produced five tons of hay. Added to this production was Westcoat's 20 acres of fresh meadows, which produced 12 tons of fresh meadow hay annually.[139]

Given Susannah's history (and the possible presence in their household of her illegitimate child), her parents were probably well-pleased to see her disposed of in marriage to Richard Crockett. Not only was he a known entity who lived locally and knew of Susannah's past, but also Richard was a relation who could be trusted. Richard Crockett seems to rise in the world financially after his marriage, so it is possible Susannah came to the marriage with a dowry of a sum of money from her parents, although William Westcoat appears to have occasionally lived beyond his means.[140] In 1769[141] and 1771[142] Westcoat was in court for unpaid debts. (In later years, after the death of his wife Dorcas Skillin, William Westcoat would have even more severe financial issues.)

Susannah's youth was marred by what appears to have been one serious

---

139. Massachusetts State Archives collection, colonial period, 1622-1788. Volume 132. Town valuations, Cape Elizabeth. P. 165. https://www.familysearch.org/ark:/61903/3:1:3Q9M-C9YR-V6Q2?i=235&cat=1055547

140. In numerous deeds executed during his lifetime William Westcoat rises (in his mind, anyway) from a simple "yeoman" (farmer) to a self-described "gentleman."

141. At the April 1769 term of the Court of Common Pleas held at Falmouth for Cumberland County, William Westcoat, yeoman of Scarborough, was the defendant in a plea of the case (with a writ on file dated March 29, 1769) brought by Stephen Woodman, gentleman of Scarborough. Westcoat was called, but did not appear. Judgment was for Woodman by default and William Westcoat was assessed damages of 2 pounds 15 shillings plus cost of suit taxed at 1 pound 18 shillings. An execution was issued July 6, 1769. Maine, Cumberland County Court of Common Pleas records. Court records, v. 3, 1768-1772, p. 107. https://www.familysearch.org/ark:/61903/3:1:3QSQ-G93S-R93Q-N?i=107&cat=1881394 Also, at the same April term of the CCP, Westcoat, gentleman of Cape Elizabeth, was the defendant v. Enoch Isley, merchant of Falmouth, plaintiff. There was another writ on file dated March 24, 1769. William was once again called, but did not appear. Judgment was for Isley by default. He was awarded damages of 26 pounds, 4 shillings and 6 pence and costs of suit taxed at 1 pound, 17 shillings and eight pence. Maine, Cumberland County Court of Common Pleas records. Court records, v. 3, 1768-1772, p. 97. https://www.familysearch.org/ark:/61903/3:1:3QS7-L93S-RBCQ?i=103&cat=1881394

142. At the April 1771 term of the Court of Common Pleas held in Falmouth for Cumberland County, William Westcoat, gentleman of Scarborough, was a defendant v. Nathan Partridge, yeoman of Falmouth. A writ on file against Westcoat was produced dated April 2, 1771. William was called, but did not appear. Judgment was for Partridge by default, who was to recover from Westcoat 2 pounds, 1 shilling and 11 pence and costs of suit in the amount of 1 pound, 14 shillings and 10 pence. Maine, Cumberland County records, Court of Common Pleas. Court records, v. 3, 1768-1772, p. 354 https://www.familysearch.org/ark:/61903/3:1:3QS7-L93S-RB47?i=363&cat=1881394

slip—that of pre-marital sex, which resulted in pregnancy.[143] According to court records, Susannah was guilty of having pre-marital sex in Cape Elizabeth on May 20, 1767. She was only fifteen at the time of the incident. The man was unknown to the jurors who "presented" her at court for fornication, and remarkably, Susanna did not give up her paramour's name to the authorities or (apparently) to the midwife during labor.[144] (This protectiveness suggests that Susannah, who was a minor, was not raped.) After giving birth to her son on the last day of February, 1768, Susannah Westcoat was legally reprimanded in April of 1768. She was brought before the Cumberland County Court of General Sessions of the Peace in Falmouth on October 18th where Susannah admitted to the crime of fornication. She was sentenced to pay a fine to the King of 20 shillings and also ordered to pay court costs and fees amounting to twenty-seven shillings and two pence.[145] (The fine and fees were large, and that fact, combined with the fact that Susannah was not threatened with the lash, speaks to her parent's wealth and status in the community.)

The language in the court records was standard for the time:

> "The Jurors for our Lord the King having on the Third Tuesday of April 1768 upon their oaths presents – That Susannah Westcoat of the District of Cape Elizabeth in the County of Cumberland single Woman on the Twentieth Day of May A.D. 1767 at Cape Elizabeth aforesaid did commit the Crime of Fornication with a Male Person to the said Jurors unknown[146] whereof, She then afterwards on or about the last Day of February A.D. 1768 had a Male bastard Child born of her Body in evil Example to Others in like Case offending against the peace of Said Lord the King and the Laws in this Case made and provided ~ To which presentment the Said Susannah Westcoat comes pursuant to her own recognizance and pleads guilty ~"[147]

---

143. Having children out of wedlock seems to have been a family failing. Susannah's uncle, Andrew Westcoat, while living in Kittery, fathered two children out of wedlock prior to his marriage. Wikitree, Andrew Wescott. https://www.wikitree.com/wiki/Wescott-504
144. During the crisis of labor with a woman carrying an illegitimate child, midwives of the period often challenged the women to name the baby's father. While sounding cruel, this was done so that the guilty man could be forced to take financial responsibility for his actions and the child would not become a charge upon the town. The Westcoats could afford an illegitimate child, however, and would not have sought financial assistance.
145. Cumberland County, Maine, records, Court of General Sessions of the Peace, Oct. 18, 1768, p. 167-168. https://www.familysearch.org/ark:/61903/3:1:3Q9M-CS73-LWRQ-8?i=88&cat=554097
146. Had the father of Susannah's child been known, he, too would have been "presented" at court for fornication and would have been court ordered to provide for the child. He could have been a soldier from Massachusetts stationed locally for a short period of time.
147. Cumberland County, Maine, records, Court of General Sessions of the Peace, Oct. 18, 1768, p. 167-168. https://www.familysearch.org/ark:/61903/3:1:3Q9M-CS73-LWRQ-8?i=88&cat=554097

Richard appears not to have been bothered by Susannah's past. He and Susannah had at least four children together, all daughters. The children were born during this nation's great battle for liberty from British tyranny. My list of their children is taken (mostly) from Candage's genealogy (from his history of the superfluous Richard Crockett)[148] and includes: Deborah, Elizabeth, Susannah, and Dorcas Crockett. Please refer to the "Genealogical Dictionary of Thomas and Ann Crockett" beginning on page 377 for more information about Richard and Susannah's family.

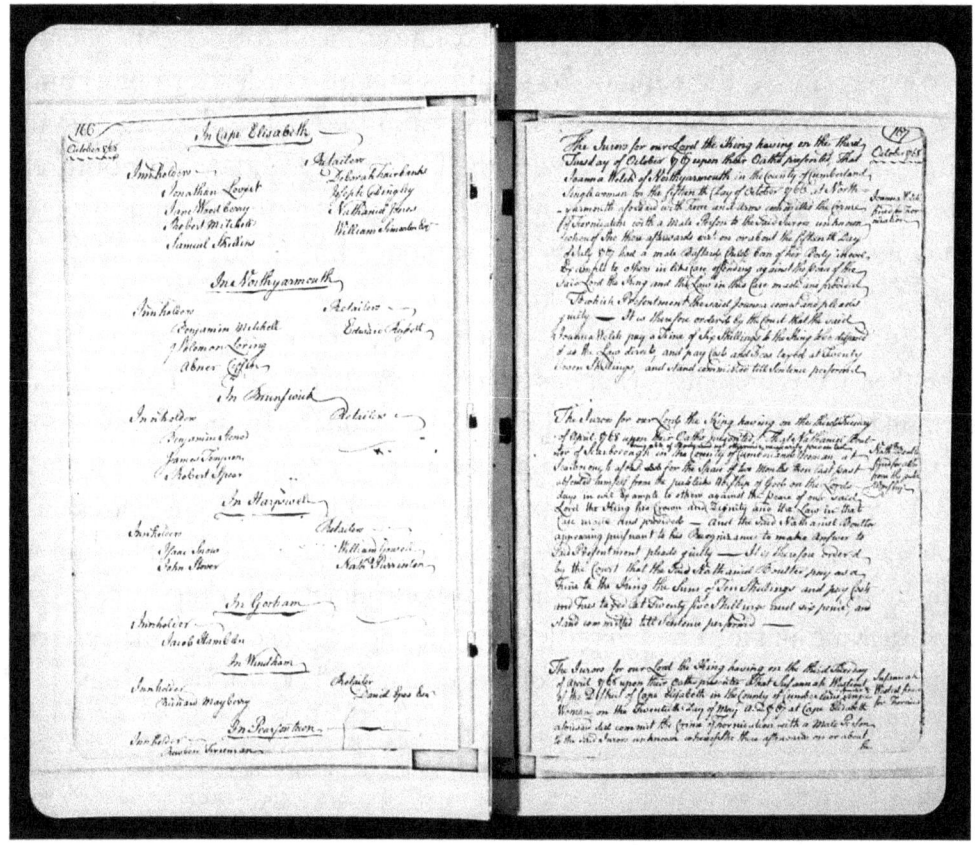

Record of Susannah Westcoat before the Cumberland County Court of General Sessions of the Peace, October 18, 1768.
During this court Susannah is charged with the crime of fornication
(right-hand page, lower paragraph).[149]
(Cumberland County, Maine, records, Court of General Sessions of the Peace, Oct. 18, 1768.)

---
148. CANDAGE, p. 36. See also the additional information about Susannah and Dorcas found in CANDAGE, p. 88.
149. Cumberland County, Maine, records, Court of General Sessions of the Peace, Oct. 18, 1768, p. 167-168. https://www.familysearch.org/ark:/61903/3:1:3Q9M-CS73-LWRQ-8?i=88&cat=554097

The Fifth Generation

Cape Elizabeth During the Revolutionary War

As the war continued to grind on through 1776 and early 1777, inflation reared its ugly head. The inflation was caused by supply shortages and price-gouging, and made for painful times in Maine and elsewhere in New England. Massachusetts attempted to deal with the situation by passing an Act to Prevent Monopoly and Oppression. On February 14, 1777, Cape Elizabeth selectmen and the local Committee of Correspondence met to consider the rates set by the new act. Believing that these fixed rates would curb inflation, the group agreed that local vendors should be forced to follow these new rates. New England rum was now to sell for 5 shillings per gallon; butter for 10 pence per pound; the price for good merchantable wood hauled right to the door at the furthermost distance was set at 12 shillings per cord (and the same price if the wood was brought by water and landed at a convenient place). The price of milk during summer was fixed at 2 pence per quart and in winter, milk was to sell for 3 pence per quart. Shoeing a horse, all around, with steel-corked heel and toes was set at 6 shillings with the same price for shoeing a yoke of oxen.

After the rates set by Massachusetts to curb inflation were adopted, it became clear that a mechanism to enforce these new rates was necessary. At a town meeting held July 8, 1777, a committee was assigned and voted upon that would execute the Act to Prevent Monopoly and Oppression in Cape Elizabeth (i.e. the committee would see that the set prices were being followed locally).[150]

Soldiers from Cape Elizabeth away fighting for liberty were never far from the thoughts and hearts of their family and friends. At a town meeting held November 5, 1777, it was voted to "make effectual provision for the families of such non-commissioned officers and privates ... as have engaged in the Continental Service." A committee was formed to see to the needs of these families. At another town meeting held in Cape Elizabeth on September 3, 1778, it was voted to raise 900 pounds—a prodigious sum, reflecting the inflation of the times—to supply the soldier's families.[151]

On February 11, 1778, after adjourning to Mrs. Jane Woodbury's inn (probably because it was too cold in the meetinghouse due to the shortage of firewood), voters "Chearfully Agree to the Articles of Confederation & Perpetual Union agreed

---
150. South Portland Town Records, 1765-1823.
151. South Portland Town Records, 1765-1823.

on by the Honorable Congress of the United States of America." (Hot buttered rum served in Mrs. Woodbury's warm tavern likely contributed to the cheerfulness, too.) Participants also voted at the same town meeting to assess a tax for the support of non-commissioned officers and privates. When the Continental Army called for more troops, the town voted April 14th (in a continuation of the annual town meeting from March 24, 1778) to raise eight men to reinforce the army and to raise a bounty of $1600, to pay the men $200 each. (This number was raised to nine new soldiers on May 20th, with an additional $200 appropriated.)[152] In November of 1780, the town voted to provide Continental soldiers with 30 shirts, 30 pair of shoes, 30 pair of stockings, and 15 blankets. To pay for this, the town voted money to purchase cloth, buttons, etc., and to pay for the shirts for the soldiers to be made.[153] In addition, the town had to raise the incredible sum of 9,000 pounds to fill Cape Elizabeth's beef levy for the Continental Army, "as their own supply [of beef] was practically non-existent."[154]

As if the financial burden of the war was not bad enough—combined with worry about a loved one away fighting the Red Coats—the winter of 1779/80 was hard in Cape Elizabeth (and elsewhere in Maine):

> "The cold was so intense that the harbor froze over as far as Simonton's Cove. In addition the snow was unusually deep, and blown by fierce winds, accumulated in tremendous drifts making travel impossible. There was great suffering throughout the area due to a lack of wood and water."[155]

By 1779, selectmen in Cape Elizabeth came to believe that the town was being taxed by Massachusetts for more polls (eligible voters) than lived in town. Due to this mistake, the town was being asked to send more recruits to the Continental Army and more money to support the war effort. Some of the men formerly on the books as a poll had relocated elsewhere; some had perished in the war; and some men were simply unaccounted for. On June 14, 1779, the town voted to send Daniel Jones, Esquire, to the Massachusetts General Court to ask for an abatement

---

152. South Portland Town Records, 1765-1823. On April 14, 1780, at a town meeting in Cape Elizabeth it was voted to pay each man that enlisted in the state's service under Brigadier General Wadsworth for the term of 8 months (as part of the town's quota) 40 shillings per month, together with their state bounty. This pay would be made in produce or silver, provided the soldiers were stationed at Camden or elsewhere out of town.
153. South Portland Town Records, 1765-1823. This vote occurred at a town meeting held Nov. 4, 1780.
154. CAPE-E, p. 50.
155. CAPE-E, p. 50.

of 100 polls.[156] Jones' attempt to get an abatement of 100 polls initially failed at the General Court, but the town continued to press for an abatement through the balance of the war, and even after:

> "Perhaps the most heartrending document that this town [Cape Elizabeth] ever drafted in any war was the petition it forwarded to the General Court in January of 1782. In it the town gave evidence of why its quota of men for the Continental service should be reduced. They stated that the town had furnished more than their quota in former times, with few of the men ever returning, which, coupled with their extraordinary losses at sea, had produced a large number of widows and orphans…Those who died in the Continental Army numbered nineteen with an additional six missing in action."[157]

(One of the six men initially reported missing in action was Richard and Elizabeth's eldest son Ephraim Crockett.)[158] The town's unflagging efforts to abate the number of polls charged by Massachusetts were eventually successful and Cape Elizabeth was abated 100 polls.[159]

In Maine, the most dramatic and disturbing event that occurred during the war (after the burning of Falmouth Neck) was the occupation of eastern Maine by the British. On July 17, 1779, British troops landed on the Bagaduce peninsular at the estuary of the Penobscot River, currently the town of Castine. The British proceeded to build a fort upon the site, once an important trading center of French Acadia, which territory had been ceded to the English at the end of the French and Indian War.

Shocked by the audacity of the British—and unwilling to surrender any territory—Massachusetts launched a joint land and sea operation comprised of more

---

156. Returns for Cape Elizabeth in 1779 reveal that the town had 292 polls. Massachusetts must have been charging the town for closer to 400 polls. Massachusetts State Archives Collections, Colonial and Post Colonial Period, 1626-1806. Vol. 323, Valuations and Taxes 1778-1787. https://www.familysearch.org/ark:/61903/3:1:3Q9M-C9YY-FQQL-6?i=869&cat =1050952 Cape Elizabeth residents voted to pay Daniel Jones $7.50 per day for his expenses; of which Jones offered to donate $1.50 per day back to the poor of Cape Elizabeth for every day that he was gone.
157. CAPE-E, p. 50.
158. Ephraim was not missing in action in the usual sense in that he had been wounded or captured during a battle, but rather he had ventured into the backcountry of the Pejepscot Patent with his uncle James Wagg. The selectmen did not know why Ephraim Crockett was missing; they only knew he was not voting in Cape Elizabeth, nor serving in the Continental Army, and yet Massachusetts was counting him as one of their polls.
159. South Portland Town Records, 1765-1823. On September 9, 1782, at a town meeting in Cape Elizabeth, residents voted to send Capt. Joseph Noyes "…to be agent to go to Boston to the General Court to get the Money for the said hundred Polls abated."

than 40 ships to retake the territory and expel the British. Nineteen warships and 25 support vessels, carrying 1,000 colonial sailors, soldiers, and supplies departed Boston on July 19th for the Bagaduce peninsula. Despite being short of able-bodied men, Cape Elizabeth raised one company to send to the regiment of Colonel Jonathan Mitchell, then being raised for Cumberland County.[160] One of the fifty-three young men to volunteer for Captain Joshua Jordan's company was Samuel Crockett,[161] youngest son of Richard and Elizabeth (Roberts) Crockett, who was then about eighteen or nineteen.

Regrettably, a squabble over who was in command of the expedition led to a disastrous defeat of the combined American forces by the British. Many of the soldiers and sailors had to make their way back to Boston (or to their homes in Maine) through the wilderness, with no food or ammunition with which to sustain themselves:

> "On August 14th the British succeeded in destroying the entire fleet engaged in the expedition thus ending Massachusetts' separate naval force. As no military success had been or could be obtained the troops commenced their disastrous withdrawal. Colonel Mitchell's regiment arrived in Falmouth about the middle of September after a long and laborious journey through the woods. In this arduous retreat one of Cape Elizabeth's leading citizens, Doctor Nathaniel Jones, died of exposure on the 4th of September. Captain Joshua Jordan's company was officially discharged the 24th of September thus ending the participation of Cape Elizabeth in the Bagaduce imbroglio."[162]

The Penobscot Expedition was the worst naval defeat in American history until Pearl Harbor. The British occupied Castine until the end of the war, during which time no civil authority existed in the area and some residents of eastern Maine (such as Richard's brother Josiah and his father in Deer Isle) were subjected to shaving-mills, as described in Chapter 4. The presence of British warships patrolling the Maine coast also amounted to a near blockade of Cape Elizabeth (and other coastal communities) that depended upon shipping for food and supplies.

One of the more interesting local characters during the war was Susannah's

---

160. CAPE-E, p. 49.
161. U.S. Revolutionary War, Pension and Bounty-Land Warrant Application Files, 1800-1900. Crockett, Samuel. Cape Elizabeth, Maine.
162. CAPE-E, p. 49.

The Fifth Generation

oldest brother William Westcoat, an innkeeper from Falmouth. He became known as "Post Wescott" because he also carried the mail from Boston to Falmouth Neck. William was more than 20 years older than Susannah, so she would not have grown up with him; however, Post Wescott was a welcome sight where ever he went, as this extract from Hugh D. McLellan's "The History of Gorham, Maine" illustrates:[163]

> "Mr. Wescott was the famous 'Post Wescott' of olden times, and during the Revolution was known to every man, woman and child on the road from Boston to Portland, and in all the region about the County of Cumberland. It is said he carried the first mail between Boston and Portland, was employed by Washington during the war in carrying dispatches, and in carrying letters to and from the soldiers in the army and their friends and family in New Hampshire and Maine... When about to start with dispatches in which the General [Washington] took much interest, [Post Wescott] was looking for a stick with which to urge forward his horse, when Washington told him to take his cane, which was more substantial than a switch, and hurry off. This cane he religiously preserved till his death and it is now an heirloom highly prized.
>
> "There are some of us yet alive who can remember the old gentleman... He was the wonder of the young, always polite and courteous, and always with something pleasant to say to all. He always attracted attention, with his erect, stately figure, and fine horsemanship, his long cane or staff, which he grasped in the old-fashioned style a few inches below the top; dressed in the old continental style, with cocked hat, single-breasted coat with large brass buttons and standing collar, with long waist and wide skirts; short breeches, high-quartered shoes with silver buckles four inches square, long stockings fastened to his breeches at the knee with large silver buckles,--this was his going-out dress, and he never abandoned it during his life."[164]

Richard and Elizabeth's sons Ephraim and Samuel Crockett both survived the American Revolution in apparent good health (although Ephraim might have experienced a hearing loss due to working with artillery). Susannah, however, lost a nephew, Joseph Westcoat, the son of her brother William "Post" Westcoat.[165]

---

163. According to McLellan, two of Post Wescott's sons relocated to Gorham. After his retirement, Wescott frequently visited his sons in Gorham, where he became a common sight in town. GORHAM, p. 819-820.
164. GORHAM, p. 819-820.
165. Joseph was the son of William Westcoat and his wife Margaret (Clement) Westcoat. He was killed in battle in Rhode

In the fall of 1781, the Continental Army under General George Washington, supported by the French (who had no love for the British), laid siege to British General Lord Charles Cornwallis' army at Yorktown, Virginia. The Americans dug trenches around the city, hauled heavy artillery into the trenches, and pounded Cornwallis into surrendering his army on October 19, 1781. Cornwallis' surrender effectively ended the fighting that occurred during Revolution, although there would be nearly two years of negotiations between the Americans and British before any treaty was inked. On March 31, 1783, word reached Cape Elizabeth that an agreement had been reached and all hostilities with Great Britian were over. When the news was officially confirmed on April 4th it prompted "...widespread rejoicing throughout the day punctuated by sporadic artillery salutes."[166] On September 3, 1783, the Treaty of Paris was signed formally ending the Revolutionary War. The treaty was ratified by the new U.S. Congress on January 14, 1784.

A New Day Dawns

After Cornwallis surrendered, a new day dawned in Cape Elizabeth and throughout the thirteen colonies. Although the treaty of Paris was not signed until 1783, life began returning to something akin to the old days after Cornwallis surrendered in the fall of 1781:

> "Almost immediately the town became engrossed in its own municipal affairs. A settlement was reached with the Reverend Ephraim Clark over his back salary, construction was started on a workhouse for the poor, the alewive fishery at Alewive Brook was closely regulated, and the ferry across the harbor at Spring Point was brought under the surveillance of a citizens committee. As in earlier times some livestock, viz., oxen, rams, sheep, and swine, were allowed to run at large under certain laws promulgated by the town."[167]

Massachusetts adopted a Constitution in 1780, which document restored the role of Governor. In April of 1781, those men in Cape Elizabeth who were eligible, voted in the gubernatorial election. Only 24 of 292 polls voted, less than 10% of

---

Island during the Revolutionary War. GORHAM, p. 819-820.
166. CAPE-E, p. 53.
167. CAPE-E, p. 53.

eligible voters. Twenty-four votes were cast for John Hancock for Governor (he won the election) and 24 votes for Thomas Cushing for Lieutenant Governor (who also won). Since Richard Crockett was a ratable poll in 1771, one assumes he was still ratable in 1781 (i.e. had an income of at least 3 pounds per year and/or an estate valued at 60 pounds or more) and so it is possible he voted. But given the low voter turnout, he probably was not one of the 10% voting. Jedidiah Preble also received 24 votes to represent Cape Elizabeth in the Massachusetts Senate.[168]

In 1781, Massachusetts asked towns and cities for a return of valuation from each. This assessment was to include the number of polls, houses, mills, livestock, ships, wharves, and much more. Cape Elizabeth complied, and reported that the town had 292 polls;[169] 175 houses, 131 barns, 9 stores, and 4 distillery houses and/or mills; and a total valuation of 2,105 pounds, 5 shillings, and 11 pence. The assessment included the acreage of English upland mowing ground (1,058 acres), tillage land (686 acres), wood and unimproved land (4,588 acres), meadow and salt marsh (850 acres); and pasturage (4,023 acres). There were 111 horses in Cape Elizabeth in 1781; 236 oxen; 600 cows; 1,164 sheep and goats; and 178 swine. An assessment was taken of other interesting items, such as the number of barrels of cider (12 barrels valued at 1 pound, 10 shillings); and the amount of goods and wares available to purchase in stores (just 24 pounds worth). For money, residents owned 100 ounces of silver (both coined and not coined) valued at 313 pounds and 16 shillings. Nobody in Cape Elizabeth owned any gold after the war.[170] And, although there were 111 horses in town, there was not a single coach or chaise for the horses to pull.[171] By comparison to Cape Elizabeth, neighboring Falmouth in 1781 was much more affluent. That town had 556 polls, 272 houses, 206 barns, 53 stores, 11 distillery houses and/or mills, and a total valuation of 4,879 pounds, 3 shillings and 2 pence. Falmouth residents also owned 25 ounces of gold; 1,500 ounces of silver; and carriages and chaises valued at 350 pounds.[172]

---

168. South Portland, Maine, Town Records, 1765-1823. The election was held in Cape Elizabeth on April 2, 1781.
169. This number is significantly less than the 402 polls Cape Elizabeth reported (or was believed by Massachusetts to have) during the war and reflects the loss of 100 polls (men who were killed, missing, or moved away), later abated by Massachusetts. See Massachusetts State Archive Collection, colonial period, 1622-1788, Vol. 161, Valuations 1777-1781. https://www.familysearch.org/ark:/61903/3:1:3Q9M-C9YR-R8FK?i=386&cat=1055547
170. Massachusetts State Archive Collection, colonial period, 1622-1788, Vol. 162 Valuations of Towns 1781-1785. https://www.familysearch.org/ark:/61903/3:1:3Q9M-C9YR-R84J?i=553&cat=1055547
171. An assessment conducted prior to this (about 1778-1779) showed that at the time there was one carriage in Cape Elizabeth. Massachusetts State Archive Collection, colonial period, 1622-1788, Vol. 161, Valuations 1777-1781. https://www.familysearch.org/ark:/61903/3:1:3Q9M-C9YR-R8FK?i=386&cat=1055547
172. Massachusetts State Archive Collection, colonial period, 1622-1788, Vol. 162 Valuations of Towns 1781-1785. https://www.familysearch.org/ark:/61903/3:1:3Q9M-C9YR-R842?i=551&cat=1055547

In the spring of 1781, Richard—then in his late forties—stepped into his first official role in town. At the annual meeting held in Cape Elizabeth on March 21, 1781, Richard was voted one of three men to collect the church tithes for the year (and keep young boys in line during the service and older men awake).[173] This was a position to which his father-in-law George Roberts had been previously elected, as well as his father. Richard would be elected tithing man the following spring, as well.

Richard Crockett's 1781 Real Estate Transactions

On April 23, 1781, Richard Crockett, chairmaker of Cape Elizabeth, purchased thirty acres of land in that town (for 30 pounds) from Samuel Mountfort, shipwright of Falmouth. This 30-acre parcel was the same land over which the heirs of Edmund Mountfort had taken Richard to court in 1771, and which he likely had been leasing or renting since.[174] The parcel was described in the deed from Samuel Mountfort (Edmund's son) as being located "… on the Southerly Side of Long Creek Stream, burred and bounded as follows, beginning at two black ash Trees, standing on One Stock, being the Northeast Bound of James Crocker's sixty acre Lot & from said two Trees to run South Southwest; One hundred and Twenty Rods to a Stake, and from thence running west Northwest Forty Rods to a stake, and from thence North Northeast, One hundred Twenty Rods to a stake, & from thence south Southeast Forty Rods to the first Bound mentioned."[175]

At the time he secured the Mountfort lot, Richard and Susanna and their children were living in the house he had built on his former father-in-law's property at Long Creek. Susannah's mother, Dorcas (Skillin) Westcoat, died in August of 1781 at 71 years of age.[176] Susannah might have inherited a sum of money from her mother because on the following month Richard purchased the balance of his former in-law's land (the Roberts' property) in Cape Elizabeth, including the land upon which his house stood.[177]

---

173. South Portland, Maine, Town Records, 1765-1823. The other two men elected "thythingmen" for Cape Elizabeth in 1781 were Humphry Richards and Samuel Dyer.
174. The 30-acre tract, which adjoined some of George Roberts' real estate as well as James Crocker's 60-acre lot, was the only parcel assigned to Edmund Mountfort at Long Creek by the Proprietors Committee of Falmouth. Samuel Mountfort was Edmund's son and one of his heirs.
175. CCROD, Book 11, p. 281. Thomas Child and Robert McDonald witnessed the deed.
176. Skillings genealogy website. https://freepages.rootsweb.com/~arlene/genealogy/Skillings/d0/i0004172.htm#i4172
177. This information is gleaned from Richard's future deed to his son Samuel, as well as from Samuel's mortgage and deed of the same property to Seth Storer. See CCROD, Book 160, p. 41.

The Fifth Generation

On September 12, 1781, George Copson Roberts and Joseph Roberts, yeomen of Cape Elizabeth, sold Richard (for 20 pounds) their right and title to all the real estate belonging to their late father and mother George and Katharine Roberts either in Cape Elizabeth or elsewhere.[178] George C. and Joseph Roberts excepted from the sale to Richard, the Roberts' former dwelling house; the two brother's rights to the corn mill (deeded to George and Katharine Roberts by Samuel Skillin) and mill privileges at Long Creek; rights to a certain thatch (grass) bed; and a tract of land commonly called the corn field.[179] Richard assigned for 2 pounds his two-fifth right to the corn field to George Copson Roberts in a deed dated the same day and obviously executed at the same time.[180]

The following day, September 13, 1781, Richard sold (for 100 pounds) 25 acres of land at Long Creek—with a dwelling house included—to his younger brother Robinson Crockett, chairmaker of Cape Elizabeth. Since Richard did not buy his late father-in-law's house,[181] the home referred to in this deed must be his own. It appears from these 1781 transactions that Richard might have planned to build a new house on the Mountfort property, and sold his original home and the Roberts' land to his brother. The property in the deed to Robinson is described as bounded: "beginning at the northerly corner of a small piece of land containing about half an acre more or less, belonging to George Roberts [the corn field], which small piece of land adjoins Josiah Westcoats[182] land, & from said northerly corner south southwest about 15 rods to land I lately purchased of Samuel Mountford, thence by said land last mentioned about thirty rods to the northerly corner thereof, thence south southwest by said last mentioned land, one hundred rods to a stake ~ thence west northwest to land of William Westcoat [Susannah's father], thence north northeast by said William Westcoat's land to the Country Road near Cumin's Bridge, thence by said Country Road to the bound first mentioned...."[183]

---

178. CCROD, Book 11, p. 408. Witnesses: David Strout and Richard's brother Robinson Crockett.
179. This field is variously described in deeds as the "corn field" and "barn field," and might be where George Roberts grew and/or stored corn for the corn mill.
180. CCROD, Book 15, p. 99. Witnesses: David Strout and Robinson Crockett.
181. Given the probable value of George Roberts' house, his sons George C. and Joseph either sold it or moved the house onto some of their land. Prior to the installation of electrical and phone lines, houses, barns, and other structures were commonly moved from location to location in Maine. In fact, on our farm here in Troy we have a shed that was formerly a small house and which over the years was moved at least twice, including down the road several miles.
182. Josiah Westcoat was Susannah's first cousin. He was the son of William Westcoat's brother Richard. Richard Westcoat had purchased 25 acres of land from George Roberts, formerly half of James Crocker's 60-acre lot that Roberts had bought from Phineas Jones. The other 5 acres of that 30 acres Roberts sold to his brother-in-law William Westcoat.
183. CCROD, Book 11, pg. 329. No dower rights signed off. Witnesses: Samuel Freeman and Enoch Freeman, Jr.

1781 deed from George Copson Roberts and Joseph Roberts to Richard Crocket, Jr. This deed is for all the real estate belonging to their late parents, excepting their dwelling house, corn mill, a thatch field, and the "corn field" previously sold to George Roberts by Richard Crockett.
(Cumberland County Registry of Deeds, Book 11, Page 408.)

But if Richard planned to build a new home on the Mountfort property, that house was never built. Instead, his brother Robinson relocated to Deer Isle with his young family by 1785,[184] if not before.[185] By then, their father and brother Josiah lived in Deer Isle, as well as two of Susannah's sisters and their husbands and families.[186] There is no deed on file from Robinson Crockett returning the house and 25-acres to his brother. That fact does not mean that a deed never existed, it simply means a deed might never have been recorded. (Richard certainly acted as though he owned the property, since he later sold his house and ten acres to his son Samuel.) It is also possible that the deed from Richard to Robinson in 1781 was not a deed of title, but rather a mortgage deed, via which Robinson lent his brother

---

184. DEERISLE, p. 103.
185. CANDAGE, p. 12.
186. Susannah's sister Mercy Westcoat was married to Job Small, and Anna married Ebenezer Webster. DEERISLE, p. 97 and 100. See also Skillings genealogy website https://freepages.rootsweb.com/~arlene/genealogy/Skillings/d0/i0004172.htm#i4172

money on the property. (Richard later executed another deed to someone else, also written up as a title deed, but which was in fact a mortgage.)

By the end of 1785, Richard owned about 55 acres of land in Cape Elizabeth (the 30-acre Mountfort lot and at least 25 acres of Roberts' land). Richard and Susannah and their family continued to live in his original house, and he probably farmed some of the Mountfort property, as well as the Roberts' land.

Susannah's Father Slides Into Debt

Less than six months after her mother's death, Susannah's father remarried. This marriage was likely one of expediency and convenience for both bride and groom. On February 7, 1782, William Westcoat and Sarah (Miller) Skillin were married at the First Congregational Church of Scarborough.[187] Sarah was the widow of Edward Skillin[188] of Scarborough. At the time of their wedding, William was about eighty-two years of age and Sarah about a decade younger. Initially, the couple (and some of their children and possibly servants) resided in Cape Elizabeth very near Richard and Susannah and their family. After Westcoat began experiencing financial difficulties, however, he removed to Scarborough where he also owned property. (Some of William Westcoat's Cape Elizabeth and Scarborough lands were adjoined, so he was still near the Crocketts.)

After the death of his first wife (Dorcas Skillin Westcoat), William Westcoat's money troubles erupted, frequently landing him in court. Most of the time Westcoat failed to show up at court (whether due to stubbornness or infirmity or both, we do not know) and thus he lost by default. No doubt some of Westcoat's economic hardship was caused by the blockade of the Maine coast by British warships during the Revolutionary War. William and his family might have lived beyond their means, too. In early deeds he is described as a "yeoman," a free-hold farmer. In later deeds (and court records) Westcoat is denoted or describes himself as a "gentleman," a significant increase in social status.

After the war, Cape Elizabeth began a slow slide downward. By 1785, Cape Elizabeth had lost population. Young people, such as Richard Crockett's sons and

---

187. Marriage intentions were recorded Jan. 10, 1782 by David Strout, Cape Elizabeth town clerk. William was then still living in Cape Elizabeth and Mrs. Skillin in Scarborough. Town and vital records, 1760-1900. Cape Elizabeth (Maine). Town Clerk; Marriage Intention: 10 Jan 1782 "Maine Vital Records, 1670-1921," database with images, FamilySearch https://www.familysearch.org/ark:/61903/3:1:3Q9M-C9BL-HXT1?cc=1803978
188. Edward Skillin was a nephew of Samuel Skillin, Sr.

Susannah's siblings, had moved away in search of land and opportunity. The town lost property valuation, too, resulting in a shrinking tax base.[189] In 1785, the town had only 208 ratable polls,[190] 84 less than in 1781. There were 132 houses (down from 175 in 1781), 104 barns (down from 131), and 7 shops separate from houses (down from 9 shops in 1781). Either the returns were inaccurate, or some of the mills had closed, for there were only 1-½ mills in 1785 compared to 4 mills in 1781. (In fact, lack of demand for the mills might have contributed to William Westcoat's financial distress.) The number of total livestock in town had increased from 1781 to 1785, suggesting that those who remained in Cape Elizabeth returned to more agrarian pursuits after the war. Horses and colts increased by 20 to 137; sheep (and goats) increased by nearly 250 to 1,392; and swine from 178 in 1781 to 263 in 1785. The number of oxen decreased by 22 (from 236 to 214), possibly because horses were now performing more of the labor in the field. Silver and gold were still in short supply. In 1785 residents only possessed 30 ounces of silver, compared to 100 ounces in 1781. As in that earlier assessment, nobody in Cape Elizabeth in 1785 owned any gold.[191]

In the fall of 1782, Martha Cotton, the widow of and executor for the late William Cotton of Falmouth, took William Westcoat to court. At the October 1782 session of the Court of Common Pleas for Cumberland County held in Falmouth, Martha said William had signed a note to her husband on March 3, 1773, promising to pay 12 pounds, 2 shillings, and 4 pence on demand. She had demanded payment of him, but had only received 11 shillings and 11 pence from Westcoat to date. William's name was called in court, but he did not appear and judgment was for Martha in the amount of 18 pounds, 4 shillings damage, and costs of suit taxed at 1 pound, 12 shillings and 10 pence. After the judgment was awarded, however, William appeared, and said he would appeal the judgment to the Supreme Court of Adjudicature at their next session.[192] There is no record of this case at the superior court, though, so Westcoat must have settled with Martha Cotton prior to the court date.

---

189. This assessment was taken in 1785, but was reported as 1786 valuations since that was the year the returns were approved by the Massachusetts legislature.
190. There were also 73 unsupported polls in town. I am not sure if these were transients or whether these men simply did not have the income and wealth necessary to be considered "ratable."
191. Massachusetts State Archive Collection, colonial period, 1622-1788, Vol. 162 Valuations of Towns 1781-1785. https://www.familysearch.org/ark:/61903/3:1:3Q9M-C9YR-RZLD?i=816&cat=1055547
192. Maine, Cumberland County Court of Common Pleas records. Court records, v. 4, March 1773-October 1785, p. 381. https://www.familysearch.org/ark:/61903/3:1:3QSQ-G93S-R93F-4?i=394&cat=1881394

The Fifth Generation

After the suit brought by Mrs. Cotton, claims against Westcoat came fast and furious. Because Westcoat could not (or would not) pay the judgments against him, he lost most of his real estate in Cape Elizabeth. (Westcoat, knowing what was coming, did manage to sell off some of his property to his relations.)[193] Eventually, all Westcoat had left of his homestead in Cape Elizabeth was his old house and four-square-rods of land. This he sold on November 3, 1788 to John Skillin.[194]

The most egregious of Westcoat's debts was to James Thompson, a yeoman of Falmouth, who won a large judgment against Susannah's father at the Court of Common Pleas held in October of 1783.[195] In April of the following year, twenty-one and a half acres of Westcoat's land in Cape Elizabeth was legally set aside by execution to Thompson by Benjamin Bailey, Deputy Sheriff.[196] Westcoat, then in his mid-eighties, apparently objected to Thompson's presence on the property, now Thompson's own, and possibly attempted to throw him off. As a result, Thompson took William to court for trespassing in October of 1784.[197] Westcoat failed to appear at the Court of Common Pleas at the October 1784 session to answer the trespass charge and Thompson was awarded another 12 pounds in damages (plus court costs). This judgment resulted in William Westcoat losing five more acres of

---

193. On July 27, 1784, William Wescot of Scarborough, gentleman, sold for 6 pounds, 13 shillings and 4 pence to Edward Doane [Dunn], yeoman of Cape Elizabeth, 2 acres and one half acre at a place called Long Creek (the land adjoins Dunn's land and also part of an island that juts out into Long Creek). CCROD, Book 13, Page 237. Witnesses: [no first name, probably Richard] Crockett and John Skillin. Also, on March 30, 1786, William Westcoat of Scarboro deeded to his "beloved son Richard" his one-quarter part of the great mill (the grist mill) at Long Creek for 300 pounds old tenor or 40 pounds lawful money. CCROD, Book 15, p. 195. Witnesses: John Green and Abigail Westcoat. And on Dec. 15, 1787, William Westcoat, gentleman of Scarborough, sold for 8 pounds to Edward Doan [Dunn] of Cape Elizabeth, yeoman, 8 acres of land at a place called Long Creek that he bought in December 1781 of Catharine Roberts and others, adjoining the County Road and running by land he lost in an execution to land of Edward Doan's; also one acre more of land he owns between said pieces of land. CCROD, Book 14, p. 291. Witnesses: Samuel and Mary Freeman. On May 16, 1788, Westcoat also sold (for 5 pounds) to George Copson Roberts a small piece of land that had formerly belonged to George Copson's father, George Roberts. CCROD, Book 16, p. 49. Witnesses: Enoch Freeman Sr. and Jr.
194. CCROD, Book 21, p. 196. Skillin paid Westcoat 15 pounds and 14 shillings for the house and small piece of land. Witnesses to the deed were John Frothingham and Benjamin Bailey, the Deputy Sheriff who had enforced James Thompson's two executions against Westcoat (apparently there were no hard feelings).
195. On October 8, 1783, at the Court of Common Pleas held in Falmouth for Cumberland County, appeared James Thompson, plt. v. William Westcoat of Scarboro, def. in a plea on the case. A writ was on file dated Oct. 8, 1783. William was called, but did not appear in court. Thompson by default was awarded 79 pounds, 18 shillings, 5 pence and 1 pound, 13 shillings, 4 pence costs of suit. Maine, Cumberland County Court records. Court of Common Pleas. Court records, Oct. 1783, p. 442. (image #448). https://www.familysearch.org/ark:/61903/3:1:3QS7-L93S-RB2V?i=447&cat=1881394
196. On April 29, 1784, William Slemons (an assessor chosen by James Thompson), Joseph Noyes (assessor chosen by Benjamin Bailey, Deputy Sheriff), John Blake (assessor chosen by Deputy Sheriff for William Westcoat), appraised William Westcoat's real estate, and set aside 21 ½ acres of land in Cape Elizabeth to the value of 86 pounds to cover the execution against him, except for a 4 by 4 rod square where his house stands. On April 24th James Thompson signed off that he had received seizen of this property and full satisfaction for the execution against Westcoat. CCROD, Book 12, p. 462. Msc. Deed.
197. Maine, Cumberland County, Court of Common Pleas. Oct. 1784, p. 510. (Image #516.) https://www.familysearch.org/ark:/61903/3:1:3QSQ-G93S-R93G-3?i=515&cat=1881394

land in Cape Elizabeth. After the five acres were determined by the assessors,[198] the land was formally "seized" by Deputy Sheriff Benjamin Bailey on July 6, 1785 and given to Thompson, who signed off that he had received satisfaction the same day. One can imagine the frustration and anger the loss of five more acres caused the curmudgeonly Westcoat!

No death record exists for William Westcoat. Susannah's father likely died in Scarborough after 1788.

The Crockett Family, 1785-1795

The decade from 1785 to 1795 was probably a happy one in Cape Elizabeth for Richard, Susannah, and their family. In 1785, Richard was about fifty-two years of age and Susannah was thirty-three. Their home was a house full of women. Even after Richard and his first wife's daughter Mary was married to James Barton in 1786,[199] there remained in the house the four young daughters of Richard and Susannah: Deborah, Elizabeth, Susannah, and Dorcas.

The first census of the United States was taken in Cape Elizabeth in December of 1790. Richard Crockett was a head of household in which lived one free white male (FWM) over sixteen years of age (Richard); one free white male under age sixteen (unknown youth, probably an apprentice or farm hand);[200] and five free white females (FWF, Susannah and the four daughters).

---

198. Per usual, three men served as assessors in the case, with one being selected by the plaintiff, one by the defendant, and one by the clerk of court. In this case, Thompson selected Joseph Noyes; Westcoat selected Thadd Broad; and clerk Enoch Freeman, J.P. selected John Quimby. The assessors appraised the value of Westcoat's five acres at 17 pounds, 8 shillings, which was the amount of Thompson's award plus all the costs of the suit, including that which was paid to the Deputy Sheriff and the assessors. CCROD, Book 13, p. 440.
199. On April 15, 1786, marriage intentions were filed in Cape Elizabeth for Mr. James Barton & Miss Mary Crocket [daughter of Richard III and Elizabeth Roberts Crockett] both of Cape Elizabeth, entered by Ebenezer Sawyer, Town Clerk. "A Book of Records For the Second Parish in The town of Falmouth containing 212 pages." New P. 32
200. This youth could not be Susannah's illegitimate son because he would have been older.

The Fifth Generation

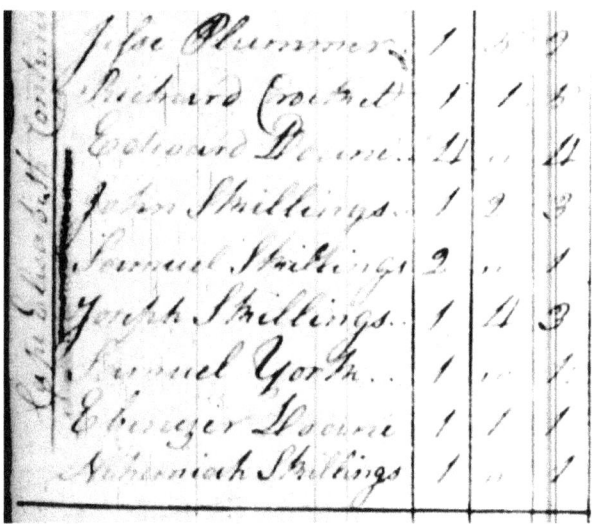

1790 U.S. Census for Cape Elizabeth, Richard Crockett.
According to this record, Richard and his family resided near Edward and Ebenezer Dunn, several Skillins, Samuel York, and Jesse Plummer.[201]

By 1790, all of Richard and his first wife's children were married, except Samuel Crockett, who is also listed as a head of household in Cape Elizabeth that year. In Samuel's house lived one free white male over sixteen (himself) and two free white females. The two women might have been Samuel's future wife Abigail Skillin and her mother or a sister. (We do not know Abigail Skillin's parents, although she was likely the daughter of one of Samuel Skillin, Jr.'s four sons.) A few months after the census was taken, on March 12, 1791, Samuel Crockett filed marriage intentions for himself and Abigail with Ebenezer Sawyer, Cape Elizabeth Town Clerk. Samuel and Abigail were then both living in Cape Elizabeth.[202] The couple was married in Cape Elizabeth on April 14, 1791, by long-time Crockett family pastor the Reverend Ephraim Clark.[203] Not long after he was married, Samuel Crockett became employed to manage a farm in Scarborough owned by Cornelius Durant. Samuel raised mules at the farm to work on a sugar plantation in St. Croix, which was also owned by Durant. Richard's grandson (and namesake) Richard Crockett was born to Samuel and Abigail on this Scarborough farm in 1795.[204]

---

201. The census taker typically visited houses in the order that he came to them, revealing often who lived next to whom. Maine Genealogy, Maine Census Guide 1790-1850. Cumberland County, Cape Elizabeth. https://www.mainegenealogy.net/census_guide.asp?censusyear=1790&county=cumberland
202. "A Book of Records For the Second Parish in The town of Falmouth containing 212 pages." New P. 42 (image 56).
203. Maine Genealogy Archives https://archives.mainegenealogy.net/2007/02/marriages-by-rev-ephraim-clark-of-cape.html See also South Portland Town Records, 1765-1823, p. 490.
204. Death notice of Captain Richard Crockett, *The Portland Daily Press*, May 24, 1880, p. 3.

From 1785 to 1795, Richard Crockett's duties and responsibilities in Cape Elizabeth increased. At the annual town meetings in 1784, 1785, and 1788, Richard was elected one of several fence viewers, field drivers, and hog reeves,[205] positions that his late father-in-law George Roberts had once filled (but never Richard's father). In March of 1791, Richard was accorded a position of more responsibility and authority when he was voted one of five constables for Cape Elizabeth (also a position filled by George Roberts). At the same meeting, his son Samuel, who had returned to town from the mule farm in Scarborough, stepped into the role of field drivers, fence viewers and hog reeve for the first time.[206] Richard would again be elected constable at annual town meetings held in 1792, 1794, and 1795.[207]

On October 18, 1786, at a town meeting in Cape Elizabeth voters considered the proposal to have the three eastern counties (i.e. the three Maine counties: York, Cumberland, and Lincoln) set off as a separate state from Massachusetts. The measure failed, with 21 votes for and 81 against.[208] (The desire to separate from Massachusetts would arise again in less than a decade.)[209]

In the spring of 1787, voters agreed to pay Josiah Westcoat (Susannah's cousin) 10 pounds and 4 shillings for having erected a beacon at Long Creek in 1777 during the Revolutionary War.[210] Despite the challenges posed by its rocky headlands, Cape Elizabeth still did not have a true lighthouse. In 1790, however, President George Washington commissioned a lighthouse to be built at Cape Elizabeth, which, after centuries of darkness along the Maine coast, must have been a spectacular sight. The lighthouse was "lighted for the first time January 10, 1791, thus making it one of the oldest lights along the Atlantic coast:

> "The stone work was seventy-two feet high topped by a 'lanthorn' fifteen feet high, making the whole tower eighty-seven feet. It was built by John Nichols and Jonathon Bryant, masons of Falmouth."[211]

---

205. South Portland Town Records, 1785-1860. In 1784 and 1785 Cape Elizabeth elected eight men to fill these positions; in 1788, the town elected nine.
206. South Portland Town Records, 1765-1823, p. 188.
207. South Portland Town Records, 1765-1823, p. 192-193; p. 200; and p.204.
208. South Portland Town Records, 1765-1823.
209. In 1795, at an adjournment of the annual town meeting held in Cape Elizabeth April 6th, there were 26 votes for separation from Massachusetts and 3 against. South Portland Town Records, 1765-1823. The separation question would crop up again after the War of 1812.
210. South Portland Town Records, 1765-1823. The vote was taken at a town meeting in Cape Elizabeth on May 14, 1784.
211. CAPE-E, p. 50.

The Fifth Generation

In the fall of 1793, Richard Crockett was a defendant at court for debt. At the November term of the Court of Common Pleas held in Portland for Cumberland County, John and Jonathan Mussey, plaintiffs, claimed that Richard owed them 2 shillings and 2 pence. This small debt was settled amicably, however, after Richard gave the Musseys a note of hand for 3 shillings and 8 pence.[212] Since the case did not arise again, we can assume the note was paid.

By the 1790s, Richard had expanded his chairmaking business to include other carpentry projects. At the adjournment of the annual Cape Elizabeth town meeting held April 4, 1796, it was voted to accept Richard Crockett's account (for payment) of 9 shillings "for a guide post and putting it up."[213] During the adjournment of the annual town meeting the following year Richard's account of 10 shillings for making a coffin for John Jonson was approved.[214]

By the end of 1795, when Richard was about sixty-two years of age, he had at least nine grandchildren, and probably many more. (Regrettably, we do not have genealogies for his daughters Anna, Sarah, Deborah, and Mary.) The eldest of Richard's (and Elizabeth Roberts') grandchildren was likely Rebecca, daughter of son Ephraim and his wife Rebecca (Stanford) Crockett, who resided in Pejepscot. Living closest to Richard were the children of son Samuel and his wife Abigail (Skillin), who lived in Cape Elizabeth. In 1795, Samuel and Abigail also had a daughter Betty, who was three, in addition to nine-month-old Richard.

Death of Susannah (Westcoat) Crockett and Marriage to Elizabeth (Lewis) Masury

Richard's second wife, Susannah, died before 1797, when Richard Crockett married for a third time. There is no death record for Susannah Crockett. Given the fact that men generally married soon after a wife's death, however, she likely died around 1796. That year, Susannah would have been forty-four, and might have died from complications related to childbirth, as did so many women of her time.

After his second wife's death, Richard was left with the care of two of their four daughters: Susannah (fifteen in 1796) and Dorcas (age unknown, but probably

---

212. Maine, Cumberland County, Court of Common Pleas records. Court records, v. 2, 1779-1793, p. 366 (image #417). https://www.familysearch.org/ark:/61903/3:1:3QS7-893S-R1WY?i=416&cat=1881394
213. South Portland Town Records, 1765-1823, p. 208.
214. South Portland Town Records, 1765-1823, p. 212.

around five or six). Daughter Elizabeth had been married in 1793 and Deborah in 1794.

On April 27, 1797, Timothy Small, town clerk, recorded "A purpose of Marriage between Mr. Richard Crockett of Cape Elizabeth & Miss Elizabeth Magerry [Masury] of Portland…"[215] Richard and Elizabeth were married in Cape Elizabeth on May 18, 1797 by the Reverend Ephraim Clark.[216] Theirs was one of Reverend Clark's last marriages. The long-time Second Parish pastor passed away in December at the age of seventy-five.[217] At the time of his third marriage, Richard was about sixty-four and Elizabeth Masury was at least forty-two.[218]

Elizabeth was the widow of John Masury,[219] a potter from Portland. Masury died after July 14, 1795, the date on which Elizabeth purchased a small lot of land on Pleasant Street in that town.[220] Masury was still alive on July 14th, but he must have been ill and/or dying because Elizabeth is described in the deed executed by David Alden, mariner of Portland, as the wife (not widow) of Masury. Only four months earlier, on March 7, 1795, John Masury had sold to Alden[221] the Portland farm Masury had owned for nearly thirty years.[222] Masury received 145 pounds from Alden from the sale of that property and (perhaps knowing that he was dying) was trying to provide a nest egg for his wife and family. Elizabeth utilized 15 pounds of the receipts to buy the new property. Although it is not stated in Alden's deed to Elizabeth, there was a house upon the small Pleasant Street lot. (Later, Richard and Elizabeth sold the house in Portland that she purchased.)

Elizabeth and John Masury had been married less than six years when the potter passed away. The couple was wed October 19, 1791 by Joseph Hooker,

---

215. South Portland Town Records, 1765-1823, p. 53.
216. "MARRIAGES IN FALMOUTH (CAPE ELIZABETH) [1756-1797], SOLEMNIZED BY REV. EPHRAIM CLARK, PASTOR 2d PARISH." Maine Genealogy Archives https://archives.mainegenealogy.net/2007/02/marriages-by-rev-ephraim-clark-of-cape.html
217. South Portland Town Records, 1765-1823, p. 381. Rev. Clark, who was the longest-serving pastor of the Congregational Church in Cape Elizabeth (Second Parish) died December 3, 1797.
218. The 1800 U.S. Census shows that Elizabeth Masury Crockett was forty-five or older that year.
219. The last name of Elizabeth's late husband, John Masury, has given genealogists plenty of headaches. I have seen the name written: Massury, Magenry, Margery, and Marjory. Since deeds executed by John and Elizabeth clearly read "Masury," and since this agrees with the spelling on their marriage record, I have used that, unless quoting an original source. In addition, although Masury was certainly rare for a family name in Maine, it was common in Massachusetts in the 18th century, where a quick search will yield several different men with the name of John Masury.
220. Elizabeth Masury paid David Alden 15 pounds for the property. CCROD, Book 23, p. 85. Witnesses: Samuel Freeman, J.P. and Anna Jones.
221. CCROD, Book 22, P. 234. Witnesses: William Finley and Dorcas Brazen.
222. John Masury purchased the property (then part of Falmouth) from Phillip Hodgkins on June 10, 1767 for 16 pounds, 13 shillings and 4 pence. CCROD, Book 5, P. 438. Masury had previously sold off two small pieces of the property. (in 1793 and 1794).

J.P.[223] Both John and Elizabeth were residing in Portland at the time of their marriage. Masury must have been in his fifties when they were wed; Elizabeth at least thirty-six. We have no idea if this was her first marriage (or his, either). Her name on the marriage record is "Elizabeth Lewis." John was probably from Massachusetts, where "Masury" was not an uncommon surname (as it was in Maine). If "Lewis" was Elizabeth's maiden name, she certainly could have been a Maine native. Given her age, however, she might well have been a widow prior to her marriage to Masury.

According to Crockett genealogist Candage, Elizabeth had a son by Masury, also named John.[224] If so, young John would have been born between 1792 and 1796. It also appears that she might have had two stepsons, Jonathan and George Masury, and a stepdaughter Rebecca Masury. My supposition about these stepchildren is supported by census data, as well as marriage records and deeds. On June 5, 1805, a "Jonathan Margrey" of Portland was married in Cape Elizabeth to Sally Roberts of Cape Elizabeth by the Reverend William Gregg (who had replaced Reverend Clark).[225] On May 9, 1811, a "Miss Rebecca Magery & Mr. Reuben Roberts," both of Cape Elizabeth, were married.[226] (Reuben, who became a baker in Portland,[227] was the son of George Copson Roberts and Deborah York.)[228] These two Roberts-Masury marriages imply a close connection between the two young Magerys (or Masurys) and Richard and Elizabeth's neighbors at Long Creek. In addition, in 1808, a "George Margery" witnessed an important deed for Richard Crockett, signifying a relationship (and that George was at least twenty-one at the time).[229]

We do not know how Richard Crockett and Elizabeth Masury met, although the name of a witness to a deed offers a potential clue. Dorcas Brazen[230] was one of the witnesses to the deed from Masury to Alden. The given name of this

---

223. Maine Marriage Records, 1713-1922. Masury, John.
224. CANDAGE, p 36.
225. South Portland Town Records, 1765-1823, p. 497.
226. South Portland Town Records, 1765-1823, p. 499.
227. Information from CCROD Roberts, Reuben. See Book 125, Page 14, for example.
228. An 1813 birth record for Raymond, Maine shows Reuben Roberts was the father of twin girls born August 18, 1813. The twins were named Elizabeth (the name of Reuben's aunt; Richard Crockett's first wife) and Deborah (the name of Reuben's mother). See Maine Birth Records, 1715-1922. Roberts, Elizabeth (or Roberts, Deborah). The record also indicates these were Reuben's first two children, which aligns with his marriage to Rebecca Masury in May of 1811. https://www.ancestry.com/imageviewer/collections/1960/images/31515_204235-04116?pId=1896145
229. CCROD, Book 160, p. 41. The other witness was the businessman William Vaughan, who also had a personal relationship with Richard Crockett. The deed was from Richard to his son Samual to Richard's house and ten acres of land.
230. The spelling of Dorcas' last name is difficult to read and could be something a bit different. See CCROD, Book 22, P. 234.

witness suggests that she was a descendant of Dorcas (Skillin) Westcoat and thus a relation to Richard's second wife Susannah Westcoat. If so, one can understand that Dorcas Brazen might have introduced Richard and Elizabeth or even played matchmaker.

Richard and his third wife made their home in Cape Elizabeth. They probably leased her house in Portland for extra income, perhaps wanting to keep it for John Masury's children. About a year after they were married, Richard and Elizabeth had a son they named William. William Crockett was baptized at the First Church of Scarborough on May 26, 1798.[231] (In 1804, Richard's son Samuel and his wife Abigail also had a child they named William.)[232]

In 1800, the second census of the United States was taken. Following is the record for Richard and Elizabeth Crockett. (Richard and his son Samuel were the only two Crockett heads of households in Cape Elizabeth in 1800.) If Elizabeth had an older stepson Jonathan Masury, he was probably apprenticed out, since he does not appear to be living with them or in the Masury home in Portland.[233]

1800 U.S. Census Cape Elizabeth, Maine

Richard Crockett (III)
FWM under 10 = 2 (Elizabeth's son John Masury and their son William Crockett)
FWM 10-15 = 1 (possibly Elizabeth's stepson George Masury or an apprentice/hired hand)
FWM 16-25 = 0
FWM 26-44 = 0
FWM 45 & older = 1 (Richard)
FWF under 10 = 0
FWF 10-15 = 1 (possibly Elizabeth's stepdaughter Rebecca Masury)
FWF 16-25 = 0
FWF 26-44 = 0
FWF 45 & older = 1 (Elizabeth)

---

231. Maine Genealogy Archives, First Church of Scarborough, Admissions and Baptisms, 1790-1842. https://archives.mainegenealogy.net/2008/06/first-church-of-scarborough-admissions_8796.html
232. CANDAGE, p. 36. William B. Crockett, son of Samuel and Abigail Crockett, was born January 4, 1804.
233. Jonathan Masury/Magenry/Magory (or other combinations of the last name) was not listed as a head of household in Portland, Falmouth or Cape Elizabeth.

After his marriage to Elizabeth, Richard continued to serve the greater community of Cape Elizabeth. On April 6, 1801, at an adjournment of the annual town meeting, Richard Crockett was added to the list of men voted as surveyors of the highways for the ensuring year, as well as field driver, fence viewer and hog reeve.[234] On May 4, 1801, the names of Richard Crockett and Enoch Dyer were drawn (from a box) for jury duty for the June term of the Court of Common Pleas held in Portland for Cumberland County.[235] At the annual meeting in 1803, Richard was once again voted a constable for Cape Elizabeth.[236] He also served that year as one of the surveyors of highways, fence viewers, field drivers and hog reeves.[237]

Leading Up to the War of 1812

The events leading up to the War of 1812 began nearly two decades before the United States formally declared war against Britain in June of 1812. In 1793, ten years after the United States won independence from England, King Louis XVI was executed during the French Revolution. This led to the rise of Napolean Bonaparte and the Napoleonic wars. Great Britain declared war against France in 1803. As a fledgling nation, the United States hoped to remain neutral during this clash of titans; however, ships from both France and Great Britain shortly began harassing American ships.

On November 21, 1806, Napolean passed a decree blockading the British Isles. In his decree, vessels from neutral countries such as the United States were warned that if headed to English ports, the ships could be seized. Britain responded to Napolean's decree the following year with its "Order in Council" (issued November 11, 1807) forbidding neutral ships from calling at French ports. Before long both French and British warships were attacking American vessels, confiscating goods, and impressing sailors. Many English sailors also defected to American vessels, giving the British Navy an excuse to board ships searching for deserters—and removing any seaman who could not prove his citizenship, including thousands of American sailors. By 1807, President Thomas Jefferson felt these attacks on Americans required drastic measures.

---

234. South Portland Town Records, 1765-1823.
235. South Portland Town Records, 1765-1823.
236. South Portland Town Records, 1765-1823. Richard was one of three constables chosen at the annual town meeting held March 17, 1803. The other two were Samuel Dunn and Caleb Dyer.
237. "A Book of Records For the Second Parish in the town of Falmouth containing 212 pages." Page 40 (image 28).

In December of 1807, the U.S. Congress at the direction of President Jefferson, responded with the Embargo Act. The Act effectively closed all U.S. ports, including those in Maine, and barred imports from Britain. The Embargo Act also forbid American ships from sailing to foreign ports.[238] In Maine (as elsewhere) this legislation was exceedingly unpopular and caused great hardship, especially in coastal communities:

> "The Embargo and other trade restrictions profoundly affected Mainers, dependent as they were upon the sea for most manufactured goods coming into the District as well as the export of their principal products, lumber and fish. All sorts of goods became scarce and inflation rose to unprecedented levels."[239]

Not only did the war make goods scarce and prices high, but the embargo imposed by the United States made it nearly impossible for Mainers to sell their goods and products abroad. The embargo, which Americans hoped would be brief, dragged on for months. Not surprisingly, the longer the embargo remained in place, the angrier Mainers and other residents along the Atlantic seaboard became. Smuggling, which had a long history in Maine, became more frequent:

> "Maine was the greatest offender [of the embargo]. Ever since the close of the Revolutionary War, to avoid burdensome restrictions, many a cargo had been transferred from an American to an English bottom in Passamaquoddy Bay, or on the shores of Campobello or some other neutral island."[240]

Although inflation was rampant, Richard Crockett appears to have survived the years leading up to the War of 1812 financially unscathed. In January of 1808 (when he was seventy-five) Richard deeded (for $100) fifteen acres of the Mountfort property to wealthy Portland entrepreneur and former Cape Elizabeth resident William Vaughan. (Vaughan was instrumental in building the new toll bridge between Portland and Cape Elizabeth that opened in 1800.)[241] Although Richard's

---

238. The War of 1812-1815: America's "Second War for Independence." (1812-1815.) Maine Secretary of State website. www.maine.gov/sos/cec/elec/voter-info/veteran/war1812.html
239. The War of 1812-1815: America's "Second War for Independence." (1812-1815.) Maine Secretary of State website.
240. Rowe, William H. "The Maritime History of Maine: Three Centuries of Ship Building & Seafaring." Gardiner, Me: The Harpswell Press, 1989. (Copyright W.W. Norton, 1948). P. 81.
241. CAPE-E, p. 54-55. "[The bridge's] total span was twenty-six hundred feet and it was built of cobb work with arches across the gaps between cobbs. A lift draw was constructed in the bridge over the river's east channel pursuant to the act of

deed to Vaughan was dated January 18, 1808, it was not recorded at the Cumberland County Registry of Deeds until after Richard's death in 1821,[242] and therefore this document should be viewed as a mortgage or a personal loan against the property. Vaughan was a close family friend, with whom Richard's grandson Richard Crockett (Samuel's son) was living and working when the deed was executed.[243] Also, on April 26, 1808, Richard raised an additional $200 by selling (or mortgaging) his home and ten acres to his son Samuel.[244] William Vaughan was one of the witnesses to this deed, which again bespeaks a close relationship between the two men. (George "Margery," probably Elizabeth's stepson, was the other witness to the deed.) Richard and his family continued to live in his house and farm the land, while Samuel, who had left Durant's farm (formerly Vaughan's) in Scarborough, probably because Durant could no longer ship his mules to his sugar plantation (because of the embargo), had taken up a farm nearby.[245]

On July 19, 1810, Richard and Elizabeth Crockett sold to Joseph Coffin Boyd of Portland a piece of land that was part of the property she purchased (as Elizabeth Masury) from David Alden in 1795. They received $33.33 for this tiny "gore"[246] of land, which was situated "one foot from the westerly corner of said Cricketts small house..."[247] For the time being, Richard and Elizabeth kept the Portland house.

In March of 1809, during the last days of Thomas Jefferson's presidency,

---

incorporation. It was quite naturally a toll bridge and when it was opened late in 1800 a detailed list of rates were posted. To cross one way on foot cost two cents, on horseback six cents, with a chaise, sulkey or sleigh drawn by two horses twelve cents and a half, with a coach, chariot, phaeton or curricle twenty-vie cents and on up until most combinations of man and beast were covered. The new bridge considerably shortened the trip to Portland ..." William Vaughan was a native of Portsmouth, N.H., a lawyer by training, who had grand visions of development in Portland around his bridge. WILLIS, p. 848-850.

242. On January 18, 1808, Richard Crockett, yeoman of Cape Elizabeth, sold for $100 to William Vaughan, gentleman of Portland, 15 acres of land in Cape Elizabeth, the southeasterly half of the 30 acres he purchased from Samuel Mountfort of Falmouth in 1781. CCROD, Book 94, p. 54. Wife Elizabeth Crockett signed off on her dower rights. Witnesses to the deed were Tristam Jordan and C.H. Vaughan. Richard Crockett died in 1821 and his deed to Vaughan was finally recorded July 24, 1822.

243. Samuel's son Richard was twelve when what amounted to a mortgage given by his grandfather Richard Crockett to William Vaughan (with whom the young Richard lived) was executed. Capt. Crockett's death notice says "...Richard's first employment away from home was in 1806, when he went to live with Wm. Vaughan, who sold his farm in Scarborough in about 1787, to [Cornelius] Durant, and moved to Portland. At one time Vaughan owned 400 acres on Bramhall's Hill. When young Crockett lived with him the whole southern slope of the hill was covered with a heavy growth of white oak." Death notice of Captain Richard Crockett, *The Portland Daily Press*, May 24, 1880, p. 3.

244. CCROD, Book 70, p. 403. See also CCROD, Book 160, p. 41, where on June 6, 1838 Samuel Crockett deeds this property to Seth Storer (who has a mortgage on it that Samuel failed to pay). In that deed Samuel describes the property as "...being the same on which my late father Richard Crockett formerly lived..."

245. Information from the Cumberland County Registry of Deeds and the death notice of Capt. Richard Crockett. Samuel did not buy a property in Cape Elizabeth, but rather he became a tenant farmer or farm manager for an absentee owner. This was common in Maine, where there were many wealthy out-of-state or absentee landowners.

246. A triangular piece of land.

247. CCROD, Book 60, p. 449. Enoch Isley and John Frothingham were witnesses to the deed. Elizabeth signed with her mark.

Congress replaced the Embargo Act with the Non-Intercourse Act. This new Act lifted trade restrictions on all shipping, except for trade with Great Britain and France. Troops were also dispatched to forts along the coast, including newly-built Fort Preble on Spring Point in Cape Elizabeth, to combat smuggling. In Maine, attempts to control smuggling were largely ineffective:

> "Cargoes were gathered, and when the auspicious moment arrived, loaded aboard a vessel in the dead of night. By morning the vessel was usually far beyond the reach of government officials. In a few particularly flagrant cases, vessels were quickly loaded and sailed away in broad daylight so rapidly, that they left the federal officials with their gunboats and forts powerless to interfere. The two harbor entrance forts, Preble and Scammel, were dubbed 'Embargo Forts,' designed more to keep American shipping in than to prevent the entrance of British naval vessels."[248]

When the 1810 U.S. Census was taken, Elizabeth's stepchildren George and Rebecca Masury appear to have been out of the house. Rebecca was married the following May, and, given her age, was likely working out. George Masury had reached the age of majority and, although not a head of household (in Portland, Cape Elizabeth, or Scarborough, anyway) was living on his own or apprenticed out, as was elder brother Jonathan Masury (also not a head of household in those three communities in 1810).

1810 U.S. Census Cape Elizabeth, Maine

Richard Crockett (III)
FWM 10-15 = 2 (Elizabeth's son John Masury and their son
  William Crockett)
FWM 45 & over = 1 (Richard)
FWF 45 & over = 1 (Elizabeth)
household members under 16 = 2
household members over 25 = 2
household members = 4

---
248. CAPE-E, p. 57.

The War of 1812

On June 18, 1812, the U.S. Congress, finding the country could no longer remain neutral, declared war on Great Britain. Most bankers and merchants in Maine (and Massachusetts), because of their dependence on foreign markets and goods, "openly sided with Britain and refused to cooperate with the federal government."[249] President James Madison responded to this defiance in 1813 by ordering "all federal garrisons in the Province of Maine to withdraw to more loyal states of the Union."[250] While the withdrawal of troops might have been greeted with glee by smugglers, the removal of a fighting force from Maine left the District unable to deter the aggression of British warships cruising Maine waters, waiting for opportunities and easy prey. After the withdrawal of soldiers to "more loyal states," William King, major general of one of the principal militia units in Maine, found the District suddenly defended only by "a few invalids ... who were retained on account of their indispositions."[251]

The withdrawal of garrisoned troops from Maine precipitated British invasion of defenseless coastal communities. Only three decades after the United States secured her independence from Great Britain, the territory in Maine east of the Penobscot River fell to the British and was once again subsumed into the British Empire.[252] Settlements along the coast dropped like dominos to the British Royal Navy. "On September first 1814, both Castine and Belfast surrendered. Shortly thereafter Bangor and Hampden were occupied; then Eastport and others."[253]

Having successfully invaded eastern Maine, British warships turned their attention to the midcoast area. There, the aggressors were less successful. A group of British marines landed on Southport Island but were beaten back by local militia.[254] (Although Maine was attacked and invaded by the British during the War of 1812, the District of Maine was only a side theater of the war.)

Despite desperate pleas for help, Massachusetts chose not to come to the defense of her residents in eastern Maine. Instead, Mainers were left to their own

---

249. The War of 1812-1815: America's "Second War for Independence." (1812-1815.) Maine Secretary of State website.
250. Woodard, Colin. "The Lobster Coast." New York, NY: Viking-Penguin, 2004. P. 151.
251. Woodard, Colin. "The Lobster Coast." New York, NY: Viking-Penguin, 2004. P. 151.
252. The War of 1812-1815: America's "Second War for Independence." (1812-1815.) Maine Secretary of State website.
253. Woodard, Colin. "The Lobster Coast." New York, NY: Viking-Penguin, 2004. P. 151.
254. Woodard, Colin. "The Lobster Coast." New York, NY: Viking-Penguin, 2004. P. 151.

devices or to the capricious mercy of the British.[255] One British commander, Captain Barry, issued the following threat to the residents of Hampden:

> "My business is to burn, sink and destroy. Your town is taken by storm, and by the rules of war, we ought both to lay your village in ashes, and put its inhabitants to the sword. But I will spare your lives, though I mean to burn your houses."[256]

On August 5, 1814, Richard's grandson Richard Crockett (Samuel's son, then nineteen) was mustered in as a private in Captain W. Rand's Company, raised at Cape Elizabeth. This company was under the command of Major George Rogers and saw service at the two forts protecting Portland harbor.[257]

At the beginning of September 1814, British war ships were spotted off the coast of Portland. Believing that an attack was imminent, calls for help were sent throughout the countryside. One of those who answered the call from afar was another of Richard's grandsons, Ephraim Crockett, Jr., who had recently settled Lee's Grant in Norway.[258] Ephraim, Jr. volunteered to serve under Captain Bailey Bodwell, who had just returned to Norway from fighting the British in Plattsburgh, N.Y. Bodwell raised a company of Norway area men, including Ephraim Crockett, Jr., to help defend Portland. [259] (Ephraim marched off with Bodwell's company, leaving his pregnant wife and their ten-month-old daughter behind.) In Portland, Bodwell's company joined up with Lieutenant Colonel W. Ryerson's regiment, where they awaited a potential British attack. The attack never materialized, however.[260] After ten days of waiting, Bodwell released the men, and most of them marched back to Norway (although we can guess that Ephraim might have visited his grandfather and other relations in Cape Elizabeth before returning home).

Richard's grandson Richard Crockett served with Captain Rand until November

---

255. The War of 1812-1815: America's "Second War for Independence." (1812-1815.) Maine Secretary of State website.
256. The War of 1812-1815: America's "Second War for Independence." (1812-1815.) Maine Secretary of State website. Fortunately, threats like Captain Barry's were rarely carried out by the British because England was loath to terrorize those whom it was hoped would become new citizens of British Canada.
257. Maine Militia, War of 1812: Capt. W. Rand's Company. Maine Genealogy Archives. https://archives.mainegenealogy.net/2009/11/maine-militia-war-of-1812-capt-w-rands.html Richard Crockett served until Nov. 5, 1814.
258. Ephraim Crockett, Jr. and his wife Sally Wentworth, and their descendants, are the subject of my companion book, "A History of the Crockett Family of Crockett's Ridge, Norway, Maine." White Wave, 2024. Ephraim was the son of Ephraim Crockett, Sr. (Richard and Elizabeth Roberts Crockett's eldest child) and Rebecca Stanford, who relocated to the Pejepscot Claim. See Chapter 7.
259. "A History of Norway, Maine." Charles F. Whitman. p. 91-92.
260. U.S. Adjutant General Military Records, 1631-1976. Records of the Massachusetts Volunteer Militia, War of 1812-1814.

5th, when he was mustered in as a private in Lieutenant O. Bray's Detached Company, under supervision of Major General Alford Richardson. This company was raised at Portland with service at Fort Burrows and Fish Point "for the protection of the forts, ordnance, and munitions of war and other property belonging to the Commonwealth."[261]

Throughout the balance of the war, young Richard served (from November 25, 1814 to January 23, 1815) as a private with Sargeant J. Lowell's Guard, under Supervision of Major Lemuel Weeks. Their duties were the same as under Major General Richardson: to protect the forts and munitions of the Commonwealth of Massachusetts.[262] The forts were never attacked and Richard Crockett's military service was as uneventful as that of his cousin's, Ephraim Crockett, Jr. of Norway.

On December 14, 1814, the Treaty of Ghent was signed in Belgium by representatives of Great Britain and the United States. The Treaty provided for the return of conquered territory (such as eastern Maine) and the establishment of a commission to settle the boundary between the United States and Canada.[263] Because of the delay in overseas communications, however, word did not reach this country until after U.S. forces under Major General Andrew Jackson had driven out the British invaders on January 6, 1815 during the Battle of New Orleans. Congress and President Madison ratified the Treaty of Ghent in February of 1815, officially ending the War of 1812. U.S. markets were once again open to trade, not only with England, but also with other foreign ports, such as the West Indies, which had been blocked by the embargo.

The failure of Massachusetts to defend the District of Maine during the War of 1812 had far-reaching consequences, however. The callousness of the powers-that-be in Boston, combined with the failure of the Massachusetts General Court to defend settlers' land rights against the greed of the Great Proprietors (covered in Chapter 7) helped spark the desire for independent statehood for Maine.

---

261. Maine Militia, War of 1812: Detached Companies Under Supervision of Gen. Alford Richardson. Maine Genealogy Archives. https://archives.mainegenealogy.net/2009/11/maine-militia-war-of-1812-detached.html
262. Maine Militia, War of 1812: Miscellaneous Detachments and Guards. Maine Genealogy Archives. https://archives.mainegenealogy.net/2009/11/maine-militia-war-of-1812-miscellaneous.html
263. Many Mainers believed that the War of 1812 was no more than an attempt by the United States to wrest Canada away from the British.

Local Effects of the War of 1812

Richard Crockett (III) weathered the financial firestorm caused by the War of 1812, as well as the years leading up to the war. He and his third wife Elizabeth must have lived a fiscally prudent life, well within their means. Richard did not hold a public office during the war. His last official duties in Cape Elizabeth were during the year 1803, when, at the age of seventy, he served as a constable, as well as one of the surveyors of highways, field drivers, fence viewers, and hog reeves.

When the war ended in February of 1815, Richard was eighty-two years of age. Elizabeth was at least sixty. Except for son Samuel, who was living in Cape Elizabeth with his growing family, Richard's children with his first two wives were scattered throughout Maine, including Portland, Limington, Pejepscot (Danville, now part of Auburn), Windham, and likely several other towns. His grandchildren were even more far flung.

But Richard's former brother-in-law George Copson Roberts was not as fortunate as he during the War of 1812. A combination of factors appears to have cost George Copson not only the homestead farm he had purchased from the heirs of Daniel Bailey, but also his late father's real estate belonging to him. Like many others in the greater Portland area, Roberts overinvested in real estate at the wrong time.

George Copson Roberts lived next to Richard Crockett on the former homestead farm of Daniel Bailey, which he had purchased in installments from 1762 to 1773 from the children[264] of the deceased Bailey.[265] Over the years, George Copson also began buying back former pieces of family property at Long Creek from extended family members.[266] George Copson also sold a small house lot to his own son, Richard Roberts (likely named for brother-in-law Richard Crockett III).

---

264. See CCROD, Book 15, p. 102; CCROD, Book 15, p. 100; CCROD, Book 14, p. 148; and CCROD, Book 14, p. 149 for the deeds from Daniel Bailey's children (and their spouses) to George Copson Roberts.
265. Daniel Bailey's homestead farm was deeded to him by his father Jonathan Bailey in 1735. YCROD, Book 17, p. 251. The Bailey lot shared a corner with the Mountfort lot purchased by Richard Crockett. The Bailey property also adjoined land owned by George Copson's father, George Roberts, as well as the thirty acres George Roberts sold to brothers Richard and William Westcoat (Richard Crockett's second father-in-law).
266. The former family land that George Copson Roberts purchased included a parcel that his late father had sold to William Westcoat, which he purchased from Westcoat's daughter (George C. Robert's cousin) Elizabeth Smith. On June 8, 1779, Roberts paid 48 pounds to Elizabeth (Westcoat) Smith (the widow of Daniel Bailey, who had remarried) for two small parcels in Cape Elizabeth. CCROD, Book 15, p. 151. This purchase occurred prior to the death of Susannah Crockett (Richard Crockett's second wife) because the deed for this 1+ acre parcel was witnessed by Susannah Crockett and Dorcas Westcoat. (Dorcas could have been either Susannah and Elizabeth Smith's sister or mother, since Dorcas Skillin Westcoat was still alive in 1779 and their sister Dorcas was not married until June 26th after the deed was witnessed on June 8th.)

The Fifth Generation

George Copson Robert's financial troubles began, however, with speculation on real estate unrelated to family land. In 1806 and 1808, Roberts invested in some of the undivided common land[267] in Cape Elizabeth.[268] The land had not been laid out because available land for the grants had not been found. Familiar as he was with Cape Elizabeth, George C. was able to parse out some open and available land between the mishmash of old grants, securing enough land from the Proprietors Committee to make up the total 30-½ acres of grants.[269] After that, George Copson might have gone into the house building business,[270] probably with his son Richard, who, as a ship's carpenter, was not getting much work due to the Embargo of 1807. (Richard Roberts had financial issues of his own, which he was able to weather.)[271]

Sadly, three court-ordered executions against George Copson Roberts in 1813 cost him his home and most of the land he owned in Cape Elizabeth[272] (except for

---

267. The "Commons" was land the ownership of which was shared by ancient and early settlers.
268. On June 28, 1806, Nathan Winslow of Falmouth, yeoman, sold for $86 to George C. Roberts, yeoman of Cape Elizabeth, 21-1/2 acres of land of common and undivided land in Falmouth where he can find it free from former grants. (This was land granted to other people, and bought up by Winslow, but the land was deeded back to the Proprietors because open and available land was not to be found). CCROD, Book 50, p. 312. Witnesses: Reuben Roberts (George C. Robert's son) and Zebulon Skillin. On January 30, 1808, Nathan Winslow again sold for $36 to George C. Roberts of Cape Elizabeth, gentleman, 9 acres of common undivided land in Falmouth in Cape Elizabeth where he can find it being free of former grants. CCROD, Book 54, p. 331. Witnesses: Thaddeus Skillin and Reuben Roberts.
269. On June 30, 1806, the Proprietors Committee for Laying Out Lands (Nathan Winslow, Benjamin Bailey, and William Winslow) laid out for George Roberts 21-1/2 acres of land (comprised of several smaller parcels) and on January 13, 1803, the Proprietors Committee (same men) laid out 9 acres (in two parcels) for George Roberts. "Copy of the Original Records of the Proprietors of Falmouth for the years 1718 to 1826." Three volumes in one. PORTLAND: Copied by F.A. Gerrish, 1861. P. 91 and p. 94. https://archive.org/details/proprietors00falmouth_202105/page/n513/mode/1up?view=theater and https://archive.org/details/proprietors00falmouth_202105/page/n516/mode/1up?view=theater
270. At the Court of Common Pleas for the first Eastern Circuit, held in Portland the third Tuesday of November 1813, Joseph Baker and John Bartels of Portland, merchants of the firm of Baker & Bartels, won a judgment against George C. Roberts of Cape Elizabeth, yeoman, *alias housewright* (emphasis mine). This suggests to me that for a short period of time, anyway, George dabbled in building houses. Because George Copson Roberts was seventy-five in 1813, I suspect the house building was performed more by his son Richard than by himself. See CCROD, Book 69, p.8-10.
271. In 1809 and 1811, Richard Roberts was a defendant at the Court of Common Pleas held in Portland for Cumberland County, where, by default (he failed to appear both times) he incurred financial judgments totaling more than $65. See Maine, Cumberland County Court records. Court records, v. 12, 1809-1811. p. 182. https://www.familysearch.org/ark:/61903/3:1:3QS7-L93S-R93D-X?i=190&cat=1881394 and Maine, Cumberland County Court records. Court records, v. 13, 1811-1812, p. 234. https://www.familysearch.org/ark:/61903/3:1:3QS7-893S-R9Q3-N?i=242&cat=1881394 The younger Roberts, who in 1807 had purchased a homestead farm from Edward Dunn, hauled in his sails and conveyed the farm back to Dunn in 1809. (See CCROD Book 54, p. 35-36 and CCROD Book 59, p. 491.) Richard Roberts probably lived after that on a house he built on the small piece of land conveyed to him by his father.
272. At the Court of Common Pleas for the first Eastern Circuit, held in Portland the third Tuesday of November last (1813) Joseph Baker and John Bartels of Portland, merchants & copartners in trade under the firm of Baker & Bartels, won a judgment against George C. Roberts of Cape Elizabeth, yeoman, alias housewright now resident in said Portland for the sum of $121.02 debt or damage and $10.75 costs of suit. Sam Freeman, Clerk (of the Court) issued an execution against Roberts on Nov. 26, 1813. Three impartial men were chosen to appraise Roberts' real estate in Cape Elizabeth: Cotton B. Brooks (chosen by Joseph Baker, one of the creditors in the suit), Joseph H. Ingraham (chosen by Roberts), and James Neal (chosen by Deputy Sheriff W.B. Peters). The three men set aside 4 acres of land with the buildings thereon (Roberts' home) to satisfy a total of $223.69 to cover the execution and the costs of the execution. On Dec. 10, 1813, the house and land were seized and handed over to Joseph Baker (for Baker & Bartels), who signed off Dec. 13, 1813 that he had received satisfaction for the execution. CCROD, Book 69, p.8-10. Also, on Nov. 26, 1813, an execution was issued against George C. Roberts,

a small parcel he was able to sell to Joseph Westcoat).[273] In a desperate attempt to keep something for himself, George Copson Roberts mortgaged to Arthur McLellan, a merchant of Portland (and real estate magnate), 38 acres of land in Cape Elizabeth that had not (yet) been taken by execution, as well as the 30+ acres of the investment property he was granted by the Falmouth Proprietors Committee. George Copson lost these properties, however, by a final execution in 1814. On October 24, 1814, Gardner Walker, deputy sheriff, auctioned off the balance of Roberts' real estate in Cape Elizabeth to cover two judgments that Susanna and Joshua Webb won at the Court of Common Pleas against George Copson Roberts. To protect his $145 investment in those parcels, McLellan, the mortgage holder, bid the highest at $52.[274]

Prior to the enforcement of the executions, Roberts had removed to Portland,[275] likely so that he did not have to witness his home and land (and real estate previously belonging to his father) being taken away. It must have been a tragically sad

---

resulting in the loss of some of his land in Cape Elizabeth. At the Court of Common Pleas in the first Eastern Circuit held at Portland the third Tuesday of November last (1813) Robert McLaughlin of Scarborough, yeoman, won a judgment against George C. Roberts of Cape Elizabeth and now of Portland in the amount of $88.25 in debt or damage and $9.64 costs of suit. Three men were selected to appraise some of Roberts' real estate: James Means (selected by the creditor McLaughlin), Joseph Ingraham (selected by Roberts, the debtor), and Ebenezer Mayo, selected by deputy sheriff W.C. Weeks. The three men appraised a tract of land belonging to George C. Roberts in Cape Elizabeth valued at $117.69 to cover the execution and the costs ($19.55) associated with levying it. The property described was to adjoin land owned by Baker and Bartels. CCROD, Book 69, p. 187. On Dec. 14, 1813, the land was awarded to McLaughlin, who signed off that he had received satisfaction for the execution. Finally, on Dec. 8, 1813, an execution was issued against George C. Roberts resulting in the loss of more of his real estate in Cape Elizabeth. At the Court of Common Pleas, the first Eastern Circuit, held in Portland the third Tuesday of November last (1813) Daniel Dole of Falmouth, yeoman, won a judgment against George C. Roberts, yeoman of Portland, in the amount of $80.70 debt or damage and $10.10 costs of suit. The execution was issued Dec. 8, 1813 by Sam Freeman, clerk, in Falmouth. Three men were chosen to impartially appraise Roberts estate: Archelaus Lewis, Esq. (chosen by Deputy Sheriff Gardner Walker), Capt. John Jones (chosen by Daniel Dole), and Joseph H. Ingraham, Esq. (chosen by Roberts). On Dec. 10th, the men appraised a parcel of land in Cape Elizabeth containing two acres and two rods to satisfy $112.47 in the whole (the execution of $91.00 and $21.47 for additional fees and charges related to levying the execution). This parcel adjoined Richard Crockett's property, and was bounded as follows: "beginning at a large stone at the easterly corner of Richard Crockett door yard by the road, thence South fifty one degrees west twenty two rods and twenty one links to a stake, thence South sixty eight degrees and thirty minets East thirty four rods to a stake standing on the Southerly side of the road leading from Stroudwater in Falmouth to Scarborough, thence by said road North twenty two degrees and fifteen mines [minutes] west twenty nine rods & fourteen links to the aforesaid rock containing two acres and twenty rods, bounded by land belonging to Richard Crockett on the Northwesterly side and on the South side and by the aforesaid road on the Easterly side ..." The land was seized by Deputy Sheriff Walker on Dec. 10th and on Dec. 18, 1813, Daniel Dole signed off that he had received seizen of the premises described and was satisfied. CCROD, Book 69, p. 76-78.

273. On Aug. 14, 1813, George C. Roberts, yeoman of Cape Elizabeth, sold for $50 to Joseph Westcoat, gentleman of Cape Elizabeth, ¾ acre of land in Cape Elizabeth bounded as follows: "beginning at the Southwest corner of Daniel Skillins Marsh which he purchased of William Doane; thence northerly by said Marsh to the Creek; thence Westerly by said Creek to Saddle Island so called; thence by said Island to the first bounds mentioned ..." CCROD Book 68, p. 309. Witnesses: M. Jordan and Daniel W. Lincoln.

274. CCROD, Book 73, p. 63. In the first suit, Susanna Webb, widow, and Joshua Webb were awarded $71.09 in debt or damages and costs of suit $6.58 by the Court of Common Pleas in Portland on the first Tuesday of March 1812. In the second suit, Joshua Webb of Falmouth, trader, received judgment against Roberts for debt or damage in the amount of $51.50, plus costs of suit $6.89 at the CCP third Tuesday in June 1814.

275. In two of the executions George C. Roberts is described as of (or formerly of) Cape Elizabeth and now of Portland.

day in the Crockett household watching the appraisers and the deputy sheriffs at their work.

George Copson Roberts returned to live in Cape Elizabeth, perhaps leasing back his house from his creditor Baker & Bartels (who were awarded the house and four acres), who appear not to have immediately sold the property. (George C. might also have lived with his son Richard.) George Copson Roberts died in Cape Elizabeth August 28, 1828 at the age of eighty-six.[276] He was buried in Long Creek cemetery with many of his extended Skillin-Roberts-Crockett relatives.

Last Years of Richard and Elizabeth Crockett

Richard turned eighty-two at the end of 1815, the year the Treaty of Ghent was ratified, officially ending the War of 1812. Given his age, he naturally would consider settling his affairs. Richard had already sold Samuel his house (although Richard and his family were living in it) and 10 acres that accompanied the home, but he still owned at least 15 acres of land (and probably more) formerly owned by his late in-laws George and Katharine Roberts. He also had the 30-acre Mountfort lot, although he had mortgaged 15 acres of this property to the toll bridge builder (and friend) William Vaughan.

On February 8, 1816, Richard Crockett, yeoman of Cape Elizabeth, sold the 30-acre Mountfort lot[277] (for $300) to his stepson John Masury (Elizabeth's son by her first marriage), yeoman of Cape Elizabeth.[278] William Vaughan, who held a deed to 15 acres of this property, was one of the witnesses to this transaction (which further corroborates my theory that the earlier deed to Vaughan was a mortgage or loan). Although John Masury was Richard's stepson and not his son, Richard had raised the boy from a young age and obviously had a close relationship with him. John was around twenty-one when this property transfer occurred. It is possible (if not probable) that part of the $300 payment from young Masury

---

276. SMALLDESC, p. 985. In her genealogy Lora Altine Woodbury Underhill says George Copson Roberts lived all his life in Cape Elizabeth. This is incorrect. For a time (probably relatively short) during the executions when his home and land was being taken away, Roberts lived in Portland.
277. It appears when writing up his deed to his stepson, Richard forgot he had previously sold (for $25) on May 24, 1814, 3-¼ acres of the Mountfort lot to Joseph Hunnewell, yeoman, of Cape Elizabeth. John "Margery," however, was one of the witnesses to this deed and so would have known when he purchased the Mountfort lot from his stepfather that this small parcel had been cut off from the 30 acres. CCROD, Vol. 70, p. 438. William Hasty was the other witness.
278. CCROD, Book 73, p. 251. Richard Roberts, George Copson's son (and Richard's namesake) was the other witness to this deed from Richard to John "Magery" (as John's last name is spelled in the deed).

was to have been paid to Vaughn (rather than to Richard) for the $100 (plus interest) Richard had received in advance from the entrepreneur.

The following month, Richard and Elizabeth sold the house in Portland that she had purchased when she was still married to young John's father. On March 8, 1816, Richard Crockett, yeomen of Cape Elizabeth, and Elizabeth his wife by right, sold (for $300) to Benjamin Leach, cordwainer of Portland, land with buildings on it, which was part of the land Elizabeth purchased from David Alden in 1785. William Vaughan was again one of the witnesses to this deed. (George Copson's son Reuben, who was married to Rebecca Masury, was the other witness.)[279]

After the war ended, the desire for independence from Massachusetts was felt in every town in Maine, including Cape Elizabeth. At a special town meeting held the first Tuesday in March 1816, Cape Elizabeth residents voted unanimously for an immediate separation of the District of Maine from old Massachusetts. The town recommended that a petition signed by the selectmen stating the outcome of the vote should be forwarded to the Legislature without delay.[280] On July 26, 1819, a District-wide election was held to consider the measure. The legal voters of Cape Elizabeth gathered to give their assent to Maine becoming a separate state, with a vote of 79 "yeas" and 17 "nays."[281] District wide, the results from July 26th were similar: approximately 17,000 Mainers voted to separate and 7,000 voted to remain with Massachusetts. A potential state constitution was drafted, and Maine formally applied to be accepted into the Union.[282]

A conundrum over the balance of power in the United States between the free states and the slave states nearly nixed Maine's chances for statehood, until the Missouri Compromise necessitated its inclusion to balance the power between free states and slave states. The U.S. Congress voted Maine into the Union (as a free state) in early March of 1820, and on March 15th Maine received a formal Act of Admission and became the 23rd state. (Missouri, a slave state, became the 24th state in 1821.) On April 3, 1820, the first elections were held in the state of Maine, during which William King (the former major general of a Maine militia during

---

279. CCROD, Book 76, p. 260.
280. South Portland Town Records, 1765-1823, p. 450.
281. South Portland Town Records, 1765-1823, p. 520.
282. "How Maine Became A State 200 Years Ago, And What That Had To Do With Slavery." Maine Public Radio host Irwin Gratz's interview with Maine historian and state representative Herb Adams. Published July 31, 2019 on the Maine Public website https://www.mainepublic.org/arts-and-culture/2019-07-31/how-maine-became-a-state-200-years-ago-and-what-that-had-to-do-with-slavery

The Fifth Generation

the War of 1812, who had spearheaded the statehood issue), was resoundingly elected the first governor.[283]

Sometime during 1819, when statehood was just around the corner, Richard received a tax bill from Massachusetts in the amount of 46¢. Like most tax-hating old-timers in Maine, Richard likely used the paper the bill was printed on to start a fire. As a result of Richard's non-payment of this miniscule (and questionable) tax, on June 18, 1819, his farm containing 26 acres was auctioned off by Massachusetts (along with the farms of some of his neighbors) for the grand total of 55¢.[284] This outrageous stunt just prior to Maine's separation from Massachusetts was likely a grift dreamed up by Jacob Quincy of Portland, a real estate speculator (and what we call a "sharper"), who purchased these dubious foreclosures (including Richard's) from W. Storer, Collector for the Seventh Collection District of Massachusetts. Quincy, after receiving deeds to his new properties from Storer (which deeds had been recorded at the registry), visited the property owners attempting (often successfully) to scare them into buying their farms back from him. (Richard Crockett was not one of those who capitulated.) Quincy sometimes netted from the true property owners up to ten times what he had paid Storer. (Quincy also bought and sold church pews, as well as the dower rights of widows.)[285] It appears, however, that no ill consequences were suffered by those who did not pay these meager sums that Massachusetts tax collectors dared to levy against Mainers just before the separation from Massachusetts occurred. (Despite having this lien against his property, Richard Crockett appears to have been legally considered the owner.)

Elizabeth Crockett, Richard's third wife, was deceased by the time the U.S. Census was taken in 1820. Richard was then in his late eighties. From the census data, it appears that still living at home were John Masury (then in his mid-twenties) and Richard and Elizabeth's son William Crockett (age twenty-two).

---

283. South Portland Town Records, 1765-1823, p. 529. In Cape Elizabeth, the vote for King for governor was 99-0.
284. CCROD, Book 86, p. 96. In this deed, Richard's property was described as "One farm containing twenty-six acres and buildings thereon, bounded N. by George C. Roberts, S. by Josiah Westcoat, E. by the Post Road from Portland to Boston, and W. by Josiah Westcoat." Quincy purchased at these shady auctions property from Maine residents in several communities in addition to Cape Elizabeth. Apparently, many Mainers felt that Massachusetts had already extracted enough money from them and disregarded these questionable tax bills.
285. See CCROD, Quincy, Jacob.

1820 U.S. Census Cape Elizabeth

Richard Crockett

FWM 16-25 = 2 (William Crockett and John Masury)

FWM 45 & over = 1 (Richard)

FWF 26-44 = 1 (unknown woman, probably young female relation or hired girl)

\# persons engaged in agriculture = 1 (probably John or William)

FW persons over 25 = 2

FW persons total = 4

Richard died in 1821 at the age of eighty-nine.[286] He would have been buried at Long Creek cemetery, with his first wife Elizabeth (Roberts) and their daughter Catharine, and probably the two other wives who predeceased him. Also buried at Long Creek were his Roberts in-laws and other extended family members, including many members of the Skillin family.

In 2014, Brenda (Daicy) Duguay mapped out Long Creek cemetery. She concluded, based on site observations and information from D.W. Clark's 19th century headstone inscription list for Long Creek, that many more people are buried in this cemetery than previously believed, possibly as many as 100 souls.[287] During my visit to Long Creek, the piece of ground upon which most of the stones are showing looks tiny for a cemetery; however, the surrounding ground is uneven and could certainly contain many more old gravesites. (See Chapter 3, page 143 for photos taken at Long Creek Cemetery, now part of South Portland.)

Wrapping Up the Life of Richard Crockett (III)

While many of the Crocketts lived fascinating lives, Richard Crockett's life—when viewed from afar—seems remarkable for the breadth of history he lived through. During the nine decades of Richard's life, he survived a multitude of wars and conflicts, including King George's War; the French and Indian War; the

---

286. CANDAGE, p. 11. There is no death record for Richard Crockett, so I have no idea where Candage found this information. His info accords with other facts I have gathered from census data and land records, except that according to my calculation, Richard would have been eighty-seven (turning eighty-eight at the end of 1821).

287. South Portland Historical Society website, The Long Creek Cemetery. https://sphistory.pastperfectonline.com/archive/B89D5F67-03D6-466D-9412-051366501517

Revolutionary War; and the War of 1812. Unlike his ancestors, Richard did not go chasing after land elsewhere, but made a commitment to one community. He appears to have dwelt in the same house at Long Creek his entire adult life, although the name of the town in which Richard resided changed (as Falmouth was chopped up), from Falmouth, to Second Parish, to Cape Elizabeth. Today, his bones lie at rest in South Portland, without having moved an inch! Richard lived under the Puritanical rule of Massachusetts Bay Colony; was subjected to taxation without representation by the British Parliament and King George III; witnessed the birth of a new nation under a Constitution as part of the Commonwealth of Massachusetts; and, finally, experienced the joy of Maine's independent statehood shortly before his death.

Richard had three wives—Elizabeth Roberts, Susannah Westcoat, and Elizabeth (Lewis) Masury—and outlived them all. He had at least thirteen children: Ephraim, Anna, Sarah, Deborah, Samuel, Mary, Lucy, and Catharine (with Elizabeth Roberts); Deborah, Elizabeth, Susannah, and Dorcas (with Susanna); and William (with Elizabeth Masury). Richard also helped raise at least one stepson, John Masury, and probably other stepchildren. At the time of his death, Richard had dozens of grandchildren and many great-grandchildren.

Many questions remain about the fate of Richard's son William and his stepson John, although we know much more about John. On September 29, 1821 (the year Richard died) marriage intentions were filed between John Masury ("Magery") of Cape Elizabeth and Ann Watts of Portland. John and Ann were married November 4, 1821.[288] The couple might have continued to reside in Richard's house (although it belonged to Richard's son Samuel, who lived in his own small home in Cape Elizabeth), while John might have continued to farm.

Events soon took a turn for the worse for Masury, however. On July 22, 1822, less than eight months after John and Ann were married, William Vaughan recorded the 1808 deed from Richard Crockett to himself for the 15 acres of Mountfort land. This might have occurred because young John failed to pay the money owed Vaughan. Had Vaughan's financial affairs not been desperate, he most likely would have written the debt off. But the entrepreneur had himself become overextended prior to and during the War of 1812 because of his real estate investments and the

---

288. Maine Marriage Records, 1713-1922.

cost of building the new Vaughan bridge. Vaughan lost nearly everything prior to his own death in Portland in 1826.[289]

Vaughan's deed for the Mountfort land, which preceded John Masury's deed from Richard Crockett, cut the amount of land John owned on the Mountfort lot to about 11-¾ acres (Richard had also previously sold 3-¼ acres from the Mountfort lot.) On July 23, 1823, John lost ten more acres from the Mountfort lot to satisfy a debt to Samuel Dunn of Dover, N.H., who recovered a judgment of $27.45 against him in June of that year. (Dunn was probably a descendant of the Dunn-Skillin family of Long Creek.) Daniel Skillin (a neighbor) and Dexter Brewer of Cape Elizabeth valued Masury's property and peeled off the 10 acres to satisfy the judgment (plus court and attachment costs).[290] This 1823 execution was the last land record I could find for John Masury/Magenry/Margery. He disappears from the Cumberland County registry of deeds, despite still owning (on paper, anyway) about 1-¾ acres of land in Cape Elizabeth. There is no evidence that John ever sold this small parcel of land; lost it; or gave the property away. John Masury also disappears from town and state records (that I have unearthed to date), and so we will say goodbye to him here.

On October 27, 1823, Richard's son Samuel Crockett (then about sixty-three)[291] mortgaged his father's house and 10 acres to Seth Storer for $90.[292] Samuel and his family did not live in his father's house, although he owned it. Why they did not live there is unclear to me. Perhaps Samuel's half-brother William was still utilizing the house or Samuel was leasing it out for extra income. Samuel and Abigail, with their sons William (seventeen) and George (thirteen),[293] resided nearby in an old shoemaker's shop, which had been converted to a tiny house. Samuel, in his 1819 application for a Revolutionary War pension,[294] states: "I own about one third of an acre

---

289. WILLIS, p. 848-850.
290. CCROD, Book 93, p. 485.
291. Samuel states in his Revolutionary War pension application, filed March 18, 1818, that he was then fifty-seven. He was thus born in 1760 or 1761. U.S. Revolutionary War Pension and Bounty=Land Warrant Application, 1800-1900. Crockett, Samuel. https://www.ancestry.com/imageviewer/collections/1995/images/MIUSA1775D_135275-00184?pId=14508
292. CCROD, Book 96, p. 361. Samuel promised to pay Storer $30 plus interest on Sept. 1, 1824; $30 plus interest on Sept. 1, 1825; and $30 plus interest Sept. 1, 1824. Although he did not make these payments, Storer did not foreclose.
293. The ages of William and George are based upon the information in Samuel's application for bounty land, to which he attested in 1820. That year William was fourteen and George was ten. Both of the boys might not still have been at home in 1823. U.S. Revolutionary War Pension and Bounty-Land Warrant Application, 1800-1900. Crockett, Samuel. https://www.ancestry.com/imageviewer/collections/1995/images/MIUSA1775D_135275-00187?pId=14508
294. In 1818, the U.S. Congress passed the first (of four) Revolutionary War Pension Acts. Samuel's application was under the Act of 1818. National Park Service website. "Revolutionary War Veteran and Widow Pensions." https://www.nps.gov/articles/000/revolutionary-war-veteran-and-widow-pensions.htm#:~:text=Quick%20guide%20to%20the%20American,62%20years%20old%20in%201818.

of sandy land in Cape Elizabeth having a small house which was once a shoemakers shop…"[295] (It is possible that this real estate was that small house/shop formerly belonging to Samuel's grandfather, Richard Crockett, Jr.; however, one would think that Samuel would have known his grandfather was a chairmaker, not a shoemaker.)

After Samuel's pension application was approved he began receiving a pension of $8 per month. (He also received $129.83 in back pension.) In 1835, the Maine legislature passed a Resolve granting long-overdue land to Revolutionary War officers and soldiers (or their widows) from the District of Maine or Massachusetts, who had served three years. Samuel, then seventy-three, met the qualifications and sent in an application for a 200-acre grant on June 27, 1835. On October 29th of that same year, he received a certificate (No. 218) stating that his claim (No. 299) had been approved. The grants were made from the "Indian Purchase"[296] in Penobscot County and from unappropriated lands in Washington County."[297] Samuel Crockett's deed was dated January 29, 1836. Lot No. 68 in Indian Purchase No. 2 was selected the same day (by a land agent),[298] and was likely immediately sold. (The Penobscot Nation had been strong-armed into selling these unorganized townships to the state of Maine in 1834. Nearly two centuries later, in 2024, the Penobscots were on track to reacquire 30,000 acres of land near Mt. Katahdin.)[299]

Samuel Crockett died July 13, 1848 at the age of eighty-seven. His wife Abigail continued to receive his Revolutionary War pension until her death November 18, 1857.

---

295. U.S. Revolutionary War Pension and Bounty-Land Warrant Application Files, 1800-1900. Crockett, Samuel. https://www.ancestry.com/imageviewer/collections/1995/images/MIUSA1775D_135275-00187?pId=14508 At the time of Samuel's pension application, the property was technically owned by John Skillin, a neighbor and relation of Abigail's. In 1824, Lemuel Skillin bought his father John's homestead, as well as twenty acres of land formerly belonging to Samuel Skillin, upon which the old shoemaker's shop apparently stood. This small property—the tiny house and 1/3 acre—Lemuel sold to Richard Crockett (Samuel's son, not the subject of this chapter) for $50 on July 26, 1828. The property where the shoemaker's shop stood was situated on the east side of the county road, and according to Lemuel's deed, was "…the same land Samuel Crockett now lives on." Another consideration of the sale from Lemuel to Richard (in addition to the $50), was that Richard agreed to "…keep and maintain a good and sufficient fence all around said land…" Possibly his father had livestock that had a habit of getting out. See CCROD, Book 287, p. 480. Witnesses: William and Mary Ann Cummings.
296. In what was largely a fraudulent transaction, the state of Maine in 1834 pushed the Penobscot tribe into selling four unorganized townships previously granted them by Massachusetts. "Changing Their Guardians: The Penobscot Indians and Maine Statehood, 1820-1849." Dorr, Jason M. (1998). Electronic Theses and Dissertations. 2746. https://digitalcommons.library.umaine.edu/cgi/viewcontent.cgi?article=3846&context=etd
297. Maine Genealogy website. "Maine Revolutionary War Bounty Land Applications, 1835-1838." https://blog.mainegenealogy.net/2016/08/maine-revolutionary-war-bounty-land.html
298. Maine Land Office, Land Grant Application, Samuel Crockett (Cape Elizabeth). Courtesy of the Maine Archives. Now available via DigitalMaine Repositories. https://digitalmaine.com/revolutionary_war_me_land_office/222/
299. The two transactions are not connected, except that land that once belonged to Maine's indigenous peoples—and of strong spiritual significance to the Penobscots—is now returning to them. "Trekking through tribal lands as the Penobscot Nation plans to reacquire 30,000 acres near Katahdin." News Center Maine website. https://www.newscentermaine.com/article/news/regional/native-america/maine-tribal-lands-katahdin-penobscot-nation-millinocket/97-ce8a8fcf-a236-4d05-9ecb-132bf4e0f377

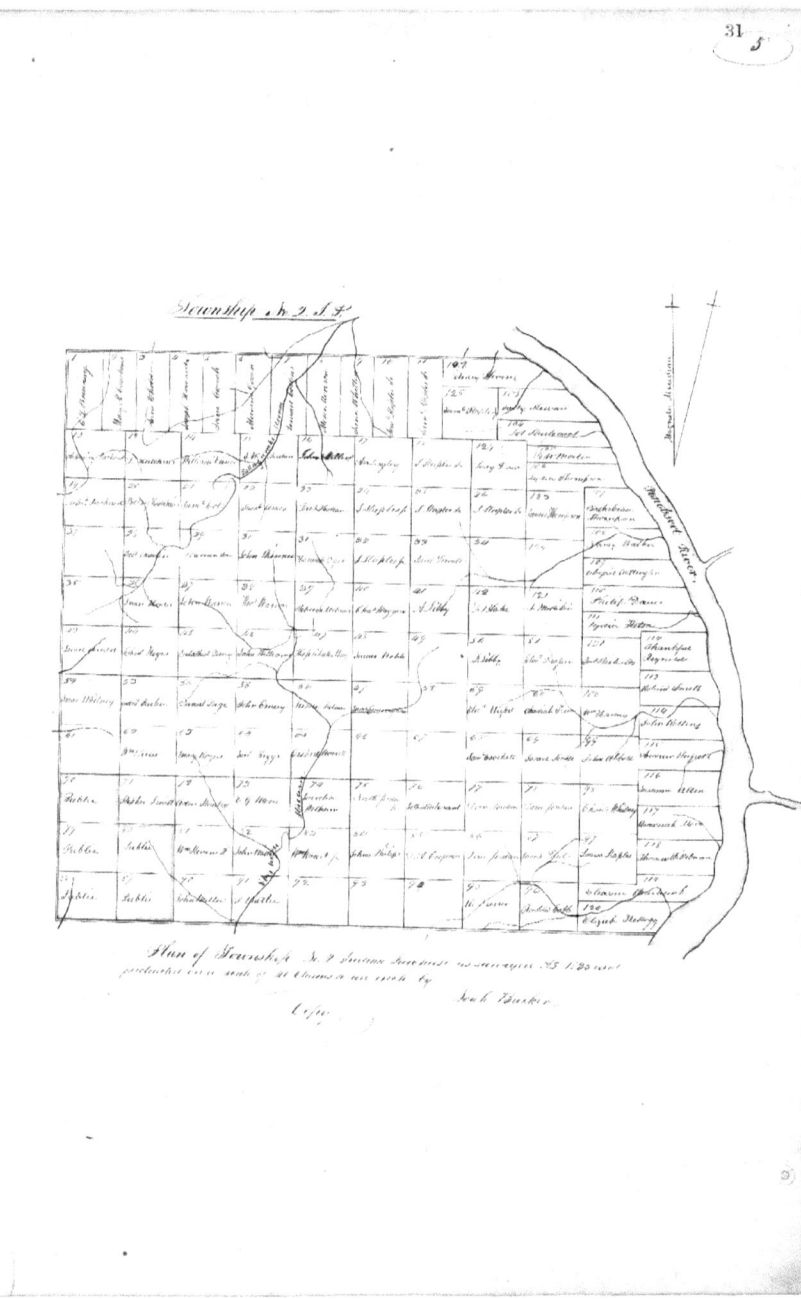

Plan of Township No. 2, Indian Purchase, 1835.
Samuel Crockett's lot is #68.
Maine Archives, Plan Book 10, p. 31.[300]

---

300. Maine Digital Repository https://digitalmaine.com/planbook_10/22/

The Fifth Generation

What happened to Richard's youngest child, William (his son with Elizabeth Lewis Masury) is most perplexing. While William seems to be living with his father when the 1820 census was taken (when William would have been twenty-two), he does not appear in census, marriage, death, or birth records after that. (By contrast, there are plenty of records for Samuel's son William Crockett, who remained in Cape Elizabeth.) A clue might be found in the 1838 deed from Samuel to Seth Storer, in which he mentions William Crockett. (Samuel never paid his mortgage to Storer, and eventually deeded him the house and ten acres that formerly belonged to his father.) Samuel described the property in the deed as "... bounded easterly by the road leading from Scarborough to Westbrook, Southerly partly by Daniel Skilling's land and partly by Joseph Westcot's land, Westerly by said Westcot's land, *northerly by land now improved by William Crockett* [emphasis the author's] and being the same on which my late father Richard Crockett formerly lived."[301] The description certainly fits Richard Crockett (III)'s property and according to my calculations there still remained at least ten acres (and likely more) of Richard's land unaccounted for. But we do not know—and cannot tell from the deed—if the William who is improving the land is Samuel's half-brother or his son. (Samuel's son William probably lived with his mother in the former shoemaker property, with which he ended up,[302] but this does not mean he did not also improve his grandfather's land.)

By 1857 (if not long before), Richard's son William Crockett must have been deceased. That year Samuel's sons Richard and William sell what appears to be the balance of their grandfather's property in Cape Elizabeth. On August 19, 1857, Richard Crockett of Portland and William Crockett of Cape Elizabeth sell for $100 to Henry Page of Portland "... a certain piece of land in Cape Elizabeth, bounded, beginning near a small fir tree at the most westerly corner of land owned by Daniel Skillin, thence southwest 41 rods; thence southeast 22 rods; thence southwest about 30 rods more or less to Scarborough line, thence southeast on said Scarborough line 35 rods to Ephraim Broad's land; thence north east by said Broad's land about 67 rods more or less to Daniel Skillin's ; thence by said Skillin's land 57 rods

---

301. CCROD, Book 160, p. 41.
302. On July 27, 1872, Samuel's son Richard Crockett sold (for $75) to his brother William "A certain tract or parcel of land in said Cape Elizabeth; being the same premises conveyed to me by Lemuel Skillin by deed dated July 26, 1828." This is the same property on which their parents had lived, which had at one point been a shoemakers shop. CCROD, Book 403, p. 29. Richard's wife Mehitable Crockett signed off on her dower rights. Witness: Augustina M. Crockett.

to the first bound mentioned containing twenty acres more or less, excepting the road across said premises."[303]

Regrettably, the 1857 map of Cape Elizabeth (part of Sidney Baker's 1857 Cumberland County map) is not helpful. While there is a William Crockett at a crossroads in Cape Elizabeth, this could be Samuel's son living with his mother (in the former shoemaker's shop) or it could be either of our two William Crocketts on Richard Crockett's property. (I think we can assume the map was drawn before William and Richard Crockett sold the balance of their grandfather's land to Page that same year.) We might never know what happened to Richard's son William or even if he survived.

Conclusion to Chapter 5

In 2017, M.M. Drymon wrote a Ph.D. thesis on paradigmatic landscape shifts in Maine. Interestingly enough (especially for our story) she focused her study area on Crockett's Corner in Cape Elizabeth. The very land, roads, and water courses that Richard Crockett (III) and his family and friends once traveled in the 18th century became in the 20th century the site of the Maine Mall in South Portland.[304] (The title of Dr. Drymon's thesis answers the question it poses: "The Forgotten Landscape: How A Place Called Crockett's Corner Became The Maine Mall.") In her thesis Dr. Drymon writes:

> "At Crockett's Corner, the immense public policy power of eminent domain accounts for more than half of the modern land use acreage in the defined Study Area ... and zoning has determined even more. The agency of individuals either had to take a back seat to sheer power or affected individuals willingly accepted the change. Within new ideas that became etched on the landscape, there may have been just enough of the old for it to feel, from the inside, like logical growth.

---

303. While this land could have been property that Abigail inherited, it seems unlikely since an inheritance would have been mentioned. Rather, the property described, adjoining Daniel Skillin, might have been the balance of the unaccounted-for land belonging to Richard Crockett (III, the subject of this chapter). CCROD, Book 281, Page 220. Abigail Crockett, who would have had a claim as Samuel's wife (if Samuel inherited the balance of his father's property), signed off on the deed, as did Mehitable Crockett (Richard's wife) and Polly Crockett (William's wife). Witnesses: Pen[?] Mitchell, J.P. and Levi Skillin. The two Crockett men took a mortgage on this property. See CCROD, Book 280, p. 340.

304. The Maine Mall was built between 1969-1971, a century and a half after Richard Crockett III's death.

The Fifth Generation

… People in the Study Area had been 'going to market' for centuries, and wasn't a mall just a reworked, somewhat more exciting, form of the old medieval marketplace done with a modern twist?"[305]

The Maine Mall, once all the rage, has become (fittingly enough) outdated in the 21st century, thanks to the rise of online shopping sites such as Amazon. When the doors to the Maine Mall will close for good, nobody knows. Ten years? Five? Even after the Maine Mall is gone, pastures and woodlots will have difficulty regenerating in the massive remnants of concrete and pavement. But … who knows? Perhaps "at a place called Long Creek"—where the Crocketts, Skillins, Roberts, Westcoats, and Dunns once roamed—Mother Earth will rise again. Let us hope so.

Drymon, in the introduction to her thesis, writes: "A strong 'quality of place' has been identified as one of the most valuable economic assets possessed by the state of Maine today."[306] I agree. We have seen in our history to date that "place" is a combination of personal (and familial) relationships and the land upon which the people dwelt. In the next chapter, "The Battle Over *Wabanaki* (Dawnland)," we will take a slight detour from following our Crockett line. In Chapter 6 we will consider the question that becomes paramount in Maine after the Revolutionary War: Who owns the land?

---

305. "The Forgotten Landscape: How A Place Called Crockett's Corner Became The Maine Mall." M.M. Drymon, Ph.D. South Portland, Maine: The Landscape History Institute, 2017. P. 21.
306. "The Forgotten Landscape: How A Place Called Crockett's Corner Became The Maine Mall." M.M. Drymon, Ph.D. South Portland, Maine: The Landscape History Institute, 2017. P. 21.

Chapter 6

THE BATTLE OVER DAWNLAND

Before we proceed with our story of Ephraim Crockett, the sixth generation in the line we are following, we need to take a short detour to consider the question: Who owned Maine? Surprisingly, the answer to that question was in flux even before Thomas Crockett stepped foot at Pascataqua in 1630 in search of freehold land.

Prior to European contact, North America was inhabited by hundreds of thousands of native peoples, including dozens of eastern Algonkian-speaking Wabanaki tribes in Maine. After the arrival of the French in the 16th century and the English in the 17th century, however, both Great Britain and France claimed ownership of North America (that territory not claimed by the Spanish in the 15th century, anyway). We have seen in our journey to date how Great Britain and France waged four major wars for dominance of this New World. In addition, during some of that time the English fought amongst themselves for control of New England. Control of Massachusetts and Maine passed between Royalists supporting the English monarchy and the Puritan faction in Parliament (and at Massachusetts Bay) for decades during the 17th century.

At the end of the French and Indian War, France ceded Maine to Great Britain. Warring Wabanaki tribes in Maine, without the aid of their French allies, could no longer continue to fight English expansionism. Most Native Americans withdrew into Canada, with the exception of peaceful tribes, such as the Penobscot and Passamoquoddy. The withdrawal from Maine of the French and hostile Indians left a vast expanse of land available in the District for exploitation and settlement by the English. This backcountry land acted as a magnet for Revolutionary War veterans from Massachusetts and coastal Maine, who had been promised land in exchange for their services.

In Chapter 7 we will learn through the story of Ephraim Crockett, a Revolutionary War veteran, how the question of "Who owned Maine?" was finally resolved, nearly four hundred years after the arrival of Thomas Crockett. There were many twists and turns along the way that could have taken Ephraim's story in an entirely different direction, however. In this chapter we will trace the important history of land ownership in Maine, which history provides necessary context for our concluding chapter in this Crockett saga.

Indigenous Understanding of Land vs. The Colonial English View

In the 17th century, Englishmen sailed to the New World by the tens of thousands. The earliest visitors to New England, who preceded permanent colonists like the Crocketts—fishermen, trappers, and traders—carried with them a host of diseases, including smallpox, bubonic plague, and various types of the flu, to which the indigenous population had no immunity or resistance. In recent years, some studies have suggested that the plague that wiped out nearly 95% of the natives in the northeast in the years just prior to the Pilgrim's arrival at Plymouth in 1620, might have been leptospirosis.

A clash of cultures and world views ensued when English colonists arrived. These Europeans considered the Indians as lesser beings or "savages," who simply occupied land belonging to Great Britain (the continent having been claimed for King Henry VII by John Cabot more than a century earlier).[1] Naturally, there was no question of purchasing the land from the native peoples since the land was at the disposal of the Crown. Later, when prudence demanded that colonists in Maine and Massachusetts deal with Native Americans (rather than fight them for the land) they were slow to understand how the indigenous view of relationship to the land conflicted with their own thinking. Ian Saxine in his excellent 2019 book, "Properties of Empire: Indians, Colonists, and Land Speculators on the New England Frontier," explains this cultural divide:

---

1. See *First Letters Patent granted by Henry VII to John Cabot, 5 March 1496* in "The Precursors of Jacques Cartier, 1497-1534." H. B. Biggar, editor. Published Ottawa, 1911; also, *A new world beckons: Columbus, Cabot, Vespucci, Verrazano.* D'Epiro & Pinkowish in "Sprezzatura: 50 Ways Italian Genius Shaped the World." New York: Anchor Books, 2001. Pp. 179–180.

The Battle Over Dawnland

"Before Europeans arrived, the people and the land shared a name: 'Wabanaki' meant people of the 'land of the dawn,' or 'Dawnland.' This shared name captured how the people thought about their relationship to where they lived. In eighteenth-century conferences with colonial leaders, Wabanaki speakers said they 'belonged' to rivers or stretches of land. In contrast, early modern English people 'belonged' to towns or other human communities rather than to the land itself. To belong to a place—or a person—implies a relationship, and the early modern English usage of the term to describe a person's residence in those terms was no accident, reflecting the web of privileges and obligations bound up in town life. The Wabanaki claims to belong to land or rivers stemmed from their view that their community privileges and obligations extended beyond the human occupants. Like other Eastern Algonquian speakers, the Wabanakis often described the land as 'Wlôgan': the Common Pot."[2]

Saxine's explanation and the "Common Pot" metaphor help us understand why indigenous people, such as the Penobscots—then and now—share the same name as the river to which their tribe is attached. The river owns them; they do not own the river. In addition, Saxine's synopsis explains why most of us of Anglo descent today describe someone as "John Smith, from Augusta, Maine," automatically linking the person to the community in which he or she resides. The primary relationship of John Smith is to his community (and his family and neighbors in that community), as we have just witnessed in our prior chapter with the life of Richard Crockett (III) of Cape Elizabeth. By contrast, the relationship of the Penobscots revolves around the Penobscot River and the land, animals, fish, and other resources connected to that water body. It is not coincidental that the Penobscot Nation today is one of the fiercest advocates for protecting this valuable natural resource.

While the English attempted via coercion and conversion to impose their world view upon the indigenous people who inhabited New England, they were largely unsuccessful.[3] Native Americans in Maine, despite having experienced severe population decline due to disease, still outnumbered by the thousands early English settlers in the area from the Saco River in the south to the St. John River in the east. In addition, warfare with the French and Indians that occurred between

---

2. EMPIRE, p. 13.
3. EMPIRE, p. 25.

1688-1713 caused the destruction of entire White settlements encroaching into Dawnland (such as the destruction of Casco or Falmouth, where Samuel Skillin's father perished in 1689). According to Saxine: "The English population of Maine plummeted from a prewar peak of 6,000 to fewer than 2,000 people by 1713, most of them clustered around the three southernmost towns of Wells, York, and Kittery" (where the Crocketts resided).[4]

Because there were more Native Americans than Englishmen in Maine, "early English arrivals had no choice but to respond. Indigenous land claims and diplomatic protocol therefore exerted a major influence on patterns of English colonization in the region."[5] Colonists began to enter into formal agreements with various native tribes and sagamores, sometimes offering annual payments for the purchase of land, even while allowing the Indians to retain the right to hunt and fish on the real estate in question (the natives not knowing of course, that the English propensity for pasturing and grazing would ruin their hunting grounds).[6] In fact, our old friend Sir Ferdinando Gorges, who gave Thomas Crockett his 188 acres on Crockett's Neck in Kittery, aware as he was that deeds and reciprocal agreements with indigenous people "had no legal standing in England, as they clashed with royal claims of sovereignty,"[7] nevertheless felt the necessity of making a show of respecting native claims to the land:

> "Bowing to this reality, Gorges directed his agents in Maine to first sign contracts with incoming colonists, then to 'give somewhat to the Adjacent Sagamore or Native, for their Consent' provided 'it be no considerable Sum,' justifying the payment as a good-will gesture that would distinguish the English from their European rivals and facilitate the spread of Christianity and 'civilization' among the Indians. The practice resembled the custom of quieting in England, by which manor lords paid squatters or other occupants a sum of money for their land without acknowledging they held a valid title to it."[8]

---

4. EMPIRE, p. 32.
5. EMPIRE, p. 25.
6. EMPIRE, p. 31.
7. EMPIRE, p. 32.
8. EMPIRE, p. 32. Gorges' belief that he held valid title to Maine and that it was the Native Americans who were the "squatters" recast the reality of the situation, and thus defined the Indians out of their land. The practice of "quieting" returns in the 19th century when Massachusetts attempted to quiet the settlers on backcountry land claimed by the Great Proprietors. More on this in the next chapter.

Trading companies (and some fur trappers and traders) also executed deeds with various Wabanaki tribal leaders. These deeds were for hunting and trapping rights, and for the right to build trading posts along the Kennebec and other rivers in Maine. Native Americans were quick to appreciate that trading posts established upriver from the coast would bring much-needed supplies closer to their people.[9] The Plymouth Company, which originated from the Pilgrim colony at Plymouth, Massachusetts, built a trading post on the Kennebec River at Augusta in 1629. By 1649, the Boston merchants Clarke and Lake Company also built trading posts along the Kennebec.[10] In addition, individuals such as Sir Ferdinando Gorges' agent Thomas Purchase, who traded with the Indians (and cheated them, some historians claim), entered into land transactions with tribal leaders along the Androscoggin River. (In 1675, during the First Indian War, Native Americans burned down Purchase's home and he and his family and crew were forced to abandon the area.)

In their deeds Native Americans intended to grant limited rights to the English intruders, while retaining specific rights for their people. A good example can be found in what is known as the "Warumbo deed" (see copy on page 299), an instrument signed in 1684 by six Wabanaki sagamores— Warumbee, Darumkin, Nimbanizett, Neonongansket, WeconDomhegon, and Wihikermett. This deed gave the Boston merchant Richard Wharton (who had bought up Thomas Purchase's prior rights from his heirs) title to land and fisheries along the Androscoggin and Kennebec rivers and Merrymeeting Bay. The text of the deed (available in the Appendix, pages 405–407) initially appears to grant Wharton traditional rights of English property ownership, but the sagamores were careful to add the caveat, "Provided nevertheless that nothing in this Deed be construed to deprive us the Sd Sagamores our Successors or People from improving our antient planting grounds nor from hunting in any of the said Land being not inclosed nor from fishing for our own provision…"[11]

Richard Wharton passed away, leaving unsettled debts behind. In 1714, Ephraim Savage of Boston was appointed administrator of Wharton's estate. To help discharge Wharton's debts, Savage liquidated his estate, including the large tract of land covered by the Warumbo deed:

---
9. EMPIRE, p. 30-31.
10. EMPIRE, p. 30-31.
11. Taken from the transcription of the Warumbo deed in "The History of Brunswick, Topsham, and Harpswell, Maine." George Augustus Wheeler, M.D. and Henry Warren Wheeler. Boston: Alfred Mudge & Son, Printers. 1878. Chapter Two.

"[Savage] sold the whole of the tract of land to Thomas Hutchinson, Adam Winthrop, John Watts, David Jeffries, Stephen Minot, Oliver Noyes, and John Ruck, of Boston, Massachusetts, and John Wentworth,[12] of Portsmouth, New Hampshire, for the sum of £140, to hold in fee as tenants in common. The conveyance was acknowledged the next day and was recorded in the York records on the nineteenth of the following November. These 'tenants in common' constituted the original company of the Pejepscot proprietors."[13]

The Pejepscot Proprietors will play a major role in the life of the next subject in our story—Ephraim Crockett—who settled on what came to be known as the Pejepscot Claim. Although the Pejepscot Claim was unable to be settled during the half century after its purchase (due to ongoing warfare with the French and Indians) the investors (and their heirs) kept their eye on the main prize: the coming days when the land could be turned into profits.

---

12. John Wentworth, one of the original Pejepscot Proprietors, was later Lt. Gov. of New Hampshire. See "The Kennebeck Proprietors, 1749-1775." Gordon E. Kershaw. Somersworth: New Hampshire Pub. Co., 1975. Wentworth was also my 8th great-grandfather, through the line of Ephraim Crockett, Jr. and Sally (Wentworth) Crockett.
13. "History of Brunswick, Topsham, and Harpswell, Maine." George Augustus Wheeler, M.D. and Henry Warren Wheeler. Boston: Alfred Mudge & Son, Printers. 1878. See Chapter Two.

The Battle Over Dawnland

The Warumbo Deed, p. 1.
In this 1684 deed, sagamores Warumbee, Darumkin, Nimbanizett, Neononganskett, WeconDomhegon, and Wihikermett deed land along the Androscoggin and Kennebec rivers and Merrymeeting Bay to Richard Wharton, a wealthy Boston merchant. (See Appendix, pages 405–407, for a full transcription of the Warumbo[14] deed.)
(Image in the public domain via Maine Memory Network.)

---

14. "Wabanaki deed to Richard Wharton, 1684." Maine Memory Network website. https://www.mainememory.net/record/20270 "Warumbo" is an alternative spelling for the name of the sagamore Warumbee.

Bostoniak: Land Speculation in Maine and the Rise of the Great Proprietors

No surprise to any Mainer of today (indigenous or otherwise), land speculation by people "from Away," blessed with deep pockets, is prevalent in the Pine Tree State. What did surprise me to learn while researching and writing this book, however, is that Native Americans were the first to discover the avarice of these land speculators, even going so far as to have a nickname for them: " *Bostoniak*—literally 'Boston people.' "[15] Early on, Indians discerned that most of the land speculation in Maine was done by wealthy Boston merchants, who, unlike the settlers, had no intention of living on the land themselves. Rather, these Bostoniak were speculators. They planned to chop up the real estate into smaller lots and peddle them to land-hungry settlers.

While the French and Indian wars that would ultimately determine which colonial power owned Maine—Great Britain or France—raged for nearly a century, Boston merchants, lawyers, and descendants of those to whom deeds had been given by native peoples did not fight to protect their interests, but rather were busy scheming how to corral large tracts of land for resale when the fighting ended. Maine settlers excoriated the Bostoniak for sitting out the French and Indian wars, telling the General Court of Massachusetts (when the settlers later defended their legal claim to their properties) that, while they were much "exposed," the absentee proprietors "Slept till the war and all danger was over and when the Inhabitants stood the brunt of it, and supported their Settlement and so made the Lands Valuable, then some of these pretended ancient proprietors started their dormant claims."[16]

During the hostilities with the French and Indians, three large land companies—the Pejepscot Proprietors, the Kennebec Proprietors, and the Waldo Proprietors—bought up individual deeds from the luckless setters who fled south for safety from the depredations that occurred during the various wars.[17] Groups of speculators also purchased native deeds (such as the men who bought the real estate conferred by the Warumbo deed), and picked up old deeds granted by or through

---
15. EMPIRE, p. 47.
16. EMPIRE, p. 121.
17. After the French and Indian warfare of 1688-1713 during which period the English population in Maine plummeted, the Bostoniak saw opportunity in the tragedy and "snapped up many of the refugee titles, then waited for the time when the frontier could again be safe for British colonization." EMPIRE, p. 36.

the authority of the British Crown or Parliament. All these deeds were then cobbled together, enabling wealthy "proprietors" to make fantastic land claims about what real estate they owned in Maine. In his illuminating 1990 book, "Liberty Men and Great Proprietors: The Revolutionary Settlement on the Maine Frontier, 1760-1820," Alan Taylor outlines the three large Maine patents (tracts) of land in Maine claimed by these Great Proprietors:

> "On the west the Pejepscot Proprietors claimed the *Pejepscot Patent*: the land four miles back on both sides of the Androscoggin River from its mouth to its 'uppermost falls.' In the center the Kennebeck Proprietors (also known as the Plymouth Company) laid claim to the *Plymouth Patent*: about three million acres located fifteen miles deep on each side of the Kennebec, Maine's central and most important river. To the east, Brigadier General Samuel Waldo and two companies of his partners, the Ten Proprietors and the Twenty Associates, claimed the *Waldo Patent*: about one million acres located between the Medomac and Penobscot rivers."[18]

Unlike the settlers to whom small parcels of land had been sold or granted (such as the Crocketts and their friends and relatives), the Bostoniak had no intention of ever living on the land they purchased. They viewed these transactions "as investments rather than homes."[19] Sometimes a proprietor would give small parcels of property away (or sell land at low prices) to tempt settlers into the Maine wilderness. The more settlers who moved into the backcountry to clear and improve land, the more the property values of the Great Proprietors increased. Ian Saxine puts it bluntly in "Properties of Empire:" "If forced to choose between creating a stable community or a profitable one," he writes, "[the Bostoniak] opted for the latter course."[20]

Going forward, our story is primarily concerned with the actions of the Boston-based Pejepscot Proprietors (and the Massachusetts General Court). After the Revolutionary War, our sixth-generation Crockett settled on land claimed by—but not legally accorded to—the Pejepscot Proprietors. By the time Ephraim Crockett arrived in the backcountry of the Pejepscot Claim the last of the Anasagunticook

---

18. LIBERTY, p. 12-13.
19. EMPIRE, p. 55.
20. EMPIRE, p. 56.

Indians living along the Androscoggin River had been defeated, pushed back into Canada with their French allies. But earlier deeds given by native chiefs to the Bostoniak did not disappear with the Indians.

It must be said that during the first hundred years of interaction between the English and indigenous people, there *were* occasional efforts to deal honorably with Native Americans. In fact, in 1721, Jeremiah Dummer, lawyer, clergyman, and London agent for Massachusetts Bay Colony, in addition to explaining why the charters of the New England colonies should not be revoked (which the British Parliament was then considering), brazenly declared that the Crown had never owned the land in the first place. Why not? Because North America "was full of Inhabitants ... and neither Queen Elizabeth by her Patents, or King James by his afterwards, could give any more than a bare Right of Preemption."[21] Dummer claimed that, while there were a few bad apples in the lot, most of the colonists had given fair value to the Indians for the land in question.[22] (Native Americans would no doubt debate this.) Predictably, Dummer's assertions about the rights of indigenous people fell upon deaf ears.

Massachusetts and Her Soldiers of the American Revolution

Hot on the heels of the French and Indian War (the Sixth Indian War, 1754-1763) came the American Revolution. The outcome of the Revolution and the creation of a new nation further complicated the issue of land ownership in Maine. Ownership of land in Maine not only had changed hands by deeds over the years, but also by defeat.

In 1763, the Treaty of Paris (not to be confused with the Treaty of Paris that ended the American Revolution) was signed between France and Great Britain and their allies (including Native Americans fighting on both sides), finally settling the bloody disputes between those two nations. The end to the French and Indian wars brought much-needed relief to the early settlers of Maine, who, having been caught

---

21. Defence of the New England Charters, Jeremiah Dummer, 1721. See also EMPIRE p. 41. Interesting to note that in the 2nd Proposition of his Defence (which is well worth reading) Dummer also blindly claims that there is little chance the American colonies will revolt and declare an independent nation. "So that I may say without being ludicrous that it would be more absurd to place two of His Majesty's Beef Eaters to watch an Infant in the Cradle that it don't rise and cut its Father's Throat, than to guard these weak Infant Colonies to prevent their shaking off the British Yoke." Of course, fifty-five years later, that is exactly what the thirteen colonies did.
22. The author is paraphrasing from EMPIRE, p. 41.

in the middle, often paid with cattle, their homes, and sometimes with their lives. From the Eastern Land Papers:

> "During the contest for supremacy in North America between French Canada and English America, Maine was caught in the middle. Occupying a strategic borderland position between the two, Maine, down to 1750, was the scene of some of the most sanguinary [bloody] battles of the war. Entire villages were destroyed, their inhabitants slaughtered by Indians who, allied with the French, viewed the English settlers as intruders."[23]

As a result of the treaty signed between Great Britain and France, Britain ended up with millions of acres of land in Maine formerly claimed by France. At the close of the Revolutionary War, these *millions* of Maine acres transferred from the ownership and control of Great Britain to the ownership and control of the Commonwealth of Massachusetts (which had purchased Sir Ferdinando Gorges' rights to the Province of Maine).[24] When Massachusetts adopted its state constitution in 1780, the new "District of Maine" was organized, encompassing the land between the Piscataqua and St. Croix rivers.[25]

According to Taylor in "Liberty Men and Great Proprietors," the Revolution was regarded by many Americans as an opportunity for great social leveling. Men like Ephraim Crockett who fought for the cause of liberty believed they were risking their lives not only to create a new, independent nation, but also to help establish a country of equals. The old world in which an inherited peerage carefully conserved lands and resources for the next generation of Upper Ten Thousand[26] would be replaced by a new nation in which a man's future would be built upon his

---

23. ELP, p. 3. https://www.sec.state.ma.us/arc/arcpdf/eastland.pdf
24. As mentioned, many of Maine's Native American tribes, such as the Anasagunticooks who lived along the Androscoggin River, were pushed back into Canada by the end of the French and Indian wars (or were absorbed by other tribes); however, remnants of the Penobscot, Passamaquoddy, and Maliseet tribes—some of whom had helped the colonists win their freedom from Great Britain—remained. It was not until 1980 and the landmark settlement with the state of Maine, approved by the U.S. Congress, that those tribes would receive some justice for their stolen lands. In that settlement the tribes received $81.5 million from the Federal government and 300,000 acres of land from the state of Maine. (A much smaller settlement with the Aroostook Band of Mi'kmaqs, a nomadic tribe that moved from Canada to the U.S., would follow.) Unfortunately, the agreement decimated some of the tribes' sovereign rights over their people and their land, including the right to control their water bodies. The reinstatement of those sovereign rights has been an ongoing consideration of the Maine legislature. See Portland Press Herald story January 14, 2020: "Sweeping recommendations would overhaul Maine's Indian land claims act."
25. "History of the District of Maine." James Sullivan, 1795. (Reprint) Augusta, ME: Maine State Museum.
26. "The Upper Ten Thousand" was a 19th century term for the British upper class (or "the Ton"). Several books of the peerage were published in England during this time, including John Debrett's "The Baronetage of England," to which Jane Austen's farcical character Sir Walter Eliott regularly refers in her novel "Persuasion."

own hard work and effort—and upon the good name he made for himself working his own freehold property. Gone forever would be the days of English tenant farming, in which a farmer was little more than a glorified laborer working a piece of land he did not own, such as Ephraim's younger brother Samuel Crockett, who (as we learned in Chapter 5) raised mules on Cornelius Durant's farm in Scarborough for work on the sugar plantations in the Caribbean. Without freehold land, Taylor says, "fathers could not pass on liberty and prosperity to their offspring; they could not retain their adolescents' labor and would suffer in old age. The New England yeomanry knew that tenancy was the unhappy lot of most of the world's peasants."[27]

As a result of the population explosion in the New World (to which the Crockett family contributed mightily), available land in Massachusetts, including the settled areas in southern and coastal Maine, had become scarce. Revolutionary War veterans, sons of old established families (and sometimes their fathers, as well) came to view the backcountry of Maine—now free from the threat of hostile French and Indians—not only as an opportunity, but also as an earned right belonging to themselves and their descendants.

The Continental Congress, to some extent, had helped create this land rush. To entice men to enlist for a period of three years (or until the end of the Revolutionary War), the new Congress passed on September 16, 1776 a Resolve promising soldiers and non-commissioned officers 100 acres of land. Massachusetts also contributed to the land scramble. Desperate to recruit and maintain soldiers—and knowing that the paper scrip with which the soldiers were paid was practically worthless—Massachusetts offered 200 acres of land as a bounty to its soldiers (with a three-year commitment required). These alluring enticements hit their mark. Small wonder that thousands of veterans—including Ephraim Crockett and other soldiers from Cape Elizabeth (and elsewhere in New England)—who flocked to the backcountry of Maine following the close of war, did so incentivized by the prospect of land. Maine's population *tripled* between the years 1775 and 1790.[28]

In addition to the promise of bounty land, real estate owned by Royalists—and abandoned by them during the Revolution (or just prior to)—was also seen as fair game. Taylor explains the mindset of the settlers regarding land formerly claimed

---

27. LIBERTY, p. 14. Today's gig economy often reminds me of the precarious position of tenant farmers of yore.
28. LIBERTY, p. 15.

by Tories, those who had fled to Nova Scotia or back to England at the outbreak of hostilities:

> "Settlers thought that the backcountry lands were free for the taking. The loyalism of the four principal Waldo heirs, the most conspicuous Kennebeck Proprietors, and a few Pejepscot Proprietors[29] inspired widespread rumors that the Commonwealth of Massachusetts would confiscate their patents to bestow free homesteads on impoverished families. Settlers insisted that loyalists' property ought to be the just reward of those who, in the words of Bristol's Williams Rogers, 'fought under the idea that they were to have the lands they were defending.'"[30]

Massachusetts, laden with war debt after the Revolution and with no money in her coffers, looked to Maine as cash cow. "The District [of Maine] seemed to offer 'exhaustless merchandize' available to exchange for the desperately needed cash."[31]

In 1781, Massachusetts created a committee to "clarify rightful land clams in Maine and identify trespassers."[32] When this committee proved unsuccessful, the General Court of Massachusetts in July of 1783 appointed a second committee charged with appraising and selling land in the District of Maine. But when it was realized that a committee of five men was not big enough to handle the entire District, in October of 1783 a separate committee was created to sell land in Lincoln County (then covering three-fifths of Maine's land to the north and east).[33] Eventually, this Lincoln committee, known as the "Committee for the Sale of Unappropriated Lands in Lincoln County," became responsible for the sale of all lands in the District of Maine.[34]

The process of parceling out land was slow and time-consuming. Ownership of the unoccupied territory had to be determined first and then surveying commenced. In the meantime, the Massachusetts General Court continued to pass numerous Resolves "in an attempt to dispose of the land in a uniform manner" (read: dispose

---

29. The claims of the Tory heirs of Hannah and Job Lewis, and Isaac Royal, important Pejepscot proprietors, affect the course of our story, as we will see in Chapter 7.
30. LIBERTY, p. 15.
31. ELP, p. 4.
32. ELP, p. 4.
33. Lincoln County, established in 1760 by the Massachusetts General Court, was the third county in Maine (after York and Cumberland). At the time of its creation, the county covered a tremendous land area, later broken up into 13 modern counties (including what is now Lincoln County).
34. ELP, p. 4.

of the land as quickly as possible so Massachusetts could get money). Cash was slow to flow into the Commonwealth's coffers, however. To speed things up the General Court even instituted a land lottery in 1786. The lottery was largely a failure, netting Massachusetts only $86,200. Potential land buyers, it turns out, were sharper than expected, and did not enter the lottery because they knew that the lands offered in the lottery "were actually left over, scattered, unsaleable tracts."[35] (In addition, veterans of the Revolution would not participate because they were awaiting their land grants.)

Eventually, money and power prevailed in the new country even as it had in the old. The wealthy Bostoniak gained control of the Massachusetts General Court. (Many of the Great Proprietors had seats in the legislature.) As a result, the wealthy proprietors who gobbled up land in Maine were given authority by the General Court to settle disputes that involved themselves and those they deemed squatters—a clear conflict of interest:

> "... in 1791 Jonathan Bridgham, a proprietor in Cumberland, complained that squatters refused to leave his land. By a resolve of March 1797, Bridgham was appointed to prosecute trespassers in the name of the Commonwealth. In other words, since an official was not available to go to Cumberland to eject the squatters, Bridgham was temporarily deputized as an official to do so."[36]

Even worse, Massachusetts, rather than confiscate the land of Loyalists who had supported Great Britain during the Revolution—which included many of the Great Proprietors and their descendants—after the war, affirmed and recognized many of their claims. Despite the fact that the British had been defeated by the upstart Americans (and that there were conflicting boundary issues and dubious title problems with these large patents, resting upon gifts from the Crown), the Great Proprietors boldly and continuously pushed for their claims to be recognized and honored by the General Court.[37] Over time, these men were successful (although the legislature did put a slight crimp in the outrageous quantity of land claimed by the Pejepscot Proprietors). Rather than making good land available to those who risked their lives to create this country, as the Continental Congress and

---

35. ELP, p. 4.
36. ELP, p. 5.
37. In an attempt to continue to milk the Maine cash cow, Tory heirs hired American lawyers to represent their claims, both to the Massachusetts General Court and to the settlers who had "squatted" on their claimed land

Massachusetts had promised, Massachusetts largely upheld the status quo of the wealthy, even acknowledging land claims of Loyalists (or their descendants) now living in England!

Some volunteer soldiers (such as Samuel Crockett, the tenant mule farmer) did finally receive the promised land in Maine (albeit decades after Maine became a state). Tragically (but typically), the four townships in Penobscot County[38] chopped up to make these belated Maine grants came—not from land belonging to Tories or from public or "open" land—but from what was known as the "Indian Purchase." The Indian Purchase was territory that the Penobscot tribe was strong-armed into selling the state of Maine in 1834. In a largely fraudulent transaction, the state pressured the Penobscots to sell for $50,000 four unorganized townships previously granted the tribe by Massachusetts.[39] (The Indians did not even get to keep or manage their money, but rather it "was to be held in the treasury of the State, and the interest of same to be paid annually by the Governor and Council through the Indian agent for the benefit of the tribe.")[40] Maine then divvyed up this deeded Native American territory into 100-acre lots, and awarded the lots to qualifying Revolutionary War veterans, often posthumously.

Many of the veterans who settled in the backcountry after the Revolution, waiting for the General Court to fulfill land promises to them, became the dreaded tenant farmer, paying rent to rapacious land managers. Settlers who tired of waiting for their land grant elected instead to purchase from the Great Proprietors (or other wealthy land speculators) the land that they themselves had cleared and settled. In the process, these settlers often discovered that they had to buy their own improved property, in effect, paying someone else for their own labor. And if they did not pay the asking price, the settlers were forcibly removed by the proprietors, endowed with that authority by the General Court.

Between the settlers and the proprietors arose a great philosophical divide. Who was responsible for creating the value of the land? Was the raw land valuable in its own right? Or did the settler create the value by clearing the land and creating

---

38. Penobscot County was taken from Hancock County, which had been part of the original Lincoln County.
39. "Changing Their Guardians: The Penobscot Indians and Maine Statehood, 1820-1849." Dorr, Jason M. (1998). Electronic Theses and Dissertations. 2746. https://digitalcommons.library.umaine.edu/cgi/viewcontent.cgi?article=3846&context=etd
40. "Report of the Joint Standing Committee on Indian Affairs on the Petition of John Attian, Governor of the Penobscot Indians, and many others of the tribe, asking for protection against money being drawn from the Indian fund by persons not authorized to receive the same." Documents printed by order of the Legislature of the State of Maine during the Session A.D. 1857. Part Second. https://lldc.mainelegislature.org/Open/Rpts/PubDocs/PubDocs1857v2/PD1857v2_S04.pdf

fields upon which crops were grown and houses built? Taylor explains the settler's point of view:

> "According to the agrarians, labor created all value, all property. In 1789, Bowdoin's settlers claimed that, when they arrived, the lands 'were only bare creation (and) by their industry they have brought them into a cultivated state, and feasted themselves with the hope that they were serving the state and laying up an inheritance for their little ones.' In 1797, (the town of) Prospect's settlers asked: 'Who made these lands more valuable than when in the state of nature? Was it not the settler?' ... Because unimproved wilderness lands were not property, proprietors had no right to sell title to them. The landed magnate who levied tolls on the settlers' access to wild land stole part of their labor."[41]

Not surprisingly, many of the settlers in Maine's backcountry—especially in the Pejepscot and Kennebec patents, but also on the Waldo Patent—fought back, like the Native Americans had done before them. On many occasions, in an ironic (but fitting) twist, settlers disguised themselves as Indians so they could not be recognized (including one of my ancestors on my Father's side who settled on land claimed by the Kennebec Proprietors)[42] and attacked the surveyors employed by the Great Proprietors. If the land could not be surveyed, they reasoned, it could not be subdivided and sold by the proprietors. Other settlers on patent lands simply refused to pay rent—and refused to leave, hiding from the law when it came in search of them. Still other backcountry settlers attempted to pay the very reasonable price per acre price set by the General Court during periods of "quieting" (attempts to 'quiet' the settlers) only to have their payments rebuffed by greedy proprietors who ignored the settlement approved by the Massachusetts legislature and demanded more money than the set price for the real estate.

What resulted from this great struggle over Dawnland following the American Revolution were decades of angst before title to thousands of acres of real estate were finally settled. A case in point is that of Ephraim Crockett, who stubbornly

---

41. LIBERTY, p. 103.
42. My 4th great-grandfather Joel Webber was one of eight men dressed as Indians who on September 15, 1809 attacked and accidentally killed surveyor Paul Chadwick, who worked for the Kennebec Proprietors. Webber absconded before he could be arrested and so was not indicted for murder; however, the other seven men stood trial. Feelings ran hot in Maine about the land disputes with the Great Proprietors and the seven who were tried were found "Not Guilty" by the jury. See the transcript of the trial prepared for Maine's bicentennial by the University of Maine, Digital Commons. https://digitalcommons.library.umaine.edu/cgi/viewcontent.cgi?article=1077&context=mainebicentennial

stayed put—despite being harassed by the Pejepscot Proprietors and their representatives—upon the sixty acres of excellent bottom land he settled along the banks of the Androscoggin River, just above Royalsborough (now Durham). The physical boundaries and ownership of the Pejepscot Patent, and thus the boundaries and ownership of the land Ephraim settled, remained in flux for more than four decades after he first landed in Pejepscot, thanks to dubious deeds, greedy proprietors with outrageous claims, and the vacillation of the Massachusetts General Court. Ephraim Crockett's story—and that of other Revolutionary War veterans who settled Pejepscot and elsewhere in Maine—loosely parallels the experience of the indigenous people of Dawnland. We will explore their story next.

1764 Plan of the Pejepscot Claim by Enoch Freeman.
While towns shown on the bottom left of the map—Brunswick and Royalsborough—were incorporated, named, and being settled by 1764, the balance of the disputed backcountry above Royalsborough was simply known as the "Pejepscot Claim" when Ephraim Crockett first arrived there in 1780. The boundaries would not be settled until 1813. (Image in the public domain, via Maine Memory Network.)[43]

---

43. "Pejepscot Claim, 1764. Maine Memory Network website. https://www.mainememory.net/record/37702

Chapter 7

"IN A PLEA OF LAND ... SAID CROCKETT PUTS HIMSELF ON THE COUNTRY" THE SIXTH GENERATION

First Generation – Thomas Crockett
Second Generation – Ephraim Crockett
Third Generation – Richard Crockett
Fourth Generation – Richard Crockett, Jr.
Fifth Generation – Richard Crockett (III, also known as Richard, Jr.)
Sixth Generation – Ephraim Crockett, 1755-1835

Revolutionary War veteran Ephraim Crockett is the sixth generation Crockett in the line we are following. He carried on the tradition of his ancestors (excepting his father Richard Crockett III) by seeking land and opportunity away from the place in which he was born. Ephraim was one of thousands of veterans, who—at the end of the Revolutionary War—flooded into Maine's backcountry looking for land. Before the conclusion of the French and Indian War, the backcountry had been unsafe to settle; however, when that war concluded France ceded Maine to Great Britain and warring Native Americans fled to Canada.

Although the area on the Androscoggin River where Ephraim settled with his uncle James Wagg, Sr. was claimed (on paper) by the Pejepscot Proprietors, those rights had not been fully accepted by the Massachusetts General Court. Equally as important, some of the Pejepscot Proprietors were Royalists who had fled the country before the Revolution. The little group of Revolutionary War veterans who settled on the banks of the Androscoggin River and created the town of Pejepscot hoped that Massachusetts would fulfill her obligation to them by awarding them the land promised in exchange for three years of military service. Other veterans, who had not signed three-year papers, also expected to be able to purchase former Tory-owned land from the Commonwealth at reasonable rates per acre.

But three decades *after* Ephraim first staked out good bottom land on the banks of the Androscoggin—after he had built a house, raised a family, paid taxes, and helped develop roads, schools, and a town there—his right and title to his land was challenged by a family of Tories who had abandoned the country before the war. In this concluding chapter of our history, we will learn what happened when Ephraim Crockett and his neighbors, many of them also Revolutionary War veterans, stubbornly fought back against those who tried to take their homesteads from them.

Ephraim's Early Years and the Influence of James Wagg, Sr. and Jr.

Ephraim Crockett was born on July 12, 1755[1] in Falmouth, York County,[2] Province of Maine, to Richard Crockett (III) and Elizabeth (Roberts) Crockett. The family lived on the south side of the Fore River in what was known as Second Parish or Cape Elizabeth District. Ephraim was the eldest of the couple's eight children. His father earned a living as a chairmaker, as did Ephraim's grandfather, Richard Crockett, Jr., who also resided in Second Parish until he relocated to Deer Isle sometime after Falmouth Neck was burned by the British in 1775.

We know little of Ephraim's early life in Cape Elizabeth, except that he and his siblings grew up in a community of extended family members. This included some of his mother's relations, the Roberts, Skillin, and Westcoat families at Long Creek, as well as his father's relations, including Ephraim's aunt Mary (Crockett) Wagg (his father's sister) and her husband, uncle James Wagg, Sr., and their children.

As a youth, Ephraim was likely apprenticed, as was the custom. Since Ephraim does not adopt a career (such as a chairmaker or shipwright), but rather becomes

---

1. There is no birth record for Ephraim Crockett. His birth date is known from Ephraim's pension application and from the record of his death. U.S. Revolutionary War Pension and Bounty-Land Warrant Application Files, 1800-1900. Crockett, Ephraim. https://www.ancestry.com/imageviewer/collections/1995/images/MIUSA1775D_135275-00084?pId=14814
2. Ephraim Crockett was born in what is today South Portland in Cumberland County, but which was then still part of Falmouth, York County. (Cumberland County was not created until 1760.) In 1898, the area in which the Crocketts resided was spun off from Cape Elizabeth to form South Portland. Today, although technically incorrect, most histories and genealogies simply note his birthplace as Cape Elizabeth, Cumberland County.

The Sixth Generation

a yeoman farmer, it is impossible to guess where he might have apprenticed during the years leading up to the Revolutionary War. The only clue we have is that his uncle James Wagg and cousin James Wagg, Jr. appear to have played an important role in the young man's life. After the conclusion of Ephraim's military service, he traveled to the Pejepscot Claim with the Waggs. Their party included James Wagg, Sr.; James Wagg, Jr.; and young James' new bride Dorcas Strout, who was a first cousin to Ephraim's wife Rebecca Stanford. Ephraim Crockett and James Wagg filed marriage intentions with Cape Elizabeth Town Clerk David Strout on the same day, March 12, 1777. (Town Clerk Stout was an uncle to both the young ladies.) This suggests an early and close relationship between the two cousins (Ephraim and James, Jr.) who married cousins (Rebecca and Dorcas).[3]

A purpose of Marriage, between Mr. Ephraim Crocket & Miss Rebecca Stanford both of Cape Elizabeth was Entered March 12th 1777 p.r David Strout Town Clerk.

A purpose of Marriage between Mr. James Wagg Jr & Miss Dorcas Strout, both of Cape Elizabeth, was enter'd March 12th 1777. p. David Strout Town Clerk

Marriage intentions filed in Cape Elizabeth with David Strout, Town Clerk, on March 12, 1777.
Mr. Ephraim Crocket and Miss Rebecca Stanford (both of Cape Elizabeth)
and Mr. James Wagg, Jr. and Miss Dorcas Strout (both of Cape Elizabeth).
(South Portland Town Records, 1765-1823.)

Regrettably, we do not know as much as we would like about James Wagg, Sr. Although he lived in Second Parish, there is no record of James owning real estate in Cape Elizabeth (or anywhere else in Maine). Wagg neither bought nor sold property, nor received a grant from the Falmouth Proprietors responsible for laying out land. As an unlanded man, Wagg was somewhat dependent upon others for his livelihood. This also suggests that (in the beginning, anyway) he was not well-connected. (Families generally helped each other rise in the world.) He might have been employed in a minor trade (such as his brother-in-law, chairmaker Richard Crockett III) or as a sailor. Or Wagg might have worked for a wealthy landowner

---

3. Rebecca was the daughter of Priscilla Strout and Joseph Stanford. Dorcas was the daughter of Priscilla Strout's brother, Christopher Strout III, and Elizabeth Smalley. Priscilla and Christopher were children of Christopher Strout, Jr. and Mary Hatch, as was David Strout, Cape Elizabeth Town Clerk. https://www.wikitree.com/wiki/Strout-2

managing a farm (as did Ephraim's younger brother Samuel Crockett). Most men of the time yearned for freehold title to land, however, and so Wagg's lack of real estate offers a clue as to why he might have decided to relocate to the backcountry in search of available land—and apparently encouraged many others to follow him.

What we know about James Wagg, Sr. comes from unpublished (and unverified) information preserved by the Androscoggin County Historical Society. By comparison to the Crocketts, James Wagg, Sr. was a late arrival to America. He was born approximately 1728 in Brighton, England and emigrated from there to Cape Elizabeth (then still part of Falmouth) before 1749, the year he filed marriage intentions with Mary Crockett.[4] According to original notes and records located at the historical society, James Wagg's descendants claim his surname was actually "Hallowell," but, because he ran away from his home in England and did not want to be found, he took his mother's maiden—"Wagg"—upon arriving in Cape Elizabeth.[5] There is no information about what James Wagg did for employment before relocating with his son, James, Jr., to the Pejepscot Claim (now part of Auburn) by 1780. (In Pejepscot, James Wagg and his son were farmers.) Nor, after scrolling through hundreds of pages of town records did I find Wagg's name, meaning that he was never elected to fill any town function in Second Parish (as was his brother-in-law Richard Crockett III). Because families of the time were generally tightknit, however, I think we can assume that the Crockett children and the Wagg children knew each other growing up, although they might have attended different schools. (There were four schools in Second Parish when the Waggs and Crocketts were young.)

Ephraim Crockett's Service in the American Revolution

The War for American Independence also played a pivotal role in Ephraim Crockett's life (as well as in that of his cousin, James Wagg, Jr.). Ephraim was nineteen when, on April 19, 1775, the British attacked Lexington and Concord. News of

---

4. This information came from various sources, including Maine marriage intentions, STARBIRD, and notes from the Wagg Family folder at AHS.
5. From STARBIRD, as well as notes on the Wagg family collected and written up by Auburn historian George Thomas Little for his history of Danville, included in "The History of Androscoggin County, Maine," Chapter XXXIX. ANDHIST, p. 691. https://www.google.com/books/edition/History_of_Androscoggin_County_Maine/yp_MEGfuKa8C?hl=en&gbpv=1&bsq=Danville%20 Little's notes also mention that some later Wagg descendants petitioned successfully to change their name to "Holland," perhaps having discovered that "Holland"—not "Hallowell"—was James Wagg's original surname.

The Sixth Generation

the attack reached Cape Elizabeth the following day.[6] This news shocked residents of Maine, then still part of Massachusetts. (Today we forget how closely Maine and Massachusetts families were once connected.) The outrage felt against the British troops who opened fire upon Massachusetts minutemen spurred many men—including Ephraim Crockett—to enlist. A biographer of William Dingley, fellow Cape Elizabeth resident and Revolutionary War veteran (who would follow Ephraim Crockett and the Waggs to the Pejepscot Claim) describes the patriotic feeling of the time and the public's animosity toward the British:

> "[William Dingley] had inherited from his ancestors and acquired through experience a hatred of England and a love for the new republic that was struggling for existence. The very year [1773] he moved from Duxbury to the new Maine colony of Cape Elizabeth[7] the famous 'Boston tea-party' was held. Two years later when William was twenty-six 'The midnight ride of Paul Revere' immortalized by the poet Longfellow (a native of Portland) had fired his patriotic heart."[8]

William Dingley, who was six years older than Ephraim Crockett, nevertheless waited to enlist until he witnessed the burning of Falmouth by Captain Mowatt and the British Royal Navy on October 17, 1775.[9] By contrast, nineteen-year-old Ephraim (along with sixty-one[10] other men from Cape Elizabeth and the greater

---

6. The information that the news of the attack on Lexington and Concord reached Cape Elizabeth on April 20, 1775 came from STARBIRD'S information collected on William Dingley, a fellow Cape Elizabethan who settled near Ephraim Crockett in Pejepscot. (Dingley settled there by 1792, per CCROD Book 36, Page 288, Daniel Sargent to William Dingley, 100 acres on the Pejepscot Claim.) WILLIS, p. 507, says news of the attack on Lexington and Concord was received at the "Neck" a day later, on April 21st.
7. Cape Elizabeth was not a new settlement or colony in 1773—it was part of Falmouth, known then as Cape Elizabeth District. When the American colonies decided to separate from Great Britain, however, Cape Elizabeth became a town in its own right, and therefore was considered "new" to some extent.
8. DINGLEY. Information from The Life and Times of Nelson Dingley, Jr. by Edward Dingley included with the Dingley Ancestry records at the AHS.
9. DINGLEY. The description of the burning of Falmouth (now Portland) is very compelling:
"Promptly at nine o'clock the signal of attack was given and the red flag of British vengeance was unfurled. It was a beautiful autumnal morning [Oct. 17, 1775] with a cloudless sky, a gentle breeze and an invigorating atmosphere. Falmouth was beautifully situated on the southern slope of a hill facing the bay. It was the largest and richest town in the state. There were four hundred dwellings, each with its garden. There were churches, a library and several public buildings. For nine hours the British stormed and shelled the doomed city. The torch was applied and the place became a roaring inferno. It was an awful spectacle. Four hundred and fourteen buildings were destroyed and the city laid in ashes. It was a most atrocious crime committed to punish the inhabitants of Falmouth for daring to thwart the British monopoly of manufacturing and trade."
10. According to historian Nathan Goold, in April 1775, Capt. Samuel Dunn of Cape Elizabeth pulled together a company of sixty-two men (including Ephraim Crockett) that would join Col. Edmund Phinney's 31st Regiment of Foot in the siege of Boston. Officers included Capt. Dunn, 1st Lieut. Ebenezer Newell of Cape Elizabeth, and 2nd Lieut. Samuel Thomas of Stroudwater. "History of Colonel Edmund Phinney's Thirty-first regiment of foot," Nathan Goold, author. Maine Society Sons of the American Revolution, Thurston Press, Portland, Maine, 1896. (GOOLD)

Falmouth area) enlisted immediately after learning of the battles of Concord and Lexington. On April 24, 1775,[11] Ephraim (and the others) joined Captain Samuel Dunn's company. Dunn (who was related to the Crocketts by marriage)[12] was a shipwright from Cape Elizabeth with some military training, and was active in town and county affairs.[13] According to the pension application of Ephraim Crockett's widow, Rebecca (Stanford) Crockett, (which gives an excellent account of Ephraim Crockett's military service)[14] Ephraim and the other men enlisted in Captain Dunn's company for an eight-month period of service beginning in April of 1775.

Captain Dunn's company would join Colonel Edmund Phinney's Massachusetts 31st Regiment of Foot, which was being organized at Falmouth. Nathan Goold's detailed history of Colonel Phinney's 31st regiment gives us insight into the time:

> "Col. Edmund Phinney's 31st Regiment of Foot, was the first regiment raised in the County of Cumberland for service in the field, in the Revolutionary war. Most of the men equipped themselves, but those who were not able were supplied by the towns where they enlisted. A large part of the men enlisted soon after the receipt of the news of the commencement of the war, and were in the service in and about Falmouth until July."[15]

According to Goold, on April 26, 1775, Colonel Phinney of Gorham was commissioned to form a regiment;[16] however, he had some difficulty getting this regiment together. In addition, a second Maine regiment was being formed to send to Massachusetts, which caused some concern in Cumberland County that the outflow of so many Maine soldiers (potentially more than 1,000 men) would leave the communities along the coast vulnerable to attacks by the British Royal Navy. To assuage this concern, Colonel Phinney was ordered to leave some of his men behind

---

11. On April 24, 1775, Captain Samuel Dunn of Cape Elizabeth mustered his company of militia, including Ephraim Crockett, into the Provincial army for active service. CAPE-E, p. 45.
12. Ephraim's mother, Elizabeth Roberts, was the daughter of George Roberts and Katharine Skillin. Samuel Dunn was married to Elizabeth's first cousin Sarah Skillin, daughter of Samuel Skillin, Jr. (Katharine's brother) and Rebecca (Sawyer) Skillin.
13. GOOLD, p. 52. Goold's bio of Capt. Dunn states: "Samuel Dunn was a shipwright, and lived in the western part of Cape Elizabeth. He married, in 1757, Sarah Skillings, daughter of Samuel Skillings; was in Capt. Samuel Cobb's training company in 1756, delegate to the county convention of September, 1774, and was prominent in the town's affairs. He died about 1784."
14. Department of the Interior, Bureau of Pensions, File 23888, Revolutionary War. Candage, in his Crockett genealogy, gives the date Ephraim joined up as May 17, 1775; however, that perhaps was the day that Ephraim was officially mustered into Capt. Dunn's company, although he had joined the prior month.
15. GOOLD, p. 3.
16. GOOLD, p. 8.

when he marched to Cambridge, Massachusetts, where the Provincial Congress and its army were situated. (It must have been gall and wormwood to the soldiers to have marched down to Massachusetts—rather than sailed—out of fear of the Royal Navy.) Colonel Phinney arrived in Cambridge July 10, 1775, with one hundred and sixty-eight of his four hundred men (probably three companies),[17] having left the balance behind to defend Falmouth and other coastal communities.[18]

When Colonel Phinney arrived in Cambridge, his regiment was stationed near the headquarters of the new Continental Army's Commander-in-Chief, General George Washington. (The Second Continental Congress appointed Washington commander on June 15, 1775, after the Congress voted to establish a national fighting force to aid the Provincial Army of Massachusetts.) Washington had arrived in Cambridge just a week earlier than Phinney, on July 3, 1775.[19] We know that Captain Dunn's company, in which Ephraim Crockett served, was one of the three companies under Colonel Phinney's command that marched to Cambridge and arrived July 10, 1775, because billeting (payment to civilians or tavern owners for a soldier's lodging) was allowed for Ephraim from May 17 to July 11.[20] (After joining the rest of the army, the soldier would require no further outsourcing of his meals and lodging.) When Ephraim arrived on the war front, he would have been a stone's throw away from General Washington, as well as from British troops. Historian Goold sets the scene:

> "On the arrival of Col. Phinney's regiment at Cambridge, they were at once in the presence of the enemy, being in sight of the British camps at Charlestown and Boston. The American camp about Boston, contained about seventeen thousand troops and was composed of habitations of every description, from the mud and log huts to the regulation canvas tents of the Rhode Islanders. Cambridge at that time had about fifteen hundred inhabitants."[21]

---

17. GOOLD, p. 15.
18. GOOLD, p. 8-11. By the end of July, all of Col. Phinney's regiment had joined him and the army in Cambridge. The departure of the troops did leave the Maine coast vulnerable, as citizens had worried. On Oct. 17, 1775 Falmouth was shelled and burned by the British.
19. GOOLD, p. 16. General Washington's headquarters were at 105 Brattle St. in Cambridge, formerly the home of John Vassell, a Tory who had fled the area before the war. This dwelling would later become the home, for half a century, of the poet Henry Wadsworth Longfellow, and is now a National Historic Site. "The Past and Present here unite..." Longfellow House Washington's Headquarters. National Park Service website. https://www.nps.gov/long/index.htm
20. Information about Ephraim's billeting taken from the section (Vol. 4, p. 128) written about Ephraim Crockett of Cape Elizabeth, in "Massachusetts Soldiers and Sailors of the Revolutionary War. A Compilation from the Archives, prepared and published by the Secretary of the Commonwealth." Wright & Potter Printing Co., [State Printers], Boston, MA, 1898.
21. GOOLD, p. 15.

Colonel Phinney's regiment was assigned to General William Heath's brigade, which, combined with General Israel Putnam's brigade, "comprised the center of the army, all under command of General Putnam."[22] Goold continues:

> "Col. Phinney's regiment at once, on their arrival in camp, assumed the dangers and responsibilities of soldiers. They participated in the skirmishes and picket firing and saw many killed and wounded about them, but during their entire service they saw no great or decisive battle."[23]

Phinney's regiment under General Putnam participated in the siege of Boston (April 19, 1775 to March 17, 1776), when New England soldiers and artillerymen successfully hemmed in the British. As a result of this siege the enemy was finally forced to abandon the city of Boston on March 17, 1776, and the Red Coats withdrew to Halifax, Nova Scotia.

Those early days in Cambridge during which the Continental Army was getting itself together as one fighting unit under General Washington, while extremely important, have not garnered the historical romance with which Revolutionary War battles—such as Bunker Hill, Saratoga, and Yorktown—have been infused. This is because General Washington, with an army comprised of inexperienced soldiers, many of whose papers would expire in December 1775 (as did Ephraim Crockett's), was loath to attack the British. Instead, Washington wisely opted for a siege. Goold gives these first volunteers in the American Revolution their due:

> "These early regiments represented the pure patriotism of the people, they had no bounties, furnished their arms and equipments and were anxious to strike the first blow for their country's liberty. They were used to hardship, and fear was unknown to them. The older men were used to warfare, as they had been accustomed from their earliest boyhood to defend their homes against a savage foe … These brave men had resolved when they entered the army that they would have liberty if it had to be purchased by their own blood…"[24]

---

22. GOOLD, p. 15. General Putnam was affectionately known as "Old Put" to his soldiers. According to GOOLD (p. 16), Gen. Putnam was a farmer-soldier who abandoned his plow mid-furrow in a field upon first hearing news the Revolutionary War had commenced.
23. GOOLD, p. 20.
24. GOOLD, p. 31.

The Sixth Generation

General Washington later wrote about the first men to serve in the Continental Army during the early days of the war:

> "They were indeed, at first, an army of undisciplined husbandmen; but it is, under God, to their bravery and attention to duty that I am indebted for that success which has procured me the only reward I wish to receive, the affection and esteem of my countrymen."[25]

At the end of 1775, the siege of Boston not yet having concluded, Colonel Phinney (and possibly Captain Dunn) re-upped for another year of service. However, Ephraim Crockett, who, like many other soldiers had signed eight-month papers (with service concluded at the end of December 1775), was anxious to return to Cape Elizabeth after the burning and destruction of Falmouth Neck by Captain Mowatt only six weeks earlier (October 18, 1775). Many soldiers did not reenlist, much to Washington's dismay. The hard-pressed general had even attempted to sweeten the pot for these soldiers to entice the men to reenlist. (In fact, on November 1, 1775 Ephraim had received an order for a bounty coat or its equivalent in money.)[26] Instead of getting out of the service altogether, however, Ephraim Crockett simply elected to enlist in a different company and regiment, one that served closer to home. On January 1, 1776, Ephraim Crockett signed up for one year[27] with Captain William Crocker's company under Colonel Mitchell's regiment, which company was stationed at Falmouth for defense of the Maine seacoast.

When his second enlistment with Captain Crocker ended (without apparently having seen any action), Ephraim enlisted a third time. On December 17, 1776, Ephraim Crockett joined Captain James Leach's company (also under Colonel Mitchell's regiment for defense of the coast) "until the first day of March next" unless discharged earlier.[28] Ephraim, along with more than forty-five other men, signed this enlistment paper (dated at Falmouth) in his own hand, spelling his

---

25. "Celebration of the centennial anniversary of the evacuation of Boston." George Edward Ellis. Boston: A. Williams & company, 1876. p. 100.
26. "Massachusetts Soldiers and Sailors of the Revolutionary War," Vol, 4, p. 129.
27. Information that Ephraim signed up for one year with Capt. Crocker's "Seacoast" company comes from his Pension Records with the Department of the Interior as noted on his widow's application for pension. Actual service was probably in two dates: service from Mar. 1, 1776 to Aug. 31, 1776 (six months—per "Massachusetts Soldiers and Sailors of the Revolutionary War") and service from Aug. 31, 1776 to Nov. 23, 1776 (three months and twenty-three days—per the widow's pension application).
28. U.S. Revolutionary War Rolls, 1775-1783 for Ephraim Crocket; from a copy of Capt. Leach's Matrosses, Mass. Militia's enlistment papers. Made available by the National Archives.

name, "Ephraim Crockit." He and the other men agreed to "engage to furnish ourselves with a good Firelock (and Bayonet fitted thereto if possible)."[29]

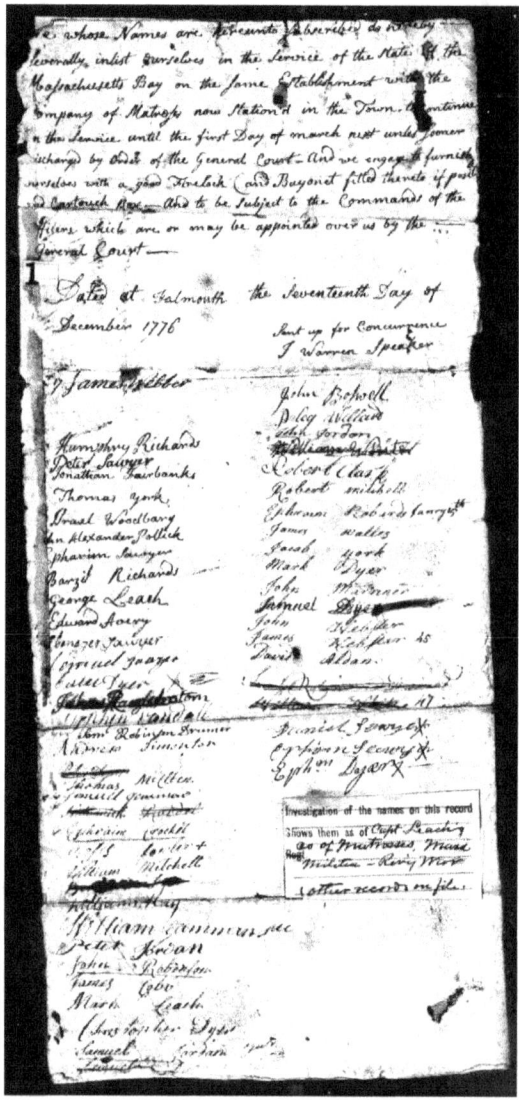

Paper signed at Falmouth December 17, 1776 by Ephraim Crockett for his third enlistment in the American Revolution.
He enlisted with Captain Leach's company of Matrosses (artillerymen). Ephraim signed in the left-hand column, about two-thirds the way down. (There is a line under his name.)
(U.S. Revolutionary War Rolls, 1775-1783. Crockett, Ephraim.)

---

29. From Capt. Leach's Matrosses, Mass. Militia's enlistment papers, via the National Archives.

This third enlistment provides valuable insight into what Ephraim Crockett was doing during a large portion of his service in the Revolutionary War. The enlistment was for a company of "Matrosses," artillerymen who ranked below a gunner. The job of a matross[30] was to "assist the gunners in loading, firing and sponging the guns."[31] Ephraim's third enlistment suggests the possibility that he might have gained some artillery experience during the siege of Boston during his first enlistment. Captain Leach's company of matrosses would have defended the local harbors against incursions by the British Royal Navy (such as Captain Mowatt's earlier invasion). It does not appear from the records, however, that the men had the opportunity to take aim at any British men-o'-war.

Ephraim's third enlistment ended March 1, 1777. By then, he had served his country two years, from April 20, 1775 to March 1, 1777. He did not enlist a fourth time. Instead, Ephraim Crockett's attention shifted to his future.

Marriage to Rebecca Stanford

Less than four months after he was released from his last enlistment, Ephraim married Rebecca Stanford. Rebecca was born in Falmouth on July 21, 1760, the daughter (and fourth child) of Joseph and Priscilla (Strout) Stanford.[32]

The Stanfords, like the Crocketts, resided in Second Parish (Cape Elizabeth). Unlike Ephraim's grandfather Richard Crockett, Jr., who immigrated to Falmouth (from Stratham, N.H.) around 1730, the Stanford family had originally come to Falmouth from Massachusetts more than half a century earlier (when Thomas Crockett and his son, the first Ephraim Crockett, were raising their families in Kittery).

In 1660, Rebecca's great-grandfather Robert Stanford[33] purchased 50 acres at Purpooduck (Cape Elizabeth) from "Mr. Jordan." (At the same time, Robert's father Thomas Stanford, a colorful character, not above swearing and drinking, also purchased 80 acres from Jordan.)[34] During the Second Indian War (King William's

---

30. From the Dutch word "matroos," a sailor who helped load and fire guns aboard ship.
31. "Matross." Encyclopædia Britannica. Volume 17. 11th edition. New York: The Encyclopædia Britannica Company, 1911.
32. Maine Birth Records, 1715-1922. Stanford, Joseph.
33. The last name is also found as: Sanford, Staniford, Standfort, and Standford. LIBBYNOYES, p. 654 and various deeds and records.
34. LIBBYNOYES, p. 654. Thomas Stanford, Rebecca Stanford's great-great grandfather, sounds like a colorful character. In 1659 Thomas was in court for swearing (an anathema to the tightly-wound Puritans of Massachusetts Bay Colony, to whom Stanford and other Mainers had recently sworn fidelity). Also, he was called "a common swearer and drunkard in 1663, and accused of breach of oath of freedom and fidelity…" LIBBYNOYES, p. 655.

War, 1688-1697), Robert Stanford fled with his family to the safety of Gloucester, Massachusetts.[35] Josiah Stanford, Robert's son (Rebecca's grandfather) returned to Falmouth, the place of his birth and youth, during the second settlement period after the Third Indian War (Queen Anne's War, 1702-1713). On March 22, 1727/28, Josiah Stanford was granted 34 acres in Falmouth on the east side of John Sawyer's tract, fronting the Fore River (near the Meeting House),[36] with "1 acre reserved on the Point to the North East of the said Stanfort's House for a Common Landing for the Town."[37] (John Sawyer operated the ferry that ran from Second Parish across the Fore River to Falmouth Neck, then the center of commerce.)

The Stanford family intermarried with other Second Parish families, including the Sawyers, Strouts, Skillins, Yorks, and Jordans. When in 1773 the rights to Thomas Stanford's land in Falmouth (granted to him posthumously in 1737 as an "ancient" proprietor of Falmouth) were sold by Thomas' heirs (for 36 pounds), twenty heirs signed the deed. Included among the heirs were ten Sawyers, three Stanfords, two Skillins, two Strouts, and two Yorks.[38]

Joseph Stanford (Josiah's son and Rebecca's father) was born in Gloucester, Massachusetts, October 3, 1724,[39] shortly before the family returned to Falmouth. Joseph was a yeoman,[40] who probably lived on or near his father's homestead. He married Priscilla Strout on April 30, 1749 in Falmouth.[41] She was the daughter of Christopher and Mary (Hatch) Strout.[42] Priscilla was born in Provincetown, Massachusetts, March 23, 1731;[43] however, her parents relocated to North Yarmouth

---

35. LIBBYNOYES, p. 654.
36. Information that Josiah Stanford's home was near the Second Parish Meeting House came from a deed (YCROD, Book 36, p. 29), when Josiah Stanford sold some of his land to Jacob Sawyer.
37. YCROD, Book 20, p. 74. Josiah was a yeoman. See YCROD, Book 28, p. 218. His son Josiah, Jr. was a mariner. (Various deeds at YCROD.)
38. CCROD, Book 17, p. 141. At a meeting of the Falmouth Proprietor's Committee for Laying Out Land in 1734, the Committee acknowledged that both Thomas and Robert Stanford had prior claims as early settlers. "Copy of the Original Records of the Proprietors of Falmouth for the years 1718 to 1826." Three volumes in one. PORTLAND: Copied by F.A. Gerrish, 1861. New Book 1, p. 31. https://archive.org/details/proprietors00falmouth_202105/page/n76/mode/1up?view=theater On December 27, 1737, the Proprietor's Committee laid out 70 acres of land to the heirs of Robert Stanford, deceased, situated on the south side of the Fore River (in Second Parish). "Copy of the Original Records of the Proprietors of Falmouth for the years 1718 to 1826." Three volumes in one. PORTLAND: Copied by F.A. Gerrish, 1861. New Book 1, p. 177. https://archive.org/details/proprietors00falmouth_202105/page/n222/mode/1up?view=theater
39. Massachusetts Town and Vital Records, 1620-1988. Gloucester births, marriages and deaths. Joseph Stanford's mother was Hannah Day.
40. See CCROD, Book 19, p. 207.
41. Maine Marriage Records, 1713-1922. Strout, Priscilla.
42. www.wikitree.com/wiki/Strout-2 Christopher Strout was named for his father and often used the suffix "Jr." because he had a son, Christopher Strout III.
43. Massachusetts Town and Vital Records, 1620-1988 for "Bersiler" (Priscilla) Strout. Provincetown Births, 1620-1845; Vol. A.

in 1737.[44] In May of 1738, Strout, a merchant, bought the homestead of Robert Means in Second Parish (near Job Sawyer's property)[45] and removed his family to Cape Elizabeth, where Priscilla was raised.

Considering that both Ephraim Crockett and Rebecca Stanford hailed from Cape Elizabeth families, it is not surprising that they decided to join their lots together. (It could be said that Ephraim married well, since the Stanfords were more affluent than the Crocketts.) The marriage, which took place on June 26, 1777, was performed by the Reverend Ephraim Clark, who was still the pastor of Second Parish (then the town of Cape Elizabeth)[46] and for whom Ephraim Crockett was named.

Ephraim was twenty-two when they wed, and Rebecca was seventeen, although both would turn a year older in a few weeks (Ephraim on July 12th and Rebecca on July 20th).[47] The couple had to wait for the feisty, long-time minister to return to town before being wed, since the Reverend Clark served as a chaplain for various regiments during the Revolutionary War and was absent from June of 1776 to June of 1777. Reverend Clark returned to his pastorate just in time to marry two other couples on June 12th, before performing the service for Ephraim and Rebecca on June 26th. These three weddings are the first Clark recorded for the year 1777.[48]

After the wedding, the couple likely lived with one of their families (probably hers), with Rebecca contributing to the household effort—cooking, weaving, sewing, doing laundry, caring for poultry, and milking cows—and Ephraim either working out or possibly helping his father, Richard (III), with his chair-making

---

44. On March 23, 1736/37, Christopher Strout, Jr., merchant of Provincetown, purchased 25 acres of land in North Yarmouth (for 200 pounds in Bills of Credit) from John Smith. YCROD, Book 18, p. 208.
45. YCROD, Book 20, p. 204. Strout, described as a "dealer" in the deed (and very well-heeled), paid 400 pounds money to Means for his homestead and 25-½ acres, situated on the water (probably the Fore River) plus 13 acres of marsh. The purchase included "... All my Housing, Out Housing, Barn, Fences, and all other Privileges." Christopher Strout also invested in real estate in Narragansett Township No. 7 (Gorham). See YCROD, Book 23, p. 112. In later records, Strout is described as "Esq." (Esquire), signifying a rise in social status. Apparently, his neighbor Job Sawyer needed to cross Strout's land for some purpose. On January 9, 1754, Sawyer signed a promissory note for "four pounds lawful money for at or before the first of July next with Lawful Entry too paid for value re'cd..." Job Sawyer did not pay up, however, and Strout charged him with trespass. The case was heard at the October 1758 session of the Court of Common Pleas for York County, where judgment was for Strout in the amount of 4 pounds, 17 shillings and 6 pence (which included fees). Maine, York County, Court of Common Pleas records, 1695-1838. Court of Common Pleas case files, Box 128. July 1578-Oct. 1758 (cont.) Folder 14-447. Christopher Strout v. Job Sawyer. https://www.familysearch.org/ark:/61903/3:1:3QS7-L93N-6X8?i=632&cat=1923498
46. Marriages in Falmouth (Cape Elizabeth), Solemnized by Rev. Ephraim Clark, Pastor 2nd Parish from the Maine Historical and Genealogical Recorder, Vol. III, p. 107 and p. 185.
47. CANDAGE, p. 36.
48. The centennial of the Cumberland Association of Congregational Ministers, at the Second Parish Church in Portland, Maine, Monday and Tuesday, May 28 and 29, 1888, p. 20 and Marriages in Falmouth (Cape Elizabeth), Solemnized by Rev. Ephraim Clark, Pastor 2nd Parish from the Maine Historical and Genealogical Recorder, Vol. III, p. 107 and p. 185.

business,[49] to raise capital for their future. At the time of Ephraim's marriage, Richard's mother was deceased, and his father's family was still living in a small dwelling near and on property belonging to Ephraim's maternal grandparents, Katharine and George Roberts, who were still alive.[50]

Although he was the eldest son, Ephraim did not rest his future hopes on inheriting his father's real estate and chair-making business. Not long before Ephraim's own marriage, his widowed father had married Susannah Westcoat (Richard Crockett's second marriage), a first cousin to Ephraim's deceased mother Elizabeth (Roberts) Crockett. Susannah had an illegitimate son who might also have joined the household, which included Richard and Susannah, and Ephraim's two younger sisters, Mary (age 13) and Lucy (about 12). Over the ensuing years, Ephraim's father and stepmother would add four more girls to the household.[51]

The first child of Ephraim and Rebecca Crockett, a daughter named Rebecca after her mother, was born in Cape Elizabeth on December 16, 1778. Ephraim, after the birth of his daughter, disappears from all written records for more than five years. He drops out of sight until 1785. In fact, Ephraim and his wife did not add to their numerous offspring until son David Crockett was born, eight years after the birth of daughter Rebecca.[52]

Where was Ephraim Crockett during this time? What was he doing?

I call the years between 1780 and 1785 the "interesting years" in Ephraim Crockett's life. Although we will likely never know for sure where he was, I have a theory about what Ephraim was doing during the period in which he leaves no trace or written record.

The Interesting Years – 1780-1785

I am not the first historian to note the eight-year gap between the first and second child of Ephraim and Rebecca Crockett and wonder what was going on with that

---

49. In a 1781 deed, Richard Crockett (then about forty-eight) was described as a "chair-maker," so we know Ephraim's father was still working in his profession in 1777, when Ephraim and Rebecca were married. CCROD, Book 11, Page 281.
50. Katherine and George Roberts probably both died around 1781. Their estate was settled by their sons George and Joseph in the fall of that year. See CCROD, Book 15, Page 99 and Book 11, Page 408.
51. CANDAGE, p. 36. Candage has Susannah Westcoat married to Richard III's son, Richard, IV; however, I do not believe that Richard IV ever existed, but rather that Richard III married Susannah Westcoat. (See Chapter 5.) The children noted for Richard IV (or Richard, Jr., as Candage calls him) therefore belong to Richard III, the chairmaker, and widower of Elizabeth Roberts.
52. David Crockett was born on January 25, 1786, in Cape Elizabeth. His older sister, Rebecca, had been born eight years earlier on December 16, 1778. CANDAGE, p. 36.

The Sixth Generation

(especially as children come fast and furious after 1786). In addition, on January 17, 1782, the selectmen of Cape Elizabeth listed Ephraim as one of the men about whom they are "not knowing whether dead or living."[53] These two historical facts combined have given rise to much romantic speculation about Ephraim's whereabouts during this time, including a "family tradition" that he was captured by the British during the Revolutionary War and spent some time at Dartmoor Prison in Devon, England.[54]

While the tradition about Ephraim being captured by the British is intriguing (and has been much noted by Crockett genealogists and other historians, thus giving it credence), the story cannot possibly be true. HMP Dartmoor was not built until 1809,[55] during the Napoleonic Wars, decades after Ephraim is listed as missing. In addition, the selectmen's list that includes Ephraim Crockett's name was simply created as an excuse for why the town had not met Cape Elizabeth's quota of soldiers for that year.[56] All towns were given a quota of soldiers they were expected to send to General Washington's new Continental Army, based upon the number of ratable polls (legal voters), and Cape Elizabeth spent years trying to convince Massachusetts that the town was being charged an extra hundred polls. (The town eventually convinced Massachusetts and received a refund from the Commonwealth.)

So, if not a prisoner at Dartmoor, where *was* Ephraim Crockett?

In my opinion, for at least five of those years, from 1780-1785, Ephraim was in the backcountry, up the Androscoggin River on the Pejepscot Claim with his uncle James Wagg, Sr., cousin James Wagg, Jr., and Dorcas (Strout) Wagg. (Aunt Mary Wagg was deceased by then.) James Wagg, Jr.'s last enlistment ended on January 1, 1780 and he returned to Maine[57] after having served out his three

---

53. Massachusetts Soldiers and Sailors of the Revolutionary War, Vol. 4, p. 128. A compilation from the Archives, prepared and published by the Secretary of the Commonwealth. Wright & Potter Printing Co., Boston, MA. 1898.
54. CANDAGE, p. 36. The story about Ephraim Crockett being imprisoned at HMP Dartmoor is also in STARBIRD'S Crockett genealogy at AHS, which Candage might have utilized.
55. HMP (His Majesty's Prison) Dartmoor was commissioned in 1806 for French soldiers captured during the Napoleonic wars. Later, during the War of 1812, the prison received some notoriety for its harsh treatment of captured American soldiers. "History of Dartmoor Prison." Dartmoor Prison Museum website. https://www.dartmoor-prison.co.uk/history_of_dartmoor_prison.php
56. In fact, one of the reasons the selectmen of Cape Elizabeth gave for not meeting their quota in 1782 was that James Wagg, Jr. (Ephraim's cousin) had moved from Cape Elizabeth "subsequent to 1776." See STARBIRD and Wagg family history, AHS, Danville files.) James served more than three years in the Continental Army and was in Pejepscot with his father by 1780. Either the Selectmen did not keep very close tabs on the men in their town, or they did keep close tabs, but used any opportunity for an excuse as to why they did not meet their quota.
57. Wagg family histories and letters included with James Wagg, Jr.'s pension and bounty-land application reveal that later family members believed James, Sr. also served in the Revolutionary War, including with Washington at Valley Forge. This

years.⁵⁸ After James, Jr. and Dorcas were married on February 24, 1780 (also by Reverend Clark),⁵⁹ the little family group headed into the backcountry, accompanied by Ephraim Crockett. (Ephraim's wife, Rebecca, remained in Cape Elizabeth with their fourteen-month-old daughter.) Winter is an excellent time to travel in Maine. Frozen water bodies can be crossed and sleds carrying supplies can be easily hauled. I believe Ephraim accompanied his uncle, not only to help him (and cousin James) clear land and build a log cabin, but also to stake out his own claim. It is not a coincidence that Ephraim settled on 60 acres on the Androscoggin River near the 100 acres claimed by the Waggs.⁶⁰ In fact, 1812 court records reveal that Ephraim claimed title to his land *through* James Wagg, Sr.⁶¹

Most histories of Danville, which at the time was part of the Pejepscot Claim, credit James Wagg, Sr. with being the first settler in what is now south Auburn, but was then known as Pejepscot. ("Pejepscot" is a Native American place name for the area near today's Brunswick, meaning "extended long rapids".)⁶² The histories note that in 1780, James Wagg Sr. and his son settled on about a hundred acres of land⁶³—good bottom country—on the Androscoggin River just north of the newly-established town of Royalsborough (incorporated 1760; later Durham).⁶⁴ One

---

has not been proved by any military service records, but Wagg, Sr. could have been a sutler or other form of camp follower, and if so, he would have returned to Cape Elizabeth with his son. The two men together returning from the war front would have created very strong impetus for getting into the backcountry as soon as possible to stake a land claim.

58. James Wagg, Jr. served three enlistments in the American Revolution. In October 1775, he enlisted as a private in Capt. Samuel Dunn's Company (the same company in which Ephraim Crockett served), Col. Phinney's Massachusetts Regiment, until December 1775. In December of 1775, James, Jr. enlisted as a private in Capt. Hart William's Company, Col. Phinney's regiment for one year. On December 31, 1776, he enlisted (for three years), with pay accounts from January 1, 1777 to December 31, 1779. During his final three years James was a private in Capt. Sewall's Company, Col. Ebenezer Sprout's regiment, and he also served in Capt. Josiah Jenkin's Company, Col. Samuel Brewer's regiment, with service at Bennington and Valley Forge. "Massachusetts Soldiers and Sailors in the Revolutionary War." Wagg, James.

59. James Wagg, Jr. and Dorcas Strout were married in Cape Elizabeth February 24, 1780 by the Rev. Ephraim Clark. Marriages in Falmouth (Cape Elizabeth), Solemnized by Rev. Ephraim Clark, Pastor 2ⁿᵈ Parish.

60. ELP. In the 1804 settlement between Massachusetts and the Pejepscot Proprietors (which the proprietors refused to honor) Ephraim Crockett and James Wagg are both shown on Range 3—Ephraim on Lot 1 and the Waggs on Lot 4.

61. Maine, Cumberland County Court of Common Pleas records, 1764-1839. Court records, v. 13, 1811-1812. March term 1812, p. 396.

62. "Indian Place Names of New England." Compiled by John C. Huden. New York: Museum of the American Indian, Heye Foundation, 1962. P. 178. The Pejepscot Proprietors claimed the land on either side of the Androscoggin River, running from Brunswick upriver to the uppermost falls.

63. STARBIRD and the Wagg family history in the possession of the AHS say the Waggs took up two lots of land. At this point, I have only found evidence at the Cumberland County registry of deeds (CCROD) that they took up one lot, although on the ELP 1804 map of the proposed settlement between the proprietors and the settlers it appears that a second lot on the east side of the Androscoggin River has Wagg's name on it. (The second lot initially taken up by Wagg, Sr. could have been parceled out to later settlers.) The accompanying ELP paperwork says that James Wagg is to pay $72.54 for one lot—ninety-three acres—situated at Range 3, Lot 4. ELP

64. ANDHIST, Chapter VII.

of the first children to be born—and to die—in Pejepscot was James and Dorcas' son Eliza (Elija), who was born December 2, 1780, and died nine days later.[65]

The quest for land was the force driving the Waggs and Ephraim Crockett into the backcountry. On September 16, 1776, the Continental Congress, to attract and retain troops, passed a Resolve offering 100 acres of land to men who signed up or reenlisted for a period of three years. (There were other inducements to get soldiers to reenlist, but none so motivating as free land.)[66] Massachusetts upped the ante for her soldiers in 1779, offering 200 acres for three years of service.[67] James Wagg, Jr., whose last day in Captain William's company, Colonel Phinney's regiment, was December 8, 1776, was one of the men enticed by the promise of land. On December 31, 1776, James, Jr. reenlisted for a period of three years. The Resolve of 1776, combined with the later offer from Massachusetts, sparked a land rush to the Maine wilderness, recently cleared of warring Native Americans by the defeat of the French. The race to the backcountry began well before the ink was dry on the peace treaty between the United States and Great Britain. The men—mostly veterans—were motivated not only to stake out their 100 (or 200) acres, but also to get the *best* land available. The first man to an unclaimed area would have the opportunity to choose the best site. The Waggs—and Ephraim Crockett—were first to arrive in unsettled Pejepscot and therefore netted the excellent bottom land along the Androscoggin River. (Today, Bell Farms still has the farmland in corn and potato production.)

The Waggs probably knew that the land they settled was claimed by the Pejepscot Proprietors. If so, they would have known that the Proprietor's title to that land was in dispute at the Massachusetts General Court. In addition, the owners of Great Lot 3 (as designated by the Proprietors), upon which the Waggs settled, were Samuel and Hannah Waterhouse, Royalists who had fled their home in Massachusetts before the war for the safety of England. Ephraim Crockett, the Waggs,

---

65. Info from the copy of an old death record for Pejepscot (via Ancestry). The death record says the child was a male named "Eliza Wagg;" however, given the fact that the handwriting on these old death records was difficult to transcribe the boy's name was likely Elijah (an Old Testament name symbolizing hope and redemption).
66. A Resolve passed by Congress later that year, on October 6, 1776, also gave the army a pay-raise and a combined clothing-cash bounty of $40. Enlisted men (such as Ephraim Crockett and James Wagg, Jr.) would receive $6.67 per month for salary, plus $20 in scrip (which would be worthless before the end of the war), and $20 worth of clothing, including "two linen hunting-shirts, two pair of stockings, two pair shoes, one pair breeches, one waistcoat, two pairs of overalls, two shirts, and one leather cap or hat, amounting in the whole to twenty dollars..." GOULD.
67. "Settling Oxford County: Maine's Revolutionary War Bounty Myth." Jean F. Hankins. Maine History. Vol. 2, No. 3. October 1, 2005. P. 141. (Via DigitalCommons@UMaine https://digitalcommons.library.umaine.edu/cgi/viewcontent.cgi?article=1164&context=mainehistoryjournal

and other veterans would have believed that Massachusetts would confiscate all Tory real estate and make the land available to the soldiers who fought and built this new nation.

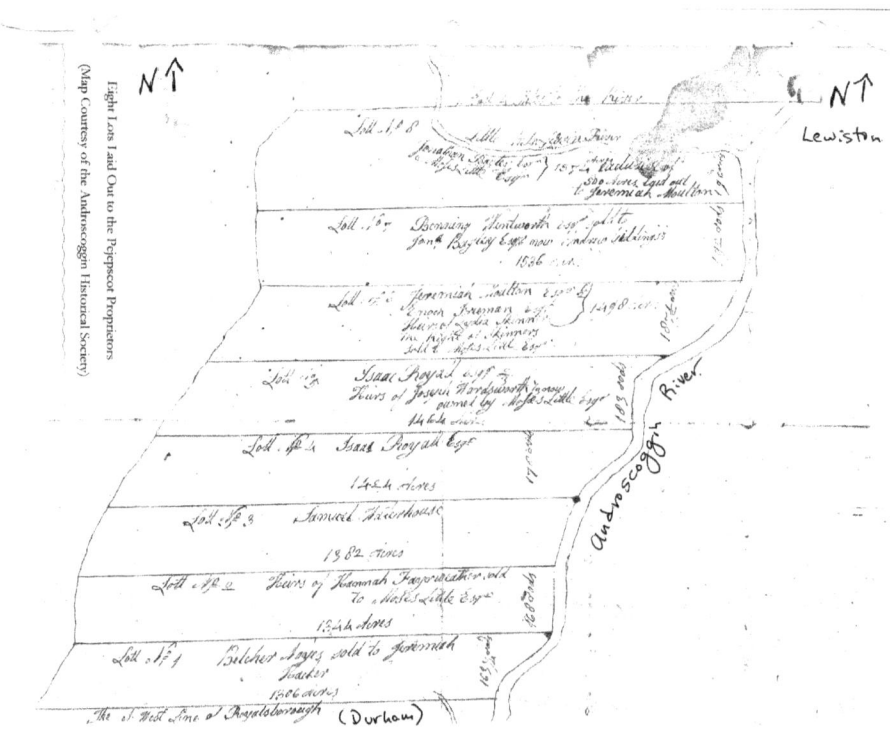

"Eight lots laid out to the Pejepscot Proprietors."
Map showing lots of land claimed by the Pejepscot Proprietors (but not confirmed by the Massachusetts General Court) along the Androscoggin River in Pejepscot. Isaac Royall (owner of Great Lots 4 and 5) and Samuel and Hannah Waterhouse (owners of Great Lot 3) were Tories, who had fled the country. Royall sold Great Lot 4 to Moses Little, who managed the Pejepscot Patent (until Little's son, Josiah took over). A real estate speculator, Little also purchased Great Lot 2, Great Lot 6, and part of Great Lot 8. The Crocketts and Waggs settled on Great Lot 3, land that had been set aside for Samuel Waterhouse (in the right of his wife Hannah, daughter of Job Lewis, founder of Lewiston) by the Pejepscot Proprietors before the war.
(Undated map obtained from the records of David C. Young and Charles Starbird, courtesy of the Androscoggin Historical Society.)
(Place names and directional indicator seen in darker ink on the map
added by the author for context.)

The Sixth Generation

Georgia Drew Merrill, editor of "The History of Androscoggin County," explains the rush to backcountry by soldiers of the American Revolution:

"The financial condition of the United States at the close of the Revolution was very poor. An enormous debt in the shape of the large issues of paper money which the exigencies of the war had brought into being was in the hands of the people demanding payment, and there was no means of payment. The soldiers had been paid with [scrip], and, on account of its great depreciation, 'a bushel of it would not buy a breakfast.' The only means of giving an equivalent was in the unappropriated lands in the several commonwealths. Massachusetts had plenty of wild land in the District of Maine, and to her unemployed citizens who had served in the army was given the opportunity of settling on 'states land' where they could develop homes for their families and give in payment at face value the colonial scrip otherwise valueless. From this offer arose a great emigration to Maine, and the Valley of the Androscoggin received its share. Although in many of the towns or settlements the claim of the state to the lands was opposed by that of the Pejepscot proprietors, still many had no faith that a conveyance made by wandering Indians could hold against the civilized claims of Massachusetts, and, pleased with the country, became settlers, and even where the disputed territory became the property of the Pejepscot proprietors, in numerous cases made their permanent homes."[68]

Like many other Revolutionary War veterans, Ephraim Crockett staked a claim in the disputed territory on Tory land. Although he had not signed three-year papers as had his cousin James Wagg, Jr., Ephraim had served from the very first days of the war. In addition, because he had been stationed next to army headquarters in Cambridge, Ephraim would have known that the home of John Vassell, a Tory, had been confiscated for the use of General Washington. It is reasonable to assume that Ephraim believed—as most soldiers did—that after the war, all real estate previously owned by those who sided with the British (and had fled the country) would be confiscated by Massachusetts. This new "states land" would be used to fulfill the promised land bounties or made available to other veterans at reasonable rates, if not for free.

---

68. ANDHIST, Chapter VII.

After his five-plus years in Pejepscot with the Waggs, Ephraim Crockett returned to Cape Elizabeth for a short period (possibly to replenish his funds) before removing his family to the backcountry permanently. Two more children were born in quick succession in Cape Elizabeth once he returned home. David was born to Ephraim and Rebecca on January 25, 1786, and Ephraim, Jr. (who settled Crockett's Ridge in Norway, Maine) was born February 7, 1788.[69] The fourth child, however—Mary Crockett (perhaps named for her late great-aunt Mary Crockett Wagg)—was born on April 21, 1790, on the Pejepscot Claim,[70] about a stone's throw from the Wagg family's log cabin.

The 1790 U.S. Census for Pejepscot shows Ephraim and Rebecca Crockett in that settlement with four children: Rebecca (almost thirteen), David (four-and-a-half), Ephraim, Jr. (two-and-a-half), and Mary (four months).[71] Altogether, Ephraim and Rebecca Crockett would have ten children: Rebecca, David, Ephraim, Jr., Mary, Sarah (Sally), Priscilla, Joseph, James, Betsey, and Eliza,[72] all but the first three born in Pejepscot. Please refer to the "Genealogical Dictionary of Thomas and Ann Crockett" beginning on page 377 for more information about Ephraim and Rebecca's children.

Life in the Backcountry of the Pejepscot Claim

When Ephraim and his family returned to the Pejepscot Claim in 1789, the Waggs had been settled on Great Lot 3 for nearly a decade. The area was still undeveloped and the first order of business for Ephraim would have been to clear the trees from a plot of land on which to build a home. He might have built a small cabin during the 1780-1785 period in preparation for bringing his family to Pejepscot, but if not, the Crocketts would have stayed with Ephraim's uncle and cousin (and young family) until their lot was cleared and the new home built. It would have been a tight fit in the small cabin in which the Waggs lived. According to a handwritten

---

69. CANDAGE, p. 36.
70. CANDAGE, p. 36.
71. The actual 1790 return for Ephraim Crockett is: Free White Males 16 and over: 1 (Ephraim); Free White Males under 16: 2 (David and Ephraim, Jr.); Free White Females: 3 (Rebecca and daughters Rebecca and Mary.) Pejepscot, Cumberland County, Maine 1790 Census Returns https://sites.rootsweb.com/~meandrhs/pej90.html The census was taken on August 2, 1790.
72. See CANDAGE p. 36 and p. 85-88. (The stories of Ephraim Crockett, Jr. and his sister Mary and their spouses and families, who settled Crockett's Ridge in Lee's Grant, are told in the author's book, "A History of the Crockett Family of Crockett's Ridge, Norway, Maine.")

Wagg family history in possession of the Androscoggin Historical Society,[73] the Waggs resided in their log cabin until 1807, when a two-story frame house (still standing on the South River Road in Auburn) was built with sawn boards. In 1789, when the Crocketts arrived with their family, James and Dorcas Wagg had five children ranging in age from newborn to seven. James and Dorcas would go on to have four more children born in their log cabin, including a set of twins.[74]

Other Revolutionary War veterans from Cape Elizabeth soon followed the Waggs and Crocketts to Pejepscot, most notably William Dingley (who had watched Captain Mowatt and the British Royal Navy shell and burn Falmouth Neck in 1775 before enlisting). In 1793, at the age of forty-four, Dingley and his family settled on the Androscoggin River south of Ephraim Crockett. Again, it cannot be a coincidence that these veterans of the Revolution—James Wagg, Jr., Ephraim Crockett, and William Dingley—settled near each other on the Pejepscot Claim, disputed territory that they likely believed would be confiscated and awarded to soldiers of the Revolution. (Keeping it all in the family, Ephraim's eldest son David would marry William Dingley's daughter, Esther, and James Wagg, Jr.'s son Samuel would marry Dingley's daughter Polly.)[75]

From one of William Dingley's ancestors, Edward Nelson Dingley, we have a detailed description[76] of life during those early years in the wilderness, including the settler's first dwelling, the log cabin:

> "… [the cabins were] simple structures of logs reared from the butts of ancient trees fallen by the pioneer's axe on the spot where they were cut down for a clearing. The walls were covered with bark or thatched. The enclosed earth was excavated for a cellar, while a primitive ladder afforded access to the garret above. The excavation was then planked over with riven logs of pine and a trap door in the center of the flooring led to the cellar. In one corner of the log walled room

---

73. This Wagg family history appears to be in a different handwriting from STARBIRD'S and might be something a Wagg descendant wrote up for him to use for his Danville genealogies.
74. STARBIRD, Wagg family history, AHS, Danville files. All of the surviving Wagg children were born in this log cabin.
75. STARBIRD, Crockett, Wagg, and Dingley family histories and genealogies, Danville files, AHS. William and Sarah Dingley had six daughters, all of whom married well. Of their sons, only one—Jeremiah Dingley—survived to carry on the family name in Pejepscot. (Ancestry lists two other sons living to maturity.)
76. "The Life and Times of Nelson Dingley, Jr." (DINGLEY). I took my information from an old, typed copy of this book in the Danville files at AHS; however, digitized copies of the book are available online. Although this interesting (to us) information about William Dingley in Pejepscot is included, the book is about Edward Dingley's father, Nelson Dingley, Jr. He was a lawyer, journalist, and Congressman on the powerful U.S. House Ways and Means Committee. Dingley, Jr. was responsible for what is known as the "Dingley Tariff," legislation that raised tariff rates and granted the President authority to invoke reciprocity when negotiating trade treaties.

was an immense fireplace. The back and one side built of stone, while a wooden post set the opposite jamb, supporting a horizontal beam for a mantlepiece."[77]

The building of a log cabin was an arduous task, especially without the aid of oxen. Sometimes, settlers had to be creative to get the job done. Auburn historian George Thomas Little[78] describes how building a roof for the log cabin was accomplished:[79]

"It was frequently the custom to select two trees 20 to 24 feet apart, build the walls [of the cabin] around them; cut [the two trees] to the height desired for the roof. To the top of these poles he secured a heavy log to form a ridge plate. His gables were then built up the desired height. Poles were then cut the needed length to extend from the topmost wall log to the ridge plate, notched to fit onto the plates. They were then pegged down."[80]

Ephraim Crockett, like most of the early settlers to Pejepscot (except for Andrew Giddings, also on the Pejepscot Claim, but closer to the town of New Gloucester) had few tools or beasts of burden to help them with their work. (In fact, Giddings, who would become prominent in town, occasionally hired out his oxen, colt, cart, and sled.)[81] Labor such as the felling and burning trees, planting corn, clearing land, and later, cutting hay, would all be done by hand. Edward N. Dingley writes:

"Plows could not be used because of stumps and logs. The implement most frequently used was a rude hoe of great weight made by the nearest blacksmith. They had no carts. Manure when used was handled with wooden shovels and carried into the field in hods. Hay and other crops were dragged into the barns

---

77. DINGLEY, AHS typed copy, p. 4. Some of the information about early life in Danville in this book by Edward Nelson Dingley is used almost verbatim by George Thomas Little in his piece on Danville (Chapter XXXIX) published in "The History of Androscoggin County," edited by Georgia Drew Merrill. (ANDHIST)
78. This might have been written by Charles Starbird and "borrowed" by Little. It is often challenging to tell which Danville/Pejepscot/Auburn historian's work is whose.
79. Unfortunately, George Thomas Little's book on the history of Androscoggin County was never published, and perhaps never finished. Nevertheless, the information he gathered for his book and his handwritten chapters provide valuable information. The section on building a log cabin came from handwritten pages that appear to match his writing in other documents attributed to him in the Danville files at AHS. The beginning of this section of his work is labeled, "Chapter V."
80. George Thomas Little, unpublished history of Androscoggin County, Chapter 5. AHS, Danville files.
81. Diary of Andrew Robinson Giddings, from 9 May 1795 to 19 Sept 1795. AHS.

on ox-sleds or 'polled in' by hand. Their heavy scythes were fastened to straight sticks or perhaps to a crooked alder cut in the swamp."[82]

According to Dingley, Indian corn would have been the staple of the Crockett's diet. Colonel Isaac Parsons of New Gloucester had recently brought into vogue a new style of growing in these clearings in the wilderness. Rather than the traditional method of planting corn in hills on newly-plowed ground (impossible because of tree stumps and roots), Parsons recommended corn seed be sown "directly upon the new land after it had been cleared and burned over and was allowed to grow without being hilled."[83] This new method enabled the settlers to provide themselves with a large quantity of corn, which would have been difficult to haul by hand from the nearest town into the backcountry, where there were no roads and falls and rapids made travel by water impractical. In addition to Indian corn, beans, and bannock (unleavened biscuits made from wheat or corn) would have been a major part of the Crockett's diet. Abundant game such as deer and moose provided the necessary protein, as well as "other wild animals of less desirable character."[84] Potatoes, root crops (particularly turnip),[85] barley, and wild berries would have rounded out their food staples. Early settlers such as the Crocketts "had no tablecloths, knives or forks, cups, or saucers. Wooden bowls and wooden spoons were, beside those furnished by nature, the utensils employed in eating. Settles[86] were used in place of chairs, and for the family to sit together at the board that served as a table, was the exception rather than the rule."[87]

There were no nearby stores, either. Instead of buying cloth to sew into clothing, wives like Rebecca Crockett would have had a small but essential variety of textiles to work with. The men grew flax for linen (and linseed oil),[88] from which the women wove coarse, heavy "tow cloth" for the men's and boy's drawers, other clothing, and sheets and towels.[89] They utilized the finer flax and linen for more important items, weaving it into "colored checks for their own and their daughters' wear on Sundays and social occasions." When sheep arrived on the scene—only

---

82. DINGLEY, AHS typed copy, p. 4.
83. ANDHIST, Chapter XXXIX. This method of growing corn was likely borrowed from Native Americans, who had employed the practice prior to contact with Europeans.
84. DINGLEY, AHS typed copy, p. 4. "Less desirable" meat might have been skunk and even gray squirrels.
85. George Thomas Little, unpublished history of Androscoggin County, Chapter 5. AHS, Danville files.
86. A settle was a long wooden bench.
87. ANDHIST, Chapter XXXIX.
88. George Thomas Little, unpublished history of Androscoggin County, Chapter 5. AHS, Danville files.
89. DINGLEY, AHS, typed copy, p. 5.

after the threat of bears and wolves had been eliminated[90]—wool became an important textile. Clipped wool was carded, combed, and spun by the women of the house, either at home or at "wool breakings" and "spinning bees."[91] The wool was used for socks, under drawers, and shirts for the men, and other warm clothing and blankets for the family. In addition, deer and moose hides provided leather and fur for coats and trousers in colder weather.[92] "Shoes and boots were not bought, but made by the cobbler, who would often spend a week at a house working up a side of leather into footwear."[93]

The early settlers to the Pejepscot Claim were almost all farmers. Even as late as 1820, 145 heads of households (including Ephraim Crockett and his eldest son David)—out of 148—were engaged in agriculture. (The other three men were engaged in commerce.)[94] The Crocketts, Waggs, and Dingleys settled on fertile ground next to the Androscoggin River, which, although excellent soil,[95] made them vulnerable to the freaks of Mother Nature. In 1785, there was a "remarkable" spring freshet, "which carried off all their bridges and was unprecedented for height."[96] This flooding caused by heavy rain and melting ice and snow would have presented a potential annual peril to the families who lived and farmed next to the river. Other farming hazards included "a great incursion of grasshoppers" in 1795[97] and a perpetual superabundance of crows, which threatened the corn crops.[98] On May 5, 1806, a bounty of twelve cents was offered for each crow (or pair of crow's feet) presented to the selectmen.[99] And when the General Court of Massachusetts passed a law in 1816 protecting crows (and other bird species), the town of Pejepscot audaciously voted to defy the law. On April 6, 1817, it was voted "that the law passed by the General Court at its last session respecting the killing of certain

---

90. DINGLEY, AHS, typed copy, p. 5.
91. DINGLEY, AHS, typed copy, p. 5. "Spinning bees and wool breakings were held for spinning and carding. When the work was done, both young and old, came in; and the affair usually closed with simple dances and merry plays."
92. DINGLEY, AHS, typed copy, p. 5.
93. ANDHIST, Chapter XXXIX.
94. ANDHIST, Chapter XXXIX.
95. The ground upon which the Crocketts and Waggs settled is still excellent farmland, nearly 250 years after James Wagg staked his claim in 1780. Today, Bell Farms on Riverside Drive in Auburn grows potatoes and sweet corn on the property. We stock up on a good supply of Bell Farm's excellent potatoes every winter. https://www.bellfarmsinc.com/
96. ANDHIST, Chapter VII.
97. ANDHIST, Chapter VII.
98. My husband and I grow heirloom Indian corn, similar in variety to what Ephraim Crockett would have grown. Each cob produces about one cub of ground cornmeal. My recipe for a pan of cornbread, which serves about nine people one serving each, requires two cups of cornmeal. My husband calculates that to feed their family of twelve for one year, the Crocketts would have had to plant (and harvest) at least one-half acre of Indian corn. (Flint corn typically produces one ear per stalk, and matures quicker than dent corn.)
99. ANDHIST, Chapter XXXIX.

birds be suspended at its operation in the town for the ensuing year."[100] There is no record that the town was reprimanded or fined by the General Court for willfully breaking this law. Worse than the crows, Mother Nature gave the farmer the cold shoulder in 1816, which was almost universally known as "the year without a summer."[101] Snow fell every month of the year in Maine and it was so cold in August that one-half inch of ice formed (presumably on puddles and small ponds).

Several diaries written by early Pejepscot settlers offer personal glimpses into the challenges of daily life in the backcountry. In 1795, Squire Andrew Giddings (the prominent early settler with the oxen for hire),[102] noted the following in his journal:[103]

"Thursday 2d July came home again [from New Gloucester] with wife Children & oxen—un well yesterday [the ox] Evg Departed this Life. I hope to enjoy a more permanent happiness than is the portion of mortals in this nether world."

"Wednesday [August] 5h—hay making. no help. Mrs. Giddings went to [New Gloucester]—borrow'd of her father 15/ [shillings] wh. was for [son] Job. [Written to the side of this entry was the notation: "paid in needle wk"].

"Tuesday [August] 27th Will Haskel. getting seed hay—very warm—PM Wm went pickg blackbury so warm could not work."

William Plummer, a Revolutionary War veteran who came to Pejepscot with his brother Edward sometime between 1787 and 1789,[104] also left a diary that provides a window into those early days in the backcountry settlement. Plummer, like James Wagg, Jr., had seen action with the Continental Army at Saratoga and had spent the winter with General Washington at Valley Forge. He was born in

---

100. ANDHIST, Chapter XXXIX.
101. "The year without a summer" (1816) occurred due to climate abnormalities that affected the entire Northern Hemisphere, causing major food shortages. The abnormalities were most likely the result of the "massive" volcanic eruption of Mount Tambora in Indonesia in April of 1815. National Park Service website. "1816 – The Year Without A Summer." https://www.nps.gov/articles/000/1816-the-year-without-summer.htm#:~:text=1816%2C%20also%20known%20as%20the,ground%20and%20the%20ocean's%20surface.
102. Squire Andrew Giddings, a descendant of the famous Pilgrim pastor at Leyden, Rev. John Robinson, was born September 22, 1763, in Gloucester, Massachusetts. He became a sailor in his youth, and on one of his sailing adventures was taken prisoner at St. Christopher in the West Indies. Eventually, he was sent to England, where an old friend got him hired onto a whaling vessel. After eighteen months of whaling, Giddings came back to New York, but made three more trips to Europe, building up his nest egg. In 1787, tired of the sailing life, he purchased a large tract of land in Pejepscot, then still wilderness. Squire Giddings lived in Pejepscot/Danville until his death (at almost eighty-four) on June 22, 1847. He was a prodigious diarist, writing in very fine, small script. AHS. Andrew Giddings folder, diaries, and other sources.
103. Squire Giddings' diaries are in the possession of AHS. Some of the entries have been made available online.
104. ANDHIST, p. 711.

Scarborough (his wife was from Cape Elizabeth), and relocated after the war to the Pejepscot Claim.[105] Plummer was a succinct, yet poignant diarist, as revealed in the following entries:[106]

"Saturday November 24 the 1804 ... youngest Child taken Sick"

"Sunday November 25th 1804 Very warm all day timothy very Sick indeed Betwixt 11 and 12 Timothy Died. Clear & pleasant evening how vain are all things hear—swift was his flight Short was his load"

"Tuesday November 26th the 1804 a Remarkable warm day Buryed my Little Son timothy. The Lord giveth and the Lord taketh"

The first physician to the area, Dr. John Thorne, did not arrive in Pejepscot until 1805.[107] As a result, deaths like that of little Timothy Plummer were far too common. The ill and injured were treated with limited medical knowledge, and such herbal remedies as the housewife had at hand. Women gave birth at home, attended by other mature females (and later, midwives). It was still not uncommon for women to die in childbirth or from complications related to giving birth (such as infection).[108] Complete and accurate death records for Pejepscot are hard to come by. We know that James and Dorcas Wagg's firstborn son died at nine days old, but we do not know how many other babies died (or from what they perished), nor how many women died in childbirth. (One could perhaps estimate how many wives a man lost to childbirth by counting the wives of child-bearing age he outlived.) Dorcas (Strout) Wagg gave birth to seven children and all but her

---

105. STARBIRD and Early Settler's List for the Pejepscot Claim and Little's Gore, edited by David C. Young of the Androscoggin Historical Society.
106. William Plummer's diary entries taken from the June 1992 Newsletter of the Androscoggin Historical Society No. 6. Here are a two more interesting entries from 1806:
"Monday June 16 the 1806 clear & cold & a Remarkable Eclipse all most total & one Star to be seen until the eclips was almost over"
"Wednesday Sepr 3th (1806) ... Rain with a Remarkable heavy gail of wind at N E—blew down trees and the corn all flat to the ground & fences all flat & some buildings—killed some cattle it was a distressing time after a great Drought Nothing more Remarkable But a man killd by the falling of a tree at cathans."
107. In ANDHIST, Chapter XXXIX, historian George Thomas Little says Dr. Thorne did not arrive until 1807; however, I found a receipt in the town of Pejepscot's miscellaneous bills folder 1803-1810 (Danville files, AHS) that suggests the doctor was in town as early as 1805. On July 10, 1805, Selectmen Andrew Giddings and Job Lane, acting as Overseers of the Poor, authorized a payment to Dr. Thorne in the amount of $11.28 for "medicine and attendance on Wm Rowe an indigent person."
108. Ephraim and Rebecca's daughter Priscilla (Crockett) Stinchfield died in 1830 at age thirty-five, possibly from childbirth (or complications resulting from giving birth). Priscilla's last living child was born in 1828 and so she would have been due to give birth again in 1830, the year she died. If so, that baby died as well.

first survived to adulthood.[109] The Crockett family was fortunate in that all seven children birthed by Rebecca on the Pejepscot Claim survived, although son James lived just three years.

Social and Religious Life in Pejepscot

Not all was back-breaking labor in the early years on the Pejepscot Claim. The Crocketts and their neighbors experienced lighter moments, as well. Women enjoyed quilting bees in addition to wool breakings and spinning bees. The entire family attended corn huskings, a neighborhood event at which everyone pitched in to help a farmer husk his corn. Volunteers were rewarded for their efforts by a day of fun and a feast that included roast lamb as the main course.[110] Men helped one another with barn raisings, and women often packed up their sewing or breadboard and took their work on a social visit to their neighbor's. Also breaking up the monotony of their laborious lives—rare, once-in-a-lifetime events, which provided delightful entertainment (and fodder for gossip for many a day). One such memorable event occurred in the summer of 1816 and was noted by William Plummer in his diary:[111]

> "Thursday 11 July ... an Elephant Passed Thrue this Town this evening
>
> Friday 12 July ... William to see the Elephant
>
> Saturday 13 July 1816 ... I went to see the Elephant"

Unfortunately, the pachyderm was "shot Dead by some Bad Person unknown In the Town of Alfred on his Return South."[112] Let us hope that the Crockett and the Wagg families had the opportunity to go see the elephant before it left the area.

Pejepscot had no settled minister until December of 1808.[113] Instead, the town was visited occasionally over the years by traveling ministers and missionaries of several different (and competing) Christian denominations, including Congregational,

---

109. STARBIRD, Wagg family history, Danville files, AHS.
110. ANDHIST, Chapter VII.
111. Diary entries taken from the June 1992 Newsletter of the Androscoggin Historical Society No. 6.
112. Diary of William Plummer, July 26, 1816. Taken from the June 1992 Newsletter of the Androscoggin Historical Society No. 6.
113. ANDHIST, Chapter XXXIX.

Universalist, and Baptist. Pejepscot was also a stop on one of the Maine tours of the well-known Methodist evangelist, the Reverend Jesse Lee, the "apostle of Methodism."[114] Because the town had no settled minister, required by Massachusetts law, Pejepscot was fined in 1808 and had to send Treasurer Lemuel Dyer to Portland to try and get the fine relieved.[115]

The lack of settled ministers was not for lack of trying, however. On November 28, 1804, Selectmen Andrew Giddings and Benning Wentworth authorized Treasurer Dyer to pay W. Thomas Barnes $16 toward hiring preachers for four sabbaths. Also, on April 3, 1805, Giddings and Job Lane (another selectman) authorized Dyer to pay himself $18 for preachers he hired in 1804 in the "predestinarian Baptist profession." On May 26, 1806, Selectmen George Leach and Benjamin Arnold authorized a payment of $12.50 to former selectman Job Lane for hiring "preachers in the Universalist Society or profession for this town."[116] (Residents of Pejepscot were apparently an eclectic Christian bunch.)

We do not know which religious meetings Ephraim Crockett and his family attended (if any); however, Ephraim's first cousin, Samuel Crockett (often mistaken by historians for Ephraim's younger brother Samuel)[117] was an ardent Free Will Baptist. For several years, Samuel Crockett was given the responsibility of securing preachers of that denomination for the community. On April 3, 1805, selectmen Andrew Giddings and Job Lane authorized a payment to Samuel Crockett in the amount of $18 out of monies approved in 1804 for the hiring of Free Will Baptist

---

114. ANDHIST, Chapter XXXIX. Born March 12, 1758, in Prince George's County, Virginia, Jesse Lee was ordained as an American Methodist Episcopal clergyman around 1789. He went on to become a well-known missionary, credited with establishing Methodism in New England from Connecticut to Maine. Rev. Lee visited Maine at least twice, in 1793 and 1795. People often traveled miles to hear him preach his fervent sermons.

115. ANDHIST, Chapter XXXIX. I am unclear what the amount of the fine was (for not having a settled minister) or if the town got off from paying it; however, it cost Pejepscot $7.40 (travel and attendance expenses) to send Lemuel Dyer to go and plead their case.

116. These three receipts for preaching in Pejepscot from 1804-1806 can be found at the AHS, Danville files, Town of Pejepscot Msc. Bills—1803-1810 folder.

117. Regrettably, it seems that Auburn historian Charles Starbird (STARBIRD), knowing Ephraim Crockett had a younger brother Samuel (also a Revolutionary War veteran), assumed that Samuel followed his older brother to Pejepscot. On the contrary, all evidence points to the fact that Ephraim's brother remained in Cape Elizabeth with his father. Rather, it is Ephraim and Samuel's first cousin Samuel who came into the backcountry. This mistake by Starbird has led to the perpetual conflating of the two Samuels—Ephraim's brother and his cousin—by other historians who took Starbird's genealogy at face value. After I realized the two Samuels must have been mixed up (the truth of which dawned on me slowly as I perused deeds, town records, and other information), I pieced together their true relationship using CANDAGE'S genealogy. Ephraim Crockett (and his brother, Samuel) and Samuel Crockett of Pejepscot share the same set of grandparents. Their fathers were brothers. Ephraim's father was Richard Crockett (III), the eldest son of Richard Crockett, Jr. and Mary (Robinson) Crockett. Cousin Samuel's father was George Crockett, the youngest son of Richard and Mary Crockett. It is unclear (to me, anyway) when cousin Samuel arrived in Pejepscot, but it was much later than when Ephraim came. Ephraim, who was eighteen years older than Samuel, might initially have housed his cousin out of family fealty when the younger man first arrived in the backcountry, thus contributing to the confusion.

preachers.[118] According to Danville historian Charles Starbird, Samuel Crockett, was "a man of deep religious convictions and a leader among the Free Will Baptists in Pejepscot." He was tasked by the Freewill Baptists (and the town, apparently) with securing preaching in that denomination for the years 1805, 1806, and 1807.[119] Cousin Samuel, a man of intense feeling (as one might expect from a Freewill Baptist), was also a bit of a rabble-rouser (as we will see).

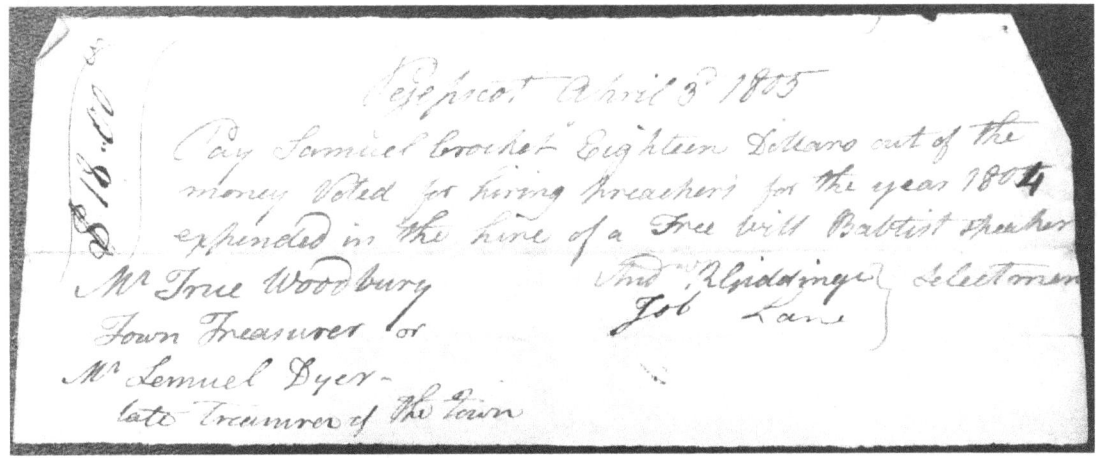

Authorization by Pejepscot selectmen for the payment of $18 to Samuel Crockett for hiring preaching in the Free Will Baptist profession for the year of 1804.
(Danville files, AHS. Jennifer Wixson photo.)[120]

Political Life in Pejepscot

In 1802, the unorganized settlements of Pejepscot Claim Plantation (where the Crockett, Wagg, and Dingley families lived) and Little's Gore (a triangle of land near New Gloucester claimed by Moses Little) officially joined together and organized to become the town of Pejepscot.[121] (In 1818, the inhabitants would petition to change the town's name to Danville.) The population in Pejepscot grew rapidly, not only because of the large number of children born per family, but also due to the flock of Revolutionary War veterans who moved with their families into the area at the conclusion of the war. The 1800 census (the second census of the United States)

---

118. AHS, Danville files, Town of Pejepscot Msc. Bills—1804-1810 folder.
119. STARBIRD. Crockett genealogy, Danville files, AHS.
120. The April 3, 1805 receipt to Samuel Crockett was found in the folder labeled "Town of Pejepscot Msc. Bills—1804-1810," located in the Danville files at AHS. Samuel was first cousin to Ephraim Crockett (and James Wagg, Jr.).
121. FamilySearch.org, Danville, Maine.

shows 701 inhabitants in Pejepscot and the Gore, nearly half of whom were under the age of ten. In 1810, the population had increased to 805 souls, and by 1820 the number of inhabitants in Danville was 1,088.[122]

The first town meeting in Pejepscot was held on April 12, 1802. According to Auburn historian George Thomas Little, at this meeting most of the business related to the building of roads.[123] A three-man commission (comprised of Squire Giddings, Solomon Larrabee, and a Captain Finson) was appointed to lay out roads, and by August of that year, the commission had planned for six public ways.[124] Many other roads would follow, all at great cost and personal labor of the citizenry:

> "The average annual [road] cost was $1,000 and each man worked out his road tax, receiving a dollar a day for his own services, 67 cents for the use of a yoke of oxen, 50 cents for a plough, and 84 cents for a cart. The charge for a plough apparently indicates a scarcity of those implements."[125]

In 1813, the town of Pejepscot voted to spend $900 on roads. Ephraim Crockett's road tax that year was $5.83. Most likely, he (as did other men) worked off his road tax. James Wagg, Sr.'s road tax in 1818 was $8.07. In 1820, Ephraim's road tax was $4.22. James Wagg, Sr. had passed away by 1820, so the tax was assessed to his two sons. James Wagg, Jr. was assessed $6.39 and his brother Samuel's share was $6.38.[126]

The town (and population) of Pejepscot was growing, but it was growing upon shifting political sands. Underlying the day-to-day activities of clearing fields, building roads, and putting food on the table was the awful truth residents faced that the bottom could drop out from under them at any moment. Why? Because the settlers on the Pejepscot Patent did not have legal title—fee simple[127]—to their land,

---

122. Population figures are taken from ANDHIST, Chapter XXXIX, written by George Thomas Little.
123. As a former selectman in Troy, Maine (and a former Budget Committee member), I can vouch for the fact that roads are still the hottest topic at our annual town meeting in March. Roads account for the second largest part of our taxes (after money spent on education), and a lively discussion always ensues, especially during a particularly challenging mud season.
124. AHS, Chapter XXXIX.
125. AHS, Chapter XXXIX.
126. Information came from Pejepscot/Danville Tax Assessment Records, Danville Files, AHS.
127. Burke and Snoe's Property: Examples and Explanations (2001, Aspen Publishers) describes fee simple as follows: "In English law, a fee simple or fee simple absolute is an estate in land, a form of freehold ownership. It is a way that real estate and land may be owned in common law countries, and is the highest possible ownership interest that can be held in real property."

or even to their improvements on that land. Freehold title was of paramount importance to these first citizens of the United States, especially the men who helped throw off the yoke of tyranny imposed by Great Britain upon her thirteen colonies. But during this time title to the Pejepscot Claim was still being debated by the Massachusetts Legislature and Supreme Judicial Court.

The Pejepscot Proprietors fought the settlers' claims to their homesteads tooth and nail, although their own claim to the same land was also built upon shaky ground. The claim of the Pejepscot Proprietors rested upon a 200-year-old grant from King James I of England, combined with a deed (with ambiguous boundaries) given in 1684 to wealthy Boston merchant Richard Wharton by the Indian sagamores Warumbee, Darumkin, Nimbanizett, Neonongansket, WeconDomhegon, and Wihikermett. (See copy of Warumbo deed on page 299, and a transcription of the deed, pages 405–407.)

Whose claim was paramount?

As early as 1798, the Massachusetts General Court attempted to work out a compromise in which settlers on the Pejepscot Patent were "quieted." I wonder how often, as Ephraim labored on the roads, working off his road assessment, he felt the shifting sands beneath his feet.

Shifting Boundaries Between the Pejepscot Proprietors and the Kennebec[128] Proprietors

The Pejepscot Proprietors felt the shifting sands long before Ephraim Crockett and other Revolutionary War veterans landed on the Pejepscot Claim. Although the Massachusetts General Court officially recognized the claim of the Pejepscot Proprietors in 1715, the court did not set or recognize the boundaries of their claim at the time.[129] Thirty years later, in the 1740s, an even larger claim (three million acres encompassing fifteen miles on either side of the Kennebec River) advanced by the Kennebec Proprietors under the Kennebec Patent[130] encroached on the territory of the Pejepscot Proprietors.[131] What ensued was a battle fought on two fronts: the battle in the Massachusetts General Court to establish the boundaries of the

---

128. I have altered the original spelling of "Kennebeck" to our present-day spelling, "Kennebec," except for quoted text.
129. ANDHIST, Chapter VI.
130. The Kennebec Patent was created in 1630 by a grant of land to the Plymouth Company from the Council of New England, under the authority of James I. (See Chapter 1.)
131. EMPIRE, p. 165.

Pejepscot Patent, and the battle with the Kennebec Proprietors, fought not only in the law courts, but also in the court of public opinion.

The struggle between the Pejepscot and Kennebec proprietors continued for more than two decades during the final throes of the French and Indian wars. According to J. G. Elder in his chapter on the Pejepscot Claim for the "Illustrated History of Androscoggin County, Maine," "The contest became intense, and the rival corporations pushed their claims with tireless energy."[132] Both sides flooded the General Court with proof of their competing claims. Likewise, the public was awash with pamphlets that mapped and described the competing patents. (These pamphlets might have given James Wagg, Sr. important information about which Great Lot to settle in the Pejepscot Claim.)

The fight continued until the Kennebec Proprietors ventured upon an unexpected legal angle—they attacked the legality of indigenous property rights,[133] the recognition of which had prevailed since the arrival of the English in the New World (albeit the English and Native Americans had different understandings of land ownership). The system of indigenous property rights had even been strengthened by Dummer's Treaty, a series of compromises from 1725 and 1729 between the English and Native Americans.[134] Now, however, the Kennebec Proprietors claimed that the English Crown—not Native Americans—had possessed the sole right to confer property ownership in New England.[135] Since many of the land transactions executed in Maine rested upon Indian deeds (including some between Native Americans and the Kennebec Proprietors themselves) this brazen claim would upset more than a century of legal precedence.

When overturning all Indian deeds proved impractical, however, the Kennebec Proprietors narrowed their efforts to attack certain individual deeds,[136] including the 1684 Warumbo deed to the Pejepscot Proprietors. If we had asked the Pejepscot Proprietors our main question from Chapter 6—"Who owned Dawnland?"—they

---

132. ANDHIST, Chapter VI.
133. EMPIRE, p. 167.
134. William Dummer, brother of Jeremiah Dummer (who had asserted indigenous property rights in his *A Defense of New England Charters*), and the Wabanaki worked with the astute and diplomatic Penobscot Chief Loron to draft a treaty successful in "bridging the divide between different cultures of ownership." Bottom line? In Dummer's Treaty the Wabanaki won reciprocity for their old land sales (i.e., they shared on-going ownership with the English, which entitled them to certain regular uses of the land, payments, and gifts). In exchange, the English got to think they "owned" the land. This détente worked well for twenty years until the Kennebec Proprietors threw a monkey-wrench into the mix by challenging the validity of Indian deeds.
135. EMPIRE, p. 167.
136. EMPIRE, p. 167.

The Sixth Generation

would have answered: "The six Indian Sagamores,"[137] who originally sold the land that became the Pejepscot Patent. In contrast to that reply, the Kennebec Proprietors would have answered the same question: "The King of England," who (via the Council of New England), originally granted the land that became the Kennebec Patent.

In 1763, King George III answered the question permanently (or so he thought). In the Proclamation of 1763, the Crown prohibited the buying of land by individuals or trading houses directly from Native Americans. Rather, land titles were now to be issued only by colonial English governments, which would enter (or had entered) into treaties with the Indians.[138] This proclamation was an attempt to extinguish any past, present, and future rights Native Americans had to their lands:

> "Since the change meant colonists obtained their land from a colonial grant, it eased the way toward an intellectual climate in which land title did not originate from the Indians at all, and these treaties were not purchases so much as gifts to pacify savage occupants rather than legitimate owners."[139]

Even before the Proclamation of 1763, the Pejepscot Proprietors had begun to feel themselves losing ground. The Kennebec Proprietors were well-heeled and well-connected, more so than the Pejepscot Proprietors. The Pejepscot Proprietors decided it was safer (and cheaper) to settle with the Kennebec Proprietors than continue to fight their opponents in court. On February 20, 1758, the Pejepscot Proprietors formed a committee to work with the Kennebec Proprietors to set a divisional line between the Pejepscot Patent and the Kennebec Patent.[140] Over the next seven years, the two companies made progress toward a settlement. On May 23, 1765, at a meeting of the Pejepscot Proprietors, members voted to award certain "partners" (shareholders) equivalent lands from "unappropriated lands belonging to

---

137. The six Sagamores were: Warumbee, Darumkin, Nimbanizett, Neonongansket, WeconDomhegon, and Wihikermett. These Indian chiefs sold the land around the Kennebec and Androscoggin Rivers and Merrymeeting Bay in 1684 to wealthy Boston merchant Richard Wharton. After his death, this real estate was purchased in 1714 for £140 by the original Pejepscot proprietors: Thomas Hutchinson, Adam Winthrop, John Watts, David Jeffries, Stephen Minot, Oliver Noyes, John Ruck, and John Wentworth. All these men were wealthy "Bostoniak," (a derogatory name given by Native Americans to Boston speculators and investors), excepting John Wentworth, who was a sea captain and church elder from Portsmouth, N.H. Later Wentworth became Lt. Governor of N.H. See "History of New Hampshire." John Norris McClintock. Boston: B.B. Russell, 1889.
138. EMPIRE, p. 193.
139. EMPIRE, p. 193. This intellectual understanding of indigenous land ownership would not change until 1980, when President Jimmy Carter signed the Maine Indian Claims Settlement Act.
140. ANDHIST, Chapter VI.

this Propriety ... in lieu of those divisions given up by [the agreement with the Kennebeck proprietors]."[141]

In the settlement, which was sealed in 1766, the Pejepscot Proprietors ceded 2,365 acres to the Kennebec Proprietors.[142] The Pejepscot Proprietors, nearly as resourceful as the Kennebec Proprietors, found a way to make up for that loss of land, however. If they could not push their boundaries to the south and east (because they would overlap the Kennebec Patent), the Pejepscot Proprietors would push their boundaries north and west.[143] The Pejepscot Proprietors latched onto the ambiguous nature of their northern boundary, which, in the underlying 17th century Warumbo deed, had simply been described as the "uppermost" falls on the Androscoggin River. What was almost certainly meant to be Ten-Mile Falls[144] (now, Lisbon Falls), was suddenly claimed by the Pejepscot Proprietors to be Twenty-Mile Falls (now, Great Falls at Lewiston-Auburn).[145] Before the northern boundary to the Pejepscot Patent could be officially set, however, the Revolutionary War intervened, stalling the debate over the patent's boundaries.

Enter the Settlers and the Little Family

The dispute between the Pejepscot Proprietors and the settlers on the Pejepscot Claim arose after thousands of land-hungry Revolutionary War veterans poured into the backcountry of central Maine prior to and following the close of the war. In the eyes of the settlers—especially the soldiers—a massive land grant that rested its validity upon a 17th century deed from long-conquered Native Americans (either exterminated or pushed north into Canada) certainly did not present as strong a

---

141. BAXTER, Vol. XXIV.
142. According to the minutes of the Meeting of the Pejepscot Proprietors on May 23, 1765 (per BAXTER) the claims to be adjusted out of "unappropriated lands" were: to the heirs of Adam Winthrop, who lost 700 acres; the heirs of Job Lewis, who lost 500 acres; J. Fairweather, who lost 665 acres; and the assigns of Cap. John Watts, who lost 500 acres.
143. ANDHIST, Chapter VI.
144. Ten-Mile Falls was so named because it was located ten miles above Brunswick on the Androscoggin River. Length in miles from a particular point was a common way of naming places, such as Twenty-five Mile Pond (now Unity Pond or Winnecook Lake), which was twenty-five miles via water from Fort Halifax in Winslow.
145. Moses Little, an elected agent for the Pejepscot Proprietors (and a notorious land speculator, who had bought into the Pejepscot Patent himself) swore that the original grantee of the land from the Indians, Thomas Purchase, had dug a cellar and built a house near Twenty-Mile Falls, not Ten-Mile Falls. During the first trial to determine the northern boundary of the Pejepscot Proprietors, the lawyers claimed that if Purchase had built a home near Twenty-Mile Falls, certainly, the boundary extended as far north as that. When the jury retired, one jurist scoffed at that claim. "What a piece of work they made in giving in their evidence about the cellar! ... I swar I dug that cellar myself about fourteen years ago when I was there loging." This ended in a mistrial being declared. A second trial to determine the northern boundary of the Pejepscot Patent was held, but that verdict was overturned, and so the saga dragged on. LIBERTY, p. 48. Later, the Pejepscot Proprietors would make the outrageous claim that the "upper falls" was even further upriver, at Livermore Falls.

claim to the land as their own. Settlers on the Kennebec Patent also felt that their claims were stronger than that of the proprietors, who rested their claim upon a grant from the now-defeated King of England. In addition, the general feeling among the populace was that all real estate previously belonging to Tories should be confiscated by Massachusetts and given to her veterans for the promised (but not yet delivered) bounty land. Any additional land should be sold or parceled out to settlers at reasonable rates.

In 1780, when Ephraim Crockett and the Wagg family first ventured onto the Pejepscot Claim, the boundaries to the Pejepscot Patent, although tentatively agreed upon by the Pejepscot and Kennebec proprietors, had yet to be legally settled with Massachusetts. In addition, several of the Pejepscot Proprietors were Tories, most notably the wealthy slave-owner Isaac Royall, Jr.[146] (for whom the neighboring town of Royalsborough, now Durham, was named). When the British were attacking American minutemen at Lexington and Concord (after which Ephraim Crockett enlisted in the Provincial Army), Isaac Royall was putting himself and his family on a boat for Halifax, Nova Scotia.[147] In 1778, Royall, who had inherited his father's extensive estate, including a sugar plantation in Antigua and dozens of slaves, was named as one of three hundred Massachusetts citizens who had "gone over to the enemy"[148]—and his estate was confiscated.

Another notable Tory, Samuel Waterhouse, who had been one of the most active members of the Pejepscot Proprietors in the 1760s, fled to England with his wife Hannah (Lewis) Waterhouse and their family (most likely before the hostilities broke out). Waterhouse was a Boston merchant and son-in-law of Job Lewis (for whom the city of Lewiston was named).[149] His wife Hannah was the sole heir of Lewis' extensive estate, including that proprietor's share of the Pejepscot Patent. (Waterhouse himself owned a partial share in the patent.) Before they absconded,

---

146. According to Elise Lemire ("Black Walden: Slavery and its Aftermath in Concord, Massachusetts." Philadelphia: University of Pennsylvania Press, 2019), Royall was born in Antigua on a sugar plantation established by his father. The plantation was completely dependent upon slave labor. Royall relocated to Massachusetts, and after inheriting his father's estate became one of the wealthiest persons in the Commonwealth. Royall's home in Medford is now a museum, the Isaac Royall House, which estate has the only slave quarters in the northeast U.S.
147. "Black Walden: Slavery and its Aftermath in Concord, Massachusetts." Philadelphia: University of Pennsylvania Press, 2019.
148. See James Henry Stark. "Banishment Act of the State of Massachusetts." The loyalists of Massachusetts and the other side of the American Revolution (1910 ed.). Salem, Mass.: Salem Press. p. 137–140.
149. LEWISTON, p. 5. Lewiston was incorporated in 1795.

however, Samuel and Hannah Waterhouse mortgaged most of their Maine real estate[150] in case the upstart colonists won the war.

With the Tory shareowners of the Pejepscot Patent out of the country, management of the patent came into the hands of Moses Little, a wealthy farmer of Newbury, Massachusetts (enslaved persons performed the actual labor on his farm).[151] Little was a representative to the General Court and a notorious land speculator. In his younger years, Moses Little had been a surveyor of the King's Woods, which opened his eyes to the potential value of backcountry lands.[152] In addition to his Massachusetts real estate, Moses Little invested in large tracts of land in Vermont, New Hampshire, and Maine.[153] Unlike his Tory counterparts, Little, had served as a captain in the French and Indian wars, and later distinguished himself as a colonel in the Revolutionary War.[154] Despite Moses Little's age (he was fifty-one in the spring of 1775), under severe fire, he led a regiment of soldiers at the Battle of Bunker Hill. According to Little's descendant and historian, George Thomas Little: "Forty of his regiment were killed or wounded; men fell on either side of him, but Colonel Little himself escaped unharmed."[155]

George Thomas Little describes his ancestor as "… a man of indomitable energy and great force of character,"[156] which is a sugar-coated way of saying Moses Little was a hard man. A commander of men, he was used to having his own way. Little's personality came across to the settlers as greedy and mean. Moses Little made the lives of backcountry settlers miserable. Viewing most of the settlers as squatters, Little constantly dunned them for rent or took them to court for cutting his (or the Pejepscot Proprietor's) trees. He also threatened to throw settlers off

---

150. LEWISTON, p. 5, 284. Also, see CCROD Book 9, p. 345, in which the document states that on June 10, 1771, Samuel Waterhouse and his wife Hannah, as sole heir to Job Lewis' estate, mortgage for £120 with interest two parcels of land in Maine, 1,150 acres in Brunswick and 1,800 acres in Royalsboro.
151. LITTLE, p. 5. In 1773, Moses Little sold a slave by the name of "Caesar" to President Eleazar Wheelock of Dartmouth College for twenty pounds. "I have determined to buy the Negro if he proves to be the Slave which you take him to be," Wheelock wrote to Little. According to the Little family historian, most of the leading families of Newbury were slaveholders at that time.
152. LITTLE, p. 4.
153. LITTLE, p. 4. In 1750, thanks to Moses Little's efforts with the Massachusetts General Court, he "succeeded in obtaining for (the proprietors of Bakerstown), a township of land in Maine in exchange for one previously granted and found to be within the borders of New Hampshire." In addition to buying into (and working for) the Pejepscot Proprietors, Little (and his son, Josiah) purchased another large grant of land in Maine, which today is comprised of Poland, Minot, and part of Auburn.
154. LITTLE, p. 5. In 1779, Col. Little turned down the position of brigadier-general due to ill health.
155. LITTLE, p. 4-5. George Washington held Col. Little in high esteem, apparently because he was one of Washington's few officers who did not complain. "[Washington] mentioned him as a model to some other officers who were complaining of the character of the provisions, saying that Colonel Little had found no time to grumble at hardships of that sort." Col. Little served in several other important battles until he was forced to resign due to ill health.
156. LITTLE, p. 4.

what he believed to be his or patent property. When Moses Little lost his ability to speak in 1781 as the result of a stroke, "settlers interpreted [the stroke] as the just desserts of his aggressive ambition."[157]

After Moses Little's stroke, his vast land interests in the District of Maine (and elsewhere), including his interest in the Pejepscot Patent, were taken over by his eldest surviving son,[158] Josiah Little, also of Newbury, Massachusetts. The younger Little, unfortunately, turned out to be just as hard and mean as his father.[159] Unlike his father, however, Josiah Little did not have the cachet of military credentials to back him up. The younger Little served in the Revolutionary War only five days (and those without seeing any action).[160] Josiah's lack of military service appears to have made him more resentful toward the Revolutionary War veterans who settled on Pejepscot Patent lands—and certainly would have made the veterans more resentful of him.[161] While there is no doubt the settlers disliked his father, Colonel Little, they at least respected the Colonel's military service. By contrast, the settlers absolutely hated Colonel Little's son. They had no reason to respect Josiah Little, especially as he—born in 1747, with a golden spoon in his mouth—was of the same generation as many of the hardscrabble veterans like Ephraim Crockett, James Wagg, Jr., and William Dingley, who had put themselves in harm's way during the Revolution.

George Little, in his flattering family history, describes Josiah as "strongly resembling" his father Moses, and a "man of great energy and business talent." With an amazing blindness to the reality of the situation, he also gives Josiah Little credit with saving the Pejepscot Patent from the claims of the settlers. George Little writes: "[Josiah Little's] influence in the legislature prevented at one time the sacrifice of state lands in Maine."[162] Nowhere in his history does Little recognize the sacrifice made by the Revolutionary War veterans in the Pejepscot Claim (and elsewhere). Nor does Little recognize that it was the settlers—not his ancestors—who cleared

---

157. LIBERTY, p. 48.
158. LITTLE, p. 5. Josiah Little was the third child (second son) of eleven born to Moses and his wife Abigail. His older brother Michael lived only a month. Two of Josiah Little's sisters (Sarah and Anna) passed away in August of 1775, bringing their father back from the war front for their funeral.
159. LIBERTY, p. 48.
160. Massachusetts Soldiers and Sailors in the War of the Revolution; Little, Josiah; Volume 9, p. 870.
161. Perhaps Josiah Little resented the Revolutionary War veterans because they were what he was not. As an educated man, Little might have been familiar with the famous quote by the 18th century English man of letters and moralist, Dr. Samuel Johnson: "Every man thinks meanly of himself for not having been a solider, or not having been at sea."
162. LITTLE, p. 6.

and improved the land; built the roads; and paid the taxes. (Pejepscot town records show that the Littles paid real estate taxes, but at a lesser, non-resident rate.)[163]

On March 8, 1787, the Massachusetts legislature passed a Resolve that declared that the "uppermost" falls described in the Warumbo deed to Richard Wharton (and the deeds underlying it) was indeed Twenty-Mile Falls.[164] This was exactly as Moses Little had claimed and should have made his son Josiah and the rest of the Pejepscot Proprietors (those who remained in this country, anyway) ecstatic. But the legislature pointed out in that Resolve that some of the other boundaries in the Pejepscot Patent were not established and therefore directed the proprietors "not to locate or dispose of any [unappropriated] land on the Androscoggin" and other areas. In addition, in 1787, the General Court "required that the Proprietors grant to the settlers 100-acre lots that encompassed their respective improvements."[165] This condition Josiah Little rigidly refused to accept and did not comply with.[166] Little continued to visit his vast acreage in Maine, harassing those whom he, too, regarded as squatters. As a result of this brazenness, on March 21, 1793, the General Court threatened to prosecute any of the Pejepscot Proprietors who continued to defy them. In this new Resolve, the legislature opened the door to "quieting" the settlers,[167] who were beginning to complain to their representatives to the Massachusetts legislature about treatment at the hands of Little.[168]

To exemplify the nature of Josiah Little's character, Alan Taylor in "Liberty Men and Great Proprietors–The Revolutionary Settlement of the Maine Frontier, 1760-1820," relates the story of the time that Little, pronouncing the rapids in the Androscoggin River between Lewiston and Auburn to be a hindrance to navigation, stubbornly (and some might say, stupidly) decided to blow them up, losing a hand in the process.[169] Nevertheless, the stiff-necked Little refused to allow his disability and advancing age slow him down. "Oblivious to threats [to his person]," Taylor continues, "he routinely visited every settlement at will to harangue the settlers about paying, to note newly-settled lots, to seek out timber trespassers, and to take depositions for use in court cases."[170]

---

163. Pejepscot town receipts, Danville files, AHS.
164. ANDHIST, Chapter VI.
165. LEWISTON, p. 7.
166. LEWISTON, p. 7.
167. ANDHIST, Chapter VI.
168. ELP, summary.
169. LIBERTY, p. 48. This incident is noted in LITTLE, as well.
170. LIBERTY, p. 48. LITTLE says: "Every year until [Josiah Little] was past eighty he used to visit his property in Maine, New Hampshire, and Vermont, driving over the rough roads alone..."

When Little could not visit Maine personally, he sent out agents on his behalf to ferret out which settlers had signed petitions of complaint against him and to strongarm squatters into buying the land from him (at extraordinarily high prices). During one such visit, Little's agent called upon William Dingley. Regarding the Revolutionary War veteran, the agent jotted in his notebook: "Offered to sell him land. says he will purchase [scribbled out word]. did not sign petition sent [to the General Court] but another. Been on [his land] 12 yrs."[171] During that same trip the agent also called on Patrick Arras (Irish),[172] who, like the Waggs, was one of the earliest settlers in Pejepscot. That visit did not even go as well as the Dingley visit. Little's agent noted in his book: "...[Arras] Said Genl Court wants [to give] them the land. [I said] not to bet on it that it was not his land but our land."[173]

Josiah Little attempted to get very high prices for his land, $6.50 to $7 per acre, according to the agent's book (and other resources). Aggrieved settlers must have felt that those were Boston prices—hardly prices for land "in a state of nature" (i.e., undeveloped)—and most refused to pay. In contrast, the Massachusetts General Court had, at one point, urged the Great Proprietors to accommodate the settlers by selling them their real estate for $1 per acre.[174]

Backlash against the perceived avarice of the proprietors, which had been

---

171. AGENTBOOK. While researching this history, I discovered an old hand-sewn booklet—containing about eleven, five-by-four-inch pages—among the Danville records at the Androscoggin Historical Society. The owner of the booklet is not identified. However, it is not Josiah Little (as he is mentioned in the book). The notebook appears to have belonged to an agent sent out by Little. Here are some other entries from the agent's record book:

"Dominicus Libby has been on [his land] 21 years, wishes to buy, had part of money by then. said they won't let Col. Little have it. [will] give what land is worth. never saw petition [to the General Court for relief] or signed it."

"John Martin, offered to sell him lot. gave no answer."

"Abner Highland, good land house & barn. offered him land for $6.50 [an acre]. said he would not buy at all. & thot he did not see petition, but told somebody to sign for him."

"Benj Alden & Joseph Sampson very good land, two good houses & barns & outbuildings. offered land as agreed in old bond between Moses Little & Alden on what it would be worth in state of nature [i.e. without improvements]. both said they never saw or signed the Petition. Sampson says was in the Western County at the time."

172. Patrick Arras/Arris was also known as Patrick "Irish" (because he was a native of County Kilkenny, Ireland). Arras, with his wife Anna, were some of the earliest settlers in Pejepscot, where probably four of their eight children were born. (ANDHIST, Chapter XL). The 1804 settlement lists Arras on Range 5, Lot 1, a lot of 39 acres with a settlement price of $58.50 ($1.50 per acre). (ELP) Patrick Arras probably held out hope until his death at the age of seventy-six in 1810 that the land would be given to him as promised by Massachusetts or, at the very least, that the state would honor the 1804 settlement. However, I can find no evidence that either Arras or any of his four sons purchased the family homestead. (See CCROD for John, Patrick, Jr., James and Thomas Arras/Arris/Irish.) Instead, the family apparently moved out of the area. Patrick Arras, Jr., as well as at least one of his siblings, died in Lisbon, where the family relocated after the patriarch's death. (Death date for Patrick Sr. and other information taken from the online resource, "ReedFamilyPages," genealogy of the Reed and Hodgkins families, Patrick Arras.)

173. AGENTBOOK.

174. ELP

simmering for years, broke into outright violence. On July 13, 1800, some unknown settlers "plunder[ed] the tools from a sawmill leased by Josiah Little of the Pejepscot Proprietors to Stephen Chase, a proprietary supporter."[175] The following night, "a shot [was] fired into the wood house belonging to Amos Davis, a surveyor for the Pejepscot Proprietors."[176] On the night of August 14th "a dozen armed settlers discharged their muskets around the house of Robert Anderson, a supporter of the Pejepscot Proprietors."[177]

Josiah Little, derisively nicknamed "the Sagamore,"[178] was the major target of the settlers' anger. On the night of September 22, 1800, about twenty settlers disguised as Indians attacked the home of Ezra Purington, where Little was then staying. Ephraim Crockett's cousin, Samuel Crockett (the leader of the Free Will Baptists in Pejepscot) was one of those imitation Indians who took shots at the house and lobbed stones through the windows. Little received minor injuries in the attack (a stone hit his lip), but otherwise was not physically harmed. He was fearful for his life (or claimed he was), writing later perhaps a bit melodramatically: "[The attackers] continued their demand to mr Purington to deliver up my body & they would send it to hell with oaths & Curses and declared on his refusal [to give up Little] that all in the house should be destroyed together."[179] During the attack, Purington hid Josiah Little in the basement and confronted the mob, which eventually dispersed. (David Hildreth, who had a mill on the Little Androscoggin River and whose voice Little had recognized, was charged in the attack. Ultimately, Hildreth had to dismantle his barn to pay his fines.)[180]

The violence continued and began to turn neighbor against neighbor in Pejepscot and Lewiston. Sides were taken. You were either with the proprietors or you were against them,[181] and as there were more *against* the proprietors, those who

---

175. LIBERTY, p. 268. Liberty notes the information came from a deposition given by Chase.
176. LIBERTY, p. 268.
177. LIBERTY, p. 269.
178. LEWISTON, p. 141.
179. LEWISTON, p. 140. This account is a quote from a source author Douglas I. Hodgkin used; however, he does not identify the source. Rather, in writing this section of his book, Hodgkin notes he has used Little's journal, deposition information, family letters, and more.
180. LIBERTY, p. 268-269 and LEWISTON, p. 140-142. Hildreth had to dismantle his barn and sell it, as well as the glass and sashes from his house, to pay his fine. LEWISTON, p. 142. In the proposed 1804 settlement, Hildreth was awarded Range 7, Lot 1; 100 acres for $185.60 ($1.86 per acre). Unfortunately for him, however, Range 7 had been allotted to Josiah Little by the Pejepscot Proprietors. Little obviously refused to sell to Hildreth (CCROD), and Hildreth disappears from Lewiston history.
181. LIBERTY, p. 264-270. Taylor adds an excellent and helpful appendix to his book documenting all incidents of "extra-legal violence" that occurred during these land controversies.

supported Josiah Little often found themselves outnumbered.[182] On November 26, 1800, five men, including Samuel Crockett, once again attacked the home of Purington (Josiah Little was not present this time) and assaulted him. In a deposition given later, Purington wrote: "I was obliged to get some of my neighbors that were friendly, to watch with me for my safty & the Safety of my Family and intrest, while in Lewistown and have since moved with my Family to Windham for Safety."[183]

Proposals to "Quiet" the Settlers

In the meantime, back in Boston, in 1798 the General Court had authorized the Attorney General to submit the land controversy to the Supreme Judicial Court, allowing for the appointment of several "disinterested persons" to referee the differences between the Pejepscot Proprietors and the Commonwealth of Massachusetts. In the proposed settlement, in exchange for lands awarded to the proprietors by the Commonwealth, Massachusetts expected a release deed *from* the proprietors for what the commissioners decided to be state land.[184] The settlers were not forgotten in the Resolve, which allowed the three commissioners to quiet any settlers on undivided patent lands.[185] According to J.G. Elder in "The History of Androscoggin County:"

> "The conditions imposed by the General Court were that these settlers should have one hundred acres of land so laid out best as to include the improvements made by them, and for such sums of money and on such terms as the commissioners should judge reasonable."[186]

The disinterested persons performed their work—but it was all in vain. The Pejepscot Proprietors failed to deliver the necessary release deed to finalize the deal with Massachusetts.[187] (Most likely, the proprietors were not in agreement with the compromise and just ignored it.) As a result, a separate Resolve was passed in 1800

---

182. Also, from LEWISTON, p. 142: "On another occasion several men assaulted (Peter) Merrill (a supporter of Little and the Pejepscot proprietors) and his horse and 'afterwards David Hildreth called to me asking if I had my Guns ready, telling me that there was Indians in the woods.'" (The quotation came from Merrill's sworn deposition given after the attack.)
183. LEWISTON, p. 142.
184. ELP. Resolves 1798, c 64.
185. ELP, Resolves 1798, c 64 and summary.
186. ANDHIST, Chapter VI.
187. ELP, Resolves 1798, c 64 and summary.

that led to the appointment of a new three-person committee of commissioners to quiet the settlers on undivided patent lands. In 1804, the three commissioners—Nathaniel Dummer, John Lord, and Ichabod Goodwin—completed their work and presented their report to the legislature. The report and accompanying maps were then filed with the Secretary of State.[188] (See the 1804 settlement map and inset map on pages 354 and 355, respectively.)

In the 1804 quieting proposal, the Pejepscot settlers were to be offered their land at very fair prices. According to the 1804 proposal, those prices ranged from $.69 per acre to $1.90 per acre, with most on the lower side.[189] (Given the price range, the commissioners appear to have taken into consideration the location and quality of the settler's land.) Following are some examples of what was proposed for settlers on the Pejepscot Claim. To each man's award—noted in bold—I have added personal information:[190]

1. **Ephraim Crockett** (Revolutionary war veteran formerly from Cape Elizabeth.) Range 3, Lot 1; **63 acres for $78.62 ($1.25 per acre).**
2. **James Wagg and James Wagg Jr.** (Wagg, Jr. was a veteran, also from Cape Elizabeth.) Range 3, Lot 4; **93 acres for $72.54 ($.78 per acre).**
3. **Samuel Crockett** (Ephraim's religious cousin and rabble rouser, not a veteran, formerly from Windham.) Range 8, Lot 3; **100 acres for $190.40 ($1.90 per acre).**
4. **William Dingley** (A veteran formerly from Cape Elizabeth.) Range 2, Lot 2; **91 acres for $129.58 ($1.42 per acre).**
5. **Charles Bisbee** (Ephraim Crockett's neighbor to the north.) Range 3, Lot 2; **77 acres for $54.51 ($.71 per acre).**
6. **James Elwell** (Ephraim Crockett's neighbor to the south, formerly from North Yarmouth.) Range 2, Lot 3; **62 ½ acres for $$73.50 ($1.18 per acre).**
7. **William Plummer** (Diarist who buried his young son Timothy, a veteran formerly from Scarborough.) NW of Lot 17 in Range 3; **100 acres for $147.20 ($1.47 per acre).**

We do not know how this 1804 settlement was received by the settlers. After

---

188. ELP summary.
189. ELP, EA7-1804. List of settlers in Pejepscot/Danville with referee awards.
190. Information about the awards noted from the 1804 settlement came from ELP, EA7-1804.

The Sixth Generation

all, the Revolutionary War veterans had been promised by the Continental Congress 100 acres for enlisting or reenlisting. Those from Massachusetts who signed up for three years were promised double that amount of land. (The soldiers did not need to serve all three years if the war ended first.)[191] The promised land had not yet materialized, although the war had ended two decades earlier. No doubt, upon seeing the compromise, many of the veterans might have felt betrayed by the state and nation they had served. But it is also possible that the settlers—veterans included—would have received the 1804 quieting proposal with a sense of relief, knowing as they did that Josiah Little and his agents were demanding $6.50 to $7 per acre.[192]

---

191. In fact, Ephraim's younger brother, Samuel Crockett, who received a Maine land grant, had reenlisted for a period of three years, but served only a fraction of that enlistment because the war ended first. Samuel's earlier years of service, however, were taken into consideration for purposes of the land grant and a pension, which he also received. (Maine Archives—Revolutionary War Land Grant Bounties, Samuel Crockett.)

192. Price per acre offered by Josiah Little was taken from various deeds he executed, as well as from the agent's book, which noted that the price given to William Dingley was $6.50 per acre.

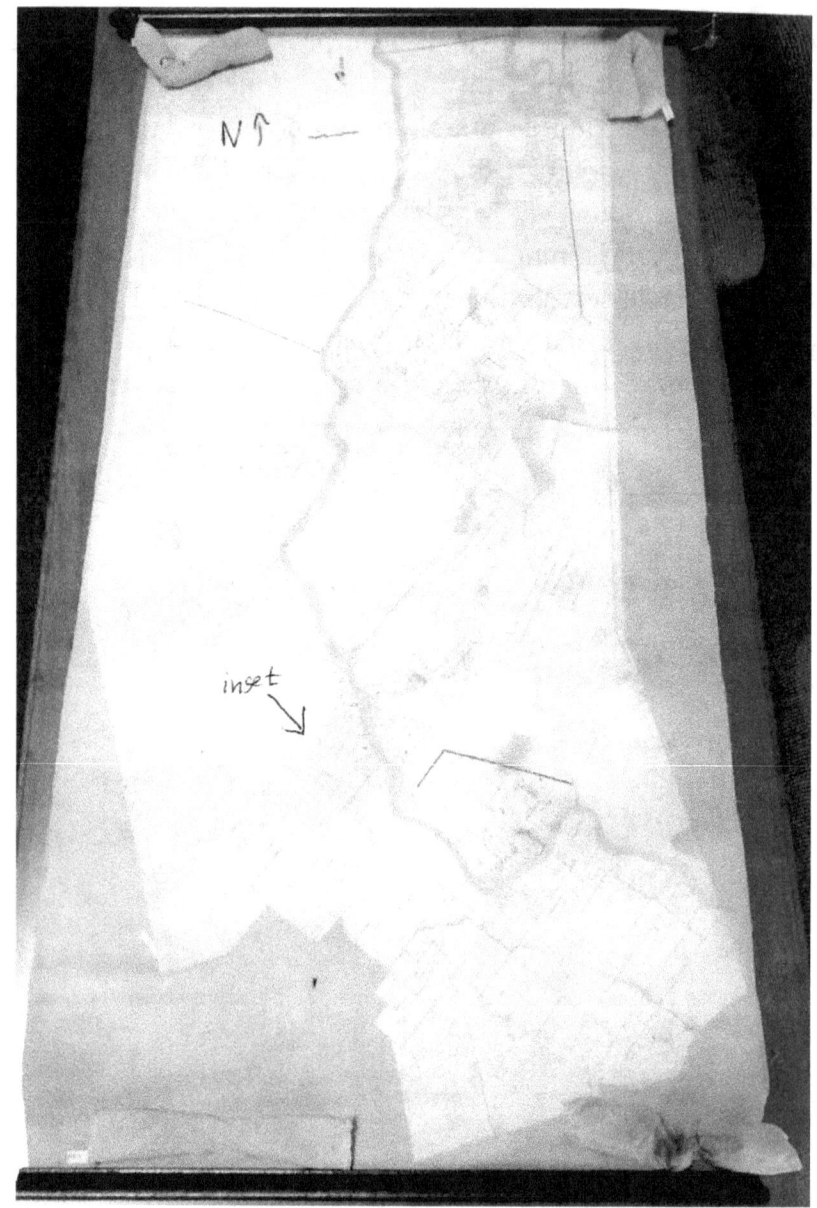

1804 map of settlers on the Pejepscot Patent presented to the Massachusetts General Court. The map was prepared by the three commissioners appointed by Governor Caleb Strong to "quiet" the settlers on the Pejepscot Patent, as provided for by the 1798 and 1800 Resolves. (See inset on opposite page for a close-up of lots settled by Revolutionary War veterans Ephraim Crockett, Jr., James Wagg, Jr., William Dingley, and others.)
(Photo courtesy of Caitlin Jones, Head of Reference, Massachusetts Archives.)[193]

---

193. Massachusetts archives. ELP, Series 85x, SC1/50 Map 1688. The directional indicator "N" and arrow showing the inset (shown in next image) were added for context by the author.

The Sixth Generation

Inset from 1804 map showing the lots proposed to "quiet" the Pejepscot settlers. The map with lots was prepared by the commissioners appointed to rectify the standoff between the proprietors and settlers. Starting at top right of map are the lots of three Revolutionary War veterans: James Wagg, Jr., who took up a lot with his father, James Wagg, Sr. (Range 3, Lot 4); three lots below the Waggs on the Androscoggin River is Ephraim Crockett (Range 3, Lot 1—his last name is mistakenly noted as "Chubb;" the handwritten correction is by the author for clarity),[194] and two lots below Ephraim is William Dingley, also on the river (Range 2, Lot 2). The proposed settlement was the result of two Resolves passed by the General Court of Massachusetts (in 1798 and 1800) to find a fair settlement between the settlers and the Pejepscot Proprietors. (Photo courtesy of Caitlin Jones, Head of Reference, Massachusetts Archives.)[195]

---

194. The accompanying handwritten list of "Settlers in Pejepscot" from the 1804 settlement clearly shows that it is "Ephraim Crockett" (not "Ephm. Chubb") on Range 3, Lot 1. ELP EA7-1804.
195. Massachusetts archives. ELP, Series 85x, SC1/50 Map 1688—close-up.

The Pejepscot Proprietors Strike Back

Incredibly, the Pejepscot Proprietors also refused to accept the 1804 settlement proposal.[196] Josiah Little ignored the report of the commissioners and continued to badger the General Court to legalize the patent's boundaries to the Pejepscot Claim. Once again, the settlers were caught in the crosshairs.

During the first decade of the 19th century, Little aggressively furthered the claims of the proprietors, in Pejepscot and Lewiston, as well as at the General Court in Boston. In addition, lawyers for some of the Tories (or their heirs) began to appear on the scene around the turn of the century, pressing the claims of *their* clients.

In 1804, Hannah Waterhouse, widow of Samuel Waterhouse and sole heir of her father, Job Lewis (a Pejepscot Proprietor), gave Boston attorney Henderson Inches power-of-attorney over her estate in Massachusetts "or elsewhere in North America."[197] (Inches, a Dickensian character, was aptly named, refusing to give an inch to the settlers.) Although Mrs. Waterhouse (and her daughters Hannah and Abigail) resided in England, having abandoned the country before the Revolutionary War—and likely had never stepped foot on Maine soil—she was nevertheless not averse to lining her pockets with Maine fleece. Before employing Attorney Inches, Mrs. Waterhouse utilized the services of Martin Brimmer, another Boston lawyer, to act as her power-of-attorney;[198] however, Brimmer appears to have been rather lackadaisical in his efforts for her in Maine and she replaced him with the indefatigable Inches.

Inches took over where his predecessor left off, with the low-hanging fruit in coastal Brunswick. After brow-beating Brunswick settlers to purchase their lots of land claimed by Mrs. Waterhouse, Inches moved up the Androscoggin River to Durham (formerly, Royalsborough).[199] Because some of those men in both Brunswick and Durham could not afford to buy their properties, Inches facilitated transactions by suggesting the settlers mortgage their real estate to him.[200] Mrs. Waterhouse's death June 7, 1807[201] appears to have stalled Inches' labor on her

---

196. ELP Summary.
197. CCROD, Book 47, Page 174. Hannah Waterhouse and her two daughters lived in Poole, England.
198. CCROD, Book 30, P. 408. Mrs. Waterhouse employed Brimmer as her POA in 1799.
199. CCROD, see 1805 deeds by Waterhouse, Hannah.
200. CCROD, see 1805 and later mortgages to Inches, Henderson.
201. The date of Mrs. Waterhouse's death was found in the court records from the CCP, March term 1812, when her daughters press their claim against Ephraim Crockett. Maine, Cumberland County Court of Common Pleas records, 1764-1839.

behalf, but he picked up his work again in late 1810 after receiving a new power-of-attorney from Mrs. Waterhouse's daughters and heirs, Hannah and Abigail Waterhouse.[202]

In one of the more egregious acts committed by Massachusetts after the war, rather than awarding the confiscated land of Tory and slave-owner Isaac Royall, Jr. to Revolutionary War soldiers, the Commonwealth returned Royall's extensive estate to his heirs after his death. (Royall died in England in 1781, of smallpox.)[203] The restoration of Royall's estate most likely occurred because, in his will, he bequeathed two thousand acres of land to Harvard College.[204] In fact, the money from the sale of that large tract of land endowed Harvard Law, the oldest law school in the nation. In 2017, Harvard finally acknowledged—with a plaque placed in front of the law school—that the labor of African American slaves created the wealth that had built the vaunted institution.[205] (In 2022, the long-time chair, the Royall Professor of Law, was finally retired.) Perhaps someday the school will acknowledge that much of the land that created Royall's wealth was tricked from Native Americans before being taken from backcountry settlers, many of whom were Revolutionary War veterans.

Final Settlements

After Attorney Inches received a power-of-attorney from the Waterhouse sisters, he worked his way further upriver to harass settlers in Pejepscot. Here, Inches met with some contumely. Not only were the settlers aware of the 1804 quieting proposal, but also these Revolutionary War veterans were not disposed to purchase the homesteads they had hewn from the wilderness from Royalists who had tucked back to England more than thirty-five years earlier.

Inches did make one early and important conquest, however: James Wagg, Sr. By 1811, when approached by Inches, James Wagg, Sr. was in his eighties. Probably

---

Court records, v. 13, 1811-1812, p. 396. (Image #406).
202. CCROD, Book 63, P. 193. Hannah and Abigail Waterhouse gave Inches their POA on November 9, 1810.
203. Royall's will allowed that the money from the sale of the 2,000 acres could be utilized for the establishment of a school of medicine or law, leaving it up to the institution to decide which. Harvard Law School, "The Legacy of Isaac Royall, Jr." https://exhibits.law.harvard.edu/legacy-isaac-royall-jr (and other sources). At one point, Royall and his father owned 64 enslaved persons, "more slaves than any other household in Massachusetts."
204. DURHAM, p. 9.
205. The Harvard Gazette, "At Law School, Honor for the Enslaved," Liz Mineo, Sept. 6, 2017. The article is about a new stone memorial with a plaque recognizing "…the enslaved whose labor created wealth that made possible the founding of Harvard Law School."

to easily secure fee simple title to his property for his heirs, the elderly Wagg paid the price that the attorney demanded on behalf of the Waterhouse sisters. After James Wagg capitulated, some other men followed suit.[206] But many did not. One of more dogged holdouts was Ephraim Crockett.

At the March 1812 term of the Court of Common Pleas held in Portland for Cumberland County, Ephraim Crockett was a defendant in a land dispute with the Waterhouse sisters (brought on their behalf by attorney Inches). Hannah and Abigail Waterhouse demanded (through the right of their mother, who had inherited the property) $1,000 in damages from Crockett, declaring that he held the land through a disseizen [207] by James Wagg. Ephraim Crockett's case is representative of many other land disputes that occurred between settlers and Great Proprietors (including others in Pejepscot). Following is the court record (edited for clarity) of Hannah and Abigail Waterhouse, spinsters of Poole, County of Poole, England v. Ephraim Crockett, yeoman of Pejepscot:[208]

> "In a plea of land wherein the said Hannah & Abigail demand against the said Crockett possession of a certain parcel or tract of land situated in said Pejepscot being a part of the great Lot numbered Three in the Pejepscott claim so called … containing sixty five acres ~ into which the said Crockett hath not entry but after a disseizen which one James Wagg under whom he claims & holds unjustly did to Hannah Waterhouse the ancestor of the descendant whose heirs they are ~ Whereupon the Demandants say that in a time of peace within fifty years last past the said Hannah Waterhouse the ancestor was seized of the demanded premises in her demesne in fee & of right, taking the profits thereof annually & every year to the value of ten dollars & being so thereof seized the said James Wagg unjustly entered into & disseized her of the same …"

Attorney Inches then declared that Hannah Waterhouse had died June 10, 1807, leaving her daughters Hannah and Abigail Waterhouse as her sole heirs. He claimed that Hannah and Abigail "… ought now to be in quiet possession of the demanded premises, but the said Crockett unjustly withholds the same ~ To the damage of the said Hannah & Abigail (as they say) the sum of one thousand Dollars."

---

206. See CCROD, deeds from Hannah and Abigail Waterhouse, 1811.
207. Illegal taking of land.
208. Maine, Cumberland County Court of Common Pleas records, 1764-1839. Court records, v. 13, 1811-1812, p. 396. (Image #406). https://www.familysearch.org/ark:/61903/3:1:3QS7-L93S-R935-G?i=405&cat=1881394

The Sixth Generation

Inches, after making his claim that Ephraim Crockett damaged the Waterhouse spinsters to the wildly inflated sum of 1,000 pounds (the disbelieving clerk of the court even felt the need to add the parenthetical remark "as they say" about its value in the record), rested his case. Ephraim Crockett then stepped up and defended himself (apparently without the use of an attorney):[209]

> " ~ And now the said Crockett comes & defends the force & injury, when to. where to. & reserving leave to waive this plea & plead anew & double at the [Supreme Judicial Court] for plea says the said James Wagg did not disseize in manner & form as the [plaintiffs] have declared against him & thereof puts himself on the country ~ "

After Ephraim Crockett "put himself on the country" for the justice of his claim to the land, Attorney Inches responded "… that the plea of said Crockett in manner & form above pleaded, is bad & insufficient in law & thereof prays Judgment & for their damage & costs." Undeterred, Ephraim responded, doubling down that *his* plea was "… good & sufficient in law, & prays Judgment for his costs."

The justices of the court considered the matter (how long we do not know) and found for Ephraim Crockett. "All which being fully seen & understood by the court," the clerk wrote in the record, "the court are of the opinion that the [Defendant's] plea is good ~ It is therefore considered by the court, that the said Ephraim Crockett recover against the said Hannah Waterhouse, & Abigail Waterhouse his costs of suit taxed at _____ ."[210]

Inches, on behalf of Hannah and Abigail Waterhouse, immediately announced his intention to appeal the decision (of behalf of his clients) at the next meeting of the Supreme Judicial Court. The Supreme Judicial Court was scheduled to meet next at Portland for Cumberland & Oxford counties in two months, on the fourth Tuesday of May [1812]. Inches posted a bond (as the law directed) "to prosecute their appeal with effect ~~"[211]

---

209. Attorney Inches' declaration after Ephraim's defense that it was "bad & insufficient in law," suggest to me that Ephraim did not use an attorney.
210. The sum for court costs and costs of suit likely would have been filled in, except that Attorney Inches immediately announced he would appeal the decision (of behalf of the Waterhouse sisters) to the Supreme Judicial Court.
211. Maine, Cumberland County Court of Common Pleas records, 1764-1839. Court records, v. 13, 1811-1812, p. 396. (Image #406). https://www.familysearch.org/ark:/61903/3:1:3QS7-L93S-R935-G?i=405&cat=1881394

396

March term A.D. 1812.

C. 290. Hannah Waterhouse & Abigail Waterhouse both of Poole in county of Poole, & Kingdom of England, Spinsters, daughters & heirs of Hannah Waterhouse late of said Poole deceased, widow of Samuel Waterhouse Plfs. vs. Ephraim Crockett of Pejepscott in the county of Cumberland, Yeoman Dft. In a plea of land wherein the said Hannah & Abigail demand against the said Crockett possession of a certain piece or tract of land situated in said Pejepscott being a part of the great Lot numbered Three in the Pejepscott claim so called and bounded as follows. Viz. beginning on the South side of Waggs brook so called at the mouth of said brook, thence running South seventeen degrees west, four & an half rods, thence South seventy five degrees west eight rods, thence North eighteen degrees West, fourteen rods, thence South west, two hundred rods, thence Northwest thirty rods to land of Moses Hanscomb thence Southwest thirty six rods, to land in possession of Stephen Sanalee thence South east sixty six rods to the dividing line between said lot numbered Three & lot numbered two in said claim thence North east on said line to the river, thence by the river to the bounds first mentioned, containing sixty five acres. Into which the said Crockett hath not entry but after a disseizen which one James Wagg, under whom he claims & holds unjustly did to Hannah Waterhouse the ancestor of the demandants whose heirs they are. Whereupon the Demandants say that in a time of peace within fifty years last past the said Hannah Waterhouse the ancestor was seized of the demanded premises in her demesne in fee & of right, taking the profits thereof annually & every year to the value of ten dollars & being so thereof seized the said James Wagg unjustly entered into & disseized her of the same & the said Hannah the ancestor being so thereof disseized thereafterwards to wit, on the tenth day of June A.D. 1807. died, seized of the right to the same leaving the demandants her children & only heirs & thereupon the same descended & came to them & they thereupon became seized thereof in fee & ought now to be in quiet possession of the demanded premises, but the said Crockett unjustly withholds the same. To the damage of the said Hannah & Abigail (as they say) the sum of one thousand Dollars. And now the said Crockett comes & defends the force & injury, when &c. where &c. & reserving leave to waive this plea & plead anew & double at the S.J.C. for plea says the said James Wagg did not disseize in manner & form as the Plfs. have declared against him & thereof puts himself on the country. And the Plfs. agreeing to the above reservation, & reserving liberty to waive this demurrer & mend & join any issue tendered in the S.J.C. says, that the plea of said Crockett in manner & form above pleaded, is bad & insufficient in law, & thereof says

Case No. 290, Cumberland County Court of Common Pleas, March term A.D. 1812.[212]
Hannah & Abigail Waterhouse, of Poole, England v. Ephraim Crockett, of Pejepscot.

212. Maine, Cumberland County Court of Common Pleas records, 1764-1839. Court records, v. 13, 1811-1812, p. 396. (Image #406). https://www.familysearch.org/ark:/61903/3:1:3QS7-L93S-R935-G?i=405&cat=1881394

March term A.D. 1812.

It is therefore considered by the court, that the said Ephraim Crockett recover against the said Hannah Waterhouse, & Abigail Waterhouse, his costs of suit taxed at —

From which Judgment, the said Hannah Waterhouse & Abigail Waterhouse appeal to the S.J.C. to be holden at Portland in the county of Cumberland, & for the counties of Cumberland & Oxford on the fourth tuesday of May next; and enter into recognizance, as the law directs, to prosecute their appeal with effect. —

C. 291. **Hannah Waterhouse & Abigail Waterhouse** both of Poole, in the county of Poole in the Kingdom of England, Spinsters, Plfs. vs. **Stephen Larrabee** of Pejepscott in the county of Cumberland, Yeoman, Dft. In a plea of land, wherein they demand against the said Stephen Larrabee possession of a certain piece or tract of land situated in Pejepscott aforesaid & is part of the great lot numbered three in the Pejepscott claim so called & bounded as follows, viz: beginning on the range or dividing line between said lot numbered three & lot numbered two in said claim at the most Easterly corner of land occupied by Humphrey Lilly on said lot numbered three, thence running Northeast one hundred & sixty four rods to land occupied by Ephraim Crockett, thence Northwest sixty six rods to land occupied by George Seach, thence Southwest one hundred & sixty four rods to Ebenezer Jordan's land, thence Southeast, sixty six rods to the first bounds containing seventy acres — into which the said Stephen hath not entry, but by disseizin which he did to Hannah Waterhouse ancester of the demandants, whose heirs they are — Whereupon the demandants say that in a time of peace, within fifty years last past the said Hannah Waterhouse the ancester was seized of the demanded premises in her demesne as of fee & right taking the profits thereof annually to the value of ten Dollars & being so thereof seized the said Stephen unjustly entered upon & disseized her of the same & being so thereof disseized, the said Hannah the ancester thereafterwards to wit on the tenth day of May A.D. 1807 died, seized of the right to the same demanded premises leaving the demandants her children & only heirs to whom the right to the same thereupon descended & came & they thereupon became seized thereof in fee & ought now to be in quiet possession of the demanded premises, but the said Stephen unjustly defoureth them thereof. To the damage of the said Hannah & Abigail (as they say) the sum of one thousand Dollars. And now the said Larrabee comes & defends the force & injury, when &c. where &c. & reserving leave to waive this plea & plead anew issued at the S.J.C. for plea says he did not disseize in manner & form as the Plfs. have declared, against him & thereof puts himself on the country — And the Plfs. agreeing to the above reservation, & reserving liberty to waive this demurrer & amend & join any issue tendered in the S.J.C. says that the

Case No. 290, Cumberland County CCP, March term, 1812 (second page).
Hannah & Abigail Waterhouse v. Ephraim Crockett.

It is small wonder that Ephraim Crockett won his case at the Court of Common Pleas. The outrageousness of Attorney Inches' claims on behalf of the Waterhouse sisters seems birdbrained and obtuse. First, the phrase "in a time of peace within fifty years last past" was probably not going to score the Boston-based attorney many points in a Maine court. Not only did James Wagg's "illegal entry" onto Great Lot No. 3 occur during a time of war with Great Britain (the American Revolution), but also within three months of this court date (June of 1812) the U.S. would again declare war upon Britain for grievances, including the impressment of thousands of American seamen into the British Royal Navy. Second, Inches' pathetic plea that Hannah Waterhouse had been taking $10 a year from the property, probably rang hollow as well. The justices of the court knew the effort required to turn wilderness into a town, and they also knew that men like Ephraim Crockett had been paying taxes all these decades and the Waterhouse sisters (or their mother) had not. (Had any money been coming *from* England, rather than the reverse, Inches would certainly have mentioned that fact in his arguments.) The only wonder in the lower court's decision is that the Waterhouse sisters (or their lawyer) decided to appeal it to the Supreme Judicial Court. But Hannah and Abigail Waterhouse (and Attorney Inches) had more than one case pending in court (in fact, they had more that day), and they could not afford to let this judgment stand or all the others might go the same route.

Because of the breaking out of hostilities between the United States and Great Britain, however, the Waterhouse sisters' appeal of this decision to the Supreme Judicial Court was *not* heard at the May term in 1812. Instead, the appeal would not appear on the docket of the Supreme Judicial Court until 1815, during the October term, after the Treaty of Ghent (ending the War of 1812) was ratified. (Possibly Inches postponed the case, suspecting it would not go well for his English clients during a time of war with Great Britain.)

During the intervening years the stalemate between Massachusetts and the Pejepscot Proprietors over boundary and settler issues continued to drag on. Josiah Little—using his wealth and position to influence the General Court—eventually prevailed. A final agreement, *which ignored the 1804 awards to the settlers*, was reached in May of 1813.[213] As a result, the settlers who had still been holding out hope (and were not financially able take their case to court, as Ephraim Crockett

---

213. Info from ELP.

had done) were forced to pay Boston prices for the land they had cleared and improved, paying not only for the real estate but also for their own improvements on that land.

Who was it who had cleared the land? Built the roads and the schools? Created towns? Who paid the taxes on the settlers' lots? It certainly was not Tories like Isaac Royall, Jr. or Hannah and Samuel Waterhouse! (Josiah Little paid taxes, but at a cheaper, non-resident rate.)[214]

Sadly, after the 1813 settlement between Massachusetts and the Pejepscot Proprietors was finalized, some of the settlers could not afford the prices demanded and were forced to abandon their long-time homes. Let us revisit our list of seven settlers (in reverse order) and discover what happened to each of these men:

7. **Revolutionary War veteran William Plummer**, who poignantly described in his diary the death of his son Timothy, eventually purchased from Hannah and Abigail Waterhouse of Poole, County of Poole, England (daughters of Tories Samuel and Hannah Waterhouse) his **94 acres for $470. At $5 per acre, this was nearly three and a half times the proposed 1804 award.**[215]

6. **James Elwell,** Ephraim Crockett's neighbor to the south, had unfortunately settled on land that was sold to Moses Little (later owned by Josiah Little) by the heirs of Hannah Fayeweather, a Pejepscot Proprietor. On December 20, 1810, Elwell bought the land on Great Lot 2 "on which he liveth" **for $426, which was almost six times his 1804 award (amounting to $6.82 per acre).** Elwell was forced to give Little a mortgage for the entire amount, $426 plus interest.[216]

5. **Charles Bisbee,** Ephraim Crockett's neighbor to the north, apparently **could not afford the price set by Henderson Inches for Hannah and Abigail Waterhouse, and Bisbee disappears from Pejepscot history**. His real estate was purchased in 1815 by John Penley,[217] a man who would play a large role in the next two generations of Crocketts, due to the proximity of the Crockett and Penley

---

214. Danville, Maine assessment records. Danville files, AHS.
215. CCROD, Book 73, Page 69.
216. CCROD, Book 62, p. 266, 360.
217. In early records this surname is spelled "Penly." Later the common spelling is "Penley." I have utilized the common spelling.

families.[218] Penley paid $348 for his 80 acres.[219] At $4.35 per acre, the price was more than six times the 1804 award to Charles Bisbee. Penley, however, could afford the price.

4. **Revolutionary War veteran William Dingley,** who joined the rag-tag Continental Army after witnessing the British Royal Navy shell and burn Falmouth, had admitted to Josiah Little's agent that he had signed a petition for relief from the proprietors. The agent also jotted down in his notebook that Dingley agreed to purchase his land from Little. But Dingley had already paid a substantial sum of money for his real estate, and most likely held out hope for relief from the General Court for some type of "quieting." In 1792, Dingley had given 32 pounds and 14 shillings to Daniel Sargent for "one hundred acres more or less on a large tract claimed by Josiah Little, Esq." In fact, Dingley never did pay Little for his land. Less than two years before his death, however, **Dingley's surviving son Jeremiah purchased the property from Little for $700. At $7 per acre, that was five times the amount Dingley would have paid had Massachusetts forced the Pejepscot Proprietors to accept the 1804 settlement.** Jeremiah Dingley only had a fraction of the purchase price at hand. He immediately gave a $500 mortgage for the property—to Josiah Little, of Newbury, Massachusetts.[220]

3. **Samuel Crockett**, Ephraim's young cousin, the Freewill Baptist and rabble rouser, **was another one of those settlers who could not afford Boston prices. He and his family eventually relocated to Stetson, where land was cheaper**. Samuel Crockett and his wife (and two of his wife's sisters and their families) were some of the earliest settlers in Stetson, where the family was active in town affairs. Samuel Crockett was the tax collector in Stetson for many years. He passed away in 1854 at the age of eighty. His wife, Olive (Swett) Crockett, died in 1861 at the age of eighty-five.[221]

2. **James Wagg and James Wagg Jr**.

    James Wagg: In 1807, James Wagg, Ephraim Crockett's uncle—runaway

---

218. Four of John Penley's children would marry four children of Ephraim Crockett, Jr., who with his wife Sally (Wentworth) settled Crockett's Ridge in Norway. The four couples buy up lots next to Ephraim and Sally, where they raise their families. Much of their land (and one old house) remains in the extended family today. See my book, "A History of the Crockett Family of Crockett's Ridge, Norway, Maine." White Wave, 2024.
219. CCROD, Book 74, p. 239. John Penley purchased the property on September 28, 1815.
220. See CCROD Book 36, p. 288; and Book 62, p. 254, 260. William Dingley died October 13, 1812, in Danville. STARBIRD, and Dingley family history, Danville files, AHS.
221. CANDAGE, p. 46.

The Sixth Generation

from England and one of the earliest settlers in the backcountry of Pejepscot—built a new frame house up where the road had been moved away from the river (due to occasional flooding). His new house, large and uniquely square, still stands today. Likely to square the family's title to their real estate before his death, the elderly **Wagg purchased on September 18, 1811, ninety-two acres from Hannah and Abigail Waterhouse for $452.**[222] **At $4.91 per acre, that was more than six times his 1804 award.** Wagg immediately mortgaged the property to Henderson Inches, the attorney for the spinster Tory sisters, for $552.

The exact date of the senior Wagg's death is unknown, although he died after 1818 when he was assessed $8.07 for his Pejepscot road tax. The author of the hand-written Wagg family history at the Androscoggin Historical Society[223] reports that James Wagg, Sr. was over ninety years of age when he died. She writes:

> "He had been to a grist mill on horseback, as the horse returned late in the day without him, search was made over the course he would take and he was found dead leaning up against a tree. To his memory we erected the $85 marker in Oct. 1823, in the old yard on the bank of the Androscoggin [River], which he gave from his farm as a public burial ground."[224]

In a strange twist of fate, in April of 1928, James Wagg's great-grandson, Howard Wagg, discovered a "gaping hole" in the cemetery while working in the field nearby. After informing the police of his shocking discovery, Chief Rowe accompanied Howard Wagg back to the burial ground, where they probed the open grave—and found no remains of the skeleton of James Wagg.[225] One hopes that his bones had simply disintegrated, "ashes to ashes, dust to dust."

Revolutionary War veteran James Wagg, Jr.: Ephraim's cousin, who served four years in the war to liberate this country from British tyranny—including

---

222. CCROD, Book 64, p. 189. See also the mortgage James Wagg gave to Henderson Inches for this property, CCROD, Book 64, P. 191. While the deed for this does not show whether it was Samuel Wagg Sr. or Jr. who had purchased the property, because there are no dower rights noted as released in the mortgage (i.e., for James Wagg, Jr.'s wife, Dorcas, who was still alive) I believe that the deed and mortgage were executed by the elder Wagg, whose wife, Mary Crockett, was deceased.
223. Wagg folder, AHS.
224. CCROD Book 64, p. 189, 191. Information on James Wagg, Sr.'s 1813 taxes came from Pejepscot Assessments for Hwys. And Town Ways, 1813, Danville files, AHS. Biographical information on the Waggs was collected by STARBIRD and can be found in the Wagg and Danville files, AHS.
225. Lewiston Journal, "50 Years Ago Today," April 20, 1978.

the 1777/78 winter at Valley Forge with General Washington—appears to have lived in the original log cabin for most of his life. His Revolutionary War pension application reveals the burden he bore because of the failure of the Massachusetts General Court to immediately honor the land promised to soldiers or to force the Pejepscot Proprietors to abide by the 1804 quieting award. Wagg, Jr. writes movingly in his pension and bounty-land application, describing his (father's) mortgaged real estate and his destitute condition:[226]

> "**Real estate**—a piece or parcel of land in Danville, formerly Pejepscot, containing ninety-two acres about the half under improvement. **The same is now and has been for nine years under a mortgage to Henderson Inches of Boston for $552.—I live on said land, but never have been able to redeem it**—the house is small—I have one horse, two sheep and two pigs—a few articles of ordinary household furniture and a few farming tools—I have no income but from my own earnings."[227]

For his service, James Wagg, Jr. was awarded in 1814 (backdated to April 28, 1813) a pension of $8 per month. In addition, in 1835, James finally received a certificate for 200 acres of land in Maine. The "Resolve in favor of certain officers and soldiers of the Revolutionary war ..." was approved on March 17, 1835, by the state of Maine in a negotiated settlement with Massachusetts. Of course, the land grant came a little late—almost sixty years after it was promised Wagg and the other soldiers! Like most veterans who received this land grant (including Ephraim's brother Samuel Crockett), James Wagg, Jr. immediately sold his award to neighbor John Penley. Penley turned around and resold the property,[228] no doubt making a profit from the sale.

James' wife Dorcas, who accompanied her husband and father-in-law to Pejepscot in 1780 (where that December she and her husband lost their nine-day-old son) predeceased her husband by twenty years. She died February

---

226. Many of these pension and bounty-land applications described conditions more pathetic than they were in actuality; however, in James Wagg, Jr.'s case we can see the devastating, long-term effect of the mortgage, necessitated by paying the Waterhouse sisters for the Wagg property.
227. U.S. Revolutionary War Pension and Bounty-Land Warrant Application Files, 1800-1900, James Wagg, Jr.
228. See copy of the deed in James Wagg's Bounty-Land application files, upon which John Penley transfers title. U.S. Revolutionary War Pension and Bounty-Land Warrant Application Files, 1800-1900, James Wagg, Jr.

11, 1825[229] at the age of 68. Dorcas is buried in the Wagg family cemetery. James, Jr. remarried immediately. On April 28, 1825, he was married to the widow Rhoda Goold (Gould) by Elder Joseph Roberts.[230] James Wagg, Jr. died in Danville on March 31, 1845. He was buried in the Wagg family cemetery with his father and first wife. What became of his second wife is unknown.

Samuel Wagg, the eldest son of James and Dorcas Wagg, was given a piece of the family farm upon his 1809 marriage to Polly Dingley, daughter of William and Sarah "Sally" (Jordan) Dingley. After Samuel's death the large, square house built by James Wagg, Sr. was sold to John Penley, who had married Samuel and Polly's daughter, Julia. (Julia was John Penley's second wife; his first wife was Julia's aunt, Desire Dingley).[231]

1. **Revolutionary War veteran Ephraim Crockett,** who enlisted after hearing of the battles at Concord and Lexington, stubbornly refused to buy his land either from Hannah Waterhouse or her daughters Hannah and Abigail Waterhouse (via attorney Henderson Inches). In November of 1809, Ephraim Crockett was a plaintiff v. Caleb Dyer, a trader from Cape Elizabeth, at the Court of Common Pleas held in Portland for Cumberland County. Ephraim won his case by default (Dyer did not appear) for a sum of money (with a writ on file) that Dyer had promised to pay Crockett. The court awarded Ephraim $126.86 in damages and costs of court taxed at $12.91.[232]

Perhaps Ephraim's 1809 victory at court gave him the impetus (and the funds) to challenge the rights claimed by the Waterhouse sisters at the Court of Common Pleas, where he won the first round against Hannah and Abigail in 1812. After winning his initial case, Ephraim prepared to fight the sisters' appeal at the Supreme Judicial Court, which was scheduled for the May term in 1812. War with Great Britain intervened, however. In 1813,

---

229. Information from Dorcas Wagg's gravestone in the Wagg family cemetery, Auburn, Maine.
230. Rhode Island Vital Extracts, 1636-1899. This record states that James was 75 when he wed Mrs. Goold; however, according to all records I have seen he would have been about 70 (as was the widow). She likely died in Rhode Island. Also, I have not researched Elder Roberts, but he probably was a relation/descendant of the Roberts family from Cape Elizabeth.
231. STARBIRD and Wagg family, Danville files, AHS. Also, Study of the Penley Family by Mrs. Harriet J. Ross, STARBIRD'S Penley file, AHS. Edward Staples, who is a descendant of John Penley (as well as a Crockett descendant) claims that Penley's second marriage to the niece of his first wife was a bit of a scandal and created some hard feelings in the family among Penley's first set of children and their spouses. (Penley had 17 children by his two wives.)
232. Maine, Cumberland County Court of Common Pleas records, 1764-1839. Court records, v. 12, 1809-1811, p. 154. In the margin of the record is the note: "Execution issued Dec. 2, 1809." This case does not again appear in court—nor was any real estate attached to make the payment—so Dyer must have paid Crockett the amount due from the execution.

prior to the cessation of hostilities, the final settlement between the General Court and the Pejepscot Proprietors was reached. This settlement did not require the quieting of settlers on the Pejepscot Claim, and was felt a severe blow to the settlers. David Crockett, the eldest son of Ephraim and Rebecca, realized after the settlement that it was useless to hold out for any type of quieting. David probably also considered the fact that if his father lost his case at the Supreme Judicial Court, Ephraim might not only have to pay a higher price per acre for the property, but also pay Henderson Inches' attorney fees and costs of court.

David, who served as a colonel in the War of 1812, had married Esther Dingley in 1809 and he and his family lived on the home farm with his parents. On August 29, 1815—shortly before his father's case was scheduled to be heard at the October term of the Supreme Judicial Court[233]—**David Crockett purchased from the spinster Waterhouse sisters the 60 acres of his father's land for $253. The $4.22 per acre was about three times the $1.25 per acre Ephraim Crockett had been awarded in the 1804 settlement.** David gave Henderson Inches a mortgage on the property for $283. His father did not let David down, though. Ephraim gave his son $200 for a half-interest in the property on April 6, 1816, in plenty of time for David to pay Inches the first of three annual payments on his mortgage.[234] David inherited his father's share of the real estate after Ephraim's death.

A review of a similar case held at the Supreme Judicial Court during the same October term suggests David made the right decision. The case of Hannah and Abigail Waterhouse, appellants, v. Samuel Achley of Pejepscot, appellee, was heard concerning 45 acres of real estate situated on Great Lot No. 3 (the same lot the Crocketts settled). Through their attorney the Waterhouse sisters claimed Achley had taken up their land under a disseizen by James Wagg (as Inches had claimed with Ephraim Crockett and various other men).[235] After hearing the facts of the case, the Supreme Judicial Court determined that the Waterhouse sisters still had a legal claim

---

233. Maine, Cumberland County Supreme Judicial Court records, 1798-1956. Court records, v. 4, 1814-1817. The case was on the docket to be heard; however, in the record it is noted "Neither Party appear," signifying that the case had been settled out of court.
234. See CCROD, Book 73, Page 75; Book 74, p. 65; and Book 120, Page 67.
235. Apparently, the elder Wagg was the one who encouraged many of these early settlers to relocate to the Pejepscot Patent, possibly claiming or staking out a large tract of land in advance for them.

upon the raw land to the value of $147 (about $3.27 per acre). The Court also determined that the value of Achley's improvements (buildings, etc.) on the land was $196 (about $4.35 per acre). The court then decided that if it was agreeable with the Waterhouse sisters (and their lawyer assured that it was) Achley was to pay Hannah and Abigail $147 plus interest over several years (to which settlement Achley agreed). Unfortunately, Achley was also stuck with the costs of court and costs of the Waterhouse sisters (the fee to attorney Inches and his expenses). These costs amounted to the staggering sum of $51.32, more than one-third the set price of the raw land![236] After learning of the disposition of the case, Ephraim Crockett probably thought his son had made the correct decision to settle with attorney Inches without the expense of going to court.

Ephraim Crockett did not receive a Maine land grant (nor did he apply for one). Although he had reenlisted twice after his first eight-month stint with Captain Dunn's company, Ephraim had not signed three-year papers as had his cousin, James Wagg, Jr. Ephraim did apply for a pension, which was approved. He passed away at nearly eighty years of age on April 9, 1835, before receiving any further reward from the Federal government for his two years of service. Ephraim Crockett was buried in the Wagg family cemetery with his uncle and cousin, and other Revolutionary War veterans who had settled nearby. Ephraim's half-interest share of his 60 acres on the banks of the Androscoggin River appears to have gone to son David after his death.

Regrettably, Ephraim's untimely death before his Revolutionary War pension was finalized complicated the matter for his widow Rebecca, who applied for—but had some difficulty getting—her husband's pension. Finally, in March of 1836, Rebecca began receiving a widow's pension of $80 per year (in a semi-annual payment of $40), which she received until her death.[237] According to *The Maine Farmer* newspaper (published December 28, 1839), Rebecca (Stanford) Crockett burned to death in her bed in December 1839. (Pension records note the date of her death as December 6, 1839.) She was seventy-nine.

Eldest son David Crockett, who purchased the property from the

---

236. Maine, Cumberland County Supreme Judicial Court records, 1798-1956. Court records, v. 4, 1814-1817, p. 209.
237. U.S. Revolutionary War Pensioners, 1801-1815, 1818-1872, Rebecca Crockett.

Waterhouse sisters, had difficulty keeping out of debt. In addition to the mortgage given to Henderson Inches, he negotiated at least two other mortgages to neighbor John Penley (hopefully using some of the money from Penley to pay off the original mortgage to Inches). Finally, on February 13, 1844, David sold the land that his father had claimed more than a half-century earlier to his own son, David Crockett, Jr., for $800. The real estate was still subject to a mortgage to John Penley for $400, and so **David Crockett passed on the original debt burden (and more) to his own son, continuing into the third generation the travesty that was afflicted by Massachusetts upon veterans of the Revolutionary War.**[238]

According to my calculations, Hannah Waterhouse and her daughters cashed out more than $7,000 in property sales from the town of Pejepscot alone. Combined with their real estate sales in Brunswick, Royalsborough, and elsewhere, this must have made them very rich women, although we have no way of knowing how much of that money ended up with them back in England, and how much lined the pockets of their Boston attorney Henderson Inches (who also held mortgages on many of these same properties).[239]

Josiah Little, the man who stubbornly refused to sacrifice to the state any of the Pejepscot Claim (no matter the cost), died the day after Christmas in 1830 at the age of eighty-three. According to George Thomas Little, he left behind him "a fortune of several hundred thousand dollars,"[240] much of it in real estate and proceeds from the sale of real estate that Little had plundered (and ensured that others, including Tories, could plunder) from the Revolutionary War veterans and early settlers on the Pejepscot Claim.

Conclusion to Our Crockett History

In Pejepscot, as elsewhere in Maine, there was a backlash against Massachusetts

---

238. CCROD, Book 133, p. 627; Book 178, p. 511; and Book 185, p. 151. According to a snapshot that appeared in the *Boston Post* on November 7, 1903, David Crockett's son, David, Jr., was still working on the farm at eighty-five years of age. The piece noted that his wife, Belinda (Hodgkins) Crockett, who was eighty-four, "does all of the housework and enjoys quite good health." The information about and accompanying photo of the Crocketts was submitted to the *Post* in the newspaper's quest to discover the oldest married couple in New England, to whom would be awarded a Morris chair and Boston rocker. At that time, David and Belinda Crockett had been married fifty-eight years, and were likely not the couple who won the contest.
239. See CCROD, Inches, Henderson.
240. LITTLE, p. 6.

The Sixth Generation

and the Great Proprietors of the Kennebec, Waldo, and Pejepscot patents for the treatment of these early settlers, especially Revolutionary War veterans. In addition, Mainers felt betrayed by Massachusetts during the War of 1812, when the Commonwealth failed to defend and protect residents in eastern Maine from British invasion. The combined backlash from these two major events contributed to the creation of Maine as a separate state.

A quick look at two votes taken in the little community of Pejepscot exemplifies this change in the hearts and minds of Mainers. In 1807, a vote taken in Pejepscot whether to separate from Massachusetts failed completely. *Not one vote was cast to leave.* At that time, settlers still clung to a hope that the Massachusetts General Court would recognize their land claims. By 1819, after the War of 1812 had ended—and when it had become abundantly clear that the Great Proprietors had prevailed against them—sentiment among voters in the town of Pejepscot (then, Danville) had so materially changed that the separationists handily won the day.[241] The following year, on March 15, 1820, Maine was admitted into the Union as the twenty-third state under the Missouri Compromise.

For two centuries we have followed the footsteps of one Maine family—the Crocketts—on a quest for land. We have traveled with Thomas Crockett (who arrived at Pascataqua as part of Captain John Mason's Laconia crew in 1630); with his son Ephraim (who lived long enough to net land grants in Kittery); with the three Richard Crocketts (who settled Falmouth, Cape Elizabeth, Deer Isle, and Stratham, N.H.); and with Ephraim Crockett (who ventured into the backcountry of Pejepscot in 1780 with his uncle and cousin). We have lived through the English claim to New England; the taking over of Sir Ferdinando Gorges' grant of Maine by the Puritans of Massachusetts Bay Colony; the restoration of the Crown and the rights of Gorges' grandson; the sale of Maine to Massachusetts; nearly a century of French and Indian warfare that destroyed Maine's indigenous people; the American Revolution; the War of 1812; the rise of the Great Proprietors; the final settlement of the backcountry; and the creation of Maine as an independent state. During war, hardship, deprivation, the loss of wives to childbirth and children to disease—six generations of Crocketts were on a perpetual quest for freehold land.

In 2020, nearly 400 years after Thomas Crockett landed at Pascataqua, the state of Maine celebrated its bicentennial.[242] During the year of our bicentennial I

---
241. ANDHIST, Chapter XXXIX.
242. As a result of the COVID-19 pandemic, however, the state's actual celebrations were postponed until 2021.

researched this final chapter in my Crockett history. I discovered then how truly our family history represented the common people of Maine. It was eye-opening to learn not only about Ephraim Crockett's life and service in the American Revolution, but also about the shameful treatment that he and other veterans received at the hands of the wealthy and powerful men of Massachusetts. The financial burden laid upon these veterans (to say nothing about the physical cost of hewing a homestead and community out of a wilderness) carried forward to drag down their ancestors (my ancestors) for at least two generations. This is not how I had hoped to conclude my Crockett history, but so it is.

Today, Ephraim Crockett lies at peace in the Wagg family cemetery in Auburn (formerly Pejepscot and Danville). This remote graveyard is situated in a serene spot on a wooded, moss-covered knoll perched on the banks of the Androscoggin River, where the Anasagunticook Indians once roamed. The several veterans buried in the Wagg cemetery—Ephraim Crockett, James Wagg, Jr., and William Dingley—receive in death the gratitude and acknowledgement they deserved in life: American flags decorate their graves, honoring the service of these "common" men in the creation of a new nation. I wonder, though, if the soldiers would have thought that was enough.

Thomas Crockett certainly would not have considered this little patch of ground enough for his descendants. On the other hand, our Wabanaki friends might think it was poetic justice.

Grave of Ephraim Crockett, Wagg family cemetery, Auburn, Maine. Directly behind his stone can be seen the flag next to the gravestone of Ephraim's cousin, James Wagg, Jr. (Jennifer Wixson photo.)

Quick Crockett Family Reference

(Names in bold show the line we are following in this book.)

<u>First Generation</u>: **Thomas and Ann** [surname unknown, possibly Lynn or Gunnison] **Crockett**

<u>Second Generation</u>: Family of **Thomas and Ann Crockett**

Ephraim	Joshua
Ann (Anne)	Joseph
Sarah	Hugh
Elihu	Mary

<u>Third Generation</u>: Family of **Ephraim and Anne (Edge) Crockett**

Ephraim, Jr.
Sarah
Mary
Richard

<u>Fourth Generation</u>: Family of **Richard and Deborah (Haley) Crockett**

Richard, Jr.	Elizabeth
Ephraim	Sarah
Samuel Haley	Mary (possible, but not definite child)
William	

<u>Fifth Generation</u>: Family of **Richard and Mary (Robinson) Crockett**

Mary	Daniel
Richard (III)	George
Joshua	Robinson
Sarah	Josiah
Hannah	Joseph (possible, but not definite child)

Sixth Generation: Family of **Richard and Elizabeth (Roberts) Crockett**

Ephraim	Samuel
Anna	Mary
Sarah	Lucy
Deborah	Catharine[1]

Seventh Generation: Family of **Ephraim and Rebecca (Stanford) Crockett**

Rebecca	Priscilla
David	Joseph
Ephraim, Jr.[2]	James
Mary	Betsey
Sarah "Sally"	Eliza

---

1. Crockett genealogist Candage lists Catharine as a daughter of Richard, Jr. and Mary (Robinson) Crockett; however, my research has led me to conclude that she was a daughter of Richard (III) and Elizabeth (Roberts) Crockett. Merton Taylor Goodrich in his CHAIRMAKERS article has a shorter list than Candage of Richard Jr. and Mary's offspring, leaving out Catharine and Joseph. This helps confirm my conclusion that Catharine was their granddaughter, not their daughter.

2. In 1814, Ephraim Crockett, Jr. and his wife Sarah "Sally" (Wentworth) Crockett settled on Lee's Grant in Norway, Maine. Their story (and that of their descendants) is told in my book: "A History of the Crockett Family of Crockett's Ridge, Norway, Maine." (White Wave, 2024.)

Genealogical Dictionary of Thomas and Ann Crockett

NOTE: This dictionary includes descendants of Thomas and Ann Crockett in the line followed in this book. For a detailed Crockett genealogy, see Charles S. Candage's "Crockett Genealogy, 1610-1988, Some Descendants of Thomas and Ann Crockett of Kittery, Maine." (Picton Press, 1990.) Also, the numbers after the Crockett names indicate their generation, with Thomas Crockett being 1, the first generation to the New World.

Crockett, Ann.1 Ann is the ancestor of all the Maine and New England Crocketts. Her parentage is unknown; however, her maiden name was reported to have been "Lynn" or "Gunnison." Ann might have been a sister to York resident and trader Henry Lynn, the first husband of Sarah Lynn Gunnison (making Ann and Sarah sisters-in-law). It is also possible that Ann was a relation of Francis Raynes of York, who posted bond for Ann at court when Thomas Crockett was absent. Ann's life is covered in Chapter 1.

Crockett, Ann (Anne).2 The eldest daughter of Thomas and Ann Crockett, Ann was married about 1673 to William Roberts.[3] The couple lived on Crockett's Neck on land she received as a marriage portion and where Roberts built a house. The couple raised four children: William, Elizabeth, Mary, and George Roberts.[4] William Roberts appears to have outlived his wife, who passed away prior to July 17, 1708, when son George Roberts (with his father's consent and stipulations) mortgaged the homestead to William Pepperell.[5] On July 5, 1715, Pepperell foreclosed, and had William Roberts' second wife, a recent widow (Anna or Nan) removed.[6]

---

3. MIGRATION, p. 497.
4. CANDAGE, p. 1.
5. On July 17, 1708, George Roberts of Ipswich (MA) sold the mortgage on the Roberts' homestead that his father William Roberts had granted him (for help paying off a bond that William Roberts owed) to William Pepperell for 16 pounds, 17 shillings. If George or William Roberts paid to Pepperell the 16 pounds 17 shillings at 6% interest by July 17, 1711, however, the deed would be voided. It was agreed before the signing that the house and land would not be claimed by George Roberts without the consent of his father William Roberts and his "now wife Anna Roberts alias Nan Roberts or ye survivor of either of them." The wording of the deed suggests that Anna or Nan was a new wife to William Roberts, not his first wife Ann (Crockett) Roberts. MEWD, Vol. 7, p. 305-306.
6. After eldest son Ephraim's unexpected death in 1688, his mother Ann Crockett, who had remarried Dygory Jeffrey, was left with the responsibility of legally settling the ownership of Crockett's Neck. On June 22, 1695, Ann Jeffrey deeded to her son-in-law William Roberts his homestead plus six more acres, with the consent of her sons Hugh and Joseph, and her daughter Ann Roberts. This real estate was adjacent to the home Thomas Crockett built on Crockett's Neck, on his grant of land from Sir Ferdinando Gorges. MEWD, Vol. 8, p. 244. In 1706, William Roberts mortgaged his homestead on Crockett's Neck to his son George (to pay off a debt of William's to Francis Wainwright of Ipswich, MA MEWD, Vol. 7, p. 304-305. In 1708, George assigned the mortgage to William Pepperell (see prior footnote). On July 5, 1715 at the Inferior Court of Common Pleas held at York (where Pepperell was one of the three magistrates on the bench), Pepperell took Anna Roberts (William Roberts' second wife) to court. She appeared as a defendant and owned a judgment for 14 pounds, 13 shillings and 5 pence due from the estate of her late husband to Pepperell, and an execution was granted to Pepperell. MPCR, Vol.

Crockett, Anna.6 Anna was a daughter of Richard (III) and Elizabeth (Roberts) Crockett. She was married to John Parker on January 29, 1777 in Portland. (No further information.)

Crockett, Betsey.7 A daughter of Ephraim6 and Rebecca (Stanford) Crockett, Betsey was born June 28, 1801 on the Pejepscot Claim. On November 16, 1820, Betsey married Asa Merrill of Lisbon. (No further information.)

Crockett, Catharine.6 Catharine was a daughter of Richard (III) and Elizabeth (Roberts) Crockett. She was born March 1759.[7] She was named for her maternal grandmother Katherine (Skillin) Roberts. She died at 22 months of age on January 11, 1761, and is buried in the Long Creek Cemetery with her great-grandfather Samuel Skillin and many other Crockett, Skillin, and Roberts relations.

Crockett, Daniel.5 Daniel was a son of Richard Crockett, Jr. and Mary (Robinson) Crockett. He was born about 1742, probably in Stratham, N.H., where his father had returned to escape his Falmouth creditors. Daniel married Mary "Molly" Noyes, who was born March 18, 1744 in Newbury, Massachusetts, a daughter of Nehemiah and Annie (Stickney) Noyes. Daniel was a veteran of the American Revolution. He and his family lived in a variety of places, including "Windham, Bucktown, Buckfield, Maine, and also in Portsmouth, N.H." Daniel and his wife and children were baptized—along with his brother George and his family—in Windham, Maine on Sept. 4, 1774.[8]

Crockett, David.7 David was the eldest son of Ephraim and Rebecca (Stanford) Crockett. He was born January 25, 1786 in Cape Elizabeth. On November 30, 1809, David married (in Pejepscot) Esther Dingley, daughter of William Dingley (a

---

5, p. 56-57. On Aug. 19, 1715, Pepperell sent the Sheriff to collect the debt due from William Roberts' widow. When Anna could not pay, Pepperell took the property on Crockett's Neck, and put the recent widow out of her home. In 1729, Henry Barter, Jr. (son of Henry Barter and Sarah Crockett, daughter of Ephraim and Ann Crockett and thus a great-grandson to Thomas Crockett) bought the property from William Pepperell for 135 pounds, about ten times the balance due on George Roberts' mortgage to Pepperell, bringing the Roberts/Crockett property back into the greater Crockett family. MEWD, Vol. 18, p. 110-111.

7. Find-A-Grave gives Catharine Crockett's birth as 1739 because the woman who added Catharine to the site believed she was 22 years old when she died; however, the gravestone clearly reads 22 months (not years), meaning Catharine was born in March of 1759. Also, the stone indicates her parents were Richard Crockett, Jr. and Elizabeth Crockett. (At the time, Richard Crockett (III) was known in Second Parish as Richard, Jr.)

8. CANDAGE, p. 12-13.

Revolutionary soldier also from Cape Elizabeth) and Sarah (Jordan) Dingley. The couple had seven children, all of whom were probably raised on the property on Great Lot 3 settled by his father.[9] David served as a colonel in the War of 1812. Esther died January 29, 1857 at age sixty-six. David died October 11, 1873 at age eighty-eight. David and Esther and (some) of their family are buried in the Penley Corner Cemetery in Auburn (formerly, Danville).

Crockett, Deborah.6 Deborah was a daughter of Richard (III) and Elizabeth (Roberts) Crockett. She was married to John Dole of Falmouth on November 24, 1773. (No further information.)

Crockett, Deborah.6 Deborah was a daughter of Richard (III) and Susannah (Westcoat) Crockett (and thus a half-sister to the Deborah Crockett above). She was married to Isaac Ingersoll either March 18, 1794, per Portland records (according to Charles Candage) or March 30, 1794, per Cumberland Center Vital Records. (No further information.)

Crockett, Dorcas.6 Dorcas was a daughter of Richard (III) and Susannah (Westcoat) Crockett. She was named for her maternal grandmother, Dorcas (Skillin) Westcoat. On April 1, 1808, Dorcas was married in Windham to Alexander Plumbly of Windham. (No further information.)

Crockett, Elihu.2 A son of Thomas and Ann Crockett, Elihu was a fisherman in Kittery. He married Mary Winnock, a daughter of Joseph Winnock. Elihu was given land on Crockett's Neck, which he sold in 1683 to Aaron Ferris.[10] In 1684, the couple had a son they named Thomas Crockett,[11] after his grandfather. In 1690, Elihu and his brother Joseph were appraisers of the estate of Elihu's father-in-law Joseph

---

9. This is the author's conjecture from later deeds and family information.
10. On June 13, 1683, "Elihew Crockett of Kittery, fisherman," sold (with the consent of his mother Ann "Geffrey" and brother Ephraim Crockett) to Aron (Aaron) Ferris of the Great Island of New Hampshire for 23 pounds, twenty acres in Spruce Creek, near the mouth of the creek, including "trees, woods, underwoods and priuledges whatsoeuer…" MEWD, Vol. 4, p. 10-12. Ephraim Crockett (and Elizabeth Hill, an unknown woman) witnessed the deed for Elihu. The property was located about four feet off Joseph Crockett's west corner. On Mar. 27, 1717, Thomas Huff deeded to Henry Barter 18-½ acres of uplands/meadows where Huff used to live, between Barter and Joseph Crockett, (almost all of) the real estate previously belonging to Huff's father-in-law, Aaron Ferris (i.e., the real estate that Elihu Crockett sold Ferris June 13, 1683). Thus, Henry Barter, husband of Sarah Crockett (daughter of Ephraim and Ann; granddaughter to Thomas and Ann) also brought Elihu's property back into the greater Crocket family. MEWD, Vol. 8, p. 378.
11. LIBBY/NOYES, p. 171. Elihu Crockett.

Winnock,¹² of Black Point (Scarborough), who was killed by Indians. Elihu's wife Mary appears to have predeceased him and he might have remarried, although Thomas Crockett was Elihu's only known child.

Crockett, Eliza.7 A daughter of Ephraim6 and Rebecca (Stanford) Crockett, Eliza was born November 30, 1803 on the Pejepscot Claim. (No further information.)

Crockett, Elizabeth.4 Elizabeth was a daughter of Richard and Deborah (Haley) Crockett. Although her birth year is unknown, Elizabeth was likely born in Kittery prior to her family's relocation to Stratham, N.H. in 1713. On May 17, 1731, Elizabeth was part of a group of young women given permission "to build up the hind sid[e] seat in the womans galliry [meeting house] pew … to have it to them selves during theire Life or there abode in the town of Stratham [N.H.]"¹³ Since two girls on this list are denoted as "dafters" of local men, Elizabeth was likely twenty-one or older at the time. If so, she was born around 1710. Elizabeth was married to John Edwards of Haverhill, Mass., December 15, 1737. He was born November 10, 1713, a son of John and Lydia (Crockett) Edwards.¹⁴ The couple had at least nine children, probably all born in Haverhill.¹⁵ When widowed, Elizabeth moved from Haverhill to Gorham, Maine, where her son Richard Edwards (and many other Crocketts, including her brother Samuel and his family) resided.¹⁶ She lived with her son Richard (probably named for his grandfather Richard Crockett) until she died.¹⁷

Crockett, Elizabeth.6 Elizabeth was a daughter of Richard (III) and Susannah (Westcoat) Crockett (Richard's second wife). She was married to John Cook. Their marriage intentions were filed February 7, 1793, per Portland Vital Records. (No further information.)

---

12. MEWD, Vol. 5, p. 92-93.
13. Stratham, N.H. Town Records via Family Search. https://www.familysearch.org/ark:/61903/3:1:3QS7-899K-DRBN?i=28&cc=1987741&cat=393768
14. Lydia (Crockett) Edwards was a daughter of Joseph and Hannah (Clements) Crockett. She and Richard Crockett were cousins, and thus their children who married each other (Elizabeth and John) were first cousins once removed or what we in Maine call "second cousins."
15. CANDAGE, p. 8.
16. GORHAM, p. 476.
17. CANDAGE, p. 8.

Crockett, Ephraim.2 The eldest child of Thomas and Ann Crockett, Ephraim was born in 1644.[18] He married Ann Edge[19] (daughter of Florence and Robert Edge) by September 19, 1671.[20] Ephraim, a tailor by trade, died less than ten years after the death of his father,[21] and only about four months after his mother deeded him the balance of Crockett's Neck,[22] the real estate not already gifted to his siblings. (Ephraim and his family are covered in Chapter 2.)

Crockett, Ephraim.4 This Ephraim was a son (possibly the eldest) of Richard and Deborah (Haley) Crockett. He was born circa 1708, probably in Kittery, before his father relocated the family to Stratham, N.H. in 1713. Ephraim married Rebecca Frink and resided in his father's homestead, where he came to be known as "Ephraim Crockett of Stratham."[23] Three of Ephraim and Rebecca's sons (Peletiah, Andrew, and Jonathan Crockett) followed their uncles Richard and Samuel Crockett (their father's brothers) back to Maine. Son David appears to have remained on the homestead, where he shows on the 1793 Phinehas Merrill Plan of Stratham, N.H. (David's house is situated near the Squamscott River between the Widow S. Wiggin and Kennison's Inn.)

Crockett, Ephraim, Jr.3 The eldest child of Ephraim and Anne (Edge) Crockett, he was not of age when his father died in 1688 (according to Ephraim Sr.'s will). There is no evidence that Ephraim, Jr. married, had children, or bought and sold real estate, and so it is likely he died before coming of age or shortly thereafter. The inheritance that would have gone to Ephraim, Jr. (had he survived) went instead to his younger brother Richard, the only other son born to Ephraim and Anne (Edge) Crockett.

---

18. On June 19, 1672, Ephraim Crockett "aged 28 years or thereabouts" gave a deposition about an issue between Francis Champernowne and Abraham Corbett. This means Ephraim was born around 1644 and confirms that he was the child whose birth was referenced by his aunt Joane Andrews (Thomas Crockett's sister) in her deposition about the ownership of Crockett's Neck. MEWD, Vol. 2, p. 222.
19. CANDAGE, p. 1.
20. At a Court of Associates held at York Sept. 19, 1671, "Ephraim Crockett's wife" is mentioned in the accounts regarding a fine and fees of 10 shillings. MPCR, Vol. 2, p. 441. MIGRATION, p. 497, says Ephraim was married to his wife in 1667, the year that Thomas Crockett removed his family to his new house on Crockett's Neck.
21. Thomas Crockett died in February or May 1679. Ephraim made his last will and testament on July 17, 1688. MEWD, Wills, p. 71-72. CANDAGE (p. 1) says the inventory of Ephraim's estate was taken Sept. 10, 1688; however, Ephraim and his wife Ann appeared in person before magistrate Francis Hook on Sept. 26, 1688 to acknowledge an instrument (a deed) as their free act and deed, so he must have passed away after that later date. MEWD, Vol. 5, p. 145.
22. MEWD, Vol. 4, p. 303.
23. CHAIRMAKERS, p. 143.

Crockett, Ephraim.6 Ephraim was the eldest son of Richard (III) and Elizabeth (Roberts) Crockett. He was born in Second Parish (Cape Elizabeth) July 12, 1755. Ephraim enlisted to fight the British during the American Revolution shortly after hearing about the battles of Concord and Lexington. When Ephraim completed his third enlistment, he returned to Cape Elizabeth and married Rebecca Stanford. Ephraim and his family relocated to the Pejepscot Claim with his uncle and cousin, Samuel Wagg, Sr. and Jr. The lives of Ephraim and Rebecca and their family are covered in Chapter 7.

Crockett, Ephraim, Jr.7 Ephraim was born February 7, 1788 in Cape Elizabeth to Ephraim Crockett6 and Rebecca (Stanford) Crockett. He married Sarah "Sally" Bartlett Wentworth. She was born in Cape Elizabeth, August 3, 1794, a daughter of Samuel Solley Wentworth and Hepsibah Hanscom. (Like the Crocketts, the Wentworth family also relocated to Pejepscot from Cape Elizabeth.) In 1812, Ephraim purchased a lot on Lee's Grant in Norway from Edward Little, son of Great Proprietor Josiah Little. The couple's first child was born in Danville, but the other twelve children (one of whom died in infancy) were born and raised on Crockett's Ridge in Norway, where Ephraim was a yeoman farmer. Ephraim died in November 12, 1856 at age 68. Sally lived for nearly two decades longer, dying May 6, 1875 at age 80. Ephraim was buried in the Crockett family cemetery next to the house. His body (and that of other family members buried there, including his wife) was exhumed and reburied at Norway Pine Grove Cemetery in South Paris.[24] Much of the land Ephraim settled is still in the family today, including the old Crockett homestead.[25]

Crockett, George.5 George was a son of Richard Crockett, Jr. and Mary (Robinson) Crockett. He was born circa 1744,[26] probably in Stratham, N.H., where his father had returned (with his family) to escape his Falmouth creditors. George married May 10, 1770, in Windham, Mary Mathews of Falmouth. George and his wife and children were baptized—along with his brother Daniel and his

---

24. Information told me by my grandmother Winona Palmer, who used to sit in her kitchen rocker by the woodstove and gaze out the window to where the old family cemetery used to be. Winona's information has since been confirmed by Norway Pine Grove Cemetery records.
25. My aunt Joyce Palmer owns the homestead. I am proud to own the ridge of land (11 acres, situated behind the house) to which Ephraim Crockett gave his name.
26. CANDAGE, p. 13.

family—in Windham, Maine on Sept. 4, 1774.[27] (They were likely Baptists.) George and Mary were the parents of Samuel Crockett, who lived in Pejepscot at the same time as our Revolutionary War ancestor Ephraim Crockett6 (son of Richard Crockett III and Elizabeth Roberts Crockett). This Samuel Crockett has often been confused by historians (understandably so) for Ephraim6's younger brother Samuel Crockett, also a Revolutionary War veteran. (More information on George and Mary's son Samuel Crockett in Chapter 7.) George Crockett died in Windham at 90 years of age.[28]

Crockett, Hannah.5 Hannah was a daughter of Richard Crockett, Jr. and Mary (Robinson) Crockett. She was born around 1740, possibly in Stratham, N.H., where her father had returned (with his family) to escape his Falmouth creditors. Hannah wed John Briant (or Bryant) of Biddeford. Their marriage intentions were filed in Falmouth, January 26, 1756. (No further information.)

Crockett, Hugh.2 A son of Thomas and Ann Crockett, Hugh lived as a youth with Sarah (Lynn) Rogers (daughter of Sarah Lynn Gunnison and her first husband Henry Lynn, and therefore a step-daughter of Hugh Gunnison) and her husband William Rogers on Gunnison's Neck.[29] In 1672, Hugh Crockett was fishing for Roger Kelly at Isle of Shoals,[30] where in 1675 or 1676 he would have met Henry Barter. Barter, a Welshman who arrived on the same boat as William Pepperell, was also a mariner,[31] and it was possibly Hugh who introduced Barter to the Crockett family. (Barter would wed Sarah Crockett, daughter of Ephraim and Ann Edge Crockett, and end up owning much of Crockett's Neck.) In 1695, Hugh, then a "mariner of Kittery" sold to his "cousin"[32] Henry Barter his "house & land lying

---

27. CANDAGE, p. 12-13.
28. CANDAGE, p. 13.
29. In a court case in 1704 between Samuel Winkley and Elihu Gunnison over a fence and boundary line, Hugh Crockett "full of years" gave testimony that "he ... did live with William Rogers thirty-six years ago ... [and] did at that time see a fence which fence run through the neck from the water side & from the main river to the water side in Spruce Creek which fence ... run about seven or eight rod below the fence now in controversy, which fence was built by William Seely." MPCR, Vol IV, p. 163. Seely and Rogers both had land on Gunnison's Neck, originally leased to them by their wives' stepfather Hugh Gunnison and later deeded to them by Gunnison's widow Sarah Gunnison (likely to protect the rights of her children with first husband Henry Lynn, and possibly in opposition to the wishes of her late husband, who might have wanted the land to revert to his own sons).
30. LIBBY/NOYES, p. 172. Hugh Crockett.
31. STACKPOLE, p. 283.
32. Henry Barter was probably not a cousin as one generally considers today. The term signified a family connection of a looser sort. Henry was the husband of Sarah Crockett, daughter of Ephraim and Ann Crockett (Hugh's niece), making Barter Hugh's nephew-in-law. Ann Crockett, Barter's grandmother-in-law, also identified Henry as "cousin." Some old-time Mainers

in the township of Kittery on my father Crockets neck of land ..."³³ In 1698, Hugh was married to Margaret _____ (surname unknown).³⁴ Hugh and Margaret had four children: Margaret/Margery, Sampson, Anne, and Elizabeth Crockett.³⁵

Crockett, James.7 A son of Ephraim and Rebecca (Stanford) Crockett, James was born Feb. 22, 1799 on the Pejepscot Claim. James lived not much more than three years. He died May 2, 1802.

Crockett, Joane. Sister of Thomas Crockett who emigrated as a young woman from Stoke Gabriel, Devon, England to Kittery by 1644, in time to be present at the birth of her nephew Ephraim. Joane married John Andrews, who was about 20 years her senior. The couple resided at Brave Boat Harbo, where they raised their family. Joane was a regular presence at court, where she was charged with a variety of infractions and often unleashed her tart tongue. Joane (Crockett) Andrew's life is covered in Chapter 1.

Crockett, Joseph.2 A son of Thomas and Ann Crockett, Joseph was born in 1653, per his deposition of April 21, 1713.³⁶ Like his father before him, Joseph was also a Constable of Kittery.³⁷ He married Hannah Clements of Haverhill, MA around 1678.³⁸ He also appears to have received land from his father on Crockett's Neck.

---

today still use the designation "cousin" as an affectionate way to cover a variety of family connections or a close relationship with a neighbor, who might have had a hand in raising children.

33. MEWD, Vol. 7, p. 192-193. The property, which Hugh appears to have been given by his father Thomas Crockett, was eight or nine acres with Hugh's house situated on it. See also MEWD, Vol. 4, p. 303, in which Ann Crockett, Thomas' widow, deeds to son Ephraim the balance of land on Crockett's Neck, bounded by Spruce Creek, land of her son Hugh Crockett, and sons-in-law William Roberts and John Parrot.

34. On July 5, 1698, at the Court of Quarter Sessions held at Wells, Hugh Crockett of Kittery and his now wife [Margaret _____] were "presented" (reprimanded) for fornication. MPCR, Vol. 4, p. 104. The infraction happened prior to July 5th; however, Hugh and Margaret were married before being presented in court. Presented at the same time were Hugh Tucker of Kittery and his now wife [Bridget _____], also for fornication. Tucker was the eldest son of Lewis Tucker and Sarah Gunnison, daughter of Hugh and Sarah Gunnison. Coincidentally, both Hugh Tucker and Hugh Crockett were likely named after Hugh Gunnison.

35. CANDAGE, p. 3.

36. MEWD, Vol 8, p. 83.

37. At a Court of Sessions held in York Aug. 12, 1684, Capt. Francis Hooke complained to the Court against Ann Billing (daughter of Thomas Crockett's sister Joane and her husband John Andrews, and wife of John Billing, Jr.) of several abuses given to himself and his wife, by "her reviling both himself and Mis Mary Hooke his wife, by very opprobrious [scornful] language, calling of her whore, thief and toad, besides other abusive speeches." Ann was brought before authority and by sufficient evidence was convicted of her crimes. She was sentenced to be carried to the post and to have 21 stripes well-laid upon her bare skin, which were administered by Joseph Crockett, her cousin, Constable of Kittery. MPCR Vol. 3, p. 198-199. (It seems that the apple did not fall too far from the tree, as Joane's daughters were much like their mother.)

38. CANDAGE, p. 2-3.

On Feb. 28, 1689, Joseph Crockett and Dennis Hicks[39] also purchased via an indenture 36 acres on Crockett's Creek in Kittery from Benjamin Woodbridge.[40] In his later years Joseph was often a witness in court (or gave depositions) about land disputes and boundaries, thanks to his early knowledge of the area and his occasional work marking property lines. Joseph and Hannah had eleven children: Joseph, Jr; Hannah; Lydia; Dorothy; Mary; John; Elizabeth; Abraham; Anna/Anne; Nathaniel; and Sarah Crockett.[41] Joseph was deceased by Jan. 3, 1716, when his widow Hannah presented a petition at the Court of General Sessions of the Peace in York "on behalf of her son Nathaniel Crockett..." to break Nathaniel's indenture to tailor John Jypson (which she successfully did).[42]

Crockett, Joseph.5 Joseph was a possible son of Richard Crockett, Jr. and Mary (Robinson) Crockett, who was reportedly born about 1750.[43] (No further information.)

Crockett, Joseph.7 Joseph was born May 23, 1797 on the Pejepscot Claim to Ephraim and Rebecca (Stanford) Crockett. On March 9, 1816, he married Elizabeth "Betsey" Jordan Wentworth, a sister of his brother Ephraim, Jr.'s wife Sally Wentworth. (Betsey was born on the Pejepscot Claim in 1796.) The couple followed her father, Samuel Solley Wentworth to Ohio. Joseph and Betsey had probably two children before her death near Chillicothe, Ohio around 1821. On April 8, 1822, Joseph married for his second wife Rachel Ferguson, who was born in

---

39. On Oct. 30, 1696, Hicks assigned any interest he had in this shared property with Joseph Crockett to Mary Ball, the future Mrs. Joseph Crockett, Jr. The couple was married Oct. 12, 1700. New England Marriages to 1700. Online database. *AmericanAncestors.org*. New England Historic Genealogical Society, 2008.
40. MPCR, Vol. 4, p. 253-255. The property purchased by Joseph Crockett and Dennis Hicks was bounded by that of Roger Deering's land on the east and land of the late Thomas Crockett on the west. Woodbridge, from whom they bought the property, was a minister in Kittery.
41. CANDAGE, p. 3.
42. MPCR, Vol. 5, p. 173-174. Young Nathaniel Crockett had been apprenticed to John Jypson of Kittery to learn the trade of tailor and learn how to read, write, and do accounts. Jypson, however, broke the terms of the indenture when he relocated (with Nathaniel) from Kittery to Rhode Island. In addition, Jypson was frequently away from home and failed to teach Nathaniel the tailor trade or his letters. Before his death, Joseph Crockett, Sr. attempted to purchase the balance of Nathaniel's indenture for 5 pounds (to keep the matter out of court); however, that settlement offer failed and the youth's mother took up the matter after her husband's death. The widow Hannah Crockett was greatly aided in her efforts (which succeeded in court to break the indenture) by William Godsoe, a surveyor and neighbor of the Crocketts, who married Elizabeth (Roberts) Surplus, widow of John Surplus, and daughter of Anne Crockett and William Roberts. (In other words, Godsoe came to the aid of the widow Hannah Crockett, who was his wife's aunt.) See MPCR, Vol V, p. 181 onward, which includes not only the record of the July 3, 1716 Court of General Sessions of the Peace held at York, in which the indenture is broken, but also related letters (including the letter of Joseph Crockett, Sr. to Jypson) and a copy of the indenture. See also LIBBY/NOYES, p. 269. (2) William Godsoe.
43. The information about Joseph Crockett is per Dr. Benjamin Lake Noyes papers, per CANDAGE, p. 7.

1803 (in Ohio). Joseph had probably four children with his second wife. No death record is available for Joseph. He is listed in the 1850 Ross County census at age 52; wife Rachel is 47.

Crockett, Joshua.2 A son of Thomas and Ann Crockett, Joshua appears to have been close in age to his brother Joseph. In order not to quarrel with eldest brother Ephraim, Joshua disowned in 1688 his right to a share of Thomas Crockett's real estate on Crockett's Neck, which he was promised by his father. Joshua sold his birthright to his brother Ephraim for 20 pounds,[44] and he and Elihu Gunnison (who was also dispossessed of his share of *his* father's estate)[45] went to Dover, N.H. where they learned the ship building trade and married daughters of Thomas and Elizabeth Trickey. (Joshua married Sarah[46] and Elihu married Martha Trickey.)[47] Joshua became a shipwright of Dover.[48] Gunnison also became a shipwright, but returned to Kittery to buy back some of his father's land, where he resided, remaining always a friend to the Crocketts, in particular a friend of Joseph Crockett. Joshua and Sarah (Trickey) Crockett had seven children: Joshua, Thomas,[49] Richard, Samuel, John/Jonathan, Elizabeth, and Deborah Crockett. Joshua died July 6, 1719. His widow was still living in 1730.[50]

---

44. MEWD, Vol. 5, p. 194. Joshua signed the deed July 10, 1688 in the presence of magistrate Francis Hooke and Hooke's wife Mary.
45. Sarah Gunnison, widow of Hugh, parceled out some of Gunnison's estate to the children (and their spouses) of her first marriage with Henry Lynn, and much of the rest was liquidated by her fourth husband Francis Morgan, a physician and spendthrift, who beat and abused her, causing Sarah in her last year(s) to throw herself upon the mercy of the Kittery selectmen for relief. Elihu Gunnison was still a minor when the liquidation of his father's estate occurred. Although Ann Crockett states she promised Hugh Gunnison before his death to help protect the rights of his two sons with Sarah (Elihu and his brother Joseph, who died young), she was unsuccessful. Elihu later bought back Gunnison's Neck. See deposition of Ann Crockett, Jan. 27, 1679. MEWD, Vol. 3, p. 248.
46. CANDAGE, p. 2.
47. MIGRATION, p. 177, Hugh Gunnison. STACKPOLE, p. 478 suggests Martha Trickey might have been a daughter of Francis Trickey, who lived next door and to whom Hugh Gunnison had sold 2 acres of land prior to his death. In 1703/04 Elihu Gunnison was taken to court by Samuel Winkley, son-in-law of Sarah Trickey (widow of Francis) and administrator of the Trickey estate, over property lines and location of an old fence. Had Winkley been Gunnison's brother-in-law it seems as though the two could have amicably worked out a solution, although Elihu was then married to his second wife, Elizabeth (Ingersol) Skillings, widow of John Skillings. Elizabeth removed to Kittery from Falmouth after her husband was killed by Indians. Elihu Gunnison and his first wife Martha Trickey had a child killed by Indians, possibly also in Falmouth. STACKPOLE, p. 478.
48. On Jan. 18, 1696/97, Joshua Crockett, shipwright of Dover, NH, sold to Richard Cutt, gentleman of Kittery, the 20 acres of land he received as a grant from the town of Kittery on July 28, 1679. The property was located between the land Cutt had recently purchased from Francis Avant and land of Joshua's brother, Ephraim Crockett, deceased. Witnesses: William Godsoe (an abutter and local surveyor and property conveyor), Richard Bryer, and Thomas Harford. MEWD, Vol. 4, p. 307-308.
49. We cannot say for sure that this child Thomas was named after his grandfather Thomas Crockett, since his maternal grandfather's given name was also Thomas.
50. CANDAGE, p. 2. Administration of Joshua Crockett's estate was given to his wife Sarah on Sept. 2, 1719. LIBBY/NOYES, p. 172. Joshua Crockett.

Crockett, Joshua.5 Joshua was a son of Richard Crockett, Jr. and Mary (Robinson) Crockett. He was born (probably in the Second District of Falmouth/Cape Elizabeth) around 1736. He married Hannah Babb (intentions filed July 8, 1757 in Falmouth), a daughter of James Babb, also of Falmouth. Joshua was a veteran of the American Revolution, rising to the rank of Lieutenant.[51] He and his wife resided in Gorham.

Crockett, Josiah.5 Josiah was one of the youngest children of Richard Crockett, Jr. and Mary (Robinson) Crockett. He was born before 1747 (either in Stratham, N.H. or Falmouth, Maine). As a young man (as early as 1768, when he was around 21), Josiah emigrated from Falmouth (probably Second District or Cape Elizabeth) to Deer Isle, where he married Sarah Dow of that settlement.[52] During the Revolutionary War the British occupied eastern Maine, which led to a time of lawlessness in that area. During this period Josiah and his father Richard (who followed his son to Deer Isle after the burning of Falmouth Neck in 1775) were both attacked and robbed by sea-faring thugs known as shaving mills. After the war was concluded, Josiah received as compensation for his suffering during the war a large grant of land in Deer Isle (as did his father and brother Robinson and many others). Josiah Crockett was described as "singular" by Deer Isle historian George L. Hosmer.[53] He died there in 1803. More information on Josiah's life can be found in Chapter 4.

Crockett, Lucy.6 Lucy[54] was a daughter of Richard (III) and Elizabeth (Roberts) Crockett. She was born June 24, 1765 in Cape Elizabeth. She married Nathaniel Abbott on October 3, 1793. Abbott was born September 30, 1764 in York, a son of Nathan Abbott and Mercy Gowan. The couple relocated in 1804 to Limington, Maine, where they made their home and raised their five children, including a son

---

51. CANDAGE, p. 11.
52. Sarah Dow was a daughter of Nathan Dow, the second person to permanently settle that area of Deer Isle, on what would become Dow's Point. DEERISLE, p.73-74 says Nathan arrived in the fall of 1767 and was believed to have been from Brunswick. Josiah Crockett arrived in Deer Isle in 1768.
53. DEERISLE, p. 103.
54. According to the genealogy, "Early Families of Limington, Maine," by Robert L. Taylor, Lucy "...was part Indian, so claimed descendants and was called a 'yellow-belly', by Lazarus Rowe, a noted Indian Hunter, who was a near neighbor." (This information is highly doubtful, given that we know Lucy's quite English genealogy; however, she might have been dark-skinned, which gave rise to this rumor, which Lucy appears not to have quashed.) "Early Families of Limington, Maine." Robert L. Taylor. Self-published. Limington, Maine: May 1984. P. 8, Abbott, Nathaniel.

named Richard after his paternal grandfather. Lucy died April 11, 1843 in Limington. Nathaniel died December 3, 1847, also in Limington.

Crockett, Mary.2 Probably the youngest child of Thomas and Ann Crockett, Mary married Elisha Barton, son of Edward and Elizabeth Barton of Cape Porpoise.[55] In 1684, Mary's brother Ephraim Crockett and her husband Elisha Barton acknowledged in court an agreement whereby Ephraim was to pay his brother-in-law over three years the sum of 12 pounds for Mary's "portion as she was a daughter to Thomas Crockett, deceased."[56] (Ephraim lived up to his agreement and Barton received his money.) Mary and Elisha both resided in Kittery in 1688.[57]

Crockett, Mary.3 A daughter of Ephraim and Anne (Edge) Crockett, Mary was likely named after her aunt Mary (Crockett) Barton. She married Francis Smart (after 1688, possibly much later). She and Francis were childless. Upon Smart's death, he willed the remainder of his estate (after Mary's death) to his "well beloved Kindred," William Barter, Sarah (Barter) Grindal, Elizabeth (Barter) Jones and Martha (Barter) Jones,[58] all of whom were children of Mary's sister Sarah (Crockett) and Henry Barter (i.e. Smart's nephew and nieces by marriage). There is no information about when Mary died.

Crockett, Mary.4 Possible daughter of Richard and Deborah (Haley) Crockett. (No further information.)

Crockett, Mary.5 Mary was the first child of Richard Crockett, Jr. and Mary (Robinson) Crockett. She was born March 28, 1732, in Falmouth, Maine. Mary married James Wagg, who lived alternately in the First and Second districts of Falmouth. (Their marriage intentions were filed in Falmouth November 11, 1749.) Mary was deceased by 1780, when James Wagg relocated to the Pejepscot Claim with their son, James Wagg, Jr. (a Revolutionary War veteran) and their nephew, Ephraim

---

55. LIBBY/NOYES, p. 79. (2) Edward Barton.
56. MPCR, Vol. 3, p. 203. On Oct. 28, 1684, at the Court of Sessions in York, Elisha Barton and Ephraim Crockett owned in court that this instrument was their free act and deed. The agreement was written into the record by Edward Rishworth. Ephraim made his payments to his sister because on May 20, 1688, his mother Ann deeded him the balance of Crockett's Neck, mentioning in this deed specifically the 12 pounds Ephraim paid to "my daughter Mary Barton." MEWD, Vol. 4, p. 303.
57. LIBBY/NOYES, p. 79. (2) Edward Barton.
58. Smart's will was dated May 10, 1743. His estate was probated Dec. 31, 1750. MEWD, Wills, p. 389-390. Elizabeth and Martha Barter married two Jones brothers.

Crockett (son of Mary's brother Richard III and his wife Elizabeth Roberts). Since the Waggs play a key role in the life of our Revolutionary War ancestor, Ephraim Crockett, their lives are covered in Chapter 7.

Crockett, Mary.6 Mary was a daughter of Richard (III) and Elizabeth (Roberts) Crockett. She was born circa 1764. Marriage intention between Mary and James Barton were filed March 20, 1786. She died October 19, 1833 and is buried in Eastern Cemetery, Portland, where she is called widow of James.

Crockett, Mary.7 Mary was a daughter of Ephraim and Rebecca (Stanford) Crockett. She was born April 21, 1790 on the Pejepscot Claim. She married Nathan Morse, Jr. of Lewiston. After her brother Ephraim, Jr.'s first partner on Lee's Grant (in Norway) backed out, he talked Mary and her husband into joining forces with him and wife Sally (Wentworth). Together, Ephraim and Nathan Morse purchased from Edward Little two contiguous lots of land on Lee's Grant, where they built homesteads next to each other and lived in harmony like brothers for the remainder of their lives. Mary and Nathan Morse had twelve children, three of whom died in childhood. In their later years, Nathan sold his homestead to a niece and nephew, and he and Mary removed to South Paris near the railroad. Mary died December 11, 1867 at age 79 and Nathan died April 20, 1870 at 82. They are buried in Norway Pine Grove Cemetery. Much of the land settled by Nathan and Mary (Crockett) Morse remains in the family today. (The lives of Mary and Nathan Morse are covered in my book, "A History of the Crockett Family of Crockett's Ridge, Norway, Maine." White Wave, 2024.)

Crockett, Priscilla.7 A daughter of Ephraim and Rebecca (Stanford) Crockett, Priscilla was born September 21, 1794 on the Pejepscot Claim. On November 5, 1812, she married Deacon John Stinchfield, Jr. (who was born on the Pejepscot Claim in 1798). The couple's eight children were all born in Pejepscot (Danville). Two of their children died very young (Rebecca, in 1818 at about four months, and "child Stinchfield," born July 6, 1824 and died two days later.) Priscilla (Crockett) Stinchfield died in Danville April 11, 1830 at age thirty-five.[59] Her husband John

---

59. It is possible that Priscilla died in childbirth (or from the results of giving birth). Her last living child was born in 1828 and so Priscilla would have been due to give birth to another child in 1830, the year she died. If so, that baby died as well.

remarried, to Sarah B. Jordan. (They also had children.) He died August 31, 1844 at fifty-five.

Crockett, Rebecca.7 Eldest child of Ephraim and Rebecca (Stanford) Crockett, Rebecca was born December 16, 1778 in Cape Elizabeth. She married James Aynes in Durham (Royalsborough) on April (or October) 26, 1797. (No further information.)

Crockett, Richard.3 Richard, the youngest son (and possibly youngest child) of Ephraim and Anne (Edge) Crockett, was only six when his father died in 1688. His elder brother Ephraim, Jr. appears not to have survived, leaving Richard (as the only remaining son) to inherit the Crockett's Neck house and property that formerly belonged to his grandfather Thomas Crockett. Richard also inherited 40 acres and a cow left to him in his father's will.[60] He and his best friend Samuel Skillin married sisters. Richard married Deborah Haley and Samuel married Rhoda (Aroda) Haley. (The women were daughters of Andrew and Deborah Wilson Haley.) Richard and his wife and family relocated to Stratham, N.H., where he became a founder of the town and was an upright and respected citizen. Deborah died young and Richard never remarried. Richard and Deborah's life is covered in Chapter 3.

Crockett, Richard, Jr.4 Richard was a son (possibly the eldest) of Richard and Deborah (Haley) Crockett. He was born 1706/1707, probably in Kittery, where his parents resided on Crockett's Neck prior to relocating to Stratham, N.H. Richard returned to Maine to live by 1731, immigrating to the greater Falmouth area where his aunt and uncle Samuel and Rhoda (Haley) Skillin, and their family, were then living. In Falmouth, Richard, Jr. met and married Mary Robinson August 20, 1731. (Mary was born January 22, 1712 in Gloucester, MA to Abraham Robinson III and Sarah York Robinson.)[61] Richard became a chairmaker and throughout

---

60. MEWD, Vol. 8, p. 105-106. Richard states in this deed of Crockett's Neck to his brother-in-law Henry Barter that the property previously belonged to Thomas Crockett and then to Richard's father Ephraim. He does not mention his elder brother Ephraim, Jr. to whom the property was left by Ephraim Sr. in his will, signifying that Ephraim, Jr. did not survive to adulthood.
61. "Massachusetts Births and Christenings, 1639-1915," database, FamilySearch https://familysearch.org/ark:/61903/1:1:V5N4-HWY There has been much confusion over Mary Robinson's parentage. Some historians and genealogists claim that her father Abraham was a descendant of the Rev. John Robinson, pastor to the Pilgrims and organizer of the Mayflower Expedition. (See Pringle's "History of the Town and City of Gloucester, Cape Ann, Massachusetts," p. 49.) According to Dr. Carol McCoy in her genealogy of Richard Crockett, Mary was the eleventh child (of fourteen) of Abraham "Peter" Robinson: "The Robinson family was Dutch in origin and had migrated to America in the early 1600's. [Mary's]

most of his life was perpetually in debt. Because of his debt (and perhaps trouble with alcoholism) Richard found it necessary to return to Stratham to live with his father for a time. After a decade or so, Richard and Mary went back to the Second District (Cape Elizabeth) of Falmouth, where they raised their family. Mary predeceased her husband (her death date is unknown). After the burning of Falmouth in 1775, Richard, Jr. emigrated to Deer Isle to live near his son Josiah. (Richard was then in his seventh decade.) He died in Deer Isle *after* March 6, 1781 (the day that Richard was the victim of a shaving mill, which he survived), but *prior to* January 1, 1786, when his heirs received a posthumous grant of land for their father. The lives of Richard and Mary Crockett are covered in Chapter 4.

Crockett, Richard (III, also known as Richard, Jr.)[5] Richard was a son of Richard Crockett, Jr. and Mary (Robinson) Crockett. He was born (probably in the Second District of Falmouth/Cape Elizabeth) around 1733. He married (first) Elizabeth Roberts, a daughter of George and Katharine (Skillin) Roberts. (Elizabeth's mother, Katharine, was a daughter of Samuel and Rhoda Haley Skillin.) Richard remained in the Second District of Falmouth where he became a leading member of Cape Elizabeth society. He was a chairmaker by trade, like his father (Richard Crockett, Jr.) After his first wife died, Richard married Elizabeth's first cousin, Susannah Westcoat (daughter of neighbor and relative William Westcoat and Dorcas Skillin Westcoat). Susannah was an unwed mother with an illegitimate son. After her death, Richard married for a third time, to the widow Elizabeth Lewis Masury (Magery), with whom he had a son William. Richard's life, and that of families (and friends) are covered in Chapter 5.

Crockett, Robinson.[5] Robinson was a son of Richard Crockett, Jr. and Mary (Robinson) Crockett. He was born before 1745, probably in Stratham, N.H., where his father had returned (with his family) to escape his Falmouth creditors. Like his father and older brother Richard, Robinson was initially a chairmaker; however, he later became a master mariner. In 1806, Robinson and "his son-in-law David

---

parents were born in MA. Her father, Abraham Peter Robinson was born in 1655 and her mother Experience Manter in 1677." (DESCENDANTS, p. 3.) Given Mary's connection to the York family, however, (Mary and Richard sold her rights of inheritance as a descendant of Samuel York) I feel confident that her mother was Sarah (York) Robinson and not Experience Manter. This would necessarily suggest that Dr. McCoy has selected the wrong Abraham Robinson for Mary's father. I am unsure whether this eliminates the connection to the Rev. John Robinson, though, not having taken my research in that direction.

Sawyer, and sons Ephraim and Richard, owned the schooner *America*."[62] Robinson married Hannah Crocker, April 23, 1764, in Cape Elizabeth or Falmouth. He and his family followed younger brother Josiah and their father to Deer Isle before 1785. Robinson eventually relocated to Little Deer Isle, and then Brooksville, where he died.

Crockett, Samuel Haley.4 A son of Richard Crockett and Deborah (Haley) Crockett, Samuel was born circa February 1717, probably in Stratham, N.H. When he was about eighteen, Samuel joined his older brother Richard and aunt and uncle Samuel and Rhoda (Haley) Skillin in Falmouth, Maine, where he worked as a chairmaker (as did Richard). Likely under the beneficent oversight of uncle Samuel Skillin (for whom Samuel was probably named), he later became a shipwright. Also, like his successful uncle Skillin, Samuel Crockett invested in real estate. Samuel married 1st Sarah Cobb; 2nd Mrs. Priscilla (Swett) Jackman; and 3rd Mrs. Mary (Cram) Whitney). Samuel's life is covered in Chapter 4.

Crockett, Samuel.6 Samuel was a son of Richard (III) and Elizabeth (Roberts) Crockett. He was born circa 1760. Like his older brother Ephraim, Samuel fought in the American Revolution. He resided in Cape Elizabeth, where he married Abigail Skillin. More information on Samuel and Abigail Crockett in Chapter 5.

Crockett, Sarah.2 A daughter of Thomas and Ann Crockett, Sarah was likely named after the couple's good friend Sarah Lynn Gunnison. She married John Parrett (or Parrott/Parrot). They resided on Crockett's Neck, where they raised their two girls (Mary and Sarah)[63] on land given them by Thomas Crockett, probably upon their marriage.[64]

Crockett, Sarah.3 A daughter of Ephraim and Anne (Edge) Crockett, she was likely named after her aunt Sarah (Crockett) Parrett (Parrot). Sarah married mariner and fisherman Henry Barter (after 1688, when she is still mentioned as "Sarah

---

62. CANDAGE, p. 12.
63. CANDAGE, p. 2.
64. On May 20, 1688, Ann Crockett Jeffrey deeded to her son Ephraim (and his heirs)—after he had paid the legacies required in his father's will—all the lands on Crockett Neck bounded by Spruce Creek, land of her son Hugh Crockett and sons-in-law William Roberts and John Parrot, containing "all the land laid out and bounded by Captn Wincoll [Winchell]..." This signifies that Sarah and John Parrot (and other Crockett children/spouses) were living on Crockett's Neck on property previously given them by their father prior to Thomas Crockett's death. MEWD, Vol. 4, P. 303.

Crockett" in her father's will) and remained on Crockett's Neck, where Barter added to his holdings and they raised their family. More information about Sarah and Henry's life is covered in Chapter 3.

Crockett, Sarah.4 Possible daughter of Richard and Deborah (Haley) Crockett of Stratham, N.H. (No further information.)

Crockett, Sarah.5 Sarah was a daughter of Richard Crockett, Jr. and Mary (Robinson) Crockett. She was born approximately 1738 (possibly earlier). Sarah was probably born in the Second District of Falmouth (Cape Elizabeth), although if the 1738 date is correct she could have been born in Stratham, N.H., to which community her father had returned (with his family) to escape his Falmouth creditors. Sarah married Richard O'Brien on September 24, 1754 in Falmouth. (No further information.)

Crockett, Sarah.6 Sarah was a daughter of Richard (III) and Elizabeth (Roberts) Crockett. She was married to Cornelius Bramhall of Falmouth on November 25, 1773 (in Falmouth). Sarah lived (for a period of her life, at least) on Vinalhaven, where she died June 1823, "age 81 years, formerly of Portland" (per *Eastern Argus* paper of June 13, 1823, per Robert Taylor 1988).

Crockett, Sarah "Sally."7 A daughter of Ephraim and Rebecca (Stanford) Crockett, Sally was born July 21, 1792 on the Pejepscot Claim. She married Joel Morse of Lewiston, a brother of Nathan Morse, who married her sister Mary Crockett (and had removed to Norway). Joel was a farmer. The couple resided in the greater Lewiston-Auburn area, where they raised their ten children, two of whom died in childhood. (Daughter Sarah died in 1819 at age seven and son James died in 1839 at age nine.) Sally (Crockett) Morse died August 13, 1850 in Auburn. Her husband Joel outlived her by eight years. Joel Morse died in Auburn August 1, 1858.

Crockett, Susannah.6 Susannah was a daughter of Richard (III) and Susannah (Westcoat) Crockett. She was born in 1781 in Cape Elizabeth, and named for her mother. At some point (possibly after her mother's death) Susannah appears to have gone to live with or visit her older half-sister Lucy (Crockett) Abbott in North

Limington (Maine). Susannah married Daniel Stone on January 20, 1800. He was of Limington, she of Falmouth (according to Candage). The couple had 10 children. Susannah (Crockett) Stone died September 16, 1863, in Limington, aged 82 years.[65]

Crockett, William.4 A son of Richard and Deborah (Haley) Crockett, William was born circa 1717/18, probably in Stratham, N.H., where his parents relocated from Kittery in 1713. In 1737, William purchased property and moved to another Exeter settlement,[66] which community broke away and became chartered as Epping in 1741. In 1749, William and his brother Samuel were gifted by their father any and all lands that Richard Crockett had coming to him by the division of the Commons in Berwick and Kittery, Maine.[67] The two brothers sold these rights in two transactions; in 1751 for 2 pounds, 2 shillings and 8 pence lawful money,[68] and, in 1758, for 160 pounds[69] old tenor.[70] According to Crockett genealogist Candage, the name of William's wife is not known. She was born circa 1719 and died in Epping, N.H. about age 64. William died in Epping August 19, 1785 at age 68.[71]

---

65. See also, "Early Families of Limington, Maine." Robert L. Taylor. Self-published. Limington, Maine: May 1984. See p. 178 and p. 8. It is from this information that I gathered that Susannah, after her mother's death, might have gone to live with or visit her older half-sister Lucy in North Limington, in which town she met her husband. It was not uncommon for unmarried women to travel around visiting relatives (and helping in their households) while in search of a husband. (In fact, the Amish continue this practice today, with both men and women travelling out of their communities in search of a spouse.)
66. On Aug. 8, 1737, Israel Gilman of Newmarket, Province of New Hampshire, sold to William Crockett (son of Richard Crockett) of Stratham, yeoman, for 225 pounds, 50 acres in Exeter that was cut off or apportioned to Moses Gilman, Jr. in 1725 according to drawing of lots. RCROD, Vol. 23, p. 77-78. Witnesses to the transaction were Ephraim Crockett (William's older brother) and John Moody.
67. On Jan 10, 1749, Richard Crockett of Stratham, yeoman, "for and in consideration of the parental love, good will & affection I have towards my well-beloved sons William Crockett of Ippen [Epping] Province of NH, husbandman, and Samuel Crockett of Falmouth in the County of York, shipwright, have granted/given all my lands & Right in Commonage in the Township of Kittery & Berwick in aforesaid County of York." RCROD, Vol. 47, p. 147-148. Richard Crockett appeared the same day before Bradstreet Wiggin, Justice of the Peace for the Province of NH, to swear the deed executed was by his free act and deed. Witnesses to the transaction were Patience and Richard Young.
68. On Oct. 8, 1751, William Crockett, yeoman of Epping, N.H. and Samuel Crockett, shipwright of Falmouth, sold for 2 pounds, 2 shillings and 8 pence to Moses Hanscom, housewright of Kittery "four rights or shares that we have in the Common Lands so called lately belonging to the Proprietors of the town of Kittery, but since divided to & among the sd. Proprietors which sd. four rights or shares lies in that part of the Proprietors Lands called Pudding hole commons and in the Division called Number Three, which Division or Part is a six acre lot & lies adjoining to lands of Nathl. Fernald on the Northerly side of said Commons." YCROD, Vol. 31, p. 165-166.
69. On Dec. 2, 1758, William Crockett, husbandman of Epping, N.H. and Samuel Crockett, shipwright of Gorham Town, Province of Maine, sold for 160 pounds old tenor in Bills of Credit, New Hampshire, to Nathan Lord, Jr. any and all of their rights to the Commons/Common Land in Berwick, Maine, which right was deeded to them by their father Richard. YCROD, Vol. 35, p. 248.
70. "Old tenor" was a nickname for paper money issued by Massachusetts Bay Colony, which was ordered (by the legislature) removed from circulation in 1751. https://nationalhumanitiescenter.org/pds/becomingamer/american/text3/oldtenor.pdf
71. CANDAGE, p. 7.

Crockett, William.6 William was a son of Richard Crockett (III) and Elizabeth Masury Crockett (Richard's third wife). He lived with his parents and stepbrother John Masury in Cape Elizabeth. William appears to have died as a young man. Since there is very limited information about William (told in Chapter 5) we must consider the possibility that he never existed, but has been mistaken for the son of Samuel (Richard III's son) and his wife Abigail, also named William.

Acknowledgements

I could not have completed a project of such wide scope without the assistance of many, many people. My deepest gratitude goes to the historians and archivists who aided me on this five-year journey, and so I will begin by thanking them.

One of the biggest challenges I faced in the third and fourth generations—with Richard Crockett, Jr. and his son, Richard (III)—was figuring out where they resided. Cape Elizabeth? Falmouth? South Portland? David Farnham of the Falmouth Historical Society (a friend of my late aunt Faith Varney) was instrumental in helping me untangle the many strands of Falmouth. Turns out, because of the way Falmouth was divided up over the past three hundred years, Richard III lived in all three towns—without moving an inch! David also gave me other sage advice and historical information via many email exchanges, for which I am grateful. I'd also like to thank Betsy Jo Whitcomb, a former President of the Falmouth Historical Society, for reviewing a first draft of "Into the Maine." There are not many people who could review such a book for accuracy and so I appreciate her knowledgeable eyes. Kathryn DiPhilippo, executive director of the South Portland Historical Society also helped me with the Falmouth/Cape Elizabeth/South Portland conundrum and Mia Sigler, Reference Assistant, Brown Research Library (MHS) researched for me many Crockett birth and marriage records (and marriage intentions) as well as family deeds.

Caitlin Jones, Head of Reference at the Massachusetts Archives, provided me with detailed information about the Pejepscot Claim from the Eastern Land Papers and a photo of the map of the lots laid out to the settlers during the 1804 proposal to "quiet" them. Thanks also to Dr. Douglas Hodgkin, Secretary of the Androscoggin Historical Society, whose books on Edward Little and the history of Lewiston (including information on the Pejepscot Proprietors) was important when I wrote the concluding chapter of the book. I enjoyed a chat with Dr. Hodgkin about the Little family one afternoon at the AHS, during which I learned nuggets of interesting information about these Great Proprietors. My gratitude to AHS for their kind assistance with my research, as well as for preserving the original documents I utilized.

I would also like to thank Paul Friday of the New Hampshire Historical Society, who helped me with early New Hampshire court records, and suggested that I gain online access to locked records via a FamilySearch center operated by the Church of Jesus Christ of Latter-Day Saints in Maine. Taking Paul's advice, I soon found my way to the Bangor FamilySearch center (which I had not known existed), where Laura and Quint Hurst not only made me feel welcome, but also helped me find Maine and New Hampshire court and town records utilizing the center's "open" computers. During every visit (and there were many), Laura graciously picked up lunch for me so that I could spend more hours at my research. In addition, after reading sections of "Into the Maine," Laura encouraged me to publish the book, assuring me that it contained valuable information about the history of our state that people would want to read. I would also like to mention friend (and distant relative) Roger Crockett. Roger gave me a copy of April Coleman's Crockett family timeline, with which I ensured I did not miss any important Crockett family events in my history.

I could not have written this book without standing upon the shoulders of historians who went before me. Special thanks go to three men whose research and books were fundamental to my story: Robert Charles Anderson and his "Great Migration Study Project" and books; Alan Taylor, author of "Liberty Men and Great Proprietors;" and Ian Saxine, author of "Properties of Empire." I am grateful for the illumination and insight (and information) provided by Anderson, Taylor, and Saxine, which helped me put a solid foundation under my Crockett history. I am also deeply indebted to Charles Candage, whose 1990 "Crockett Genealogy, 1610-1933" I would have been lost without. I cannot forget, also, how much I owe to those historians no longer with us, but who also lighted my way, including Sibyl Noyes, Charles Thornton Libby, Walter Goodwin Davis, Wilbur D. Spencer, Charles Edward Banks, Everett S. Stackpole, James Phinney Baxter, Hugh D. McLellan, William Willis, and William B. Jordan, Jr. I am especially grateful to the Maine Historical Society for publishing its six-volume set of the "Province and Court Records of Maine," and to the men who edited those consequential volumes, including C.T. Libby; Robert E. Moody (whose personal set of these records I now own, complete with his pencil notations in the margins); and Neal W. Allen, Jr. Finally, I must also acknowledge the contribution of historical websites to which I turned for useful information (and often photos and maps), especially the Old Berwick Historical Society and Maine Memory Network.

A special thanks goes to the members of the Maine Air National Guard in

Acknowledgements

South Portland (formerly Cape Elizabeth), who allowed me to visit (and accompanied me to) the ancient Long Creek cemetery (located behind the guard facility), where many Crocketts are buried, as well as their Skillin, York, and Roberts relations. This was particularly kind of the Guard as I arrived on their doorstep on a Friday afternoon (during the COVID pandemic) when they were busy gathering for weekend drills.

I am much indebted to John Goldfine of Swanville, who edited the first—and then the final—draft of this book. Thanks to John's light, but deft touch, I am a better writer today than I was when I began this journey. As a result, "Into the Maine" is a better book.

The beautiful front cover was created by Peter Harris of Spofford, N.H., the eighth cover Peter has done for me. Thanks also to Clark Kenyon of Camp Pope Publishing for another outstanding typesetting job, and to Leigh Ann Laney for her incredibly thorough (and so important!) indexing.

Finally, I would like to recognize the contributions of my husband Stanley Luce. His love and support kept me balanced and focused while researching and writing this book. Yes, dear—it is finally DONE.

Thank you everyone. Truly, I could not have completed this project without you all.

Jennifer Wixson
Troy, Maine
April 19, 2025

Appendix

List of Appendix Items

Inventory of the estate of Thomas Crockett, 20 March 1678/79.	402
Last Will and Testament of Ephraim Crockett, 17 July 1688 – p. 1.	403
Last Will and Testament of Ephraim Crockett, 17 July 1688 – p. 2.	404
Transcription of the Warumbo Deed, negotiated 7 July 1684.	405
Petition of Josiah Crockett to the General Court of Massachusetts 11 April 1781	408

From York Deeds Book 5.

An Inventory of the Estate formerly Thomas Crockett, now deceased as it was shewd unto vs whose names are vnderwritten, this 20th day March 1678-9

Imprs one Necke of land, neare unto Spruse Cricke, bounded at the head with a little Island, & doth Containe as we Judg one hundred eighty eight Acres, or yr abouts at 50s p Acre

	L	s	d
	141	00	0
It one horse, one Heiffer at three pounds........	005	10	0
It To six acres Marsh or yr abouts at ten pounds	10	00	0
It to Iron Potts, a potthooke, & Crookes at......	1	00	0
It 3 Chests & things in them 12s, Earthern & wooden ware 13s	01	05	0
It a spitt, twoold axes betle rings and other Iron.	000	10	0
It a frinpann 4s, & other severall ould Calkes 6s	00	10	0
It 4 pewter dishes, one cupp, bason & Candlestick	00	11	00
It one grindstone & too basketts 3s6d, a Cubbard 2s 6d	01	06	00
It too Wedges 2s6d, Cloathing lining and Woolen 40s	02	2	6
It a debt due from Ephriam Crockett	07	00	0
It an ould Connow at 16s	00	16	0

Apraised by us the day & yeare above written

FRANCIS HOOKE, WILLIAM SCRIUINE

Ann Crockett gives vpon her oath in Court, that this is a true Inventory of her husbands Estate, & if more appeare afterwards shee vpon the same oath will give it in. taken in Court: of April 1679: as Attes: Edw: Rishworth ReCor:

See also:

York Deeds Book v.

July 10, 1688—Joshua Crockett to Ephraim Crockett—Folio 109
Quit Claim to all right to Crocketts neck.

Apr. 27, 1686. Deed of Ephraim Crockett to Richard White of land at Broad Boat Harbor.

Inventory of the estate of Thomas Crockett, 20 March 1678/79.
York Deeds, Book 5.

Maine Wills.

Probate Office, I, 10.

The Last Will and Testament of Ephraim Crocket being weak in body but of perfect memory being Sencible of the Dept I ow to nature p death the which I am in dayly expectacōn off, and for the prevention of distraccōn after my decease am willing to settle my little Estate God hath given me in this world/

viz: I comitt my Soule to God and my body to y⁰ Earth to be decently buried att the discretion of my wife and my Estate to be disposed in manner and forme as followeth./

viz I Will and determin that all my just and honest debts and funerall charges shall be wel and truly satisfied and paid

2 I Will that all my Estate both Lands and moveables remaine in the hands of my well beloved wife An Crocket till my Son Ephraim Crocket shall come to age

3 I will give and bequeath to my Son Ephraim Crockett all my house and Land where now I dwell as alsoe all that peece of Salt Marsh at Broadboate harbour which I bought of Captn Champernown for an Inheritence to him & his heires for ever

4 I will that my now wife Anna Crockett shall have possesse and quietly enjoy the one halfe of this my house and Land and Marsh dureing her Naturall life/

5 I will that my Son Ephraim Crockett shal enter into possession of the one halfe of my house Land & Marsh abovesaid when he comes to age and the other halfe to returne to him y⁰ sd Ephraim Creckett att the decease of my wife./

6 I give and bequeath to my wife all my moveables as Cattle Sheep horses Swine or any other thing either abroad or att home wthin doores or wthout for her support and maintenance dureing her life here and that w^{t}soever shall remayne of my moveables att her decease shall retorne to my Son Ephraim Crockett./

7 I give and bequeath to my son Richard Crockett forty

Last Will and Testament of Ephraim Crockett, 17 July 1688 – p. 1.

Acres of Land lyeing neare the Mast way to him and his Heires for ever./ And one Cow

8 I will and bequeath to my daughters Sarah and Mary Crockett twenty pounds a peece to be paid to them by my Eldest son Ephraim Crocket att the decease of my wife./

9 That Whereas my ffather Thomas Crockett did in his life tyme give Lay out and bound a peece of his Neck of Land which was in his owne possession to my sister An Roberts as alsoe a peece of sd Neck of Land to my Sister Sarah Parrett as their Marriage portions my Will is the said Land thus given by my father shall stand good to my Sisters and their Heires for ever/

10 I Will choose and appoint my trusty and faithfull friends Bro^r Joshua Crockett Richard Cutt and William Scrivener as Overseers of this my Last Will and Testament In Wittnes whereof I have hereunto sett my hand and Seale this 17th of July in the year of our Lord 1688

Signed and Sealed in ye Ephraim Crocket
  p^{r}sence of us   E   (seal)
  William Screven   his mark
  Richard Cutt
  Humphrey Churchwood

Sworn to and Recorded March 13th, 1688-9. Inventory returned Sept., 10, 1688 at £49: 01: 08, by Nicholas Weekes William ffernald, appraisers.

Last Will and Testament of Ephraim Crockett, 17 July 1688 – p. 2.

Appendix

Transcription of the Warumbo Deed,[1] negotiated 7 July 1684.

"To ALL People to whom these presents shall come, Know Yee that whereas near three score years since M` Thomas Purchase deceas'd came into this Countrey as wee have been informed and did as well by Power or Patent derived from the King of England as by consent contract & agreement with Sagamores & Proprietors of all the Lands lying on the Easterly Side of Casco Bay & on, the both sides of Androscoggen River & Kennebeck River, enter upon & take possession of all the Lands lying four Miles Westward from the uppermost Falls in Sd Androscoggan River to Maquoit in Casco Bay & in the Lands on the other side Androscoggan River from above sd Falls down to Pejepscot and Merrymeeting Bay to be bounded by a South West & North East Line to run from the upper part of sd Falls to Kennebeck River & all the Lands from Maquoit to Pejepscot & to hold the same Breadth where the Land will bear it down to a place called Atkins his Bay near to Sagadahock or the Westerly side of Kennebeck River & all the Islands in the Sd Kennebeck River & Land between the said Atkins his Bay & Small Point Harbour the Lands & Rivers & Pond interjacent containing in breadth about three English Miles more or less, And whereas we are well assured that Majr Nicholas Shapleigh in his lifetime was both by purchase from the Indian Sagamores our Ancestors and consent of Mr. Gorges Commissioner possessed & dyed Seized of the remainder of all the Lands lying & adjoining upon the Maine & all the Islands between the said Small Point Harbour & Maquoit afores'd & particularly of a Neck of Land Merryconege & an Island called Sebasco Diggin. And whereas the Relicts & Heirs of said Mr Purchase and Majr Nicholas Shapleigh have reserved accommodations for their several Families sold all the remainder of the aforesaid Lands & Islands to Richard Wharton of Boston Mercht, And for asmuch as the said Mr. Purchase did personally possess improve & inhabit at Pejepscot aforesd near the Centre or Middle of all the Lands aforesd for near fifty years before the Late unhappy War, And Whereas the sd Richard Wharton hath desired an enlargement upon and between the sd Androscoggen & Kennebec Rivers & to encourage the Said Richard Wharton to settle an English Town & promote the Salmon and Sturgeon Fishing by which we promise our Selves great Supplyes & Relief. Therefore & for other good causes & consideration, & especially for & in consideration of a Valuable

---

1. Transcription taken from The History of Brunswick, Topsham, and Harpswell, Maine. George Augustus Wheeler, M.D. and Henry Warren Wheeler. Boston: Alfred Mudge & Son, Printers. 1878. Chapter Two.

Sum received from the Sd Wharton in Merchandize. Wee Warumbee, Darumkine, Wihikermet, Wedon-Domhegon, Neonongasset, & Nimbanewet Chief Sagamores of all the aforesaid and other Rivers & Land Adjacent have in conformation of the said Richard Whartons Title & Propriety fully freely and absolutely given granted ratify ed & confirmed to him the said Richard Wharton all the aforesd Lands from the uppermost part of ANDROSCOGGAN FALLS FOUR MILES Westward & so down to MAQUOIT & by Said, River of Pejepscot & from the other side of Androscoggan Falls all the Land from the Falls to Pejepscot & Merrymeeting Bay to Kenebeck & towards the Wilderness to be bounded by a SOUTH WEST & NORTH EAST LINE to extend from the upper part of the said Androscoggan UPPERMOST FALLS to the said River of KENEBECK & all the Land from Maquoit to Pejepscot & to run & hold the same Breadth Where the Land will bear it unto ATKINS his BAY in Kenebeck River & SMALL POINT HARBOUR in Casco Bay and all ISLANDS in Kenebeck & Pejepscot Rivers & Merrymeeting Bay & within the aforesd Bounds. Especially the aforesaid Neck of Land called MERRYCONEGE & Island called SEBASCO DEGGIN Together with all Rivers Rivulets Brooks Ponds Pools Waters Watercourses. All wood Trees of Timber or other Trees & all Mines Mineralls & Quarries and especially the Sole & absolute use & benefit of Salmon and Sturgeon Fishing in all the Rivers Rivulets or Bays aforesd & in all Rivers Brooks Creeks or Ponds within any of the Bounds aforesaid. And also Wee the Said Sagamores have upon the considerations aforesaid given granted bargained & sold enfeoffed & confirmed & do by these presents give grant bargain sell aliene enfecooffe & confirm to him the said Richard Wharton all the Land lying FIVE MILES ABOVE the uppermost of the said Androscoggan Falls in Breadth & Length holding the same Breadth from Androscoggan Falls to Kenebeck River & to be bounded by the aforesd South West and North East Line & a parcell of Land at Five Miles Distance to run from Androscoggan to Kennebeck River as aforesd Together with all the Profits Priviledges Commodities Benefits & Advantages & particularly the Sole Propriety Benefit & Advantage of the Salmon & Sturgeon Fishing within the Bounds & Limits aforesaid To have & to hold to him the said Richard Wharton his heirs & assignes for ever all the aforenamed Lands Priveledges & Premises with all benefits rights appurtenances or advantages that now do or hereafter shall or may belong unto any part or parcell of the Premises fully freely & absolutely acquitted & discharged from all former & other gifts grants bargains sales mortgages & Incumbrances whatsoever, And Wee the said Warumbee Derumkine Wihiketmet Wedon-Domhegon, Neonongasset & Numbenewet do covenant & grant to & with the said Richard Wharton that we have in our selves good right & full power thus to confirm & convey the premises & that we our heirs and successors shall & will warrant & defend the said Richard Wharton his heirs & assignes for ever in the peaceable enjoyment of the Premises & every part thereof against all and every person or persons that may legally claim any right Title Interest or Propriety in the Premises by from or under us the abovenamed Sagamores or any of our Ancestors or Predecessors, Provided nevertheless that nothing in this Deed be construed to deprive us the Sd Sagamores our Successors or People from improving our antient planting grounds nor from hunting in any of the said Land being not inclosed nor from fishing for our own provision so long as no Damage shall be to the English Fishery, Provided also that nothing herein contained shall prejudice any of the. English Inhabitants or Planters being at present actually possessed of any of the Premises & legally deriving right from Sd Mr. Purchase &c or Ancestors. In witness hereof we the aforenamed Sagamores well understanding the Purport hereof do set to our hands & Seales at Pejepscot the seventh Day of July in the thirty fifth year of the Reign of our Sovereign Lord King Charles the Second One Thousand Six hundred eighty four."

Sealed and Delivered In presence of

JOHN BLANEY
JAMES ANDREWS
HENRY WALTERS
JOHN PARKER
GEO. FELT

THE MARK OF WARUMBEE

THE MARK OF DARUMKINE

THE MARK OF WIHIKERMET

THE MARK OF WEDON DOMHEGON

THE MARK OF NEHONONGASSET

THE MARK OF NUMBENEWET

Petition of Josiah Crockett[2] to the General Court of Massachusetts
11 April 1781

To the Honourable the Senate and house of Representatives of the Commonwealth of Massachusetts Humbly Sheweth Josiah Crockett of Deer Island in the County of Lincoln that on the failure of the expedition to Penobscott in the year 1779, the inhabitants of Deer Island, especially those who had taken up arms with their brethren of this Commonwealth (among whom was your petitioner) were compelled by the British Commander at Majorbigwaduce [another name for Fort George] to take the oath of Allegiance to the King of Great Britain, as the condition upon which alone they might peaceably enjoy their estates, with the assurance however that they should not be called upon to bear arms against those under the banners of America. That on the eighteenth day of April A.D. 1780 General Wadsworth Commander of the American forces in the County of Lincoln, by his proclamation of that date, in tenderness and justice to the inhabitants of said Deer Island and other places adjacent to Majorbigwaduce, (whose critical and uncomfortable situation was not owing to their want of affection to, or zeal for, the Government of Massachusetts, but to a contingency of events needless to be mentioned) did order and direct the inhabitants aforesaid to consider themselves as neutrals in regard of aiding or assisting either party; allowing them an intercourse with the subjects of this Commonwealth, and declaring that they should always have proper passes for their return home from the Commander at the American post: That on the 7th day of October 1779, the house of Representatives requested the Honble Council to direct the Commanding Officer of the County of Lincoln not to suffer small scouting parties to molest or disturb the inhabitants of Penobscott; By all which the spirits of the people have been supported under their sufferings, reflecting, that although a wise Providence has seen fit to exercise their patience by an ostensible submission to his Britannic Majesty, (which can only be considered as temporary, and during the present constraint they are under), yet the inhabitants of Deer Island could never doubt your Honours confidence in their heart affection and zeal for the cause and interest of the United States as having never by any voluntary act forfeited the protection of the laws and Government of this Commonwealth, Yet in addition to their distress as though it were not already sufficient, in total disregard

---
2. Petition of Josiah Crockett to the General Court of Massachusetts, April 11, 1781. BAXTER2, p. 195.

of the feelings of humanity, prompted by avarice and a desire of plunder a certain Nathaniel Thomson of Falmouth in the County of Cumberland in a boat with fifteen men from said Falmouth on the sixth day of March last past landed at said Deer Island abused robbed and plundered some of the inhabitants thereof. They entered the house of your petitioner, struck and abused his wife there being, broke in the window where a child was laying then dangerously sick and thereby greatly hazarded its life;–They took and carried away from your petitioners store rum tobacco &c and meeting your petitioner as they left his house as he returned from his neighbours they insulted and abused him; took from him eleven gallons of molasses he then had with him, and forced him on board their boat, where they detained him a considerable time. They also entered the house of Mr. Richard Crockett your petitioners father, being above 75 years of age, and with a loaded gun placed at his breast threatened to take away his life, they otherwise insulted him, and beat and wounded him so that he was unable to follow his business for the space of fourteen days. More insults and outrages were offered to others his neighbours by said Thompson and his men which 'tis probable will be laid before your Honours. Your Petitioner as soon as conveniently he could repaired to Falmouth, to obtain satisfaction of the Capt and crew of the boat aforesaid; but received only abuse and insult, yea two of the crew and they the most guilty swore that if he prosecuted them they would burn and destroy all the interest and estate he had on Deer Island. Your petitioner therefore, reposing the highest confidence in the wisdom, justice, liberality and goodness of this Commonwealthy, looks up to your Honours as the avengers of injuries done to the subjects thereof, and begs his case may be taken into your wise consideration, and such order taken thereon as may be for the security of the subject from such injuries in future, and that the perpetrators of the injuries and inormities set forth in this petition may be punished. And as your petitioner is employed by many neighbours on Deer Island to purchase corn for their necessary support, he prays a permit may be granted him to transport the same without danger of being taken by Privateers, or robbed and plundered by parties of men from boats or hindered and delayed unnecessarily in ports & harbours as has heretofore been his case, And your Petitioner as in duty bound shall every pray

Josiah Crockett
Falmouth 11th of April 1781

Bibliography

For ease of use I have divided the Bibliography into four groups:
Original records
Periodicals, Journals, Website Articles, and Theses
Family Histories and Genealogies (Published and Self-Published)
Reference Books

<u>Original records</u>

_____. Record book belonging to an agent of the Pejepscot Proprietors. Danville files. Androscoggin Historical Society.

_____. "Study of the Penley Family." Typed family history and genealogy of the Penley family of Danville, Maine. Penley folder. Androscoggin Historical Society.

_____. "Wagg family history." Hand-written history and genealogy of the Wagg family of Danville, Maine. Wagg folder. Androscoggin Historical Society.

Andrews, Joan. "Deposition of Joan Andrews, 2 Feb. 1665." (Crockett-Thomas land dispute. EMWD, Vol. 2, p. 27. Made available online by *American Ancestors*, New England Historic Genealogical Association.)

Cape Elizabeth, Maine, Vital Records. (Via FamilySearch and Ancestry.com.)

Cape Elizabeth, Maine, Town and Vital records, 1760-1900. "Meeting minutes, 1760-1765, of the Second Parish of the Town of Falmouth; town and vital records of Cape Elizabeth: town officers, strays, intentions of marriage and marriage records 1773-1865, births and deaths prior to 1879 arranged in families." (Via FamilySearch.)

Church records, 1728-1859, First Church in **Scarborough**, Me. Congregational Library & Archives. (Via New England's Hidden Histories website.)

Clark, Rev. Ephraim. "Marriages by Rev. Ephraim Clark of Cape Elizabeth, 1756-1797." (Via Maine Genealogical Archives.)

Crockett, Ann. "Deposition of Ann Crockett, 27 Jan. 1679." (Dispute over ownership of Gunnison's Neck. MEWD, Vol. 3, p. 248. Made available online by *American Ancestors*, New England Historic Genealogical Association.)

Crockett, Ephraim. "Deposition of Ephraim Crockett, 19 June 1672." (Champernowne and Corbett case. MEWD, Vol. 2, p. 222. Made available online by *American Ancestors*, New England Historic Genealogical Association.)

Crockett, Ephraim. "Last Will and Testament of Ephraim Crockett, 17 July 1688." (MEWD, Wills, p. 71-72. Made available online by *American Ancestors*, New England Historic Genealogical Association.)

Crockett, Josiah. "Petition of Josiah Crockett to the General Court of Massachusetts, 11 April 1781." (Shaving Mill, Deer Isle. Deposition published in BAXTER2. "Documentary history of the state of Maine, Volume XIX.")

Crockett, Samuel. "Land Grant Application, Samuel Crockett (Cape Elizabeth)." Maine Land Office. Courtesy of the Maine Archives.

Crockett, Thomas. "Deposition of Thomas Crockett, 22 April 1654." (The Gunnison-Shapleigh Case. Published in "Documentary history of the state of Maine, Volume IV, containing the Baxter Manuscripts.")

Cumberland County Registry of Deeds. Various deeds, mortgages, and other instruments.

Cumberland County records, Court of General Sessions of the Peace, and Court of Common Pleas. Records as noted. (Via FamilySearch.)

Danville/Pejepscot, Maine. Danville files. Danville/Pejepscot Town records (including tax assessment and valuation records), original notes, family histories, various receipts, and other information relating to Danville and its early settlers. As noted. Androscoggin Historical Society.

England Marriages, 1538-1973. (Via FamilySearch.)

England Births and Christenings, 1538-1975. (Via FamilySearch.)

Eyre, Thomas. "An original letter from Thomas Eyre, one of the adventurers or company of Laconia, to Mr. Gibbins, their factor." (Published in BELKNAP, Appendix. Letter No. 2.)

Falmouth, Maine, Vital Records. (Via FamilySearch and Ancestry.com.)

Falmouth, Maine Town Records, Book 2, 1728-1773. (Via Archive.org.)

Falmouth, Maine. "Falmouth Militia Members, 1757." (Via Maine Genealogical Archives.)

Falmouth, Proprietors of. "Copy of the Original Records of the Proprietors of Falmouth [Maine] for the years 1718 to 1826." Three volumes in one. Portland: Copied by F.A. Gerrish, 1861. (Via Archive.org.)

Find-A-Grave. (Various cemetery records, online database.)

First Church of Boston. "Boston, MA: Church Records 1630-1895." (Made available online by *American Ancestors*, New England Historic Genealogical Association.)

First Church of Falmouth. "Baptisms and Admission from the Records of First Church in Falmouth." (See KING under References.)

First Church of Scarborough. "First Church of Scarborough, Admissions and Baptisms, 1790-1842." (Via Maine Genealogy Archives.)

Frost, Nicholas. "Deposition of Nicholas Frost given to Magistrate Nicholas Shapleigh, 4 April

Bibliography

1658." (Crockett-Thomas land dispute. MEWD, Vol 2, p. 26. Made available online by *American Ancestors*, New England Historic Genealogical Association.)

Gibbons, Ambrose. "Letter from Ambrose Gibbons to John Mason, Newichwanicke, 13 July 1633." (Published in BELKNAP, Appendix, Letter No. 5.)

Giddings, Andrew. Diaries. Early Pejepscot/Danville settler. Giddings folder, Androscoggin Historical Society.

Gorges, Sir Ferdinando and **Mason**, Captain John. "Letter from Sir Ferdinando Gorges and Capt. John Mason to Messrs. Wannerton and Gibbins, 5 May 1634." (Published in BELKNAP, Appendix, Letter No. 7.)

Gorham (Maine) Town Records, 1770-1805. (Via FamilySearch.)

Hancock (Maine) County Registry of Deeds. Various deeds, mortgages, and other instruments.

Laconia Company. "Letter from the company to Ambrose Gibbins, London, 5th December, 1632." (Published in BELKNAP, Appendix, Letter No. 3.)

Little, George Thomas. (Unpublished.) "History of Androscoggin County." Chapter 5. Danville files. Androscoggin Historical Society.

Maine, Cumberland County Court of Common Pleas, Court of General Sessions of the Peace, and Superior Court of Judicature records. Records as noted. (Via Family Search.)

Maine, Cumberland County census records. "Maine Census Guide 1790-1850." Cumberland County, Cape Elizabeth. Records as noted. (Via Maine Genealogy website.)

Maine: Early Wills and Deeds, 1640-1760. CD-ROM. Boston, Massachusetts: New England Historic Genealogical Society, 2006. As noted.

Maine Militia. War of 1812: Capt. W. Rand's Company. (Via Maine Genealogy Archives.)

Maine Militia. War of 1812: Detached Companies Under Supervision of Gen. Alford Richardson. (Via Maine Genealogy Archives.)

Maine Militia. War of 1812: Miscellaneous Detachments and Guards. (Via Maine Genealogy Archives.)

Maine State Archives:

Plan Book 11. Page 50. "**Plan of Deer Isle, 1785**" by John Peters, Jonathan Stone, Samuel Titcomb, Jonathan Mathews. (Via DigitalMaine Repository.)

Plan Book 10. "**Plan of Township No. 2, Indian Purchase**, 1835." (Via DigitalMaine Repository.)

Maine Vital Records. (Via FamilySearch and Ancestry.com.)

Maine, York County. Inferior Court of Common Pleas and General Sessions of the Peace records as noted. (Via FamilySearch.)

Mason, Captain John. "Letter from Capt. John Mason to Ambrose Gibbins, 5 May 1634.) (Published in BELKNAP, Appendix, Letter No. 8.)

Mason, Captain John. "Answer to the foregoing, Letter from Ambrose Gibbons to John Mason. Newichawannock, the 6th of August 1634." (Published in BELKNAP, Appendix, Letter No. 9.)

Massachusetts Archives:

Eastern Land Papers, Records, 1717-1860. Secretary of the Commonwealth, Massachusetts Archives. Various boxes, including ELP, Series 85x, SC1/50 Map 1688 (1804 map for quieting settlers on the Pejepscot Claim); and ELP EA7-1804 (handwritten list of "Settlers in Pejepscot" to accompany the map of the 1804 settlement proposal).

Valuations of towns, 1760; 1771. Massachusetts State Archives collection, colonial period 1622-1788. Vol.130, Vol. 132, Vol. 161 and 162.

Valuations of towns, 1779. Massachusetts State Archives collection, colonial and post colonial period, 1626-1806. Vol. 323, Valuations and Taxes 1778-1787.

Index to French and Indian War Muster Rolls Massachusetts State Archive collection, 1603-1799.. Mass. Archives. Vol 91-99. Film #008731870.

Massachusetts Births and Christenings, 1639-1915. (Via FamilySearch and Ancestry.com.)

Massachusetts Deaths and Burials, 1795-1910. (Via FamilySearch and Ancestry.com.)

Massachusetts, Superior Court of Judicature records, Suffolk County, Massachusetts. Records as noted. (Various records via FamilySearch.)

Massachusetts, Town and Vital Records, 1620-1988. (Via FamilySearch and Ancestry.com.)

Mayberry, S.P. "Deposition of S.P. Mayberry, sworn before Enoch Freeman, J.P., in Falmouth, 13 April 1781." (Taken from, "Deposition in the Time of the Revolutionary War. Deer Isle." *Bangor Historical Magazine*, Vol. 2, 1887.)

Mendum, Robert. "Deposition of Robert Mendum given to Magistrate Thomas Withers, 29 April 1658." (MEWD, Vol. 2, p. 26-27. Made available online by *American Ancestors*, New England Historic Genealogical Association.)

Munns, Mark. "Deposition of Mark Munns, 15 March 1654." (The Gunnison-Shapleigh Case. Published in BAXTER3, "Documentary history of the state of Maine, Volume IV, containing the Baxter Manuscripts.")

New England Historic Genealogical Society. "New England Marriages Prior to 1700." Online database. *AmericanAncestors.org*. New England Historic Genealogical Society, 2008. Originally published as: *New England Marriages Prior to 1700*. Boston, Mass.: New England Historic Genealogical Society, 2015.

New Hampshire Vital Records. (Via FamilySearch and Ancestry.com.)

New Hampshire, Colonial Records of, 1638-1772. Rockingham County, Inferior Court of Common Pleas records as noted. (Via FamilySearch.)

Pejepscot. Plan of the Pejepscot Claim, 1764. Maine Memory Network.

Bibliography

Plummer, William. Diary. Early Pejepscot/Danville settler. (Entries taken from the June 1992 Newsletter of the Androscoggin Historical Society, No. 6.)

Raynes, Francis. "Will of Francis Raynes." (MEWD, Wills, p. 95. Made available online by *American Ancestors*, New England Historic Genealogical Association.)

Rockingham (N.H.) County Registry of Deeds. Various deeds, mortgages, and other instruments.

Rhode Island Vital Extracts, 1636-1899. (Via Ancestry.com.)

Second Parish (Maine) records. (See Cape Elizabeth and South Portland.)

Skillin, Samuel and **Crockett**, Richard. "Deposition of Samuel Skillin and Richard Crockett, 4 April 1704." (Gunnison-Winkley case. Records from Maine, York County Court of Common Pleas, April term, 1704.)

South Portland (Maine). "A Book of Records For the Second Parish in The town of Falmouth containing 212 pages." South Portland, Maine Town Records, 1765-1823. (Via FamilySearch.)

South Portland, Maine, Vital Records. (Via FamilySearch and Ancestry.com.)

Starbird, Charles. Various genealogies of Danville, Maine families (Crockett, Wagg, Penley, Dingley, etc.) assembled by the historian. Androscoggin Historical Society. (Various files and folders, AHS.)

Starbird, Charles and **Young**, David C. "Eight lots laid out to the Pejepscot Proprietors." Undated map obtained from the records of David C. Young and Charles Starbird. Androscoggin Historical Society.

Stoke Gabriel (Devon) Parish Church Records; Church and Social History; The Yew Tree; and Pirates of the Maghreb. Online access provided by Church of St. Mary and St. Gabriel.

Stoke Gabriel (Devon) Parish Registers, Baptism Records. (Via RootsWeb.)

Stratham (N.H.) Cemetery Records. (via Family Search).

Stratham (N.H.) Town Records. "State's Copy of Records of Stratham. State's Vol. 1. Stratham's Vol. 1 & 2." (Via FamilySearch.)

Thomas, Nathaniel. "Affidavit of Nathaniel Thomas presented to the General Court of Massachusetts. Taken in Falmouth, 13 April 1781." (Shaving Mill, Deer Isle. Published in BAXTER2.)

United States Archives. "Revolutionary War Pension and Bounty-Land Warrant Application Files, 1800-1900." (Via Ancestry.com.)

United States. Census data, 1790, 1800, 1810, 1820, 1830, 1840. (Via Ancestry.com.)

United States. Department of the Interior, Bureau of Pensions, File 23888, Revolutionary War.

United States. U.S. Revolutionary War Rolls, 1775-1783. Ephraim Crocket; from a copy of Capt. Leach's Matrosses, Mass. Militia's enlistment papers. Made available by the National Archives.

Vines, Richard. "Lease agreement on patent owned by Gorges and Mason, Kittery, 1637." (Via Maine Memory Network.)

"**Warumbo**" Deed. Maine Memory Network. (For transcription of this deed see **Wheeler**, George Augustus in References.)

White, John. "Deposition of John White, 24 June 1669." (Crockett-Pendleton land dispute. MEWD, Vol. 2, p. 212. Made available online by *American Ancestors*, New England Historic Genealogical Association.)

York County Registry of Deeds. Various deeds, mortgages, and other instruments.

Young, David C., editor. "Early Settler's List for the Pejepscot Claim and Little's Gore." Androscoggin Historical Society.

Periodicals, Journals, Website Articles, and Theses

Aten, Carol Walker. "Exeter is a Seaport." Exeter (N.H.) Historical Society website.

Barrows, Mandy. "Candlemas Day (the Christian Festival of Lights)." Project Britain. British Life and Culture. Project Britain website.

(Old) Berwick Historical Society. "South Berwick's First People." Old Berwick Historical Society website.

(Old) Berwick Historical Society. "Berwick Begins: 1631-1713." Old Berwick Historical Society website.

Betlock, Lynn. "New England's Great Migration." *New England Ancestors* 4 (2003): 2:22-24.

Bilodeau, Christopher J. "Creating an Indian Enemy in the Borderlands: King Philip's War in Maine, 1675-1678." *Maine History*. Vol. 47, Number 1. Jan. 1, 2013.

Brooks, Rebecca Beatrice. "History of King William's War." History of Massachusetts blog.

Butman, John. "Sir Ferdinando Gorges and His Impossible Dream of Maine." MaineBoats.com. The Website of the Coast.

Christy, Miller, Esq. "Attempts toward Colonization : the Council for New England and the Merchant Venturers of Bristol, 1621-1623." *The American Historical Review*, Vol. 4, No. 4 (July, 1899).

Chu, Jonathan M. "The Social and Political Contexts of Heterodoxy: Quakerism in Seventeenth-Century Kittery." *The New England Quarterly*. Vol. 54, No. 3. (Sep., 1981).

Clark, D.W. "Transcription list of Long Creek Cemetery." (Via South Portland Historical Society website.)

Cumberland Association of Congregational Ministers. "The centennial of the Cumberland Association of Congregational Ministers, at the Second Parish Church in Portland, Maine, Monday and Tuesday, May 28 and 29, 1888." (Via N.H. Historical Society.)

Dartmoor Prison website. "History of Dartmoor Prison."

Bibliography

DePaoli, Neill. "Beaver, Blankets, Liquro, and Politics Pemaquid's Fur Trade, 1614, 1760." *Maine History*. Volume 33, Number 3 (1994).

Dorr, Jason M. "Changing Their Guardians: The Penobscot Indians and Maine Statehood, 1820-1849." (1998). (Electronic Theses and Dissertations. 2746. DigitalCommons, University of Maine.)

Digital History website. "Regional Contrasts." Digital History ID 3580.

Dreamstress, The. "Terminology: What is calamanco?" 18th Century, Textiles & Costume. The Dreamstress website.

Drymon, Ph.D., M.M. "The Forgotten Landscape: How a Place Called Crockett's Corner Became The Maine Mall." South Portland Maine: The Landscape History Institute, 2017. (Ph.D. thesis.)

Dummer, Jeremy. "Defence of the New England Charters." 1721. (Via National Humanities Center online.)

Eckstrom, Fannie Hardy. "The Attack on Norridgewock, 1724." *The New England Quarterly*, Vol.7, No. 3, (Sept. 1934).

Falmouth [Maine], Town of. "History of Falmouth, Maine." 2019. *Maine History Documents*. 191. (University of Maine, Digital Commons.)

Farber, Hannah. "The Rise and Fall of the Province of Lygonia, 1643-1658." *The New England Quarterly*, Vol. LXXXII, no. 3 (September 2009).

First Congregational Church, United Church of Christ, South Portland, Maine. (Articles and info from their website.)

Getchell, Sylvia Fitts. "Piscataqua Area Place Names and History." Privately printed. Undated.

Gilder Lehrman Institute of American History. "The Stamp Act, 1765." (Via their website.)

Goodrich, Merton Taylor, M.A. "The Case of the Chairmakers: A Problem in the Crockett Family." *The American Genealogist*, Vol XVII, No. 3, January 1941, p. 138-143.

Hammon, Otis Grant. "The Mason Title and Its Relations to New Hampshire and Massachusetts." *American Antiquarian Society*. October 1916.

Harvard Law School. "The Legacy of Isaac Royall, Jr." Exhibit Addenda. HLS website.

Hathaway, Nate. "Trekking through tribal lands as the Penobscot Nation plans to reacquire 30,000 acres near Katahdin." News Center Maine website.

Heritage Newfoundland & Labrador. "The English Migratory Fishing and Trade in the 17th Century." Newfoundland and Labrador Heritage Web Site Project, 1997.

Higgins, Pat. "Ann Mitton Brackett—Needlewoman to the Rescue." Website, The Maine Story.

Historic Ipswich. "Great Sorrows, the Deadly 'Throat Distemper' of 1735" and "The Tithingman at the Ipswich Meetinghouse." Historic Ipswich website.

Howe, Edward T. "Early Church Bell Founders." Connecticuthistory.org.

Hull, John T. "The Siege and Capture of Fort Loyall, Destruction of Falmouth, May 20, 1690 (O.S.). A paper read before the Maine Genealogical Society, June 2, 1885." Printed by Order of City Council of Portland. Portland, ME: Owen, Strout & Co., Printers, 1885.

Johnson, Marian Peabbles, "History of Cape Elizabeth Maine." Major Project in Partial Fulfillment of Requirements for the Degree of Master of Education, 1954. Boston University.

Lewiston Journal. "50 Years Ago Today." April 20, 1978.

Little, Charles Thomas. "Danville." Published in "The History of Androscoggin County, Maine." Chapter XXXIX. County, Maine. (See **Merrill**, Georgia Drew in References.)

Macy-Colby House. "The Winthrop Fleet in 1630." The Macy-Colby House, Amherst, Massachusetts (via their website.)

Maine Genealogy Trails. "The Northeast Coast Campaign of Queen Anne's War." Queen Anne's War. Maine Genealogy Trails website.

Maine Historic Preservation Commission website. State of Maine. "Maine Native American Pre-European History (or Maine Pre-History)."

Maine Public Radio. "How Maine Became A State 200 Years Ago, And What That Had To Do With Slavery." MPR host Irwin Gratz's interview with Maine historian and state representative Herb Adams. Published July 31, 2019 on the Maine Public website.

Maine. "Maine Revolutionary War Bounty Land Applications, 1835-1838." (Via Maine Genealogy website.)

Maine Secretary of State. "The War of 1812-1815: America's 'Second War for Independence.' (1812-1815.)" Maine Secretary of State website.

Mineo, Liz. "At Law School, Honor for the Enslaved." *The Harvard Gazette*, Sept. 6, 2017.

Micheneur, Ron. "Money in the American Colonies." Economic History Association website.

National Humanities Center. "The 'Old Tenor' Affair: Massachusetts Bay Colony, 1751." National Humanities Center Resource Toolbox online.

National Park Service website. "The Past and Present here unite…" Longfellow House Washington's Headquarters. National Park Service website.

National Park Service website. "King Philip's War (1675-1678)." Roger Williams National Memorial, Rhode Island.

National Park Service website. "Revolutionary War Veteran and Widow Pensions."

National Park Service website. "1816 – The Year Without A Summer."

New England Historical Society. *The New England and Historical Genealogical Recorder*. (Online database, info. as noted.)

New Hampshire Historical Society website. "Timeline of New Hampshire History, 1676."

Nissenbaum, Stephen W. "Christmas in Early New England, 1620-1820: Puritanism, Popular Culture, and the Printed Word." *American Antiquarian Society*, 1996.

Norton, Mary Beth. " 'The Ablest Midwife That Wee Knowe in the Land': Mistress Alice Tilly and the Women of Boston and Dorchester, 1649-1650." *William and Mary Quarterly*, 3d Series, Volume LV, Number 1, January 1998.

Pike, Rev., Richard. "Building and Occupancy of Fort Pownall." A paper read before the New England Historic-Genealogical Society, Oct. 5, 1859. By Rev. Richard Pike of Dorchester, Mass. The New England Historical and Genealogical Register, Volume XIV, p. 6. Boston: Samuel G. Drake, Publisher, 1860.

Portland Daily Press. "Death notice of Captain Richard Crockett." May 24, 1880.

Portland Press Herald . "Sweeping recommendations would overhaul Maine's Indian land claims act." Published January 14, 2020.

Portsmouth Peace Treaty of 1713 website. "Treaty of Portsmouth, 1713."

Ridgeway, Claire. "Candlemas." The Tudor Society website.

Robinson, J. Dennis. "How New Hampshire Was Settled By Mistake." Excerpt from his book published on SeaCoastNH.com.

Rosier, James. "True Relations of Waymouth's Voyage, 1605. (See Books, Burrage, Henry S., editor.)

Smith, Rev., Thomas. Journals of. (See Willis, William for publication information.)

South Portland Historical Society. "The Long Creek Cemetery." (Via their website.)

Stratham, N.H., Town of. "History of Stratham" and "Facts & Firsts." Town of Stratham website.

Thompson, David. "David Thompson's Indenture, 1622." *The New Hampshire Genealogical Record*. Vol. II, July 1904-April 1905.

University of Nottingham (U.K.) "Wives, Widows and Wimples: Inheritance." University of Nottingham website.

U.S. Fish & Wildlife Service. "The King of Fish." Life Cycle of Atlantic Salmon. U.S. Fish and Wildlife Service website.

U.S. Secretary of State, Office of the Historian website. "Treaty of Paris, 1763."

Wabanaki Alliance. "Penobscot Nation, *penawahpkekeyek*." Wabanaki Alliance website article.

Family Histories and Genealogies (Published and Self-Published)

Ackerman, Arlene L. Brown. "Descendants of Thomas and Deborah (?) *Skillings* of Cumberland Co., Maine." (Via Rootsweb.com.)

Candage, Charles Samuel. " *Crockett* Genealogy 1610-1988: Some Descendants of Thomas and Ann Crockett of Kittery, Maine (with 1990 Addendum). Rockport, Maine: Picton Press, 1990.

Coleman, April. "A Time Line for the *Crockett* Family of Maine." Privately printed. Undated.

Crockett, Leon O. "The *Crockett* Family of New England, 1632-1943." Camden: The Camden Herald Publishing Company, 1943.

Davis, Walter Goodwin. "The Ancestry of Joseph *Waterhouse*, 1754-1837, of Standish Maine." Portland, Maine: Anthoesen Press, 1949. (Various other Maine families.)

Davis, Walter Goodwin. "Massachusetts and Maine Families in the Ancestry of Walter Goodwin Davis (1885-1966)." Introduction by Gary Boyd Roberts. Reprint. Baltimore, Maryland: Genealogical Publishing Company, 1996. (*Various families* relevant to our story.)

Dingley, Edward Nelson. "The life and times of Nelson *Dingley*, jr." Kalamazoo, Michigan: Ihling Bros. & Everard, 1902.

French, Janie Preston Collup and **Armstrong**, Zela. "Notable Southern Families, Volume 5, The *Crockett* Family and Connecting Lines." Bristol, Tenn: The King Printing, Col, 1928.

Goldthwaite, Charlotte. "Goldthwaite genealogy: descendants of Thomas *Goldthwaite*, an early settler of Salem, Mass., with some account of the Goldthwaite Family in England." Hartford: Hartford Press, 1899.

Gunnison, George. "A Genealogy of the Descendants of Hugh *Gunnison*, of Boston, Mass., covering the period from 1610-1876." Boston: George A. Foxcroft, 1880.

McCoy, Carol P., Dr. "Descendants of Richard *Crockett*, Including Notes of Dr. David Crockett." June 2007.

Scott, Donna Hopkins. "The *Crockett* Family of Maine: Following mainly the descendants of David Crockett who migrated to Utah in 1849." Jan. 1, 1968.

Preble, George Henry, Captain, U.S.N. "Genealogical Sketch of the First Three Generations of Prebles in America: with an account of Abraham *Preble*, the Emigrant, their Common Ancestor and the grandfather of Brigadier General Jedidiah Preble and his Descendants." Boston: Printed for Family Circulation, David Clapp & Son, 1868.

Shapleigh Family Association. "Alexander Shapleigh's Family Tree – the first four generations in America." *Shapleigh* Family Association website.

Taylor, Robert L. "Early Families of Limington, Maine." Self-published. Limington, Maine: May 1984. (Info. on *Abbott* family.)

Underhill, Lora Altine Woodbury. "Descendants of Edward *Small* of New England : and the allied families with tracings of English ancestry." Volume II. Cambridge: The Riverside Press (Privately Printed), 1910. (Includes information about the *Roberts* family.)

Wentworth, John, LL.D. "The *Wentworth* Genealogy: English and American." In three volumes. Boston: Little, Brown and Company, 1878.

Reference Books

Allen, Neal W., Jr., Ph.D., editor. "Province and Court Records of Maine, Vol. 4." Portland: Maine Historical Society, 1958.

Allen, Neal W., Jr., Ph.D., editor. "Province and Court Records of Maine, Vol. 5." Portland: Maine Historical Society, 1964.

Allen, Neal W., Jr., Ph.D., editor. "Province and Court Records of Maine, Vol. 6." Portland: Maine Historical Society, 1975.

Anderson, Robert Charles. "The Great Migration Begins: Immigrants to New England, 1620-1633. Volume 1, A-F." Boston: New England Historic Genealogical Society, 1995.

Anderson, Robert Charles; Sanborn, Jr., George G.; and Sangorn, Melinda Lutz. "The Great Migration, Immigrants to New England, 1634-1635, Volume I, A-B." Boston: New England Historic Genealogical Society, 1999.

Anderson, Robert Charles. "The Great Migration, Immigrants to New England, 1634-1635. Volume VII." Boston: New England Historic Genealogical Society, 2011.

Banks, Charles Edward. "History of York, Maine, Successively known as Bristol (1632), Agamenticus (1641), Gorgeanna (1642), and York 1652)." Vol. I.

Banks, Charles Edward. "History of York, Maine, Successively known as Bristol (1632), Agamenticus (1641), Gorgeanna (1642), and York 1652)." Vol. II.

Banks, Charles Edward. "The Planters of the Commonwealth." Boston: Riverside Press (for Houghton Mifflin), MDCCCCXXX.

Banks, Charles Edward. "Topographical Dictionary of 2885 English Emigrants to New England, 1620-1650." Baltimore: Southern Book Company, 1957.

Banks, Charles Edward. "Edward Godfrey: His Life, Letters, and Public Service, 1584-1664." Privately printed, 1887.

Baxter, James Phinney. "Documentary History of the State of Maine, Vol, III, Containing the Treelawny Papers." Portland: Hoyt, Fogg, and Donham, 1884.

Baxter, James Phinney, A.M. "Documentary History of the State of Maine, Vol. IV, Containing the Baxter Manuscripts." Portland: Brown Thurston & Company, 1889.

Belknap, Jeremy, D.D. "The History of New Hampshire." Vol. I. Dover: S.C. Stevens and Ela & Wadleigh, 1831.

Belknap, Jeremy, A.M. "The History of New Hampshire." Vol. II. Dover, N.H.: F.K. Remich & F. Mann, Printers, 1812.

Bicheno. H. "Redcoats, and Rebels: The American Revolutionary War." London: Harper Collins, 2003.

Bigar, Henry Percival, editor. "The Precursors of Jacques Cartier, 1497-1534." Ottawa: Government Printing Bureau, 1911.

Burrage, Henry S., D.D. "The Beginnings of Colonial Maine, 1602-1658." Portland, Maine: Marks Printing House, 1914.

Burrage, Henry S., editor. "Early English and French Voyages, Chiefly from Hakluyt, 1534-1608." New York: Charles Scribner's Sons, 1906.

Chisholm, Hugh, editor. "Encyclopaedia Britannica, Vol. 16." (11th ed.). Cambridge: Cambridge University Press, 2017.

Clayton, W. Woodford. "History of Cumberland Col, Maine, with Illustrations and Biographical Sketches and a list of Its Prominent Men and Pioneers." Philadelphia: Everts & Peck, 1880.

D'Epiro, Peter & **Pinkowish**, Mary Desmond. "Sprezzatura: 50 Ways Italian Genius Shaped the World." New York: Anchor Books, 2001.

Douglas-Lithgow, Robert Alexander. "Dictionary of American-Indian Place and Proper Names in New England." Boston: Harvard University Press, 1909.

Ellis, George Edward. "Celebration of the centennial anniversary of the evacuation of Boston." Boston: A. Williams & company, 1876.

Goold, Nathan. "History of Col. Edmund Phinney's 31st Regiment of Foot." Portland, Maine: Press of the Thurston Print, 1896.

Grenier, John. "The First Way of War: American War Making on the Frontier." Cambridge: Cambridge University Press, 2005.

Hodgkin, Douglas I. "Frontier to Industrial City: Lewiston Town Politics, 1768-1863." Topsham: Just Write Books, 2008.

Hodgkin, Douglas I. "Dear Parent: A Biography and Letters of Edward Little." Published by the Androscoggin Historical Society. Portland, Maine: Walch Printing, 2017.

Hosmer, George L. "An Historical Sketch of the Town of Deer Isle, Maine: with Notices of Its Settlers and Early Inhabitants." Boston, Mass: The Fort Hill Press, 1905.

Hubbard, William. F., Rev. "A General History of New England From the Discovery to MDCLXXX." Second edition, collated with the original MS. Boston: Charles C. Little and James Brown, MDCCCXLVIII.

Hubbard, William. "A narrative of the Indian wars in New-England, from the first planting thereof in the year 1607, to the year 1677. : Containing a relation of the occasion, rise and progress of the war with the Indians, in the southern, western, eastern and northern parts of said country." Boston: Printed and sold by John Boyle in Marlborough-Street, 1775.

Huden, John C., compiler. "Indian Place Names of New England." New York: Museum of the American Indian, Heye Foundation, 1962

Hutchinson, Vernal. "When Revolution Came: The Story of Old Deer Isle In the Province of Maine During the War For American Independence." Ellsworth, Maine: The Ellsworth American, 1972.

Jewett, Sarah Orne. "Selected Stories and Sketches." 1884. Barnes and Noble, electronic edition.

Jordan, William B., Jr. "A History of Cape Elizabeth Maine." Berwyn Heights, MD: Heritage Books, Inc., 2014.

Kershaw, Gordon E. "The Kennebeck Proprietors, 1749-1775." Somersworth: New Hampshire Pub. Co., 1975.

King, Marquis F., Compiler. "Baptisms and Admission from the Records of First Church in Falmouth, now Portland, Maine, with Appendix of Historical Notes." Portland, Maine: Maine Genealogical Society, 1898.

Lemire, Elise. "Black Walden: Slavery and its Aftermath in Concord, Massachusetts." Philadelphia: University of Pennsylvania Press, 2019

Libby, Charles Thornton, editor. "Province and Court Records of Maine, Vol. 1." Portland: Maine Historical Society, 1928.

Libby, Charles Thornton, editor. "Province and Court Records of Maine, Vol. 2." Portland: Maine Historical Society, 1931.

Little, George Thomas, A.M., Litt.D., editor and compiler. "Genealogical and Family History of the State of Maine." New York: Lewis Historical Publishing Company, 1909. (Via Internet Archive.)

Massachusetts, Commonwealth of. "Massachusetts Soldiers and Sailors of the Revolutionary War." A Compilation from the Archives, prepared and published by the Secretary of the Commonwealth. Wright & Potter Printing Co., [State Printers], Boston, MA, 1898. Vol. 4.

McIntyre, Sheila and **Travers**, Len, editors. "The Correspondence of John Cotton, Jr." Published by the Colonial Society of Massachusetts, 2009.

Maine Historical Society. "The Maine Bicentennial Atlas: An Historical Survey." Portland, Maine; MHS, 1976.

Maine, State of. "Note By the Commissioner on the Sources of Land Titles in Maine." "Fourth Revision. The Revised Statutes of the State of Maine, passed August 29, 1883, and taking effect January 1, 1884." Portland: Loring, Short and Harmon and William Marks, Printer, 1884.

Maine State Legislature. "Report of the Joint Standing Committee on Indian Affairs on the Petition of John Attian, Governor of the Penobscot Indians, and many others of the tribe, asking for protection against money being drawn from the Indian fund by persons not authorized to receive the same." Documents printed by order of the Legislature of the State of Maine during the Session A.D. 1857. Part Second.

McClintock, John Norris. "History of New Hampshire." Boston: B.B. Russell, 1889.

McLellan, Hugh D. "The History of Gorham, Maine." A facsimile of the 1903 edition with a new foreword by William David Barry. Somersworth: New England History Press, 1980.

Merrill, Georgia Drew, editor. "History of Androscoggin County, Maine. (Illustrated.)" Boston, Mass: W.A. Fergusson & Co. (Lewiston, Me: Journal Press), 1891.

Merrill, Nancy Carnegie. "Exeter, New Hampshire: 1888-1933." Portsmouth, N.H.: Peter E. Randall, 1988.

Moody, Robert. E, Ph.D., editor. "Province and Court Records of Maine, Vol. 3." Portland: Maine Historical Society, 1947.

Nelson, Charles B. "History of Stratham, New Hampshire, 1631-1900." Stratham, NH: Town of Stratham, 1987.

Noyes, Sibyl; **Libby**, Charles Thornton; **Davis**, Water Goodwin. "Genealogical Dictionary of Maine and New Hampshire." Boston, Massachusetts: New England Historic Genealogical Society, 2012.

Pearson, Gardner W. "Massachusetts Volunteer Militia Called out by the Governor of Massachusetts to suppress a threatened invasion during the War of 1812-14." Published by Brig. Genl. Gardner W. Pearson, The Adjutant General of Massachusetts, 1913. Reprinted for Clearfield Company Inc. Baltimore, Maryland: Genealogical Publishing Co., Inc., 1993.

Pringle, James R. "History of the Town and City of Gloucester, Cape Ann, Massachusetts." Gloucester, Mass: Published by the Author, 1892.

Rowe, William H. "The Maritime History of Maine: Three Centuries of Ship Building & Seafaring." Gardiner, Me: The Harpswell Press, 1989. (Copyright W.W. Norton, 1948).

Saxine, Ian. "Properties of Empire: Indians, Colonists, and Land Speculators on the New England Frontier." New York: New York University Press, 2019.

Schlich, Victor A. "Maine Parks Campgrounds and Historic Sites." Portland, Maine: J. Weston Walch, Publisher, 1974.

Sheraton, Thomas. "The Cabinet Dictionary, containing An Explanation of all the Terms used in the Cabinet, Chair, and Upholstery Branches." London: W. Smith, 1803.

Spencer, Wilbur D. "Pioneers on Maine Rivers with Lists to 1651." Portland, Maine: Lakeside Printing Company, 1930.

Stackpole, Everett S. "Old Kittery and Her Families." Lewiston, Maine: Press of Lewiston Journal Company, 1903.

Stark, James Henry. "Banishment Act of the State of Massachusetts: *The loyalists of Massachusetts and the other side of the American Revolution.*" Salem, Mass.: Salem Press, 1910.

Bibliography

Sullivan, Jeremy. "History of the District of Maine." 1795. (Reprint) Augusta, ME: Maine State Museum.

Taylor, Alan. "Liberty Men and Great Proprietors: The Revolutionary Settlement on the Maine Frontier, 1760-1820." Chapel Hill & London: The University of North Carolina Press, 1990.

Vietze, Andrew. "White Pine: American History and the Tree that Made a Nation." Guilford, Connecticut: Globe Pequot, 2018.

Wheeler, George Augustus, M.D. and Wheeler, Henry Warren. "The History of Brunswick, Topsham, and Harpswell, Maine." Boston: Alfred Mudge & Son, Printers. 1878.

Whitman, Charles F. "A History of Norway, Maine, from the Earliest Settlements to the Close of the Year 1922." Lewiston, Maine: Lewiston Journal Printshop and Bindery, 1924.

Willis, William. "The History of Portland, From 1632 to 1861: With a Notice of Previous Settlements, Colonial Grants, and Changes of Government in Maine." Second Edition. Portland: Bailey & Noyes, 1865.

Willis, William. "Journals of the Rev. Thomas Smith, and the Rev. Samuel Deane, Pastors of the First Church in Portland with Notes and Biographical Notices: and a Summary History of Portland." Portland: Joseph S. Bailey, 1849.

Woodard, Collin. "The Lobster Coast." New York, NY: Viking-Penguin, 2004.

Index

In this index, *italicized page numbers* denote images, while **bold page numbers** denote maps. Numbers following "n" after a page number denote footnotes. Persons bearing identical names are differentiated by parentage, recorded in brackets following the name; where parentage is unknown, an alternate relationship or identifier is supplied in brackets. Maiden names are given in parentheses.

NOTE: Please see "Genealogical Dictionary of Thomas and Ann Crockett" (p. 377–395) for more unindexed Crockett info.

A

Abenaki (Native American tribe), 9–10, 21, **22**, 39, 80n45, 130–131, 133

Acadia (French settlement), 101, 130, 253

Achley, Samuel, 368–369

Act to Prevent Monopoly and Oppression, 251

Adams, Joseph, 139–140

Adiawando (Native American), 152

alarm lists, 178–179, *180*, 224

Alden, David, 268, 269, 273, 282

Algonkian-speaking tribes (Eastern), 2n5, 21, 56, 293. *See also* Wabanaki

Allen, Benjamin, 153, 211, 213n25, 214n29, 219

Allen, Hannah, 213n25

Allen, Priscilla, 214n29

Ambreas, Nathaniel, 149n13

American Revolution, 239–246
  Battle of Bunker Hill, 243
  Boston, siege of, 318
  Boston Port Act, 241
  Boston Tea Party, 240, 241
  Continental Army, 243–244, 247, 252, 253, 256, 318–319, 325, 335
  Fort George, building of, 243

American Revolution (*continued*)
  George Washington, 243n127, 244, 245, 256, 317, 318–319
  Intolerable Acts, 241
  land bounties promised to soldiers of, 287, 293–294, 304, 307, 312, 327–329, 344–345, 353
  Matrosses (artillerymen), *320*, 321
  Penobscot Expedition, 253–254
  "shot heard round the world," 242
  Stamp Act (1765), 239
  Sugar Act (1764), 243
  Townsend Acts (1766), 239
  Treaty of Paris (1783), 196, 256
  Yorktown, siege of, 256

Amherst, Jeffrey, 229

Amoret (Native American), 9, 10

Anasagunticook (Native American tribe), 301–302, 303n24, 372

Anderson, Robert, 350

Andrews, Ann, 91–92

Andrews, Joane (Crockett). *See* Atwell, Joane (Crockett) Andrews

Andrews, John
  children of, 91, 114
  estate of, 55

427

Andrews, John (*continued*)
  legal troubles of, 40n156, 40n157
  marriage to Joane Crockett, 6, 35n142, 36, 54
  submission to Massachusetts Bay Colony, 41
Andrews, John, Jr., 55, 56
Andrews, Margaret, 215n35
Andrews, Sarah, 56n228, 114
Andros, Edmund, 88, 101, 102, 103
Androscoggin/Ammoscogon (Native American tribe), **22, 54**, 80, 83, 84, 88, 152
Anglicans, 5, 15–16, 30
Anne, Queen of England, 113, 130. *See also* Queen Anne's War
Archangel (ship), 1, 8–9
Arnold, Benjamin, 338
Arras (Irish), Patrick, 349
Arrowsick, 132
Atkinson, Theodore, 124
Atwell, Joane (Crockett) Andrews
  birth of, 5
  Brave Boat Harbor, move to, 36
  character of, 6, 35n142
  children of, 91, 114
  emigration to New England, 6, 35n141
  Frances White legal case, witness to, 32n126
  legal troubles of, 6n22, 40–41, 40n156, 72–73, 74
  marriage to Philip Atwell, 55–56
  social status of, 54–56
  Thomas Crockett, close relationship with, 34–35
Atwell, Philip, 55–56
Atwood, Samuel, 176n126
Avant, Francis, 65n265

B

Babb, Hannah, 224
Bailey, Benjamin, 263, 264, 279n269
Bailey, Daniel, 278
Bailey, Deborah, 243
Bailey, Jonathan, 278n265
Baker, Joseph, 279n270, 279n272
Baker & Bartels, 279n270, 279n272, 281
Bangs, Joseph, 177n132
Banks, Charles Edward, 4, 16–17, **39, 61,** *102,* 105
Barbour Farm, 3n7, 202–203. *See also* Crockett's Cove (Deer Isle)
Barefoot, Walter, 56n228, 63, 72n11, 75
Barker, Joseph, 144n162, 184n161
Barnes, W. Thomas, 338
Barry (British Captain in War of 1812), 276
Bartels, John, 279n270, 279n272
Barter, Eleanor, 62n248
Barter, Elizabeth, 62n248
Barter, Henry
  children of, 62n248, 97n98, 110
  Crockett's Neck and, 50, 95n90
  as Deacon of Kittery church, 129
  house as "defencible" housing, 97
  as Kittery selectman, 110
  land grants of, 65n265, 113n58
  marriage to Sarah Crockett, 50n203, 109, 110
  real estate transactions of, 63, 65n265, 98, 98n104, 110, 119
  relationship with Richard Crockett, 109, 110
Barter, Henry, Jr., 62n248, 97n98
Barter, Martha, 62n248
Barter, Richard, 62n248

Index

Barter, Sarah (Crockett), 50n203, 62n248, 97n98, 109, 110
Barter, Sarah [Henry Barter and Sarah Crockett], 62n248, 110
Barter, William, 62n248
Barter's Creek, 46n188, 110. *See also* Crockett's Creek
Barton, Elisha, 33n133, 94n87
Barton, James, 264
Barton, Mary (Crockett), 51, 94n87
Battle of Bunker Hill, 243
Battle of Damariscotta, 108
Battle of Falmouth, 104
Battle of Fort Loyal, 104
Battle of New Orleans, 277
Battle of Port Royal, 104
Battle of Quebec, 187, 228–229
Battle of the Plains of Abraham, 187, 228–229
Belcher, Jonathan, 151–152
Berry, George, 228
Billing, Ann (Andrews), 91–92
Billing, Elizabeth, 42n165
Billing, John, 33, 42n165, 92n73
Billing, John, Jr., 42n165, 73
Bisbee, Charles, 352, 363–364
Bitman, Benjamin, 168n96
Black Point (Scarborough), 114
Blake, John, 263n196
Blower, Alice (Frost), 32n129
Blower, Sarah. *See* Morgan, Sarah Lynn Gunnison Mitchell
Blower, Thomas, 32n129
Boaden, Ambrose, 91–92
Boaneo, Elizabeth, 36n143
Bodwell, Bailey, 276

Bonaparte, Napoleon, 271
Boston Port Act, 241
Boston Tea Party, 240, 241
Bostoniak, 300, 306, 343n137. *See also* Great Proprietors
Boyd, Joseph Coffin, 273
Brackett, Ann (Mitton), 86
Brackett, Anthony, 85–86
Bradbury, Thomas, 29n118
Brave Boat Harbor, 29, 36, **50**, 52, 63, 73, 94, 95, 96
Bray, John, 55, 93n79, 93n80, 156n228
Bray, O. (Lieutenant), 277
Brazen, Dorcas, 268n221, 269, 270
Brewer, Dexter, 286
Brewer, Samuel, 326n58
Briant, John, 178n137
Bridgham, Jonathan, 306
Brimmer, Martin, 356
Broad, Thadd, 264n198
Broad, William, 95n88
Brooking, Henry, 93n80
Brooks, Cotton B., 279n272
Brooks, Robert, 155
Brunswick, 105, **310**, 370
Bryant, Jonathon, 266
Bucknam, William, 223
Burgess, Richard, 49n201
Burrin, George, 63, 93n79

C

Cabot, John, 8, 294
Campbell, John, 197
Campbell, Mary, 197, 199, 200
Candlemas Day Massacre, 64, 106–107

Cane, Mary, 189
Cape Elizabeth, District of
   American Revolution and, 240–246
   creation of, 205, 229–230
   road taxes in, 236
   school districts of, 230
   township of, 244
   See also Falmouth; Second Parish
Cape Elizabeth, town of
   abatement of polls, 252–253
   American Revolution and, 251–256, 261–262
   attempt to separate from Massachusetts, 266
   census records of, 265, 270, 274, 284
   Declaration of Independence and, 245, *246*
   lighthouse erected at, 266
   town valuation in 1781, 257
   township of, 244
   See also Falmouth; Second Parish
Cape Porpus, 114
Cape Sable (Native American tribe), 57n230, 172
Cargill, James, 228
Carpenter, Philip, 114
Casco Bay, 84, 85–87, 103, 105, 114, 212, 296
census records, 188, 264, 265, 270, 274, 283, 284, 330, 339–340
Champernowne, Arthur, 29n118
Champernowne, Francis, 29–30, 29n118, 48, 69n6
Champernowne's Island, 29n118
Champlain, Samuel de, **81**, 82
Charles I, King of England, 2n3, 48, 76, 77, 78
Charles II, King of England, 77–78
Chase, Jonathan, 122

Chase, Stephen, 350
Child, Thomas, 258n175
Church, Benjamin, 105
Church of St. Mary and St. Gabriel, 4, 5, 14–15
Churchward/Churchwood, Alse "Anne," 4, 6
Churchwards of Stroke Gabriel, 4, 6–7
Clark, Ephraim, 219–221, 224, 247, 256, 265, 268, 326
Clark, George, 124, 125, *126*
Clark, John, 122n100
Clark, Samuel, 172
Clark and Lake Company, 297
Cleeves, George, 63n11
Cobb, Jonathan, 164
Cobb, Joseph, Jr., 235
Cobb, Samuel, 316n13
Cobb, Sarah, 164, 169, 172n106
Cocheco, 87, 88n61. *See also* Dover, New Hampshire
Coercive Acts, 241
Coffin (Colonel), 200
Committee of Correspondence, 240, 241, 251
Committee of Eastern Claims and Settlements, 132
Committee of Inspection, 243
Continental Army, 243–244, 247, 252, 253, 256, 318–319, 325, 335
Continental Congress, 243n127, 245, 304, 306, 317, 327
Cook, Thomas, 172, 176
Corbett, Abraham, 51–52, 69n6, 73n19
Cornwallis, Charles, 256
Cotton, Martha, 262
Cotton, William, 223, 262

Index

Couch, Joseph, 56n228
Council of New England, 11–12, 118n86, 243, 341n130
County of Cumberland Congress, 242
Court of Common Pleas, 104–105, 105–106, *112*, 166, *167,* 182, 184
Court of General Sessions (Maine), Day of Solemn Fasting and Prayer, 104–105, 106
Cow Cove, 27–28
Cowasuck (Native American tribes), **22**
Cox, John, 77, 213n26
Crechet/Crechett, Thomas. See Crockett, Thomas
Crechet/Crechett/Crockett, Clement, 5
Crechet/Crechett/Crockett, Elnore, 5
Crechet/Crechett/Crockett, Joan. See Atwell, Joane (Crockett) Andrews
Crechet/Crechett/Crockett, John, 5
Crechet/Crechett/Crockett, Thomas, Sr., 4, 5, 6, 7
Crocker, James, 213, 213n26, 258n174, 259n182
Crocker, William, 319
Crockett, Abigail [Samuel and Priscilla Swett Jackman], 189
Crockett, Abigail (Skillin), 267, 270, 286, 287, 290n303
Crockett, Abraham, 179
Crockett, Andrew, 188–189
Crockett, Ann
  birth of, 70
  character of, 33
  children of, 4, 51, 69
  Crockett's Neck management and rights to, 33n132, 33n134, 59–60, 62, 63, 95

Crockett, Ann (*continued*)
  death of, 62, 70
  descendants of, 50n203, 70–71
  final years of, 62–65
  identity of, 31–32, 32n128, 32n129, 35n141
  Kittery, return to, 42
  legal issues of, 7, 32n126, 33n130, 33n131, 40, 44–45, 50n203
  marriage to Dygory (Digory) Jeffrey, 62–63
  marriage to Thomas, 70
  promise to Hugh Gunnison, 386n46
  York (Gorgeana), move to, 36
Crockett, Ann [Thomas and Ann], 62n245, 62n248, 96, 100n2, 137, 210–211
Crockett, Anna, 237, 246
Crockett, Anne (Edge)
  birth of, 70
  Brave Boat Harbor and, 63, 94, 95, 96
  children of, 76, 100
  death of, 70, 97–98, 97n103
  inheritance from Ephraim, 62, 96, 97–98
  marriage to Ephraim, 70, 74
Crockett, Augustina M., 289n302
Crockett, Belinda (Hodgkins), 370n238
Crockett, Betsey, 330
Crockett, Betty, 267
Crockett, Catharine, 142, 237, *238,* 285
Crockett, Daniel, 185
Crockett, David, 324, 330, 331, 368, 369–370
Crockett, David, Jr., 370n238
Crockett, Davy, 2n4
Crockett, Deborah (Haley)
  birth of, 70
  children of, 116, 119, 124, 247n138
  Crockett's Neck and, 98

Crockett, Deborah (Haley) (*continued*)
   death of, 70, 123–124, 144
   Exeter, relocation to, 117–118
   marriage to Richard Crockett, 70, 111, 116
   Stratham, life in, **121**, 123
Crockett, Deborah [Richard III and Elizabeth Roberts], 237, 285
Crockett, Deborah [Richard III and Susannah Westcoat], 250, 264, 268, 285
Crockett, Dorcas, 250, 264, 267–268, 285
Crockett, Elihu, 34n124, 51, 120n93
Crockett, Eliza, 330
Crockett, Elizabeth "Betty" [Samuel and Sarah Cobb], 169
Crockett, Elizabeth Lewis Masury, 206, 268–270, 282, 283
Crockett, Elizabeth [Richard and Deborah Haley], 124
Crockett, Elizabeth [Richard III and Susannah Westcoat], 250, 264, 268, 285
Crockett, Elizabeth (Roberts)
   children of, 142, 230–231, 237, *238*, 285
   death of, 71, 238
   family of, 206, 214, 219, 316n12
   marriage to Richard Crockett III, 71, 137n142, 178n137, 219
   Reverend Clark, support of, 220
Crockett, Ephraim, Jr. [Ephraim and Anne Edge], 76, 99
Crockett, Ephraim, Jr. [Ephraim and Rebecca Stanford], 67n1, 276, 330
Crockett, Ephraim [Richard and Deborah Haley]
   birth of, 116, 124
   children of, 141, 188–189

Crockett, Ephraim [Richard and Deborah Haley] (*continued*)
   inheritance of father's property, 146, 184n161
   Stratham minister controversy, 139
   vote against Massachusetts Bay Colony control, 138
Crockett, Ephraim [Richard III and Elizabeth Roberts]
   American Revolution, service in, 243, 245, 311–312, 314–321
   as backcountry settler, 311–312, 313, 326–328, 329–330
   birth of, 67, 71, 208, 237, 285, 311, 312
   Caleb Dyer, case against, 367
   children of, 276n258, 330, 337
   death of, 67, 71, 311
   grave of, 372, *373*
   inheritance to son David, 368
   James Wagg Sr. and Jr., influence of, 313
   land dispute with Hannah Waterhouse heirs, 358–362, 367–368
   marriage to Rebecca Stanford, 71, *313*, 321, 323–324
   missing in action, report of, 253
   missing years of, 324–330
   Pejepscot Proprietors and quieting settlement, 308–309, 352, **355**
   pension of, 369
   road tax in 1813, 340
Crockett, Ephraim [Thomas and Ann]
   Aunt Joane, relationship with, 54, *55*, 73, 73n16
   birth of, 51, 67, 69, 70, 99
   Brave Boat Harbor, life at, *52*, 94

Crockett, Ephraim [Thomas and Ann] (*continued*)
  character of, 90–92
  children of, 76, 100
  as Constable and juryman of Kittery, 92–93
  Crockett's Neck and, 62, 63, 95
  death of, 10, 56, 67, 68, 70, 95, 99
  land and property inheritance, 94, 96–97, 97–98, 100
  last will and testament of, 95–97
  legal troubles of, 89–90, 92n74
  marriage to Anne Edge, 70, 74
  occupation of, 72, 92
  real estate transactions of, 51–52, 72n9, 73, 94–95
Crockett, Esther (Dingley), 368
Crockett, George [Richard Jr. and Mary Robinson], 154, 185
Crockett, George [Samuel and Abigail Skillin], 286
Crockett, Hannah (Babb), 224
Crockett, Hannah [Richard Jr. and Mary Robinson], 154, 178
Crockett, Hannah [wife of Joseph Crockett], 64n264
Crockett, Hugh, 51, 65n265, 95, 98n103, 100n2, 113n58
Crockett, James, 330, 337
Crockett, Joane. *See* Atwell, Joane (Crockett) Andrews
Crockett, John, Jr. [nephew of Thomas Crockett], 5n19
Crockett, John [brother of Thomas Crockett], 5

Crockett, John "Jonathan" [Joshua and Sarah Trickey], 179n147, 215n35
Crockett, Jonathan [Ephraim and Rebecca Frink], 139n146, 188–189
Crockett, Joseph, Jr., 65n265, 113n58
Crockett, Joseph, Sr. [Thomas and Ann], 51, 64, 65n265, 92n77, 113n58, 114
Crockett, Joseph [Ephraim and Rebecca Stanford], 330
Crockett, Joseph [Richard Jr. and Mary Robinson], 154, 185
Crockett, Joshua, 215n35
Crockett, Joshua [Richard Jr. and Mary Robinson], 154, 179, 224
Crockett, Joshua [Thomas and Ann], 65n265
Crockett, Josiah
  Crockett's Cove and, 3n7, **194**, **195**
  Deer Isle, life in, 191, 192, **194**, **195**, 244, 260
  land grant as proprietor of Deer Isle, 201–202
  parents of, 154, 185
  petition to Massachusetts General Court for relief, 199–201
  "shaving mill" attack on, 197–201
Crockett, Lucy, 237, 238, 247, 285, 324
Crockett, Mary [Ephraim and Anne Edge], 76, 96
Crockett, Mary [Ephraim and Rebecca Stanford], 330
Crockett, Mary (Knight), 179n147, 215n35
Crockett, Mary [Richard and Deborah Haley], 124
Crockett, Mary [Richard III and Elizabeth Roberts], 237, 247, 264, 285, 324

Crockett, Mary [Richard Jr. and Mary Robinson], 150, 151, 153, 154, 312, 314, 325
Crockett, Mary (Robinson)
  birth of, 70, 149
  children of, 3n7, 150, 154
  confusion over parentage, 149n17
  Congregational Church in Scarborough, 153
  death of, 70, 184
  Falmouth land, sale of, 174
  marriage to Richard Crockett, Jr., 70, 137, 147, 149
  mourning fabric, purchase of, 160–162
  Second Parish, life in, 154–155
Crockett, Mary [Thomas and Ann], 51, 94n87
Crockett, Mehitable, 289n302, 290n303
Crockett, Nathaniel, 215n35
Crockett, Olive (Swett), 364
Crockett, Peletiah, 139n146, 188–189
Crockett, Polly, 290n303
Crockett, Priscilla, 189, 330, 336n108
Crockett, Rebecca [Ephraim and Rebecca Stanford], 267, 324, 330
Crockett, Rebecca (Frink), 139n146, 141, 188–189
Crockett, Rebecca (Stanford), 67n1, 71, 276n285, 313, 321, 323–324, 330, 337, 369
Crockett, Richard, III [Richard Jr. and Mary Robinson]
  birth of, 67, 71, 154, 205
  Cape Elizabeth, roles in, 258, 266, 271, 278
  census records of, 264, *265*, 270, 274, 284
  chairmaking and other carpentry, 267
  children of, 142, 230–231, 237, *238*, 250, 270, 285, 324

Crockett, Richard, III [Richard Jr. and Mary Robinson] (*continued*)
  death of, 67, 71, 205, 284
  debts and legal troubles, 231–233, 236–237, 267
  George Roberts, influence of, 210
  grandchildren of, 267
  lien against property by Massachusetts tax collectors, 283
  list of polls and estates, 234, *235*
  marriage to Elizabeth Masury, 268, 269–270
  marriage to Elizabeth Roberts, 71, 137n142, 178, 219
  marriage to Susannah Westcoat, 137n142, 206, 209–210, 246–248
  real estate transactions of, 207n2, 212, 231, 258–261, 272–273, 281, 281–282
  Reverend Clark controversy, 220
  Richard IV, confusion with, 207–210
  summary of life, 284–285
  war services of, 179, 216, *217*, 224, 226
Crockett, Richard, IV, non-existence of, 207–210
Crockett, Richard, Jr. [Richard and Deborah Haley]
  alarm lists, 178–180, 224
  birth of, 67, 70, 116, 124, 145, 146
  children of, 3n7, 150, 154, 185
  Congregational Church in Scarborough, 153
  death of, 67, 70, 145, 201
  debts and financial difficulties of, 145, 146, 154, 155–156, *162*, 163–169, *171*, 176, 181–184
  Deer Isle, relocation to, 191–192, 244
  Falmouth land, 174, 175, 184

Index

Crockett, Richard, Jr. [Richard and Deborah Haley] (*continued*)
  as field driver, 149
  Gorham, debatable move to, 177–178
  grave of, 202
  list of polls and estates, 185–186, 191, *235*
  marriage to Mary Robinson, 70, 137, 147, 149
  occupations of, 148, 163, 192
  posthumous land grant, 201–202
  "shaving mill" attack on, 192n189, 197–201
  Stratham, life in, 139, 154, 163
  as surveyor of highways, 176, 235
  as tithingman, 176
Crockett, Richard [Ephraim and Anne Edge]
  assistance with Richard Jr.'s debts, 169, 176
  birth of, 67, 70, 76, 100
  children of, 116, 119, 124
  death of, 67, 70, 144, 181, 214
  Gunnison's Neck, dispute of boundary-line on, 110–111, *112*
  inheritance from father Ephraim, 94, 96, 99
  Kittery land grant, 65n265, 113
  marriage to Deborah Haley, 70, 116
  New Hampshire, relocation to, 113, 117–118
  property rights left to children, 144, 146
  proprietor of Bow, New Hampshire, 144
  real estate transactions of, 98, 116, 118–120, 119–120, 122, 124–125, 127, **128**, 129–130, 144, 169
  sale of oxen to George Clark, 1*25*, *126*
  Stratham, life in, 100, 120–123, 127, 139
  vote against Massachusetts Bay Colony control, 138
Crockett, Richard [Robinson and Hannah Crocker], 3n7, 202
Crockett, Richard [Samuel and Abigail Skillin], 265, 276, 276–277, 289
Crockett, Robinson, 3n7, 154, 185, 201–202, 207n2, *227*, 228, 259, 260
Crockett, Sally (Wentworth), 276n257, 298n12, 364n218
Crockett, Samuel [George and Mary Matthews], 338–339, 350, 351, 352, 364
Crockett, Samuel Haley
  alarm list, *180*
  birth of, 119, 124
  children of, 169
  Falmouth, arrival in, 147–148
  influence of aunt and uncle, 147, 170
  marriage to Mary (Cane) Whitney, 189
  marriage to Priscilla (Swett) Jackman, 175
  marriage to Sarah Cobb, 163–164
  occupations of, 148, 169–170
  payments made to Phineas Jones shop, 163
  private in Captain Cushing's list, 179, *180*
  promissory note to Phineas Jones, *171*
  real estate transactions of, 164, 172, 176, 177, 183–184
  shop in business district of Falmouth, 172
Crockett, Samuel [Richard III and Elizabeth Roberts]
  American Revolution, service in, 196, 254
  birth of, 237, 258
  Cape Elizabeth, roles in, 266
  children of, 267, 270
  confusion with Crockett, Samuel [George and Mary Matthews], 338
  death of, 287

Crockett, Samuel [Richard III and Elizabeth Roberts] (*continued*)
    land grants of, 188n167, 287, **288**, 353n191
    marriage to Abigail Skillin, 265
    real estate transactions of, 273, 281, 286–287, 289
Crockett, Sarah (Cobb), 164, 169, 172n106
Crockett, Sarah (Dow), 192, 198–199
Crockett, Sarah [Ephraim and Anne Edge], 76, 96
Crockett, Sarah [Richard and Deborah Haley], 124
Crockett, Sarah [Richard III and Elizabeth Roberts], 237, 285
Crockett, Sarah [Richard Jr. and Mary Robinson], 154, 178
Crockett, Sarah "Sally" [Ephraim and Rebecca Stanford], 330
Crockett, Sarah [Samuel Haley and Sarah Cobb], 164
Crockett, Sarah [Thomas and Ann], 96–97
Crockett, Susanna [Samuel Haley and Sarah Cobb], 169
Crockett, Susannah [Richard III and Susannah Westcoat], 250, 264, 267
Crockett, Susannah (Westcoat), 137n142, 206, 209–210, 213, 247–250, 267, 278n266, 324
Crockett, Thomas
    arrival in the New World, 2–3, 3n10, 14–15, 16, 17, 20, **121**
    birth of, 5, 5n18, 67, 70
    children of, 51, 69
    Crockett's Neck and, 34, 46–49, 73
    death of, 58, 67, 70

Crockett, Thomas (*continued*)
    descendants of, 67, 70, 70–71
    estate of, 59–60
    ferry work in Kittery Point, 30–31, 43
    Gibbons' house work, 29
    Gunnisons, connection to, 31–32
    Kittery, return to, 42
    land grants of, 17n63, 36, 39, **61**
    legal issues, 7, 40, 45
    marriage to Ann, 70
    Massachusetts Bay Colony, oath of allegiance to, 36–38
    missing years of, 29
    Newichawannock House work, 23, 25, 26, 28
    real estate transactions of, 17, 33, 36n146, 51–52, 59, 73n19
    York, move to, 36
Crockett, Thomas [Elihu and Mary Winnock], 120n93
Crockett, Thomas Sr., 4, 5, 6, 7
Crockett, William [Richard and Deborah Haley], 124, 144, 164–165, 166, 176, 183–184
Crockett, William [Richard III and Elizabeth Masury], 270, 274, 283, 284, 285, 289–290
Crockett, William [Samuel and Abigail Skillin], 270, 286, 289
Crockett's Back Creek, 110
Crockett's Corner, 3, 290–291
Crockett's Cove (Deer Isle), 3, 192, **194**, **195**, 202–203
Crockett's Cove (Kittery), **46**
Crockett's Creek, **46**, 110

Index

Crockett's Mill, **195**
Crockett's Neck
  descendants on, 95, 100, 116
  dispute over ownership, 34, 46–49, 69n8
  land granted to Thomas Crockett, 34
  land on given to Thomas' daughters, 96–97
  management of after Thomas' death, 33n132, 33n133, 59–60, 62, 63, 95
  real estate transactions on, 97–98, 110, 119
  Thomas' family on, 3, 73, 74, 116
Crockett's Plain, 65n265
Crockett's Ridge, 3, 67n1, 364n218
Cromwell, Oliver, 48
Cumberland County Congress, 234
Cummings, Mary Ann, 287n295
Cummings, William, 287n295
Cummins, Thomas, 213
Curtis, Joseph, 113n58
Cushing, Ezekiel, 218, 220, 221, 223
Cushing, Loring, 178, *180,* 223
Cushing, Thomas, 257
Cushnoc, 78

D

Damariscotta, battle of, 108
Danville, 278, 325–326, 339–340, 366, 367, 371, 372. *See also* Pejepscot, town of
Dart (river in Devon, England), 4, 7, 24, 29–30
Dartmouth and Devon Fishing Industry, 7–8
Dartmouth (city in Devon, England), 7, 8
Darumkin (Native American), 297, 299, 341
Davenport, Richard, 43n172
Davis, Amos, 350
Davis, John, 102
Davis, Joseph, 7n27, 44, 45–46, 72n13, 89

Davis, Nicholas, 40n157, 72
Dawnland, 2, 135n132, 293–298, 308–309
Day of Public Humiliation, 105–106
Day of Public Thanksgiving, 106
Day of Solemn Fasting and Prayer, 106
Dearborn, Jonathan, 122
Dearing, Roger, 110n47
Declaration of Independence, 245, 246
Deer Isle
  early settlers of, **194, 195,** 201–202
  food and supply shortages during American Revolution, 193
  Richard Jr. and Josiah on, 191–192, 202, 244, 260
  shaving mill attacks, 197–201
  See also Crockett's Cove (Deer Isle)
deer reeves, 235
Deering/Dearing, Henry, 55n223, 95n88, 95n89
Dehamda (Native American), 10
Derby, Richard, Jr., 245
Dingley, Desire, 367
Dingley, Edward Nelson, 331–332
Dingley, Esther, 331, 368
Dingley, Jeremiah, 331n75, 364
Dingley, Nelson, Jr., 331n76
Dingley, Polly, 331, 367
Dingley, Sarah "Sally" (Jordan), 367
Dingley, William, 315, 331, 349, 352, 353n192, **355,** 364, 367, 372
diseases brought to the New World, 21, 294, 295
Doane/Dunn, Edward, 263n193
Dole, Daniel, 280n272
Door, Richard, 120n93

437

Dover, New Hampshire, 85, 87, 88n61
Dow, Sarah, 192, 387n53
Downing, Dennis, 108
Downing, Joshua, 76n34, *109*
Dudley, Joseph, 130
Duely, Samuel, 168
Duguay, Brenda (Daicy), 284
Duke D'Anville, 173–174
Duke of York, 88, 89. *See also* James II, King of England
Dummer, Jeremiah, 302, 342n134
Dummer, Nathaniel, 352
Dummer, Shubael, 64n259, 106
Dummer, William, 134n131, 342n134
Dummer's Treaty (1726), 175, 216, 342
Dummer's War, 101, 133–135, 172n108, 175
Dunn, Deborah (Bailey), 243
Dunn, Ebenezer, *265*
Dunn, Edward, *265*, 279n271
Dunn, Nathaniel, 243
Dunn, Samuel, 235, 242–243, 244, 271n236, 286, 316
Durant, Cornelius, 265
Durham, 309, 326, 345, 356. *See also* Royalsborough
Dyamont/Diamond, John (of Kittery), 93n80
Dyamont/Diamond, John (of Stoke Gabriel), 10–11, 14
Dyer, Caleb, 271n236, 367
Dyer, Enoch, 271
Dyer, Henry, 240n114
Dyer, Isaac, 235
Dyer, Lemuel, 337

E

Eastern Land Papers, 303
Edge, Anne. *See* Crockett, Anne (Edge)
Edge, Florence "Grandma," 74–76, 97, 100
Edge, Peter, 75
Edge, Robert, 74–76
Elwell, James, 352, 363
Embargo Act (1807), 272
Emery, James, *109*
English Civil War, 30
English settlements, early, 10–13
Eyre, Thomas, 19–20

F

Fairweather, J., 344n142
Falmouth
    ancient and new settlers, distinction between, 148n11
    boycott of British goods, 190
    Fifth Indian War in, 173, 175
    food shortage, winter 1765, 189
    French and Indian War in, 222–223, 223
    Native American raids on, 134
    population explosion of, 147
    Proprietor's Committee, 148, 212–213
    resettlement of, 136–138
    selectmen of, 132, 223
    "terrible distemper," 160–161
    valuation of (1781), 257
    wolf bounty, 156–157
    See also Second Parish
Falmouth Neck, 172, 175, 177, 190–191, 218, 244
Father Rasles' War, 101, 133–135, 172n108, 175

Fayeweather, Hannah, 363
fence viewers, 236, 266, 271, 278
Fergison, John, 92n78
Fernald, John, 116
Fernald, William, *109*
field drivers, 149, 149n13, 149n14, 236, 266, 271, 278
Fifth Indian War, 101, 172–175, 215–218
Finely, William, 268n221
Finson (Captain), 340
First Church of Falmouth, 150, 150–151, 153, 160, 169, 173n111, 187, 211
First Church of Scarborough, 160, 270
First Indian War, 57–58, 79–89, 101, 297
Follet, John, 129n120
Folsom, Jeremy, 122, 124n104
Folson, John, 168n92
Fort George, 193
Fort Loyal, 64n259, 136n135
Fort Pejepscot, 105
Fort Point, 228. *See also* Fort Pownall
Fort Pownall, 225, 228
Fourth Indian War, 101, 133–135, 172n108, 175
Free Will Baptists, 338–339
Freeman, Enoch, 199n203, 259n183, 263n193, 264n198, **310**
Freeman, Enoch, Jr., 263n193
Freeman, Mary, 263n193
Freeman, Sam, 279n272, 280n272
Freeman, Samuel, 259n183, 263n193
French, William, 120n93, 122n100, 124n105
French and Indian War, 101, 173n111, 178, *180,* 187–188, 218, 221–229, 293
French settlements, early, 10–11

Frink, George, 137n139, 189n174
Frink, Rebecca, 141, 188–189
Frink, Rebecca (Skillin), 137n139, 189n174
Frontenac, Louis de Baude de, 104
Frost, Charles, 87, 92n74, 107–108, 213n27
Frost, Dorothy (Mendum), 119n88
Frost, Joanna, 213n27
Frost, Nicholas (beaver trader), 92n74
Frost, Nicholas (depositions for Thomas Crockett), 47, 49
Frothingham, John, 273n247
Fryer, Nathaniel, 91, 92n73

G

Gage, Edmund, 56
Gardiner, Thomas, 84
George III, King of Great Britian, 188, 343
Georgiana/Gorgeana (plantation), **19**
Gibbons, Ambrose, 15, 19–20, 23, 24, 25, 26–27, 26n102, 29
Gibbons, Rebecca, 20, 32n129
Giddings, Andrew, 332, 335, 336n107, 337, 338, 340
Gilbert, John, 118n87
Gilbert, John, Jr., 119n90
Glorious Revolution, 101n5, 102
Godfrey, Ann, 33n130
Godfrey, Edward, 15, 15n58, 26n102, 29, 33n130, 36n150, 40, 90
Godfrey, Elizabeth, 40
Godsoe, William, 65n265, 129, 385n43
Goodwin, Ichabod, 352
Goold/Gould, Rhoda, 367
Gorgeana (York), **39**

Gorges, Ferdinando (grandson of English knight), 48, 63, 77
Gorges, Sir Ferdinando (English knight), 9–10, 12–13, 15, 16, **19**, 24n92, 26, 29n118, 296
Gorges, Thomas, 34
Gorham, 177, 323n45
Grand Inquest, 110, 129
Great Island, 31, *55*, 91
Great Lot No. 3, 327, **328**, 330, 358, 362, 368
Great Migration, 16
The Great Migration Study Project, 68–69
Great Mill, 206, 214, 263n193
Great Proprietors, 2, 277, 300–301, 306, 307–309, 371. *See also* Kennebec Proprietors; Pejepscot Proprietors; Waldo Proprietors
Great Swamp Massacre, 57n229
Green, John, 263n193
Greenland, Henry, 95n88
Greenleaf, Jonathan, 200
Gregg, William, 269
Grievance Committee, 240
Gunnison, Deborah, 54n218, 72–73
Gunnison, Elihu, 103, *109*, 110–111, 112, 115, 117, 129, 182, 386n46
Gunnison, Elizabeth [first wife of Hugh Gunnison], 36n143, 73
Gunnison, Elizabeth (Ingersol) Skillin, 103, 115, 137n141
Gunnison, George, 115
Gunnison, Hugh, 5n18, 31–32, 35–36, 41–43, 52n208, 53, 73, 103n13, 386n46
Gunnison, Joseph, 114–115
Gunnison, Martha (Trickey), 103n13
Gunnison, Sarah [Hugh and Sarah Lynn], 114
Gunnison, Sarah Lynn. *See* Morgan, Sarah Lynn Gunnison Mitchell
Gunnison-Shapleigh case, 5n18, 31n125, 41–42
Gunnison's Neck, 111
Gutteridge, Jeremiah, 91

H

Haley, Andrew, 111, 129
Haley, Andrew, Jr., 113n58
Haley, Deborah. *See* Crockett, Deborah (Haley)
Haley, Deborah (Wilson), 111, 113, 114
Haley, Hannah, 247n138
Haley, Rhoda, 111, 113, 117n77, 129, 137, 155, 206, 210–211, 247n138
Hall, Charles, 178n134
Hammond, Joseph, 107
Hancock, John, 257
Hanscom, Moses, 176
Harbert, Sylvester, 72n11
Harmon, Johnson, 135, 152n34
Hart, William, 326n58
Harvard College, 357
Hasty, William, 281n277
Hatch, Mary, 313n3
Heard, John, 108
Heath, William, 244, 318
Henry VII, King of England, 294
Hertel, Francois de, 104
Hildreth, David, 350
Hilton, William, 40n155, 41n162, 43n173
Hoag, Benjamin, 118n87, 119n90
Hoag, Joseph, 119n90
Hodgkins, Belinda, 370n238

Index

Hodgkins, Phillip, 268n222
hog reeves, 149n14, 266, 271, 278
Holyoke, Eleazer, 220
Hooke, Francis, 55, 58, 93n80, 95–96, 384n38
Hooker, Joseph, 268–269
Hopewell (ship), 74
Howard, Robert, 43n172
Hubbard, William, 79–80, 83, 85–86
Hunnewell, Joseph, 281n277
Hutchins, Enoch, 108n39
Hutchinson, Thomas, 298, 343n137

I
Ilsley, Isaac, 223
Inches, Henderson, 356–357, 357–358, 358–359, 362, 365, 365n222, 368
Indian corn, 333
Indian Purchase No. 2, 188n167, 287, **288**, 307
Indian Wars in Maine (chart), 101
Inferior Court of Common Pleas, 124–125, 148n8, *162, 167,* 232
Ingersoll, Elizabeth, 103, 137n141
Ingraham, Joseph H., 279n272, 280n272
Intolerable Acts, 241
Isle of Shoals, 29, 33, 110
Isley, Enoch, 248n141, 273n247

J
Jackman, Priscilla (Swett), 175, 189
Jackson, Andrew, 277
James I, King of England, 10, 11, 341
James II, King of England, 89, 102. *See also* Duke of York
Jefferson, Thomas, 271–272

Jeffrey, Ann Crockett. *See* Crockett, Ann
Jeffrey, Dygory (Digory), 56n228, 62–63, 93n79, 94, 95n88, 110
Jeffrey, James, 120n92, 127
Jeffries, David, 298, 343n137
Jeffry, Cyrprian, 122n96
Jeffry, James, 122n96
Jenkin, Josiah, 326n58
Jewel (slave owned by James Millers), 129n116
Jewett, Benjamin, 125, 144n161, 169
Jocelyn, Henry, 26, 26n102
Jones, Benjamin, 122n100
Jones, Daniel, 252–253
Jones, John, 280n272
Jones, Nathaniel, 240n114, 254
Jones, Phineas
    lawsuits with Richard Crockett, Jr., 165–166, *167,* 168
    promissory note from Richard and Samuel Crockett, 164–165, *171*
    real estate transactions of, 155, 172, 176, 212, 259n182
    shopkeeper, 148, 160, *162,* 163
Jones, Stephen, 164–165, 168
Jonson, John, 267
Jordan, Clement, 242
Jordan, Dominicus, 156
Jordan, Dominicus (Captain), 223
Jordan, Jeremiah, 157
Jordan, John, Jr., 157n57
Jordan, Joshua, 254
Jordan, M., 280n273
Jordan, Mary, 157
Jordan, Nathaniel, Jr., 242
Jordan, Robert, 157

Jordan, Samuel, 155–156, 163, 166, *167,* 168
Jordan, Tristam, 273n242

K
Keats, Richard, 116n76
Kelley, Holdridge, 122
Kene, Nathaniel, 94n85, 129
Kenison, James, 120n92
Kennebec Patent, 308, 341–344, 371
Kennebec Proprietors, 300–301, 305, 308, 341–344. *See also* Plymouth Company
Kennebec River, 10, 57, 78, 130, 134, 297, 341
Kennebis/Kennebecs (Native American tribe), **22,** 57, 80, 88, 130–131
King, Richard, *109*
King, William, 275, 282–283
King George's War, 101, 172–175, 215–218
King Philip (Native American), 56, 79, 85
King Philip's War, 56–58, 79–89, 101, 297
King William's War, 64, 100, 101, 104–109
Kittery, town of, 46–49, **50,** 94–95, 104, 107–109, 110, 113, 129
Kittery Point, 29, 30–31, **46,** 51–52
Kittery Selectmen, 108, *109,* 110, 114
Knight, Francis, 43n172
Knight, George, 181–182
Knight, Mary, 179n147, 215n35
Knight, Samuel, 93n79

L
Laconia Company, 13, 14–15, 16, 17–18, 19–20, 20–21, 23–24, 25–26
Laconia patent, 12, 12n48
Lake of the Iroquois, 14, 19

land ownership, Indigenous *vs.* English concepts, 294–297
land speculation, 300–309. *See also* Great Proprietors
Lander, John, 33
Lane, Job, 336n107, 338
Larrabee, Solomon, 340
Larraby, Benjamin, 149n13
Laud, William, 17n61
Lawton, Henry, 84
Leach, Benjamin, 282
Leach, George, 338
Leach, James, 245, 319–321
Leavitt, Dudley, 139
Lee, Jesse, 338
Lee's Grant, 67n1, 276, 330n72
Leverdure, John, 84
Levett, John, 127n112
Lewis, Archelaus, 280n272
Lewis, Elizabeth, 206, 268–270, 282, 283
Lewis, Hannah, 305n29
Lewis, Job, 305n29, **328,** 344n142, 345, 356
Lidden, Edward, 113n61
Lidden, Elizabeth, 113n61
Lidden, Mary, 113n61
Lincoln, Daniel W., 280n273
Lincoln County, committee to appraise and sell land in, 305–306
Little, Abigail, 347n158
Little, Anna, 347n158
Little, Josiah, **328,** 347–351, 353, 356, 362, 363, 364, 370
Little, Michael, 347n158
Little, Moses, **328,** 344n143, 346–347, 363
Little, Sarah, 347n158

Index

Little Harbor, 18, 26, 26n102, 27
"little ice age," 68–69
Little's Gore, 339, 340
Livermore, Matthew, 165, 168, 169
Lockwood, Deborah (Gunnison), 54n218, 72–73
Lockwood, Richard, 54, 73n16, 75
Lombard, Solomon, 188n173
Long Creek, Falmouth, 137–138
Long Creek cemetery, 142, *143,* 238, *238,* 281, 284
Long Creek (settlement), 206–207
Long Reach, attack on, 107
Longfellow, Henry Wadsworth, 317n19
Longfellow, Stephen, 129n116, 178n137, 209n10, 219, 228n74
Lord, John, 352
Lord, Nathan, Jr., 184n160
Loron (Native American), 152, 342n134
Louis XVI, King of France, 271
Lowell, J. (Sargeant), 277
Lynn, Elizabeth, 43, 73
Lynn, Ephraim, 31n124, 32n128, 32n129, 53
Lynn, Henry, 31, 32, 32n129, 35n141
Lynn, Sarah. *See* Morgan, Sarah Lynn Gunnison Mitchell
Lynn, Sarah [Henry and Sarah], 43

M

Madison, James, 275
Madockawando (Native American), 64, 101, 106
Maine, District of
  British invasion during War of 1812, 275–276

Maine, District of (*continued*)
  British occupation during American Revolution, 192–193, 253–254
  British tax on, 189–191
  Indian Wars in, 101
  land grants for American Revolution soldiers, 327–329
  land speculation, 300–309
  ownership, battle over, 2, 293–298
  population of, 188, 296
  raids on residents of after the American Revolution, 196–201
Maine, Province of
  cows arrive in, 27–28
  Massachusetts purchase of, 63, 76–78
  settlements of, 10–13
  settlers of, 16–17, 90
  Wabanaki Confederacy in, **22**
Maine, state of, 277, 282–283, 371
Maine Mall, 290–291
Maliseet (Native American tribe), **22**, 97, 303n24
Maneddo (Native American), 10
Manter, Experience, 149n17
Margery, George, 269, 273
Mariner, Joseph, 240n114
Marshall, Robert, 93n79
Marston, James, 165
Marston, John, 182, 183, 184
Mary II, Queen of England, 102
Mason, John, 12–13, 15, 16, **19**, 24, 24n92, 25, 26
Massachusetts
  Committee for the Sale of Unappropriated Lands in Lincoln County, 305–306

Massachusetts (*continued*)
  Constitution of, 1780, 256–257, 303
  failure to help Maine during War of 1812, 275–276, 277
  land grants promised to American Revolution soldiers, 304, 306, 327–329
  land lottery of 1786, 306
  Provincial Army, 242, 243, 243n127, 316n11, 317, 345
  purchase of Maine, 63, 77–78
  tax bills to Mainers in 1819, 283

Massachusetts Bay Colony
  attacks on Montreal and Quebec during Second Indian War, 105
  Father Rasles demands on, 133
  Ferdinando Gorges' real estate, theft and purchase of, 76–78
  petition to govern New Hampshire, 138
  submission to, 36–38, **39**, 41
  Winthrop Fleet, 16–17, 18

Massachusetts General Court
  Act to Prevent Monopoly and Oppression, 251
  bounties on Native American scalps, 173, 215
  Committee of Eastern Claims and Settlements, 132
  creation of Narragansett Township No. 7, 177
  Deer Isle residents petition for relief, 199–201
  Pejepscot Proprietors, settlement with, 368
  petition for relief of taxation and aid, 108–109

Massachusetts General Court (*continued*)
  "quieting" of backcountry settlers, 308, 341, 348, 351–352, **354, 355**, 364
  raises taxes for war effort, 114
  Second Parish petition as separate township from Falmouth, 229

Massachusetts Provincial Army, 242, 243, 243n127, 316n11, 317, 345

Massachusetts Provincial Congress, 196, 205, 243, 244, 317

Masury, Elizabeth Lewis, 206, 268–270, 282, 283

Masury, George, 269, 270, 274

Masury, John, 268–269

Masury, John [John Masury and Elizabeth Lewis], 269, 270, 274, 281, 284, 285, 285–286

Masury, Jonathan, 269, 270, 274

Masury, Rebecca, 269, 270, 274

Matrosses (artillerymen), *320*, 321

Mayo, Ebenezer, 280n272

Mayo, Noah, 213n28

McFarland, Joanna R., 202–203

McFarland, Phillip, 3n7, 192

McLaughlin, Robert, 280n272

McLellan, Arthur, 280

Means, James, 280n272

Medaganesset (Ameriscoggon/Androscoggin tribal leader), 152

Meeting House Hill, 153

Mendum, Dorothy, 119n88

Mendum, Jonathan, 119n88

Mendum, Nathaniel, 119n88

Mendum, Robert, 36, 42, 47

Index

Mendum, Robert [grandson of Robert Mendum], 119n88
Metacom (Native American), 56, 79, 85
Micmac/Mi'kmaq (Native American tribe), **22**, 97, 130, 225n67, 303n24
Miles, Joseph, 36n146
Milk, James, 223
Millers, James, 129n116
Minot, Stephen, 298, 343n137
Missiqoi (Native American tribe), **22**
Missouri Compromise, 282
Mitchell, Christopher, 55, 93
Mitchell, John, 44
Mitchell, Jonathan, 254
Mitchell, J.P., 290n303
Mitchell, Robert, 149n13
Mitchell, Sarah. *See* Morgan, Sarah Lynn Gunnison Mitchell
Mitchell, Sarah (Andrews), 56n228, 114
Mitchell (Colonel), 319
Mitton, Ann, 86
Mohawk (Native American tribe), 88, 135
Monhegan Island, 1, 8
Montcalm, Louis-Joseph de, 229
Montcalm, Marquis de, 187
Montreal, attack on, 105
Morgan, Francis, 52–53, 54, 386n46
Morgan, Sarah Lynn Gunnison Mitchell
  children of, 32n128, 43, 73, 103n13
  description of, 41n159
  identity of, 32n129
  legal issues of, 31n145, 52
  liquidation of Hugh Gunnison's estate, 386n46
  marriages of, 31, 32, 32n129, 35–36, 43–44, 52–53

Morgan, Sarah Lynn Gunnison Mitchell (*continued*)
  Thomas and Ann Crockett, connection to, 31–32, 35
Morrill, John, 90
Morse, Nathan, 67n1
Morton, Bryant, 216
Moulton, Jeremiah, 135, 152n34
Mount Pleasant Cemetery, 153
Mountfort, Edmund, 231, 258
Mountfort, Edmund, Jr., 231–232, *233*
Mountfort, Elizabeth, 231–232, *233*
Mountfort, Esther (Rogers), 231–232, *233*
Mountfort, Samuel, 207n2, 258, 259
Mowatt, Henry, 190–191, 244
Mussey, John, 267
Mussey, Jonathan, 267

N

Narragansett (Native American tribe), 57n229, 79, 87
Narragansett Township No.7 (Gorham), 177, 323n45
Nason, Sarah, 107
Native American population decline, 21, 294, 295
Neal, Andrew, 114
Neal, James, 279n272
Neal, Walter, 15, 18–19, 24–25
Neonongansket (Native American), 297, 299, 341
New Dartmouth, raid on, 101
New England
  colonization of, 10–13, 14–15, 17–20

New England (*continued*)
   longevity in "New" England *vs.* "Old" England, 68–69
   money in (old tenor and new tenor), 139n145
   shifting powers within, 16–17, 102 (*See also* Massachusetts Bay Colony)

New France, 104, 130, 134, 135

New Hampshire
   Inferior Court of Common Pleas, 124–125, 148n8, *162, 167, 232*
   naming of by John Mason, 12
   petition to be put under the government of Massachusetts Bay Colony, 138
   "terrible distemper," 160

New Somersetshire, 12

Newfoundland, 7, 8

Newfoundland fishery, 7

Newichawanncok House, 20–28, *26*

Newichawannock (Native American tribe), 20, 21

Newichawannock (region), **19**

Nicholas, John, 266

Nimbanizett (Native American), 297, *299*, 341

Nine Year's War. *See* King William's War; Second Indian War

Nipmuck (Native American tribe), 87

Noble, James, 157–159, 163, 165, 168

Non-Intercourse Act, 274

Norridgewock, Native American settlement, destruction of, 133–134

Norridgewock (Native American tribe), 97, 133–135, 152, 175

North Yarmouth, 132, 232n44, 322

Northeast Coast Campaign of 1688, 102n8

Northeast Coast Campaign of 1724, 134

Northwest Passage, 12–13, 14–15

Nova Scotia Native tribes, 187–188, 229

Noyes, Joseph, 263n196, 264n198

Noyes, Oliver, 298, 343n137

O

Obrion, Richard, 178n137

Odanak (Native American tribe), **22**

Ogrado(e)/O'Grady, Charles, 72n9, 94

Old French War, 178. *See also* French and Indian War; Sixth Indian War

P

Palmer, George, 95n88

Palmer, Rowena, *203*

Palmer, William, 93n80

Parker, Isaac, 157–158

Parker, John, 246

Parret/Parrot, Sarah (Crockett), 96–97, 100n2

Parrot/Parrett, John, 95

Parsons, Isaac, 333

Partridge, Nathan, 248n142

Pascataqua, 17–18, **19**, 20, **121**

Passamaquoddy (Native American tribe), **22**, 187–188, 229, 293, 303n24

Paul, Catherine, 93n79

Paul, Stephen, 93n79

Peace of Ryswick (1697), 108

Peace of Utrecht (1713), 130

peace talks between Native Americans and English
   Cocheco 1676, 87–88
   Falmouth 1732, 151–152
   Falmouth 1749, 174–175

peace talks between Native Americans and English (*continued*)
   Portsmouth 1713, 130–131
Pearce, Joseph, 93, 93n80
Pejepscot, town of, 339–341
Pejepscot Claim
   1764 plan of, **310**
   census records of, 330
   daily life in, 330–337
   early settlers of, 301–302, 326–327
   "quieting" the settlers of, 351–355
   social and religious life in, 337–339
Pejepscot Patent
   early settlers of, 308, **354, 355**
   Great Lot No. 3, 327, **328**, 330, 358, 362, 368
   and Josiah Little, 347–351
   land description of, 301
   Moses Little and, 345–346
   "quieting" of settlers of, 348, 351–356
   shifting boundaries of, 309, 341–344
Pejepscot Proprietors
   claims to land, 300–301, 305, 306, 311–312, 327, **328**, 329, 341
   harassment of Ephraim Crockett, 308–309
   order to grant settlers lots by Massachusetts General Court, 348
   original members of, 343n137
   proposed settlement with Massachusetts, 351–355, 356
   settlement with Kennebec Proprietors, 341–344
   settlement with Massachusetts, 362–370, 368
Penacook (Native American tribe), 87
Penas, Sias (Native American), 223

Pendleton, Bryan, 47–48, 60n241
Pendleton, James, 49n202
Penhallow, Samuel, 117n83
Penley, Desire (Dingley), 367
Penley, John, 363–364, 366, 370
Penley, Julia (Wagg), 367
Penley, Sampson, 53n213
Penobscot Expedition, 196, 253–254
Penobscot (Native American tribe)
   conference with Massachusetts Bay, 152
   Fifth Indian War, 172, 175
   First Indian War, 80, 88
   forced sale of land to Maine in 1834, 287, 307
   location of, **22**
   relationship with river, 295
   remain in Maine after Fall of Quebec, 187–188, 229
   settlement with government, 1980, 303n24
   Treaty of Portsmouth, 130–131
Pepperrell, Andrew, 119n91
Pepperrell, Margery, 116n76
Pepperrell, Sir William, Jr., 65n265, 98n104, 119n91, 182
Pepperrell, William, Sr., 62, 65n265, 97n98, *109,* 110n43, 113n58, 116n76, 117n83, 119n91
Perryman, Nicholas, 168
Peters, W.B., 279n272
Pett, Jonathan, 93n79
Phillis (slave owned by James Millers), 129n116
Phinney, Edmund, 243, 244, 245, 316–318, 319, 326n58
Phips, William, 104

Pickering, Thomas, 29
Pied Cow (ship), 3n9, 15n56, 20, 27–28
Pigwacket/Pequawaket (Native American tribe), **22**, 80, 88, 152, 180
Pike, Richard, 225n67
Pilgrims, 18, 149n17, 294, 297. *See also* Plymouth Colony
Piper, Samuel, 118, 119
Piscataqua Plantations, *19,* 20
Piscatoquake (Native American tribe), 117n79
Plummer, Edward, 335
Plummer, Jesse, *265*
Plummer, Timothy, 336
Plummer, William, 335–336, 337, 352, 363
Plymouth Colony, 56, 78, 105
Plymouth Company, 10, 297, 301, 341n130
Plymouth Patent, 301
Pomeroy, Richard, 149n13
Ponwall, William, 225, 228
Popham, George, 10
Popham, Sir John, 10
Popham Colony, 10–11
"Post Westcott," 255
Pownall, Thomas, 225
Pray, Joseph, 108n39
Preble, Jedidiah, 181–182, 231, *232,* 240, 243, 257
Preble, Jedidiah, Jr., 181
Preble, Mehitable (Bangs) Roberts, 181
Pring, Martin, 10, 23n89
Pritchard, John, 147n6
privateers, attacks by, 197–201, 254
Proclamation of 1763, 343
Proprietors Committee, 212, 258n174, 279, 280

Purchase, Thomas, 297, 344n143
Purington, Ezra, 350, 351
Puritans, 16–17, 18, 29, 48, 76–77, 78, 102, 293
Purpooduck, 105, 147, 153, *154,* 211–212, 230, 321. *See also* Falmouth; Second Parish
Putnam, Israel, 318

Q

Quamscott House, 118n85
Quartering Act, 241
Quebec, attack on (1690), 105
Quebec, fall of (1759), 187–188
Queen Anne's War, 64, 101, 113–114, 130
"quieting"
 of backcountry settlers, 308, 341, 348, 351–352, **354, 355,** 364
 definition of, 296
 of Native Americans, 296
Quimby, John, 264n198
Quincy, Jacob, 283

R

Rand, W. (Captain), 276
Randles, Stephen, 212
Rasles, Sébastien, 133–135, 152n34. *See also* Father Rasles' War
Raynes, Ellen, 33n130, 40, 41, 42
Raynes, Francis, 33n130, *38,* 40, 45, 59, **61,** 89–90
Raynes, Nathaniel, 59n238
Raynes Neck, **61**
Reed, Robert, 116
Revolutionary War. *See* American Revolution
Richardson, Alford, 277

Index

Richmond Island, 33
Riggs, Wheeler, 178n131
Rindage, Captain, 127
Rishworth, Edward, 34, 47n193, 51n204, 53n213, 58n234, 92n74
River Dart (England), 4, 7, 24, 29–30
Roberts, Ann (Crockett), 62n245, 62n248, 96, 100n2, 210–211
Roberts, Benjamin, 214, 224, 224–225, 228
Roberts, Catharine, 263n193
Roberts, Deborah [Rueben Roberts and Rebecca Masury], 269n228
Roberts, Deborah (York), 228, 269
Roberts, Elizabeth. *See* Crockett, Elizabeth (Roberts)
Roberts, Elizabeth [Reuben Roberts and Rebecca Masury], 269n228
Roberts, George
  birth of, 62n248, 210
  Cape Elizabeth, roles in, 236, 266
  children of, 137n142, 150, 206, 214
  death of, 324n50
  as Lieutenant in French and Indian War, 179, 224
  life in Falmouth, 210–212
  list of polls and estates, 234–235
  real estate transactions of, 96n98, 137, 212–214, 278n265
Roberts, George Copson
  children of, 269
  death of, 281
  financial troubles of, 278–281
  in French and Indian War, 224–225, 228
  friendship with Richard Crockett III, 214
  marriage to Deborah York, 228

Roberts, George Copson (*continued*)
  Portland, move to, 281
  real estate transactions of, 207n2, 259, *260*, 263n193, 280
Roberts, John, Jr., 181
Roberts, Joseph, 207n2, 214, 224, *260*
Roberts, Katharine (Skillin), 137, 137n142, 150, 206, 210–214, 234–235, 324n50
Roberts, Lydia, 214
Roberts, Mehitable (Bangs), 181
Roberts, "Nan" (Anna/Ann), 97n98
Roberts, Reuben, 269, 279n268, 282
Roberts, Rhoda, 150, 211
Roberts, Richard, 278, 279, 281n278
Roberts, Sally, 269
Roberts, Sarah (Creasey), 210
Roberts, William, I, 65n265, 95, 96n98, 97n103, 110n46, 113n58, 210
Roberts, William, II [William Roberts I and Ann Crockett], 62n248, 97n103, 114, 210
Roberts, William [George Roberts and Katharine Skillin], 214
Robinson, Abraham III, 149, 174n119
Robinson, David, Jr., 122
Robinson, David (town clerk), 138–139, 150n20
Robinson, John, Jr., 174, 223
Robinson, John [Abraham Robinson III and Sarah York], 174n117
Robinson, John (creditor to Richard Crockett III), 223, 236–237
Robinson, John (pastor to Pilgrims), 149n17, 335n102, 390n62
Robinson, Mary. *See* Crockett, Mary (Robinson)

Robinson, Samuel, 174
Robinson, Sarah (York), 149, 174n119
Roebuck (ship), 197, 198
Rogers, Esther, 231–232, *233*
Rogers, George, 276
Rogers, Gersom, 231–232
Rogers, Sarah (Lynn), 43
Rogers, William, 43, 111n51
Rollins, Thomas, 122
Rosier, James, 1, 8–9
Royalists, 16, 29, 48, 78, 293, 304–305, 312, 327–328, 344–345
Royall, Isaac, 305n29, **328**, 345
Royall, Isaac, Jr., 345, 357, 363
Royalsborough, 309, **310**, 326, 345, 356, 370
Ruck, John, 298, 343n137
Rust, Henry, 122, 138–140
Ryerson, W. (Lieutenant Colonel), 276

S

Saco, town of, 114, 132
Saco (Native American tribe), 54, 79–84, 88
Saffacomoit (Native American), 10
Sagadahock (region), 10, 80
Saint-Castin, Baron Jean Vincent de, 64, 101, *102*, 103
Salmon Falls, 27, 104
Salmon Falls River, **19**, 23n88, 23n89, 28
Sanders' Point, 18, 25, 26, 29
Sargeant, Diamond, 119n91
Sargeant, Fitzwilliam, 166, 169n97
Sargent, Daniel, 364
Saunders, Edward, 35n141
Savage, Ephraim, 297–298
Sawyer, Ebenezer, 230, 264n199, 265
Sawyer, Jacob, 147, 157, 322n36
Sawyer, Job, 323n45
Sawyer, John, 147, 150n22, 154–155, 157, 175, 322
Sawyer, John, Jr., 175, 184, 208n4
Sawyer, Joseph, 149n13
Sawyer, Rebecca, 141n155, 150–151, 150n27, 175n122, 243, 316n12
Scammon, William, 122
Scossaway (Native American), 84
Scriven/Screven/Scrivine, William, 58, 59–60
Second Continental Congress, 245
Second Indian War, 64, 100, 101, 104–109
Second Parish
  Crocketts and Skillins in, 137–138, 147
  establishment of, 211
  meeting houses, 153, *154,* 211
  mid-18th century, 153, 218–219
  petition to be set off from Falmouth, 229–230
  "terrible distemper," 160
  See also Cape Elizabeth, District of; Falmouth
Seely, Elizabeth (Lynn), 43, 73
Seely, William, 43, 111n51
Selemons, William, 263n196
Seven Years War, 178n138, 187–188, 221–229. *See also* French and Indian War
Sewall, Captain, 326n58
Shapleigh, Alexander, 29n117, 30n119
Shapleigh, John, *109*
Shapleigh, Nicholas, 29–30, 30n119, 41–42, 44, 48, 49, 63
shaving mills (attacks by privateers), 197–201, 254

Index

Shephard, John, 94n85
Shirley, William, 174–175, 216
Simon the Yankee Killer, 85
Simonton, William, 218, 220
Sinkler, John (Jonathan), 124, 124n106, 125n109
Sixth Indian War, 101, 173n111, 178, *180*, 187–188, 218, 221–229, 293
Skicowaros (Native American), 9, 10
Skillin, Abigail, 265
Skillin, Benjamin [Thomas Skillin, Jr.], 132
Skillin, Benjamin [Thomas Skillin, Sr.], 132n126
Skillin, Daniel, 286, 289
Skillin, Deborah, 132n126
Skillin, Dorcas. *See* Westcoat, Dorcas (Skillin)
Skillin, Elizabeth (Ingersoll), 103, 137n141
Skillin, Joanna, 155, 228
Skillin, John, 263, 287n295
Skillin, John, Jr., 137n139, 137n141
Skillin, John, Sr., 103, 113n59, 132n126, 137n139, 137n141, 206, 212–213
Skillin, Josiah [brother of Samuel Skillin], 117n77
Skillin, Josiah [Samuel Skillin, Jr. and Rebecca Sawyer], 150–151
Skillin, Katharine, 137, 137n142, 150, 206, 210–214, 234–235, 324n50
Skillin, Lemuel, 287n295
Skillin, Levi, 290n303
Skillin, Rebecca [Samuel Skillin, Jr. and Rebecca Sawyer], 151n28
Skillin, Rebecca (Sawyer), 141n155, 150–151, 150n27, 175n122, 243, 316n12
Skillin, Rhoda (Haley), 111, 113, 117n77

Skillin, Rhoda (Haley) (*continued*) 129, 137, 155, 189n174, 206, 210–211, 247n138
Skillin, Rhoda [Samuel Skillin, Jr. and Rebecca Sawyer], 151
Skillin, Samuel, Jr.
  Cape Elizabeth, roles in, 235
  captain of company in Stroudwater, 141n155, 179, 224
  children of, 150–151, 151n28, 243, 316n13
  Committee of Correspondence, service on, 241
  First Church of Falmouth, 150, 150–151
  list of polls and estates, 235
Skillin, Samuel, Sr.
  children of, 137, 155, 206, 210–211
  death of, 142, 181, 214
  descendants of, 137n142, 189n174
  friendship with Richard Crockett, 99
  gravestone of, *143*
  grist and saw mills, 137, 155n46, 206, 259
  Gunnison's Neck, dispute of boundary-line fence, 110–111, *112*
  influence on nephew Samuel Crockett, 170
  Kittery, roles in, 129
  land given to daughter Katharine, 213–214
  land grants of, 113n59
  marriage to Rhoda Haley, 113
  occupation as shipwright, 117
  ownership of enslaved African Americans, 129
  real estate transactions of, 113n61, 118–119, 129–130, 137, 141
  relocation to Falmouth, 104n19, 136–137, 206
  relocation to New Hampshire, 117

451

Skillin, Samuel, Sr. (*continued*)
   service in local militia, 141–142
Skillin, Samuel III [Samuel Skillin Jr. and Rebecca Sawyer], 141n155
Skillin, Sarah, 243, 316n12, 316n13
Skillin, Sarah (Miller), 261
Skillin, Thaddeus, 279n268
Skillin, Thomas, Jr., 132
Skillin, Thomas, Sr., 103n11, 132, 142n156
Skillin, Zebulon, 279n268
slavery, 84, 87, 107, 129, 345, 346, 357
Small, Job, 260n186
Small, Timothy, 268
Smalley, Elizabeth, 313n3
Smith, Elizabeth (Westcoat) Bailey, 278n266
Smith, Israel, 122n100
Smith, Thomas, 150, 173n111, 178n137, 187, 189, 215–216
smuggling in Maine, 272
Sokoki (Native American tribe), **22**
Somerset County, 2n3
South Berwick, *28*, 104
Spencer, Wilbur, 15, 21, 22, 29
Sprout, Ebenezer, 326n58
Spruce Creek, 72n9, 107, 111, 114, 118–119, 137
Spurwink, 114, 223, 230
Squamscott Patent, 118, 120, 141
Squamscott River, 118
Squando (Native American), 79–81, 83, 84
St. Croix (French colony), 10, 265
St. John (Native American tribe), 130–131, 172, 187–188, 229
Stamp Act, 1765, 239
Stanford, Joseph, 313n3, 321, 322
Stanford, Josiah, 322
Stanford, Priscilla (Strout), 313n3, 321, 322–323
Stanford, Rebecca. *See* Crockett, Rebecca (Stanford)
Stanford, Robert, 321–322, 322n38
Stanford, Thomas, 321–322, *322*
Stileman, Mary, 72n9, 94n85
Stileman, Richard, 72n9, 94n85
Stinchfield, Priscilla (Crockett), 330, 336n108
Stoke Gabriel Church, 4, 6. *See also* Church of St. Mary and St. Gabriel
Stoke Gabriel Clock Tower, 13–14
Stoke Gabriel (Devon, England), 2, 4, 7, 14–15
Stoke Gabriel yew tree, 13–14
Storer, Seth, 258n177, 273n244, 286, 289
Storer, W., 283
Stover, Elizabeth, 42n166
Stover, John, 42n166
Stover, Sylvester, 42n166
Stratham, New Hampshire
   First Church of, 122–123
   meeting house bell, 127
   minister controversy, 138–140
   new township, formerly Squamscott Patent, 120
   Reverend Henry Rust, call of, 122
   schools, 140–141
   wolf bounty, 127
Stratham Meeting House, seat assignments, 122–123
Strawbery Banke, 18, 29, 43
Strong, Caleb, **354**
Stroudwater (Westbrook, Maine), 141n155, 179, 185, 222, 224

Index

Strout, Christopher, 322n42
Strout, Christopher, III, 313n3, 322n42
Strout, Christopher, Jr., 177, 313n3, 322–323, 323n44, 323n45
Strout, David, 208–209, 228n74, 242, 259n178, 259n180, 261n187, 313, 313n3
Strout, Dorcas, 313, 325–326, 331, 336–337, 366–367
Strout. Mary (Small), 322
Strout, Priscilla, 313n3, 321, 322–323
Strout, Will, 213n28
Sugar Act, 1764, 239
Sumner, Increase, 200
surveyors of highways, 155n46, 176, 235, 236, 271, 278
Swett, John, 175
Swett, Martha (Noyes), 175
Swett, Olive, 364
Swett, Priscilla, 175, 189

T
Tahanedo (Native American), 9, 10
Tarratine (Native American tribe), 97, 130, 225, 303n24
Tea, Jesse, 202–203
Ten Proprietors, 301
Ten-Mile Falls, 344
tenant farming, 273n245, 307
Third Indian War, 64, 101, 113–114, 130
Thomas, James, 136n136
Thomas, Nathaniel, 192n188, 198, 199, 200
Thomas, Richard "Rice," 34, 36n146, 40n155, 40n156, 46–49
Thompson, James, 263–264
Thompson, Nathaniel, 197–201

Thompson, Samuel, 190n181
Thomson, David, 18
Thorne, John, 336
Thornes, Joseph, 149n13
Thury, Louis-Pierre, 64n259, 106
Tilley, Alice (Frost) Blower, 32n129
Tilley/Tilly, William, 32n129, 36n144, 43n172
Titcom, General, 200
tithingman, 176, 236, 258
Tories. See Royalists
Townsend, Charles, 239
Townsend Acts, 239
Toxus (Native American), 152
treaties, between foreign powers
    Peace of Ryswick (1697), 108
    Peace of Utrecht (1713), 130
    Treaty of Aix-la-Chapelle (1748), 174, 216
    Treaty of Ghent (1814), 277
    Treaty of Paris (1763), 188, 302
    Treaty of Paris (1783), 256
treaties, between Massachusetts Bay Colony and Native Americans
    Dummer's Treaty (1726), 175, 216, 342
    Pemaquid (1696), 130
    Treaty of Casco (1678), 88–89, 100
    Treaty of Portsmouth (1713), 130–131, 132–133
Trelawny Plantation, 33
Treworgy, James, 29n117, 30n119
Trickey, Francis, 43n171, 111n51
Trickey, John, 93n80
Trickey, Martha, 103n13
Trickey, Mary, 215n35
Trickey, Sarah, 93n80, 179n147, 215n35
Tucker, Bridget, 117n83, 384n35

Tucker, Hugh, 117n83, 384n35
Tucker, Lewis, 114, 155n47
Tucker, Nicholas, 110n46, 117
Tucker, Sarah (Gunnison), 114
Tucker, William, 117
Turf and Twig, 33–34
Twenty Associates, 301
Twenty-Mile Falls, 344, 348

U
Usher, John, 64n258, 77

V
Vassell, John, 317n19, 329
Vaughn, C.H., 273n242
Vaughn, George, 120
Vaughn, William, 269n229, 272–273, 281, 282, 285–286
Veasey, Thomas, 122
Vines, Richard, 49n201

W
Wabanaki Confederacy, 9n33, **22**, 80, 101
Wabanaki (Native American tribe)
"common pot" understanding of land, 294–295
definition of, 2n5
First Indian War, 57–58, 79, 80, 84
language of, 21
peace talks, 89, 150–152, 216
Second Indian War, 100, 101
Warumbo deed, 297
withdrawal into Canada after French and Indian War, 293
See also Dawnland

Wadsworth, (General), 252n152
Wagg, Desire (Dingley), 367
Wagg, Dorcas (Strout), 313, 325–326, 331, 336–337, 366–367
Wagg, Eliza/Elija, 327
Wagg, Howard, 365
Wagg, James, 253n158, 368
Wagg, James, Jr.
American Revolution, service in, 325–326, 327
children of, 331, 336–337
grave of, 372, *373*
influence on Ephraim Crockett, 313
marriage to Dorcas Strout, *313*
marriage to Rhoda Goold, 367
on Pejepscot Claim, 325, 365–366
pension and certificate of land, 366
"quieting" settlement, 352, **355**
Wagg, James, Sr.
birth of and possible original surname of, 314
death of, 365
grave of, 371
influence on Ephraim Crockett, 312, 313
on Pejepscot Claim, 311, 325, 326, 364–365
"quieting" settlement, 352, **355**
real estate of, lack of, 313–314
road tax (1813), 340
settlement with Waterhouse heirs, 357–358, 365
Wagg, Julia, 367
Wagg, Mary (Crockett), 150, 151, 153, 154, 312, 314, 325
Wagg, Polly (Dingley), 367
Wagg, Samuel, 331, 340, 367

Wagg Family Cemetery, 367, 369, 372, *373*
Wahway (Native American), 152
Wainwright, Francis, 96n987
Waite, John [John/Jonathan Waite], 187n165
Waite, John/Jonathan, 164, 182–184, *184*
Wakely, Thomas, 83
Waldo, Samuel (Brigadier General), 225n66, 301
Waldo, Samuel [Brigadier-General Samuel Waldo], 239n109
Waldo Patent, 255n66, 301, 308, 371
Waldo Proprietors, 300–301
Waldron, Richard, 83, 85, 87–88, 107
Walker, Gardner, 280, 280n272
Wampanoag (Native American tribe), 56–57, 79, 87
Wannerton, Thomas, 25n94, 25n95
War of 1812, 271–274, 275–281
War of Austrian Succession, 101, 172–174, 215–218
War of Spanish Succession, 64, 101, 113–114, 130
War of the League of Augsburg, 108. *See also* King William's War; Second Indian War
Warehouse Point, 30n119
Warrens, James, 92n78
Warumbee (Native American), 297, *299*, 341
Warumbo Deed, 297, *299*, 342, 344, 348
Warwick (ship), 3n9, 15, 17–18, 20
Washington, George, 243n127, 244, 245, 255, 256, 317, 318–319
Waterhouse, Abigail, 356, 357, 358–362, 362, 363, 365, 368–369, 370
Waterhouse, Hannah (Lewis), 327, **328**, 345–346, 356, 358, 362, 370
Waterhouse, Hannah [Samuel Waterhouse and Hannah Lewis], 356, 357, 358–362, 362, 363, 365, 368–369, 370
Waterhouse, Samuel, 327, **328**, 345–346, 363
Watts, Ann, 285
Watts, John, 298, 343n137, 344n142
Wawenock (Native American tribe), 175
Waymouth, George, 1, 8–9
Waymouth, James, 113n61
Waymouth, Katherine, 113n61
Webb, Joshua, 280
Webb, Susanna, 280
Webster, Anna (Westcoat), 260n186
Webster, Ebenezer, 260n186
WeconDomhegon (Native American), 297, 299, 341
Weeks, Lemuel, 277
Weeks, W.C., 280n272
Wehanownowit (Native American), 117n79
Welch, George, 157
Wells, attack on, 107, 114
Wentworth, Benning, 338
Wentworth, Grace, 114–115
Wentworth, Hunking, *171*
Wentworth, John, 298, 343n137
Wentworth, Sally, 276n257, 298n12, 364n218
Wentworth, William, 115
Westbrook, Thomas, 134, 137n139
Westcoat, Abigail, 263n193
Westcoat, Andrew, 249n143
Westcoat, Anna, 260n186
Westcoat, Dorcas (Skillin), 206, 210n12, 213, 247, 248, 258, 261, 270, 278n266
Westcoat, Dorcas [William Westcoat and Dorcas Skillin], 247, 278n266

Westcoat, Elizabeth, 137n142, 278n266
Westcoat, Joseph, 255, 280, 280n273, 289
Westcoat, Josiah, 259n182, 266
Westcoat, Mercy, 260n186
Westcoat, Richard, 213, 247n137, 259n182
Westcoat, Sarah (Miller) Skillin, 261
Westcoat, Susannah, 137n142, 206, 209–210, 213, 247–250, 267, 278n266, 324
Westcoat, William
    children of, 206, 247, 254–255
    financial and legal troubles of, 261, 262–264
    inheritance of, 247–248
    marriage to Sarah (Miller) Skillin, 261
    real estate transactions of, 213, 259n118, 259n182, 263, 278n266
Westcoat, William "Post Wescott" [Susannah's brother], 255
Wharton, Richard, 297, 299, 341, 343n137
Wheelwright, John, 117n79
Whipple, Martha, 118n85
Whipple, Mathew, 118n85
White, Frances, 7, 43, 43n173, 44–45, 44n179, 45
White, John, 48
White, Richard, 7, 43, 44–45, 44n179, 45, 95, 96
Whitney, Abel, 188n171, 189
Whitney, Mary (Cane), 189
Wiggin, Andrew, 122, 124n104, 144n62
Wiggin, Chase, 124n106
Wiggin, Dorothy, 144n162
Wiggin, Hannah, 118
Wiggin, James, 32n126
Wiggin, Jonathan, 118n85, 122, 144n162
Wiggin, Magdeline, 32n126
Wiggin, Mary (Emery), 118n85
Wiggin, Simon, 118, 119n90
Wiggin, Thomas, 118, 122, 124n106
Wiggins, Simon, 127, *128*
Wihikermett (Native American), 297, *299*
William III, King of England, 104, 113. *See also* William of Orange
William of Orange, 102
Williams, Roger, 57n229
Wilson, Deborah, 111, 113, 114
Wilson, Gowen, 6, 111
Wilson, Joseph, 110n50
Wilson, William, 113n59
Wincoll (Winchell), John, 94
Winkley, Samuel, 110–111, 112
Winnock, Joseph, 379–380
Winslow, Nathan, 279n268, 279n269
Winslow, William, 279n269
Winter Harbor, 114
Winthrop, Adam, 298, 343n137, 344n142
Winthrop, John, 16
Winthrop Fleet, 16, 18
Wiswell, Rev., 190n181
Wiwurna (Native American), 152
Wixson, Cheryl, 3n7, 192
Wixson, Lori, 144n162
Wixson, Wesley E., 144n162
Wolfe, James, 187, 229
Wolinak (Native American tribe), *22*
Woodbury, Jane, 251–252
Woodbury, Joshua, Jr., 174n116
Woodbury, Joshua, Sr., 174n116
Woodman, Stephen, 248n141
Wormwood, William, 33
Wright, Mrs, Jr., 123

Index

Y

Yarmouth, raid on, 101

"year without a summer," 335

York, Benjamin, 136, 136n137, 149–150, 151, 155

York, Deborah, 228, 269

York, Joanna (Skillin), 155, 228

York, Mary (Dutch), 161n69

York, Mary (wife of Benjamin), 151

York, Rufus, 195n191

York, Samuel [Benjamin York], 155, 228, *265*

York, Samuel [brother of Benjamin], 135n135

York, Samuel [father of Benjamin York], 136, 137

York, Samuel [Mary Crockett's uncle], 161n69

York, Samuel [Samuel York and Mary Dutch], 161n69

York, Thomas, 174n118

York, town of, 39n153, **61**, 64, 106–107

Young, Richard, 144n161

About the Author

Maine farmer and writer Jennifer Wixson is a descendant of Thomas Crockett (and his wife Ann), who arrived at Pascataqua in 1630. She currently lives with her husband Stanley Luce in Troy (Maine), where they garden, keep bees, and produce maple products.

Other Books by Jennifer Wixson

Fiction
Hens and Chickens
Peas, Beans and Corn
The Songbird of Sovereign
The Minister's Daughter
Maggie's Dilemma

Non-Fiction
Learning to SOAR!
Under the Apple Tree
The History of the Crockett Family of Crockett's Ridge, Norway, Maine

www.ingramcontent.com/pod-product-compliance
Lightning Source LLC
Chambersburg PA
CBHW051349070526
44584CB00025B/3697